Lecture Notes in Computer Science 5947

Commenced Publication in 1973
Founding and Former Series Editors:
Gerhard Goos, Juris Hartmanis, and Jan van Leeuwen

Editorial Board

David Hutchison
  Lancaster University, UK
Takeo Kanade
  Carnegie Mellon University, Pittsburgh, PA, USA
Josef Kittler
  University of Surrey, Guildford, UK
Jon M. Kleinberg
  Cornell University, Ithaca, NY, USA
Alfred Kobsa
  University of California, Irvine, CA, USA
Friedemann Mattern
  ETH Zurich, Switzerland
John C. Mitchell
  Stanford University, CA, USA
Moni Naor
  Weizmann Institute of Science, Rehovot, Israel
Oscar Nierstrasz
  University of Bern, Switzerland
C. Pandu Rangan
  Indian Institute of Technology, Madras, India
Bernhard Steffen
  TU Dortmund University, Germany
Madhu Sudan
  Microsoft Research, Cambridge, MA, USA
Demetri Terzopoulos
  University of California, Los Angeles, CA, USA
Doug Tygar
  University of California, Berkeley, CA, USA
Gerhard Weikum
  Max-Planck Institute of Computer Science, Saarbruecken, Germany

Amir Pnueli   Irina Virbitskaite
Andrei Voronkov (Eds.)

Perspectives of Systems Informatics

7th International Andrei Ershov Memorial Conference, PSI 2009
Novosibirsk, Russia, June 15-19, 2009
Revised Papers

 Springer

Volume Editors

Amir Pnueli (1941-2009)
The Weizmann Institute of Science, Rehovot, Israel
New York University, NY, USA

Irina Virbitskaite
A.P. Ershov Institute of Informatics Systems
Siberian Division of the Russian Academy of Sciences
6, Acad. Lavrentiev pr., 630090, Novosibirsk, Russia
E-mail: virb@iis.nsk.su

Andrei Voronkov
University of Manchester
Department of Computer Science
Oxford Road, Manchester, M13 9PL, UK
E-mail: voronkov@cs.man.ac.uk

Library of Congress Control Number: 2009943004

CR Subject Classification (1998): F.3, D.3, D.2, D.1

LNCS Sublibrary: SL 1 – Theoretical Computer Science and General Issues

ISSN 0302-9743
ISBN 978-3-642-11485-4 Springer Berlin Heidelberg New York

This work is subject to copyright. All rights are reserved, whether the whole or part of the material is
concerned, specifically the rights of translation, reprinting, re-use of illustrations, recitation, broadcasting,
reproduction on microfilms or in any other way, and storage in data banks. Duplication of this publication
or parts thereof is permitted only under the provisions of the German Copyright Law of September 9, 1965,
in its current version, and permission for use must always be obtained from Springer. Violations are liable
to prosecution under the German Copyright Law.

springer.com

© Springer-Verlag Berlin Heidelberg 2010

Typesetting: Camera-ready by author, data conversion by Scientific Publishing Services, Chennai, India
Printed on acid-free paper   SPIN: 12829361   06/3180   5 4 3 2 1 0

Preface

This volume contains the final proceedings of the 7th International Andrei Ershov Memorial Conference on Perspectives of System Informatics Akademgorodok (Novosibirsk, Russia), June 15–19, 2009.

PSI is a forum for academic and industrial researchers, developers and users working on topics relating to computer, software and information sciences. The conference serves to bridge the gaps between different communities whose research areas are covered by but not limited to foundations of program and system development and analysis, programming methodology and software engineering, and information technologies.

PSI 2009 was dedicated to the memory of a prominent scientist, academician Andrei Ershov (1931–1988), and to a significant date in the history of computer science in the country, namely, the 50th anniversary of the Programming Department founded by Andrei Ershov. Initially, the department was a part of the Institute of Mathematics and later, in 1964, it joined the newly established Computing Center of the Siberian Branch of the USSR Academy of Sciences. Andrei Ershov, who was responsible for forming the department, gathered a team of young graduates from leading Soviet universities. The first significant project of the department was aimed at the development of ALPHA system, an optimizing compiler for an extension of Algol 60 implemented on a Soviet computer M-20. Later, the researchers of the department created the Algibr, Epsilon, Sigma, and Alpha-6 programming systems for the BESM-6 computers. The list of their achievements also includes the first Soviet time-sharing system AIST-0, the multi-language system BETA, research projects in artificial intelligence and parallel programming, integrated tools for text processing and publishing, and many others. The scope of problems facing the Programming Department was widening in time, its organizational structure changed and new research directions appeared, including school informatics and mixed computation. Founded in 1990, the Institute of Informatics Systems is justly considered to be the successor of the Programming Department, preserving its main research directions and maintaining its best traditions.

The first six conferences were held in 1991, 1996, 1999, 2001, 2003 and 2006, and proved to be significant international events. The seventh conference followed the traditions of the previous ones and preserved the style of the PSI conferences: the program of PSI 2009 included invited papers in addition to contributed regular and short papers.

This time 67 papers were submitted by researchers from 26 countries. Each paper was reviewed by four experts, at least three of them from the same or closely related discipline as the authors. The reviewers generally provided a high-quality assessment of the papers and often gave extensive comments to the authors for the possible improvement of the presentation. The Program

Committee selected 26 regular and 4 short papers for presentation at the conference. A range of hot topics in system informatics was covered by five invited talks given by prominent computer scientists.

We are glad to express our gratitude to all the persons and organizations who contributed to the conference – to the authors of all the papers for their effort in producing the materials included here, to the sponsors for their moral, financial and organizational support, to the Steering Committee members for their coordination of the conference, to the Program Committee members and the reviewers who did their best to review and select the papers, and to the members of the Organizing Committee for their contribution to the success of this event and its great cultural program. Finally, we would like to mention the fruitful cooperation with Springer during the preparation of this volume.

The Program Committee work and the volume preparation were done using the EasyChair conference management system.

During the last stages of preparation of this volume, we received the sad news that Amir Pnueli has passed away. We offer our condolences to his friends and family.

November 2009   Irina Virbitskaite
                                                                            Andrei Voronkov

Organization

Steering Committee

Members

Manfred Broy (Munich, Germany)
Bertrand Meyer (Zurich, Switzerland)
Andrei Voronkov (Manchester, UK)

Honorary Members

Tony Hoare (Cambridge, UK)
Niklaus Wirth (Zurich, Switzerland)

Conference Chair

Alexander Marchuk (Novosibirsk, Russia)

Sponsoring Organizations

- Russian Foundation for Basic Research
- Intel Corporation
- HP Labs
- Google
- Microsoft Research
- Formal Methods Europe
- Semantic Technology Institute (STI) Innsbruck
- EMC R&D Center
- Sun Microsystems
- Office of Naval Research Global
  The content of the proceedings does not necessarily reflect the position or the policy of the United States Government and no official endorsement should be inferred.

Program Committee

Janis Barzdins (Riga, Latvia)
Frédéric Benhamou (Nantes, France)
Stefan Brass (Halle, Germany)
Mikhail Bulyonkov (Novosibirsk, Russia)
Gabriel Ciobanu (Iasi, Romania)

Igor Belousov (Moscow, Russia)
Eike Best (Oldenburg, Germany)
Kim Bruce (Claremont, USA)
Albertas Čaplinskas (Vilnius, Lithuania)
Javier Esparza (Munich, Germany)

Jean Claude Fernandez (Grenoble, France)

Jan Friso Groote (Eindhoven, The Netherlands)

Victor Ivannikov (Moscow, Russia)

Joost-Pieter Katoen (Aachen, Germany)

Nikolay Kolchanov (Novosibirsk, Russia)

Rustan Leino (Redmond, USA)

Pericles Loucopoulos (Loughborough, UK)

Andrea Maggiolo-Schettini (Pisa, Italy)

Dominique Méry (Nancy, France)

Bernhard Möller (Augsburg, Germany)

Peter Mosses (Swansea, UK)

Fedor Murzin (Novosibirsk, Russia)

Nikolaj Nikitchenko (Kiev, Ukraine)

Francesco Parisi-Presicce (Rome, Italy)

Jaan Penjam (Tallinn, Estonia)

Alexander Petrenko (Moscow, Russia)

Vladimir Polutin (Moscow, Russia)

Viktor Sabelfeld (Bern, Switzerland)

Timos Sellis (Athens, Greece)

Klaus-Dieter Schewe (Massey, New Zealand)

Nikolay Shilov (Novosibirsk, Russia)

Mark Trakhtenbrot (Rehovot, Israel)

Andrei Voronkov (Manchester, UK)

Tatyana Yakhno (Izmir, Turkey)

Chris George (Macau)

Heinrich Herre (Leipzig, Germany)

Victor Kasyanov (Novosibirsk, Russia)

Alexander Kleshchev (Vladivostok, Russia)

Gregory Kucherov (Lille, France)

Johan Lilius (Turku, Finland)

Audrone Lupeikiene (Vilnius, Lithuania)

Klaus Meer (Cottbus, Germany)

Torben Mogensen (Copenhagen, Denmark)

Hanspeter Mössenböck (Linz, Austria)

Peter Müller (Redmond, USA)

Valery Nepomniaschy (Novosibirsk, Russia)

José R. Paramá (A Coruña, Spain)

Wojciech Penczek (Warsaw, Poland)

Peter Pepper (Berlin, Germany)

Amir Pnueli (New York, USA)

Wolfgang Reisig (Berlin, Germany)

Donald Sannella (Edinburgh, UK)

Alexander Semenov (Novosibirsk, Russia)

David Schmidt (Manhattan, USA)

Alexander Tomilin (Moscow, Russia)

Irina Virbitskaite (Novosibirsk, Russia)

Alexander L. Wolf (London, UK)

Wang Yi (Uppsala, Sweden)

Reviewers

Anureev I.
Athanasiou S.
Auer P.
Barzdins G.
Barzdins J.
Belousov I.
Bourdon J.
Brass S.
Brazdil T.
Bruce K.
Bulyonkov M.
Cameron N.
Campbell B.
Čaplinskas A.
Caravagna G.
Cats Th.
Chong S.
Ciobanu G.
Claude Fernandez J.
Demakov A.
Dubtsov R.
Emelyanov P.
Esparza J.
Fahland D.
George C.
Giannopoulos G.
Gierds Ch.
Glück R.
Glukhankov M.
Grall H.
Groote J.F.
Gross R.
Herre H.
Hilscher M.
Hoefner P.
Idrisov R.
Jarocki M.
Johnstone A.
Kahrs S.
Karaulov A.
Katoen J.-P.
Kleeblatt D.
Kleshchev A.
Kolchanov N.
Kucherov G.
Lanotte R.
Lazard S.
Leino R.
Levy A.
Liagouris J.
Lilius J.
Loucopoulos P.
Lupeikiene A.
Luttenberger M.
Meer K.
Méry D.
Meyer R.
Milazzo P.
Möller B.
Mössenböck H.
Mogensen T. Æ.
Monfroy E.
Mosses P.
Motik B.
Müller P.
Murzin F.
Mutilin V.
Nazim B.
Nepomniaschy V.
Nguyen V.Y.
Niewiadomski A.
Nikitchenko N.
Nõmm S.
Opmanis M.
Pahikkala T.
Parama Gabia J.R.
Parisi-Presicce F.
Patroumpas K.
Penabad M.
Penczek W.
Penjam J.
Pepper P.
Petrenko A.
Pliuskevicius R.
Polutin V.
Pyzhov K.
Rakow A.
Reisig W.
Rikacovs S.
Rybin P.
Sabelfeld V.
Sannella D.
Schewe K.-D.
Schmidt D.
Schmitt I.
Schneider S.-A.
Schult Ch.
Semenov A.
Shilov N.
Shkurko D.
Skiadopoulos S.
Stasenko A.
Stigge M.
Suermeli J.
Suwimonteerabuth D.
Szreter M.
Tini S.
Trakhtenbrot M.
Van Weerdenburg M.
Vityaev Eu.
Voronkov A.
Wilkeit E.
Willemse T.
Wolf A.
Yakhno T.
Yi W.

Table of Contents

Invited Talks

Regular Papers

Games, Interaction and Computation

Samson Abramsky

Oxford University, UK

Our current understanding of computation has widened enormously beyond the original closed world picture of numerical calculation in isolation from the environment. In the age of the Internet and the Web, and now of pervasive and ubiquitous computing, it has become clear that interaction and information flow between multiple agents are essential features of computation. The standard unit of description or design, whether at a micro-scale of procedure call-return interfaces or hardware components, or a macro- scale of software agents on the Web, becomes a process or agent, the essence of whose behaviour is how it interacts with its environment across some defined interface.

These developments have required the introduction of novel mathematical models of interactive computation. The traditional view whereby a program is seen as computing a function or relation from inputs to outputs is no longer sufficient: what function does the Internet compute? One of the compelling ideas which has taken root is to conceptualize the interaction between the System and the Environment as a two-person game. A program specifying how the System should behave in the face of all possible actions by the Environment is then a strategy for the player corresponding to the System.

Over the past 15 years, there has been an extensive development of Game Semantics in Computer Science. One major area of application has been to the semantics of programming languages, where it has led to major progress in the construction of fully abstract models for programming languages embodying a wide range of computational effects, and starting with the first semantic construction of a fully abstract model for PCF, thus addressing a famous open problem in the field. It has been possible to give crisp characterizations of the shapes of computations carried out within certain programming disciplines: including purely functional programming, stateful programming, general references, programming with non-local jumps and exceptions, non-determinism, probability, concurrency, names, and more.

More recently, there has been an algorithmic turn, and some striking applications to verification and program analysis. We shall give an introduction and overview of some of these developments.

A. Pnueli, I. Virbitskaite, and A. Voronkov (Eds.): PSI 2009, LNCS 5947, p. 1, 2010.
© Springer-Verlag Berlin Heidelberg 2010

Rôle of Domain Engineering in Software Development

Why Current Requirements Engineering Is Flawed !

Dines Bjørner

Fredsvej 11, DK-2840 Holte, Danmark
bjorner@gmail.com
www.imm.dtu.dk/~db

Abstract. We introduce the notion of domain descriptions (D) in order to ensure that software (S) is right and is the right software, that is, that it is correct with respect to written requirements (R) and that it meets customer expectations (D). That is, before software can be designed (S) we must make sure we understand the requirements (R), and before we can express the requirements we must make sure that we understand the application domain (D): the area of activity of the users of the required software, before and after installment of such software. We shall outline what we mean by informal, narrative and formal domain descriptions, and how one can systematically — albeit not (in fact: never) automatically — go from domain descriptions to requirements prescriptions. As it seems that domain engineering is a relatively new discipline within software engineering we shall mostly focus on domain engineering and discuss its necessity. The paper will show some formulas but they are really not meant to be read, let alone understood. They are merely there to bring home the point: Professional software engineering, like other professional engineering branches rely on and use mathematics. And it is all very simple to learn and practise anyway ! We end this paper with, to some, perhaps, controversial remarks: Requirements engineering, as pursued today, researched, taught and practised, is outdated, is thus fundamentally flawed. We shall justify this claim.

1 The Software Development Dogma

1.1 The Dogma

The dogma is this: Before software can be designed we must understand the requirements. Before requirements can be finalised we must have understood the domain.

We assume that the reader knows what is meant by software design and requirements. But what do we mean by "the domain" ?

A. Pnueli, I. Virbitskaite, and A. Voronkov (Eds.): PSI 2009, LNCS 5947, pp. 2–34, 2010.
© Springer-Verlag Berlin Heidelberg 2010

1.2 What Do We Mean by 'Domain' ?

By a domain we shall loosely understand an 'area' of natural or human activity, or both, where the 'area' is "well-delineated" such as, for example, for physics: mechanics or electricity or chemistry or hydrodynamics; or for an infrastructure component: banking, railways, hospital health-care, "the market": consumers, retailers, wholesalers, producers and the distribution chain.

By a *domain* we shall thus, less loosely, understand a universe of discourse, small or large, a structure (i) of simple entities, that is, of "things", individuals, particulars some of which are designated as state components; (ii) of functions, say over entities, which when applied become possibly state-changing actions of the domain; (iii) of events, possibly involving entities, occurring in time and expressible as predicates over single or pairs of (before/after) states; and (iv) of behaviours, sets of possibly interrelated sequences of actions and events.

1.3 Dialectics

Now, let's get this "perfectly" straight ! Can we develop software requirements without understanding the domain ? Well, how much of the domain should we understand ? And how well should we understand it ?

Can we develop software requirements without understanding the domain ? No, of course we cannot ! But we, you, do develop software for hospitals (railways, banks) without understanding health-care (transportation, the financial markets) anyway ! In other engineering disciplines professionalism is ingrained: Aeronautics engineers understand the domain of aerodynamics; naval architects (i.e., ship designers) understand the domain of hydrodynamics; telecommunications engineers understand the domain of electromagnetic field theory; and so forth.

Well, how much of the domain should we understand ? A basic answer is this: enough for us to understand formal descriptions of such a domain.

This is so in classical engineering: Although the telecommunications engineer has not herself researched and made mathematical models of electromagnetic wave propagation in the form of Maxwell's equations: Gauss's Law for Electricity, Gauss's Law for Magnetism, Faraday's Law of Induction, Ampéres Law:

$$\oint \vec{E} \cdot d\vec{A} = \frac{q}{\varepsilon_0} \quad \oint \vec{B} \cdot d\vec{A} = 0 \quad \oint \vec{E} \cdot d\vec{s} = -\frac{d\Phi_B}{dt} \quad \oint \vec{B} \cdot d\vec{s} = \mu_0 i + \frac{1}{c^2}\frac{\partial}{\partial t}\int \vec{E} \cdot d\vec{A}$$

the telecommunications engineer certainly understands these laws.

And how well should we understand it ? Well, enough, as an engineer, to manipulate the formulas, to further develop these for engineering calculations.

1.4 Conclusion

It is about time that software engineers consult precise descriptions, including formalisations, and establish, themselves or by consultants, such descriptions, of the application domains for software. These domain models may have to be developed by computing scientists. Software engineers then "transform" these into requirements prescriptions and software designs.

2   The Triptych of Software Development

We recall the dogma: before software can be designed we must understand the requirements. Before requirements can be finalised we must have understood the domain.

We conclude from that, that an "ideal" software development proceeds, in three major development phases, as follows:

- **Domain engineering**: The results of domain engineering include a domain model: a description, both informal, as a precise narrative, and formal, as a specification. The domain is described as it is.
- **Requirements engineering**: The results of requirements engineering include a requirements model: a prescription, both informal, as a precise narrative, and formal, as a specification. The requirements are described as we would like the software to be, and the requirements must be clearly related to the domain description.
- **Software design**: The results of software design include executable code and all documentation that goes with it. The software design specification must be correct with respect to the requirements.

2.1   Technicalities: An Overview

Domain Engineering. Section 3 outlines techniques of domain engineering. But just as a preview: Based on extensive domain acquisition and analysis an informal and a formal domain model is established, a model which is centered around sub-models of: intrinsics, supporting technologies, management and organisation, rules and regulations, script [or contract] languages and human behaviours, which are then validated and verified.

Requirements Engineering. Section 4 outlines techniques of requirements engineering. But just as a preview: Based on presentations of the domain model to requirements stakeholders requirements can now be "derived" from the domain model and as follows: First a domain requirements model is arrived at: projection of the domain model, instantiation of the domain model, determination of the domain model, extension of the domain model and fitting of several, separate domain requirements models; then an interface requirements model, and finally a machine requirements model. These are simultaneously verified and validated and the feasibility and satisfiability of the emerging model is checked. We show only the briefly explained specifications of an example "derivation" of (and in this case only of, and then only some aspects of) domain requirements.

Software Design. We do not cover techniques of software design in detail — so only this summary. From the requirements prescription one develops, in stages and steps of transformation ("refinement"), first the system architecture, then the program (code) organisation (structure), and then, in further steps of development, the component design, the module design and the code. These stages and step can be verified, model checked and tested with respect to the previous phase of requirements prescription, respectively the previous software design stages and steps. One can then assert that the $\mathcal{S}$oftware design is correct with respect to the $\mathcal{R}$equirements in the context of the assumptions expressed about the $\mathcal{D}$omain:

$$\mathcal{D}, \ \mathcal{S} \models \mathcal{R}$$

3   Domain Engineering

We shall focus only on the actual modelling, thus omitting any treatment of the preparatory administrative and informative work, the identification of and liaison with domain stakeholders, the domain acquisition and analysis, and the establishment of a domain terminology (document). So we go straight to the descriptive work. We first illustrate the ideas of modelling domain phenomena and concepts in terms of simple entities, operations, events and behaviours, then we model the domain in terms of domain facets. Also, at then end, we do not have time and paper space for any treatment of domain verification, domain validations and the establishment of a domain theory.

3.1   Simple Entities, Operations, Events and Behaviours

Without discussing our specification ontology, that is, the principles according to which we view the world around us, we just present the decomposition of phenomena and concepts into simple entities, operations, events and behaviours. All of these are "first class citizens", that is, are entities.

We now illustrate examples of each of these ontological categories.

Simple Entities. A *simple entity* is something that has a distinct, separate existence, though it need not be a material existence, to which we apply functions. With simple entities we associate attributes, i.e., properties modelled as types and values. Simple entities can be considered either continuous or discrete, and, if discrete then either atomic or composite. It is the observer (that is, the specifier) who decides whether to consider a simple entity to be atomic or composite. Atomic entities cannot meaningfully be decomposed into sub-entities, but atomic entities may be analysed into (Cartesian) "compounds" of properties, that is, attributes. Attributes have name, type and value. Composite entities can be meaningfully decomposed into sub-entities, which are entities. The composition of sub-entities into a composite entity "reveals" the, or a mereology of the composite entity: that is, how it is "put together".

─────── Example 1: Transport Entities: Nets, Links and Hubs — Narrative ───────

1. There are hubs and links.
2. There are nets, and a net consists of a set of two or more hubs and one or more links.
3. There are hub and link identifiers.

4. Each hub (and each link) has an own, unique hub (respectively link) identifiers (which can be observed from the hub [respectively link]).

_____ Example 2: Transport Entities: Nets, Links and Hubs — Formalisation _____

type
  1 H, L,
  2 N = **H-set** × **L-set**
axiom
  2 ∀ (hs,ls):N • **card** hs≥2 ∧ **card** hs≥1
type
  3 HI, LI
value
  4a obs_HI: H → HI, obs_LI: L → LI
axiom
  4b ∀ h,h':H, l,l':L •
        h≠h'⇒obs_HI(h)≠obs_HI(h') ∧ l≠l'⇒obs_LI(l)≠obs_LI(l')

Operations. By an *operation* we shall understand something which when *applied* to some entities, called the *arguments* of the operation, *yields* an entity, called the *result* of the operation application (also referred to as the operation invocation). Operations have signatures, that is, can be grossly described by the Cartesian type of its arguments and the possibly likewise compounded type of its results. Operations may be total over their argument types, or may be just partial. We shall consider some acceptable operations as "never terminating" processes. We shall, for the sake of consistency, consider all operation invocations as processes (terminating or non-terminating), and shall hence consider all operationdefinitions as also designating process definitions.

We shall also use the term **function** to mean the same as the term operation.

By a *state* we shall loosely understand a collection of one or more simple entities whose value may change. By an *action* we shall understand an operation application which applies to and/or yields a state.

_____ Example 3: Link Insertion Operation _____

5. To a net one can insert a new link in either of three ways:
  (a) Either the link is connected to two existing hubs — and the insert operation must therefore specify the new link and the identifiers of two existing hubs;
  (b) or the link is connected to one existing hub and to a new hub — and the insert operation must therefore specify the new link, the identifier of an existing hub, and a new hub;

(c) or the link is connected to two new hubs — and the insert operation must therefore specify the new link and two new hubs.

(d) From the inserted link one must be able to observe identifier of respective hubs.

6. From a net one can remove a link. The removal command specifies a link identifier.

type

5 Insert == Ins(s_ins:Ins)

5   Ins = 2xHubs | 1x1nH | 2nHs

5a   2xHubs == 2oldH(s_hi1:HI,s_l:L,s_hi2:HI)

5b   1x1nH == 1oldH1newH(s_hi:HI,s_l:L,s_h:H)

5c   2nHs == 2newH(s_h1:H,s_l:L,s_h2:H)

axiom

5d ∀ 2oldH(hi',l,hi''):Ins • hi'≠hi'' ∧ obs_LIs(l)={hi',hi''} ∧
   ∀ 1old1newH(hi,l,h):Ins • obs_LIs(l)={hi,obs_HI(h)} ∧
   ∀ 2newH(h',l,h''):Ins • obs_LIs(l)={obs_HI(h'),obs_HI(h'')}

7. If the Insert command is of kind 2newH(h',l,h'') then the updated net of hubs and links, has
   - the hubs hs joined, ∪, by the set {h',h''} and
   - the links ls joined by the singleton set of {l}.
8. If the Insert command is of kind 1oldH1newH(hi,l,h) then the updated net of hubs and links, has
   8.1 : the hub identified by hi updated, hi', to reflect the link connected to that hub.
   8.2 : The set of hubs has the hub identified by hi replaced by the updated hub hi' and the new hub.
   8.2 : The set of links augmented by the new link.
9. If the Insert command is of kind 2oldH(hi',l,hi'') then
9.1–.2   : the two connecting hubs are updated to reflect the new link,
   9.3 : and the resulting sets of hubs and links updated.

int_Insert(op)(hs,ls) ≡

$\star_i$ **case** op **of**

7   2newH(h',l,h'') → (hs ∪ {h',h''},ls ∪ {l}),

8   1oldH1newH(hi,l,h) →

8.1   **let** h' = aLI(xtr_H(hi,hs),obs_LI(l)) **in**

8.2   (hs\{xtr_H(hi,hs)}∪{h,h'},ls ∪{l}) **end**,

9   2oldH(hi',l,hi'') →

9.1   **let** hsδ = {aLI(xtr_H(hi',hs),obs_LI(l)),

9.2   aLI(xtr_H(hi'',hs),obs_LI(l))} **in**

9.3 $(hs\setminus\{xtr\_H(hi',hs),xtr\_H(hi'',hs)\}\cup hs\delta,ls \cup\{l\})$ **end**
$\star_j$ **end** $\star_k$ **pre** pre_int_Insert(op)(hs,ls)

Events. Informally, by an *event* we shall loosely understand the occurrence of "something" that may either trigger an action, or is triggered by an action, or alter the course of a behaviour, or a combination of these.

An *event* can be characterised by a predicate, p and a pair of ("before") and ("after") of pairs of states and times: $p((t_b,\sigma_b),(t_a,\sigma_a))$. Usually the time interval $t_a - t_b$ is of the order $t_a \simeq (t_b) + \delta_{\text{tiny}}$.

_____ Example 4: Transport Events _____

(i) A link, for some reason "ceases to exist"; for example: a bridge link falls down, or a level road link is covered by a mud slide, or a road tunnel is afire, or a link is blocked by some vehicle accident. (ii) A vehicle enters or leaves the net. (iii) A hub is saturated with vehicles.

Behaviours. By a *behaviour* we shall informally understand a strand of (sets of) actions and events. In the context of domain descriptions we shall speak of behaviours whereas, in the context of requirements prescriptions and software designs we shall use the term processes.

By a *behaviour* we, more formally, understand a sequence, q of actions and/or events $q_1, q_2, \ldots, q_i, q_{i+1}, \ldots, q_n$ such that the state resulting from one such action, q_i, or in which some event, q_i, occurs, becomes the state in which the next action or event, q_{i+1}, if it is an action, is effected, or, if it is an event, is the event state.

_____ Example 5: Transport: Traffic Behaviour _____

10. There are further undefined vehicles.
11. Traffic is a discrete function from a 'Proper subset of Time' to pairs of nets and vehicle positions.
12. Vehicles positions is a discrete function from vehicles to vehicle positions.

type
    10 Veh
    11 TF = Time $\underset{m}{\rightarrow}$ (N × VehPos)
    12 VehPos = Veh $\underset{m}{\rightarrow}$ Pos

13. There are positions, and a position is either on a link or in a hub.
    (a) A hub position is indicated just by a triple: the identifier of the hub in question, and a pair of (from and to) link identifiers, namely of links connected to the identified hub.
    (b) A link position is identified by a quadruplet: The identifier of the link, a pair of hub identifiers (of the link connected hubs), designating a

direction, and a real number, properly between 0 and 1, denoting the relative offset from the from hub to the to hub.

type
   13 Pos = HPos | LPos
   13a) HPos == hpos(s_hi:HI,s_fli:LI,s_tli:LI)
   13b) LPos == lpos(s_li:HI,s_fhi:LI,s_tli:LI,s_offset:Frac)
   13b) Frac = {|r:**Real**•0<r<1|}

3.2 Domain Facets

By a domain facet we mean one amongst a finite set of generic ways of analysing a domain: a view of the domain, such that the different facets cover conceptually different views, and such that these views together cover the domain

We shall postulate the following domain facets: intrinsics, support technologies, management & organisation, rules & regulations, script languages [contract languages] and human behaviour. Each facet covers simple entities, operations, events and behaviours.

We shall now illustrate these.

Intrinsics. By *domain intrinsics* we mean those phenomena and concepts of a domain which are basic to any of the other facets (listed earlier and treated, in some detail, below), with such domain intrinsics initially covering at least one specific, hence named, stakeholder view.

———————————— Example 6: Intrinsics, I ————————————

    The links, hubs, hence the nets, and the identifiers of links and hubs are intrinsic phenomena, respectively concepts.

So are:

———————————— Example 7: Intrinsics, II ————————————

14. From any link of a net one can observe the two hubs to which the link is connected.
    (a) We take this 'observing' to mean the following: From any link of a net one can observe the two distinct identifiers of these hubs.
15. From any hub of a net one can observe the one or more links to which are connected to the hub.
    (a) Again: by observing their distinct link identifiers.
16. Extending Item 14: the observed hub identifiers must be identifiers of hubs of the net to which the link belongs.
17. Extending Item 15: the observed link identifiers must be identifiers of links of the net to which the hub belongs.

value
    14a obs_HIs: L → HI-set,
    15a obs_LIs: H → LI-set,
axiom
    14b ∀ l:L • **card** obs_HIs(l)=2 ∧
    15b ∀ h:H • **card** obs_LIs(h)≥1 ∧
    ∀ (hs,ls):N •
    14a)   ∀ h:H • h ∈ hs ⇒ ∀ li:LI • li ∈ obs_LIs(h) ⇒
                ∃ l':L • l' ∈ ls ∧ li=obs_LI(l') ∧ obs_HI(h) ∈ obs_HIs(l') ∧
    15a)   ∀ l:L • l ∈ ls ⇒
                ∃ h',h'':H • {h',h''}⊆hs ∧ obs_HIs(l)={obs_HI(h'),obs_HI(h'')}
    16 ∀ h:H • h ∈ hs ⇒ obs_LIs(h) ⊆ iols(ls)
    17 ∀ l:L • l ∈ ls ⇒ obs_HIs(h) ⊆ iohs(hs)
value
    iohs: H-set → HI-set, iols: L-set → LI-set
    iohs(hs) ≡ {obs_HI(h)|h:H•h ∈ hs}
    iols(ls) ≡ {obs_LI(l)|l:L•l ∈ ls}

Support Technologies. By *domain support technologies* we mean ways and means of concretesing certain observed (abstract or concrete) phenomena or certain conceived concepts in terms of (possibly combinations of) human work, mechanical, hydro mechanical, thermo-mechanical, pneumatic, aero-mechanical, electromechanical, electrical, electronic, telecommunication, photo/opto-electric, chemical, etc. (possibly computerised) sensor, actuator tools.

In this example of a support technology we shall illustrate an abstraction of the kind of semaphore signalling one encounters at road intersections, that is, hubs. The example is indeed an abstraction: we do not model the actual "machinery" of road sensors, hub-side monitoring & control boxes, and the actuators of the green/yellow/red sempahore lamps. But, eventually, one has to, all of it, as part of domain modelling.

—————————— Example 8: Hub Sempahores ——————————

To model signalling we need to model hub and link states.

A hub (link) state is the set of all traversals that the hub (link) allows. A hub traversal is a triple of identifiers: of the link from where the hub traversal starts, of the hub being traversed, and of the link to where the hub traversal ends. A link traversal is a triple of identifiers: of the hub from where the link traversal starts, of the link being traversed, and of the hub to where the link traversal ends.

A hub (link) state space is the set of all states that the hub (link) may be in. A hub (link) state changing operation can be designated by the hub and a possibly new hub state (the link and a possibly new link state).

type

   LΣ' = L_Trav-**set**

   L_Trav = (HI × LI × HI)

   LΣ = {| lnkσ:LΣ' • syn_wf_LΣ\{lnkσ\} |}

   HΣ' = H_Trav-**set**

   H_Trav = (LI × HI × LI)

   HΣ = {| hubσ:HΣ' • wf_HΣ\{hubσ\} |}

   HΩ = HΣ-**set**, LΩ = LΣ-**set**

value

   obs_LΣ: L → LΣ, obs_LΩ: L → LΩ

   obs_HΣ: H → HΣ, obs_HΩ: H → HΩ

axiom

   $\forall$ h:H • obs_HΣ(h) $\in$ obs_HΩ(h) $\land$ $\forall$ l:L • obs_LΣ(l) $\in$ obs_LΩ(l)

value

   chg_HΣ: H × HΣ → H, chg_LΣ: L × LΣ → L

   chg_HΣ(h,hσ) **as** h$'$

     pre hσ $\in$ obs_HΩ(h) **post** obs_HΣ(h$'$)=hσ

   chg_LΣ(l,lσ) **as** l$'$

     pre lσ $\in$ obs_LΩ(h) **post** obs_HΣ(l$'$)=lσ

Well, so far we have indicated that there is an operation that can change hub and link states. But one may debate whether those operations shown are really examples of a support technology. (That is, one could equally well claim that they remain examples of intrinsic facets.) We may accept that and then ask the question: How to effect the described state changing functions ? In a simple street crossing a semaphore does not instantaneously change from red to green in one direction while changing from green to red in the cross direction. Rather there is are intermediate sequences of, for example, not necessarily synchronised green/yellow/red and red/yellow/green states to help avoid vehicle crashes and to prepare vehicle drivers. Our "solution" is to modify the hub state notion.

type

   Colour == red | yellow | green

   X = LI×HI×LI×Colour [crossings **of** a hub]

   HΣ = X-**set** [hub states]

value

   obs_HΣ: H → HΣ, xtr_Xs: H → X-**set**

   xtr_Xs(h) $\equiv$

      \{(li,hi,li$'$,c)|li,li$'$:LI,hi:HI,c:Colour•\{li,li$'$\}$\subseteq$obs_LIs(h)$\land$hi=obs_HI(h)\}

axiom

   $\forall$ n:N,h:H • h $\in$ obs_Hs(n) $\Rightarrow$ obs_HΣ(h)$\subseteq$xtr_Xs(h) $\land$

     $\forall$ (li1,hi2,li3,c),(li4,hi5,li6,c$'$):X •

       \{(li1,hi2,li3,c),(li4,hi5,li6,c$'$)\}$\subseteq$obs_HΣ(h) $\land$

       li1=li4 $\land$ hi2=hi5 $\land$ li3=li6 $\Rightarrow$ c=c$'$

We consider the colouring, or any such scheme, an aspect of a support technology facet. There remains, however, a description of how the technology that supports the intermediate sequences of colour changing hub states.

We can think of each hub being provided with a mapping from pairs of "stable" (that is non-yellow coloured) hub states ($h\sigma_i$, $h\sigma_f$) to well-ordered sequences of intermediate "un-stable' (that is yellow coloured) hub states paired with some time interval information $\langle (h\sigma', t\delta'), (h\sigma'', t\delta''), \ldots, (h\sigma'^{\cdots'}, t\delta'^{\cdots'}) \rangle$ and so that each of these intermediate states can be set, according to the time interval information,[1] before the final hub state ($h\sigma_f$) is set.

type
    TI [time interval]
    Signalling = $(H\Sigma \times TI)^*$
    Sema = $(H\Sigma \times H\Sigma) \xrightarrow{\sim}{_m}$ Signalling
value
    obs_Sema: H → Sema
    chg_HΣ: H × HΣ → H
    chg_HΣ_Seq: H × HΣ → H
    chg_HΣ(h,hσ) **as** h′ **pre** hσ ∈ obs_HΩ(h) **post** obs_HΣ(h′)=hσ
    chg_HΣ_Seq(h,hσ) ≡
        let sigseq = (obs_Sema(h))(obs_Σ(h),hσ) **in** sig_seq(h)(sigseq) **end**

    sig_seq: H → Signalling → H
    sig_seq(h)(sigseq) ≡
        if sigseq=$\langle\rangle$ **then** h **else**
        let (hσ,tδ) = **hd** sigseq **in**
        let h′ = chg_HΣ(h,hσ); **wait** tδ;
        sig_seq(h′)(**tl** sigseq) **end end end**

Management and Organisation

Management. By *domain management* we mean people (i) who determine, formulate and thus set standards (cf. rules and regulations, a later lecture topic) concerning strategic, tactical and operational decisions; (ii) who ensure that these decisions are passed on to (lower) levels of management, and to "floor" staff; (iii) who make sure that such orders, as they were, are indeed carried out; (iv) who handle undesirable deviations in the carrying out of these orders cum decisions; and (v) who "backstop" complaints from lower management levels and from floor staff.

Organisation. By *domain organisation* we mean the structuring of management and non-management staff levels; the allocation of strategic, tactical and operational concerns to within management and non-management staff levels; and hence the "lines of command": who does what and who reports to whom — administratively and functionally.

Examples. Formalisation of the next example is found in Sect. 3.2, Pages 18–21.

─────────── Example 9: Bus Transport Management & Organisation ───────────

In Sect. 3.2, Pages 18–21, we illustrate what is there called a contract language. "Programs" in that language are either contracts or are orders to perform the actions permitted or obligated by contracts. The language in question is one of managing bus traffic on a net. The **management & organisation** of bus traffic involves contractors issuing contracts, contractees acting according to contracts, busses (owned or leased) by contractees, and the bus traffic on the (road) net. Contractees, i.e., bus operators, `"start"` buses according to a contract timetable, `"cancel"` buses if and when deemed necessary, `"insert"` rush-hour and other buses if and when deemed necessary, and, acting as contractors, `"sub-contract"` sub-contractees to operate bus lines, for example, when the issuing contractor is not able to operate these bus lines, i.e., not able to fulfill contractual obligations, due to unavailability of buses or staff. Clearly the programs of bus contract languages are "executed" according to **management** decisions and the sub-contracting "hierarchy" reflects **organisational** facets.

Rules and Regulations. Human stakeholders act in the domain, whether clients, workers, managers, suppliers, regulatory authorities, or other. Their actions are guided and constrained by rules and regulations. These are sometimes implicit, that is, not "written down". But we can talk about rules and regulations as if they were explicitly formulated.

The main difference between rules and regulations is that rules express properties that must hold and regulations express state changes that must be effected if rules are observed broken.

Rules and regulations are directed not only at human behaviour but also at expected behaviours of support technologies.

Rules and regulations are formulated by enterprise staff, management or workers, and/or by business and industry associations, for example in the form of binding or guiding national, regional or international standards[2], and/or by public regulatory agencies.

Domain Rules. By a *domain rule* we mean some text which prescribes how people or equipment are expected to behave when dispatching their duty, respectively when performing their functions.

Domain Regulations. By a *domain regulation* we mean some text which prescribes what remedial actions are to be taken when it is decided that a rule has not been followed according to its intention.

─────────

[2] Viz.: ISO (International Organisation for Standardisation, www.iso.org/iso/-home.htm), CENELEC (European Committee for Electrotechnical Standardization, www.cenelec.eu/Cenelec/Homepage.htm), etc.

Two Informal Examples. The two informal examples will be followed up by sketches of formalisation.

――――― Example 10: Trains at Stations: Available Station Rule and Regulation ―――――

– Rule: In China the arrival and departure of trains at, respectively from, railway stations is subject to the following rule:

> In any three-minute interval at most one train may either arrive to or depart from a railway station.

– Regulation: *If it is discovered that the above rule is not obeyed,* then there is some regulation which prescribes administrative or legal management and/or staff action, as well as some correction to the railway traffic.

――――― Example 11: Trains Along Lines: Free Sector Rule and Regulation ―――――

– Rule: In many countries railway lines (between stations) are segmented into blocks or sectors. The purpose is to stipulate that if two or more trains are moving along the line, then:

> There must be at least one free sector (i.e., without a train) between any two trains along a line.

– Regulation: *If it is discovered that the above rule is not obeyed,* then there is some regulation which prescribes administrative or legal management and/or staff action, as well as some correction to the railway traffic.

A Formal Example. We shall develop the above example (11, Page 14) into a partial, formal specification. That is, not complete, but "complete enough" for the reader to see what goes on.

――――― Example 12: Continuation of Example 11 Page 14 ―――――

We start by analysing the text of the rule and regulation. The rule text: *There must be at least one free sector (i.e., without a train) between any two trains along a line.* contains the following terms: free (a predicate), sector (an entity), train (an entity) and line (an entity). We shall therefore augment our formal model to reflect these terms. We start by modelling sectors and sector descriptors, lines and train position descriptors, we assume what a train is,, and then we model the predicate free.

type
    Sect$'$ = H × L × H,
    SectDescr = HI × LI × HI
    Sect = {|(h,l,h$'$):Sect$'$ • obs_HIs(l)={obs_HI(h),obs_HI(h$'$)}|}
    SectDescr = {|(hi,li,hi$'$):SectDescr$'$ •
                        ∃ (h,l,j$'$):Sect•obs_HIs(l)={obs_HI(h),obs_HI(h$'$)}|}

$Line' = Sect^*,$

$Line = \{|line:Line' \cdot wf\_Line(line)|\}$

$TrnPos' = SectDescr^*$

$TrnPos =$

$\quad \{|trnpos':TrnPos' \cdot \exists\ line:Line \cdot conv\_Line\_to\_TrnPos(line)=trnpos'|\}$

value

wf_Line: $Line' \rightarrow$ **Bool**

wf_Line(line) $\equiv$

$\quad \forall\ i:$**Nat** $\cdot\ \{i,i+1\} \subseteq$ **inds**(line) $\Rightarrow$

$\qquad$ **let** $(\_,l,h)=line(i),(h',l',\_)=line(i+1)$ **in** $h=h'$ **end**

conv_Line_to_TrnPos: $Line \rightarrow TrnPos$

conv_Line_to_TrnPos(line) $\equiv$

$\quad \langle(obs\_HI(h),obs\_LI(l),obs\_HI(h'))|1 \leq i \leq$ **len** $line \wedge line(i)=(h,l,h')\rangle$

The function lines yield all lines of a net.

value

lines: $N \rightarrow Line$-**set**

lines(hs,ls) $\equiv$

$\quad$ **let** lns $= \{\langle(h,l,h')\rangle|h,h':H,l:L \cdot proper\_line((h,l,h'),(hs,ls))\}$

$\qquad\qquad \cup\ \{ln\hat{\ }ln'|ln,l':Line \cdot \{ln,ln'\} \subseteq lns \wedge adjacent(ln,ln')\}$ **in**

$\quad$ lns **end**

The function lines makes use of an auxiliary function:

adjacent: $Line \times Line \rightarrow$ **Bool**

adjacent$((\_,l,h),(h',l',\_)) \equiv h=h'$

$\quad$ **pre** $\{obs\_LI(l),obs\_LI(l')\} \subseteq obs\_LIs(h)$

We reformulate traffic in terms of train positions.

type

$TF = T \ \overrightarrow{m} \ (N \times (TN \ \overrightarrow{m} \ TrnPos))$

We formulate a necessary property of traffic, namely that its train positions correspond to actual lines of the net.

value

wf_TF: $TF \rightarrow$ **Bool**

wf_TF(tf) $\equiv$

$\quad \forall\ t:T \cdot t \in$ **dom** tf $\Rightarrow$

$\qquad$ **let** $((hs,ls),trnposs) = tf(t)$ **in**

$\qquad \forall\ trn:TN \cdot trn \in$ **dom** trnposs $\Rightarrow$

$\qquad\quad \exists\ line:Line \cdot line \in lines(hs,ls)\ \wedge$

$\qquad\qquad trnposs(trn) = conv\_Line\_to\_TrnPos(line)$ **end**

Nothing prevents two or more trains from occupying overlapping train positions. They have "merely" – and regrettably – crashed. But such is the domain. So wf_TF(tf) is not part of an axiom of traffic, merely a desirable property.

value

has_free_Sector: $TN \times T \to TF \to$ **Bool**
has_free_Sector(trn,(hs,ls),t)(tf) $\equiv$
    let ((hs,ls),trnposs) = tf(t) **in**
    (trn $\notin$ **dom** trnposs $\lor$ (tn $\in$ **dom** trnposs(t) $\land$
    $\exists$ ln:Line • ln $\in$ lines(hs,ls) $\land$
        is_prefix(trnposs(trn),ln))(hs,ls)) $\land$
        $\sim\exists$ trn′:TN • trn′ $\in$ **dom** trnposs $\land$ trn′$\neq$trn $\land$
           trnposs(trn′)=conv_Line_to_TrnPos($\langle$follow_Sect(ln)(hs,ls)$\rangle$))
    end
    pre exists_follow_Sect(ln)(hs,ls)

is_prefix: $Line \times Line \to N \to$ **Bool**
is_prefix(ln,ln′)(hs,ls) $\equiv$ $\exists$ ln″:Line • ln″ $\in$ lines(hs,ls) $\land$ ln⌢ln″=ln′

The test ln″ $\in$ lines(hs,ls) in the definition of is_prefix is not needed for the cases where that function is invoked as only shown here.

    The function follow_Sect yields the sector following the argument line, if such a sector exists.

exists_follow_Sect: Line $\to$ Net $\to$ **Bool**
exists_follow_Sect(ln)(hs,ls) $\equiv$
    $\exists$ ln′:Line•ln′ $\in$ lines(hs,ls)$\land$ln⌢ln′ $\in$ lines(hs,ls)
    pre ln $\in$ lines(hs,ls)
follow_Sect: Line $\to$ Net $\overset{\sim}{\to}$ Sect
follow_Sect(ln)(hs,ls) $\equiv$
    let ln′:Line•ln′ $\in$ lines(hs,ls)$\land$ln⌢ln′ $\in$ lines(hs,ls) **in hd** ln′ **end**
    pre line $\in$ lines(hs,ls)$\land$exists_follow_Sect(ln)(hs,ls)

We doubly recursively define a function free_sector_rule(tf)(r). tf is that part of the traffic which has yet to be "searched" for non-free sectors. Thus tf is "counted" up from a first time t till the traffic tf is empty. That is, we assume a finite definition set tf . r is like a traffic but without the net. Initially r is the empty traffic. r is "counted" up from "earliest" cases of trains with no free sector ahead of them. The recursion stops, for a given time when there are no more train positions to be "searched" for that time; and when the "to-be-searched" traffic is empty.

type
    TNPoss = T $\underset{m}{\to}$ (TN $\to$ TrnPos)
value
    free_sector_rule: $TF \times TF \to$ TNPoss

free_sector_rule(tf)(r) ≡
   if tf=[ ] **then** r **else**
   let t:T•t ∈ **dom** tf∧smallest(t)(tf) **in**
   let ((hs,ls),trnposs)=tf(t) **in**
   if trnposs=[ ] **then** free_sector_rule(tf\{t})(r) **else**
   let tn:TN•tn ∈ **dom** trnposs **in**
   if exists_follow_Sect(trnposs(tn))(hs,ls)
          ∧∼has_free_Sector(tn,(hs,ls),t)(tf)
       then
          let r′ = **if** t ∈ **dom** r **then** r **else** r ∪ [t↦[ ]] **end in**
          free_sector_rule(tf†[t↦((hs,ls),trnposs\{tn})])
                         (r†[t↦r(t)∪[tn↦trnposs(tn)]]) **end**
       else
          free_sector_rule(tf†[t↦((hs,ls),trnposs\{trn})])(r)
   end end end end end end

smallest(t)(tf) ≡ ∼∃ t′:T• t′isin **dom** tf∧t′<t **pre** t ∈ **dom** tf

---

Script Languages [Contract Languages]. By a *domain script language* we mean the definition of a set of licenses and actions where these licenses when issued and actions when performed have morally obliging power.

By a *domain contract language* a domain script language whose licenses and actions have legally binding power, that is, their issuance and their invocation may be contested in a court of law.

A Script Language. The next examples exemplify narrative and formal description of syntax of bus timetables as well as formal description of semantics of bus timetables.

_____ Example 13: Narrative Syntax of a Bus Timetable Script Language _____

18. Time is a concept covered earlier. Bus lines and bus rides have unique names (across any set of time tables). Hub and link identifiers, HI, LI, were treated from the very beginning.
19. A TimeTable associates to Bus Line Identifiers a set of Journies.
20. Journies are designated by a pair of a BusRoute and a set of BusRides.
21. A BusRoute is a triple of the Bus Stop of origin, a list of zero, one or more intermediate Bus Stops and a destination Bus Stop.
22. A set of BusRides associates, to each of a number of Bus Identifiers a Bus Schedule.
23. A Bus Schedule a triple of the initial departure Time, a list of zero, one or more intermediate bus stop Times and a destination arrival Time.

24. A Bus Stop (i.e., its position) is a Fraction of the distance along a link (identified by a Link Identifier) from an identified hub to an identified hub.
25. A Fraction is a **Real** properly between 0 and 1.
26. The Journies must be well-formed in the context of some net.

_____ Example 14: Formal Syntax of a Bus Timetable Script Language _____

type
18. T, BLId, BId
19. TT = BLId $\overrightarrow{m}$ Journies
20. Journies$'$ = BusRoute × BusRides
21. BusRoute = BusStop × BusStop* × BusStop
22. BusRides = BId $\overrightarrow{m}$ BusSched
23. BusSched = T × T* × T
24. BusStop == mkBS(s_fhi:HI,s_ol:LI,s_f:Frac,s_thi:HI)
25. Frac = {|r:**Real**•0<r<1|}
26. Journies = {|j:Journies$'$•∃ n:N • wf_Journies(j)(n)|}

_____ Example 15: Semantics of a Bus Timetable Script Language _____

type
  Bus
value
  obs_X: Bus → X
type
  BusTraffic = T $\overrightarrow{m}$ (N × (BusNo $\overrightarrow{m}$ (Bus × BPos)))
  BPos = atHub | onLnk | atBS
  atHub == mkAtHub(s_fl:LIs_hi:HI,s_tl:LI)
  onLnk == mkOnLnk(s_fhi:HI,s_ol:LI,s_f:Frac,s_thi:HI)
  atBSt == mkAtBS(s_fhi:HI,s_ol:LI,s_f:Frac,s_thi:HI)
  Frac = {|r:**Real**•0<r<1|}
value
  gen_BusTraffic: TT → BusTraffic-**infset**
  gen_BusTraffic(tt) **as** btrfs
    post ∀ btrf:BusTraffic • btrf ∈ btrfs ⇒ on_time(btrf)(tt)

We omit definition of several functions, including the interesting on_time predicate.

A Contract Language. We shall, as for the timetable script, just hint at a contract language.

─────── Example 16: Informal Syntax of Bus Transport Contracts ───────

An example contract can be 'schematised':

con_id: **contractor** corn **contracts contractee** ceen
    to perform operations "start","cancel","insert","subcontract"
    with respect to bus timetable tt.

─────── Example 17: Formal Syntax of a Bus Transport Contracts ───────

type
    CId, CNm
    Contract = CId × CNm × CNm × Body
    Body = Op-**set** × TT
    Op == "conduct" | "cancel" | "insert" | "subcontract"

an example contract:

    (cid,cor,cee,({"start","cancl","insrt","subcon"},tt))

─────── Example 18: Informal Syntax of a Bus Transport Actions ───────

Example actions can be schematised:

(a)   cid: **start bus ride** (blid,bid) **at time** t
(b)   cid: **cancel bus ride** (blid,bid) **at time** t
(c)   cid: **insert bus ride like** (blid,bid) **at time** t

The schematised license (Page 19) shown earlier is almost like an action; here is
the action form:

(d)   cid: **contractee** cee **is granted a license** cid$'$
           to perform operations {"start","cancel","insert",subcontract" }
           with respect to timetable tt$'$.

─────── Example 19: Formal Syntax of a Bus Transport Actions ───────

type
    Action = CNm × CId × (SubLic | SmpAct) × Time
    SmpAct = Start | Cancel | Insert
    DoRide == mkSta(s_blid:BLId,s_bid:BId)
    Cancel == mkCan(s_blid:BLId,s_bid:BId)

Insert = mkIns(s_blid:BLId,s_bid:BId)
SubCon == mkCon(sci:ConId,sce:CNm,sbd:(sos:Op-set,stt:TT))

examples:
(a) (cee,cid,mkRid(blid,id),t)
(b) (cee,cid,mkCan(blid,id),t)
(c) (cee,cid,mkIns(blid,id),t)
(d) (cee,cid,mkCon(cid′,({″start″,″cancl″,″insrt″,″subcon″},tt′),t))

where: cid′ = generate_ConId(cid,cee,t)

──────── Example 20: Semantics of a Bus Transport Contract Language, I ────────

type
  Body = Op-set × TT
  ConΣ = RcvConΣ×SubConΣ×CorBusΣ
  RcvConΣ = CNm $\overrightarrow{m}$ (CId $\overrightarrow{m}$ (Body×TT))
  SubConΣ = CNm $\overrightarrow{m}$ (CId $\overrightarrow{m}$ Body)
  BusNo
  BusΣ = FreeBusesΣ × ActvBusesΣ × BusHistsΣ
  FreeBusesΣ = BusStop $\overrightarrow{m}$ BusNo-set
  ActvBusesΣ = BusNo $\overrightarrow{m}$ BusInfo
  BusInfo = BLId×BId×CId×CNm×BusTrace
  BusHistsΣ = Bno $\overrightarrow{m}$ BusInfo*
  BusTrace = (Time×BusStop)*
  CorBusΣ = CNm $\overrightarrow{m}$ (CId $\overrightarrow{m}$ ((BLId×BId) $\overrightarrow{m}$ (BNo×BusTrace)))
  AllBs=CNm $\overrightarrow{m}$ BusNo-set

──────── Example 21: Semantics of a Bus Transport Contract Language, II ────────

value
  cns:CNm-set, busnos:BNo-set, ibσ:IBΣs=CNm $\overrightarrow{m}$ BusΣ,
  rcor,icee:CNm • rcor $\notin$ cns∧icee $\in$ cns, itr:BusTraffic,
  rcid:ConId, iops:Op-set={″subcontract″}, itt:TT, t$_0$:Time
  allbs:AllBs • **dom** allbs=cns ∪ {rcor}∧∪ **rng** allbs=busnos,
  icon:Contract=(rcid,rcor,icee,(iops,itt)),
  icσ:ConΣ=([icee $\mapsto$ [rcid $\mapsto$ [icee $\mapsto$ icon]]]
                    ∪ [cee $\mapsto$ [] | cee:CNm • cee $\in$ cnms\{icee}],[],[]),
  system: **Unit** → **Unit**
  system() ≡
    cntrcthldr(icee)(ilσ(icee),ibσ(icee))
    ‖(‖{cntrcthldr(cee)(ilσ(cee),ibσ(cee))|cee:CNm•cee $\in$ cns\{icee}})

$\|(\|\{\text{bus\_ride}(b,cee)(rcor,''\texttt{nil}'')$
    $\mid cee:CNm,b:BusNo\bullet cee \in \textbf{dom} \text{ allbs} \wedge b \in \text{allbs}(cee)\})$
$\|\text{time\_clock}(t_0) \parallel \text{bus\_traffic}(itr)$

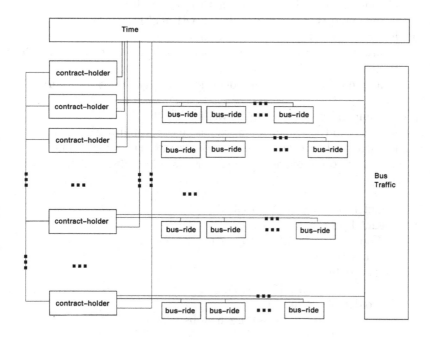

Fig. 1. An organisation

The thin lines of Fig. 1 denote communication "channels".

Human Behaviour. By *human behaviour* we mean any of a quality spectrum of carrying out assigned work: from (i) **careful, diligent** and **accurate**, via (ii) **sloppy** dispatch, and (iii) **delinquent** work, to (iv) outright **criminal** pursuit.

──────────── Example 22: A Diligent Operation ────────────

The int_Insert operation of Page 7 was expressed without stating necessary pre-conditions:

27. The insert operation takes an Insert command and a net and yields either a new net or **chaos** for the case where the insertion command "is at odds" with, that is, is not semantically well-formed with respect to the net.
28. We characterise the "is not at odds", i.e., is semantically well-formed, that is: pre_int_Insert(op)(hs,ls), as follows: it is a propositional function which applies to Insert actions, op, and nets, (hs,ls), and yields a truth value if the

below relation between the command arguments and the net is satisfied.
Let (hs,ls) be a value of type N.

29. If the command is of the form 2oldH(hi′,l,hi′) then
    ⋆1 hi′ must be the identifier of a hub in hs,
    ⋆2 l must not be in ls and its identifier must (also) not be observable in
       ls, and
    ⋆3 hi″ must be the identifier of a(nother) hub in hs.
30. If the command is of the form 1oldH1newH(hi,l,h) then
    ⋆1 hi must be the identifier of a hub in hs,
    ⋆2 l must not be in ls and its identifier must (also) not be observable in
       ls, and
    ⋆3 h must not be in hs and its identifier must (also) not be observable in
       hs.
31. If the command is of the form 2newH(h′,l,h″) then
    ⋆1 h′ — left to the reader as an exercise (see formalisation !),
    ⋆2 l — left to the reader as an exercise (see formalisation !), and
    ⋆3 h″ — left to the reader as an exercise (see formalisation !).

value
    28′ pre_int_Insert: Ins → N → **Bool**
    28″ pre_int_Insert(Ins(op))(hs,ls) ≡
    ⋆2   s_l(op)∉ ls ∧ obs_LI(s_l(op)) ∉ iols(ls) ∧
           case op **of**
    29   2oldH(hi′,l,hi″) →
              {hi′,hi″}⊆iohs(hs),
    30   1oldH1newH(hi,l,h) →
              hi ∈ iohs(hs)∧h∉ hs∧obs_HI(h)∉ iohs(hs),
    31   2newH(h′,l,h″) →
              {h′,h″}∩ hs={}∧{obs_HI(h′),obs_HI(h″)}∩ iohs(hs)={}
           end

These must be carefully expressed and adhered to in order for staff to be said
to carry out the link insertion operation accurately.

┌──────── Example 23: A Sloppy via Delinquent to Criminal Operation ────────┐

We replace systematic checks (∧) with partial checks (∨), etcetera, and
obtain various degrees of sloppy to delinquent, or even criminal behaviour.

value
    28′ pre_int_Insert: Ins → N → **Bool**
    28″ pre_int_Insert(Ins(op))(hs,ls) ≡
    ⋆2   s_l(op)∉ ls ∧ obs_LI(s_l(op)) ∉ iols(ls) ∧
           case op **of**
    29   2oldH(hi′,l,hi″) →
              hi′ ∈ iohs(hs)∨hi″isin iohs(hs),

30   1oldH1newH(hi,l,h) →
                hi ∈ iohs(hs)∨h∉ hs∨obs_HI(h)∉ iohs(hs),
31   2newH(h',l,h'') →
                {h',h''}∩ hs={}∨{obs_HI(h'),obs_HI(h'')}∩ iohs(hs)={}
        end

Dialectics. So now you should have a practical and technical "feel" for domain engineering: What it takes to express a domain model.

But there is lots' more: We have not shown you (i) the rôle of domain stakeholders: (i.1) how to identify them, (i.2) how to involve them and (i.3) how they help validate resulting domain descriptions. (ii) the domain (ii.1) knowledge acquisition and (ii.2) analysis processes, (ii) the domain (ii.1) model verification and (ii.2) validation and processes, and (iii) the domain theory R&D process.

Can we agree that we cannot, as professional software engineers, start on gathering requirements, let alone prescribing these before we have understood the domain ? Can we agree that, "ideally", we must therefore first R&D the domain model before we can embark on any requirements prescription process ?

By "ideally" we mean the following: Ideally domain engineering should fully precede requirements engineering, but for many practical reasons[3] we must co-develop domain descriptions "hand-in-hand" with requirements prescriptions. And that is certainly feasible, when done with care. So we shall, for years assume this to be the case.

Pragmatics. While the software industry "humps along": co-developing domain descriptions and requirements with their clients, or, for COTS, with their marketing departments, private and public research centres should and will embark on large scale (5–8 manyears/year), long range projects (5–8 year) foundational research and development (R&D) of infrastructure component domain models of the financial service industry: banking (all forms); insurance (all forms); portfolio management; securities trading: brokers, traders, commodities and stock etc. exchanges; transportation: road, rail, air, and sea; healthcare: physicians, hospitals, clinics, pharmacies, etc.; "the market": consumers, retailers, wholesalers, and the supply chain; etcetera.

3.3   Further on the Modelling of Domains

[6] Part IV, Chaps. 8–16 covers techniques of domain modelling.

---

[3] Among the many practical reasons for not first fully developing a domain model are: (a) it takes literally "ages" to develop a complete domain model, (b) in fact one will never achieve complete domain models, and (c) software houses and their clients cannot wait for this software!

4 Requirements Engineering

We cannot possibly, within the confines of a seminar talk and a reasonably sized paper cover, however superficially, both informal and formal examples of requirements engineering.

Instead we shall just briefly mention the major stages and sub-stages of requirements modeling:

- **Domain Requirements:** those which can be expressed sôlely using terms from the domain description;
- **Interface Requirements:** those which can be expressed using terms both from the domain description and from IT; and
- **Machine Requirements:** those which can be expressed sôlely using terms from IT.

_____ IEEE Definition of Requirements _____

By IT requirements we understand (cf. IEEE Standard 610.12): *"A condition or capability needed by a user to solve a problem or achieve an objective on a computing machine"*.

By computing *machine* we shall understand a, or the, combination of computer (etc.) *hardware* and *software* that is the target for, or result of the required computing systems development.

4.1 Domain Requirements

_____ Domain Requirements _____

By *domain requirements* we mean such which can be expressed sôlely using terms from the domain description

To construct the domain requirements the domain engineer together with the various groups of requirements stakeholder "apply" the following "domain-to-requirements" operations to a copy of the domain description: **projection, instantiation, determination, extension** and **fitting**. First we briefly characterise these.

The Domain-to-Requirements Operations. The 'domain-to-requirements' operations cannot be automated. They increasingly "turn" the copy of the domain description into a domain requirements prescription.

Projection removes, from that emerging requirements document all the domain phenomena and concepts for which the customer does not need IT support.

_____ Simple Linear Road: Projection _____

Our requirements is for a simple road: a linear sequence of links and hubs:

type

N, L, H, LI, HI
value
   obs_Hs: N → H-set, obs_Ls: N → L-set
   obs_HI: H → HI, obs_LI: L → LI
   obs_HIs: L → HI-set, obs_LIs: H → LI-set
axiom
   See Items 14–17 Pages 9–9

Instantiation makes a number of entities: *simple, operations, events and behaviours*, less abstract, more concrete.

────────────── Simple Linear Road: Instantiation ──────────────

The linear sequence consists of eaxtly 34 links.

type
   H, L,
   $N' = H \times (L \times H)^*$
   $N'' = \{|n{:}N'\bullet wf(n)|\}$
value
   wf_N'': N' → **Bool**
   wf_N''(h,(l,h)^lhl) ≡
     len lhl = 33 ∧
     obs_HI(l)=obs_HI(h) ∧
     ∀ i,j:**Nat** • {i,i+1,j}⊆**inds** lhl ⇒
       let (li,hi)=lhl(i),(li',hi')=lhl(i+1),(lj,hj)=lhl(j) **in**
       h≠hi∧i≠j⇒li≠lj∧hi≠hj∧
       obs_HIs(li')={obs_HI(hi),obs_HI(hi')}∧
       obs_LIs(hi)∩ obs_LI(li)≠{}∧obs_LIs(hi')∩ obs_LI(li')≠{} **end**
   obs_N: N'' → N
   obs_N(h,lhl) ≡
     ({h}∪{hi|(hi,li):(L×H)•(hi,li)∈ **elems** lhl},
       {li|(hi,li):(L×H)•(hi,li)∈ **elems** lhl})

wf_N' secures linearity; obs_N allows abstraction from more concrete N'' to more abstract N.

Determination makes the emerging requirements entities more determinate, that is, removes undesired non-determinism.

────────────── Simple Linear Road: Determination ──────────────

All links and all non-end hubs are open in both directions; we leave end-hub states undefined — but see below, under 'Extension'.

type
   LΣ = (HI×HI)-set, LΩ

$H\Sigma = (LI{\times}LI)\text{-}\mathbf{set},\ H\Omega$

value

   obs_LΩ: L $\rightarrow$ LΩ

   obs_HΩ: H $\rightarrow$ HΩ

axiom

   $\forall$ (h,$\langle$(l1,h2)$\rangle$^lhl):N'' •

     obs_LΣ(l1)={obs_HI(h),obs_HI(h2)}$\wedge$

     $\forall$ i,i+1:**Nat** • {i,i+1}$\subseteq$**inds** lhl $\Rightarrow$

       let (li,hi)=lhl(i),(li′,hi′)=lhl(i+1),(lj,hj)=lhl(j) **in**

       obs_LΩ(li′)={{(obs_HI(hi),obs_HI(hi′)),(obs_HI(hi′),obs_HI(hi))}}$\wedge$

       obs_HΩ(hi)={{(obs_LI(li),obs_LI(li′)),(obs_LI(li′),obs_LI(li))}} **end**

The last two lines of the axiom express that links are always open two ways and that hubs are always open for through traffic.

Extension introduces new, computable entities that were not possible in the non-IT domain.

———————————— Simple Linear Road: Extension ————————————

We extend the model of linear roads by introducing the concept of a Hub-Plaza: this is an area "around" each hub from where and into where there is always access onto, respectively from the hub:

type

   HP, HPI

   $H\Sigma' = (LI{\times}LI)\text{-}\mathbf{set} \cup (LI{\times}HPI)\text{-}\mathbf{set} \cup (HPI{\times}LI)\text{-}\mathbf{set}$

   $H\Omega' = H\Sigma'\text{-}\mathbf{set}$

value

   obs_HΩ': H $\rightarrow$ HΩ'

   obs_HP: H $\rightarrow$ HP

   obs_HPI: HP $\rightarrow$ HPI

axiom

   $\forall$ h,h′:H • h$\neq$h′ $\Rightarrow$

     obs_HP(h)$\neq$obs_HP(h′)$\wedge$obs_HPI(obs_HP(h))$\neq$obs_HPI(obs_HP(h′)),

   $\forall$ (h,(l,h)^lhl):N'' •

     $\forall$ i,j:**Nat** • {i,i+1,j}$\subseteq$**inds** lhl $\Rightarrow$

       let (li,hi)=lhl(i),(li′,hi′)=lhl(i+1),(lj,hj)=lhl(j) **in**

       obs_HΩ'(h)=

         {{(obs_LI(l),obs_HPI(obs_HP(h))),(obs_HPI(obs_HP(h)),obs_LI(l))}}

       $\forall$ i,i+1:**Nat** • {i,i+1}$\subseteq$**inds** lhl $\Rightarrow$

        let (_,hi)=lhl(i),(_,hi′)=lhl(i+1),(_,hj)=lhl(j) **in**

        obs_HΩ'(hi)=

          {{(obs_LI(li),obs_LI(li′)),

             (obs_LI(li′),obs_LI(li)),

           (obs_HPI(obs_HP(hi)),obs_LI(li)),

             (obs_HPI(obs_HP(hi)),obs_LI(li′))

(obs_LI(li),obs_HPI(obs_HP(hi))),
 (obs_LI(li′),obs_HPI(obs_HP(hi)))}}
end end

The obs_HΩ' lines of the axiom with respect to that of 'Determination' express plaza access.

Fitting merges the domain requirements prescription with those of other, more-or-less independent IT developments.

• • •

The domain requirements examples are necessarily "microscopic". The very briefly outlined domain requirements methodology has many fascinating aspects — more fully covered in [4,5,6] and the upcoming [7].

4.2 Interface Requirements

—————————————— Interface Requirements ——————————————

By *interface requirements* we mean such which those which can be expressed using terms from both the domain description and from IT, that is, terminology of hardware and of software.

When phenomena and concepts of the domain are also to be represented by the machine, these phenomena and concepts are said to be shared between the domain and the machine; the requirements therefore need be expressed both in terms of phenomena and concepts of the domain and in terms of phenomena and concepts of the machine.

Shared Phenomena and Concepts. A shared phenomenon or concept is either a simple entity, an operation, an event or a behaviour.

Shared simple entities need to be initially input to the machine and their machine representation need to be regularly, perhaps real-time refreshed.

Shared operations need to be interactively performed by human or other agents of the domain and by the machine.

Shared events are shared in the sense that their occurrence in the domain (in the machine) must be made known to the machine (to the domain).

Shared behaviours need to occur in the domain and in the machine by alternating means, that is, a protocol need be devised.

For each of these four kinds of interface requirements the requirements engineers work with the requirements stakeholders to determine the properties of these forms of sharing. These interface requirements are then narrated and formalised. They are always "anchored" in specific items of the domain description.

• • •

The very briefly outlined interface requirements methodology has many fascinating aspects — more fully covered in [4,5,6] and the upcoming [7].

4.3 Machine Requirements

_____ Machine Requirements _____

By *machine requirements* we mean those which can be expressed sôlely using terms from the machine, that is, terminology of hardware and of software.

We shall not cover any principles or techniques for developing machine requirements, but shall just list the very many issues that must be captured by a machine requirements.

- Performance
  - Storage
  - Time
  - Software Size
- Dependability
  - Accessibility
  - Availability
  - Reliability
- Robustness
  - Safety
  - Security
- Maintenance
  - Adaptive
  - Corrective
  - Perfective
  - Preventive
- Platform (P)
  - Development P
  - Demonstration P
  - Execution P
  - Maintenance P
- Documentation Requirements
- Other Requirements

The machine requirements are usually not so easily, formalised, if at all, with today's specification language tools. Extra great care must therefore be exerted in their narration. Some formal modelling calculations, like fault (tree) analysis, can be made in order to justify quantitative requirements.

4.4 Further on the Modelling of Requirements

[6, Part V, Chaps. 17–24] and the upcoming [7] covers techniques of requirements modelling, including machine requirements in far more detail than here enumerated.

5 Why "Current" Requirements Engineering (RE) Is Flawed

Current, conventional requirements engineering has no scientific basis. The requirements engineering sketched in this paper starts with a domain model. The domain model provides the scientific basis. "Derivation" of domain and interface requirement provides a further scientific basis. The fact that the requirements engineering models advocated in this paper also are formalised provides a final scientific basis. The separation of concerns: (the formalised) domain model, in-and-by-itself, and the (the formalised) requirements projection, instantiation, determination, extension and fitting operations provide a basis for scientific analysis. Current, conventional RE does not have these bases. If we are to pursue Software Engineering in a professionally responsible manner then requirements engineering must be pursued in a scientifically responsible manner.

6   Conclusion

6.1   Summary — A Wrap Up

We have illustrated the triptych concept: from domains via requirements to software. We spent most time on domain engineering. We just sketched major requirements engineering concepts. And we assumed you know how to turn formal requirements into correct software designs !

6.2   Dialectics

So, are we clear on this: (i) that we must understand the domain before we express the requirements; (ii) that we can "derive" major parts of the requirements prescription from the domain description; (iii) that domains are far more "stable" than requirements; (iv) that prescribing requirements with no prior domain description is thoroughly unsound; (v) that describing [prescribing] domains [requirements] both informally (narratives) and formally (formal specifications) helps significantly towards consistent specifications; and (vi) that we must therefore embrace the triptych: from domains via requirements to software.

Implication: Theory-work. So, get on with it ! Pick up one or another of the new domain engineering ideas: business processes, facets, domain theories, etc., or the new requirements engineering ideas: projection, instantiation, determination, extension and fitting, research them, write papers about it.

Implication: Engineering-work — Extrovert Applications. But do it in connection with real life, actual domains: banking, insurance, stock exchange and brokerage, hospitalisation, bus & tax transport, rail transport, container line shipping, etcetera. That is, "build" some impressive domain theories !

Implication: Engineering-work — Introspective Applications. By introspective applications we mean such as providing software for, or such as the Internet, the Web, operating systems database management, data communication, etcetera, etcetera, Also these are lack proper domain descriptions.

6.3   For More on Domain and Requirements Engineering

For details on domain and requirements engineering we refer to:

> *Software Engineering [6]:*
> *Vol. 3: Domains, Requirements and Software Design,* XXX+766 pages.
> Texts in Theoretical Computer Science, EATCS Series, 2006 Springer

and the upcoming book:

> *From Domain to Requirements, [7]*
> *The Triptych Approach to Software Engineering*

This book (draft) has been and is the basis for lectures at (i) Univ. Henri Poincaré/INRIA, Nancy, France, Oct.-Dec. 2007; (ii) Techn. Univ. of Graz, Austria Nov.-Dec. 2008; (iii) Univ. of Saarland, Germany March 2009; (iv) Univ. of Edinburgh, Scotland, Sept.–Oct. 2009; (v) Univ. of Tokyo, Japan Fall (Oct.-Nov.) 2009.

6.4 For More on Extrovert Applications

We refer to some indicative Internet-based reports — from: www.imm.dtu.dk/~db/

- air traffic: brisbane.pdf and airtraffic.pdf;
- container line industry: container-paper.pdf;
- the 'Market': themarket.pdf;
- IT security: 5lectures/it-system-security-IS0.pdf;
- oil industry and pipelines: de-p.pdf and pipeline.pdf;
- railways: www.railwaydomain.org/;
- transportation (in general): tseb.pdf;
- logistics: logistics.pdf
- et cetera.

6.5 Software Engineering Archeology

In general I would prefer to see precise domain models of the Internet, the Web, 'Cloud Computing', Windows Vista, Linux and idealised SQL[4] as the basis for requirements and software that claim that they are "based" on the Internet, the Web, 'Cloud Computing', Windows Vista, Linux and/or SQL.

Here is clearly a fascination engineering task.

I see the Internet as an instantiation of 'Cloud Computing'.

6.6 For More on Research Topics

A number of research topics of domain theory has been outlined in [8]:

Domain Theory: Practice and Theories, Discussion of Possible Research Topics. In *ICTAC'2007*, volume 4701 of *Lecture Notes in Computer Science (eds. J.C.P. Woodcock et al.)*, pages 1–17, Heidelberg, September 2007. Springer.

Excursions in 'Philosophy of Informatics' are covered in [12,13]:

On Mereologies in Computing Science. Festschrift for Tony Hoare, Springer UK, History of Computing (ed. Bill Roscoe), 2009
An Emerging Domain Science – A Rôle for Stanisław Leśniewski's Mereology and Bertrand Russell's Philosophy of Logical Atomism. Higher-order and Symbolic Computation, Fall 2009.

---

[4] By idealised SQL I mean an SQL where relations are indeed sets, and hence that all results of SQL queries are sets. To my knowledge ORACLE SQL does not satisfy this simple property, but the FRONTBASE SQL92 system does (http://www.frontbase.com/cgi-bin/WebObjects/FrontBase)

Acknowledgements

The author thanks the organisers, the steering and the programme committee for PSI'09 for inviting me to present this paper and for funding my stay in Akademgorodok. The author also thanks Prof. Victor Ivannikov, Director, Institute of Systems Programming, Russian Academy of Science, Moscow, for funding my domestic travel in the Russian Federation, my stay in Moscow, and for inviting me to give two talks at ISPRAS. The author finally thanks Formal Methods Europe for covering my international travel, visa expenses and further miscellaneous expenses.

Bibliographical Notes

Specification languages, techniques and tools, that cover the spectrum of domain and requirements specification, refinement and verification, are dealt with in Alloy: [36], ASM: [52,53], B/event B: [1,2], CSP [31,55,56,32], DC [60,61] (Duration Calculus), Live Sequence Charts [17,27], Message Sequence Charts [33,34,35], RAISE [21,23,4,5,6,20] (RSL), Petri nets [37,47,50,49,51], Statecharts [26,28], Temporal Logic of Reactive Systems [40,41,46,48], TLA+ [38,39,42,43] (Temporal Logic of Actions), VDM [10,11,19,18], and Z [57,58,59,30,29]. Techniques for integrating 'different' formal techniques[5] are covered in [3,24,15,14,54]. The recent book on Logics of Specification Languages [9] covers ASM, B/event B, CafeObj, CASL, DC, RAISE, TLA+, VDM and Z.

References

1. Abrial, J.-R.: The B Book: Assigning Programs to Meanings. Tracts in Theoretical Computer Science. Cambridge University Press, Cambridge (1996)
2. Abrial, J.-R.: Modeling in Event-B: System and Software Engineering. Cambridge University Press, Cambridge (2009)
3. Araki, K., Galloway, A., Taguchi, K. (eds.): IFM 1999: Integrated Formal Methods. LNCS, vol. 1945. Springer, Heidelberg (1999)
4. Bjørner, D.: Software Engineering. Abstraction and Modelling. Texts in Theoretical Computer Science, the EATCS Series, vol. 1. Springer, Heidelberg (2006)
5. Bjørner, D.: Software Engineering. In: Specification of Systems and Languages, ch. 12-14 are primarily authored by Christian Krog Madsen. Specification of Systems and Languages. Texts in Theoretical Computer Science, the EATCS Series, vol. 2. Springer, Heidelberg (2006)
6. Bjørner, D.: Software Engineering. In: Domains, Requirements and Software Design. Texts in Theoretical Computer Science, the EATCS Series, vol. 3. Springer, Heidelberg (2006)
7. Bjørner, D.: From Domains to Requirements: The Triptych Approach to Software Engineering. Submitted to Springer for evaluation in 2009. Slightly incomplete draft version, approximately XXVII+160+25 pages (frontmatter, main text, appendices) (2009), http://www.imm.dtu/~db/de+re-p.pdf

---

[5] The 'difference' is primarily in the semantic types of the formal specification languages and in the proof systems of these 'different' formal techniques.

8. Bjørner, D.: Domain Theory: Practice and Theories, Discussion of Possible Research Topics. In: Jones, C.B., Liu, Z., Woodcock, J. (eds.) ICTAC 2007. LNCS, vol. 4711, pp. 1–17. Springer, Heidelberg (2007)

9. Bjørner, D., Henson, M.C. (eds.): Logics of Specification Languages. EATCS Monograph in Theoretical Computer Science. Springer, Heidelberg (2008)

10. Bjorner, D., Jones, C.B. (eds.): The Vienna Development Method: The Meta-Language. LNCS, vol. 61. Springer, Heidelberg (1978)

11. Bjørner, D., Jones, C.B. (eds.): Formal Specification and Software Development. Prentice-Hall, Englewood Cliffs (1982)

12. Bjørner, D.: On Mereologies in Computing Science Festschrift for Tony Hoare. In: Roscoe, B. (ed.) History of Computing. Springer, UK (2009)

13. Bjørner, D.: An Emerging Domain Science – A Rôle for Stanisław Leśniewski's Mereology and Bertrand Russell's Philosophy of Logical Atomism. In: Higher-order and Symbolic Computation. Springer, Heidelberg (2009)

14. Boiten, E.A., Derrick, J., Smith, G.P. (eds.): IFM 2004. LNCS, vol. 2999. Springer, Heidelberg (2004)

15. Butler, M., Petre, L., Sere, K. (eds.): IFM 2002. LNCS, vol. 2335. Springer, Heidelberg (2002)

16. Cansell, D., Méry, D.: Logical Foundations of the B Method. Computing and Informatics 22(1-2) (2003)

17. Damm, W., Harel, D.: LSCs: Breathing life into Message Sequence Charts. Formal Methods in System Design 19, 45–80 (2001); Early version appeared as Weizmann Institute Tech. Report CS98-09, April 1998. An abridged version appeared in Proc. 3rd IFIP Int. Conf. on Formal Methods for Open Object-based Distributed Systems (FMOODS 1999), pp. 293–312. Kluwer, Dordrecht (1999)

18. Fitzgerald, J.S.: The Typed Logic of Partial Functions and the Vienna Development Method. In: Logics of Specification Languages [9], pp. 453–487. Springer, Heidelberg (2008)

19. Fitzgerald, J.S., Larsen, P.G.: Developing Software using VDM-SL. Cambridge University Press, Cambridge (1997)

20. George, C., Haxthausen, A.E.: The Logic of the RAISE Specification Language. In: Logics of Specification Languages [9]. Springer, Heidelberg (2008)

21. George, C.W., Haff, P., Havelund, K., Haxthausen, A.E., Milne, R., Nielsen, C.B., Prehn, S., Wagner, K.R.: The RAISE Specification Language. The BCS Practitioner Series. Prentice-Hall, Hemel Hampstead (1992)

22. George, C.W., Haxthausen, A.E.: The Logic of the RAISE Specification Language. Computing and Informatics 22(1-2) (2003)

23. George, C.W., Haxthausen, A.E., Hughes, S., Milne, R., Prehn, S., Pedersen, J.S.: The RAISE Method. The BCS Practitioner Series. Prentice-Hall, Hemel Hampstead (1995)

24. Grieskamp, W., Santen, T., Stoddart, B. (eds.): IFM 2000. LNCS, vol. 1945. Springer, Heidelberg (2000)

25. Hansen, M.R.: Duration Calculus. In: Logics of Specification Languages [9], pp. 299–347. Springer, Heidelberg (2008)

26. Harel, D.: Statecharts: A visual formalism for complex systems. Science of Computer Programming 8(3), 231–274 (1987)

27. Harel, D., Marelly, R.: Come, Let's Play – Scenario-Based Programming Using LSCs and the Play-Engine. Springer, Heidelberg (2003)

28. Harel, D., Naamad, A.: The STATEMATE semantics of Statecharts. ACM Transactions on Software Engineering and Methodology (TOSEM) 5(4), 293–333 (1996)

29. Henson, M.C., Deutsch, M., Reeves, S.: Z Logic and Its Applications. In: Logics of Specification Languages [9], pp. 489–596. Springer, Heidelberg (2008)
30. Henson, M.C., Reeves, S., Bowen, J.P.: Z Logic and its Consequences. Computing and Informatics 22(1-2) (2003)
31. Hoare, T.: Communicating Sequential Processes. C.A.R. Hoare Series in Computer Science. Prentice-Hall International, Englewood Cliffs (1985)
32. Hoare, T.: Communicating Sequential Processes. Published electronically (2004), http://www.usingcsp.com/cspbook.pdf Second edition of [31], http://www.usingcsp.com/
33. ITU-T. CCITT Recommendation Z.120: Message Sequence Chart (MSC) (1992)
34. ITU-T. ITU-T Recommendation Z.120: Message Sequence Chart (MSC)(1996)
35. ITU-T. ITU-T Recommendation Z.120: Message Sequence Chart (MSC)(1999)
36. Jackson, D.: Software Abstractions Logic, Language, and Analysis. The MIT Press, Cambridge (2006)
37. Jensen, K.: Coloured Petri Nets. In: Kurt Jensen. EATCS Monographs in Theoretical Computer Science, vol. 1: Basic Concepts (234 pages + xii), vol. 2: Analysis Methods (174 pages + x), vol. 3: Practical Use (265 pages + xi). Springer, Heidelberg (1985); revised and corrected second version (1997)
38. Lamport, L.: The Temporal Logic of Actions. Transactions on Programming Languages and Systems 16(3), 872–923 (1995)
39. Lamport, L.: Specifying Systems. Addison–Wesley, Boston (2002)
40. Manna, Z., Pnueli, A.: The Temporal Logic of Reactive Systems: Specifications. Addison Wesley, Reading (1991)
41. Manna, Z., Pnueli, A.: The Temporal Logic of Reactive Systems: Safety. Addison Wesley, Reading (1995)
42. Merz, S.: On the Logic of TLA+. Computing and Informatics 22(1-2) (2003)
43. Merz, S.: The Specification Language TLA$^+$. In: Merz, S. (ed.) Logics of Specification Languages [9], pp. 401–451. Springer, Heidelberg (2008)
44. Mossakowski, T., Haxthausen, A., Sannella, D., Tarlecki, A.: Casl – the Common Algebraic Specification Language. In: Logics of Specification Languages [9], pp. 241–298. Springer, Heidelberg (2008)
45. Mossakowski, T., Haxthausen, A.E., Sanella, D., Tarlecki, A.: CASL — The Common Algebraic Specification Language: Semantics and Proof Theory. Computing and Informatics 22(1-2) (2003)
46. Moszkowski, B.C.: Executing Temporal Logic Programs. Cambridge University Press, Cambridge (1986)
47. Petri, C.A.: Kommunikation mit Automaten. Institut für Instrumentelle Mathematik, Schriften des IIM Nr. 2, Bonn (1962)
48. Pnueli, A.: The Temporal Logic of Programs. In: Proceedings of the 18th IEEE Symposium on Foundations of Computer Science, IEEE CS FoCS, Providence, Rhode Island, pp. 46–57. IEEE CS, Los Alamitos (1977)
49. Reisig, W.: A Primer in Petri Net Design, 120 pages. Springer, Heidelberg (1992)
50. Reisig, W.: Petri Nets: An Introduction. EATCS Monographs in Theoretical Computer Science, vol. 4. Springer, Heidelberg (1985)
51. Reisig, W.: Elements of Distributed Algorithms: Modelling and Analysis with Petri Nets, xi + 302 pages. Springer, Heidelberg (1998)
52. Reisig, W.: The Expressive Power of Abstract State Machines. Computing and Informatics 22(1-2) (2003)
53. Reisig, W.: Abstract State Machines for the Classroom. In: Logics of Specification Languages [9], pp. 15–46. Springer, Heidelberg (2008)

54. Romijn, J.M.T., Smith, G.P., van de Pol, J. (eds.): IFM 2005. LNCS, vol. 3771. Springer, Heidelberg (2005)
55. Roscoe, A.W.: Theory and Practice of Concurrency. C.A.R. Hoare Series in Computer Science. Prentice-Hall, Englewood Cliffs (1997), http://www.comlab.ox.ac.uk/people/bill.roscoe/publications/68b.pdf
56. Schneider, S.: Concurrent and Real-time Systems — The CSP Approach. Worldwide Series in Computer Science. John Wiley & Sons, Ltd., Baffins Lane (2000)
57. Spivey, J.M.: Understanding Z: A Specification Language and its Formal Semantics. Cambridge Tracts in Theoretical Computer Science, vol. 3. Cambridge University Press, Cambridge (1988)
58. Spivey, J.M.: The Z Notation: A Reference Manual, 2nd edn. Prentice Hall International Series in Computer Science (1992)
59. Woodcock, J.C.P., Davies, J.: Using Z: Specification, Proof and Refinement. Prentice Hall International Series in Computer Science (1996)
60. Zhou, C.C., Hansen, M.R.: Duration Calculus: A Formal Approach to Real–time Systems. Monographs in Theoretical Computer Science. An EATCS Series. Springer, Heidelberg (2004)
61. Zhou, C.C., Anthony, C., Hoare, R.: A Calculus of Durations. Information Proc. Letters 40(5) (1992)

Compositional and Quantitative Model Checking
(Extended Abstract)*

Kim G. Larsen

Dept. of Computer Science, Aalborg University, Denmark
kgl@cs.aau.dk

Abstract. This paper gives a survey of a composition model checking methodology and its succesfull instantiation to the model checking of networks of finite-state, timed, hybrid and probabilistic systems with respect to suitable quantitative versions of the modal μ-calculus [Koz82].

The method is based on the existence of a quotient construction, allowing a property φ of a parallel system $A|B$ to be transformed into a sufficient and necessary quotient-property φ/A to be satisfied by the component B. Given a model checking problem involving a network $P_1|\ldots|P_n$ and a property φ, the method gradually move (by quotienting) components P_i from the network into the formula φ. Crucial to the success of the method is the ability to manage the size of the intermediate quotient-properties by a suitable collection of efficient minimization heuristics.

1 Model Checking

During more than twenty years efficient methods and heuristics model checking algorithms have been devised for finite-state systems. More recently substantial effort has been made toward quantitative model checking where the model (as well as the properties to be checked) include timing, hybrid or probabilistic and stochastic aspects.

In all cases the main obstacle is that of the so-called *state-space-explosion problem*, which refers to the fact that the size of the state-spaces to be analyzed grow exponentially in the number of components of the model to be analysed. In fact for all of the above models (and logics) the model checking of composite systems are complexity-wise hard problems, e.g. either PSPACE-complete or EXPTIME-complete.

Thus, effort has been focused on the development of a variety of heuristics have been proposed to overcome this problem at least for the analysis of large ranges of *realistic* systems. The heuristics developed include symbolic model-checking, on-the-fly techniques, guided model checking, bounded model checking, partial order techniques.

---

* This paper has been partly supported by the VKR Center of Excellence MT-LAB.

A. Pnueli, I. Virbitskaite, and A. Voronkov (Eds.): PSI 2009, LNCS 5947, pp. 35–42, 2010.
© Springer-Verlag Berlin Heidelberg 2010

2   Compositional Model Checking

An alternativ technique for overcoming the problem of state-space explosion is the *compositional model checking* introduced by Andersen [And95] in 1995 for finite-state systems and later extended to real-time [LL98a, LL98b, KLL+97, LL95] and hybrid systems [CL00]. The method is based on the notion of *quotienting* for parallel composition: given a property φ and a parallel system $A|B$ the quotient property φ/A should satisfy the following equivalence:

$$A|B \models \varphi \text{ if and only if } B \models A/\varphi \tag{1}$$

Depending on the specification formalims used for specifying φ, the modeling formalism used to describe A and B as well as the particular notion of parallel composition, $|$, the quotient-formula φ/A may, or may not, be expressible in the specification formalism. We shall see examples of this when instantiating the compositional model checking methodology to probabilistic systems.

Now consider the following typical model checking problem $(P_1|\ldots|P_n) \models \varphi$ involving a network of n components (finite state, timed automata, hybrid automata or probabilistic systems). Assuming the existence of a quotient construction, we may verifty that the parallel composition of the n components satisfies the formula φ without having to construct the complete state space of the network $(P_1|\ldots|P_n)$: we simply remove the components P_i one by one while simultaneously transforming the formula according. Thus, when removing the component P_n we will transform the formula φ into the quotien formula φ/P_n such that:

$$(P_1|\ldots|P_n) \models \varphi \text{ if and only if } (P_1|\ldots|P_{n-1}) \models \varphi/P_n \tag{2}$$

Now clearly, if the quotient is not much larger the original formula, we have succeeded in simplifying the problem. Repeated application of quotienting yields:

$$(P_1|\ldots|P_n) \models \varphi \text{ if and only if } 1 \models \varphi/P_n/P_{n-1}/\ldots/P_1 \tag{3}$$

where 1 is the unit with respect to parallel composition. However, based on quotienting alone, (3) provides no solutoin ot the problem as the explosion will now occur in the size of the final quotient formula instead. The crucial and experimentally "verified" observation by Andersen was that each quotienting should be followed by a *minimization* of the formula based on a collection of few, efficiently implementable strategies.

3   Finite State Systems

In this section we give a detailed instatiation of the described compositional model checking technique in the setting of finite state systems. First we introduce the (well-known) notion of a (finite) labelled transition system:

Table 1. Satisfaction relation for the modal μ-calculus

$$P \models \text{tt}$$
$$P \models \varphi_1 \wedge \varphi_2 \text{ iff } P \models \varphi_1 \text{ and } P \models \varphi_2$$
$$P \models \varphi_1 \vee \varphi_2 \text{ iff } P \models \varphi_1 \text{ or } P \models \varphi_2$$
$$P \models \langle a \rangle \varphi \text{ iff } \exists P'.P \xrightarrow{a} P' \wedge P' \models \varphi$$
$$P \models [a]\varphi \text{ iff } \forall P'.P \xrightarrow{a} P' \Rightarrow P' \models \varphi$$
$$P \models X_i \text{ iff } P \models \varphi_i \text{ where } (X = \varphi_i) \in \mathcal{E}.$$

Definition 1. *A (finite) labelled transition system $\mathcal{P}$ over a set of labels or actions* Act *consists of a finite set of processes (or states)* Proc *and a transition relation* $\rightarrow \subseteq$ Proc $\times$ Act $\times$ Proc *is the transition relation. Whenever* $(P, a, P') \in \rightarrow$ *we write* $P \xrightarrow{a} P'$. *None*

Now properties are specified in the following version of the modal μ-calculus [Koz82]:

$$\varphi ::= \text{tt} \mid \text{ff} \mid \varphi_1 \wedge \varphi_2 \mid \varphi_1 \vee \varphi_2 \mid \langle a \rangle \varphi \mid [a]\varphi \mid X$$

Here X belongs to a set of formula-variables $\{X_1, \ldots, X_m\}$ each having a defining equation $\mathcal{E} : \{X_i = \varphi_i | i = 1 \ldots n\}$, where $\sigma_i \in \{\mu, \nu\}$. The notion of satisfaction $P \models \varphi$ satisfies the equivalences of Table 1[1]. We recall that the modal μ-calculus provides a characterization of bisimulation in the sence that $P \sim Q$ if and only if $\forall \varphi.P \models \varphi \Leftrightarrow Q \models \varphi$.

Quotienting

Networks or composite systems over a labelled transition systems $\mathcal{P}$ are terms of the form $(P_1 | \ldots | P_n)[f]$, where $P_i \in$ Proc for all $i \in \{1 \ldots n\}$ and $f : (\text{Act} \cup \{0\}) \rightharpoonup$ Act is a synchronization function combining actions from each of the n components – with 0 indicating inaction, i.e. $P \xrightarrow{0} P$ – into an action of the composite system in the obvious way:

$$\frac{[P_i \xrightarrow{a_i} P_i']\ _{i=1..n}}{(P_1, \ldots, P_n)[f] \xrightarrow{a} (P_1', \ldots, P_n')[f]} \quad f(a_1, \ldots, a_n) = a$$

Note that the synchronization functions given by $f_{int}(0, \ldots, a, \ldots, 0) = a$ respectively $f_{sync}(a, \ldots, a) = a$ provides pure interleaving and synchonous composition respectively.

Now, let f be a binary synchronization function. Then – for non-variable formula – the quotient construction is defined by structural induction according to Table 2. Quotienting a formula-variable X_i with defining equation $X_i =_{\sigma_i} = \varphi_i$ is defined as $X_i/P = X_i^P$ where X_i^P is a new formula variable with defining equation $X_i^P =_{\sigma_i} = \varphi_i/P$.

---

[1] $\models$ is actually the the maximal or minimal relation satisfying Table 1 depending on whether $\sigma_i = \mu$ (minimal) or $= \nu$ (maximal).

Table 2. Structural definition of quotient formula φ/P

$$\mathrm{tt}/P = \mathrm{tt}$$
$$\mathrm{ff}/P = \mathrm{ff}$$
$$\varphi_1 \vee \varphi_2/P = \varphi_1/P \vee \varphi_2/P$$
$$\varphi_1 \wedge \varphi_2/P = \varphi_1/P \wedge \varphi_2/P$$
$$\langle a\rangle\varphi/P = \bigvee\nolimits_{P\xrightarrow{b}P',f(c,b)=a}\langle c\rangle(\varphi/P')$$
$$[a]\varphi/P = \bigwedge\nolimits_{P\xrightarrow{b}P',f(c,b)=a}[c](\varphi/P')$$

Theorem 1. *Let P and Q be processes and φ a formula. Then $P|Q \models \varphi$ if and only if $Q \models \varphi/P$.* *None*

3.1 Simplifications

Now after quotienting the number of new (quotient) formula variables X_i^P is obviously $n \cdot |\mathsf{Proc}|$. Thus in order to avoid explosion in the number of formula variables, efficient heuristic methods for simplifying formulas and reducing the number of variables must be provided. The heuristics below are suggested in [And95] with reported good effect on a number of case-studies including Milner's Scheduler:

Boolean Simplification: A number of simple boolean simplifications may be performed, e.g. $\varphi \vee \mathrm{tt} \equiv \mathrm{tt}$, $\varphi \wedge \mathrm{tt} \equiv \varphi$ and $\varphi \wedge \varphi \equiv \varphi \wedge \varphi \equiv \varphi$. Also, $\langle a\rangle\mathrm{ff} \equiv\equiv \mathrm{ff}$ and $[a]\mathrm{tt} \equiv \mathrm{tt}$.

Reachability Analysis: Removal of variables X^P unreachable from X_0/P_0, where P_0 is the initial process.

Constant Propagation: Remove trivial variables $X =^d \mathrm{tt}$ and $X =^d \mathrm{ff}$. Obviously, after constant propagation the formulas in which X occurs are subject to boolean simplification.

Trivial Equation Elimination: Replace $X =^d \varphi$ with $X =^d \mathrm{tt}$ if $\varphi[\mathrm{tt}/X] \equiv \mathrm{tt}$.

Equation Reduction: Collapse X and Y if $X =^d \varphi, Y =^d \psi$ and $\varphi[Y/X] \equiv \psi[Y/X]$.

4   Timed Automata

In this section we review the quotient-based compositional model checking method applied to timed automata, a formalism introduced by Alur and Dill [AD94, AD90] which by now established itself as a classical formalism for describing the behaviour of real-time systems.

The set $\Phi(C)$ of *clock constraints* φ over a finite set (of *clocks*) C is defined by the grammar $\varphi ::= x \bowtie k \mid \varphi_1 \wedge \varphi_2$ where $x \in C, k \in \mathbb{N}, \bowtie \in \{\leq, < \text{ and } \geq, >\}$.

Definition 2. *A* timed automaton *is a tuple* $(L, \ell_0, F, C, \mathsf{Act}, I, E)$ *consisting of a finite set L of locations, an initial location $\ell_0 \in Q$, a set $F \subseteq Q$ of final locations, a finite set C of clocks, a finite set Act of actions, a location invariants mapping $I : L \to \Phi(C)$, and a set $E \subseteq L \times \Phi(C) \times \mathsf{Act} \times 2^C \times L$ of edges. None*

We shall denote an edge $(\ell, \varphi, a, r, \ell') \in E$ by $\ell \xrightarrow{\varphi, a, r} \ell'$.

Definition 3. *The* zone *of a clock constraint in $\Phi(C)$ is a set of clock valuations $C \to \mathbb{R}_{\geq 0}$ given inductively by*

$$[\![x \bowtie k]\!] = \{ v : C \to \mathbb{R}_{\geq 0} \mid v(x) \bowtie k \}$$
$$[\![\varphi_1 \wedge \varphi_2]\!] = [\![\varphi_1]\!] \cap [\![\varphi_2]\!]$$

We shall write $v \models \varphi$ instead of $v \in [\![\varphi]\!]$.   *None*

Definition 4. *The* semantics *of a* timed automaton $A = (L, \ell_0, F, C, \Sigma, I, E)$ *is the transition system $[\![A]\!] = (S, s_0, \Sigma \cup \mathbb{R}_{\geq 0}, T = T_s \cup T_d)$ given by*

$$S = \{ (\ell, v) \in L \times \mathbb{R}_{\geq 0}^C \mid v \models I(\ell) \} \qquad s_0 = (\ell_0, v_0)$$
$$T_s = \{ (\ell, v) \xrightarrow{a} (\ell', v') \mid \exists \ell \xrightarrow{\varphi, a, r} \ell' \in E : v \models \varphi, v' = v[r] \}$$
$$T_d = \{ (\ell, v) \xrightarrow{d} (\ell, v + d) \mid \forall d' \in [0, d] : v + d' \models I(\ell) \} \qquad \text{None}$$

Now properties are specified in the logic L_ν [LLW95] being a timed extension of the modal μ-calculus, given a finite set of formula clocks K:

$$\varphi ::= \mathsf{tt} \mid \mathsf{ff} \mid Z \mid$$
$$\varphi_1 \wedge \varphi_2 \mid \varphi_1 \vee \varphi_2 \mid \langle a \rangle \varphi \mid [a] \varphi \mid$$
$$\exists \varphi \mid \forall \varphi \mid x \text{ in } \varphi \mid x \sim n \mid x - y \sim n$$

where $x \in K$. Now given a timed automaton A Table 3 provides some of the structural defintions of the interpretion of L_ν over extended states $\langle (l, u), v \rangle$, where (l, u) is a state of A and v is a clock valuation over K. When A is a timed automata and φ a formula we write $A \models \varphi$ if and only if $\langle (l_0, u_0), v_0 \rangle \models \varphi$, where l_0 is the initial location of A, u_0 and v_0 are clock valuations assigning 0 to all clocks.

Quotienting

Assuming disjoint sets of clocks C_i, parallel composition of timed automata $A_1, \ldots, A_n$ are semantically parallel compositions of states $s_i = (l_i, u_i)$ of the respective timed automata with synchronization of discrete actions Act given by a synchronization function f. The rules for discrete and delay transitions are given below:

$$\frac{[s_i \xrightarrow{a_i} s_i'] \quad i = 1..n}{(s_1, \ldots, s_n)[f] \xrightarrow{a} (s_1', \ldots, s_n')[f]} \quad f(a_1, \ldots, a_n) = a$$

Table 3. Interpretation of L_ν

$$\langle(l,u),v\rangle \models \langle a\rangle\varphi \ \text{ iff } \ \exists(l,u) \overset{a}{\to} (l',u').\langle(l',u'),v\rangle \models \varphi$$
$$\langle(l,u),v\rangle \models \exists\varphi \ \text{ iff } \ \exists d.\langle(l,u+d),v+d\rangle \models \varphi$$
$$\langle(l,u),v\rangle \models x \text{ in } \varphi \ \text{ iff } \ \langle(l,u),v[x=0]\rangle \models \varphi$$

Table 4. Timed Quotient

$$c/n = c$$
$$(\varphi_1 \wedge \varphi_2)/n = \varphi_1/n \wedge \varphi_2/n$$
$$(x \text{ in } \varphi)/n = x \text{ in } (\varphi/n)$$
$$(\forall\varphi)/n = \forall(\varphi/n)$$
$$X/n = X_n \text{ where } X_n = \varphi_X/n$$
$$([a]\varphi)/n = \bigwedge\nolimits_{n \overset{gar}{\to} m}(g \Rightarrow [a](r \text{ in } \varphi_m))$$

Table 5. Constraint Propagation

$$\text{ff} \Rightarrow \varphi \equiv \text{tt}$$
$$D \Rightarrow C \equiv \text{tt if } D \subseteq C$$
$$D \Rightarrow ([a]\varphi) \equiv [a](D \Rightarrow \varphi)$$
$$D \Rightarrow (\varphi_1 \wedge \varphi_2) \equiv (D \Rightarrow \varphi_1) \wedge (D \Rightarrow \varphi_2)$$
$$\cdots$$
$$D \Rightarrow (\forall\varphi) \equiv \forall(D^\uparrow \Rightarrow \varphi) \text{ if } D^\downarrow \subseteq D$$

$$\frac{[s_i \overset{\varepsilon(d)}{\to} s_i'] \ _{i=1..n}}{(s_1,\ldots,s_n)[f] \overset{\varepsilon(d)}{\to} (s_1',\ldots,s_n')[f]} \quad \text{Urg. Constr.}$$

Now let B be a timed automaton over clock set C and let φ be an L_ν formula over clock set K, then we define the *quotient* formula φ/n over $C \cup K$ inductively as indicated in Table 4. Then the following theorem holds:

Theorem 2. *Let B be a timed automaton over clock-set C and let φ be a formula over clock set K. Then for any timed automaton A, $(A|B) \models \varphi$ if and only if $A \models \varphi/n_0$, where n_0 is the initial location of B.*   *None*

Simplification

In addition to the simplification rules for boolean simplification, constant propogation, reachability analysis, trivial equation elimination and equation reduction a number of simplification rules for propagating constraints are used as illustrated in Table 5.

The quotient construction and simplification rules have been implemented in the tool CMC [LL98a, KLL$^+$97] which allows for compositional model checking of networks of timed automata.

5   Concluding Remarks

Quotient constructions has been provided for both linear hybrid systems [CL00] and probabilistic systems [LS92]. In the latter case it turns out that the natural probabilistic extension of the modal μ-calculus is not expressive enough for quotienting to exist. The least expressive extension of this logic is characterized.

Also quotienting for timed automata with respect to reachability properties has been considered in [ABL98, ABBL98]. Obviously, reachability properties are not closed under quotienting and the above papers characterizes logical properties which may be obtained as the quotient of a reachability property with respect to some (test) timed automata.

References

[ABBL98]   Aceto, L., Bouyer, P., Burgueño, A., Larsen, K.G.: The power of reachability testing for timed automata. In: Arvind, V., Sarukkai, S. (eds.) FST TCS 1998. LNCS, vol. 1530, pp. 245–257. Springer, Heidelberg (1998)

[ABL98]   Aceto, L., Burgueño, A., Larsen, K.G.: Model checking via reachability testing for timed automata. In: Steffen, B. (ed.) TACAS 1998. LNCS, vol. 1384, pp. 263–280. Springer, Heidelberg (1998)

[AD90]   Alur, R., Dill, D.: Automata for modeling real-time systems. In: Paterson, M. (ed.) ICALP 1990. LNCS, vol. 443, pp. 322–335. Springer, Heidelberg (1990)

[AD94]   Alur, R., Dill, D.: A theory of timed automata. Theoretical Computer Science (TCS) 126(2), 183–235 (1994)

[And95]   Andersen, H.R.: Partial model-checking (extended abstract). In: Proc. 10th IEEE Symp. on Logic in Computer Science (LICS 1995), pp. 398–407. IEEE Computer Society Press, Los Alamitos (1995)

[CL00]   Cassez, F., Laroussinie, F.: Model-checking for hybrid systems by quotienting and constraints solving. In: Emerson, E.A., Sistla, A.P. (eds.) CAV 2000. LNCS, vol. 1855, pp. 373–388. Springer, Heidelberg (2000)

[KLL$^+$97]   Kristoffersen, K.J., Laroussinie, F., Larsen, K.G., Pettersson, P., Yi, W.: A compositional proof of a real-time mutual exclusion protocol. In: Bidoit, M., Dauchet, M. (eds.) CAAP 1997, FASE 1997, and TAPSOFT 1997. LNCS, vol. 1214, pp. 565–579. Springer, Heidelberg (1997)

[Koz82]   Kozen, D.: Results on the propositional μ-calculus. In: Nielsen, M., Schmidt, E.M. (eds.) ICALP 1982. LNCS, vol. 140, pp. 348–359. Springer, Heidelberg (1982)

[LL95]   Laroussinie, F., Larsen, K.G.: Compositional model-checking of real-time systems. In: Lee, I., Smolka, S.A. (eds.) CONCUR 1995. LNCS, vol. 962, pp. 27–41. Springer, Heidelberg (1995)

[LL98a]   Laroussinie, F., Larsen, K.G.: CMC: A tool for compositional model-checking of real-time systems. In: Proc. IFIP Joint Int. Conf. on Formal Description Techniques & Protocol Specification, Testing, and Verification (FORTE-PSTV 1998), pp. 439–456. Kluwer Academic, Dordrecht (1998)

[LL98b]   Laroussinie, F., Larsen, K.G.: Cmc: A tool for compositional model-checking of real-time systems. In: Budkowski, S., Cavalli, A.R., Najm, E. (eds.) FORTE. IFIP Conference Proceedings, vol. 135, pp. 439–456. Kluwer, Dordrecht (1998)

[LLW95]   Laroussinie, F., Larsen, K.G., Weise, C.: From timed automata to logic – and back. In: Hájek, P., Wiedermann, J. (eds.) MFCS 1995. LNCS, vol. 969, pp. 529–539. Springer, Heidelberg (1995)

[LS92]   Larsen, K.G., Skou, A.: Compositional verification of probabilistic processes. In: Cleaveland, W.R. (ed.) CONCUR 1992. LNCS, vol. 630, pp. 456–471. Springer, Heidelberg (1992)

Invariants, Modularity, and Rights*

Ernie Cohen[1], Eyad Alkassar[2], Vladimir Boyarinov[3], Markus Dahlweid[4],
Ulan Degenbaev[2], Mark Hillebrand[3], Bruno Langenstein[3], Dirk Leinenbach[3],
Michał Moskal[4], Steven Obua[2], Wolfgang Paul[2], Hristo Pentchev[2],
Elena Petrova[2], Thomas Santen[4], Norbert Schirmer[3], Sabine Schmaltz[2],
Wolfram Schulte[5], Andrey Shadrin[2], Stephan Tobies[4], Alexandra Tsyban[2],
and Sergey Tverdyshev[2]

[1] Microsoft Corporation, Redmond, WA, USA
ernie.cohen@microsoft.com
[2] Saarland University, Computer Science Dept., Saarbrücken, Germany
{eyad,ulan,obua,wjp,pentchev,petrova,sabine,shadrin,azul,
deru}@wjpserver.cs.uni-sb.de
[3] German Research Center for Artificial Intelligence (DFKI), Saarbrücken, Germany
{Vladimir.Boyarinov,mah,langenstein,Dirk.Leinenbach,
Norbert.Schirmer}@dfki.de
[4] European Microsoft Innovation Center, Aachen, Germany
{markus.dahlweid,michal.moskal,thomas.santen,
stephan.tobies}@microsoft.com
[5] Microsoft Research, Redmond, WA, USA
schulte@microsoft.com

Abstract. The quest for modular concurrency reasoning has led to recent proposals that extend program assertions to include not just knowledge about the state, but rights to access the state. We argue that these
rights are really just sugar for knowledge that certain updates preserve
certain invariants.

1   Introduction

Over the years, many approaches to reasoning about concurrent systems have
been proposed. At their core, most of these approaches are based on *invariants*.
Invariance reasoning is conceptually simple, and compositional across concurrent composition. But invariance reasoning also has a downside: to check an
update to the state, you have to check all of the invariants that the update
might break. This is not usually a problem when reasoning about concurrent
algorithms, where you can afford to see all of the invariants. Nor is it usually
a problem when reasoning about concurrent hardware or distributed systems,
where the sharing of data and invariants across components is typically static.

---

* Work partially funded by the German Federal Ministry of Education and Research
(BMBF) in the framework of the Verisoft XT project under grant 01 IS 07 008. Work
of the sixteenth author was funded by the German Research Foundation (DFG)
within the program 'Quality Guarantees for Computer Systems'.

A. Pnueli, I. Virbitskaite, and A. Voronkov (Eds.): PSI 2009, LNCS 5947, pp. 43–55, 2010.
© Springer-Verlag Berlin Heidelberg 2010

But it is a big problem when reasoning about large concurrent programs, where sharing is dynamic, and code might break invariants that are out of scope (or, indeed, might not have even been written when the code is verified).

The modern attack on this problem is to strengthen the specification language to specify not only a thread's *knowledge*[1] (about the state) but also its *rights* (what it is allowed to do to the state), the combination of which we call a thread's *stuff*. For example, the stuff of a thread typically includes exclusive access to its local data (that is, right to modify the data and knowledge of its exact value), and lesser rights and knowledge about shared data (e.g., one thread might be allowed only to increase a counter and another only to decrease it; the former thread can possess knowledge about its maximum value, the latter about its minimum).

In rely-guarantee reasoning [5], the stuff in a thread is static over its lifetime. In more recent approaches, stuff can move in and out of threads, e.g., through shared objects such as resources. A procedure specification describes the stuff provided to the procedure on entry, and the stuff returned on exit (or, depending on methodology, how the stuff can change). (Fork and join are conceptually similar to procedure call and return.)

The usual way to represent stuff, typified by Concurrent Separation Logic (CSL) [7], is to describe stuff using a linear logic. This elegant approach has led to some very beautiful proofs of programs. However, it is not without drawbacks:

1. Rights and knowledge are very different things, governed by very different mathematics. Knowledge follows the rules of ordinary logic and can be freely created or destroyed, while rights have to follow some conservation principles to avoid unsoundness (e.g., from duplicating and distributing an exclusive right) or resource leakage (e.g., if you forget about your exclusive right to a chunk of memory). The introduction of linearity features into the logic produces a substantial jump in computational complexity (e.g., for separation logic see [1, 2]).

2. There are many ways to form a linear space of rights. For example, in CSL, one might use either fractional permissions or counting permissions; there are also other possibilities, such as a tree-like structuring of permissions, or permission accounting using infinitesimals (as in Chalice [6]), not to mention more expressive approaches, such as relational permissions [4]. So it seems odd to build such a commitment into the programming logic.

The point of this paper is that once we have a program logic that provides ghost state and two-state invariants (which we need anyway to do internal simulation reasoning[2]), we no longer need rights within the logic; rights can be represented as the knowledge that certain updates don't break certain invariants. (In order to

---

[1] We use knowledge here in the usual sense of what the thread can deduce about the state or changes thereto, not in the sense as in logics of knowledge.

[2] To show that a program simulates some abstract specification, we make this specification a (two-state) invariant of an explicit ghost object, with a 1-state coupling invariant linking it to the concrete state. The ghost object is then updated (either implicitly or explicitly) so as to maintain these invariants.

make knowledge – and rights – first class, we use objects as the carriers of knowledge.) This might seem odd; since knowledge can be freely duplicated, what makes an exclusive right exclusive? The trick is to view threads as objects. The invariant of a thread is given implicitly by the annotation one would put on the thread (i.e., a disjunction with disjuncts of the form "if control is here, then this predicate holds"). So if thread T uses its exclusive right to a variable to deduce (in its assertion) that the value of the variable has some value at some point in its execution, another thread can't change the value without breaking T's invariant. Since threads are verified without access to what code might be running in other threads, this means that exclusive rights effectively prevent modifications by other threads.

The price we pay is that to move rights around, we have to manipulate ghost state. But this is to be expected, given the complexity gap between validity checking in ordinary logic and linear logics; the use of linear logics amounts to folding these manipulations of ghost state into the programming logic. One advantage to our approach is that, by building rights on top of ghost code and invariants, the "logic" of rights can be extended by just adding more code; the substitution of code verification for metatheory is usually a good trade. Equally important, software engineers understand code and invariants, whereas they are likely to reject fancy program logics. Nevertheless, our approach is compatible with the use of fancier linear rights.

The ideas here were developed in the context of the design of the Verifying C Compiler (VCC) [3], an automatic verifier for concurrent C code. However, many of the ideas are realized somewhat differently in VCC; we point out some of these differences in the footnotes.

2   Local Invariance Reasoning

Assume a state consisting of an addressable heap (containing both real state and ghost state). When we speak of a variable, we mean a heap address, and when we speak of the value of a variable a, we mean the value $[a]$ stored at the address a in a given state. Define $[A]$, where A is a set of addresses, to be the partial (heap) map restricted to the addresses in A. On top of the state, we imagine a collection of *objects*,[3] each with a unique identifier (so that we can store object references on the heap), and each with a fixed collection of invariants (two-state predicates on the heap).[4] If o denotes an object identifier,

---

[3] An alternative (but essentially equivalent) approach, used in VCC, is to start with objects and fields, and to use only ownership between objects. However, we then need additional system invariants to prevent aliasing objects from existing at the same time and to make sure that there is always some existing object for each bit of memory (to prevent memory leakage). Moreover, because it should be possible to change the owner of an object without having to check the object's invariant, the ownership bit for an object has to be treated specially.

[4] Note that we are assuming a fixed grain of atomicity; all objects share the same notion of system step. This might seem inelegant, but has the enormous practical advantage of allowing invariants of different objects to be freely combined with conjunction when reasoning about the state.

define $inv(o)$ to be the conjunction of the invariants of o; intuitively, we expect each object invariant should hold across each state transition (pair of consecutive states) in every execution of the program. In two-state predicates, $old(e)$ gives the value of the (single-state) expression e in the prestate, while e gives the value in the poststate. Define $unch(e) \equiv (e = old(e))$. Define the single-state invariant $inv1(o)$ to hold in a state s iff $inv(o)$ holds across the transition from s to s (the *stuttering* transition from s). Finally, define the single-state predicate $\langle p \rangle$ ("necessarily p") to mean that every possible state transition from the current state satisfies the two-state invariant p.

To enable modular checking that a state update preserves all invariants, we introduce an ownership policy on state, as follows. We add to ghost state a map *owner* from addresses to objects[5]; if $owner(a) = o$, we say that o owns a. Define $span(o) \equiv [\{a \mid owner(a) = o\}]$, i.e., the span of o consists of the set of locations owned by o and the values of the heap at these locations. We require the object invariants to satisfy the following *admissibility condition*, for every object o, over every possible state transition:

$$(\forall o' : old(inv1(o'))) \wedge$$
$$(\forall o' : unch(span(o')) \vee inv(o'))$$
$$\Rightarrow inv(o)$$

This condition says that to check that an update preserves all invariants, we only have to check the invariants of those objects who own an updated location or who acquired or released ownership of a location, i.e., whose span has changed. It thus provides the desired modularity when checking an update: we need only to find a set of objects whose spans cover the updated data, and check the invariants of these objects (assuming that all single-state invariants hold in the prestate). Admissibility checking itself is modular – we can check admissibility of an object invariant without knowing all of the object invariants (although it usually depends on some of them). Note that admissibility requires in particular that all invariants are preserved under stuttering.

To allow objects to be created and destroyed, the heap contains for each object o a (ghost) Boolean variable $exists(o)$ that says whether that object actually exists. We think of each object invariant as implicitly containing a hypothesis that the object exists in the prestate or the poststate. In addition, o has an invariant that says that it owns $exists(o)$, whether o exists or not[6].

To allow object invariants to assert the invariants of other objects, we allow invariants to contain terms of the form $inv(o)$, as long as such terms occur

---

[5] We are here assuming that *owner* is not on the heap, to avoid giving it an owner; equivalently, we could put it on the heap, making its owner a system object whose only invariant is that it owns *owner*.

[6] It is important for o to own $exists(o)$ even when it doesn't exist to avoid having to worry about breaking the invariant of the old owner of $exists(o)$ when truthifying $exists(o)$.

only with positive polarity; this polarity constraint guarantees a consistent interpretation of which invariants hold across any state transition[7]. Let I be the conjunction of all object invariants; if $I \wedge old([exists(o)]) \Rightarrow p$ (across every possible pair of states), we say that o *claims* p.

3   Structuring Invariants

Some forms of invariants are trivially admissible. For example, an invariant of object A that can be written as a predicate on $span(A)$ is admissible as long as it is invariant under stuttering. More generally, any invariant of the form $unch(span(A)) \vee p$ is admissible. However, invariants that depend on data owned by other objects sometimes require help from the owning objects.

Suppose that an invariant of an object B depends on some variable a in the span of an object A. For example, A might be a lower-level object forming part of the representation of B, and a might hold some part of the abstract state of A. Typically, an update to a requires checking some condition on B, or even concurrent update to B, to avoid breaking B's invariant. Without some precaution, this will make B's invariant inadmissible. We don't want to put B's particular invariant in A, because the implementation of B is not in A's scope. (Moreover, in most cases, the particular object dependent on A is state-dependent, e.g., given by some ghost variable of A, such as its owner.)

One approach is to turn the relevant state of B into an existentially quantified variable. For example, if B's invariant is a single-state invariant p that relates $[a]$ with the value of a variable b in the span of B, we can replace B's invariant with the invariant $(\exists c : p')$, where p' is p with $[b]$ replaced by c. This approach is suitable only when we don't need to constrain updates to A, and only need to mirror them by updating b appropriately[8].

An approach that we have found more useful is to allow changes to a only when some condition on the ghost heap holds, with an invariant (in A) of the form $(unch([a]) \vee p)$ (which itself is necessarily admissible). For example, p might be simply $[b]$, where b is a state bit owned by B, allowing B to inhibit updates to a by keeping b false; this right can move around with ownership of b. More sophisticated predicates are also possible; for example, p might require a more complex test on the state, or even a particular simultaneous update of the state. The form that we have found most useful is where p is of the form $inv(B)$, which essentially requires a check of B's invariant (without saying what that invariant is) when updating a; we say that B *approves* changes to a. This

---

[7] There are various ways to weaken the polarity constraint. For example, one can stratify the objects according to a static well-founded relation (e.g., on object types), so that the invariant of object o can use $inv(o')$ with negative polarity only if $o' < o$, or stratify on the basis of the time when $exists(o)$ becomes true.

[8] Another issue is that if other objects refer to b, replacing these references with existential loses the coherence between the instances. We have considered adding to VCC existential variables that are defined by such existential formulas, but the defining formulas of such variables have to be suitably stratified to guarantee consistency.

automatically gives B's invariants admissible use of a. We can allow this power of approval to move around by replacing the constant B with a state expression, have multiple approvers by using a conjunction of such invariants, or approve a more restricted class of changes (e.g., changes that increase a).

The simplest case of approval arises where B claims that (under some condition) A exists. There are many ways to make such a B admissible. One is for A to keep track of such "clients" with the invariant that A isn't destroyed while this set is nonempty and that taking an object out of the set requires approval of the object. (Note that this doesn't have to be done for all objects that claim the existence of A, just for those whose admissibility cannot be established in other ways.) Because B is a full-fledged object, the existence of B can be claimed by other objects, creating a graph-like information structure. Another way to structure this is to extend ownership to objects, and to give each object an implicit invariant that its owner approves its destruction or ownership changes. Yet another is to assign a fraction in the range $(0, 1]$ to each claimant, with the invariant that these claims sum to 1, which simulates fractional permissions of CSL. These can all be mixed together in the same system.

4 Threads

Because the system state is stored on the heap, the continuation of each thread has to likewise be stored on the heap, and we think of the thread as owning the locations used to represent its continuation. (For example, in a higher-order language, we would have a location for each thread that stores its continuation.) In a standard hardware architecture, we can think of the thread owning (memory locations corresponding to) the local registers (in particular, the program counter), the register data saved in the stack frames on the control stack, and any stack memory reserved beyond the current stack top. Stack variables are owned by the thread when they are allocated and when they are released, but in between ownership might pass out of the thread; this is necessary for languages like C that allow references to stack variables to be stored in data structures.

Checking admissibility of a thread means checking that updates that don't change the span of the thread don't break its (implicit) invariants. This amounts to checking that any assertion we attach to a control location is stable under any action that preserves all invariants of updated objects. This stability is normally proved using the invariants of objects mentioned in the assertion.

The invariant of a thread (like the invariant of any object) can admissibly talk about any data the thread owns. Similarly it can talk admissibly about any data whose update is approved by the thread. Note that in contrast to other approaches, where threads can only update locations that they own exclusively, nothing logically prevents a thread from changing state owned by another thread (even its program counter). However, the possibility of such updates do not effect the verification of the potentially modified thread. Moreover, as a practical matter, threads typically don't have access to the actual invariants of other threads, so we cannot verify threads that change state owned by other threads.

5 Claims

An object that owns no interesting data can nevertheless provide useful knowledge about the state (or how the state may change), through its invariant. Useful knowledge is almost never permanent; for example, knowledge about a data structure is destroyed when the structure is torn down. Thus, the admissibility of such knowledge depends on its approving destruction of the relevant parts of the state, as described in the last section. We call such an object a *claim.*

Why would we wish to use a claim to pass information around, as opposed to an ordinary assertion within program code? The answer is that code assertions can only speak sensibly about state that is owned by the thread running the code, whereas shared objects (e.g., locks) are usually not owned by the thread. Even if some property of a shared object is known to hold at some point in a program, any write to nonlocal state can destroy such information. Verifying that such information is not destroyed typically requires using invariants of objects that are out of scope (e.g., because they are invariants of lower level data objects whose implementation is hidden). Even if the invariants are in scope, this would force the properties being maintained to be proved over and over again, which would be a disaster for practical reasoning. Conversely, the knowledge carried within a claim is guaranteed to stay around until the claim itself is destroyed; because the claim is typically owned by the thread, this can only happen if the thread itself destroys the claim. Thus, claims allows knowledge to be broken up into logical units, these units moved around as necessary (put into data structures, passed in and out of procedures, etc.).

The admissibility check when forming a claim amounts to checking that its invariant is stable (i.e., cannot be falsified) as long as the claim exists; it is essentially analogous to the check of an assertion associated with a program location, except that it cannot assume the constancy of data owned by the thread. Of course the two-state invariant of the claim must hold over the transition in which the claim is "created" (i.e., when it goes from nonexistence to existence).

It is often convenient to use claims to build new claims. In order to do this, claims themselves must keep track of these *dependent* claims, so that the dependents can approve destruction of the claim. Such claims can be destroyed only when all of its dependents have been destroyed (or are simultaneously destroyed). A program using such a claim thus has to maintain (through program assertions or object invariants) information about the possible dependents that might still exist.

Claims are often passed as ghost arguments to procedures[9]. Typically, a precondition of the procedure guarantees that the claim exists and is owned by the thread executing the procedure (so that it remains in existence until the thread destroys it or gives up its ownership). There are several possible idioms for what the procedure can do with the claim. The most usual is that the precondition

---

[9] It is also possible to simply assert as a precondition the existence of a claim with the suitable properties, but passing it as a ghost argument has the advantage of immediately giving it a name to which it can be referred to in ghost code.

guarantees that the claim is returned with the same dependents as upon entry[10]. In some cases, the procedure has to be able to destroy the claim (e.g., if it is destroying an object referenced by the claim)[11]; in this case, the precondition also specifies the claimants that might exist on entry.

Procedures that operate on shared synchronization objects (such as locks) typically take as a ghost argument a claim that claims that the target object exists. From these initial claims, a thread can deduce the existence of other objects (possibly claims themselves). For example, acquisition procedures typically return an object with ownership of the object transfered to the calling thread; for exclusive access (as in a writer lock) this object is the very object protected by the lock, whereas for shared access (as in a reader lock), the object is a claim claiming the existence of the protected object.

6   Permissions

We return to the question of what it means to have permission to perform an action. Suppose we want to update the heap at some location, say by atomically setting it to 0. What would justify such an update?

If the thread owns the updated location, the thread's invariant is all that has to be checked. By the form of the thread invariant, this means just checking that if performing the update from a state satisfying the program assertion preceding the update results in a state satisfying the program assertion following the update. This is just ordinary sequential program reasoning.

On the other hand, if the updated location is owned by some object, we have to check that object's invariant (as well as that of the thread). The obvious thing to do is to use the prestate to deduce which object owns the location, and that the state is such that the update preserves this object's invariant. Often this approach is possible. For example, in the code implementing a concurrent object, the procedures updating some private part of the object state usually have enough local information to do this check. The majority of atomic updates in commercial code can be checked in this way (if the hardware intrinsics are treated as primitives).

However, there are cases where this approach is insufficient. First, procedures that serve as low-level wrappers of atomic hardware intrinsics (e.g., interlocked increment,) cannot talk about all possible objects that might own (or refer to) the updated location. Second, even if code updating the heap knows the object that owns the data and can see its invariant, this object might use approval or similar mechanisms that require checking the invariants of other objects; since these other objects are typically at higher levels, their invariants are likely to be out of scope (as well they should be).

---

[10] This corresponds to returning the same "amount" of claim in logics based on fractional permissions.

[11] To make this more convenient, claims in VCC have the property that once destroyed they can never again be recreated, allowing the destroyer of a claim to assert that the claim doesn't exist on procedure return.

Let us consider a typical example, where an object A has an invariant $unch([a]) \vee inv(B)$. We'd like to pass to the code updating a a claim c that it can use to check the update to a. When updating a, we cannot soundly assume the invariant of c holds across the update, even if the update doesn't destroy c. However, we can safely assume that the invariant of c holds over the transition that stutters from the prestate of the update. To get from this information about a nonstuttering transition from the prestate (such as the update to a, we use a claim with a (single-state) invariant that talks about all possible transitions from the prestate. To allow the code to update a without breaking B, we pass to it a claim that claims $\langle p \Rightarrow inv(B) \rangle$. For example, if B has the invariant $[a] \leq [b]$, then from a claim that claims that $[b] = 5$ we can construct a dependent claim claiming $\langle unch(span(B)) \wedge [a] \leq 5 \Rightarrow inv(B) \rangle$, which says that any change that doesn't change B and satisfies $[a] \leq 5$ preserves the invariant of B.

Note that this technique is more modular than a rely-guarantee condition, because A might have other approvers besides B (that the client might not even know about). The claim doesn't claim that an update satisfying p will satisfy all invariants (which would be impossible without breaking information hiding), only that it will not break B's invariant.

Now, just as we don't want to expose information about B to the code, we also don't want to expose details of the update to the client providing the claim (since the update to a might need to simultaneously update other data belonging to A. All that p has to specify (beyond the change to a) is that the update doesn't update the span of B. For example, if the whole invariant of B (beyond ownership of b) is $([exists(A)] \wedge [a] < [b])$, a suitable claim would be one that claims $\langle old([a]) \geq [a] \wedge unch(span(B)) \Rightarrow inv(B) \rangle$ (which can be read as: from the current state, any state change that doesn't increase a and doesn't change B preserves the invariant of B). In general, we can view any claim of the form $\langle p \rangle$ as giving information about the effects of potential updates, and therefore a form of partial permission.

7   Read Permissions

So far, we have talked about permissions that allow a thread to change the state. Fractional permissions or counting permissions (as described in the implementation of claims) are often used in logics such as CSL to allow reading part of the state.

In the view presented here, reading a location requires no permission at all; the reason for having a read permission is to allow the thread reading the location to make a subsequent assertion about the location (such as its having the same value that was read). That is, the read permission is just an invariant that makes the subsequent assertion admissible. In the CSL tradition, a read permission specifically guarantees that the location isn't changing, which can be expressed in an ordinary invariant.

A natural objection is that this means we would be certifying programs that read possibly "invalid" regions of memory (which would, of course, result in a page fault on typical hardware). One response would be that such reads are not really "reads", but calls to lower level reading procedures that require that the memory being read is valid[12].

8   Superposition

In some cases, permission isn't enough. In some cases, b must be updated along with a, e.g., to preserve an invariant in B of the form $[a] = [b]$. Note that in real software, this situation would only arise when b was a ghost variable, whereas a could be either real or ghost. We call the required update to b that restores an invariant a *compensation*. The need for compensation creates a dilemma: we can't update b within the code that knows about a (because b is out of scope), nor in the code that knows about b (since any required updates to private parts of A would not be possible).

What we need to do is to pass a suitable compensation to the code updating a; the compensation thus looks like a callback that is called within the atomic action that updates b. This is a bit tricky, because the compensation has to "run" starting from a state (after the update of a, but still within the atomic action) where object invariants might no longer hold (not even for objects that haven't been modified). So validation of the callback usually needs to know something about the update that preceded it. Dually, the atomic action needs to know some properties of the callback.

We could pass the compensation as an explicit (mathematical) function from states to states, but since the compensation updates only ghost state, it is sufficient to know that a state representing the result of the compensation exists. So we can pass a compensation in the form of a claim that claims

$$(\forall S : p(S_0, S) \Rightarrow (\exists S' : q(S, S') \wedge r(S_0, S')))$$

where S_0 denotes the current state. Here, p describes what the caller (or whoever justifies the compensation) knows about the update, q describes what the code performing the atomic action needs to know about the compensation, and r describes what it needs to know about the combined effect. So in the case of the invariant $[a] = [b]$, we could define $p \equiv unch(span(B))$, $q \equiv unch(span(A))$, and $r \equiv inv(B)$. The claim can be constructed[13] by defining S' to be the state obtained by applying the update $b := a$ to the state S. Within the atomic action, the code updates a, then simply moves to an arbitrary state S' satisfying the condition given by the claim.

---

[12]   In VCC, in the name of efficacy we dispense with these explicit memory access procedures, and simply keep track of which memory locations are valid according to the rules of C, checking that all memory accesses are to valid memory locations.

[13] An automatic verifier can hardly be expected to guess the witnessing Skolem function $S'(S_0, S)$ automatically, so the code constructing the compensation claim gives explicit code performing the necessary compensation, i.e., the code snippet $b := a$. Note that, like all ghost code, this code has to be guaranteed to terminate to ensure soundness, and any nondeterminism can be considered angelic rather than demonic.

9 Automata

The claim used to provide permission in the last section allows an update to be done an arbitrary number of times. Sometimes, we want to allow an update to happen only once. For example, if we are simulating a step of a processor, we might in a single step write to memory while simultaneously updating the (virtual) program counter. This permission can only be used once – we don't want execution of a single machine instruction to result in multiple writes to shared memory.

We can get this effect in two ways. One is for the compensation to require the destruction of the permission as part of the atomic action. (Note that because permissions are objects, they are effectively additive – if a thread gains two permission objects, he can use them for two separate updates.) The other approach is to use a more complex form of permission that, instead of being based on claims, is based on more general objects that can own additional "local" state that is updated when the permission is used. Such an object can represent more complex permissions that allow operations to be performed only according to some (arbitrarily complex) protocol (given by the invariant of the object). Moreover, the local state can be used to make sure that the client has actually used the permission when it returns. (In the case of simulating the processor step, this allows the caller to ascertain that the virtual program counter has actually moved forward.)

10 Implementation

The development of VCC has been driven by the verification of the Microsoft Hypervisor (the core component of Hyper-V^{TM}) as part of the Verisoft XT project[14]. The hypervisor, consisting of 100KLOC of concurrent C and about 6KLOC of x64 assembler, runs directly on multiprocessor x64 hardware, turning it into a number of virtual multiprocessor x64 machines (with an extra level of virtual address translation, to allow each machine to be given the illusion of 0-based contiguous memory). Except for moderate size, it is fairly representative of low-level commercial system software: it contains a small operating system (albeit without devices), complete with kernel, memory manager, scheduler, debugger, etc. The most complex part of the system (which uses shadow page tables to provide a virtual TLB) uses a number of very subtle concurrent algorithms, with a quite complex simulation relation.

In VCC, most objects correspond to structured type declarations within the code. That is, for each struct declaration, we provide annotations giving its invariants; these invariants apply to each instance of the type. By default, each object owns its fields (except for fields of compound types, which are considered separate objects; large structs can be broken up by introducing ghost substructures). The type declarations are proved admissible using only type information

---

[14] http://www.verisoftxt.de

(they don't need to examine the code). Claims are treated differently from ordinary type definitions, because most claims are local to the code of a single procedure. So the admissibility of a claim is checked at the point at which the claim is formed in the code.

In VCC, there are actually two levels of object construction. The first level merely gives an object ownership of some memory; it guarantees that, in any state, the heap is interpreted in a consistent way. Whenever code accesses memory using a structured type, it requires existence of the structured object. The second level of existence is called "closing" an object; it is only while an object is closed that its declared invariants hold.

In C, there is an important difference between access to variables that are owned by a thread and those that might be concurrently accessed by another thread; in the former case, the compiler can safely reorder operations, while in the latter it cannot. In C, accesses of the later type must be marked as *volatile*, to prevent such optimizations. Only volatile data is update in explicit atomic actions; nonvolatile updates are treated using ordinary sequential reasoning. Nonvolatile fields of an object can only be updated when the object is open and owned by the updating thread.

11   Conclusion

In the world of security, the rights abstraction was introduced for a very practical reason: it provides a simple characterization of what a principal (such as a thread) might do, one that can be simply understood and can be enforced with simple hardware and software mechanisms in a small trusted computing base. It also provided a degree of modularity: a thread can check that it has the rights it needs so that it doesn't get stuck, and can keep certain rights to itself to make sure that other threads don't interfere.

The main lesson of this paper is that rights are a natural derivative of knowledge and invariance, rather than a fundamental notion. From a methodological standpoint, this is enabled by an alternative approach (admissibility) to the required modularity of invariance reasoning. In our approach, the expressiveness of rights grows naturally with the expressiveness of knowledge, and that new rights abstractions can be introduced through programming rather than through extensions to the logic and metatheory. From an implementation standpoint, it allows reuse of the substantial infrastructure built up to reason about knowledge, without the need to introduce new program logics.

These observations do not mean that expressive logics combining knowledge and rights are not a good idea; they provide useful abstractions and guidance for how proofs of programs can be structured. We have even considered including such notations in VCC, as syntactic sugar. But we are very conservative when it comes to extending the program logic itself, and our general policy is to avoid doing so when the desired functionality can be built at the program level. We have not yet found such extensions necessary.

References

1. Brochenin, R., Demri, S., Lozes, E.: On the almighty wand. In: Kaminski, M., Martini, S. (eds.) CSL 2008. LNCS, vol. 5213, pp. 323–338. Springer, Heidelberg (2008)
2. Calcagno, C., Yang, H., O'Hearn, P.W.: Computability and complexity results for a spatial assertion language for data structures. In: APLAS, pp. 289–300 (2001)
3. Cohen, E., Dahlweid, M., Hillebrand, M., Leinenbach, D., Moskal, M., Santen, T., Schulte, W., Tobies, S.: VCC: A practical system for verifying concurrent C. In: Urban, C. (ed.) TPHOLs 2009. LNCS, vol. 5674, pp. 1–22. Springer, Heidelberg (2009) (invited paper)
4. Dodds, M., Feng, X., Parkinson, M., Vafeiadis, V.: Deny-guarantee reasoning. In: Castagna, G. (ed.) ESOP 2009. LNCS, vol. 5502, pp. 363–377. Springer, Heidelberg (2009)
5. Jones, C.B.: Specification and design of (parallel) programs. In: IFIP Congress, pp. 321–332 (1983)
6. Rustan, K., Leino, M.: A basis for verifying multi-threaded programs. In: Castagna, G. (ed.) ESOP 2009. LNCS, vol. 5502, pp. 378–393. Springer, Heidelberg (2009)
7. O'Hearn, P.W.: Resources, concurrency, and local reasoning. Theor. Comput. Sci. 375(1-3), 271–307 (2007)

Distributed Embedded Systems: Reconciling Computation, Communication and Resource Interaction

Lothar Thiele

Swiss Federal Institute of Technology Zurich (ETH), Zurich, Switzerland
thiele@tik.ee.ethz.ch
http://www.tik.ee.ethz.ch/~thiele/

Extended Abstract

Embedded systems are typically reactive systems that are in continuous inter-action with their physical environment to which they are connected through sensors and actuators. Examples are applications in multimedia processing, automatic control, automotive and avionics, and industrial automation. This has as result that many embedded systems must meet real-time constraints, i. e. they must react to stimuli within a time interval dictated by the environment.

The embedding into a technical environment and the constraints imposed by a particular application domain often require a distributed implementation of embedded systems, where a number of hardware components communicate via some interconnection network. The hardware components in such systems are often specialized and aligned to their local environment and their functionality. And also the interconnection networks are often not homogeneous, but may instead be composed of several interconnected sub-networks, each with its own communication protocol and topology. And in more recent embedded systems, the architectural concepts of heterogeneity, distributivity and parallelism can even be observed on single hardware components themselves: they become system characteristics that can be observed on several abstraction layers.

It becomes apparent that heterogeneous and distributed embedded real-time systems as described above are inherently difficult to design and to analyze. During the system level design process of an embedded system, a designer is typically faced with questions such as whether the timing properties of a certain system design will meet the design requirements, what architectural element will act as a bottleneck, or what the memory requirements will be. Consequently it becomes one of the major challenges in the design process to analyze specific characteristics of a system design, such as end-to- end delays, buffer require-ments, or throughput in an early design stage, to support making important design decisions before much time is invested in detailed implementations. This analysis is generally referred to as system level performance analysis.

Based on the above discussion we can summarize that embedded systems are characterized by a close interaction between computation, communication, the associated resources and the physical environment. The solution of the above

A. Pnueli, I. Virbitskaite, and A. Voronkov (Eds.): PSI 2009, LNCS 5947, pp. 56–57, 2010.
© Springer-Verlag Berlin Heidelberg 2010

complex analysis and design problems relies on our abilities to properly deal with some of the following challenges:

- *Challenge 1:* Designing component models whose interfaces talk about extra-functional properties like time, energy and resource interaction.
- *Challenge 2:* Designing models of computation that talk about functional component properties and resource interaction.
- *Challenge 3:* Developing system design methods that lead to timing-predictable and efficient embedded systems.

It will be necessary to (re)think the classical separation of concerns which removed very successfully physical aspects from the concept of computation. It will be necessary to (re) combine the computational and physical view of embedded software.

The presentation we will cover the following aspects:

- Component-based performance analysis of distributed embedded systems (Modular Performance Analysis): basic principles, methods and tool support.
- Real-time Interfaces: from real-time components to real-time interfaces, adaptivity and constraints propagation.
- Application examples that show the applicability of the concepts and their use in embedded system design.

References

1. Thiele, L., Chakraborty, S., Naedele, M.: Real-time calculus for scheduling hard real-time systems. In: Proc. Intl. Symposium on Circuits and Systems, vol. 4, pp. 101–104 (2000)
2. Chakraborty, S., Kunzli, S., Thiele, L.: A general framework for analysing system properties in platform-based embedded system designs. In: Proc. 6th Design, Automation and Test in Europe (DATE), pp. 190–195 (2003)
3. Thiele, L., Wandeler, E., Stoimenov, N.: Real-time interfaces for composing real-time systems. In: International Conference on Embedded Software EMSOFT 2006, Seoul, Korea, pp. 34–43 (2006)
4. Wandeler, E., Thiele, L.: Interface-based design of real-time systems with hierarchical scheduling. In: Proc. 12th IEEE Real-Time and Embedded Technology and Applications Symposium (RTAS), San Jose, CA, USA, April 2006, pp. 243–252 (2006)
5. Wandeler, E., Thiele, L., Verhoef, M., Lieverse, P.: System architecture evaluation using modular performance analysis — a case study. Software Tools for Technology Transfer (STTT) 8(6), 649–667 (2006)
6. Perathoner, S., Wandeler, E., Thiele, L., Hamann, A., Schliecker, S., Henia, R., Racu, R., Ernst, R., González Harbour, M.: Influence of different system abstractions on the performance analysis of distributed real-time systems. In: Proc. 7th International Conference on Embedded Software (EMSOFT), Salzburg, Austria, pp. 193–202 (2007)
7. Wandeler, E., Thiele, L.: Real-Time Calculus (RTC) Toolbox (2008), http://www.mpa.ethz.ch/Rtctoolbox

Simulation of Kohn's Molecular Interaction Maps through Translation into Stochastic CLS+

Roberto Barbuti[1], Daniela Lepri[2], Andrea Maggiolo-Schettini[1],
Paolo Milazzo[1], Giovanni Pardini[1], and Aureliano Rama[1]

[1] Dipartimento di Informatica, Università di Pisa
{barbuti,maggiolo,milazzo,pardinig,rama}@di.unipi.it
[2] Institutt for Informatikk, Universitetet i Oslo
leprid@ifi.uio.no

Abstract. Kohn's Molecular Interaction Maps (MIMs) are a graphical notation for describing bioregulatory networks at the molecular level. Even if the meaning of Kohn's diagrams can be often easily understood, in many cases, due to the lack of a precise mathematical semantics, the notation can be ambiguous. By this paper we achieve two goals. Firstly, we give a precise meaning to MIMs by their translation into a formalism, the Stochastic Calculus of Looping Sequences (SCLS+), with a mathematical semantics. Further, by this translation we provide MIMs with all the tools developed for SCLS+, namely analysers and simulators. The ability of SCLS+ to specify compartments allows us to easily translate MIMs descriptions also when membranes are involved in the interactions.

1 Introduction

The definition of a diagrammatic graphical language able to describe biochemical networks in a clearly visible and unambiguous way is an important step towards the understanding of cell regulatory mechanisms. One of the most well designed and rigidly defined proposals of graphical language are Kohn's Molecular Interaction Maps (MIMs) [1,2,3]. In these maps, biochemical components of bioregulatory networks are depicted using a notation similar to the "wiring diagrams" used in electronics, and various types of interactions that may occur between the components can be represented. Interactions include complex formations, phosphorylations, enzyme catalysis, stimulation and inhibition of biochemical reactions, DNA transcription, etc.

The use of a single MIM diagram to describe all the interactions in a biochemical network allows the tracing of pathways within the network, for instance with the aid of computer simulation. However, even if the meaning of MIM symbols is clear and easy to understand, there is a lack of univocal interpretation when symbols are combined, hence some diagrams cannot be used directly as an input for a simulation tool. This is confirmed by the distinction made by Kohn in [2] between *heuristic maps*, which may have more than one interpretation, and *explicit maps*, that are less expressive but unambiguous. The conclusion of Kohn

A. Pnueli, I. Virbitskaite, and A. Voronkov (Eds.): PSI 2009, LNCS 5947, pp. 58–69, 2010.
© Springer-Verlag Berlin Heidelberg 2010

is that only the latters should be used to perform simulations, by translating them into a list of chemical reactions.

In this paper we face the problem of allowing the simulation of a set of diagrams larger than the explicit ones. In particular, we consider the Stochastic CLS formalism [4], that is a formal language based on term rewriting for the description of biochemical systems. We recall its definition by adopting the syntax of CLS+ [5,6] (we call this variant Stochastic CLS+). We translate MIMs into Stochastic CLS+ by exploiting (i) the similarities between biochemical reactions and rewrite rules and (ii) the capability of Stochastic CLS+ to model compartments. We show that with this translation we can simulate more diagrams than the set of explicit ones.

As regards related work, in [7] a simple example of MIM has been modeled using the Beta–binders formalism [8]. Another translation of MIMs in a formal syntax (concurrent constraint programming) can be found in [9]. Moreover, other graphical languages for biochemical networks have been defined [10,11,12]. Among these, the notation introduced in [10] (which has been compared with MIMs in [13]) seems to be another promising proposal, as it has been used to model a real complex example of signalling pathway [14] and it is supported by useful software tools [15]. A different approach to the graphical description of biochemical networks based on graph rewriting is proposed in [16,17]. Finally, present work is based on the approach proposed in [18].

2   Stochastic CLS+

In this section we recall the definition of the Stochastic Calculus of Looping Sequences (SCLS for short) and the syntax of an extension called CLS+, to define a variant we call Stochastic CLS+. For the sake of brevity we omit some technical details. Missing details of the calculus can be found in [4,5,6].

The Stochastic CLS+ formalism is basically a term rewriting framework including some typical features of process calculi for concurrency. A model in the Stochastic CLS+ is composed by a term describing the inital state of the modeled system, and a finite set of rewrite rules to be applied to terms, describing the events that may occur in the system. In the definition of Stochastic CLS+ terms, that follows, we assume an alphabet of elements $\mathcal{E}$ ranged over by $a, b, c, \ldots$.

Terms T, branes B and sequences S of the Stochastic CLS+ are given by the following grammar:

$$T \ ::= \ S \ | \ (B)^L \rfloor T \ | \ T \,|\, T \qquad B \ ::= \ S \ | \ B \,|\, B \qquad S \ ::= \ \epsilon \ | \ a \ | \ S \cdot S$$

We denote with $\mathcal{T}$, $\mathcal{B}$ and $\mathcal{S}$ the sets of all terms, all branes and all sequences, respectively. Note that $\mathcal{E} \subset \mathcal{S} \subset \mathcal{B} \subset \mathcal{T}$. A term can be either (i) a sequence of symbols in $\mathcal{E}$ with ϵ as the empty sequence and $\cdot$ as the sequencing operator, or (ii) a looping sequence $(B)^L$ (that is a parallel composition of sequences, with $|$ as the parallel composition operator) containing another term T, with $\rfloor$ as the containment operator, or (iii) the parallel composition (the juxtaposition) of two terms.

The calculus comes with structural congruence relations on sequences $\equiv_S$, on branes $\equiv_B$ and on terms $\equiv$ such that $\equiv_S \subseteq \equiv_B \subseteq \equiv$. The first, $\equiv_S$, is defined as the least congruence on $\mathcal{S}$ for which $(S, \cdot, \epsilon)$ is a monoid. The second, $\equiv_B$, is the least congruence such that $(\mathcal{B}, \mid, \epsilon)$ is a commutative monoid. The third, $\equiv$, is the least congruence closed under $(\cdot)^L \rfloor \cdot$ and such that $(\mathcal{T}, \mid, \epsilon)$ is a commutative monoid. A rewrite rule is essentially a pair of terms with variables (called *patterns*) P_1, P_2 representing a portion of the described system before and after the occurrence of the modeled event. A rewrite rule can be applied to a term T if there exists a subterm of T which is structurally equivalent to an instantiation of P_1, by replacing the subterm with the corresponding instantiation of P_2. Variables $\mathcal{V}$ are of different kinds. *Element variables* $x, y, \ldots \in \mathcal{X}$, which can be instantiated by elements in $\mathcal{E}$, *sequence variables* $\tilde{x}, \tilde{y}, \ldots \in \mathcal{SV}$, for sequences in $\mathcal{S}$, *brane variables* $\overline{X}, \overline{Y}, \ldots \in \mathcal{BV}$ for branes in $\mathcal{B}$, and *term variables* $X, Y, \ldots \in \mathcal{TV}$ for terms in $\mathcal{T}$. Formally, patterns are defined as follows:

$$P \; ::= \; SP \; \mid \; (BP)^L \rfloor P \; \mid \; P \mid P \; \mid \; X \qquad BP \; ::= \; SP \; \mid \; BP \mid BP \; \mid \; \overline{X}$$
$$SP \; ::= \; \epsilon \; \mid \; a \; \mid \; SP \cdot SP \; \mid \; \tilde{x} \; \mid \; x$$

We denote by $\mathcal{P}$ the set of all Patterns and by Σ the set of all instantiation functions $\sigma : \mathcal{V} \mapsto \mathcal{T}$. Instantiation functions are required to preserve the types of the variables. Formally, a *rewrite rule* is a triple (P', P'', f), where $P', P'' \in \mathcal{P}$ and $f : \Sigma \mapsto \mathbb{R}^+$, such that $P' \not\equiv \epsilon$ and $Var(P'') \subseteq Var(P')$.

In what follows, we will use the notation $P' \stackrel{f}{\mapsto} P''$ for a rewrite rule (P', P'', f), and we will call f the *rate function* of the rewrite rule. Such a function gives the rate value of the rule, depending on the actual term used for the instantiation of the variables in P'. We say that a rewrite rule (P', P'', f) is ground if both P' and P'' contain no variables.

Now, a Stochastic CLS+ model consisting of a set of rewrite rules $\mathcal{R}$ and of an initial ground term T_0, evolves by means of a sequence of application of rewrite rules in $\mathcal{R}$ to term T_0. After each application, a new term is obtained which describes the state of the system after the occurrence of the event modeled by the applied rule. At each step, the rule to be applied is randomly chosen with a probability which depends on an *actual application rate*. Such an actual rate is the value obtained by the rate function multiplied by the number of possible positions in the term where the rule can be applied. The actual application rate is used also as the parameter of an exponential distribution to determine the quantity of time spent by the occurrence of the described event.

More precisely, at each step a set of *applicable ground rewrite rules* $AR(\mathcal{R}, T)$ is computed which contains all the ground rules that can be applied to T and that are obtained by instantiating variables in the rules in $\mathcal{R}$. In each of these ground rules we have $r = f(T)$, where f is the rate function of the rewrite rule from which it was istantiated. By the finiteness of $\mathcal{R}$ and of T we have that $AR(\mathcal{R}, T)$ is a finite set of ground rewrite rules. For each ground rule R in $AR(\mathcal{R}, T)$ and for each possible term T' that can be obtained by the application R, the number of different application positions in T where R can be applied producing T' is computed. Such a number, called the *application cardinality* of

R leading from T to T', is denoted as $AC(R, T, T')$, and is the number that must be multiplied by the rate constant of R to obtain the actual application rate.

The semantics of the Stochastic CLS+ can now be given as a labeled transition system, in which a transition corresponds to the application of a rule and its label contains a reference to the applied rule and the actual application rate. In the definition of the semantics we use a notion of *context* to express the position in the term where a rewrite rule is applied.

Formally, *Term Contexts* C_T and *Brane Context* C_B are given by:

$$C_T ::= \square \mid C_T \mid T \mid T \mid C_T \mid (B)^L \rfloor C_T$$
$$C_B ::= \square \mid C_B \mid T \mid T \mid C_B \mid (C_B')^L \rfloor T \mid (B)^L \rfloor C_B$$
$$C_B' ::= \square \mid C_B' \mid T \mid T \mid C_B'$$

where $T \in \mathcal{T}$, $B \in \mathcal{B}$ and $S \in \mathcal{S}$. Context $\square$ is called the *empty context*. C_T is the set of all the Term Contexts and C_B is the set of all Brane Contexts.

With $C[T]$ we denote the term obtained by replacing $\square$ with T in C. The structural congruence relation can be easily extended to contexts.

Definition 1 (Semantics). *Given a finite set of rewrite rules $\mathcal{R}$, the semantics of the Stochastic CLS+ is the least labeled transition relation satisfying the following inference rules:*

$$\frac{R = T' \overset{r}{\mapsto} T'' \in AR(\mathcal{R}, C[T']) \quad C \in \mathcal{C}_T}{C[T'] \xrightarrow{R, r \cdot AC(R, C[T'], C[T''])} C[T'']} \qquad \frac{R = B' \overset{r}{\mapsto} B'' \in AR(\mathcal{R}, C[B']) \quad C \in \mathcal{C}_B}{C[B'] \xrightarrow{R, r \cdot AC(R, C[B'], C_B[B''])} C[B'']}$$

The semantics of the calculus is a transition relation describing all the possible evolutions of the modeled system. From such a relation a Continuous Time Markov Chain (CTMC) can be easily derived, allowing the verification of properties of the system. However, since the whole CTMC describing the system has often a huge number of states, hence its construction is often unfeasible, we can follow a standard simulation procedure that corresponds to Gillespie's simulation algorithm [19]. A complete simulator for Stochastic CLS has been already implemented in F#, based on this simulation strategy [20].

3   Molecular Interaction Maps

In this section we recall the definition of Kohn's Molecular Interaction Maps (MIMs) and we show how they can be translated into Stochastic CLS+. Since several definitions of MIMs are available, we refer to the definition that can be found in [3]. We present both MIMs and their translation incrementally, by showing first the diagrams for basic molecular interactions and then their extension with contingency symbols.

A species in a MIM is depicted as a box containing the species name (Fig. 1.a). In the case of a DNA site, the box is placed over a thick line representing a DNA strand, and more than one site can be placed over the same line (Fig. 1.c). A bullet (Fig. 1.b) is used to denote both a species when it is the result of a reaction and different instances of the same species (see the dimer *AB:AB* in Fig. 4).

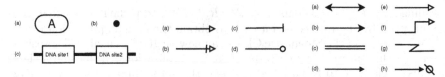

Fig. 1. Species in MIMs   **Fig. 2.** Contingency arrows   **Fig. 3.** Reaction symbols

Basic Diagrams. Basic MIM diagrams are composed by species and DNA fragments related each other by some reaction symbols. Reaction symbols are arrows, and they are listed in Fig. 3. In the figure, arrow (a) connects two species and denotes the reversible binding of them; (b) points to one species and denotes a covalent modification (phosphorylation, acetylation, etc.), the type of the modification is usually written at the tail of the arrow; (c) connects two species and denotes a covalent binding; (d) connects two species and denotes a stoichiometric conversion, namely the species at the tail of the arrow disappears while the pointed one appears; (e) is like (d) without the loss of the species at the tail of the arrow; (f) connects a DNA strand and a species and denotes DNA transcription; (g) represents the cleavage of a covalent bond; finally, (h) is connected to a single species and represents its degradation. Every reaction symbol in a MIM diagram is associated with a kinetic constant (to be obtained from biological experiments) representing its occurrence rate. Arrow (a) is associated with two kinetic constants: one describing the rate of binding and the other describing the rate of unbinding.

Extended Diagrams. MIM diagrams can be extended with reaction modifiers, called "contingencies". Contingency arrows start from a species (or a compound of species) and point to a reaction, meaning that the presence (or absence) of the species influences the reaction. This influence is expressed as a change in the rate at which the reaction can happen. Contingency arrows are listed in Fig. 2. In the figure, arrow (a) stimulates the reaction pointed (increase its reaction rate) if the species is present in the environment; (b) is the necessity contingency and means that the reaction can happen only if the species is present (if not present, the reaction rate drops to zero); inhibition contingency (c) is dual to the previous one in that the reaction is allowed only if the species at hand is not present in the environment; finally, (d) is the catalysis arrow which means that the reaction have a much higher reaction rate if the species is present than if it is not.

Example. Here we show a small example of a real life MIM. In Figure 4 one can see a MIM depicting a process of RNA synthesis inside the cell nucleus, activated by the presence of a species (B) outside the outer membrane of the cell through interaction with a membrane channel (species A). Species B can bind to species A that is present onto the plasma membrane forming complex $A{:}B$. Two such complexes can bind together, forming compound $AB{:}AB$, which allows the phosphorilation of a third A, denoted A_p, which can then migrate inside the nucleus membrane. There, compund species A_p can bind to a DNA fragment and together they stimulate the synthesis of a fragment of RNA.

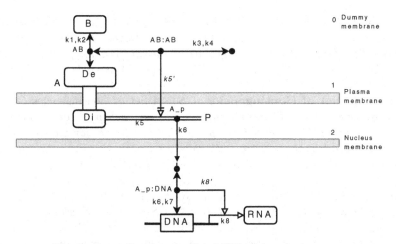

Fig. 4. Example of an explicit MIM with rate constants

4   Translating Maps into Stochastic CLS+

In this section we provide a precise semantics for MIMs by its translation into
Stochastic CLS+. Since there is no formal description of MIMs, we introduce
an *intermediate encoding* of MIMs, that allows us to formally specify the source
of our translation. This intermediate encoding is sufficiently high level to allow
a straightforward construction of the encoding from a diagram. Since we are
interested in the possibility of simulating the MIMs, we need additional information about the initial number and position of the molecules of each species.
This information, which is not provided by MIM diagrams, has to be included
in the intermediate encoding.

4.1   Intermediate Encoding of MIM

An intermediate encoding is composed of a *Membrane Structure*, a *Set of Species*,
and a *Set of Reactions*. The first specifies the (static) membrane structure, the
second describes position and initial number of the molecules of each species, the
third captures the interaction capabilities of the species and their contingencies.
We assume that membranes are uniquely identified by natural numbers in $\mathbb{N}$. We
represent each different species (simple or compound) that appears in a MIM
diagram as a simple CLS+ sequence S.

Definition 2 (Membrane Structure of a MIM). *A Membrane Structure
MS is a set of tuples of the form $\langle i, I \rangle \in \mathbb{N} \times \mathscr{P}(\mathbb{N})$, where i is the membrane
number, that uniquely identifies it, and I contains the identification numbers of
the membranes which are immediately contained in membrane i.*
We denote with $\mathcal{MS}$ the set of all possible Membrane Structures.

Definition 3 (Set of Species). *A Set of Species SS is a set of tuples of the
form $\langle S, (i, j), q \rangle \in \mathcal{S} \times (\mathbb{N} \times \{0, 1\}) \times \mathbb{N}$ where each tuple corresponds to a CLS+*

sequence S (representing a species), whose position in the membrane hierarchy is described by (i, j), and whose quantity is q. In particular, i is the membrane id and j specifies if S is either on the surface of the membrane, $(j = 0)$, or inside the membrane, $(j = 1)$. We denote by SS the set of all possible Sets of Species.

Definition 4 (Set of Contingencies, CS). *A Set of Contingencies CS is a set of pairs of the form $\langle C, k \rangle \in SS \times \mathbb{R}$, where each pair corresponds to a contingency symbol, C is the Set of Species that must exist for the contingency to be verified and k is the reaction rate constant.*
We denote with $\mathcal{CS}$ the set of all possible Sets of Contingencies.

Definition 5 (Set of Reactions, RS). *Given a MIM, its Set of Reactions RS is a set of tuples of the form $\langle CS, R, P \rangle \in \mathcal{CS} \times SS \times SS$ where each tuple corresponds to a reaction symbol in the MIM. In particular, CS are the contingencies, and R and P specify reactants and products of the reaction, respectively. We denote with $\mathcal{RS}$ the set of all possible Sets of Reactions.*

The construction of an intermediate encoding of a MIM diagram is almost straightforward. First of all, assuming to identify each membrane with a natural number, and each species with a simple CLS+ sequence S, we can construct a Membrane Structure and a Set of Species by inspecting the MIM diagram. Please note that in the Set of Species we have to specify the initial quantity of each molecular species in each position where they appear. To simplify the translation, we assume the existence of a dummy outer membrane with $id = 0$ that contains the whole system.

For each reaction symbol of the MIM diagram, we create one or two tuples in the Set of Reactions specifying contigency species, reactants and products. Reactants specify the species that are needed for the reaction to happen, and are replaced by the product species once the reaction occurs. This representation is sufficient to describe the behavior of any MIM reaction symbol (fig. 3). For instance in fig. 4 the reversible binding between A and B is described by tuples $\langle \langle \varnothing, k_1 \rangle, R, P \rangle$ and $\langle \langle \varnothing, k_2 \rangle, P, R \rangle$ where $R = \{ \langle A, (1, 0), 1 \rangle, \langle B, (0, 1), 1 \rangle \}$ and $P = \{ \langle AB, (1, 0), 1 \rangle \}$.

As regards contingencies, the intermediate representation treats uniformly the different MIM symbols available (fig. 2), by modeling each contigency as a set of species whose presence in the environment affects the (constant) basal rate of the reaction. First of all, the basal reaction rate to use when no contingency is involved is also represented in the Set of Contingencies, by a tuple of the form $\langle \varnothing, k_0 \rangle$. We call it *neutral contingency*, and assume that each reaction has one. To avoid ambiguity in determining the basal rate of a reaction for which more than one contingency is verified, we impose some constraints on the Set of Contingencies. In particular, we require that, for any two contingencies $\langle C_1, k_1 \rangle, \langle C_2, k_2 \rangle \in CS$ there exists a contingency $\langle C_1 \cup C_2, k_3 \rangle$ specifying the rate to use (k_3) when all the species of C_1 and C_2 are present. In this way, we can determine the basal reaction rate as the one given by the *most specific* contingency, i.e. the one for which biggest set of contingency species are present.

4.2 From the Intermediate Encoding to Stochastic CLS+

The translation is composed of two parts. The first concerns translation of the initial state of the MIM system, described by its Membrane Structure and a Set of Species, into a CLS+ term. The second deals with the interaction symbols, by translating the Set of Reactions of the MIM into a set of rewrite rules.

Translation of the initial state. In the following, we need to extract, from a Set of Species SS, its subset of species appearing on a precise position, i.e. on the surface or inside a given membrane. We denote this subset as $SS^{ij} \in SS$, where i is the membrane id and j specifies if we need the elements on the surface of the membrane, if $j = 0$, or those inside, if $j = 1$. Formally, $SS^{ij} = \{\langle S, (i, j), q \rangle \in SS\}$. Moreover, we denote by $membrane(SS) \subset \mathbb{N}$ the ids of the membranes appearing in a given SS, i.e. $membrane(SS) = \{i \in \mathbb{N} | \langle S, (i, j), q \rangle \in SS\}$.

The following definitions formally describe the construction of the initial CLS+ term corresponding to a MIM.

Definition 6 (Set of species Translation Function, ϕ). *Given a set of species SS, the function $\phi : SS \rightarrow \mathcal{T}$ gives the corresponding CLS+ term formed by the parallel composition of all species with their multiplicities, i.e. $\phi(\{\langle S_1, p_1, q_1 \rangle, \dots, \langle S_n, p_n, q_n \rangle\}) = q_1 \odot S_1 | \cdots | q_n \odot S_n$, where $n \odot T$ stands for a parallel composition of n times T, that is $T | \dots | T$ of length n $(0 \odot T \equiv \epsilon)$.*

Note that the term produced by the function ϕ is always a brane $\mathcal{B}$ since it never contains a looping sequence operator.

Definition 7 (Term Translation Function, $[\![\cdot]\!]$). *Given a Membrane Structure $MS \in \mathcal{MS}$ and a Set of Species $SS \in SS$, the Term Translation Function $[\![\cdot]\!]$ is defined by the following rule schema:*

$$\frac{\langle j_k, C_k \rangle \in MS \qquad [\![\langle j_k, C_k \rangle]\!] \mapsto T_k \qquad k = 1, \dots, n}{[\![\langle i, \{j_1, \dots, j_n\}\rangle]\!] \mapsto (i | \phi(SS^{i0}))^L \rfloor (\phi(SS^{i1}) | T_1 \dots | T_n)}$$

Note that SS^{i0} is the set of species present on the surface of the membrane i while SS^{i1} contains the species inside membrane i.

Definition 8 (Initial Term of a MIM). *Given a Molecular Interaction Map, described by a Membrane Structure $MS \in \mathcal{MS}$ and a Set of Species SS, the initial CLS+ term is $T_0 = [\![\langle 0, C \rangle]\!]$, where $\langle 0, C \rangle \in MS$.*

The initial term is constructed by Term Translation Function applied to the outer membrane with $id = 0$. This translation computes a CLS+ term, where each membrane of the MIM is represented by a looping sequence, and their containment hierarchy is preserved. The species appearing on the surface and inside the membranes are put in the correct position in the corresponding looping sequences. Finally, a special symbol i is present on each looping sequence, denoting the membrane id from which it has been constructed.

Translation of the interactions. Given a membrane structure MS and a set of nodes N, we denote by $subtree(MS, N) \in \mathcal{MS}$ the smallest subtree of MS induced by the nodes N, that is the minimal tree containing all the nodes in N. We also assume the function $root : \mathcal{MS} \rightarrow (\mathbb{N} \times \mathscr{P}(\mathbb{N}))$ that gives the root node of the membrane structure (where a node is the pair of its id and the set of ids of the nodes immediately contained in it).

Each reaction of a MIM, represented by an element of a Set of Reactions RS, is translated into a stochastic CLS+ rewrite rule. This translation is performed by the reaction translation function, which uses an auxiliary function, the parallel pattern builder, for constructing the patterns which compose the rewrite rule.

Definition 9 (Parallel Pattern Builder Function, $[\![\cdot]\!]_{pp}$). *Given a membrane structure MS, the* parallel pattern builder function $[\![\cdot]\!]_{pp} : (\mathbb{N} \times \mathscr{P}(\mathbb{N})) \times (\mathcal{SS} \times \mathcal{SS}) \rightarrow \mathcal{P} \times \mathcal{P}$ *is defined as follows:*

$$X_0 = new(\mathcal{BV}) \qquad X_1 = new(\mathcal{TV})$$

$$\langle c_j, C_j \rangle \in MS \qquad [\![\langle c_j, C_j \rangle, (SS_1, SS_2)]\!]_{pp} \mapsto (P1_j, P2_j) \qquad j = 1, 2, \dots, k$$

$$\phi(SS_1^{i0}) = T1_{i0} \quad \phi(SS_1^{i1}) = T1_{i1} \qquad \phi(SS_2^{i0}) = T2_{i0} \quad \phi(SS_2^{i1}) = T2_{i1}$$

$$[\![\langle i, \{c_1, c_2, \dots c_k\} \rangle, (SS_1, SS_2)]\!]_{pp} \mapsto ((i \,|\, T1_{i0} \,|\, X_0)^L \,\rfloor\, (T1_{i1} \,|\, P1_1 \,|\, \dots \,|\, P1_k \,|\, X_1),$$
$$(i \,|\, T2_{i0} \,|\, X_0)^L \,\rfloor\, (T2_{i1} \,|\, P2_1 \,|\, \dots \,|\, P2_k \,|\, X_1))$$

where $X_i = new(\dots)$ means that the term variable X_i has not previously been used in the current application of $[\![\cdot]\!]_{pp}$, $P_i \in \mathcal{P}$ and $T_i \in \mathcal{T}$.

The parallel pattern builder function takes as arguments a root membrane (and its children), two sets of species (the reactants and the products of a reaction) and it gives as a result the pair of reactants-products expressed as CLS+ terms. The $[\![\cdot]\!]_{pp}$ function is used in the definition of the function for translating a reaction into a stochastic CLS+ rewrite rule.

The reaction translation function also uses the following function xc to deal with contingencies. Function xc is applied to a pattern, obtained by the parallel pattern builder, and a set of species SS, representing the contingencies of the reaction. It associates, with each term variable X appearing in P, a term containing the species from SS that can be instantianted in the variable X. In this way, we can keep track of the variables in which the contigency species can appear. Formally, function $xc : \mathcal{P} \times \mathcal{SS} \rightarrow \mathscr{P}(\mathcal{BV} \cup \mathcal{TV} \times \mathcal{T})$ is defined as:

$$xc((i \,|\, B_1 \,|\, \overline{X_1})^L \,\rfloor\, (P_2 \,|\, X_2), \, SS) = \{\langle \overline{X_1}, \phi(SS^{i0}) \rangle, \langle X_2, \phi(SS^{i1}) \rangle\} \cup xc(P_2, SS)$$
$$xc(P1 \,|\, P2, SS) = xc(P_1, SS) \cup xc(P_2, SS) \qquad xc(T, SS) = \varnothing$$

Definition 10 (Reaction Translation Function, $[\![\cdot]\!]_r$). *Let MS be the Membrane Structure of a MIM. Given a reaction $\langle CS, RS, PS \rangle$, the Reaction Translation Function $[\![\cdot]\!]_r : (\mathcal{CS} \times \mathcal{SS} \times \mathcal{SS}) \rightarrow \Re$ is defined as follows:*

$$(P_1, P_2) = [\![root(MS'), (CS, RS, PS)]\!]_{pp} \qquad MS' = subtree(MS, N)$$
$$N = membrane((\textstyle\bigcup_{j=1}^{n} C_j) \cup RS \cup PS) \qquad CS = \{(C_1, k_1), (C_2, k_2), \dots, (C_n, k_n)\}$$
$$xc(P_1, C_i) \mapsto \{\langle X_1, T_1^i \rangle, \langle X_2, T_2^i \rangle, \dots, \langle X_m, T_m^i \rangle\} \quad i = 1, \dots, n$$
$$[\![\langle CS, RS, PS \rangle]\!]_r = (P_1, P_2, f)$$

where P_1, P_2 are CLS+ patterns, and the rate function f is defined as follows:

$$f(P_1\sigma) = basalRate(\sigma) \cdot \prod_{\langle S,(i,j),q\rangle \in RS} \left(\frac{occ(P_1\sigma, (i,j), S)}{q} \right)$$

$$basalRate(\sigma) = \begin{cases} k_1 & if \; \exists U_1,\ldots,U_m. \quad \sigma(X_1) \equiv T_1^1 \,|\, U_1 \wedge \ldots \wedge \sigma(X_m) \equiv T_m^1 \,|\, U_m \\ k_2 & if \; \exists U_1,\ldots,U_m. \quad \sigma(X_1) \equiv T_1^2 \,|\, U_1 \wedge \ldots \wedge \sigma(X_m) \equiv T_m^2 \,|\, U_m \\ \vdots & \qquad \vdots \\ k_n & if \; \exists U_1,\ldots,U_m. \quad \sigma(X_1) \equiv T_1^n \,|\, U_1 \wedge \ldots \wedge \sigma(X_m) \equiv T_m^n \,|\, U_m \end{cases}$$

The function f computes the rate of the application of the rewrite rule as the product of a basal rate and of the number of different reactions represented by this application. The basal rate is a constant rate that depends on the contingencies. In the definition of $basalRate$ we are assuming that, if more than one condition is satisfied (i.e. more than one contingency is applicable), then the most specific one is used. The constraints we imposed on the set of contincencies (see Sec.4.1) ensure that the definition of $basalRate$ is unambiguous.

The number of different reactions represented by the application of a rewrite rule takes into account the reactions involving molecules of a same species S. Considering a single compartment i, j, the reaction can happen among any subset of molecules of that species S, having the right cardinality. Therefore, for each reactant species S in each compartment i, j, described by a tuple in RS, the number of reactions corresponds to the binomial coefficient of q, i.e. the number of molecules required, and $occ(P_1\sigma, (i, j), S)$, i.e. the number of molecules present in compartment (i, j) in the actual term $P_1\sigma$.

Definition 11 (Set of Rewrite Rules of a MIM, RR). *Given a Molecular Interaction Map, described by a Membrane Structure MS and whose reactions are encoded in the Set of Reactions $RS = \{R_1,\ldots,R_n\}$, the Set of Rewrite Rules $RR \subset \Re$ of the corresponding Stochastic CLS+ model is $RR = \{[\![R_1]\!]_r, [\![R_2]\!]_r, \ldots, [\![R_n]\!]_r\}$.*

5 Applications

Now we show a small example of the translation process we defined by translating part of MIM of Fig.4 which showed a process of RNA synthesis. In the first phase of the process, protein A binds to protein B thus forming the complex $A{:}B$ on the plasma membrane. Then two complexes can form a dimer which can be phosphorilated. In the following, we show these two reactions translated as Stochastic CLS+ terms and rewrite rules.

Firstly, we define the membrane structure: $MS = \{\langle 0, \{1\}\rangle, \langle 1, \{2\}\rangle, \langle 2, \varnothing\rangle\}$.

Then we want to formalize the reaction where B binds to A ($A \mid B \overset{k_1}{\underset{k_2}{\rightleftharpoons}} AB$).

To do so, we need to describe two reaction tuples for this reaction, one for the complexation and another one for the de-complexation:

$$R_1 = \langle \{\langle \varnothing, k_1 \rangle\}, \{\langle A, (1,0), 1\rangle, \langle B, (0,1), 1\rangle\}, \{\langle AB, (1,0), 1\rangle\}\rangle$$
$$R_2 = \langle \{\langle \varnothing, k_2 \rangle\}, \{\langle AB, (1,0), 1\rangle\}, \{\langle A, (1,0), 1\rangle, \langle B, (0,1), 1\rangle\}\rangle$$

As one can see, no contingency influences these reactions, hence the only one present is the neutral one. We place the product on membrane 1, since the complex should be still connected to the membrane. The resulting rewrite rules for these reactions are:

$(R_1) \quad (0 \,|\, X_0)^L \,\rfloor\, (B \,|\, (1 \,|\, A \,|\, X_2)^L \,\rfloor\, X_3 \,|\, X_1) \stackrel{f_1}{\mapsto} (0 \,|\, X_0)^L \,\rfloor\, ((1 \,|\, AB \,|\, X_2)^L \,\rfloor\, X_3 \,|\, X_1)$

$(R_2) \quad (0 \,|\, X_0)^L \,\rfloor\, ((1 \,|\, AB \,|\, X_2)^L \,\rfloor\, X_3 \,|\, X_1) \stackrel{f_2}{\mapsto} (0 \,|\, X_0)^L \,\rfloor\, (B \,|\, (1 \,|\, A \,|\, X_2)^L \,\rfloor\, X_3 \,|\, X_1)$

where the $basalRate$ of both f_1 and f_2 have constant results, resp. k_1 and k_2.

Now we describe the phosphorylation of the A component allowed by the presence of the dimer $AB{:}AB$ on the plasma membrane. This modification will be described by a single reaction tuple since it is not reversible. The presence of a "necessity" contingency pointing to the reaction will be a tuple in the Set of Contingencies of the Reaction Set. Thus, we will formalize the following (mutually exclusive) reactions $A \stackrel{k_5}{\rightleftharpoons} pA$ and $AB{:}AB \,|\, A \stackrel{k'_5}{\rightleftharpoons} AB{:}AB \,|\, pA$. A single reaction tuple will model both reactions:

$$R_3 = \langle \{\langle \varnothing, k_5\rangle, \langle \{\langle AB{:}AB, (0,1), 1\rangle\}, k'_5\rangle\}, \{\langle A, (1,0), 1\rangle\}, \{\langle pA, (1,0), 1\rangle\}\rangle$$

where k_5 is equal to zero in our example (since the phosphorylation needs the presence of $AB{:}AB$). The resulting rewrite rule for this reaction tuple is:

$(R_3) \quad (0 \,|\, X_0)^L \,\rfloor\, ((1 \,|\, A \,|\, X_2)^L \,\rfloor\, X_3 \,|\, X_1) \stackrel{f}{\mapsto} (0 \,|\, X_0)^L \,\rfloor\, ((1 \,|\, pA \,|\, X_2)^L \,\rfloor\, X_3 \,|\, X_1)$

$$basalRate(\sigma) = \begin{cases} k'_5 & \text{if } \sigma(X_1) \equiv AB{:}AB \,|\, T \\ k_5 & \text{otherwise} \end{cases}$$

6   Conclusions

In this paper we have given a formal definition of the semantics of Kohn's Molecular Interaction Maps by providing a translation into a variant of the Stochastic Calculus of Looping Sequences (called Stochastic CLS+). Such a definition allows unambiguous understanding and reasoning on Kohn's maps. Moreover, the translation into SCLS+ provides MIMs with simulators and other tools and methodologies developed for CLS+. We plan to implement our translation and to perform some simulations in order to validate the obtained CLS+ model with respect to biological observations. Future work will involve the contruction of graphical interfaces allowing the input of Molecular Interaction Maps and the automatic translation of them into CLS+ terms and rules. This will allow biologists to use the tools for CLS+ with MIMs as interfaces.

References

1. Aladjem, M.I., Pasa, S., Parodi, S., Weinstein, J.N., Pommier, Y., Kohn, K.W.: Molecular Interaction Maps–A Diagrammatic Graphical Language for Bioregulatory Networks. Sci. STKE 2004 (222), 8 (2004)
2. Kohn, K.W.: Molecular Interaction Maps as Information Organizers and Simulation Guides. CHAOS 11(1), 84–97 (2001)
3. Kohn, K.W., Aladjem, M.I., Weinstein, J.N., Pommier, Y.: Molecular Interaction Maps of Bioregulatory Networks: A General Rubric for Systems Biology. Molecular Biology of the Cell 17, 1–13 (2006)
4. Barbuti, R., Maggiolo-Schettini, A., Milazzo, P., Tiberi, P., Troina, A.: Stochastic CLS for the Modeling and Simulation of Biological Systems. Trans. on Comput. Syst. Biol. IX 5121, 86–113 (2008)
5. Milazzo, P.: Qualitative and Quantitative Formal Modeling of Biological Systems. PhD thesis, Computer Science Department - University of Pisa (2007)
6. Milazzo, P.: Formal Modeling in Systems Biology. An approach from Theoretical Computer Science. VDM - Verlag Dr. Muller, Saarbrucken (2008)
7. Ciocchetta, F., Priami, C., Quaglia, P.: Modeling Kohn Interaction Maps with Beta-Binders: An Example. Trans. on Comput. Syst. Biol. III 3737, 33–48 (2005)
8. Priami, C., Quaglia, P.: Beta Binders for Biological Interactions. In: Danos, V., Schachter, V. (eds.) CMSB 2004. LNCS (LNBI), vol. 3082, pp. 20–33. Springer, Heidelberg (2005)
9. Bortolussi, L., Fonda, S., Policriti, A.: Constraint-Based Simulation of Biological Systems Described by Molecular Interaction Maps. In: IEEE International Conference on Bioinformatics and Biomedicine, vol. 0, pp. 288–293 (2007)
10. Kitano, H.: A Graphical Notation for Biochemical Networks. BIOSILICO 1(5), 169–176 (2003)
11. Pirson, I., Fortemaison, N., Jacobs, C., Dremier, S., Dumont, J.E., Maenhaut, C.: The Visual Display of Regulatory Information and Networks. Trends in Cell Biology 10, 404–408 (2000)
12. Systems Biology Graphical Notation, http://sbgn.org
13. Kohn, K.W., Aladjem, M.I.: Circuit Diagrams for Biological Networks. Molecular Systems Biology 2 (2006)
14. Oda, K., Matsuoka, Y., Funahashi, A., Kitano, H.: A Comprensive Pathway Map of Epidermal Growth Factor Receptor Signaling. Molecular Systems Biology 1 (2005)
15. Funahashi, A., Morohashi, M., Kitano, H.: CellDesigner: a Process Diagram Editor for Gene–Regulatory and Biochemical Networks. BIOSILICO 1(5), 159–162 (2003)
16. Danos, V., Laneve, C.: Formal molecular biology. Theor. Comp. Sci. 325(1), 69–110 (2004)
17. Faeder, J.R., Blinov, M.L., Hlavacek, W.S.: Graphical rule-based representation of signal-transduction networks. In: Symposium on Applied Computing (SAC), pp. 133–140 (2005)
18. Lepri, D.: A formal semantics for Molecular Interaction Maps. Master Thesis in Computer Science, University of Pisa (2008)
19. Gillespie, D.T.: Exact stochastic simulation of coupled chemical reactions. Journal of Physical Chemistry 81(25), 2340–2361 (1977)
20. CLSm: simulation tool, http://www.di.unipi.it/~milazzo/biosims

A Two-Level Approach for Modeling and Verification of Telecommunication Systems

Dmitry Beloglazov and Valery Nepomniaschy

A.P. Ershov Institute of Informatics Systems
Siberian Division of Russian Academy of Sciences
6, Lavrentiev ave., Novosibirsk 630090, Russia
dmitry.beloglazov@gmail.com, vnep@iis.nsk.su

Abstract. For modeling, specification and verification of telecommunication systems, the models such as finite automata, Petri nets and their generalizations are usually applied. The goal of our paper is to represent a new two-level approach for modeling, specification and verification of telecommunication systems. On the first level, telecommunication systems are specified by communicating extended finite automata, while on the second level the automata systems are translated into coloured Petri nets (CPN). Correctness of the translation algorithm is justified by proving bisimilarity between the resulting CPN and the automata system. This method is applied to investigation of two case studies: ring protocols (RE-protocol and ATMR-protocol) and the feature interaction problem in telephone networks. CPN Tools [9] are used for modeling these telecommunication systems and constructing reachability graphs of CPN. We used the Petri Net Verifier [11] for verification of the net models with respect to properties expressed in mu-calculus by the model checking method.

1 Introduction

The development of methods and tools for analysis, validation and verification of telecommunication systems is an important problem. Formal description technique SDL based on extended finite automata (EFA) is widely used to represent telecommunication systems. It should be noted that a high expressive power of SDL complicates analysis and verification of telecommunication systems.

A natural approach to overcome the problem is to use the models like EFA [12] or high level Petri nets. Coloured Petri Nets (CPN) [8] should be distinguished among Petri nets, because CPN have significant expressive power, a wide application, and the simulation and analysis tool available called CPN Tools [9]. A method for translation from SDL into CPN, as well as the STSV tool (SDL Telecommunications Systems Verifier) which implements this method, have been described in [15]. However, formal justification of such translators is an open difficult problem. STSV extends CPN Tools with our model checker PNV (Petri Net Verifier) [11] that allows us to verify net model properties represented by mu-formulas.

Note that communicating EFA are useful for initial specification of telecommunication systems from some classes, such as ring protocols and telephone networks. For example, natural compact specifications of RE-protocol and ATMR-protocol are

A. Pnueli, I. Virbitskaite, and A. Voronkov (Eds.): PSI 2009, LNCS 5947, pp. 70–85, 2010.
© Springer-Verlag Berlin Heidelberg 2010

represented as communicating EFA in [4] and [16], respectively. Telephone networks are specified in this way in [1, 3].

The goal of our paper is to represent a new two-level approach for modeling, specification and verification of telecommunication systems. On the first level, telecommunication systems are specified by communicating EFA, while on the second level the automata systems are translated into CPN. Correctness of the translation algorithm is justified. This method is applied to investigation of two case studies: ring protocols (RE-protocol and ATMR-protocol and the feature interaction problem in telephone networks [10]. CPN Tools are used for modeling these telecommunication systems and constructing reachability graphs of CPN. We used the Petri Net Verifier for verification of the net models by the model checking method.

The paper consists of 7 sections. Communicating EFA are defined in Section 2. Section 3 represents the translation algorithm specification. Section 4 is devoted to justification of this translation algorithm. Section 5 and 6 describe the application of our method to ring protocols and telephone networks, respectively. The results and perspectives of our approach are discussed in Section 7.

This work is partly supported by Russian Foundation for Basic Research under the grant 07-07-00173.

2 Communicating Extended Finite Automata

Our goal is to define the system of communicating Extended Finite Automata (EFA). For this, we took definitions from [12] as the basis and made the following significant change: instead of reading and writing symbols, the automaton gets an incoming signal of a predefined format from an environment and sends output signals to the environment. Also, along with the local variables, the automaton can use global system variables. Integer, boolean, enumeration, record and list types are accepted as the types of local and global variables.

Definition. The Extended Finite Automaton (EFA) is a tuple

$\alpha = <S, V, G, I, O, T>$, where

- S is a set of states.
- V is a set of local variables of the automaton. It includes a special integer variable *id* which denotes the automaton identifier used for communication with other automata.
- G is a set of global variables.
- I is a set of incoming signals.
- O is a set of outgoing signals. Incoming and outgoing signals have the following format: *[Src, Dest, Type, Param]*, where *Src* is the identifier of the sender, *Dest* – the identifier of the recipient, *Type* – the enumeration type of the signal and *Param* is an optional parameter of the signal.
- T is a set of transitions. Each transition from T is a tuple
  $t = \{Ss, Se, Os(G,V,I_0), P(G,V,I_0)), E(G,V, I_0)\}$, where
  - Ss is an initial state,
  - Se is a resulting state,

  – I_0 is an incoming signal from *Env*,
  – $Os(G,V,I_0)$ is a subset of the set *O*.
  – $P(G,V,I_0)$ is a predicate,
  – $E(G,V,I_0)$ is a set of assignment expressions on global and local variables.

The incoming signal I_0 may be empty meaning that the transition is independent from the incoming signal.

Definition. The system of communicating EFA (or EFA system) is a tuple
   $\Sigma = <A, G, Env, Init>$, where
   - *A* is a set of Extended Finite Automata.
   - *G* is a set of global variables of all automata in the system.
   - *Env* is the set of the signals awaiting reception in the system.
   - *Init* is an initialization function defined on *G* and *A* which defines the initial states and the initial values for the local variables of all EFA from the set *A*, the initial values for the global variables from the set *G*, and initializes the set *Env*. If the initialization function is not defined then no assignments to the variables will be made and the *Env* set will be empty initially.

All sets in the definitions, i.e. states, transitions and variables, should be finite. The namespace of global variables should not intersect the namespace of local variables of automata. The system execution is defined with respect to global time, i.e. the set of steps expressed by positive integer numbers.

Definition. The configuration of the automaton α of the system Σ at a step *k* is the pair $<S(k), V(k)>$, i.e. the state of the automaton and the values of its local variables at the step *k*. The configuration of the system at the step *k* is the set of configurations of all automata, the set of all global variables values and the value of *Env* at this step.

Definition. The transition *t* of EFA α of the system Σ is enabled if the automaton is in the state *Ss* and $P(G,V,I_0)$ is true for some signal I_0 from *Env*. Occurrence of the enabled transition means
   - changing the state from *Ss* to *Se*,
   - if I_0 is specified, removing an incoming signal I_0 from the environment *Env*,
   - changing the values of the variables according to $E(G,V, I_0)$,
   - putting the output signals $Os(G,V,I_0)$ to the environment *Env*.

We say that an automaton executes a transition when some of its enabled transitions occurs (nondeterministic choice). We say that the system executes a step *k* when some automaton of the system executes a transition at this step (nondeterministic choice).

Example. Consider the following simple example of the communicating EFA system – the "Sender-Receiver" system. This system consists of two interacting EFA – the Sender automaton and the Receiver automaton. Sender sends a message to Receiver and awaits the reception of acknowledgment. Receiver receives the message and returns the acknowledgement to Sender.

   Initially Sender is in *IDLE* state. Its algorithm is as follows.
   1. If the current state is *IDLE*, then send the signal of type *msg* (message) to Receiver and go to *AWAITING_ACK* (awaiting acknowledgement) state.

2. If the current state is *AWAITING_ACK* and the incoming signal of type *ack* (acknowledgement) is received, then return to the initial *IDLE* state.

The algorithm of Receiver consists of the following rule: if the message (a signal of type *msg*) is received, the *ack* signal is returned to its sender.

Thus, according to EFA definition, for Sender we have

a_s = <*S, V, G, I, O, T*>, where
S = {*IDLE, AWAITING_ACK*}, *V* = {*Receiver_id*}, *G* = {}, *T* = {t_1, t_2},
t_1 = {*IDLE, AWAITING_ACK, [id, Receiver_id, msg, null], -, -*},
t_2 = {*AWAITING_ACK, IDLE, -, I_0.type = ack, -*}.

The Receiver automaton is a_r, where

S = {*IDLE*}, *V* = {}, *G* = {}, *T* = {t_1},
t_1 = {*IDLE, IDLE, [id, I_0.src, ack, null], I_0.type = msg, -*}.

The corresponding EFA system is Σ = <*A, G, Env, Init*>, where

A = {a_s, a_r}, *G* = {}, *Env* = {}, *Init* = {a_s.*id* = 1, a_s.*Receiver_id* = 2, a_r.*id* = 2}.

The graphical representation of the system is given on Figure 1.

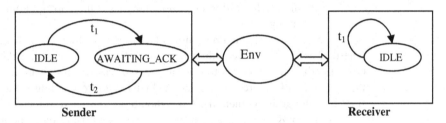

Fig. 1. Sample EFA system: Sender-Receiver

3 Translation of EFA Systems to Coloured Petri Nets

Below we define the rules for the translation of EFA systems (EFAS) to coloured Petri nets [8,9]. The main idea is the following: for each state of an automaton, integer coloured (typed) places are created, where each *1'x* token represents an automaton with *id* = *x*. The transition of an automaton from one state to another becomes a transition of the corresponding token from one place to another.

The translation should be done step-by-step according to the following algorithm.

Algorithm EFAS→CPN
1. Build the auxiliary data types (colours):
    - *sType = enum {...}* – enumeration for signal types,
    - *Signal = record [int Src, int Dest, sType Type, int Param]* – for signals.
2. For all variables in the system (global and local), build the corresponding data types. For arrays, create the record data types of the format
    [int ind, <array type>], where *ind* denotes the array index.
3. For each global variable g_i of type *Ti*, create a place with the name g_i and color *Ti*.

4. For *Env*, build a place *Env* of color *Signal*.
5. For each automaton α from *A*, perform the following actions.
    5.1. For each local variable l_i of type *Ti* (except for *id*), build a place named α_l_i of color *Record[int, Ti]*.
    5.2. For each state *s* from *S*, build an integer place α_s.
    5.3. For each transition *t* from *T*, build a transition named α_t in CPN as follows.
        5.3.1. Build an incoming arc from α_Ss to α_t with the expression *id*.
        5.3.2. Build an outgoing arc from α_t to α_Se with the expression *id*.
        5.3.3. If the predicate *P* is defined for the transition, then
            5.3.3.1. Create the incoming and outgoing arcs to the places corresponding to the variables used in *P* (g_i and α_l_i). For arc expressions, create the variables of the corresponding types.
            5.3.3.2. If *P* contains the condition on the incoming signal I_0, add the incoming arc from the place *Env* with the following expression: *[Src, id, Type, Param]*.
            5.3.3.3. Translate *P* into the guard function on the transition, replacing the variables by the expressions from the corresponding incoming arcs.
            A special case is the translation of expressions like *M[x]* = *y*, where *M* is an array. According to 5.3.3.1, there is an arc from the corresponding place to this transition. The expression on this arc has the format *[i, v]*, where *i* is an index and *v* is the corresponding value. If *M* is a global array, then *M[x]* = *y* should be translated to the conjunction *i* = *x* & *v* = *y*. Local arrays are translated using the similar technique.
        5.3.4. If $E(G,V,I_0)$ is defined for the transition, then for each evaluation $v = f(G,V,I_0)$ create
            5.3.4.1. Incoming arcs for all variables from $f(G,V,I_0)$. For arc expressions, define the variables of the corresponding color.
            5.3.4.2. An outgoing arc to the place corresponding to the variable *v* with the expression $f(G,V,I_0)$, where all occurrences of variables are substituted by expressions from the corresponding incoming arcs. Also, if an outgoing arc to this place already exists (it was created at some preceding step), it should be deleted. The evaluation for arrays is translated similar to 5.3.3.3: the check for equality is added for the array index and the argument, and then the array value is placed to the corresponding outgoing arc.
        5.3.5. If the outgoing signals *Os* are set, build the incoming and outgoing arcs to the corresponding places of the variables used (g_i and α_l_i). For arc expressions, define the variables of the corresponding types. Then build the outgoing arc to the *Env* with the expression
            [id, Dest, Type, Param], where each variable should be replaced by the corresponding variable retrieved from the incoming arcs.

6. The initial CPN marking based on the initialization function of the EFA system is defined as follows.

    6.1. For the automaton α with the identifier *id* which is in its initial state *s*, put a token with the value *id* to the place α_s.

    6.2. For each global variable assignment $g_i = x_i$, place the x_i token to the place g_i.

    6.3. For each automaton α with the identifier *id* and for each local variable assignment $l_i = y_i$, put *[id, y_i]* token to the place α_l_i. For global and local arrays, the values should be initialized for all possible indexes that are going to be used by the automata during the system execution.

    6.4. For each signal in *Env*, put the corresponding token to the place *Env*.

Example. For the sample from the previous chapter, let us build a coloured Petri net using the translation algorithm. Fulfilling it step by step, we need to do the following:

1. Build the auxiliary data types. The *sType* will have the following definition: *sType = typedef {msg, ack}*.

2. There is one global variable *Receiver_id* in the system and it has the default color (integer), so we skip this step.

3. Create the place *Receiver_id* with *int* color.

4. Build the place *Env* with *Signal* color.

5. Build the following elements for the Sender transitions.

    • For transition t_1=*{IDLE, AWAITING_ACK, [id, Receiver_id, msg, null], -, -}* create

        – *Sender_t1* transition,

        – *Sender_IDLE* and *Sender_AWAITING_ACK* places and the arcs *Sender_IDLE →Sender_t1* and *Sender_t1 →Sender_AWAITING_ACK* with the expression *id*,

        – Incoming and outgoing arcs for the place *Receiver_id* (as we use this variable) with the corresponding expressions,

        – The outgoing arc to the *Env* place with the expression *[id, receiver_id, msg, null]*.

    • For the transition t_2 = *{AWAITING_ACK, IDLE, -, I_0.Type = ack, -}* we build the following elements:

    • Sender_t2 transition,

        – *Sender_AWAITING_ACK→ Sender_t2* and *Sender_t2 →Sender_IDLE* arcs with the expression id,

        – An arc from *Env* with the expression *[Src, id, Type, Value]* and the guard function I_0.*Type = ack* (or the expression *[Src, id, ack, Value]*).

    We build the Receiver transitions in the similar manner.

6. Assuming that the Sender has *id = 1* and the Receiver has *id = 2*, the initial marking of the CPN will be as follows:
    Sender_IDLE = {1'1}, Sender_AWAITING_ACK = {},
    Receiver_IDLE = {1'2}, Receiver_id = {1'2}, Env = {}.

The resulting CPN is shown on Fig. 2.

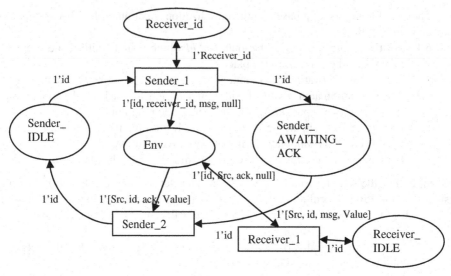

Fig. 2. The resulting CPN

4 Justification of the EFAS→CPN Algorithm

Below we define bisimilarity between EFA system and CPN and justify the EFAS→CPN algorithm by proving that it preserves this bisimilarity.

Definition. Let us define bisimilarity between a EFA system configuration and a CPN marking. The EFA system configuration consists of global variables values, *Env* value and configurations of all EFA in the system. We will call the EFA system configuration bisimilar to CPN marking if

- for each global variable g_i, $g_i = x_i$ iff in CPN there is a token in the place g_i with the value x_i;
- for each automaton α with the identifier *id*, the automaton α is in state *Sk* iff the place α_Sk contains the token with the value *id*;
- for each local variable l_i of each automaton α with the identifier *id*, $l_i = y_i$ iff in CPN there is a token in the place α_l_i with the value *[id, y_i]*;
- for each signal from *Env*, there is a corresponding token in the place *Env* in CPN.

We call CPN bisimilar to EFA system if

1. the initial marking of CPN is equivalent to the initial configuration of the EFA system;
2. if at some step *k* the CPN marking is equivalent to the EFA configuration, then the equivalence is preserved after the occurrence of any transition, i.e. the state graphs of CPN and EFA system coincide.

The following theorem justifies the EFAS→CPN algorithm.

Theorem. The EFAS→CPN algorithm builds a CPN which is bisimilar to the initial EFA system.

Proof. According to the translation rules, in particular, point 6, the initial configuration of the EFA system is bisimilar to the initial CPN marking.

Assuming that at some step k the EFA system configuration is bisimilar to the CPN marking, let us prove that after any transition to the step $k+1$ bisimilarity is preserved. We consider the transition from k to $k+1$ which is the result of the occurrence of some transition t of an automaton a with the identifier id. The transition has the following format: $t = \{Ss, Se, Os(G,V,I), P(G,V,I), E(G,V, I)\}$, where

$$E(G,V,I) = g_i = fg_i(G,V,I),\ i=1..n;\ l_k = fl_k(G,V,I),\ k=1..m.\ Os(G,V,I) = o_i(G,V,I)$$
$$= [Src_i(G,V,I),\ Dest_i(G,V,I),\ Type_i(G,V,I),\ Param_i(G,V,I)],\ i=1..k.$$

Here g_i are the global variables of the automaton a, l_i are its local variables and fg_i, fl_i, $Src_i(G,V,I)$, $Dest_i(G,V,I)$, $Type_i(G,V,I)$, $Param_i(G,V,I)$ are functions of the corresponding data types on the global variables, local variables of the automaton and the incoming signal.

Assume that at step k the configuration was as follows.

- The environment Env contained the signal $I_0 = [Src, id, Type, Param]$,
- The automaton α was in the state Ss,
- The global variables g_i had values x_i, respectively,
- The local variables l_i of the automaton α had the values y_i, respectively.

The bisimilar marking of CPN has the form:

- The place Env contains the token $I_0 = [Src, id, Type, Param]$,
- The place α_Ss contains the token id,
- The places g_i contain the tokens x_i, respectively,
- The places α_l_i contain tokens y_i, respectively.

As a result of translation, the transition t becomes the transition α_t in CPN, where

- The transition α_t has the incoming arc from α_Ss with the expression id.
- The transition α_t has the outgoing arc to α_Se with the expression id.
- The transition has the incoming arcs from the places g_i, α_l_i and Env with the corresponding expressions: g_i, α_l_i, $[Src, id, Type, Param]$.
- The guard function on the transition coincides with $P(G,V,I)$ with the only difference: the α_l_i variables are used instead of the local variables l_i.
- The outgoing arcs to the places g_i and l_i are supplied by the expressions $fg_i(G,V,I_0)$ and $fl_i(G,V,I_0)$, correspondingly. In these expressions, again, all variables have values from the incoming arcs.
- The outgoing arc to the place Env has the following expressions: $o_i(G,V,I_0) = [Src_i(G,V,I_0),\ Dest_i(G,V,I_0),\ Type_i(G,V,I_0),\ Param_i(G,V,I_0)]$.

The above means that the conditions on the occurrence of the automaton transition coincide with the equivalent conditions on the occurrence of the CPN transition.

As a result of occurrence of t in EFA system, the following happens.

- The signal $I_0 = [Src, id, Type, Param]$ is removed from Env.
- Signals $o_i(G,V,I_0)$ are placed to Env.
- The automaton α enters the Se state.
- The global variables g_i change their values from x_i to $fg_i(G,V,I_0)$.
- The local variables l_i change their values from y_i to $l_i(G,V,I_0)$.

As a result of occurrence of the corresponding transition α_t of CPN, the following happens:

- The token $I_0 = [Src, id, Type, Param]$ is removed from the place Env.

- Tokens $o_i(G,V,I_0)$ are put to the Env place.
- The token id leaves the Ss place and enters the Se place.
- The token x_i is removed from the place g_i.
- The token $fg_i(G,V,I_0)$ is put to the place g_i.
- The token y_i is removed from the place a_l_i.
- The token $fl_i(G,V,I_0)$ is put to the place a_l_i.

Finally we can see that the CPN marking preserved bisimilarity with the EFSA system configuration after the transition from step k to step $k+1$. This means that the resulting CPN preserves bisimilarity for all transitions, i.e. the state graphs of EFA system and CPN coincide. Thus, the resulting CPN is bisimilar to the EFA system.

5 Case Study: Ring Protocols

In this section two ring protocols are modeled and verified – RE-protocol and ATMR-protocol. They were studied before in [15] based on the given SDL specifications translated to CPN, but the verification was not complete as there is no proof for the translation algorithm correctness.

5.1 RE-protocol

The ring RE-protocol which was introduced in [4] is used in the slotted-ring network, where the data transfer is performed within the regular time periods in synchronous mode for all stations.

The frame of the fixed length travels through the ring from station to station. The frame is split into slots. For simplicity we'll assume that frame equals to slot (see [4]).

The main principle of ring networks is that each station receives the frame from its upstream neighbor (the previous station in the ring) and sends it to the downstream neighbor (the next station). If the station has some data to send, it waits for the frame labeled as *empty*, changes this label to *full* and loads its data into the frame. The station which received the *full* frame, transmits it unaltered, and in case when the destination address equals to the station address, it copies the frame data into the local buffer.

RE-protocol uses 2 bits for labeling and the structure of the frame is as follows:

R	E	DEST	SRC	DATA	RESP

- R and E – are the auxiliary label bits,
- $DEST$ – the field which stores the destination station address,
- SRC – the field which stores the sender address,
- $DATA$ – the field for the data being transferred,
- $RESP$ – the checksum field.

In the RE-protocol one of the stations controls the protocol functionality and corrects it in case of errors in bits R and E, as these bits are not protected by the checksum. This special station is called the *monitor*.

Let us apply the concept of the communicating EFA to the RE-protocol modeling. Actually the original model presented in [4] has the form of finite automata. We just need to formally specify it according to our definition and define the communication mechanism.

The states are obviously preserved, i.e. the station automaton will have the *LISTEN, RESET* and *RECOVERY* states, and the monitor will have *NORMAL, RESET* and *RESTORE* states. For simplicity let the signal type be a *RE* pair value. Thus the system will have 4 types of signals: *00, 01, 10* and *11*. So the RE-protocol will have *sType = {00, 01, 10, 11}*. The frame fields *SRC* and *DEST* should be put to the signal parameter *Param*, as the record of two corresponding variables.

The communication will be organized in a following natural way: the stations will have the identifiers from 1 to N, and the monitor will have the $id = N+1$. For the stations and the monitor we define the local variable n_id, dedicated for storing the identifier of the downstream neighbor. For example, the station with $id = 1$ will have $n\_id = 2$. The monitor will have $n\_id = 1$, and thus the ring is enclosed.

We use *[1, 2, 00, [null, null]]* as the initial signal value which means that in our system the station number 1 sends the frame to the station number 2 and the SRC and DEST fields are empty (null).

Here is the sample transition of the station:

t = {LISTEN, LISTEN, [id, n_id, 11, I_0.Param], I_0.Type = 11, -}

The following table illustrates the EFA station model for the RE-protocol.

Table 1. RE-protocol station model

	Ss	Se	P	Os
1.	LISTEN	LISTEN	I_0.Type = 11	[id, n_id, 11, I_0.Param]
2.	LISTEN	LISTEN	I_0.Type = 01	[id, n_id, 01, I_0.Param]
3.	LISTEN	LISTEN	I_0.Type = 00	[id, n_id, 00, I_0.Param]
4.	LISTEN	ACTIVE	I_0.Type = 00	[id, n_id, 01, [id, Rnd x]]
5.	ACTIVE	LISTEN	I_0.Type = 01 & I_0.Param.Src = id	[id, n_id, 00, [null, I_0.Param.Dest]]
6.	ACTIVE	LISTEN	I_0.Type = 10	[id, n_id, 10, I_0.Param]
7.	ACTIVE	RECOVERY	(I_0.Type = 00 I I_0.Type = 01) & I_0.Param.Src != id	[id, n_id, 00, [null, I_0.Param.Dest]]
8.	ACTIVE	RECOVERY	I_0.Type = 10	[id, n_id, 10, I_0.Param]
9.	LISTEN	RECOVERY	I_0.Type = 10	[id, n_id, 10, I_0.Param]
10	RECOVERY	LISTEN	I_0.Type = 11	[id, n_id, 11, I_0.Param]
11	RECOVERY	RECOVERY	(I_0.Type = 00 I I_0.Type = 01 I I_0.Type = 10)	[id, n_id, 10, I_0.Param]

In Table 1 *Rnd x* denotes a random station number. This expression is used to model message sending to random recipient. To model this we use an additional *STATIONS_POOL* place and in the transition where the signal parameter is *Rnd x* we add an incoming arc with the integer expression *x* from the *STATIONS_POOL* to this transition and a condition "*x* is not equal *id*" so the station doesn't send a message to itdelf. The *STATIONS_POOL* place is initialized with the full set of tokens corresponding to identifiers of the stations in the ring.

After applying the EFAS→CPN algorithm to the EFA system model the equivalent CPN was built. For this CPN we performed simulation using the CPN Tools [9]. Using this system we studied the general behavior of the protocol and check some basic properties such as the absence of deadlocks and the presence of loops.

Using CPN Tools together with the special module of the STSV system [15] we built the reachability graph for the CPN and prepared it for the further analysis (model checking). The RE-protocol was studied for cases of reliable and unreliable medium with up to 10 stations and a monitor. It was checked to be satisfying the following properties [15]:

1. *Presence of deadlocks.* RE-protocol in cases studied has no deadlocks.
2. *Safety.* This property holds in systems where it is possible to receive all sent messages. This property holds for RE-protocol in all cases studied.
3. *Extended safety.* This property means "all sent messages are received". This property holds only for cases with reliable medium.
4. *Repeating messages.* This property was discovered in our earlier studies, when the RE-protocol was specified using ESTELLE language and then simulated. We found that if the medium is unreliable, the message sent by one station to another may eventually come more than one time to its recipient. Our program verification confirmed that in case of unreliable medium the repetition of messages appears. This is not happening for models with reliable medium. The corrections were introduced to solve this problem.

Table 2. RE-protocol verification results

Network type	Deadlocks	Extended safety	Repeating messages
Reliable medium	false	**true**	false
Unreliable medium	false	false	**true**
Unreliable medium, corrected	false	false	false

The results for different types of medium and for the corrected protocol are shown in the Table 2. Compared to [15] we were able to check the properties of the RE-protocol for more stations (up to 10), because models were significantly smaller. Also we made the complete verification of the above properties, as the translation from EFA from CPN is justified.

5.2 ATMR Protocol

It is also a ring protocol similar to RE-protocol in its basics, however there is no special station to control the correctness of network functioning. The ATMR-protocol is a high-speed protocol and it has no unreliable medium handler. It is supposed that high-level protocols should take care of re-sending messages. That is why we studied ATMR-protocol for cases with reliable medium.

Table 3. ATMR-protocol station model

	Ss	Se	P	Os	E
1.	IDLE	IDLE	I_0.Type = D & I_0.Param.DST = id	[id, n_id, E, [0, I_0.Param.BA]]	-
2.	IDLE	IDLE	I_0.Type = D & I_0.Param.DST != id	[id, n_id, D, I_0.Param]	-
3.	IDLE	IDLE	I_0.Type = R	[id, n_id, R, I_0.Param]	C = MaxCr
4.	IDLE	IDLE	I_0.Type = E & I_0.Param.BA != id	[id, n_id, E, I_0.Param]	-
5.	IDLE	SEND	Has_data & C > 0	-	-
6.	IDLE	RESET	I_0.Type = E & I_0.Param.BA = id	[id, n_id, R, I_0.Param]	-
7.	IDLE	WAIT	Has_data & C <= 0	-	-
8.	SEND	IDLE	I_0.Type = E	[id, n_id, D, [Rnd x, id]]	C = C - 1
9.	SEND	IDLE	I.Type = R	[id, n_id, R, I_0.Param]	C = MaxCr
10.	SEND	SEND	I_0.Type = D & I_0.Param.DST = id	[id, n_id, E, [0, id]]	-
11.	SEND	SEND	I_0.Type = D & I_0.Param.DST != id	[id, n_id, D, [I_0.Param.DST, id]]	-
12.	RESET	IDLE	I_0.Type = R	[id, n_id, D, [I_0.Param.DST, id]]	C = MaxCr
13.	RESET	RESET	I_0.Type = D & I_0.Param.DST = id	[id, n_id, E, [0, I.Param.BA]]	-
14.	RESET	RESET	I_0.Type = D & I_0.Param.DST != id	[id, n_id, D, I_0.Param]	-
15.	RESET	RESET	I_0.Type = E	[id, n_id, E, I_0.Param]	-
16.	WAIT	IDLE	I_0.Type = R	[id, n_id, R, I_0.Param]	C = MaxCr
17.	WAIT	RESET	I_0.Type = E & I_0.Param.BA = id	[id, n_id, R, I_0.Param]	-
18.	WAIT	WAIT	I_0.Type = D & I_0.Param.DST = id	[id, n_id, E, [0, I_0.Param.BA]]	-
19.	WAIT	WAIT	I_0.Type = D & I_0.Param.DST != id	[id, n_id, D, I_0.Param]	-
20.	WAIT	WAIT	I_0.Type = E & I_0.Param.BA != id	[id, n_id, E, I_0.Param]	-

The ATMR protocol operates cells instead of frames. Each cell can be of 3 types: *Empty (E)*, *Data (D)*, *Reset (R)*. When the station has some data to send and it receives an *Empty* cell, it can fill it with the data changing its type to *Data* and puts the recipient address to the *DST* field. Each station has a certain number of *Credits (C)*, which corresponds to the number of messages the station can send in a row. Each time a station sends a message it subtracts 1 from its *Credits* value. When it has no credits left, it waits for a *Reset* cell to refill its *Credits* to the maximum value. The *Reset* cell is sent by one of the stations, which identifies that it's the only active station in the ring (using the *Busy Address (BA)* field containing the address of last active station).

The specification was given in [16] in a form of EFA, and we only had to adjust this specification to meet our format. The station automaton has *IDLE*, *SEND*, *RESET* and *WAIT* states, the signal types are *E*, *D* and *R*. The *DST* and *BA* field is modeled as the record of two corresponding variables in the signal parameter. The communication was organized the same way as for the RE-protocol, using the n_id variable. The Table 3 illustrates the ATMR-protocol station specification in terms of EFA.

We used the EFAS→CPN algorithm to build the CPN models and we studied the models for up to 5 stations. We checked the same properties as for the RE-protocol. ATMR-protocol appeared to have no deadlocks, satisfy safety and extended safety as well as have no repeating messages. And that was quite expected, since the medium was reliable. Comparing to [15] we were able to model ring networks with more stations and perform the justified verification of the properties.

6   Case Study: Feature Interaction Problem in Telephone Network

In this part of our work we present a model for feature interaction problem (FIP).

Basic Call State Model. The basic interaction of the subscribers and the station is defined by the so-called Basic Call State Model (BCSM). This is the model of the Basic Call Service (BCS) which allows subscribers to communicate – dial a number, answer calls, etc.

We model the subscribers and the telephone station as separate automata, separating the logic of the subscriber from the station logic. The subscribers send the requests to the station which processes the requests and returns results to the subscribers.

The additional features (or services) are modeled by the separate element – the Feature Manager – which becomes a mediator between the subscribers and the BCS. This element processes the signals coming from the subscribers according to which features the caller (and/or callee) has enabled. Feature Manager either responds to the subscribers directly or it passes the control to the Basic Call Service.

As the result, we built a model with 3 different automaton types: the Subscriber (in multiple instances), the Basic Call Service and the Feature Manager. The Subscriber automation has the states corresponding to what subscribers can do: Idle, Dialling, Calling, Talking, etc. Both Basic Call Service and the Feature Manager have only one state: they process the incoming signals, change the values of the variables and send the outgoing signals to Subscribers and to each other. The signal types that Subscribers send to Feature Manager are *offhook*, *onhook* and *dial*. In return, they receive the signals of types: *dialtone*, *busytone*, *incoming_call*, etc.

We modeled the following 3 features considered in [15]: Direct Connect (DC), Denied Termination (DT), Call Forwarding when Busy (CFB). In addition, we modeled the following two features:

1. Originating Call Screening (OCS). If x subscribes to OCS and puts y to the OCS screening list then any outgoing call to y from x is restricted, while any other call to z from x is allowed. Suppose the x receives dial tone. At this time, even if x dials y, x receives busy tone instead of calling y.
2. Terminating Call Screening (TCS). If x subscribes to TCS and puts y to the TCS screening list then any incoming call from y to x is restricted, while any other call from z to x is allowed. Suppose the y receives dial tone. At this time, even if y dials x, y receives busy tone instead of calling x.

Using the CPN Tools and the EFAS→CPN algorithm, we built the coloured Petri net first for Basic Call State Model and then for the whole system (with the Feature Manager).

Using this model we performed the simulation and the program verification of the interesting properties for the models with up to 5 subscribers.

The simulation was made using the CPN Tools. For verification we used the STSV system [15]. For the models (reachability graphs) built with STSV we checked the following properties: the presence of deadlocks, loops, nondeterminism and conditions violation [15].

Here are some comments on the results. If the subscriber has enabled CFB and DT simultaneously than the nondeterminism occurs and it is not clear which feature should occur: should the incoming call be dropped or should it be forwarded? Another example of nondeterminism is DT + TCS, as both of them trigger on an incoming call, and it is not clear which one should occur if both of them are enabled. In case of CFB + CFB the loop is present in the system if two subscribers had pointed this feature to each other (forward the incoming calls to each other).

The results are shown on Table 4.

Table 4. Feature Interaction model checking results

Features	Deadlocks	Loops	Nondeterminism	Condition Violation
CFB + DC	false	false	false	false
CFB + DT	false	false	true	false
DC + DT	false	false	false	false
CFB + CFB	false	true	false	false
CFB + OCS	false	false	true	false
CFB + TCS	false	false	true	false
DC + OCS	false	false	false	false
DC + TCS	false	false	false	false
DT + OCS	false	false	true	false
DT + TCS	false	false	true	false
All Features	false	true	true	false

7 Conclusion

To the best of our knowledge, our approach using communicating EFA and high-level Petri nets for modeling, specification and verification of telecommunication systems is a new approach. Our approach has the following advantages:

- Initial specification of telecommunication systems by means of communicating EFA is compact and natural for some classes such as ring protocols and telephone networks.
- CPN models are constructed from communicating EFA by the proposed correct algorithm.
- Combination of different means for modeling, analysis and verification of CPN models that have been implemented in CPN Tools [9] and STSV [15] plays an important role.

The described case studies illustrate these advantages allowing to perform justified verification of some telecommunication systems such as ring protocols and telephone networks with interacting features. Verification of ATMR-protocol described in [16] is performed using the model-checker SPIN which is applied to its specification in the Promela language, but this specification is not justified with respect to its initial EFA specification in [16].

Modeling and verification of telephone networks with interacting features has been considered in the interesting papers [1,2,3,5,13,14,17], where communicating EFA or related models are used in [1,3,5,17] and high-level Petri nets are used in [2,13,14]. It should be noted that different kinds of EFA are used in [1,3], but there are no appropriate tools for their direct analysis and verification. For verification of telephone networks with respect to properties represented by LTL formulas and mu-formulas, model checking method is used in [1] and [17], respectively. Note that some verified service properties are expressed in mu-calculus using fixed point operator [17] which is not expressed in the logic LTL. In contrast to [1], we performed more justified verification of telephone networks with interacting features, because along with EFA specifications Promela specifications are used in [1]. We detected new undesirable feature interactions as comparing with [15].

A method to check the preservation of safety properties under the addition of features in telephone networks is described in [6]. It is supposed to use this method in our approach. Moreover, we are going to extend our EFA systems in order to investigate the feature interaction problem for mobile telephone networks using CPN Tools and STSV.

We are grateful to anonymous reviewers for helpful remarks.

References

1. Calder, M., Miller, A.: Using SPIN for Feature Interaction Analysis – A Case Study. In: Dwyer, M.B. (ed.) SPIN 2001. LNCS, vol. 2057, pp. 143–162. Springer, Heidelberg (2001)
2. Capellmann, C., Dibold, H., Herzog, U.: Using High-Level Petri Nets in the Field of Intelligent Networks. In: Billington, J., Díaz, M., Rozenberg, G. (eds.) APN 1999. LNCS, vol. 1605, pp. 1–36. Springer, Heidelberg (1999)
3. Cavalli, A., Maag, S.: A New Algorithm for Service Interaction Detection. In: George, C.W., Miao, H. (eds.) ICFEM 2002. LNCS, vol. 2495, pp. 371–382. Springer, Heidelberg (2002)
4. Cohen, R., Segall, A.: An Efficient Reliable Ring Protocol. IEEE Transactions on Communications 39(11), 1616–1623 (1991)
5. Gibson, P., Hamilton, G., Mery, D.: Integration Problems in Telephone Feature Requirements. In: Proc. of the 1st Intern. Conf. on Integrated Formal Methods, York (IFM 1999), pp. 129–148. Springer, Heidelberg (1999)
6. Guelev, D., Ryan, M., Schobbens, Yv.: Model-checking the Preservation of Temporal Properties upon Feature Integration. Int. J. on Software Tools for Technology Transfer 9(1), 53–62 (2007)
7. Imai, K., Ito, T., Kasahara, H., Morita, N.: ATMR: Asynchronous transfer mode ring protocol. Computer Networks and ISDN Systems 26, 785–798 (1994)
8. Jensen, K.: Coloured Petri Nets: basic concepts, analysis methods and practical use, vol. 1, 2, 3. Springer, Heidelberg (1996)
9. Jensen, K., Kristensen, L.M., Wells, L.: Coloured Petri Nets and CPN Tools for modeling and validation of concurrent systems. Int. J. on Software Tools for Technology Transfer 9, 213–254 (2007)
10. Keck, D.O., Kuehn, P.J.: The Feature and Service Interaction Problem in Telecommunications Systems: A Survey. IEEE Trans. on Software Eng. 24(10), 779–796 (1998)
11. Kozura, V.E., Nepomniaschy, V.A., Novikov, R.M.: Verification of Distributed Systems Modelled by High-level Petri Nets. In: Proc. Intern. Conf. on Parallel Computing in Electrical Engineering, Warsaw, Poland, pp. 61–66. IEEE Comp. Society, Los Alamitos (2002)

12. Lee, D.: Principles and methods of testing finite state machines. Proc. IEEE 84(8), 1090–1123 (1996)
13. Lorentsen, L., Tuovinen, A., Xu, J.: Modelling Feature Interaction Patterns in Nokia Mobile Phones using Coloured Petri Nets and Design/CPN. In: Proc. 3rd Workshop on Practical Use of Coloured Petri Nets (CPN 2001), Aarhus Univ., DAIMI PB-554, pp. 1–14 (2001)
14. Nakamura, M.: Design and Evaluation of Efficient Algorithms for Feature Interaction Detection in Telecommunication Services. PhD dissertation, Osaka University (1999)
15. Nepomniaschy, V., Beloglazov, D., Churina, T., Mashukov, M.: Using Coloured Petri Nets to Model and Verify Telecommunications Systems. In: Hirsch, E.A., Razborov, A.A., Semenov, A., Slissenko, A. (eds.) Computer Science – Theory and Applications. LNCS, vol. 5010, pp. 360–371. Springer, Heidelberg (2008)
16. Peng, H., Tahar, S., Khendek, F.: SPIN vs. VIS: A Case Study on the Formal Verification of the ATMR Protocol. Int. J. on Software Tools for Technology Transfer 4(2), 234–248 (2003)
17. Schatz, B., Salzmann, C.: Service-based systems engineering: Consistent combination of services. In: Dong, J.S., Woodcock, J. (eds.) ICFEM 2003. LNCS, vol. 2885, pp. 86–104. Springer, Heidelberg (2003)

SVM Paradoxes

Jean Beney[1] and Cornelis H.A. Koster[2]

[1] LCI, Département Informatique, INSA de Lyon F69621 Villeurbanne
Université de Lyon
`jean.beney@insa-lyon.fr`
[2] Radboud University, ICIS, Nijmegen
`kees@cs.ru.nl`

Abstract. Support Vector Machines (SVM) is widely considered to be the best algorithm for text classification because it is based on a well-founded theory (SRM): in the separable case it provides the best result possible for a given set of separation functions, and therefore it does not require tuning. In this paper we scrutinize these suppositions, and encounter some paradoxes.

In a large-scale experiment it is shown that even in the separable case SVM's extension to non-separable data may give a better result by minimizing the confidence interval of the risk. However, the use of this extension necessitates the tuning of the complexity constant.

Furthermore, the use of SVM for optimizing precision and recall through the F function necessitates the tuning of the threshold found by SVM. But the tuned classifier does not generalize well. Furthermore, a more precise definition is given to the notion of training errors.

1 Introduction and Related Work

Support Vector Machines (SVM) is the most popular and successfull algorithm for classification. Apart from its use in text classification, SVM has been used sucessfully in many other classification tasks: in the classification of speech patterns [7], plasma discharge [14], cancers [16,1] as well as various kinds of images.

In text classification its success is relative: compared to other methods, SVM gives the best accuracy but in some cases this accuracy is not very good ([5,2,11]), too low for practical use.

The problem lies in the number of features. There may be as few as 8 parameters in plasma discharge classification to a few hundred pixels, but in document classification we may encounter over 500,000 word forms to be used as features. This problem is linked to the bound of the generalization error ([19], pages 77-81) which increases with the number of features.

But this large number of features has an advantage: it is always possible to find enough words to built a separator between two classes [8]. Thus, the data is linearly separable, and any kernel (polynomial, RBF) can be used as well. As no properties of the vector space can be derived from the construction of this space, there is no way to choose the *best* kernel. We may as well work with a linear separator and use a method for linearly separable data.

A. Pnueli, I. Virbitskaite, and A. Voronkov (Eds.): PSI 2009, LNCS 5947, pp. 86–97, 2010.
© Springer-Verlag Berlin Heidelberg 2010

The elegant theorical foundation of SVM proves that this method gives the best error expectation and therefore it is often said that it is not subject to overfitting. As a corollary, it is also claimed that it has the advantage to have no parameter that should be tuned [8].

Even in the separable case, many authors prefer the SVM variant for non-separable data [12], or even the skew variant that attaches different weights to false negatives and false positives [20]. In order to explain this paradox, we report on an experiment with SVM on a large set of patent applications and we analyze the results of the tuning of the complexity constant (section 4).

Another paradox is that SVM was defined to minimize the number of errors whereas it is often used with another accuracy measure such as precision, recall and the $F1$ function. Its result may not necessarily be optimal in terms of these other accuracy measures.

In particular, precision and recall are often very different, which makes it likely that the $F1$-value is not optimal because it is far from the break-even point. In section 5 we discuss how to optimize $F1$ by modifying the threshold in order to reach this break-even point.

Other authors have written on the optimization of SVM parameters in relation to other measures, such as Mean Average Precision [20], $F1$: Li-CoNLL [13], or more sophisticated methods (derivative-free method APPSPACK: [6], Genetic Programming: [4]). These methods cannot be used with our huge document set because of the large amount of training they require. But previous experiments have shown that the optimal parameters may have rather different values when working with a small subset [9].

In the next sections, we first recapitulate the theory of SVM and then describe the experiments we have performed.

2   SVM and Structural Risk Minimization

SVM is based on the method of Structural Risk Minimization (SRM) as introduced by Vapnik [19]. It consists in the search for that function, belonging to a given set of functions, that minimizes the functional risk. If the function set is characterized by parameters α, this risk can be defined by:

$$R(\alpha) = \int Q(z, \alpha) dF(z)$$

where $Q(z, \alpha)$ is a measure of the *loss* between the true function and the estimated function and $F(z)$ is the distribution of the data in the given space. When $F(z)$ is not known, but only l points (train examples) are given, the empirical risk is used:

$$R_{emp}(\alpha) = \sum_{i=1}^{l} Q(z_i, \alpha)$$

These two risks are linked by the inequality:

$$R(\alpha) \leq R_{emp}(\alpha) + \Phi(\alpha)$$

where $\Phi(\alpha)$ is the confidence interval.

In the classification problem, given a set of functions (e.g. the linear functions, hyperplanes), every exact separator of the train set is a function that minimizes the empirical risk (to zero). In general, it is advisable to look for the function that minimizes the confidence interval, in order to minimize the upper bound of the functional risk.

The optimal function is the separator for which the margin between positive and negative examples is maximal. Support Vector Machines compute this separator, even when it is not linear, or when the train data is not separable.

2.1   The Optimal Hyperplane

In this brief introduction to SVM, we follow [3]. Let there be given a set of labeled training examples $x_i \in \mathbb{R}^n$:

$$E = \{< x_i, y_i > | 1 \leq i \leq M\}, y_i = \pm 1$$

is said to be linearly separable if:

$$y_i(\langle w.x_i \rangle + b) \geq 1 \tag{1}$$

where $\langle . \rangle$ is the inner product. The optimal hyperplane:

$$\langle w_0.x \rangle + b_0 = 0$$

is the unique one that separates the examples with a maximal margin. This margin is:

$$\rho(w, b) = \frac{2}{|w|} = \frac{2}{\sqrt{\langle w.w \rangle}}$$

The problem is then to find w_0 that minimizes $w.w$ under the constraints (1).

With the Lagrange multipliers method, it is easy to show that the vector w_0 can be written as a combination of the training vectors :

$$w_0 = \sum_{i=1}^{M} \alpha_i y_i x_i \tag{2}$$

Since the multipliers α_i are zero for many training examples, w_0 depends only on the *Support Vectors* (those vectors that are near to the margin). The maximal margin also depends only on the SV because:

$$\langle w_0.w_0 \rangle = \sum_{i=1}^{M} \alpha_i$$

The quadratic programming problem (called *dual*) to be solved is to maximize:

$$L(\Lambda) = \sum_{i=1}^{M} \alpha_i - \frac{1}{2} \sum_{i=1}^{M} \sum_{=1}^{M} \alpha_i \alpha_j y_i y_j \langle x_i \cdot x_j \rangle \tag{3}$$

subject to the constraints:

$$\sum_{i=1}^{M} \alpha_i y_i = 0 \tag{4}$$

$$\alpha_i \geq 0, \; i = 1, M \tag{5}$$

2.2 Non-separable Data: The Soft Margin Hyperplane

When the train set is not linearly separable, the preceding problem and its dual have no solution. In that case, *training errors* should be allowed for, but their number should be minimized. This is done by introducing slack variables $\xi_i \geq 0$ to relax the constraints:

$$y_i(\langle w.x_i \rangle + b) \geq 1 - \xi_i \quad i = 1, ..., M$$

and using:

$$\sum_{i=1}^{M} \xi_i$$

as a measure of the number of errors[1] that should be minimized. In fact, this sum is an upper bound of the number of errors.

As we now must optimize two functions, they are combined in one with the use of a constant C that expresses the relative importance of the 2 optima.

$$R = \frac{1}{2} \langle w.w \rangle + C \sum_{i=1}^{M} \xi_i$$

The constant C is called the *complexity constant*.

The Lagrange multipliers method leads to the following dual problem: minimize $L(\Lambda)$ (equation 3) subject to the constraints (4) and :

$$C \geq \alpha_i \geq 0, \; i = 1, M \tag{6}$$

2.3 Kernel Functions

As the above objective functions only depend on the inner products between pairs of data vectors, these inner products can be replaced by a *Kernel function* $K(u, v)$, that is a symmetric positive definite function, which leads to the minimization of:

$$L(\Lambda) = \sum_{i=1}^{M} \alpha_i - \frac{1}{2} \sum_{i=1}^{M} \sum_{=1}^{M} \alpha_i \alpha_j y_i y_j K(x_i, x_j)$$

under the constraints (4) and (4) (or (6) for non-separable data). This method allows to look for non-linear separators, for example a polynomial or exponential (radial or potential) function. Since our data is linearly separable, we will not use such kernel functions.

---

[1] The real number of errors cannot be used because it is not derivable. Other functions may be used instead.

2.4   Solving the Quadratic Programming Problem

Due to the large number of training data x_i, and consequently the large number of Lagrange multipliers to compute, it may be too time consuming to solve the dual problem. Several investigations have led to efficient methods to solve quadratic programming problems by working on subsets of the variables to be computed. *Sequential Minimal Optimization* [15] considers two variables in each step. In SVM^{light} [18], each step is not limited to two variables.

3   Experimentation Setup

We briefly describe the software and data sets used in the experiments.

3.1   The Programs

In the experiment we made use of SVM^{light} implemented by Thorsten Joachims [18]. This program proceeds by solving sub-problems (several vectors are selected and their multipliers are moved towards the solution) until all Lagrange multipliers have been computed.

The data were preprocessed by term selection (selecting 105 000 out of 558 000 terms according to the Simplified ChiSquare criterion). The strength of the terms (raw words) in the documents were computed using the LTC formula, followed by a cosine normalization.

Due to the large size of the corpus EPO2F and the high number of runs to perform (44 classes, many parameter values) we did not use cross-validation but a single shuffle of the given example into 80% for training and 20% for testing.

3.2   The Data

EPO2F is a corpus of patent applications selected by the European Patent Office for the evaluation of classification programs [10]. The documents were chosen by EPO, from one year of input, in such a way that each of the training sets corresponding to the 44 classes (called *directorates*) contains at least 2000 documents. Each patent was labeled by EPO with one or more classes (up to 7 in practice), so that we chose to classify each directorate separately.

Some statistics of EPO2F are given in the table 1.

3.3   The Quality Measures

The patent applications that arrive at EPO must be sent only to the relevant directorate(s) (EPO calls this *preclassification*) and within each directorate to the relevant *examiner*(s) that will check that the invention is really new. When a document is sent to a wrong directorate, it costs time; therefore a high precision is required.

The examiners need to search in a database, to find all the related patents already registered. At this stage, a very high recall is needed.

Table 1. Statistics of the data set EPO2F

number of documents	68 418
number of classes	44
classes/doc : mean	1,43
classes/doc : maximum	7
docs/class : mean	2 227
docs/class : minimum	2 000
docs/class : maximum	2 947
words/doc : mean	59 528
words/doc : minimum	357
words/doc : maximum	163 261
unique words	557 790

As well as the number of errors (E), we will compute the precision (P), the recall (R) and the F_1 measure that combines them giving equal weight to both:

$$F_1 = \frac{2PR}{P + R}$$

It is known that at the point where the precision equals the recall (*break-even point*), F1 is approximately maximal.

In other applications, where precision is more important than recall or vice versa, a more general measure F_γ can be used, where γ controls the relative importance of precision and recall. In that case, a variant of SVM for unbalanced data can be used which includes two parameters C^+ and C^-, expressing the cost of false positives and false negatives, in place of the C parameter of SVM for the non-separable data.

4   Tuning the Complexity Constant

Although the data are linearly separable with a large margin for each classification (directorate), we have experimented with different values for the C parameter (the *complexity constant*). For smaller C values, the errors have less importance in the goal function, errors are allowed provided that at the same time the margin is enlarged.

We first consider the case of one class, then of 44 (the number of directorates).

4.1   Results on 1 Class

Table 2 gives the results obtained on the directorate number 01. Figure 1 shows F(1) on dir01 and its average on the 44 directorates.

These results call for the following remarks:

 – When C is greater than or equal to 50, we get a perfect classifier of the train data (no errors) but the results on test data are not optimal. The limit on the Lagrange multipliers (condition 6) allows to improve the results.

Table 2. Varying C (dir01)

C		train set				test set		
	P	R	F1	E	P	R	F1	E
0.3	92.75	70.58	80.16	830	88.89	63.05	73.77	1065
0.5	94.01	79.29	86.02	612	87.70	67.43	76.24	998
0.7	94.94	84.51	89.42	475	86.52	69.70	77.20	978
0.9	96.01	88.13	91.90	369	85.50	71.28	77.74	970
1	96.38	89.65	92.89	326	85.24	71.80	77.94	965
1.2	97.33	92.05	94.61	249	85.15	72.33	78.21	957
1.3	97.66	92.93	95.23	221	84.80	72.33	78.07	965
1.4	97.81	93.86	95.79	196	84.41	73.03	**78.30**	961
1.5	98.16	94.40	96.24	175	84.18	72.68	78.00	974
1.7	98.45	96.13	97.27	128	83.84	72.68	77.86	982
2	98.85	97.35	98.09	90	83.20	72.85	77.68	995
3	99.54	99.49	99.51	23	81.60	73.03	77.07	1032
5	99.79	99.83	99.80	9	80.19	73.03	76.44	1059
10	99.96	99.87	99.91	4	80.27	73.38	76.67	1061
20	100.00	99.96	99.97	1	79.96	73.38	76.52	1069
50	100.00	100.00	100.00	0	80.19	73.03	76.44	1069
100	100.00	100.00	100.00	0	80.15	72.85	76.32	1074
150	100.00	100.00	100.00	0	80.15	72.85	76.32	1074
200	100.00	100.00	100.00	0	80.15	72.85	76.32	1074

- When C is lower, we have a few errors on train data () and a better result on test data (+2% on F(1), -10% on the number of errors).
- The difference between the results on train and test data is very large.

These phenomena can be explained by the following arguments:

- The so-called training errors (2.2) are not necessarily errors: they are vectors that are either on the wrong side of the separation hyperplane or on the right side but inside the margin. They should rather be called *marginal errors*.
- Allowing marginal errors can give a larger margin and a better generalization error, because the confidence interval of the risk is decreased.
- The train data is not perfectly representative of the test set. This is always the case with documents when the terms are the words (raw or lemmatized) because it is known that every document brings a lot of new words.
  In this situation, every method (including SVM) is subject to *overfitting*: obtaining much better results on train data than on test data. When the method includes certain parameters (C for SVM, promotion factor and number of iterations for Winnow or Perceptron [9]), they sometimes can be used to reduce the effect of overfitting. When the method has no such parameters (Rocchio, SBC), there is no way to reduce overfitting.

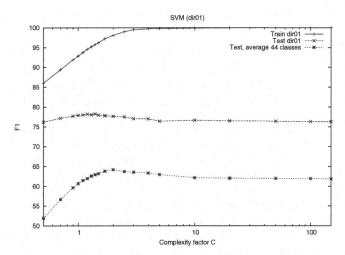

Fig. 1. Accuracy as a function of C

4.2   Results on the 44 Classes

We have trained each of the 44 directorates using the strategy *one against all*. The values given are the micro-averaged F1. As in EPO2F the number of examples is stable across the classes, the macro-averaged values are very similar.

With a good choice of C, the possible gain for each class varies from 0.37% to 6.16% with an average value of 2.43%. Unfortunately, the maximum is obtained for different value of C for the different classes (between 1 and 150), which means that tuning is necessary for each class separately.

However, by choosing $C = 2$ for all the classes, the gain is 2.20% (F(1)=64.20) compared to the case $C = 200$ (perfect classifier of the train data).

5   Tuning the Threshold

When the result hyperplane:

$$\langle w_0.x_i \rangle + b_0 = 0$$

is used for the classification of new data, a document (vector) is said to belong to the class when:

$$\langle w_0.x_i \rangle \geq -b_0$$

Then b_0 is called the threshold. It is computed using one (unbounded[2]) support vector x_i, y_i because such a vector lies on the margin:

$$b_0 = y_i - \langle w_0.x_i \rangle$$

---

[2] A support vector x_i is bounded if $\alpha_i = C$; it is unbounded when $\alpha_i < C$.

Table 3. Threshold tuning (dir01, C=1.4)

b	train				test			
	P	R	F1	Nb Err	P	R	F1	Nb Err
0.5	94.45	98.78	96.56	167	70.10	87.04	77.65	286
0.6	95.22	98.15	96.66	161	74.05	84.94	79.12	256
0.65	95.68	97.77	96.71	158	75.12	84.06	79.33	250
0.66	95.75	97.73	96.72	157	75.55	83.89	79.50	247
0.67	95.82	97.69	**96.74**	156	75.99	83.71	79.66	244
0.68	95.82	97.56	96.68	159	76.57	83.54	79.90	240
0.69	95.82	97.52	96.66	160	77.02	83.36	80.06	237
0.7	95.90	97.43	96.65	160	77.45	83.01	**80.13**	235
0.75	96.32	96.93	96.62	161	78.89	79.86	79.37	237
0.8	96.71	96.55	96.62	160	80.54	78.28	79.39	232
0.85	97.14	95.79	96.46	167	81.60	76.88	79.16	231
0.9	97.50	95.08	96.27	175	82.82	75.13	78.78	231
0.99830698	97.81	93.86	95.79	196	84.41	73.03	78.30	231
1	97.81	93.77	95.74	198	84.38	72.85	78.19	232
1.1	98.26	92.42	95.25	219	86.39	70.05	77.36	234

The above results (table 2) are not at the break-even point (3.3): the precision is always much larger than the recall. Therefore, we may expect that it is possible to get a larger F1 value. One possible method is to use the SVM variant for unbalanced data (3.3) with $C^+ > C^-$, which is also paradoxal because we are looking for a balanced result.

We have experimented with another method: to chose a smaller threshold whose result will be to select more documents, then enlarging the recall and probably decreasing the precision.

5.1   Results on 1 Class

Table 3 and figure 2 show that setting the threshold at 0.67 improves F1 on the train data by .95% above the result given in table 2. The threshold at the break-even point is different (about 0.8) but F1 is rather stable between these two points.

The corresponding F1 increase on test data is even larger (+1.36%) but this is still not the maximum possible (+1.83% for a threshold 0.7).

This improvement causes also a decrease of the number of errors on train documents (196 to 156), which may be surprising as SVM is already supposed to minimize the number of errors. But, as before, we must consider that SVM minimizes the number of marginal errors while we are interested in the number of true errors.

5.2   Results on the 44 Classes

Unfortunately, the positive result obtained on the class dir01 cannot be repeated on all other classes: the tuning of the threshold on the train data does not

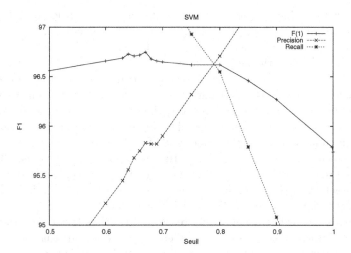

Fig. 2. Accuracy on unseen data as a function of the threshold (dir01)

Table 4. F1 on unseen data after tuning of the threshold

	dir01		average 44 classes	
	b_0 SVM	best b_0	b_0 SVM	best b_0
C>100	72.85		61.80	
C=2	76.32	78.82	64.20	64.00
best C for each class	78.30	79.33	64.23	63.50

necessarily improve F1 on the test data. The micro-averaged effect on F1 may even be negative as shown in table 4, where we compare the best C value for each class with a *standard* value C=2.

Note that for a perfect classifier of the train data (C>100), no tuning is possible since there are no errors to remove.

It means that the result given by SVM, even if it not the best possible on train data, has a very good generalization capacity. In most cases, trying to reduce the number of *true train errors* leads to overfitting, and therefore a worse result on test data.

6   Conclusions and Further Work

In this paper, we have addressed a number of paradoxes and common misunderstandings associated with the SVM classification method.

To begin with, we have shown experimentally that SVM is subject to overfitting just like many other classification methods. It is not perfect in this respect.

The basic method for separable data generalizes rather well. But the use of the variant for non-separable data (which would seem useless) allows the reduction of overfitting by reducing the confidence interval, at the price of a less than perfect separation of the train data (the empirical risk is not null).

Then, the complexity constant must be chosen carefully for each class by trying several values, with the possible help of the gradient.

The large difference between the accuracy on train and test documents is due to the many new terms that appear with new documents. When we build a test set independent from the training set, they are not identically distributed. Therefore, the train data cannot be said to belong to the same distribution as the whole document set, and the same holds for the test set.

SVM is not defined to optimize F1 so that it is possible to increase the value of this measure on the train data by moving the threshold in order to be nearer from the break-even point (precision equals recall). But the classifier obtained by this process does not generalize as well as the one given by SVM.

We have also seen that, when we decrease the risk (less true errors and better F1 on train data), we often increase its confidence interval; this *improvement* leads to overfitting. In this situation, the direct SVM result is the best and must be taken as it is, even if the method was not designed to optimize F1..

Incidently, this result suggest that optimizing F1 on the train data is not the best strategy because the classifier obtained does not generalize very well on a train set.

In consequence of these results, we are working on the following ideas:

- is it possible to design a better problem setting based on true errors instead of marginal errors?
- how can we establish a theory of overfitting, based on statistics of new words in each documents?

Aknowledgement. The experimentation was performed on the Large Data Collider of the Information Retrieval Facility.

References

1. Ayat, N.E., Cheriet, M., Suen, C.Y.: Kmod-a two parameter svm kernel for pattern recognition. In: ICPR, pp. 30331–30334 (2002)
2. Basu, A., Watters, C., Shepherd, M.: Support vector machines for text categorization. In: HICSS 2003: Proceedings of the 36th Annual Hawaii International Conference on System Sciences (HICSS 2003) - Track 4, Washington, DC, USA, p. 103. 3. IEEE Computer Society, Los Alamitos (2003)
3. Cortes, C., Vapnik, V.: Support-vector networks. Machine Learning 20(3), 273–297 (1995)
4. Cummins, R., O'Riordan, C.: Evolved term-weighting schemes in Information Retrieval: an analysis of the solution space. Artificial Intelligence Review, 35–47 (November 2007)
5. Dumais, S., Platt, J., Heckerman, D., Sahami, M.: Inductive learning algorithms and representations for text categorization. In: CIKM 1998: Proceedings of the seventh international conference on Information and knowledge management, pp. 148–155. ACM Press, New York (1998)

6. Eitrich, T., Lang, B.: Efficient optimization of support vector machine learning parameters for unbalanced datasets. J. Comput. Appl. Math. 196(2), 425–436 (2006)
7. Huang, J.: Face recognition using component-based svm classification and morphable models. In: SVM, pp. 334–341 (2002)
8. Joachims, T.: Text categorization with support vector machines: learning with many relevant features. In: Nédellec, C., Rouveirol, C. (eds.) ECML 1998. LNCS, vol. 1398, pp. 137–142. Springer, Heidelberg (1998)
9. Koster, C.H.A., Beney, J.G.: On the importance of parameter tuning in text classification. In: Virbitskaite, I., Voronkov, A. (eds.) PSI 2006. LNCS, vol. 4378, pp. 270–283. Springer, Heidelberg (2007)
10. Krier, M., Zaccà, F.: Automatic categorisation applications at the european patent office. World Patent Information 24, 187–196 (2002)
11. Lauser, B., Hotho, A.: Automatic multi-label subject indexing in a multilingual environment. In: Koch, T., Sølvberg, I.T. (eds.) ECDL 2003. LNCS, vol. 2769, pp. 140–151. Springer, Heidelberg (2003)
12. Li, Y., Bontcheva, K., Cunningham, H.: Svm based learning system for information extraction. In: Proceedings of Sheffield Machine Learning Workshop. LNCS. Springer, Heidelberg (2005)
13. Li, Y., Bontcheva, K., Cunningham, H.: Using Uneven Margins SVM and Perceptron for Information Extraction. In: Proceedings of Ninth Conference on Computational Natural Language Learning, CoNLL 2005 (2005)
14. Lukianitsa, A.A., Zhdanov, F.M., Zaitsev, F.S.: Analyses of iter operation mode using the support vector machine technique for plasma discharge classification. Plasma Physics and Controlled Fusion 50(6), 065013, 14 p. (2008)
15. Platt, J.: Sequential minimal optimization: A fast algorithm for training support vector machines. In: Schölkopf, B., Burges, C., Smola, A. (eds.) Advances in Kernel Methods - Support Vector Learning. MIT Press, Cambridge (1998)
16. Rifkin, R., Mukherjee, S., Tamayo, P., Ramaswamy, S., Yeang, C.h., Angelo, M., Reich, M., Poggio, T., Eric, S.L., Golub, T.R., Mesirov., J.P.: An analytical method for multiclass molecular cancer classification. SIAM Review 45, 706–723 (2003)
17. Sebastiani, F.: Classification of text, automatic. In: The Encyclopedia of Language and Linguistics, pp. 457–463. Elsevier Science Publishers, Amsterdam (2006)
18. Thorsten, J.: Making large-scale svm learning practical. In: Schölkopf, B., Burges, C., Smola, A. (eds.) Advances in Kernel Methods – Support Vector Learning, ch. 11, pp. 41–56. MIT Press, Cambridge (1999)
19. Vapnik, V.: The nature of Statistical Learning Theory, 2nd edn. Springer, New York (2000)
20. Yue, Y., Finley, T.: A support vector method for optimizing average precision. In: Proceedings of SIGIR 2007 (2007)

Indexing Dense Nested Metric Spaces for Efficient Similarity Search*

Nieves R. Brisaboa, Miguel R. Luaces, Oscar Pedreira,
Ángeles S. Places, and Diego Seco

Database Lab., Universidade da Coruña
Facultade de Informática, Campus de Elviña s/n, 15071 A Coruña, Spain
{brisaboa,luaces,opedreira,asplaces,dseco}@udc.es

Abstract. Searching in metric spaces is a very active field since it offers methods for indexing and searching by similarity in collections of unstructured data. These methods select some objects of the collection as reference objects to build the indexes. It has been shown that the way the references are selected affects the search performance, and several algorithms for good reference selection have been proposed. Most of them assume the space to have a reasonably regular distribution. However, in some spaces the objects are grouped in small dense clusters that can make these methods perform worse than a random selection. In this paper, we propose a new method able to detect these situations and adapt the structure of the index to them. Our experimental evaluation shows that our proposal is more efficient than previous approaches when using the same amount of memory.

1   Introduction

Similarity search has become a necessary operation for a large number of applications that deal with data without a semantically clear structure. For instance, multimedia databases manage unstructured objects as images, sound, or video. Content-based retrieval of the most similar images to another one given as a query is an example of similarity search. Applications related to strings and documents are present in systems that range from text editors to big search engines: finding words similar to another one for spelling correction, near-duplicate detection of documents, query rewriting, or spam detection are some examples. We can find more applications in areas such as computational biology (retrieval of DNA or protein sequences), or pattern recognition (where a pattern can be classified from similar, previously classified patterns) [1,2].

Similarity search can be formalized through the concept of metric space. A *metric space* is a pair (X, d) composed of a *universe* of objects X and a *metric*

---

* This work has been partially supported by "Ministerio de Educación y Ciencia" (PGE y FEDER) ref. TIN2006-16071-C03-03 and by "Xunta de Galicia" ref. PGIDIT05SIN10502PR., and by "Dirección Xeral de Ordenación e Calidade do Sistema Universitario de Galicia, da Consellería de Educación e Ordenación Universitaria-Xunta de Galicia" for Diego Seco.

A. Pnueli, I. Virbitskaite, and A. Voronkov (Eds.): PSI 2009, LNCS 5947, pp. 98–109, 2010.
© Springer-Verlag Berlin Heidelberg 2010

$d : X \times X \longrightarrow \mathbb{R}^{+}$, a function that satisfies the properties of *strictly positiveness* $(d(x, y) \geq 0$, and $d(x, y) = 0 \Leftrightarrow x = y)$, *symmetry* $(d(x, y) = d(y, x))$, and the *triangle inequality* $(d(x, y) \leq d(x, z) + d(z, y))$. The value $d(x, y)$ is called the distance from x to y with respect to the metric d, and it represents the dissimilarity between them [3]. The *database* or *collection* of objects where the searches are carried out is represented by a finite subset $U \subseteq X$ of size $n = |U|$.

A *query* is expressed as a query object $q \in X$ and a criterion of similarity on that object. The *result set* is the subset of objects of the collection that satisfy that criterion of proximity. There are two main queries of interest in metric spaces: *(i) range search* retrieves all the objects of the collection up to a certain distance r to the query object q; *(ii) k-nearest neighbors search* retrieves the k most similar objects to the query. Range search is the most important, since it is the more general and other queries can be implemented in terms of it [1].

Vector spaces are a particular case of metric spaces, where each object is a tuple of real numbers. In this case, we can use any of the metrics of the L_p family, defined for $\mathbb{R}^l$ as $L_p(x, y) = \left(\sum_{1 \leq i \leq l} |x_i - y_i|^p \right)^{1/p}$. For instance, L_1 is the Manhattan distance, L_2 the Euclidean distance (the usual choice), and $L_\infty = max_{1 \leq i \leq l} |x_i - y_i|$ is the maximum distance. The set of all the strings of a given alphabet with the edit distance (computed as the number of symbols we need to add, remove, or replace to transform one string into another) is another example of a metric space. The dictionaries of different languages are possible databases, and we could be interested in retrieving all the words up to a certain distance of the query to correct spelling errors.

The naive way of implementing similarity search consists in sequentially comparing the query object with all the objects of the database. However, this solution is not feasible in practice since the comparison of two objects is supposed to involve a high computational cost and the database may have a large number of objects. This has motivated the development of methods for indexing and searching that make this operation more efficient by trying to reduce the number of comparisons of objects needed to solve a query. This can be achieved by building indexes that store information that, during the search, permits to directly discard a significant amount of objects from the result set without directly comparing them with the query object.

Although reducing the number of evaluations of the distance function is the main goal of these methods, there are other issues to take in account. Some methods can only work with discrete distance functions, while others can work with continuous distances too. This constraint limits the range of problems in which the algorithm can be applied. Processing the information stored in the index for solving a query involves an extra CPU time that also affects the overall search performance. The possibility of efficiently storing the index in secondary memory and the number I/O operations needed to process it is other important aspect.

Methods for searching in metric spaces use a set of objects from the collection as reference points that are used to obtain the information stored in the index to speed-up the search. It has been shown that the specific set of reference objects affects the final search cost [4,5] and several techniques have been proposed for their effective selection. These references are selected without caring about the topology of the space, assuming that it is reasonably regular. However, in some cases the spaces present irregularities that may cause these techniques to perform worse than even a random selection.

In this paper we propose *Sparse Spatial Selection for Nested Metric Spaces* (SSS-NMS), a new method for searching in metric spaces that adapts the index structure to the distribution of the collection. The rest of the paper is organized as follows: Section 2 introduces some concepts and related work we use in this paper. Section 3 presents SSS-NMS. In Section 4 we describe the experimental evaluation we carried out and the results we obtained. Finally, in Section 5 we present the conclusions of this work and possible lines of future work.

2   Background and Related Work

Methods for searching in metric spaces can be grouped in two classes [1]: *pivot-based* methods, and *clustering-based* methods. In pivot-based methods, the index is a data structure that stores precomputed distances from the objects of the database to a subset of objects used as pivots. When given a query (q, r), the query object is compared with the pivots. For every $x \in U$ and every pivot $p \in U$, we know (by the triangle inequality) that $d(p, x) \leq d(p, q) + d(q, x)$, and therefore $d(q, x) \geq |d(p, x) - d(p, q)|$. If $|d(p, x) - d(p, q)| > r$, then $d(q, x) > r$ and x can be discarded from the result set without comparing it with the query. The simplest index consists in a table storing the distances from all the objects of the database to all the pivots. Well-known pivot-based methods are BKT [6], FQT [7], VPT [8], AESA [9] and LAESA [10].

Clustering-based methods partition the metric space in a set of clusters, each of them represented by a cluster center $c \in U$ and the covering radius $r_c \in \mathbb{R}^+$: the distance from the center to its furthest object in the cluster. When given a query (q, r), the query object is compared with the cluster centers. For each cluster (c, r_c), the whole cluster can be directly discarded if $d(q, c) - r_c > r$, since in this case, the intersection of the cluster and the result set is empty. Well-known clustering-based methods are BST [11], GHT [12], GNAT [5] and M-Tree [13].

In both cases, the objects that could not be discarded make up the candidate list and have to be directly compared with the query. The search complexity is given by the sum of the comparisons of the query with pivots or centers (internal complexity) and the comparisons with candidate objects (external complexity).

Selection of Reference Objects

Both pivot-based and clustering-based methods use some objects of the collection as references for building the index: pivots in the case of pivot-based methods and cluster centers in the case of clustering-based methods.

It has been shown that the specific set of objects used as references affects the search performance of the method [4,5]. The number of references, and their

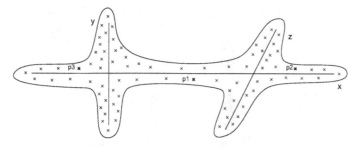

Fig. 1. Dense subspaces nested in a general metric space

location with respect to other references and to the objects of the database determine the effectiveness of the index for discarding objects. Several techniques have been proposed for selecting references. [10,5,8] proposed different techniques for selecting references far away from each other. [4] formally analyzed the problem of reference selection, and proposed a criterion for comparing the effectiveness of two sets of pivots and several techniques based on the iterative optimization of that criterion. [14,15,16] are also based on defining a criterion for measuring the effectiveness of the set of reference objects and select the references by trying to optimize that criterion.

Sparse Spatial Selection (SSS) [17] selects a set of pivots well distributed in the space. In contrast to previous techniques, SSS is dynamic, this is, the database is initially empty and new references are selected as needed when new objects are inserted in the database. When a new object is inserted, it is selected as a reference if its distance to the other references is greater or equal than $M\alpha$, being M the maximum distance between any two objects, and α a constant that usually takes values around 0.4. The object becomes a reference if it is far enough from the already selected references.

[17] shows that the optimal values of α are in the range $[0.35, 0.40]$ and the search cost is virtually the same for all the values in that interval. Other important feature of SSS is that it is not necessary to specify the number of references to select. SSS selects more references as needed when the database grows, adapting the number of objects to the complexity of the collection. Although it was originally proposed for selecting pivots, it can be applied for selecting cluster centers without changes.

Nested Metric Spaces

Most methods for searching in metric spaces assume that the topology of the collection of objects is reasonably regular. However, some spaces present irregularities that can affect their behavior and degrade the search performance they achieve.

In many applications the objects of the collection are grouped in different clusters or subspaces, in such a way that different dimensions or variables explain the differences between objects inside each subspace.

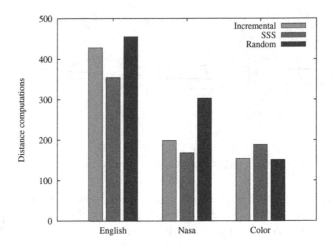

Fig. 2. Average search cost for the collections for English, Nasa, and Color, with Incremental, SSS, and random pivot selection

Figure 1 shows an example of this situation. The database is a subset of $\mathbb{R}^3$. This space has three explicit dimensions: the main corresponds to the x axis, and the other two correspond to the y and z axis. In this example, there are two subspaces with a large number of objects along the axes y and z. The objects inside a subspace are almost equal according to the main dimension, but different according to the specific dimensions of the subspace they belong to. In this example, the maximum distance between two objects is given by the main dimension. If working with SSS, after selecting the pivots p_1, p_2, and p_3, no more pivots could be selected. However, a random pivot selection has the chance of putting pivots inside each subspace since they have a large number of objects.

Figure 2 shows the average search cost for solving a query in the collections English, Nasa, and Color (the details of each collection are described in Section 4). SSS gets the best result in English and Nasa. However, in Color it is worse than even a random selection. Most the coordinates of the feature vectors of Color take the value 0 or are very close to 0, so a large number of objects is grouped near the origin of coordinates. The irregularity of this collection makes SSS to obtain this result.

3   Sparse Spatial Selection for Nested Metric Spaces

Sparse Spatial Selection for Nested Metric Spaces (SSS-NMS) is a new method for searching in metric spaces that identifies dense clusters of objects in the collection and adapts the structure of the index to this situation.

The index built by SSS-NMS is structured in two levels. In a first level, SSS-NMS selects a set of reference objects with SSS and uses them as cluster centers to create a Voronoi partition of the space. In a second phase, those clusters

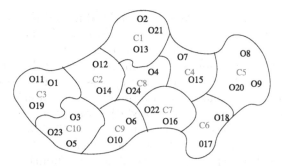

Fig. 3. At the first level, the space is partitioned using reference objects selected with SSS as cluster centers

considered dense are further indexed by applying SSS in each of them. Following this procedure, SSS-NMS is able to detect complex groups of objects in the database and to index them according to their complexity.

3.1 Construction

The construction of the index is carried out in two phases. Since SSS is used in each of them, we will call α and β the constants that control the selection of reference objects with SSS in each phase respectively.

Voronoi Partition of the Space with SSS

In the first phase SSS is applied to obtain a set of reference objects used as cluster centers $\{c_1, \ldots, c_m\}$. To create a Voronoi partition of the collection, each object is assigned to the cluster corresponding to its nearest cluster center: $C_i = \{x \in U / \forall j \neq i, d(x, c_j) \geq d(x, c_i)\}$, where C_i is the cluster associated to the center c_i (see Figure 3).

The value of α should be small in this first phase. Having few cluster centers could result in dense clusters that contain also objects that do not belong to the real dense cluster of objects. However, a small value of α can also result in empty clusters. Those empty clusters are removed, and their corresponding centers are added to the rest of clusters as any other object of the collection.

Indexing Dense Clusters with SSS

In the second phase, those clusters considered dense are further indexed using a set of references obtained with SSS as pivots. We compute the density of each cluster as the number of elements in the cluster divided by the maximum distance between them:

$$density(C_i) = \frac{|C_i|}{max\{d(x, y)/x, y \in C_i\}}$$

Computing the density of all clusters could be very costly if the maximum distance of each of them is obtained by comparing all the objects of the cluster with all the rest of objects. To avoid this overhead in the construction time, we obtain an approximation of the maximum distance. To do this, an object of the cluster is picked at random and compared with the rest of objects of the cluster. Its furthest object is then compared with all the objects of the cluster, to obtain it furthest object too. After repeating the process for a few iterations, a good approximation of the maximum distance (if not the actual maximum distance) is obtained. This approximation is also used when applying SSS in the first level.

We consider that the cluster C_i has a high density if $density(C_i) > \mu + 2\sigma$, where μ and σ are the mean and the standard deviation of the densities of all clusters. For each dense cluster, a set of objects is obtained with SSS to be used as pivots, and the table of distances from all the objects of the cluster to the pivots is computed and stored. In this second phase the index stores more information for the dense complex subspaces. In this case, the value of β should be around 0.4, as indicated in [17].

3.2   Search

Given a query (q, r), the query object is compared with all the cluster centers of the first level. Those clusters $C_i = (c_i, r_c)$ for which $d(q, c_i) - r_c > r$ are directly discarded from the result set, since the intersection of the cluster and the result set is empty. For the clusters that could not be discarded there are two possibilities. If the cluster does not have associated a table of distances from its objects to pivots, the query has to be directly compared with all the objects of the cluster. If the cluster has associated a table of distances, the query is compared with the pivots and the table is processed to discard as many objects as possible, as described in 2. The objects that can not be discarded are directly compared with the query.

4   Experimental Evaluation

Test Environment

For the experimental evaluation of our method we used three collections of real data available in the Metric Spaces Library [18]: English is a collection of 69,069 words extracted from the English dictionary, and compared using the standard edit distance; Nasa is a collection of 40,150 images extracted from the archives of image and video of the NASA, and represented by feature vectors of dimension 20; Color is a collection of 112,544 color images represented by feature vectors of dimension 112. Both in Nasa and Color the images are compared using the Euclidean distance of their feature vectors. As usual, the experimental evaluation focused in range search, using the number of distance computations as the measure of the search cost.

Construction and Search

Our initial hypothesis was that, when working with real collections, we can not assume a regular distribution of the objects in the space, and that they are usually

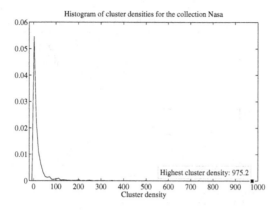

Fig. 4. Histogram of clusters density for Nasa

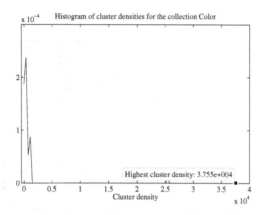

Fig. 5. Histogram of clusters density for Color

grouped in dense subspaces nested into a more general metric space. With these experiments we also obtained the densities of the clusters obtained in the first phase of the construction. Figures 4 and 5 show the histograms of cluster densities for the collections Nasa and Color. As we can see, most of the clusters have more or less the same density, although some of them have a much higher density. The number of clusters with a too high density is small, and these are the ones indexed in the second level of the index. The results are similar for English, and for other values of α (we do not include the graphics for reasons of space).

The construction of SSS-NMS depends on the parameters α and β, that control the number of reference objects selected by SSS in the first and second levels of the index respectively. Since these parameters affect the structure of the index and the information it stores, they also affect the search performance. In the previous section we indicated that the value of α should be small for selecting a significant number of cluster centers in the first level, and that the value of β should be around 0.4, as indicated in [17].

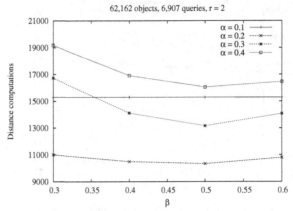

Fig. 6. Search cost in terms of α and β for **English**

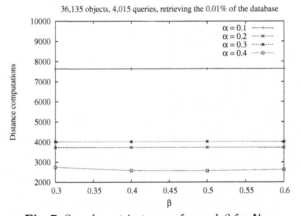

Fig. 7. Search cost in terms of α and β for **Nasa**

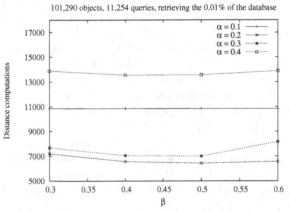

Fig. 8. Search cost in terms of α and β for **Color**

In our first set of experiments we indexed the three collections for values of α between 0.1 and 0.4, and values of β between 0.3 and 0.6. In each case, the 90% of objects of the database were indexed, and the other 10% were used as queries. The search radius for English was $r = 2$, and for Nasa and Color we used search radius that retrieve a 0.01% of the objects of the collection. Figure 6, 7, and 8 show the results we obtained. As we can see in these results, the optimal search cost is obtained for $\alpha = 0.2$ and $\beta = 0.5$. Although in Nasa the best result is obtained for $\alpha = 0.4$, the difference with the result obtained for $\alpha = 0.2$ is small. These results are consistent with [17], since the optimal β for each space is always around 0.4, and the search cost for all those values is virtually the same.

Comparison

We evaluated the search efficiency of SSS-NMS by comparing it with existing state-of-art methods. Particularly, we compared it with SSS [17], Incremental [4] and LAESA with random pivots [10]. All of them are pivot-based methods. Comparing SSS-NMS with clustering-based methods would not make sense, since it uses a cluster approach at a first level, to which it adds more information in the second level.

Pivot-based algorithms achieve better results as more space for storing the index is given to them. However, this is only possible for small collections, since in large collections their optimal result can require an index of several gigabytes. Thus, the comparison was carried out configuring the methods to use the same amount of space for storing the index.

Again, 90% of the objects of each collection were indexed and 10% were used as queries, retrieving an average of 0.01% of objects of the database for each query in the case of Nasa and Color, and using a search radius $r = 2$ for English.

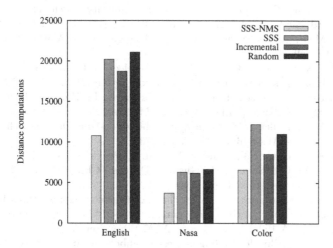

Fig. 9. Comparison of SSS-NMS with LAESA with random pivots and SSS pivots

Figure 9 shows the results we obtained. For each collection and method we show the average distance computations needed for solving a query. These results show that SSS-NMS is more efficient in terms of distance computations than the other methods when using the same amount of space.

5 Conclusions

In this paper we propose a new method for searching in metric spaces called *Sparse Spatial Selection for Nested Metric Spaces* (SSS-NMS). The main feature of SSS-NMS, is that it assumes that the data does not necessarily have a regular distribution, and it adapts the index structure to the actual distribution of the space. SSS-NMS indexes the dataset in two levels: the first one creates a Voronoi partition of the Space using SSS; in the second level, those clusters considered to have a high density of objects are further indexed with pivots selected with SSS too. Thus, SSS-NMS obtains more information for the complex regions of the space.

The paper also presents experimental results with collections of words and images from the Metric Spaces Library [18], that show the efficiency of SSS-NMS against other methods.

There are still some open questions for future work. As in pivot-based methods is possible to gain efficiency by adding more space, we are studying ways of making possible SSS-NMS to use more space and thus be even more efficient when the characteristics of the application allow that use of additional memory.

References

1. Chávez, E., Navarro, G., Baeza-Yates, R., Marroquín, J.L.: Searching in metric spaces. ACM Computing Surveys 33(3), 273–321 (2001)
2. Zezula, P., Amato, G., Dohnal, V., Batko, M.: Similarity search. The metric space approach. Advances in Database Systems, vol. 32. Springer, Heidelberg (2006)
3. Searcóid, M.O.: Metric Spaces. Springer Undergraduate Mathematics Series. Springer, Heidelberg (2007)
4. Bustos, B., Navarro, G., Chávez, E.: Pivot selection techniques for proximity searching in metric spaces. Pattern Recognition Letters 24(14), 2357–2366 (2003)
5. Brin, S.: Near neighbor search in large metric spaces. In: Proc. of 21st conference on Very Large Databases (VLDB 1995). ACM Press, New York (1995)
6. Burkhard, W.A., Keller, R.M.: Some approaches to best-match file searching. Communications of the ACM 16(4), 230–236 (1973)
7. Baeza-Yates, R., Cunto, W., Manber, U., Wu, S.: Proximity matching using fixed-queries trees. In: Crochemore, M., Gusfield, D. (eds.) CPM 1994. LNCS, vol. 807, pp. 198–212. Springer, Heidelberg (1994)
8. Yianilos, P.: Data structures and algorithms for nearest-neighbor search in general metric spaces. In: Proc. of the fourth annual ACM-SIAM Symposium on Discrete Algorithms (SODA 1993), pp. 311–321. ACM Press, New York (1993)
9. Vidal, E.: An algorithm for finding nearest neighbors in (approximately) constant average time. Pattern Recognition Letters 4, 145–157 (1986)

10. Micó, L., Oncina, J., Vidal, R.E.: A new version of the nearest-neighbor approximating and eliminating search (aesa) with linear pre-processing time and memory requirements. Pattern Recognition Letters 15, 9–17 (1994)
11. Kalantari, I., McDonald, G.: A data structure and an algorithm for the nearest point problem. IEEE Transactions on Software Engineering 9, 631–634 (1983)
12. Uhlmann, J.K.: Satisfying general proximity/similarity queries with metric trees. Information Processing Letters 40, 175–179 (1991)
13. Ciaccia, P., Patella, M., Zezula, P.: M-tree: An efficient access method for similarity search in metric spaces. In: Proc. of the 23rd International Conference on Very Large Data Bases (VLDB 1997), Athens, Greece, pp. 426–435. ACM Press, New York (1997)
14. Vleugels, J., Veltkamp, R.C.: Efficient image retrieval through vantage objects. Pattern Recognition 35(1), 69–80 (2002)
15. van Leuken, R.H., Veltkamp, R.C., Typke, R.: Selecting vantage objects for similarity indexing. In: Proc. of the 18th International Conference on Pattern Recognition (ICPR 2006), pp. 453–456. IEEE Press, Los Alamitos (2006)
16. Venkateswaran, J., Kahveci, T., Jermaine, C.M., Lachwani, D.: Reference-based indexing for metric spaces with costly distance measures. The VLDB Journal 17(5), 1231–1251 (2008)
17. Brisaboa, N.R., Fariña, A., Pedreira, O., Reyes, N.: Similarity search using sparse pivots for efficient multimedia information retrieval. In: Proc. of the 8th IEEE International Symposium on Multimedia (ISM 2006), San Diego, California, USA, pp. 881–888. IEEE Press, Los Alamitos (2006)
18. SISAP: Metric spaces library, http://sisap.org/metric_space_library.html

On the Containment Problem for Queries in Conjunctive Form with Negation

Victor Felea

"Al.I.Cuza" University of Iasi
Computer Science Department, 16 General Berthelot Street, Iasi, Romania
felea@infoiasi.ro
http://www.infoiasi.ro

Abstract. We consider the problem of query containment for conjunctive queries with safe negation property. A necessary and sufficient condition for two queries to be in containment relation is given. Using this condition a class of queries is emphasized and a characterization of containment problem for this class using certain maximal sets is specified. The time complexity of containment problem for this class of queries is studied.

Keywords: query containment, negation, safeness, sets of equality relations.

1   Introduction

The problem of query containment is very important in database management, including query optimization, checking of integrity constraints, data sources in data integration, verification of knowledge bases, finding queries independent of updates, rewriting queries using views. The problem of query containment has already captivated many researchers. In [24] J. D. Ullman presents an algorithm based on canonical databases, using an exponential number of such databases. In [16] and [25] F. Wei and G. Lausen propose an algorithm that uses containment mappings defined for two queries. This algorithm increases the number of positive atoms from the first query in the containment problem. Many authors study the problem of query containment under constraints. Thus, in [10] C. Farre et al. specify a constructive query containment method to check query containment with constraints. N.Huyn et al. consider the problem of incrementally checking global integrity constraints [15]. Some authors approach the containment problem for applications in Web services, e. g. A. Deutsch et al. in [8], X. Dong et al. in [9] , Li Chen in [18] and B. Ludascher et al. in [19]. D. Florescu et al. in [13] give a syntactic criteria for query containment, based on a notion of query mappings, which extends containment mappings for conjunctive queries. In [21] T. Millstein et al. define relative containment, which formalizes the notion of query containment relative to the sources available to a data-integration system. The containment problem of conjunctive queries using graph homomorphisms giving necessary or sufficient conditions for query containment is investigated by

A. Pnueli, I. Virbitskaite, and A. Voronkov (Eds.): PSI 2009, LNCS 5947, pp. 110–123, 2010.
© Springer-Verlag Berlin Heidelberg 2010

M. Leclere and M. L. Mugnier in [17]. The reduction of the containment problem to equivalence for queries with expandable aggregate functions is treated by S. Cohen et al. in [6,7]. The containment query problem is used for rewriting queries using views by F. Afrati et al. in [1] and [2]. In [14] A. Halevy studies the problem of answering queries using views and different applications of this problem as query optimization, containment problem and so on. In a recent paper the author introduces and studies a notion of strong containment that implies classical containment problem for two queries in conjunctive form with negation [11]. In [12] the author studies the containment problem for a special class of queries, where the first query has a single literal in his negated part.

Checking containment of conjunctive queries without negation (called positive) is an NP-complete problem (A. K. Chandra [5]). It can be solved by testing the existence of a containment mapping corresponding to the two queries. For queries with negation, query containment problem becomes Π_2^P-complete.

In this paper we give a necessary and sufficient condition for two queries to be in the containment relation. Using this condition we study a special class of queries. The time complexity for the containment problem of queries from this class is discussed.

The paper is organized as follows: in Section 2 we give some definitions and notations used in the following. In Section 3 we give a necessary and sufficient condition for the containment problem. In Section 4 we consider a special class of queries and characterize the containment problem for this class using certain maximal sets. In Section 5 we specify a method to calculate the sets of equality relations used by the conditions formulated in Section 4. In Section 6 some aspects of time complexity for the containment problem associated to the class specified in Section 4 are given. Finally, a conclusion is presented.

2   Preliminaries

Consider two queries Q_1 and Q_2 having the following forms:

$$Q_1 : H(\overline{x}) : -R_1(\overline{w}_1), \ldots, R_h(\overline{w}_h), \neg R_{h+1}(\overline{w}_{h+1}), \ldots, \neg R_{h+p}(\overline{w}_{h+p}) \quad (1)$$

$$Q_2 : H(\overline{x}) : -S_1(\overline{w}'_1), \ldots, S_k(\overline{w}'_k), \neg S_{k+1}(\overline{w}'_{k+1}), \ldots, \neg S_{k+n}(\overline{w}'_{k+n}) \quad (2)$$

where $\overline{x}$ is a variable vector consisting of all free variables from Q_1 and Q_2, $\overline{w}_i, \overline{w}'_i$ are variable vectors, the symbols R_i and S_j are relational symbols, $1 \leq i \leq h+p$, $1 \leq j \leq k+n$.

Let us denote by X the set of all variables from $\overline{x}$. The vectors $\overline{w}_i$ can contain other variables beside the variables from X, that are called nondistinguished in Q_1 and implicitly they are existentially quantified in Q_1. Let us denote the set of these variables by: $Y_1 = \{y_1, \ldots, y_m\}$. Let $Y = X \cup Y_1$. The vectors $\overline{w}'_j$ can contain other variables beside the variables from X, that are called nondistinguished in Q_2 and implicitly they are existentially quantified in Q_2, and we denote by Z the set of these variables. Each variable from X occurs in at least $\overline{w}_i$ and in at least $\overline{w}'_j$. Moreover, we assume that all variables occurring

in the negated subgoals also occur in the positive ones (safe negation property).
Let us denote by $f_1(X, Y_1)$ the right part of Q_1 and by $f_2(X, Z)$ the right part
of Q_2.

Definition 1. *Let Dom be a domain of values, that can be constants or variables. A database D is a set of atoms defined on Dom. We say that D is a
database on Dom. For a query Q_1 having the form as in (1) and a database D
we define the answer of Q_1 for D, denoted $Q_1(D)$ as the set of all $H(\tau\overline{x})$, where
τ is a substitution for variables from X such that there is a substitution τ_1 that
is an extension for τ to all variables from Y_1 such that D satisfies the right part
of Q_1 for τ_1. Formally,*

$$Q_1(D) = \{H(\tau\overline{x}) \mid \exists \tau_1 \text{ an extension of } \tau \text{ so that } D \models \tau_1 f_1(X, Y_1)\} \qquad (3)$$

where $f_1(X, Y_1)$ denotes the right part of Q_1.
  We say that D satisfies $\tau_1 f_1(X, Y_1)$ denoted $D \models \tau_1 f_1(X, Y_1)$ if

$$\tau_1 R_j(\overline{w}_j) \in D, 1 \le j \le h, \text{ and } \tau_1 R_{h+i}(\overline{w}_{h+i}) \notin D, 1 \le i \le p. \qquad (4)$$

Definition 2. *We say that the query Q_1 is contained in Q_2, denoted $Q_1 \subseteq Q_2$,
if for each value domain Dom and a database D on Dom, the answer of Q_1 for
D is contained in the answer of Q_2 for D, that means $Q_1(D) \subseteq Q_2(D)$.*

Definition 3. *A query Q_1 having the form as in (1) is satisfiable if there are a
domain Dom and a database D such that $Q_1(D) \ne \emptyset$, otherwise it is unsatisfiable.*

Proposition 1. *[25] A query Q_1 as in (1) is unsatisfiable iff there is $R_j(\overline{w}_j)$,
$1 \le j \le h$ and $R_{h+i}(\overline{w}_{h+i})$, $1 \le i \le p$ such that these atoms are identical, that
means $R_j = R_{h+i}$ and $\overline{w}_j = \overline{w}_{h+i}$.*

In case where $f_1(X, Y_1)$ satisfies the condition of unsatisfiability from Proposition
1 , we denote this by $f_1(X, Y_1) = \bot$. Since in case when $f_1(X, Y_1) = \bot$, we have
$Q_1(D) = \emptyset$, it is sufficient to consider the case when $f_1(X, Y_1) \ne \bot$.
  We need to consider the equality relations defined on the set $Y = \{x_1, \ldots x_q,
y_1, \ldots, y_m\}$, where $x_j, 1 \le j \le q$ are all variables from X and $y_i, 1 \le i \le m$
are all variables from Y_1. Let us denote by M a set of equality relations on Y.
We express M as: $M = \{(t_{\alpha_1}, t_{\beta_1}), \ldots, (t_{\alpha_s}, t_{\beta_s})\}$, $t_{\alpha_i}, t_{\beta_i} \in Y$. Let us denote
by M^* the reflexive, symmetric and transitive closure of M. Thus, M^* pro-
duces a set of equivalence classes denoted $Classes(M)$. We denote by $\hat{y}_i$ the
class that contains y_i. We must consider a total order on Y, let us define this
order as $x_1 < \ldots < x_q < y_1 < \cdots < y_m$. We denote by M_0 the empty set of
equality relations. Intuitively, the significance of the $Classes(M)$ is the following: all elements belonging to a class will be considered equal and two elements
belonging to a different classes will be considered distinct. Let us consider a
conjunction of literals like those from $f_1(X, Y_1)$. We define the conjunction denoted $\psi_M f_1(X, Y_1)$ by replacing in $f_1(X, Y_1)$ each variable t_j with a, where a
is the minimum element from the class $\hat{t}_j$ with respect to "$<$" order defined

on the set Y. If $f_1(X, Y_1)$ is a conjunction of literals that is satisfiable, then it could exists a set M such that $\psi_M f_1(X, Y_1)$ is unsatisfiable. For example, let $f_1(X) = a(x_1, x_2), \neg a(x_1, x_3)$, where $X = \{x_1, x_2, x_3\}$. Evidently, we have $f_1(X) \neq \perp$. If we take $M = \{(x_2, x_3)\}$, then $\psi_M f_1(X) = \perp$. By $pos(f_i)$ we mean the set of all atoms from positive part of f_i, $neg(f_i)$ means the set of all atoms from negated part of f_i. By $Rel(pos(f_i))$ we mean the set of all relational symbols from $pos(f_i)$ and $Rel(neg(f_i))$ denotes all relational symbols from $neg(f_i)$. We denote by $Rel(f_i)$ the set of all relational symbols from f_i. Moreover, we consider $Rel(neg(f_2)) \subseteq Rel(f_1)$, because otherwise we can easily construct a database D such that $Q_1(D) \not\subseteq Q_2(D)$.

3   A Necessary and Sufficient Condition for the Containment Query Problem

In this section we give a necessary and sufficient condition for two queries to be in the containment relation. For this we consider the following formula:
$\quad F(Y) = (\forall M)(M$ a set of equality relations on $Y)(\forall D_0)$
$(D_0$ a database on $\psi_M(Y))(\exists \theta)[(D_0 \models \psi_M f_1) \Rightarrow ((D_0 \models \theta f_2) \wedge (\theta \overline{x} = \psi_M \overline{x}))]$,
where θ is a mapping from $X \cup Z$ into $\psi_M(Y)$. The notation $(\theta \overline{x} = \psi_M \overline{x})$ means $\theta(x_j) = \psi_M(x_j)$ for each $j, 1 \leq j \leq q$. Since the sets X, Y and Z are finite, the problem "$F(Y)$ is a tautology" is decidable. For the queries from Example 1 we give the corresponding formula $F(Y)$.

Theorem 1. *Let Q_1 and Q_2 be two queries. We have $Q_1 \subseteq Q_2$ iff $F(Y)$ is a tautology.*

Proof.   Firstly, assume that $Q_1 \subseteq Q_2$. Let M be a set of equality relations defined on Y and D_0 a database on $\psi_M(Y)$ such that $D_0 \models \psi_M f_1$. From Definition 1 we have $H(\psi_M \overline{x}) \in Q_1(D_0)$. Using the hypothesis, we obtain $H(\psi_M(\overline{x})) \in Q_2(D_0)$. This means, there exists a mapping θ from $X \cup Z$ into $\psi_M(Y)$ such that $D_0 \models \theta f_2$ and $\theta \overline{x} = \psi_M \overline{x}$.
Inversely, we assume that $F(Y)$ is a tautology. We must show that $Q_1 \subseteq Q_2$. Let Dom be a value domain, D a database on Dom and λ_1 be a mapping from Y into Dom such that $D \models \lambda_1 f_1$. This means $H(\lambda_1 \overline{x}) \in Q_1(D)$. We need to show that $H(\lambda_1 \overline{x}) \in Q_2(D)$ that is equivalent to:

$$\exists \theta : X \cup Z \to Dom, \text{ such that } D \models \theta f_2 \text{ and } \theta \overline{x} = \lambda_1 \overline{x} \qquad (5)$$

We do not restrict the generality if we consider $Y \cap Dom = \emptyset$. Let $Y = \{t_1, \ldots, t_{q+m}\}$ and $\lambda_1(t_j) = v_j$, $1 \leq j \leq q + m$. Corresponding to λ_1 we define a set of equality relations M as follows: $M = \{(t_\alpha, t_\beta) | t_\alpha < t_\beta$ and $\lambda_1(t_\alpha) = \lambda_1(t_\beta)\}$. Let $w_1, \ldots, w_p$ be all distinct elements from the string $v_1, \ldots, v_{q+m}$, considered in the order from this string. Let $W = \{w_1, \ldots, w_p\}$. Let $i_j = min\{l, 1 \leq l \leq q + m, w_j = v_l\}$, $1 \leq j \leq p$. We define a new mapping denoted λ_2 as follows: $\lambda_2(t_{i_j}) = v_{i_j}$, $1 \leq j \leq p$. Let $Y' = \{t_{i_1}, \ldots, t_{i_p}\}$. We note that $Y' = \psi_M(Y)$. In this manner, λ_2 is a one to one mapping from Y' into

W and $\lambda_1 = \lambda_2 \psi_M$. We split the database D into two databases denoted D_1 and D_2, where $D_1 = \{R(\overline{u}) | R(\overline{u}) \in D$ and $\overline{u}$ contains values only from $W\}$ and $D_2 = D - D_1$. Let $D_1' = \{R(\lambda_2^{-1}(\overline{u})) | R(\overline{u}) \in D_1\}$. If the vector $\overline{u}$ has the form: $\overline{u} = (v_1, \ldots, v_r)$, then we define $\lambda_2^{-1}(\overline{u}) = (\lambda_2^{-1}(v_1), \ldots, \lambda_2^{-1}(v_r))$. Since we have: $D \models \lambda_1 f_1$, we obtain: $D_1 \models \lambda_1 f_1$, hence we get: $D_1 \models \lambda_2 \psi_M f_1$, which implies $\lambda_2^{-1}(D_1) \models \psi_M f_1$. The database $D_0 = \lambda_2^{-1}(D_1)$ is defined on Y' and therefore applying the hypothesis we obtain:

$$\exists \theta' \text{ from } X \cup Z \text{ into } Y', \text{ such that } D_0 \models \theta' f_2 \text{ and } (\theta' \overline{x} = \psi_M \overline{x}) \qquad (6)$$

From the first assertion of (6) we obtain $D_1 \models \theta f_2$, where $\theta = \lambda_2 \theta'$. Moreover, we have: $\theta \overline{x} = \psi_M \overline{x}$. From the properties of D_1 and D_2 and the safe negation property of Q_2 we obtain: $D = D_1 \cup D_2 \models \theta f_2$, hence (5) is true. $\qquad \square$

In the following we need to specify several notations. For a set of equality relations M on Y, let us denote by D_M^0 and D_M^{max} the following databases:

$$D_M^0 = \psi_M pos(f_1) \qquad (7)$$

$$D_M^{max} = \{\psi_M \ R(\overline{w}) | R \in Rel(f_1), \overline{w} \text{ is a vector on } Y\} - \psi_M \ neg(f_1) \qquad (8)$$

Intuitively, the database D_M^0 is minimum database defined on $\psi_M(Y)$ with respect to the inclusion relation between sets, that satisfies the condition $D_M^0 \models \psi_M f_1$ and D_M^{max} is maximum with the same property.
For each subset S from D_M^{max} we define the following set of substitutions:

$$\mathcal{F}_M(S) = \{\theta | \theta : X \cup Z \to \psi_M(Y), \theta \ pos(f_2) \subseteq S, \text{ and } \theta \overline{x} = \psi_M \overline{x}\} \qquad (9)$$

We need to consider another set of substitutions denoted $\mathcal{N}_M$ and defined as follows:

$$\mathcal{N}_M = \{\sigma | \sigma : X \cup Z \to \psi_M(Y), \sigma \ neg(f_2) \subseteq \psi_M \ neg(f_1),$$

$$\sigma \ pos(f_2) \cap \psi_M \ neg(f_1) = \emptyset \text{ and } \sigma \overline{x} = \psi_M \overline{x}\}$$

For each substitution $\sigma \in \mathcal{N}_M$ we define a subset S_σ from D_M^{max}, where $S_\sigma = \psi_M pos(f_1) \cup \sigma \ pos(f_2)$. Let $\mathcal{P}_M = \{S_\sigma | \sigma \in \mathcal{N}_M\}$, $\mathcal{S}_M = \{S | D_M^0 \subseteq S \subseteq D_M^{max}\}$ and $\mathcal{Q}_M = \{S | S \in \mathcal{S}_M, \exists \theta \in \mathcal{F}_M(S) \text{ such that } \theta \ neg(f_2) \subseteq \psi_M \ neg(f_1)\}$.

Example 1. Let us consider the following two queries:
$\quad Q_1 : H : -a(y_1, y_2), a(y_2, y_3), \neg a(y_1, y_3), \neg a(y_2, y_2)$
$\quad Q_2 : H : -a(A, B), a(C, D), \neg a(A, C), \neg a(B, D)$
We have $X = \emptyset, Y = Y_1 = \{y_1, y_2, y_3\}$. The sets M_0 and $M_1 = \{(y_1, y_3)\}$ are all sets that satisfy $\psi_M f_1 \neq \perp$ (see Example 5).We have: $\psi_{M_1} f_1 = a(y_1, y_2)$, $a(y_2, y_1), \neg a(y_1, y_1), \neg a(y_2, y_2)$, $D_{M_0}^0 = \{a(y_1, y_2), a(y_2, y_3)\}$, $D_{M_0}^{max} = \{a(y_i, y_j) | 1 \le i, j \le 3\} - \{a(y_1, y_3), a(y_2, y_2)\}$, $D_{M_1}^0 = D_{M_1}^{max} = \{a(y_1, y_2), a(y_2, y_1)\}$. For the set M_0 the statement $D_0 \models f_1$ is equivalent to $D_{M_0}^0 \subseteq D_0 \subseteq D_{M_0}^{max}$ ($\psi_{M_0} f_1 = f_1$) and for the set M_1 the statement $D_0 \models \psi_{M_1} f_1$ is equivalent to $D_{M_1}^0 \subseteq D_0 \subseteq D_{M_1}^{max}$. Hence, the formula $F(Y)$ is the following:
$F(Y) = (\forall D_0)[D_{M_0}^0 \subseteq D_0 \subseteq D_{M_0}^{max}](\exists \theta)[D_0 \models \theta f_2] \wedge (\exists \theta)[D_{M_1}^0 \models \theta f_2]$.

The set $\mathcal{N}_{M_0}$ consists of the substitutions $\sigma_1, \sigma_2, \sigma_3$, where $\sigma_1(A, B, C, D) = (y_1, y_1, y_3, y_3)$, $\sigma_2(A, B, C, D) = (y_1, y_2, y_3, y_2)$ and $\sigma_3(A, B, C, D) = (y_2, y_1, y_2, y_3)$. We order the elements of $D_{M_0}^{max}$ so that $a(i, j)\tau a(k, l)$ if $(i, j)\rho(k, l)$, where ρ is the ascending lexicography order defined on $\{1, 2, 3\} \times \{1, 2, 3\}$. Thus, the set $D_{M_0}^{max}$ consists of $u_i, 1 \leq i \leq 7$, where $u_1\tau \ldots \tau u_7$ and $u_1 = a(y_1, y_1)$, $u_7 = a(y_3, y_3)$. We get: $D_{M_0}^0 = \{u_2, u_4\}$, $S_{\sigma_1} = \{u_2, u_4, u_1, u_7\}$, $S_{\sigma_2} = \{u_2, u_4, u_6\}$, $S_{\sigma_3} = \{u_2, u_4, u_3\}$.

Proposition 2. *The classes $\mathcal{P}_M$ and $\mathcal{Q}_M$ satisfy the inclusion: $\mathcal{P}_M \subseteq \mathcal{Q}_M$ and for all $S \in \mathcal{Q}_M$, there exists $S_\theta \in \mathcal{P}_M$ such that $S_\theta \subseteq S$.*

For a set of equality relations M such that $\psi_M f_1(X, Y_1) \neq \bot$ we need to consider all subsets S from $\mathcal{S}_M$. Let us define a function denoted $MARK$. We consider the following conditions:
(C0) $\mathcal{F}_M(S) = \emptyset$. In this case we consider $MARK(S) = 0$.
(C1) There exists $\theta \in \mathcal{F}_M(S)$ such that $\theta \, neg(f_2) \subseteq \psi_M \, neg(f_1)$. In this case we take $MARK(S) = 1$.
(C2) The condition $(C1)$ is not satisfied, but there is $\theta \in \mathcal{F}_M(S)$ such that $\theta \, neg(f_2) \cap S = \emptyset$. In this case we take $MARK(S) = 2$.
(C3) For every $\theta \in \mathcal{F}_M(S)$ we have $\theta \, neg(f_2) \cap S \neq \emptyset$. Then $MARK(S) = 3$.

Remark 1. (i) We have $MARK(S_\sigma) = 1$ for all database S_σ from $\mathcal{P}_M$.
(ii) The elements S from $\mathcal{P}_M$ are minimal in $\mathcal{S}_M$ with respect to the inclusion relation between sets having the property $MARK(S) = 1$.

Proposition 3. *In the case when $MARK(S) = 1$ we have: there exists θ from $\mathcal{F}_M(S)$ such that $S' \models \theta f_2$ for each subset S' with the property: $S \subset S' \subseteq D_M^{max}$.*

Proof.   From $(C1)$ we obtain: for the subset S there exists θ from $\mathcal{F}_M(S)$ such that $S \models \theta f_2$. Since $S' \cap \psi_M neg(f_1) = \emptyset$ and $MARK(S) = 1$, we obtain $S' \models \theta f_2$. Moreover, we have $MARK(S') = 1$. This statement justifies the deletions in step 2 from the function $COMP(M)$ specified in the following. $\square$

We order the elements of $\mathcal{S}_M$ in the form $\mathcal{S}_M = (E_1, \ldots, E_m)$ such that if $E_i \subset E_j$ then $i < j$ (a topological order).
We denote by $COMP(M)$ a function that computes the values of the function $MARK$. The function $COMP(M)$ is computed using the following steps:
1. If $\mathcal{F}_M(D_M^0) = \emptyset$ Then $MARK(D_M^0) = 0$; return 0; EndIf
2. For all $S_\sigma \in \mathcal{P}_M$ do $MARK(S_\sigma) = 1$;
    While $\exists S_2 \in \mathcal{S}_M$ and $S_\sigma \subset S_2$ delete S_2 from $\mathcal{S}_M$; EndWhile
    Endfor
3. For all $S \in \mathcal{S}_M$ do
    If S satisfies $(C3)$ Then $MARK(S) = 3$; return 3; EndIf
    If S satisfies $(C2)$ Then $MARK(S) = 2$; EndIf
    EndFor
4. return 1;

Remark 2. By Proposition 2, the function $COMP(M)$ in step 2 deletes all elements from $\mathcal{Q}_M$, that are not minimal with respect to " $\subseteq$ " relation.

The following propositions specifies some properties of the functions $MARK$ and $COMP$.

Proposition 4. (i) If $COMP(M) = 0$ then we have $MARK(D_M^0) = 0$, hence $Q_1 \not\subseteq Q_2$.

(ii) If $COMP(M) = 3$ then there is a set S having $MARK(S) = 3$ such that $S \not\models \theta f_2$, for each θ from $\mathcal{F}_M(S)$, hence $Q_1 \not\subseteq Q_2$.

(iii) If $MARK(S) = 2$ then we have: there exists $\theta \in \mathcal{F}_M(S)$ such that $S \models \theta f_2$.

(iv) If $MARK(S) = 1$ then we have: there exists θ from $\mathcal{F}_M(S)$ such that $S \models \theta f_2$ and θ $neg(f_2) \subseteq \psi_M$ $neg(f_1)$.

(v) $S \models \psi_M$ $pos(f_1)$, for each $S \in \mathcal{S}_M$.

Proof. If $MARK(D_M^0) = 0$ then there is no containment mappings $(\mathcal{F}_M(D_M^0) = \emptyset)$, hence $Q_1 \not\subseteq Q_2$. If $MARK(S) = 3$, then we get:

$$(\forall \theta)(\theta_j \in \mathcal{F}_M(S))(\exists l_j)(1 \leq l_j \leq n)[\theta_j \ S_{k+l_j}(\overline{w}'_{k+l_j}) \in \ S] \tag{10}$$

This statement implies $S \not\models \theta f_2$, for each θ from $\mathcal{F}_M(S)$.

If $MARK(S) = 1$ then we have the following two assertions:

$$\exists \theta \in \mathcal{F}_M(S) \text{ such that } \theta S_{k+l}(\overline{w}'_{k+l}) \in \ \psi_M neg(f_1) \text{ for each } l, 1 \leq l \leq n \tag{11}$$

$$\text{and } \theta S_l(\overline{w}'_l) \in \ S \text{ for each } l, 1 \leq l \leq k \tag{12}$$

From relations (11) and (12) we obtain $S \models \theta f_2$.

If $MARK(S) = 2$ then we have:

$$\exists \theta \in \mathcal{F}_M(S) \text{ such that } \theta \ S_{k+l}(\overline{w}'_{k+l}) \notin \ S \text{ for each } l, 1 \leq l \leq n \tag{13}$$

This statement implies $S \models \theta \ f_2$. $\qquad\square$

Proposition 5. Let $M_0 = \emptyset$ and M_1 be a set of equality relations such that $\psi_{M_1} f_1(X, Y_1) \neq \bot$. We have: $(MARK(D_{M_0}^0) \neq \emptyset)$ implies $(MARK(D_{M_1}^0) \neq \emptyset)$, or equivalently $COMP(M_0) \neq 0$ implies $COMP(M_1) \neq 0$.

Proposition 6. Let M be a set of equality relations such that $\psi_M f_1(X, Y_1) \neq \bot$. The following two assertions are equivalent:

(i) for each S such that $D_M^0 \subseteq S \subseteq D_M^{max}$, there exists θ from $\mathcal{F}_M(S)$ such that $S \models \theta f_2$.

(ii) $COMP(M) = 1$.

Proof. From Propositions 3, 4 and the steps of the function $COMP$. $\qquad\square$

In the following proposition we specify that $MARK(D_M^{max}) = 1$ is a necessary condition for $Q_1 \subseteq Q_2$.

Proposition 7. Let Q_1 and Q_2 be two queries. If $Q_1 \subseteq Q_2$ then for each set M of equality relations on Y such that $\psi_M f_1(X, Y_1) \neq \bot$ we have:

$$MARK(D_M^{max}) = 1 \tag{14}$$

Proof. Since $D_M^{max} \models \psi_M f_1$ and $Q_1 \subseteq Q_2$, using Theorem 1 we obtain: there exists $\theta \in \mathcal{F}_M(D_M^{max})$ such that $D_M^{max} \models \theta \ f_2$ and $\theta \ neg(f_2) \subseteq \psi_M \ neg(f_1)$, hence the relation (14) holds. $\qquad\square$

Now we specify the main result of this section, that gives a necessary and sufficient condition for the containment problem.

Theorem 2. *Let Q_1 and Q_2 be two queries having the form as in (1) and (2), respectively. We have $Q_1 \subseteq Q_2$ iff the following statement yields:*
(i) for each set of equality relations M such that $\psi_M f_1(X, Y_1) \neq \perp$ we have $COMP(M) = 1$.

Proof. From Theorem 1 and Proposition 6. $\qquad\square$

Example 2. Let us consider the queries from Example 1. From Propositions 2 and 3 we obtain: $MARK(S_{\sigma_i}) = 1$, for all $i, 1 \leq i \leq 3$. After the execution of step 2 from the function $COMP(M_0)$, the class $\mathcal{S}_{M_0}$ contains beside $D_{M_0}^0$ and $S_{\sigma_i}, 1 \leq i \leq 3$, the databases S_j, $1 \leq j \leq 5$, where $S_1 = \{u_2, u_4, u_1\}$, $S_2 = \{u_2, u_4, u_7\}$, $S_3 = \{u_2, u_4, u_5\}$, $S_4 = \{u_2, u_4, u_1, u_5\}$, $S_5 = \{u_2, u_4, u_7, u_5\}$. For these databases we have: $MARK(S_j) = 2$. Moreover, we have (see Example 1)$D_{M_1}^0 = D_{M_1}^{max}$. On the other hand, we get: $MARK(D_{M_1}^{max}) = 1$ and $MARK(D_{M_0}^{max}) = 1$. So, using the function $COMP$ and Theorem 2 we obtain $Q_1 \subseteq Q_2$.

Example 3. Let us consider the following two queries:
   $Q_1 : H : -a(y_1, y_2), a(y_2, y_3), \neg a(y_1, y_3)$
   $Q_2 : H : -a(A, B), a(C, D), \neg a(A, D), \neg a(B, C), \neg a(A, C)$
For $M_0 = \emptyset$ we have: $D_{M_0}^0 = \{a(y_1, y_2), a(y_2, y_3)\}$. Let us consider the following subset $S = \{a(y_1, y_2), a(y_2, y_3), a(y_2, y_2)\}$. We have: for all $\theta \in \mathcal{F}_{M_0}(S)$, $\theta a(A, D) \in S$ or $\theta a(B, C) \in S$ or $\theta a(A, C) \in S$ which implies $S \not\models \theta f_2$, for each θ from $\mathcal{F}_{M_0}(S)$. This means $Q_1 \not\subseteq Q_2$. We have $MARK(S) = 3$, and $COMP(M_0) = 3$.

4   A Special Class of Queries

In this section we point out a class of queries for what the containment problem is expressed using maximal sets of equality relations on Y. Let us give some notations for this section. For a set M of equality relation let us define the set denoted $\overline{Y}_M$, where $\overline{Y}_M = \{t | t \in Y$ and t occurs in $\psi_M neg(f_1)\}$. For two sets M_1 and M_2 such that $M_1 \leq M_2$ we define a mapping denoted ψ_{M_1, M_2} from $\psi_{M_1}(Y)$ into $\psi_{M_2}(Y)$ and defined by: $\psi_{M_1, M_2}(t) = \psi_{M_2}(t)$, for each $t \in \psi_{M_1}(Y)$. In the following we consider the queries Q_1, Q_2 specified in (1) and (2) such that Q_1 has the property:

$$(\forall M_1)(\exists M_2)(M_1 \leq M_2)(\forall t \in \overline{Y}_{M_2})[|\psi_{M_1, M_2}^{-1}(t)| = 1] \qquad (15)$$

and the query Q_2 satisfies the following restriction:

$$(\forall i, j)(1 \leq i < j \leq k)[(S_i(\overline{w}_i'), S_j(\overline{w}_j')) \in pos(f_2)) \Rightarrow (pr_Z(\overline{w}_i') \cap pr_Z(\overline{w}_j') = \emptyset)] \qquad (16)$$

where $pr_Z(\overline{w}_i')$ denotes the set of all variables from Z that occur in $\overline{w}_i'$ and M_2 is a maximal set of equality relations and $M_1 \leq M_2$ is given in the following definition. Moreover, we consider the restriction of ψ_{M_2} on the set X as a one-to-one mapping. The notation $|S|$ means the cardinality of S.

Definition 4. *We consider two partial order relations on sets of equality relations denoted " $<$ " and " $\leq$ ". They are defined as follows: $M_1 < M_2$ if $M_1^* \subset M_2^*$, that means the set M_1^* is strictly included in M_2^*. We say that $M_1 \leq M_2$ if $M_1 < M_2$ or $M_1^* = M_2^*$.*

Firstly, let us emphasize the relations between the sets of substitutions corresponding to different sets of equality relations.

Proposition 8. *Let M_1 and M_2 be two sets of equality relations such that $M_1 \leq M_2$. Let ψ_{M_2} be the mapping from Y into Y defined by M_2. We have:*

$$\psi_{M_2}\mathcal{F}_{M_1}(S) = \mathcal{F}_{M_2}(\psi_{M_2}(S)), \text{ for each subset } S \text{ of atoms of the form } R(\overline{w}),$$
$$(17)$$

where R is a relational symbol from $Rel(f_1)$ and $\overline{w}$ is a vector on Y.

Proof. In general, for the sets of substitutions from (17) we have $\psi_{M_2}\mathcal{F}_{M_1}(S) \subseteq \mathcal{F}_{M_2}(\psi_{M_2}(S))$, but using the condition specified in (16) we obtain the equality between the two sets of substitutions.   □

In the following proposition we establish a relation between $COMP(M_1)$ and $COMP(M_2)$ in case when $M_1 < M_2$.

Proposition 9. *Let M_1 and M_2 be two sets of equality relations such that $M_1 < M_2$ and (M_1, M_2) satisfies (15). If $COMP(M_1) = 3$ then $COMP(M_2) = 3$.*

Proof. Let M_1 be with the property $COMP(M_1) = 3$. This means there exists S that satisfies $D_{M_1}^0 \subseteq S \subseteq D_{M_1}^{max}$ such that $S \not\models \theta_1 f_2$, for each θ_1 from $\mathcal{F}_{M_1}(S)$. The condition (15) assures that $S \in \mathcal{S}_{M_1}$ implies $\psi_{M_2}(S) \in \mathcal{S}_{M_2}$. Let θ be a substitution from $\mathcal{F}_{M_2}(\psi_{M_2}(S))$. By Proposition 8 there exists a substitution θ_1 from $\mathcal{F}_{M_1}(S)$ such that $\theta = \psi_{M_2}\theta_1$. Since $S \not\models \theta_1 f_2$, we have:

$$\theta_1 S_l(\overline{w}_l') \in S, \text{ for every } l, 1 \leq l \leq k \text{ and } (\exists r)(1 \leq r \leq n)\, \theta_1 S_{k+r}(\overline{w}_{k+r}') \in S$$
$$(18)$$

Applying ψ_{M_2} to the formulas from (18) we obtain:

$$\psi_{M_2}\theta_1 S_l(\overline{w}_l') \in \psi_{M_2}(S), 1 \leq l \leq k \text{ and}$$

$$(\exists r)(1 \leq r \leq n)\, \psi_{M_2}\theta_1 S_{k+r}(\overline{w}_{k+r}') \in \psi_{M_2}(S) \qquad (19)$$

Since we have $\theta = \psi_{M_2}\theta_1$, the relation (19) implies $\psi_{M_2}(S) \not\models \theta f_2$, for each θ from $\mathcal{F}_{M_2}(\psi_{M_2}(S))$. Hence $MARK(\psi_{M_2}(S)) = 3$ and $COMP(M_2) = 3$.   □

Theorem 3. *Let Q_1 and Q_2 be two queries having the form as in (1) and (2), respectively and the two queries satisfy the restrictions from (15) and (16). We have $Q_1 \subseteq Q_2$ iff the following three conditions are satisfied:*

a) $COMP(M_0) \neq 0$ *and*

b) The relation (14) *yields for every set of equality relations* M *on* Y *such that* $\psi_M f_1(X, Y_1) \neq \perp$ *and*

c) $COMP(M_s) = 1$ *for all maximal sets* M_s *of equality relations on* Y *such that* $\psi_{M_s} f_1(X, Y_1) \neq \perp$.

Proof.   If $Q_1 \subseteq Q_2$, then using Theorem 2, Proposition 6 from Section 3 and Lemma 2.1 from [25] we obtain the statements from $a), b), c)$. Inversely, assume that the statements from $a), b), c)$ are satisfied, let us show the assertion (i) from Theorem 2. Assume the contrary, then there exists M such that $COMP(M) \in \{0, 3\}$. Let M_s be the maximal set having the property $\psi_{M_s} f_1(X, Y_1) \neq \perp$ such that $M \leq M_s$ and M, M_s satisfy (15). If $COMP(M) = 3$ then, using Proposition 9, we obtain $COMP(M_s) = 3$, which contradicts the hypothesis. If $COMP(M) = 0$, since $M_0 \leq M$ from Proposition 5 we have $COMP(M_0) = 0$, which contradicts the condition $a)$.   □

Example 4. Let us consider two queries Q_1 and Q_2 as follows:
$Q_1 : H : -a(y_1, y_2), a(y_2, y_3), \neg a(y_2, y_2)$, $Q_2 : H : -a(A, B), a(C, D), \neg a(A, D)$. The sets of equality relations M such that $\psi_M f_1(X, Y_1) \neq \perp$ are $M_0 = \emptyset$ and $M_1 = \{(y_1, y_3)\}$ (as in Example 5). The second is maximal with the property specified. We have:
$D_{M_0}^0 = \{a(y_1, y_2), a(y_2, y_3)\}$, $D_{M_1}^0 = \{a(y_1, y_2), a(y_2, y_1)\}$, $D_{M_0}^{max} = \{a(y_i, y_j) | 1 \leq i, j \leq 3\} - \{a(y_2, y_2)\}$, $D_{M_1}^{max} = \{a(y_1, y_2), a(y_2, y_1), a(y_1, y_1)\}$. If we consider the substitutions denoted θ_1 and θ_2 and defined by: $\theta_1(A, B, C, D) = (y_2, y_3, y_1, y_2)$, $\theta_2(A, B, C, D) = (y_2, y_1, y_1, y_2)$, then we have: θ_1 satisfies (14) for $D_{M_0}^{max}$ and θ_2 satisfies (14) for $D_{M_1}^{max}$. Moreover, $COMP(M_0) = 1$ and $COMP(M_1) = 1$, hence by Theorem 2 (and by Theorem 3 as well) we have $Q_1 \subseteq Q_2$. The conditions from (15) and (16) are satisfied for Q_1 and Q_2.

5   Maximal Sets of Equality Relations

In this section we specify a method to obtain all maximal subsets M of equality relations such that $\psi_M f_1(X, Y_1) \neq \perp$. We define a boolean function denoted φ_M for pairs of elements from Y, pairs of vectors on Y, and for expressions constructed with conjunction and disjunction operations having pairs of elements from Y and pairs of vectors as components of expressions:

(i) $\varphi_M(y_i, y_j) = TRUE$ if $\psi_M(y_i) = \psi_M(y_j)$, $y_i, y_j \in Y$,

(ii) $\varphi_M(p_1 \wedge p_2) = \varphi_M(p_1) \wedge \varphi_M(p_2)$, $\varphi_M(p_1 \vee p_2) = \varphi_M(p_1) \vee \varphi_M(p_2)$, where p_1 and p_2 are pairs of elements from Y,

(iii) If $\overline{w} = t_1 \ldots t_s$ and $\overline{w}' = t_1' \ldots t_s'$, then $\varphi_M(\overline{w}, \overline{w}') = TRUE$ if $\psi_M(t_i) = \psi_M(t_i')$ for each $i, 1 \leq i \leq s$, $t_i, t_i' \in Y$,

(iv) $\varphi_M(q_1 \wedge q_2)$ and $\varphi_M(q_1 \vee q_2)$ are defined as in (ii), where q_1 and q_2 are pairs of vectors on Y.

Now for two expressions E_1 and E_2 we define an equivalence relation between them with respect to φ_M:

$$E_1 \equiv_M E_2 \text{ if } \varphi_M(E_1) = \varphi_M(E_2).$$

Let $R_j(\overline{w}_j)$ be an atom from $neg(f_1)$, where $h+1 \leq j \leq h+p$. For the relational symbol R_j we consider all atoms from $pos(f_1)$, that have R_j as relational symbol. Let us denote these atoms by $R_j(\overline{w}_{\alpha_1}), \ldots, R_j(\overline{w}_{\alpha_r})$. Associated to $R_j(\overline{w}_j)$ we consider an expression denoted E_j and defined as follows:

$$E_j = (\overline{w}_j, \overline{w}_{\alpha_1}) \vee \ldots \vee (\overline{w}_j, \overline{w}_{\alpha_r}) \tag{20}$$

In case when $r = 0$ we define $E_j = FALSE$. We take the disjunction of all expressions E_j, $h+1 \leq j \leq h+p$, denoted E, i.e.

$$E = E_{h+1} \vee \ldots \vee E_{h+p} \tag{21}$$

Let r be the number of vector pairs from E. We consider a certain order on these pairs and let $(\overline{w}_l, \overline{w}'_l)$, $1 \leq l \leq r$ be all pairs from E. Thus, we take expression E as follows:

$$E = (\overline{w}_1, \overline{w}'_1) \vee \ldots \vee (\overline{w}_r, \overline{w}'_r)$$

It is clear that $\varphi_M(E) = TRUE$ iff $\psi_M f_1(X, Y_1) = \perp$. $\tag{22}$

From the statement (22) we obtain:

$$\psi_M f_1(X, Y_1) \neq \perp \text{ iff } \varphi_M(\neg E) = TRUE \tag{23}$$

where the symbol $"\neg"$ represents the logic negation. But the expression $\neg E$ is equivalent to the following expression:

$$\neg E \equiv_M \neg(\overline{w}_1, \overline{w}'_1) \wedge \ldots \wedge \neg(\overline{w}_r, \overline{w}'_r) \tag{24}$$

If $\overline{w}_l = (t_1, \ldots, t_s)$ and $\overline{w}'_l = (t'_1, \ldots, t'_s)$ then

$$\neg(\overline{w}_l, \overline{w}'_l) \equiv_M \neg(t_1, t'_1) \vee \ldots \vee \neg(t_s, t'_s) \tag{25}$$

Using the assertions from (24) and (25) and the distributivity of conjunction with respect to disjunction we obtain an expression E' that is equivalent to $\neg E$ with respect to φ_M and E' is in a disjunctive form:

$$E' \equiv_M F_1 \vee \ldots \vee F_m \tag{26}$$

where F_i has the form $[\neg(t_{\alpha_1}, t'_{\alpha_1}) \wedge \ldots \wedge \neg(t_{\alpha_q}, t'_{\alpha_q})]$ $\tag{27}$

For an expression F_i we define a graph $G_{F_i} = (Y, E_{F_i})$, so its vertex set is Y and its edge set is denoted E_{F_i} and defined as follows:

$$E_{F_i} = \{(t, t')|t, t' \in Y\} - \{(t_{\alpha_1}, t'_{\alpha_1}), \ldots, (t_{\alpha_q}, t'_{\alpha_q})\} \tag{28}$$

To find a maximal set M of equality relations defined on Y such that $\psi_M f_1(X, Y_1) \neq \perp$ is equivalent to find a maximal set M from $Y \times Y$ such that there exists an integer $i, 1 \leq i \leq m$ having the property: $M^* \subseteq E_{F_i}$. Let $C_1, \ldots, C_p$ be all maximal cliques from the graph G_{F_i}. We also consider a clique as the set of all its edges, hence as a subset of $Y \times Y$. If the vertex set of the clique C_l is $V_l = \{t_1, \ldots, t_r\}$, then the edge set of V_l is $U_l = \{(t_\alpha, t_\beta), 1 \leq \alpha, \beta \leq r\}$, $1 \leq l \leq p$. We consider all union of pair-wise disjoint subsets of different U_l. Let us denote by $Cl_1(G_i)$ the obtained class of sets. Let $Cl_2(G_i)$ be the class that consists of all elements from $Cl_1(G_i)$ that are maximal. Let $Cl_j = \cup\{Cl_j(G_i)|1 \leq i \leq m\}$, $j = 1, 2$. Concerning these classes we have the following result:

Theorem 4. *Let M be a set of equality relations on Y. We have:*
(i) $M^* \in Cl_1$ iff $\psi_M f_1(X, Y_1) \neq \perp$.
(ii) $M^* \in Cl_2$ iff M is maximal such that $\psi_M f_1(X, Y_1) \neq \perp$.

Proof. Let us consider M such that $\psi_M f_1(X, Y_1) \neq \perp$. From the relation (22) we have $\varphi_M(\neg E) = TRUE$, hence $\varphi_M(E') = TRUE$. Therefore, there exists i, $1 \leq i \leq m$ such that $\varphi_M(F_i) = TRUE$. This implies the statements:

$$\varphi_M(t_{\alpha_j}, t'_{\alpha_j}) = FALSE \text{ for each } j, 1 \leq j \leq q \text{ and} \tag{29}$$

$$\varphi_M(t, t') = TRUE \text{ for each } (t, t') \in E_{F_i} \tag{30}$$

The set M^* is a union of equivalence classes on Y as follows: $M^* = T_1 \cup \ldots \cup T_n$, where $T_i \cap T_j \neq \emptyset$, for each $1 \leq i \neq j \leq n$. We intend to show that T_l, $1 \leq l \leq n$, is a clique in the graph G_{F_i}. By definition of the application ψ_M we have $\psi_M(t) = \psi_M(t')$ for each t and t' from T_l, which implies $\varphi_M(t, t') = TRUE$. Let us denoted by $Node(T_l)$ the set of all vertex from T_l. If $Node(T_l) = \{t_1, \ldots, t_m\}$ then we have:

$$\varphi_M(t_i, t_j) = TRUE \text{ for each } i, j \text{ such that } 1 \leq i, j \leq m \tag{31}$$

Using the statements from (29), (30) and (31) we obtain T_l is a clique in the graph G_{F_i}. Hence, we obtain: $M^* \in Cl_1(G_i)$. If M is maximal with the property $\psi_M f_1(X, Y_1) \neq \perp$, it results that $M^* \in Cl_2(G_i)$. The inverse part follows similarly. □

Example 5. Let us consider the query Q_1 from Example 1. We must compute all sets M so that $\psi_M f_1 \neq \perp$. The symbol a is the only relational symbol from f_1. We rewrite f_1 as follows: $f_1 = a(\overline{w}_1), a(\overline{w}_2), \neg a(\overline{w}_3), \neg a(\overline{w}_4)$, where $\overline{w}_1 = y_1 y_2$, $\overline{w}_2 = y_2 y_3$, $\overline{w}_3 = y_1 y_3$, $\overline{w}_4 = y_2 y_2$. We get the expressions E_1 and E_2 as follows: $E_1 = (\overline{w}_3 = \overline{w}_1) \vee (\overline{w}_3 = \overline{w}_2)$ and $E_2 = (\overline{w}_4 = \overline{w}_1) \vee (\overline{w}_4 = \overline{w}_2)$. Hence, we obtain $\neg E \equiv \neg(y_2 = y_3) \wedge \neg(y_1 = y_2)$. This implies $M_0 = \emptyset$ and $M_1 = \{(y_1, y_3)\}$.

6   Some Aspects of Time Complexity

To our best knowledge, only two algorithms for the queries in conjunctive form with negation were proposed, one of them was studied by J. D. Ullman in [24] and the other one by Wei and Lausen in [25]. For a database S let us denote by $|S|$ its cardinality. Let $R_1, \ldots, R_r$ be all distinct relational symbols from $Rel(f_1)$. Let n_j be the arity of R_j. Let $y_M = |\psi_M(Y)|$, $s = n_1 + \ldots + n_r$, $h = |\psi_M pos(f_1)|$, $p = |\psi_M neg(f_1)|$, $k = |pos(f_2)|$, $n = |neg(f_2)|$ and $x = |X|$. We have: $|D_M^{max}| \leq y_M^{n_1} + \ldots + y_M^{n_r} - p$. The time complexity to compute the set $\mathcal{P}_M$ is $O(s_1)$, where $s_1 = n + x * k * p^{n+1}$ The time complexity for $COMP(M)$ is $O(r_M)$, where $r_M = n * (h^k + C(n' - h, 1) * (h+1)^k + \ldots + C(n' - h, n' - h) * n'^k)$, $n' = |D_M^{max}|$, and $C(i, j)$ denotes the number of all j−combinations of i elements. So in the worst case the conditions from Theorem 2 imply the same performance as the algorithm proposed in [24]. However, the existence of sets S with $MARK(S) = 1$ implies fewer operations in $COMP(M)$.

For the class of queries specified in Section 4, for a certain M the time complexity to test the relation (14) is $O(n^p)$. Hence, if $n_M = |\{M|\psi_M f_1(X, Y_1) \neq \bot\}|$, then the time complexity to verify (14) is $O(n_M * n^p)$. The time complexity to test $COMP(M_0) \neq 0$ is $O(k^h)$. The time complexity to compute all maximal cliques of a graph with l vertices is $O(3^{l/3})$ ([20, 23]). Let $m_1 = |Y|$ and $C_1, \ldots, C_{p_i}$ be all maximal cliques from G_i. Let $s_i = max\{|V_l|, 1 \leq l \leq p_i\}$. We obtain: $p_i \leq 3^{m_1/3}$, $s_i \leq m_1$. If r_i denotes the time complexity of $Cl_1(G_i)$ and q_i the time complexity for $Cl_2(G_i)$, then we get: $r_i \leq 2^{p_i * s_i}$ and $q_i \leq r_i^2$. Hence, we obtain the time complexity for Cl_j is $O(t_j)$, where $t_1 = m * 2^{t_3}$, $t_2 = m * 2^{2*t_3}$, and $t_3 = m_1 * 3^{m_1/3}$. Let $M_1, \ldots, M_v$ be all maximal sets from the class Cl_2 and r_{M_j} be the time complexity for $COMP(M_j)$, $1 \leq j \leq v$. The time complexity to test the condition c) from Theorem 3 is $O(t)$, where $t = t_2 * r_{M_1} * \ldots r_{M_v}$. In [22] N. Tamas and C. Gabor give some functions to compute all or maximal cliques in a graph. The problem of the enumeration of maximal cliques in a graph is studied by E. A. Akkoyunlu in [3] and I. M. Bomze et al. in [4].

7   Conclusion

In this paper we have given a characterization for the containment problem for two conjunctive queries. A special class of queries was studied with respect to the containment problem. We have used sets of equality relations defined on the set of all universally and existentially quantified variables from the first query. For the future work, we intend to use the results of this paper for the problem of rewriting queries using views with negation.

References

1. Afrati, F., Pavlaki, V.: Rewriting Queries Using Views with Negation. AI Communications 19, 229–237 (2006)
2. Afrati, F., Mielikainen, T.: Advanced Topics in Databases, University of Helsinki (2005)
3. Akkoyunlu, E.A.: The enumeration of maximal cliques of large graphs. SIAM Journal of Computing 2, 1–6 (1973)
4. Bomze, I.M., Budinich, M., Pardalos, P.M., Pelillo, M.: The maximum clique problem. In: Handbook of Combinatorial Optimization, vol. 4, pp. 1–74 (1999)
5. Chandra, A.K., Merlin, P.M.: Optimal implementations of conjunctive queries in relational databases. In: ACM Symp. on Theory of Computing (STOC), pp. 77–90 (1977)
6. Cohen, S.: Containment of Aggregate Queries. ACM SIGMOD 34(1), 77–85 (2005)
7. Cohen, S., Nutt, W., Sagiv, Y.: Containment of Aggregate queries, http://www.macs.hw.ac.uk/~nutt/Publications/icdt03.pdf
8. Deutsch, A., Tannen, V.: XML queries and constraints, containment and reformulation. Theoretical Computer Science 336(1), 57–87 (2005)
9. Dong, X., Halevy, A.Y., Tatarinov, I.: Containment of Nested XML Queries, http://data.cs.washington.edu/papers/nest-vldb.pdf

10. Farre, C., Teniente, E., Urpi, T.: Checking query containment with CQC method. Data and Knowledge Engineering 53(2), 163–223 (2005)
11. Felea, V.: A Strong Containment Problem for Queries in Conjunctive Form with Negation. In: Proceedings on The First DBKDA 2009, Cancun, Mexico, March 1-6 (2009), http://profs.info.uaic.ro/~felea/FeleaVictor-DB09.pdf
12. Felea, V.: On the Containment Problem for Queries with Safe Negation. In: Proceedings of the 33 Annual Congress of the American Romanian Academy of Arts and Sciences, Sibiu, June 2-7, vol. II, pp. 201–205 (2009)
13. Florescu, D., Levy, A., Suciu, D.: Query containment for conjunctive queries with regular expressions. In: ACM Symp. on Principles of Database Systems (PODS), pp. 139–148 (1998)
14. Halevy, A.Y.: Answering Queries Using Views: A survey. VLDB Journal 10(4), 270–294 (2001)
15. Huyn, N.: Efficient Complete Local Tests for Conjunctive Query Constraints with Negation, http://dbpubs.stanford.edu/pub/1966-26
16. Lausen, G., Wei, F.: On the containment of conjunctive queries. In: Klein, R., Six, H.-W., Wegner, L. (eds.) Computer Science in Perspective. LNCS, vol. 2598, pp. 231–244. Springer, Heidelberg (2003)
17. Leclere, M., Mugnier, M.L.: Some algorithmic improvements for the containment problem of conjunctive queries with negation. In: Schwentick, T., Suciu, D. (eds.) ICDT 2007. LNCS, vol. 4353, pp. 404–418. Springer, Heidelberg (2006)
18. Chen, L.: Testing Query Containment in the Presence of Binding Restrictions, technical report (1999)
19. Ludascher, B., Nash, A.: Web service composition through declarative queries: the case of conjunctive queries with union and negation. In: Proc. 20th Intern.Conf. on Data Engineering, pp. 840–860 (2004)
20. Makino, K., Uno, T.: New algorithms for enumerating all maximal cliques. In: Hagerup, T., Katajainen, J. (eds.) SWAT 2004. LNCS, vol. 3111, pp. 260–272. Springer, Heidelberg (2004)
21. Millstein, T., Levy, A., Friedman, M.: Query Containment for Data Integration Systems. In: Proc. of Symp. on Principles of Database Systems, pp. 67–75 (2000)
22. Tamas, N., Gabor, C.: http://cneurocvs.rmki.kfki.hu/igraph/doc/R/cliques.html
23. Tomita, E., Tanaka, A., Takahashi, H.: The worst-case time complexity for generating all maximal cliques. In: Proc. 10th Int. Computing and Combinatorics Conf. (2004); also in Theoretical Computer Science 363(1), 28–42 (2006)
24. Ullman, J.D.: Information integration using logical views. In: International Conference on Database Theory (ICDT), pp. 19–40 (1997)
25. Wei, F., Lausen, G.: Containment of Conjunctive Queries with Safe Negation. In: Calvanese, D., Lenzerini, M., Motwani, R. (eds.) ICDT 2003. LNCS, vol. 2572, pp. 346–360. Springer, Heidelberg (2002)

Towards a Scalable, Pragmatic Knowledge Representation Language for the Web

Florian Fischer, Gulay Unel, Barry Bishop, and Dieter Fensel

Semantic Technology Institute (STI) Innsbruck,
University of Innsbruck, Austria
firstname.lastname@sti2.at

Abstract. A basic cornerstone of the Semantic Web are formal languages for describing resources in a clear and unambiguous way. Logical underpinnings facilitate automated reasoning about distributed knowledge on the Web and thus make it possible to derive only implicitly available information.

Much research is geared to advancing very expressive formalisms that add increasingly complex modelling constructs. However, this increase in language expressivity is often intrinsically linked to higher computational cost and often leads to formalisms that have high theoretical complexity and that are difficult to implement efficiently.

In contrast, reasoning in the context of the Web has a distinct set of requirements, namely inference systems that can scale to planetary-size datasets. A reduced level of expressivity is often sufficient for many practical scenarios and crucially, absolutely necessary when reasoning with such massive datasets. These requirements have been acknowledged by active research towards more lightweight formalisms and also by industrial implementations that often implement only tractable subsets of existing standards.

In this paper we aim to explore this trend and formulate a basic language, called $L2$, layered upon RDF as the data-model, that is inherently tractable, easy to implement on common rule engines and motivated by pragmatic considerations concerning the use of language constructs and the means to implement them.

1 Introduction

The next evolutionary step for the Web, the Semantic Web [1], envisions human-readable content enriched with meta-data that has machine-understandable semantics for the purpose of sharing and interconnecting commercial, scientific, personal, and other data. Using a well defined formal language for this purpose enables machine interpretability and in turn automated processing. This vision leads to a Semantic Web, in which content has a well defined meaning and can be reasoned with in order to derive implicit knowledge.

The Web has made tremendous amounts of information available that can be processed based on the formal semantics attached to it, e.g. as a product

A. Pnueli, I. Virbitskaite, and A. Voronkov (Eds.): PSI 2009, LNCS 5947, pp. 124–134, 2010.
© Springer-Verlag Berlin Heidelberg 2010

of the Linking Open Data (LOD)[1] [2] community. A number of languages have been developed that use logic for the purpose of defining these formal semantics. However, the initial sets of standards for this purpose, e.g. OWL [3], have very high worst-case complexity results for key inference problems (usually ExpTime or higher).

The inherent trade-off between the expressiveness of a logical representation formalism and scalability of reasoning has been clearly observed from a theoretical point of view [4] and has also been shown to have a very practical impact on possible use-cases. While worst-case complexity results might not always reflect the practical behavior of an implementation they become increasingly important when faced with the sheer size of the data that is involved in reasoning at a Web scale. Furthermore, data found on the Web is not only special in terms of size, but also in terms of diversity, and in turn inconsistency. Consequently, since completeness in the traditional sense might be a hopeless endeavor, it makes sense to focus only on a pragmatically selected subset of inferences that

- provide a useful level of additional semantics for end-users on the web, falling in line with language constructs that are actually employed,
- are inherently tractable in terms of computational complexity,
- can be practically implemented without major obstacles, or that are already supported by existing tools.

As a contribution towards this goal, we propose $L2$, a very lightweight formalism that supports tractable inferences by both omitting "expensive" language constructs and in certain cases "weakening" the semantics of them. $L2$'s intended semantics is defined as set of "entailment rules" that operate directly on RDF triples, and are thus independent of any particular high level syntax.

This paper is structured as following: Section 2 motivates our approach and describes related work. Section 3 outlines the features of $L2$. Section 4 extends this high-level view with the relevant formal underpinnings in the form of entailment rules that operate directly on a set of RDF triples, and specify $L2$'s intended semantics. Finally, Section 5 concludes and summarizes this paper.

2   Motivation and Related Work

RDF as a data-model represents a labeled, directed multi-graph. Layered upon this are more expressive languages such as RDF Schema [5] and OWL [3], which were introduced to provide a greater degree of expressive power. A fundamental result is that even small increases in the expressive power of a language can have a severe impact on the associated reasoning complexity that leads to the intractability of inference. However, as [6] and others point out, a large portion of Semantic Web data is often only described using a limited subset of existing standards, i.e. RDFS plus certain elements from OWL. Moreover, an important

---

[1] http://esw.w3.org/topic/SweoIG/TaskForces/CommunityProjects/
LinkingOpenData

observation is that while resources on the Web are likely to be annotated with relatively lightweight ontologies, the number of resources annotated with these ontologies is likely to be very large [7].

Practical computational efficiency is important and is reflected both by active research on tractable, lightweight formalisms such as DL-Lite [8], EL++ [9], pD* [10], ELP [11], ... as well as the adoption of tractable profiles within the upcoming OWL 2 standard [12].

Aside from the theoretical work in this area, it is notable that existing implementations of large-scale, RDF-based inference engines often support only a specific subset of current standards in order to scale to very large data-sets. These inference engines give an indication of what modeling primitives are useful and are usually a combination of primitives with low complexity overhead or are based on practical user requirements. In other words, language features are not considered purely in terms of their theoretical characteristics, but also in terms of:

1. The relevance of specific language constructs for users.
2. The practicability of implementing certain language features efficiently.

The subsets implemented, e.g. in OWLIM[2], Oracle 11g[3], or AllegroGraph RDF-Store[4] all support a very similar set of language primitives, usually with the aim of avoiding inferences that derive disjunctions or the existence of anonymous individuals. The features supported usually include support for the basic features available in RDFS and additionally specific parts of the OWL vocabulary along the lines of [10]. More particularly, all of these products support (to various extents) class and property hierarchies, equivalence (of properties, classes and individuals), and additional qualitative statements about properties (denoting transitivity, symmetricity, etc).

3   Language Overview

In this section we describe the language primitives of $L2$, which are selected based on (i) practical considerations outlined in the previous section, (ii) theoretical complexity results. This selection mostly consists of the RDFS vocabulary and a limited sub-set of OWL that is still inherently tractable. As $L2$ could be considered an OWL fragment, in the sense that it allows a restricted set of inferences to be made, we can use the OWL 2 functional-style[5] as high-level syntax. However, any surface syntax with an appropriate mapping to the underlying RDF primitives can be used, e.g. [13], because the fundamental design aspects of the language are independent of the particular syntax employed. This achieves two goals: First of all, it automatically aligns $L2$ with existing standards and at the same time facilitates easy end-user adoption.

---

[2] http://www.ontotext.com/owlim/index.html
[3] http://www.oracle.com/technology/tech/semantic_technologies/index.html
[4] http://agraph.franz.com/allegrograph/
[5] http://www.w3.org/TR/owl2-syntax/

We will now briefly enumerate the features in $L2$, explain why they are included and provide informal descriptions.

Class definitions. (`rdfs:Class`) A class defines a set of individuals that belong together because they share common properties. Only partial class definitions are supported and not complete class definitions, because they allow the emulation of several other language features that are not explicitly included, e.g. class intersection.

Subclass descriptions. (`rdfs:subClassOf`) $L2$ allows the definition of class hierarchies in the same way as RDFS. Thus the intended meaning is exactly the same: If class C_1 is defined to be the subclass of a class C_2 then the set of individuals that "belong to" (are in the class extension of) C_1 should be a subset of those that belong to C_2. Furthermore, subclass relations are transitive and a class is a subclass of itself.

Property definitions. (`rdf:Property`) Properties can be used to state specific relations, either between individuals or between individuals and plain data values.

Subproperty descriptions. (`rdfs:subPropertyOf`) In the same fashion as for classes it is also possible to organize properties in hierarchies by stating that a property is a sub-property of a number of other properties. Obviously, as subclassing, `rdfs:subPropertyOf` has transitive behavior.

Domain and Range restrictions. (`rdfs:domain` and `rdfs:range`) The domain of a property restricts what individuals the property can be applied to, while the range restricts the set of values that a property can take. Both domain and range restrictions impose *global* constraints on a property independently of which specific class a property is applied to. It needs to be noted that for both domains and ranges, it is possible to give two different kinds of interpretations, namely inferring and constraining. For example, assume an individual x that is related to another individual y via a certain property p, with a class C_1 as domain and another class C_2 as the range. Applying an inferring interpretation, it is possible to conclude that x belongs to C_1 and furthermore that y belongs to C_2. A constraining interpretation on the other hand, would actually *check* that the individual is of the correct type, as a condition, and otherwise raise this as an error. Both semantics of domain and ranges are valid and a choice should be made depending on the requirements of an application.

Class equivalence. (`owl:equivalentClass`) Two classes may be stated to be equivalent, in which case they also have the same set of instances and moreover also share common super and subclasses. This functionality is useful to perform basic schema mapping. Class equivalence is a symmetric, reflexive, and transitive property. Furthermore, class equivalence between two classes C_1 and C_2 simply requires two implications stating that C_1 is a subclass of C_2 and vice versa. In this sense it is cleanly layered on top of RDFS, where this functionality is already available, but with no explicit syntax.

Transitive properties. (`owl:TransitiveProperty`) Transitivity of properties has the usual meaning that if a property p holds for a pair of individuals (x, y) and another pair (y, z), then it also holds for (x, z).

Symmetric properties. (owl:SymmetricProperty) A symmetric property is a property that is true in both directions. *L2* allows for the specification of symmetric properties with the usual meaning; if a property p holds for a pair (x, y), then it also holds for (y, x).

Inverse properties. (owl:inverseOf) Furthermore, properties can be stated to be the inverse of another property, i.e. hasParent and hasChild. If p_1 is the inverse of p_2 and an individual x is related to another individual y by p_1, then y is related by p_2 to x.

Property equivalence. (owl:equivalentProperty) Two properties may be stated to be equivalent in the same fashion as classes can. Equivalent properties relate one individual to the identical set of other individuals.

Individual equivalence. (owl:sameAs) Individual equality is included in the language for practical purposes since two distinct URIs can identify the same resource. While individual equality slightly raises the computational complexity (see [14] for an in-depth treatment) it can still be dealt with in practical implementations by various means.

4   Formal Semantics

4.1   Basic Definitions

In this section we give a formal definition of the language primitives outlined in the previous section using specific *entailment rules*. To do so, we briefly recall the required basic terminology as in [15], as a slight extension of the notions in [16].

First, let U denote the set of *URI references*, B denote the (infinite) set of *blank nodes*, and L denote the set of literals, i.e. data values such as strings, booleans, or XML documents. L is partitioned into the set L_p of *plain literals* and the set L_t of *typed literals*. A *typed literal l* consists of a lexical form s and a datatype URI t; l can then be denoted as the pair $l = (s, t)$. The sets U, B, L_p, and L_t are pairwise disjoint. A *vocabulary* is a subset of $U \cup L$. Any symbol t in $U \cup B \cup L$ is called a *RDF term* and the set of RDF terms is denoted by T.

The basic notion of RDF graphs [17,16] only allows URI references in the place of predicates, however, *generalized RDF graphs*, which also allow properties to be blank nodes, were introduced in [15] to solve the problem that the standard set of entailment rules for RDFS [17] is incomplete.

Definition 1 (Generalized RDF Graph). *An RDF graph G is a subset of the set $(U \cup B) \quad \times \quad (U \cup B) \times \quad (U \cup B \cup L)$.*

The elements (s, p, o) of an RDF graph are called *triples*, which consist of a subject s, a predicate (or property) p, and an object o, respectively. We write triples as s p o .

The set $T(G)$ of *RDF terms of an RDF graph G* is the set of all elements that occur in the graph, and the set $bl(G)$ of *blank nodes of an RDF graph G* is in turn defined as $bl(G) = T(G) \cap B$. A graph is ground if it does not contain any blank nodes, that is if $bl(G) = \emptyset$.

Definition 2 (Vocabulary of an RDF graph). *Based on this, the* vocabulary of an RDF graph G *is defined by* $V(G) = T(G) \cap (U \times L)$.

An interpretation of an RDF graph is intrinsically tied to this notion of a specifc *vocabulary* (RDF, RDFS, ...), as in [17], starting with *simple interpretation*, as following:

Definition 3 (Simple Interpretation). *An interpretation I of a vocabulary V is a tuple $I = (R_I, P_I, E_I, S_I, L_I, LV_I)$, where R_I is a nonempty set, called the set of resources, P_I is the set of properties (not required to be disjoint from resources), LV_I is the set of literal values, which is a subset of R_I that contains at least all plain literals in V, and where E_I , S_I and L_I are functions:*

- $E_I : P_I \rightarrow 2^{R_I \times R_I}$
- $S_I : (V \cap U) \rightarrow (R_I \cup P_I)$
- $L_I : (V \cap L_t) \rightarrow R_I$

4.2 Entailment Rules

We then use *entailment rules*, as in [15]. An entailment rule is considered as a pair of generalized RDF graphs where variables can occur as predicate, subject and object in triples. In other words, a rule consists of two sets of triple patterns[6].

For any rule $\rho = (\rho_l, \rho_r)$, we call ρ_l the body of the rule ρ and ρ_l the head of the rule. Syntactically such rules take the following simple form:

$$\text{IF } \rho_l \text{ THEN } \rho_r$$

Informally, a proper entailment rule describes under which conditions ρ_l the statements ρ_r must hold. From this, the statements ρ_r can be inferred whenever we detect the situation specified by ρ_l – it characterizes the expected inferences over a domain vocabulary.

Given a rule ρ, the set of *variables of ρ* is denoted by $var(\rho) = var(\rho_l)$, the set of *blank nodes of ρ* by $bl(\rho) = bl(\rho_r)$, and the *vocabulary of ρ* by $V(\rho) = V(\rho) \cup V(\rho_r)$.

If R is a set of rules, then $V(R) = \bigcup_{\rho \in R} V(\rho)$. An entailment rule ρ is said to *introduce blank nodes* if $bl(\rho) \neq \emptyset$. A rule ρ is called *finite* if the rule head ρ_r and the rule body ρ_l are both finite. A rule ρ is called a *proper rule* if the rule head ρ_r and the rule body ρ_l are both nonempty.

From the above, it is possible to define the meaning of entailment rules in a model-theoretic sense, by defining when a rule is satisfied by an interpretation, and secondly by defining what statements (triples) are entailed by a specific set of rules R, i.e. the notion of simple R-entailment.

---

[6] In the sense defined by the RDF Data Access Group, W3C, http://www.w3.org/2001/sw/DataAccess/

4.3   Definition of $L2$ Language Features

We are now in a position to give a concise, formal definition of the semantics of $L2$ by defining (i) its vocabulary, and (ii) the corresponding set of entailment rules, as described in the previous sections. $L2$'s vocabulary is constructed as an extension of the RDF and RDFS vocabulary (see [17]) and adds the following selected constructs from OWL:

Definition 4 ($L2$ Vocabulary). $V_{L2} = \{$ `owl:sameAs`,
`owl:SymmetricProperty`, `owl:TransitiveProperty`, `owl:inverseOf`,
`owl:equivalentClass`, `owl:equivalentProperty` $\} \cup V_{RDFS} \cup V_{RDF}$

$L2$'s set of entailment rules is then defined on top of RDFS entailment (omitting literal generalization) and several additional rules covering the OWL primitives as depicted in Table 1. The semantics defined for them via the listed entailment rules are slightly weaker than their OWL counterparts, mostly for performance reasons, and in this sense $L2$ is a semantic subset. In the following, we point out some important characteristics of the chosen rule set.

- For performance reasons $L2$ has only "if-conditions" for e.g.
  `rdf:range`, `rdf:domain`, `rdf:subClassOf`, `rdf:subPropertyOf`,
  `owl:TransitiveProperty`, etc. instead of the stronger extensional
  "if and only if conditions" as in OWL.
- In order to capture the intended semantics of class and property hierarchies, including reflexivity and transitivity, rules are included to make this notion explicitly visible.
- Axiomatic triples are not considered during inference.
- Class equivalence is cleanly layered on top of RDFS in the sense that two classes are considered equivalent if and only if they are both a subclass of each other, whereas in OWL only their extensions have to be equal. The same reasoning applies for property equivalence. This style of modeling the semantics of equivalence is rooted in the fact that equivalence, e.g. between classes, can already be indirectly expressed in RDFS in this way, only the vocabulary to make this explicit was not available.
- Furthermore OWL treats `owl:sameAs` strictly as equivalence whereas $L2$ slightly weakens its interpretation and only treats it as an equivalence relation. In order to recapture a set of essential inferences several additional rules are added.

Common reasoning tasks, such as query answering, reduce to entailment between two generalized RDF graphs. Due to its close relationship with pD* [10] known complexity and tractability carry over to $L2$, i.e. ground entailment can be checked in polynomial time. Moreover, we ensure tractability by restricting entailment rules to Horn rules (see [18] for relevant complexity results).

For the specific rule-set of $L2$ we additionally give relevant complexity measures in Table 1. These include for each rule, the time complexity T for detecting a required rule application and the space complexity Δ for the number of triples inferred (the number of nodes needed to construct the closure graph in terms

Table 1. Intended semantics for $L2$ given by means of first-order implications / entailment rules. Rule (1) and (2) cover symmetry and transitivity of properties. Rules (3a) and (3b) formalize the notion that an individual can be considered to be equal to itself. Rule (4) captures reflexivity and respectively and rule (5) transitivity of individual equivalence. Rule (6) and (7) cover the semantics of inverse properties, including its reflexivity. Rules (8) and (9) denote that individuals that are classes or properties are considered sub-classes or sub-properties of themselves. These rules are important to facilitate basic meta-modelling in the language. Rule (10) denotes that existing relations are preserved when renaming nodes. Rules (11a), (11b) and (11c) express the semantics of class equivalence, while (12a), (12b) and (12c) do the same for property equivalence.

Rule No.	IF	THEN	$\mathcal{T}$	Δ
1	`?p type SymmetricProperty` `?v ?p ?w`	`?w ?p ?v`	$O(n^2)$	$O(n)$
2	`?p type TransitiveProperty` `?u ?p ?v` `?v ?p ?w`	`?u ?p ?w`	$O(n^3)$	$O(n^2)$
3a	`?v ?p ?w`	`?v sameAs ?v`	$O(n)$	$O(n)$
3b	`?v ?p ?w`	`?w sameAs ?w`	$O(n)$	$O(n)$
4	`?v sameAs ?w`	`?w sameAs ?v`	$O(n)$	$O(n)$
5	`?u sameAs ?v` `?v sameAs ?w`	`?u sameAs ?w`	$O(n^2)$	$O(n^2)$
6	`?p inverseOf ?q` `?v ?p ?w`	`?w ?q ?v`	$O(n^2)$	$O(n)$
7	`?p inverseOf ?q` `?v ?q ?w`	`?w ?p ?v`	$O(n^2)$	$O(n)$
8	`?v type Class` `?v sameAs ?w`	`?v subClassOf ?w`	$O(n^2)$	$O(n)$
9	`?p type Property` `?p sameAs ?q`	`?p subPropertyOf ?q`	$O(n^2)$	$O(n)$
10	`?u ?p ?v` `?u sameAs ?w` `?v sameAs ?q`	`?w ?p ?q`	$O(n^3)$	$O(n)$
11a	`?v equivalentClass ?w`	`?v subClassOf ?w`	$O(n)$	$O(n)$
11b	`?v equivalentClass ?w`	`?w subClassOf ?v`	$O(n)$	$O(n)$
11c	`?v subClassOf ?w` `?w subClassOf ?v`	`?v equivalentClass ?w`	$O(n^2)$	$O(n)$
12a	`?v equivalentProperty ?w`	`?v subProperty ?w`	$O(n)$	$O(n)$
12b	`?v equivalentProperty ?w`	`?w subProperty ?v`	$O(n)$	$O(n)$
12c	`?v subPropertyOf ?w` `?w subPropertyOf ?v`	`?v equivalentProperty ?w`	$O(n^2)$	$O(n)$

Table 2. Omitted rules and the associated scalability with respect to the to the increase in the size of the computed closure and the effort needed to apply them

Rule No.	IF	THEN	$\mathcal{T}$	Δ
N1	?p type FunctionalProperty ?u ?p ?v ?u ?p ?w	?v sameAs ?w	$O(n^3)$	$O(n)$
N2	?p type InverseFunctionalProperty ?u ?p ?w ?v ?p ?w	?u sameAs ?w	$O(n^3)$	$O(n)$
N3	?v hasValue ?w ?v onProperty ?p ?u ?p ?w	?u type ?w	$O(n^3)$	$O(n)$
N4	?v hasValue ?w ?v onProperty ?p ?u type ?v	?u ?p ?w	$O(n^3)$	$O(n)$
N5	?v someValuesFrom ?w ?v onProperty ?p ?u ?p ?x ?x type ?w	?u type ?v	$O(n^4)$	$O(n)$
N6	?v allValuesFrom ?w ?v onProperty ?p ?u type ?v ?u ?p ?x	?x type ?w	$O(n^4)$	$O(n)$

of the size of the initial graph). To contrast this with more computationally expensive entailment rules, we show the same information for additional rules from [10] in Table 2.

As shown the highest time complexity for the rules we included in $L2$ is $O(n^3)$, whereas it is $O(n^4)$ for the omitted rules in Table 2. The most complex rule covers transitive properties (Rule 2), which poses the same challenges as existing RDFS vocabulary. As a practical solution, the application of this rule on a graph can be mapped to a well studied problem, graph reachability, where efficient optimization algorithms exist see [19] [20] [21].

5   Conclusion

In this paper we presented $L2$, a lightweight and tractable language for the description of resources on the Semantic Web for which rule based and efficient reasoning methods are directly applicable. For that purpose we considered related work concerning theoretical research results as well as practical implementations that are similar in spirit to our approach. We gave a high level explanation of the modeling primitives supported, that (i) are implementable in a scalable way and (ii) useful in practical settings. Lastly, we gave a formal definition of entailment rules that capture the semantics of $L2$ and from which it is straightforward to establish the tractability of $L2$.

It should be noted, that the definition of the formal semantics of $L2$ by restricted entailment rules is not the only possible approach and should not necessarily be taken as a direct algorithmic evaluation procedure. However, this approach can be understood as a basis for defining a minimal, useful and implementable language that is in line with existing Web standards, and also allows for extension with custom rule sets.

Acknowledgments

This research has been partially supported by the LarKC EU-funded project (FP7-215535). For more information visit http://www.larkc.eu.

References

1. Berners-Lee, T., Hendler, J., Lassila, O., et al.: The Semantic Web. Scientific American 284(5), 28–37 (2001)
2. Bizer, C., Heath, T., Ayers, D., Raimond, Y.: Interlinking Open Data on the Web. In: Demonstrations Track, 4th European Semantic Web Conference, Innsbruck, Austria (2007)
3. McGuinness, D., van Harmelen, F., et al.: OWL Web Ontology Language Overview. W3C Recommendation 10, 2004–03 (2004)
4. Brachman, R., Levesque, H.: The tractability of subsumption in frame-based description languages. In: Proc. of the 4th Nat. Conf. on Artificial Intelligence (AAAI 1984), pp. 34–37 (1984)
5. Brickley, D., Guha, R.: RDF Vocabulary Description Language 1.0: RDF Schema. W3C Recommendation 2 (2004)
6. Wang, T., Parsia, B., Hendler, J.: A Survey of the Web Ontology Landscape. In: Cruz, I., Decker, S., Allemang, D., Preist, C., Schwabe, D., Mika, P., Uschold, M., Aroyo, L.M. (eds.) ISWC 2006. LNCS, vol. 4273, pp. 682–694. Springer, Heidelberg (2006)
7. Weithoner, T., Liebig, T., Luther, M., Bohm, S.: What's Wrong with OWL Benchmarks? In: Second International Workshop on Scalable Semantic Web Knowledge Base Systems, SSWS 2006 (2006)
8. Calvanese, D., De Giacomo, G., Lembo, D., Lenzerini, M., Rosati, R.: DL-Lite: Tractable Description Logics for Ontologies. In: Proceedings of the National Conference on Artificial Intelligence, vol. 20(2), p. 602 (2005)
9. Baader, F., Brandt, S., Lutz, C.: Pushing the EL Envelope Further. In: Proceedings of the OWLED Workshop (2008)
10. ter Horst, H.J.: Combining RDF and part of owl with rules: Semantics, decidability, complexity. In: Gil, Y., Motta, E., Benjamins, V.R., Musen, M.A. (eds.) ISWC 2005. LNCS, vol. 3729, pp. 668–684. Springer, Heidelberg (2005)
11. Krötzsch, M., Rudolph, S., Hitzler, P.: Elp: Tractable rules for owl 2. In: Sheth, A.P., Staab, S., Dean, M., Paolucci, M., Maynard, D., Finin, T., Thirunarayan, K. (eds.) ISWC 2008. LNCS, vol. 5318, pp. 649–664. Springer, Heidelberg (2008)
12. Grau, B., Horrocks, I., Parsia, B., Patel-Schneider, P., Sattler, U.: Next Steps for OWL. OWL Experienced and Directions (2006)
13. Horridge, M., Drummond, N., Goodwin, J., Rector, A., Stevens, R., Wang, H.: The Manchester OWL Syntax

14. Volz, R.: Web Ontology Reasoning with Logic Databases. PhD thesis, Universität Karlsruhe (TH), Universität Karlsruhe (TH), Institut AIFB, D-76128 Karlsruhe (2004)
15. ter Horst, H.J.: Completeness, decidability and complexity of entailment for RDF schema and a semantic extension involving the owl vocabulary. J. Web Sem. 3(2-3), 79–115 (2005)
16. Klyne, G., Carroll, J., McBride, B.: Resource Description Framework (RDF): Concepts and Abstract Syntax. W3C Recommendation 10 (2004)
17. Hayes, P., McBride, B.: RDF Semantics. W3C Recommendation 10 (2004)
18. Dantsin, E., Eiter, T., Gottlob, G., Voronkov, A.: Complexity and expressive power of logic programming. ACM Computing Surveys (CSUR) 33(3), 374–425 (2001)
19. Schenkel, R., Theobald, A., Weikum, G.: Efficient Creation and Incremental Maintenance of the HOPI Index for Complex XML Document Collections. In: Proceedings of the International Conference on Data Engineering, 1998, vol. 21, p. 360. IEEE Computer Society Press, Los Alamitos (2005)
20. Schenkel, R., Theobald, A., Weikum, G.: HOPI: An Efficient Connection Index for Complex XML Document Collections. In: Bertino, E., Christodoulakis, S., Plexousakis, D., Christophides, V., Koubarakis, M., Böhm, K., Ferrari, E. (eds.) EDBT 2004. LNCS, vol. 2992, pp. 237–255. Springer, Heidelberg (2004)
21. Wang, H., He, H., Yang, J., Yu, P., Yu, J.: Dual labeling: Answering graph reachability queries in constant time. In: Proceedings of the 22nd International Conference on Data Engineering (ICDE), p. 75 (2006)

An Experiment with
the Fourth Futamura Projection

Robert Glück[*]

DIKU, Dept. of Computer Science, University of Copenhagen,
DK-2100 Copenhagen, Denmark
glueck@acm.org

Abstract. We have experimentally validated the theoretical insight, that a compiler generator is an Ershov generating extension of a program specializer, by showing that an existing offline partial evaluator can perform the fourth Futamura projection. Specifically, an online and an offline partial evaluator for an imperative flowchart language were transformed into two new compiler generators by Romanenko's classical partial evaluator Unmix. The two partial evaluators are described, as is a novel recursive method for polyvariant specialization. The new compiler generators are demonstrated by converting a universal parser into a parser generator. These results strongly indicate that existing partial evaluation techniques can be put to work on several new applications. To date, all previous compiler generators based on partial evaluation were either generated by self-application or handwritten. None of these works considered the generation of one compiler generator by another.

1 Introduction

The three Futamura projections stand as a cornerstone in the development of partial evaluation. The observation by Futamura, that the self-generation of a compiler generator is due to a fourth projection [6], and the insight by Klimov and Romanenko, that Futamura's abstraction scheme can be continued beyond his third projection [19], were recently investigated, and several new applications for compiler generators were identified [10].

Computer experiments are needed to test these theoretical results and to determine whether existing partial evaluation technology is strong enough for this task. This paper describes and assesses such experiments. The focus is not on introducing new specialization methods geared towards solving the transformation challenges, but on determining whether and in what way existing partial evaluators can computationally realize some of the theoretical predictions. For our experiments, we chose Romanenko's partial evaluator *Unmix* for a first-order subset of Scheme [21], a direct descendant of the first offline partial evaluator *Mix* [18], which is the basis for practically all offline partial evaluators today. The results obtained for Unmix should therefore be applicable to many of the later

---

[*] Part of this work was performed while the author was visiting the National Institute of Informatics (NII), Tokyo.

A. Pnueli, I. Virbitskaite, and A. Voronkov (Eds.): PSI 2009, LNCS 5947, pp. 135–150, 2010.
© Springer-Verlag Berlin Heidelberg 2010

and more developed partial evaluators and to hand-written compiler generators based on the offline approach, though the technical details and programming languages may vary from case to case (*e.g.* Similix, C-Mix, Tempo, PGG, Logen).

We investigate the structure and organization of partial evaluators needed for their conversion into compiler generators by the fourth Futamura projection. For this purpose, we wrote two partial evaluators for the imperative flowchart language of Gomard and Jones [14], one employing online and one employing offline techniques. The two partial evaluators are functionally equivalent to Hatcliff's online and offline partial evaluators [15], disregarding block order and renaming of labels in the residual programs. An important advantage is that partial evaluation for this language has been very well documented (*e.g.*, [1,14,17,15,3,2]), which should make our results easily accessible and comparable.

The main contribution of this paper is to experimentally validate the application of the fourth Futamura projection: *the generation of one compiler generator by another*. The results demonstrate that this can be performed by existing partial evaluators and gives reasonable results. We also show a novel recursive method for polyvariant specialization, which allows the generation of a compiler generator based on online partial evaluation, producing generating extensions that are as efficient as those produced by its offline counterpart. This result is remarkable because partial evaluation folklore has indicated that online techniques unavoidably lead to overgeneralized generating extensions [17, Ch. 7.3.2]. The quality of our generating extensions is demonstrated by staging Bulyonkov's universal parser for regular languages [1]. The new compiler generators have an interesting property, in that they can turn interpreters into cross-compilers.

Throughout this paper, we assume that readers are familiar with the basics of partial evaluation, *e.g.*, as presented by Jones *et al.* [17, Part II].

2   The Fourth Futamura Projection

We begin with a brief review of the third and fourth Futamura projections, using a notation adapted from Jones *et al.* [17]; see also [9]. An L-program s is an N/L-*specializer* iff $\forall p \in P_N$ and $\forall x, y \in D$: $[\![[\![s]\!]_L (p, x)]\!]_N y = [\![p]\!]_N (x, y)$.

Futamura noticed [5] that a compiler generator cog produced by his third projection, that is by double self-application of an L/L-specializer s, generates a copy of itself when applied to s. Starting with the *third Futamura projection* (3.) and apply s once more to abstract from the second argument in the projection, where the second argument ($\underline{s}$) is underlined for clarity:

	Abstract:			Instantiate:
3.		$[\![s]\!]_L (s,\ \underline{s})$	$= \text{cog}$	
4.	$[\![s]\!]_L (s,\ s)$		$= \text{cog}$	$[\![\text{cog}]\!]_L\ \underline{s} = \text{cog}$

It follows from the correctness of the specializer s applied in (4.) that the application of its residual program cog to $\underline{s}$, $[\![\text{cog}]\!]_L\ \underline{s}$, returns the same result as $[\![s]\!]_L (s, \underline{s})$ in (3.). Thus, cog is *self-generating* when applied to $\underline{s}$, a finding first observed for the compiler generator of the partial evaluator Mix [18].

A residual program produced by a specializer can be applied to many different arguments; in particular, the residual program cog produced by the fourth projection can be applied to many different specializers (s_0, s_1, ...), not only to $\underline{s}$, and each specializer is turned into a compiler generator (cog_0, cog_1, ...):

$$[\![cog]\!]_L s_0 = cog_0, \quad [\![cog]\!]_L s_1 = cog_1, \quad [\![cog]\!]_L s_2 = cog_2, \quad \ldots . \qquad (1)$$

At first glance, the *fourth Futamura projection* (4.) appears disappointing, since it seems to produce nothing new. But the situation is different when applying cog to different specializers. Since these specializers can have different characteristics, *e.g.*, concerning specialization methods and subject languages, several new application scenarios emerge [10]. In general, a compiler generator turns a program with two arguments into a generating extension. Since a specializer is a two-argument program that is turned into a compiler generator, there is good reason to add to Ershov's generating extensions [4] an important case: *the generating extension of a specializer is a compiler generator.*

2.1   The Experiment: Generating a New Compiler Generator

Experimental validation is required to determine whether existing specialization methods can turn specializers into compiler generators without self-application. A compiler generator, cog_{OLD}, for a language S, which may be written by hand or obtained by self-application, can be characterized by the equation

$$[\![[\![[\![cog_{OLD}]\!]_S p]\!]_S x]\!]_S y = [\![p]\!]_S (x, y). \qquad (2)$$

If we write a new N/S-specializer s_{NEW}, where N may or may not be identical to S, application of cog_{OLD} to s_{NEW} produces a compiler generator cog_{NEW} in one step:

$$[\![cog_{OLD}]\!]_S s_{NEW} = cog_{NEW}. \qquad (3)$$

This new compiler generator can be described by the equation

$$[\![[\![[\![cog_{NEW}]\!]_S q]\!]_S x]\!]_N y = [\![q]\!]_N (x, y). \qquad (4)$$

This indicates that cog_{NEW} is implemented in S, along with the generating extension that it produces, $genq = [\![cog_{NEW}]\!]_S q$. Application of the generating extension $genq$ to x produces an N-program that consumes the remaining input y. The equations assert that N/S-specializers can be turned into compiler generators in one step and without self-application [10]. This is interesting for several reasons:

1. The *language* N may be a *domain-specific language*, which is not well suited for implementing a program specializer, or N may *not be Turing-complete*. Nevertheless, we obtain a compiler generator cog_{NEW}, which turns N-programs into generating extensions implemented in S that produce N-programs.
2. The *specializer* s_{NEW} may *not be self-applicable* for formal reasons, because $N \neq S$, or for practical reasons, even when $N = S$, because s_{NEW} may employ online specialization techniques for which self-applicability has not been definitely determined. These include online partial evaluation [15, 22], Turchin's supercompilation [24, 13], and Futamura's generalized partial computation [7].

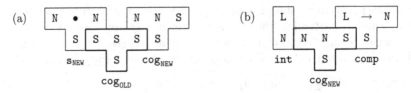

Fig. 1. Transformation of a specializer into a compiler generator, $[\![\text{cog}_{\text{OLD}}]\!]_S \, s_{\text{NEW}} = \text{cog}_{\text{NEW}}$, and transformation of an interpreter into a cross-compiler, $[\![\text{cog}_{\text{NEW}}]\!]_S \, \text{int} = \text{comp}$

To illustrate the involved languages, it is convenient to use a variant of the T-diagrams familiar from compiler construction. The specializer and the two compiler generators are shown in Fig. 1a. The figure shows the subject language N, the target language N, and the implementation language S of the N/S-specializer s_{NEW}. The bullet (•) in the center distinguishes its T-diagram from that of a compiler. The two compiler generators have an additional language, written in the center of their T-diagrams, namely the target language of the generating extensions that they produce (S in the case of cog_{OLD}, N in the case of cog_{NEW}).

In our experiments, S was the functional language Scheme, a statically-scoped version of Lisp, well suited for symbol manipulation, whereas N was an unstructured imperative language with assignments and jumps, called FCL. The semantics of FCL is identical to those that have been formalized and published [15, 17]. The compiler generator cog_{OLD} was obtained by self-application of the offline partial evaluator Unmix [21]. Utilizing the partial evaluation methods by Gomard and Jones [14] and Hatcliff [15], we wrote two FCL/S-partial evaluators, an online partial evaluator s_{ON} and an offline partial evaluator s_{OFF}. Both partial evaluators work on a Scheme representation of FCL-programs (Fig. 2). They are examples for the second case above (N $\neq$ S). Scheme is also better suited for implementing the partial evaluators than FCL, which illustrates the first case.

When we performed an experiment with an interpreter written in FCL for the while-language MP [18], we found that both compiler generators produced efficient MP-to-FCL-compilers written in Scheme. In general, cog_{NEW} turns an L-interpreter int written in N into an L-to-N-compiler comp written in S (Fig. 1b). A *cross-compiler* can therefore be obtained in two steps: $[\![[\![\text{cog}_{\text{OLD}}]\!]_S \, s_{\text{NEW}}]\!]_S \, \text{int} = \text{comp}$.

3   A Universal Parser and Its Generating Extension

To show the quality of the new compiler generators, we present a complete example. Application of the compiler generator cog_{NEW} to a universal parser parse written in FCL, yields a parser generator parsegen written in Scheme:

$$[\![\text{cog}_{\text{NEW}}]\!]_S \, \text{parse} = \text{parsegen}. \tag{5}$$

One of the first programs to which polyvariant specialization was applied is a *universal parser for regular languages* over the two-character alphabet $\{a, b\}$ [1]. The universal parser parse written in FCL is shown in Fig. 3, where ta and tb

$$
\begin{array}{lll}
p ::= ((x^*)\ (l)\ (b^+)) & & \text{(program)} \\
b ::= (l\ a^*\ j) & & \text{(basic block)} \\
a ::= (x := e) & & \text{(assignment)} \\
j ::= (\textbf{goto}\ l) & & \text{(unconditional jump)} \\
\quad |\ (\textbf{if}\ e\ l\ l) & & \text{(conditional jump)} \\
\quad |\ (\textbf{return}\ e) & & \text{(program return)} \\
e ::= (o\ u^*) & & \text{(simple expression)} \\
o ::= \textbf{car}\ |\ \textbf{cdr}\ |\ \textbf{cons}\ |\ \textbf{+}\ |\ \textbf{-}\ |\ \textbf{=}\ |\ \textbf{<}\ |\ \dots & & \text{(primitive operator)} \\
u ::= x\ |\ \textbf{'}v & & \text{(operator argument)} \\
x \in Name \quad v \in Value \quad l \in Label & &
\end{array}
$$

Fig. 2. Scheme representation of the flowchart language FCL

```
((s ta tb) (init) ((init (q := '0)              Example FSA and its tabular form:
  start state
            (goto loop))                              start
  (loop (if (= s '()) end isab))
  (isab (c := (car s))      ; next char
        (s := (cdr s))      ; rest string
        (if (= c 'a) doa dob))
  (doa   (q := (ith ta q)) ; next state
         (goto loop))
  (dob   (q := (ith tb q)) ; next state
         (goto loop))
  (end   (return q)) ))
```

$$
\begin{array}{c|cc}
q & a & b \\
\hline
0 & 1 & 0 \\
1 & 0 & 1 \\
\end{array}
$$

Fig. 3. A universal parser for regular languages over alphabet $\{a, b\}$ written in FCL and a finite state automaton (FSA) that accepts strings with an even number of a

```
((s) (init) ((init (if (= s '()) end0 isab0))
  (isab0 (c := (car s))   ; state 0       (isab1 (c := (car s))   ; state 1
         (s := (cdr s))                          (s := (cdr s))
         (if (= c 'a)  doa0 dob0))               (if (= c 'a)  doa1 dob1))
  (doa0  (if (= s '()) end1 isab1))       (doa1  (if (= s '()) end0 isab0))
  (dob0  (if (= s '()) end0 isab0))       (dob1  (if (= s '()) end1 isab1))
  (end0  (return '0))                     (end1  (return '1)) ))
```

Fig. 4. Specialized parser for strings with an even number of a (see FSA in Fig. 3)

is the tabular representation of the corresponding *finite state automaton* (FSA), q is the state of the automaton, c is the current character, and s is the string. The program returns the last state as the result, which indicates whether the string given to the parser has been accepted. The three input parameters (s, ta, tb) and the initial label (init) are written at the beginning of the FCL-program. As is customary, the set of values in FCL is that of the Lisp S-expressions, where '() is the empty list. The string s is a list of characters. The operator ith

```
(define (pefcl-1 tab)    ; The parser generator inputs a table tab = (ta tb)
  (pestmts-1 0 (car tab) (cadr tab) (mkHEAD ' (s)  ' init  ' (ta tb)  tab)))
(define (pestmts-1 q ta tb code)
  (pepoly-2 q ta tb
    (pepoly-1 q ta tb
      (mkBLOCK ` (if (= s '()) (end  (q ta tb) ( ,q ,ta ,tb  ))
                     (isab (q ta tb) ( ,q ,ta ,tb  )))  . ,code))))
(define (pepoly-1 q ta tb code)
  (if (done? 'end '(q ta tb) `(,q ,ta ,tb) code) code
    (mkBLOCK ` ( (return ' ,q ) (end (q ta tb) ( ,q ,ta ,tb  ))  ,code))))
(define (pepoly-2 q ta tb code)
  (if (done? 'isab '(q ta tb) `(,q ,ta ,tb) code) code
    (pepoly-4 q ta tb
      (pepoly-3 q ta tb
        (mkBLOCK ` ( (if (= c 'a) (doa (q ta tb) ( ,q ,ta ,tb  ))
                         (dob (q ta tb) ( ,q ,ta ,tb  )))
                    (s := (cdr s)) (c := (car s))
                    (isab (q ta tb) ( ,q ,ta ,tb  ))  ,code))))))
(define (pepoly-3 q ta tb code)
  (if (done? 'doa '(q ta tb) `(,q ,ta ,tb) code) code
    (pestmts-1 (list-ref ta q) ta tb
               ` ( (doa (q ta tb) ( ,q ,ta ,tb  ))  ,code))))
(define (pepoly-4 q ta tb code)
  (if (done? 'dob '(q ta tb) `(,q ,ta ,tb) code) code
    (pestmts-1 (list-ref tb q) ta tb
               ` ( (dob (q ta tb) ( ,q ,ta ,tb  ))  ,code))))
```

Fig. 5. Parser generator produced in Scheme by the new compiler generators

returns the ith element of a list; `car` and `cdr` return the head and tail of a list, respectively.

As an example consider the regular language that contains all strings with an even number of a. The language is accepted by the FSA, which starts and accepts in state 0 (Fig. 3). State 1 indicates non-acceptance. The tabular description of the FSA is `ta = (1 0)` and `tb = (0 1)`.

Parser Generator. Application of the parser generator `parsegen` (Fig. 5) to the tabular description of an FSA generates a parser for that language. For example, the specialized parser in Fig. 4 was generated for the FSA in Fig. 3. Its control flow resembles the FSA. The parser generator is remarkably compact and readable, in part because cog_{NEW} inherited the Unmix postprocessor, including the *arity raiser* [20], improving the quality of the generating extension. It was generated automatically and consists of specialized versions of the procedures in the partial evaluators described below (`pefcl`, `pepoly`, `pestmts`). The program shown in the figure was obtained by hand-editing which consisted only of name changes because machine-produced names are uninformative. The boxes indicate the program code that is generated. Code generation makes liberal use of the Scheme "backquote" notation. For example, `pepoly-1` contains a code template for a return statement in which the value of `q` is inserted as a constant (the specialized parser in Fig. 4 contains two such return statements).

Some operations originating from the universal parser can be performed when the parser generator is running, whereas others are placed into the generated parser. Operations that depend only on the given tables (`ta`, `tb`) can be performed by the parser generator. These include the table lookups in procedures `pepoly-3` and `pepoly-4` by the Scheme procedure `list-ref`, which returns the ith element of a list. Operations that may depend on the unknown string `s`, such as taking the next character by `car`, are performed in the specialized parser (Fig. 4).

The program in Fig. 5 is the *complete* parser generator, except for three auxiliary procedures. These are `mkHEAD`, which creates the head of an FCL-program with parameters and initial label; `mkBLOCK`, which adds a new block to `code`; and `done?`, which determines whether a block that needs to be generated already exists in `code`. The three procedures take 12 lines of Scheme text.

Two technical points, however, require further explanation: (1) Statements are *pushed* onto `code`. This explains the reversed order in which they appear, *e.g.*, `(s := (cdr s)) (c := (car s))` in `pepoly-2`. When a block is completed, `mkBLOCK` adds the reversed list to the generated parser. (2) The syntax of FCL allows S-expressions as labels. The labels produced by the parser generator take the form ⟨*source-label static-names static-values*⟩, *e.g.*, `(doa (q ta tb) (0 (1 0) (0 1)))`. For readability, these were later replaced by shorter labels (*e.g.*, by `doa0`; Fig. 4).

4   The Online and Offline Partial Evaluators

This section presents the online and offline partial evaluators for FCL that we designed and implemented in Scheme. Our aim was not to discuss the advantages of using online compared with offline strategies. Rather, we sought to assess the *organization and structure* of the two partial evaluators, allowing an 'off-the-shelf' compiler generator to turn these into compiler generators that produce efficient generating extensions from FCL-programs. More specifically, we transformed the partial evaluators, s_{ON} and s_{OFF}, into two new compiler generators, cog_{ON} and cog_{OFF}, using Unmix's compiler generator cog_{UNMIX}, where S denotes Scheme:

$$[\![cog_{UNMIX}]\!]_S \; s_{ON} \; = \; cog_{ON}, \tag{6}$$

$$[\![cog_{UNMIX}]\!]_S \; s_{OFF} \; = \; cog_{OFF}. \tag{7}$$

Recursive Polyvariant Specialization   The two partial evaluators are based on *polyvariant block specialization* [1]: each block in an FCL-program may give raise to several specialized versions in the residual program. Each block in a residual program is a specialization of a block in the subject program with respect to different variable divisions and/or different values for the static variables.

A main difficulty during the specialization of a partial evaluator with respect to an FCL-program is to obtain enough static information about the pending list, which is a dynamic data structure. In an offline partial evaluator this important information, the labels of blocks and their divisions, can be determined beforehand (*offline*) by a *binding-time analysis* (BTA) and made available to the partial evaluator via the annotations of the subject program. When an offline partial evaluator is specialized with respect to an *annotated* FCL-program, the information about the pending list can be recovered by a binding-time improvement, called 'The Trick', which is the key to the generation of efficient generating extensions [17, Ch. 4.8.3]. This programming trick cannot be used in an online partial evaluator that has no BTA and determines the necessary information incrementally during the specialization (*online*) of an *unannotated* FCL-program.

Using a recursive method, we can perform polyvariant specialization *without a pending list*. This avoids the need for an accumulating parameter (the pending list). We use a procedure pepoly that specializes a block 1 in an FCL-program p with respect to the *static names* sn and the *static values* sv. The procedure takes as last argument the current residual program in code and adds to it the specialized version of block 1, unless that version already exists in code. The type is pepoly :: *Label* × *Program* × *Names* × *Values* × *Code* → *Code*. Representing the static store of a block by two lists (sn, sv) allows to give them different binding times. This binding-time improvement is well known in partial evaluation. To represent the *division* of variables, it is sufficient to know the names of the static variables sn; all others are regarded as dynamic.

A conditional jump (if e l_1 l_2) with a dynamic test expression e gives raise to two new tasks for block specialization, the specialization of the target blocks l_1 and l_2. To specialize the blocks, we nest two calls to pepoly:

```
(pepoly l₂ p sn sv
  (pepoly l₁ p sn sv code)).
```

This method can be used regardless of whether the specialization of statements in a block l_i is performed online or offline. We therefore use the same recursive polyvariant specialization method in both partial evaluators. The nesting of the two calls can be seen in the case of a dynamic conditional jump in Figs. 7 and 8. Note that the specialization of a block l_i can lead to further block specializations.

When the two calls to pepoly are specialized with respect to l_i, p, and sn, two code generators are produced, one for each block (*e.g.*, the pepoly-1 and pepoly-2 in Fig. 5, where Unmix's arity raiser [20] split the list sv into the three variables q, ta, tb; note also the nested calls to pepoly-1 and pepoly-2 in pestmts-1).

The Partial Evaluators. Common to both partial evaluators is the main program in Fig. 6. Offline specialization is performed by replacing onpestmt by offpestmt in procedure pestmts. The underlines represent the annotation by a monovariant BTA and will be explained later. The main procedure pefcl takes as input an FCL-program program (an annotated FCL-program in the offline case) and the static names sn and the static values sv of the program. These FCL-programs are assumed to be syntactically correct. Specialization begins by using initcode to make the header of the residual program with the residual parameters (all variables xs except those in sn) and the start label, followed by generation of the residual blocks with peblock. The procedure peblock looks up the statement list of block 1 in program p and specializes the list by pestmts. To avoid generating

```
(define (pefcl program sn sv)                    ; PE of program
   (with (( ( xs ( l ) p )   program ))
     (peblock l p sn sv (initcode xs l sn sv)))))

(define (peblock l p sn sv code)                 ; PE of block
   (pestmts (lookupstmts l p) p sn sv code))

(define (pestmts stmts p sn sv code)             ; PE of statements
   (onpestmt (car stmts) (cdr stmts) p sn sv code))

(define (pepoly l p sn sv code)                  ; polyvariant specialization
   (if (done? l sn sv code) code
       (peblock l p sn sv (mkLABEL l sn sv code)))))
```

Fig. 6. Main program of the FCL-partial evaluators

the same specialized version of a block twice, the procedure done? in pepoly determines whether the desired block already exists in code.

A partial evaluator takes values for the static parameters of a program and tries to precompute as many statements as possible. Statements that cannot be precomputed are placed into the residual program. A specialization strategy is said to be *online* if the values computed at the time of specialization can affect the choice of action taken; otherwise a strategy is said to be *offline* [17, Ch. 4.4.7]. We will briefly explain the online and offline strategies for the partial evaluation of FCL-statements (Figs. 7 and 8). The pattern matching expression select in the figures improves readability and is expanded into Scheme by Unmix.

Online Partial Evaluation of Statements. The online strategy for specializing an *assignment* $x := e$ is simple: if e depends only on static names, as tested by static?, the static store is updated with the value of e; otherwise, variable x is removed from the static store. This makes x dynamic. Procedure mkASG generates an assignment $x := e'$, in which e' is obtained from e by replacing every occurrence of a static name by its value. An expression $e = $ (gen x) is always considered as dynamic, even when x is static, and may be used in an FCL-program to avoid possible finite or infinite code explosion during partial evaluation [15].

One of the most interesting aspects of the online strategy and one that distinguishes online from offline strategies is specializing a *conditional jump* if e l_1 l_2. If e depends only on static names, the conditional jump is replaced by the statements obtained by specializing the block l_i selected by the value of e. This unfolding decision depends on the actual static values. If e is not static, however, either branch may be executed when the residual program is run. A conditional jump with residual labels is generated by mkIF, completing the current block specialization. The blocks l_1 and l_2 are then specialized by pepoly, as described above.

An *unconditional jump* goto l can be replaced by the statements obtained by specializing block l. A *return statement* return e is replaced by return e', where e is reduced to e' in the current static store.

```
(define (onpestmt stmt stmts p sn sv code)
 (select (stmt)
  ((x ':= e)      => (if (static? e sn)
                         (pestmts stmts p (updsn x sn) ; static assign
                                  (updsv x (evalop e sn sv) sn sv) code)
                         (pestmts stmts p (delsn x sn) ; dynamic assign
                                  (delsv x sn sv) (mkASG x e sn sv code))))

  (('IF e l₁ l₂) => (if (static? e sn)
                        (if (evalop e sn sv)                ; static if
                            (peblock l₁ p sn sv code)
                            (peblock l₂ p sn sv code))
                        (pepoly l₂ p sn sv                  ; dynamic if
                                (pepoly l₁ p sn sv
                                        (mkIF e l₁ l₂ sn sv code)))))

  (('GOTO l)      => (peblock l p sn sv code))             ; goto
  (('RETURN e)    => (mkRETURN e sn sv code)) ))           ; return
```

Fig. 7. Online partial evaluation of FCL-statements by s_{ON}

```
(define (offpestmt stmt stmts p sn sv code)
 (select (stmt)
  ((x ':=S e)     => (pestmts stmts p (updsn x sn)      ; static assign
                             (updsv x (evalop e sn sv) sn sv) code))
  ((x ':=D e)     => (pestmts stmts p (delsn x sn)      ; dynamic assign
                             (delsv x sn sv) (mkASG x e sn sv code)))

  (('IFS e l₁ l₂) => (if (evalop e sn sv)               ; static if
                         (peblock l₁ p sn sv code)
                         (peblock l₂ p sn sv code)))
  (('IFD e l₁ l₂) => (pepoly l₂ p sn sv                 ; dynamic if
                             (pepoly l₁ p sn sv
                                     (mkIF e l₁ l₂ sn sv code))))

  (('GOTO l)      => (peblock l p sn sv code))          ; goto
  (('RETURN e)    => (mkRETURN e sn sv code)) ))        ; return
```

Fig. 8. Offline partial evaluation of FCL-statements by s_{OFF}

As an example, consider the specialization of the universal parser in Fig. 3 with respect to $sn = $ (ta tb) and $sv = $ ((1 0) (0 1)). This produces the residual program in Fig. 4, in which the label names have been rewritten for readability.

Offline Partial Evaluation of Statements. Decisions taken by the offline strategy do not depend on the actual static values, but *only* on the annotations of the

```
(define ($pefcl program sn)        ; staging of program
  (with (( ( xs ( l ) p ) program ))
    `[(|CALL ($peblock ,l ,p ,sn) [sv (initcode '],xs ['],l ['],sn [sv))])
```

```
(define ($peblock l p sn)          ; staging of block
  ($pestmts (lookupstmts l p) p sn))
```

```
(define ($pestmts stmts p sn)      ; staging of statements
  ($onpestmt (car stmts) (cdr stmts) p sn))
```

```
(define ($pepoly l p sn)           ; staging of polyvariant
specialization
  `[(if (done? '],l ['],sn [sv code) code]
        [(|CALL ($peblock ,l ,p ,sn) [sv (mkLABEL '],l ['],sn [sv code)))])
```

Fig. 9. Compiler generator for FCL: specializing polyvariant specialization

FCL-program. A dynamic conditional, ifD e l_1 l_2, and a dynamic assignment, x :=D e, are always treated as dynamic regardless of whether e is actually static or not. The handling of goto and return is the same as in the online case.

The offline strategy in Fig. 8 works with any congruent annotation of an FCL-program. It can be used together with a monovariant, pointwise or polyvariant BTA. In the case of a polyvariant BTA, a polyvariant expansion of the subject program is used to represent the different divisions of a block. In the case of a monovariant BTA, which means that the same division is valid for *all* blocks, the handling of assignments in Fig. 8 can be simplified by omitting the procedures calls that change the division (updsn, delsn, delsv).

Annotation of the Partial Evaluators. Unmix is an offline partial evaluator with a monovariant BTA [21]. The annotation of our programs by Unmix's BTA is shown in Figs. 6–8 by underlining the <u>dynamic</u> expressions. The classification of the three parameters of the main procedure pefcl in Fig. 6: the FCL-program program and the name list sn are *static* and the value list sv is *dynamic*. Operations that depend only on program and sn can be static, while all other operations that may depend on sv are underlined. In particular, the first three parameters of pepoly in Fig. 6 remain static and only sv and code are dynamic. The recursive method of polyvariant block specialization kept the essential information static (l, p, sn), providing the key to a good specialization of our partial evaluators.

Procedures that carry no annotation are *fully evaluated* when the partial evaluators are specialized with respect to an FCL-program and do not occur in the generating extensions produced by Unmix. As an example, the important tests static? in Fig. 7 are evaluated when the online partial evaluator is specialized. They will thus never occur in the generating extensions (*cf.*, Fig. 5). Also, a change of the transition compression strategy does not affect the binding time separation. The Unmix-inserted call annotation rcall is not shown in Figs. 6–8.

```
(define ($onpestmt stmt stmts p sn) (select (stmt)
  ((x ':= e) => (if (static? e sn)
                  `[(CALL ($pestmts ,stmts ,p ,(updsn x sn)) ; stat.assign
                   ,($updsv x sn ($evalop e sn)) [code])
                  `[(CALL ($pestmts ,stmts ,p ,(delsn x sn)) ; dyn.assign
                   ,($delsv x sn) [(mkASG '],x ['],e ['],sn [sv code)])))

  (('IF e l₁ l₂) => (if (static? e sn)
                  `[(if] ,($evalop e sn)                         ; static if
                     [(CALL ($peblock ,l₁ ,p ,sn) [sv code]
                     [(CALL ($peblock ,l₂ ,p ,sn) [sv code])
                  `[(CALL ($pepoly ,l₂ ,p ,sn) [sv]              ; dynamic if
                     [(CALL ($pepoly ,l₁ ,p ,sn) [sv]
                        [(mkIF '],e ['],l₁ ['],l₂ ['],sn [sv code)])))

  (('GOTO l)    => `[(CALL ($peblock ,l ,p ,sn) [sv code]])      ; goto
  (('RETURN e)  => `[(mkRETURN '],e ['],sn [sv code]) ))         ; return
```

Fig. 10. Online staging of FCL-statements by cog_{ON}

```
(define ($offpestmt stmt stmts p sn) (select (stmt)
  ((x ':=S e) => `[(CALL ($pestmts ,stmts ,p ,(updsn x sn)) ; stat. assign
                 ,($updsv x sn ($evalop e sn)) [code]])
  ((x ':=D e) => `[(CALL ($pestmts ,stmts ,p ,(delsn x sn)) ; dyn. assign
                 ,($delsv x sn) [(mkASG '],x ['],e ['],sn [sv code)]])

  (('IFS e l₁ l₂) => `[(if] ,($evalop e sn)                    ; static if
                     [(CALL ($peblock ,l₁ ,p ,sn) [sv code]
                     [(CALL ($peblock ,l₂ ,p ,sn) [sv code])])
  (('IFD e l₁ l₂) => `[(CALL ($pepoly ,l₂ ,p ,sn) [sv]         ; dynamic if
                     [(CALL ($pepoly ,l₁ ,p ,sn) [sv]
                        [(mkIF '],e ['],l₁ ['],l₂ ['],sn [sv code)]])

  (('GOTO l)    => `[(CALL ($peblock ,l ,p ,sn) [sv code]])    ; goto
  (('RETURN e)  => `[(mkRETURN '],e ['],sn [sv code]) ))       ; return
```

Fig. 11. Offline staging of FCL-statements by cog_{OFF}

5 The Two New Compiler Generators

The online and offline partial evaluators described in the previous section can be specialized by Unmix with respect to an FCL-program, thereby producing a generating extension of the FCL-program written in Scheme, or they can be turned by Unmix's compiler generator into compiler generators that produce the same generating extensions as the specialization of the partial evaluators, but faster.

Partial evaluation folklore has suggested that online strategies *unavoidably* lead to overgeneralized "crazy" generating extensions [17, Ch. 7.3.2]. The compact and efficient generating extension shown in Fig. 5, which was produced by cog_{ON}, demonstrates that this is not necessarily the case. In fact, inspection of cog_{ON} reveals that its generating extensions *never* suffer from this deficiency. An online strategy cannot discover extra static values in the universal parser (Fig. 3) and both compiler generators produce the *same* parser generator (Fig. 5). In general, an online strategy can propagate more static values than an offline strategy with a monovariant BTA. This can lead to a deeper specialization by cog_{ON}, but may also lead to the generation of larger programs than cog_{OFF}. An important practical advantage is that both compiler generators inherit the postprocessor of Unmix, which improves the quality of the generating extensions.

The Compiler Generators. The staging transformations performed by the two compiler generators, cog_{ON} and cog_{OFF}, are shown in Fig. 9–11. Pattern matching was added for readability. The figures do not show the main loop that was inherited from Unmix and that controls the polyvariant specialization by a conventional pending list [17, Ch. 5.4]. The difference between the compiler generators is immediately visible: the online staging of FCL-statements (Fig. 10) takes all decisions based on division sn, that is, the handling of assignments (:=) and conditional jumps (IF), while the corresponding part in Fig. 11 follows the annotations (:=S, :=D, IFS, IFD). Aside from the decision taking, the generated Scheme code is the same for each statement, as shown by comparing Figs. 10 and 11. The quality of the generating extensions produced by cog_{OFF} thus depends only on the accuracy of the BTA. If the BTA is maximally polyvariant, both compiler generators produce the same generating extensions. This is consistent with the finding that an offline partial evaluator can be as accurate as an online partial evaluator for FCL, provided the BTA is *maximally polyvariant* [2].

We now explain the staging in more detail. The compiler generators consist of procedures of Unmix specialized with respect to procedures of the FCL-partial evaluators. Procedures that generate Scheme code are prefixed with $. They produce parts of the generating extension. Procedures that have no prefix, such as static?, are the same as in the partial evaluators. Procedures $onpestmt in Fig. 10, and likewise $offpestmt in Fig. 11, have only four parameters. The static values sv and the residual program code, which are known to the partial evaluators, are unknown to the compiler generators.

If the expression e in an *assignment* $x := e$ is static, x is added to sn by updsn, whereas $updsv generates Scheme code that can update sv with the value of e when the generating extension is run. Otherwise, x is removed from sn by delsn and a call to mkASG is placed into the generating extension. Calls to simple non-recursive procedures are unfolded by Unmix's postprocessor, *e.g.*, a call such as (mkASG 'c '(car s)) is replaced by the FCL-code that it generates: '(c := (car s)).

If e in a *conditional jump* if e l_1 l_2 is static, a *Scheme-conditional* (if ...) is emitted that can generate FCL code for either target block when the generating extension is run and e can be computed. Procedure $evalop places into the

Scheme-conditional a test expression that implements e in Scheme. This therefore translates simple FCL-expressions into Scheme-expressions. The strategy for staging a conditional jump is inherited from the FCL-partial evaluator.

The staging of the partial evaluators into compiler generators by Unmix's compiler generator follows the principles outlined for the staging of annotated Scheme programs into generating extensions [17, Ch. 5.8]. This explains the structural similarities between the partial evaluators and the compiler generators.

The compiler generators inherit the specialization method for Scheme procedures from Unmix. This method is well known and documented [17, Ch. 5.4]. Before emitting a new Scheme procedure, the main loop of the compiler generator scans the procedure body and replaces every (CALL ($fname v_1 ... v_m) . es) by a Scheme procedure call (fname$_{v_1...v_m}$. es), and invokes the code generator $fname with the values v_1, ..., v_m to generate the specialized procedure fname$_{v_1...v_m}$.

6   Related Work

Compiler generators have been generated by self-application of specializers, which is the approach followed by Mix [18] and Unmix [21], or written by hand, which is the more recent *cogen-approach*. A compiler for MP has also been produced by specializing a small online partial evaluator with respect to an interpreter by a stronger online specializer [22]. Amix is a self-applicable offline partial evaluator that has different subject and target languages [16]. None of these, however, considered the generation of one compiler generator by another. A *higher-order* pending list, which was used by a breadth-first inverse interpreter to allow good specialization by Similix [12, p. 15], is an alternative to the lifting of the pending list into a recursion on the meta-level, as illustrated here. This method could not be used because Unmix is a partial evaluator for a first-order subset of Scheme.

7   Conclusions and Future Work

At first, the step beyond the third Futamura projection does not appear to make sense, but the situation is different when specializers are used in a mixed fashion. We have shown that existing partial evaluation methods can be used for several novel applications, such as the staging of online partial evaluators and the generation of cross-compilers. From the compiler generators that we obtained, it appears that writing online compiler generators by hand is also feasible (*cf.* [23]), possibly taking advantage of an efficient representation for the generating extensions [11], including the compiler generators themselves.

An intriguing question is whether the step can be repeated by writing in FCL a new partial evaluator, thereby continuing the bootstrapping that we started by writing an FCL-partial evaluator in Scheme. Based on our previous investigation [9], we expect that Jones optimality plays an essential role in the quality of those compiler generators, especially since Unmix is Jones-optimal [8], whereas FCL-partial evaluation is not [14].

Acknowledgements. It is a great pleasure to thank Akihiko Takano for hosting the author at the National Institute of Informatics (NII), Tokyo, and for providing excellent working conditions, and Neil Jones, Sergei Romanenko, and Lars Hartmann for insightful comments on an earlier version of this paper.

References

1. Bulyonkov, M.A.: Polyvariant mixed computation for analyzer programs. Acta Informatica 21(5), 473–484 (1984)
2. Christensen, N.H., Glück, R.: Offline partial evaluation can be as accurate as online partial evaluation. ACM TOPLAS 26(1), 191–220 (2004)
3. Debois, S.: Imperative-program transformation by instrumented-interpreter specialization. Higher-Order and Symbolic Computation 21(1-2), 37–58 (2008)
4. Ershov, A.P.: On the partial computation principle. Information Processing Letters 6(2), 38–41 (1977)
5. Futamura, Y.: Partial computation of programs. In: Goto, E., Nakajima, R., Yonezawa, A., Nakata, I., Furukawa, K. (eds.) RIMS 1982. LNCS, vol. 147, pp. 1–35. Springer, Heidelberg (1983)
6. Futamura, Y.: Partial evaluation of computation process, revisited. Higher-Order and Symbolic Computation 12(4), 377–380 (1999)
7. Futamura, Y., Konishi, Z., Glück, R.: WSDFU: Program transformation system based on generalized partial computation. In: Mogensen, T.Æ., Schmidt, D.A., Sudborough, I.H. (eds.) The Essence of Computation. LNCS, vol. 2566, pp. 358–378. Springer, Heidelberg (2002)
8. Gade, J., Glück, R.: On Jones-optimal specializers: a case study using Unmix. In: Kobayashi, N. (ed.) APLAS 2006. LNCS, vol. 4279, pp. 406–422. Springer, Heidelberg (2006)
9. Glück, R.: An investigation of Jones optimality and BTI-universal specializers. Higher-Order and Symbolic Computation 21(3), 283–309 (2008)
10. Glück, R.: Is there a fourth Futamura projection? Partial Evaluation and Program Manipulation. Proceedings, pp. 51–60. ACM Press, New York (2009)
11. Glück, R., Jørgensen, J.: Efficient multi-level generating extensions for program specialization. In: Hermenegildo, M., Swierstra, S.D. (eds.) PLILP 1995. LNCS, vol. 982, pp. 259–278. Springer, Heidelberg (1995)
12. Glück, R., Kawada, Y., Hashimoto, T.: Transforming interpreters into inverse interpreters by partial evaluation. In: Proceedings of Partial Evaluation and Semantics-Based Program Manipulation, pp. 10–19. ACM Press, New York (2003)
13. Glück, R., Klimov, A.V.: Occam's razor in metacomputation: the notion of a perfect process tree. In: Cousot, P., Falaschi, M., Filé, G., Rauzy, A. (eds.) WSA 1993. LNCS, vol. 724, pp. 112–123. Springer, Heidelberg (1993)
14. Gomard, C.K., Jones, N.D.: Compiler generation by partial evaluation: a case study. Structured Programming 12, 123–144 (1991)
15. Hatcliff, J.: An introduction to online and offline partial evaluation using a simple flowchart language. In: Hatcliff, J., Mogensen, T. Æ., Thiemann, P. (eds.) DIKU 1998. LNCS, vol. 1706, pp. 20–82. Springer, Heidelberg (1999)
16. Holst, C.K.: Language triplets: the Amix approach. In: Bjørner, D., et al. (eds.) Partial Evaluation and Mixed Computation, pp. 167–185. North-Holland, Amsterdam (1988)

17. Jones, N.D., Gomard, C.K., Sestoft, P.: Partial Evaluation and Automatic Program Generation. Prentice-Hall, Englewood Cliffs (1993)
18. Jones, N.D., Sestoft, P., Søndergaard, H.: Mix: a self-applicable partial evaluator for experiments in compiler generation. Lisp and Symbolic Computation 2(1), 9–50 (1989)
19. Klimov, A.V., Romanenko, S.A.: Metavychislitel' dlja jazyka Refal. Osnovnye ponjatija i primery (A metaevaluator for the language Refal. Basic concepts and examples). Preprint 71, Keldysh Institute of Applied Mathematics, Academy of Sciences of the USSR, Moscow (1987) (in Russian)
20. Romanenko, S.A.: Arity raiser and its use in program specialization. In: Jones, N.D. (ed.) ESOP 1990. LNCS, vol. 432, pp. 341–360. Springer, Heidelberg (1990)
21. Romanenko, S.A.: The specializer Unmix (1990), Program and documentation, `ftp://ftp.diku.dk/pub/diku/dists/jones-book/Romanenko/`
22. Ruf, E., Weise, D.: On the specialization of online program specializers. Journal of Functional Programming 3(3), 251–281 (1993)
23. Sumii, E., Kobayashi, N.: Online-and-offline partial evaluation: a mixed approach. In: Proceedings of Partial Evaluation and Semantics-Based Program Manipulation, pp. 12–21. ACM Press, New York (2000)
24. Turchin, V.F.: The concept of a supercompiler. ACM TOPLAS 8(3), 292–325 (1986)

Extracting the Essence of Distillation

G.W. Hamilton

School of Computing
Dublin City University
Ireland
hamilton@computing.dcu.ie

Abstract. In this paper, we give a re-formulation of our previously defined *distillation* algorithm, which can automatically transform higher-order functional programs into equivalent tail-recursive programs. Our re-formulation simplifies the presentation of the transformation and hopefully makes it easier to understand. Using distillation, it is possible to produce superlinear improvement in the run-time of programs. This represents a significant advance over deforestation, partial evaluation and positive supercompilation, which can only produce a linear improvement.

1   Introduction

It is well known that programs which are written using lazy functional programming languages often tend to make use of intermediate data structures, and are therefore inefficient. A number of program transformation techniques have been proposed which can eliminate some of these intermediate data structures; for example *partial evaluation* [1], *deforestation* [2] and *supercompilation* [3]. *Positive supercompilation* [4] is a variant of Turchin's supercompilation which was introduced in an attempt to study and explain the essentials of Turchin's supercompiler. Although positive supercompilation is strictly more powerful than both partial evaluation and deforestation, Sørensen has shown that positive supercompilation (and hence also partial evaluation and deforestation) can only produce a linear speedup in programs [5]. A more powerful transformation algorithm should be able to produce a superlinear speedup in programs.

Example 1. Consider the function call *nrev xs* shown in Fig. 1. This reverses the list *xs*, but the recursive function call (*nrev xs'*) is an intermediate data structure, so in terms of time and space usage, it is quadratic with respect to the length of the list *xs*. A more efficient function which is linear with respect to the length of the list *xs* is the function *arev* shown in Fig. 1. A number of algebraic transformations have been proposed which can perform this transformation (e.g. [6]) by appealing to a specific law stating the associativity of the *app* function. However, none of the generic program transformation techniques mentioned above are capable of performing this transformation.

Previously, we defined a transformation algorithm called *distillation* [7] which will allow transformations such as the above to be performed. In our previous

A. Pnueli, I. Virbitskaite, and A. Voronkov (Eds.): PSI 2009, LNCS 5947, pp. 151–164, 2010.
© Springer-Verlag Berlin Heidelberg 2010

$$nrev\ xs$$
where
$$nrev = \lambda xs.\textbf{case}\ xs\ \textbf{of}$$
$$[]\qquad \Rightarrow []$$
$$|\ x' : xs' \Rightarrow app\ (nrev\ xs')\ [x']$$
$$app\ = \lambda xs.\lambda ys.\textbf{case}\ xs\ \textbf{of}$$
$$[]\qquad \Rightarrow ys$$
$$|\ x' : xs' \Rightarrow x' : (app\ xs'\ ys)$$

$$arev\ xs$$
where
$$arev\ = \lambda xs.arev'\ xs\ []$$
$$arev' = \lambda xs.\lambda ys.\textbf{case}\ xs\ \textbf{of}$$
$$[]\qquad \Rightarrow ys$$
$$|\ x' : xs' \Rightarrow arev'\ xs'\ (x' : ys)$$

Fig. 1. Alternative Definitions of List Reversal

work, the definition of distillation was dependent upon that of positive supercompilation. In this paper, we give a definition of distillation which is not dependent upon positive supercompilation, thus simplifying the algorithm and hopefully making it easier to understand.

The distillation algorithm was largely influenced by positive supercompilation, but also improves upon it. Both algorithms involve *driving* to produce a *process tree* representing all the possible states in the symbolic execution of a program, and *folding* to extract a (hopefully more efficient) program from this process tree. *Generalization* may also be required to ensure the termination of the algorithm. The extra power of the distillation algorithm over positive supercompilation is obtained through the use of a more powerful matching mechanism when performing folding and generalization. In positive supercompilation, folding and generalization are performed on flat terms; terms are considered to match only if they use the same functions. In distillation, folding and generalization are performed on process trees, so terms are considered to match only if they have the same recursive structure.

The remainder of this paper is structured as follows. In Section 2 we define the higher-order functional language on which the described transformations are performed. In Section 3 we define the driving rules for this language which perform symbolic execution to produce a process tree. In Section 4 we define generalization on terms in this language and also on process trees. In Section 5 we show how folding can be performed on process trees to extract corresponding programs. In Section 6 we give some examples of the application of distillation and Section 7 concludes.

2   Language

In this section, we describe the higher-order functional language which will be used throughout this paper. The syntax of this language is given in Fig. 2.

$$prog ::= e_0 \text{ where } f_1 = e_1 \ldots f_k = e_k \qquad \text{Program}$$

$$
\begin{aligned}
e \quad ::= \; & v & & \text{Variable} \\
& | \; c \; e_1 \ldots e_k & & \text{Constructor} \\
& | \; f & & \text{Function Call} \\
& | \; \lambda v.e & & \text{λ-Abstraction} \\
& | \; e_0 \; e_1 & & \text{Application} \\
& | \; \textbf{case } e_0 \textbf{ of } p_1 \Rightarrow e_1 \; | \cdots | \; p_k \Rightarrow e_k & & \text{Case Expression}
\end{aligned}
$$

$$p \quad ::= c \; v_1 \ldots v_k \qquad\qquad\qquad\qquad\qquad\quad \text{Pattern}$$

Fig. 2. Language Syntax

Programs in the language consist of an expression to evaluate and a set of function definitions. The intended operational semantics of the language is normal order reduction. It is assumed that erroneous terms such as $(c \; e_1 \ldots e_k) \; e$ and **case** $(\lambda v.e)$ **of** $p_1 \Rightarrow e_1 \; | \cdots | \; p_k \Rightarrow e_k$ cannot occur. The variables in the patterns of **case** expressions and the arguments of λ-abstractions are *bound*; all other variables are *free*. We use $fv(e)$ and $bv(e)$ to denote the free and bound variables respectively of expression e. We write $e \equiv e'$ if e and e' differ only in the names of bound variables. We require that each function has exactly one definition and that all variables within a definition are bound. We define a function *unfold* which replaces a function name with its definition.

Each constructor has a fixed arity; for example *Nil* has arity 0 and *Cons* has arity 2. We allow the usual notation $[]$ for *Nil*, $x : xs$ for *Cons x xs* and $[e_1, \ldots, e_k]$ for *Cons $e_1 \ldots (Cons \; e_k \; Nil)$*.

Within the expression **case** e_0 **of** $p_1 \Rightarrow e_1 \; | \cdots | \; p_k \Rightarrow e_k$, e_0 is called the *selector*, and $e_1 \ldots e_k$ are called the *branches*. The patterns in **case** expressions may not be nested. No variables may appear more than once within a pattern. We assume that the patterns in a **case** expression are non-overlapping and exhaustive.

We use the notation $\{v_1 := e_1, \ldots, v_n := e_n\}$ to denote a *substitution*, which represents the simultaneous substitution of the expressions $e_1, \ldots, e_n$ for the corresponding variables $v_1, \ldots, v_n$, respectively. We say that an expression e is an *instance* of expression e' if there is a substitution θ such that $e \equiv e' \; \theta$. We also use the notation $[e'_1/e_1, \ldots, e'_n/e_n]$ to denote a *replacement*, which represents the simultaneous replacement of the expressions $e_1, \ldots, e_n$ by the corresponding expressions $e'_1, \ldots, e'_n$, respectively.

3   Driving

In this section, we define *driving* rules similar to those for positive supercompilation to reduce a term (possibly containing free variables) using normal-order reduction and produce a *process tree*. We define the rules for driving by identifying the next reducible expression (*redex*) within some *context*. An expression which cannot be broken down into a redex and a context is called an *observable*. These are defined as follows.

Definition 1 (Redexes, Contexts and Observables). Redexes, contexts and observables are defined as shown in Fig. 3, where *red* ranges over redexes, *con* ranges over contexts and *obs* ranges over observables (the expression $con\langle e \rangle$ denotes the result of replacing the 'hole' $\langle \rangle$ in *con* by e).

Definition 2 (Normal Order Reduction). The core set of transformation rules for distillation are the normal order reduction rules shown in Figure 4 which defines the map $\mathcal{N}$ from expressions to ordered sequences of expressions $[e_1, \ldots, e_n]$. The rules simply perform normal order reduction, with information propagation within **case** expressions giving the assumed outcome of the test.

$$
\begin{aligned}
red ::=\ & f \\
| \ & (\lambda v.e_0)\ e_1 \\
| \ & \textbf{case}\ (v\ e_1 \ldots e_n)\ \textbf{of}\ p_1 \Rightarrow e_1'\ |\cdots|\ p_k \Rightarrow e_k' \\
| \ & \textbf{case}\ (c\ e_1 \ldots e_n)\ \textbf{of}\ p_1 \Rightarrow e_1'\ |\cdots|\ p_k \Rightarrow e_k' \\
| \ & \textbf{case}\ (\textbf{case}\ e_0\ \textbf{of}\ p_1 \Rightarrow e_1\ |\cdots|\ p_n \Rightarrow e_n)\ \textbf{of}\ p_1' \Rightarrow e_1'\ |\cdots|\ p_k' \Rightarrow e_k'
\end{aligned}
$$

$$
\begin{aligned}
con ::=\ & \langle \rangle \\
| \ & con\ e \\
| \ & \textbf{case}\ \langle \rangle\ \textbf{of}\ p_1 \Rightarrow e_1\ |\cdots|\ p_k \Rightarrow e_k
\end{aligned}
$$

$$
\begin{aligned}
obs ::=\ & v\ e_1 \ldots e_n \\
| \ & c\ e_1 \ldots e_n \\
| \ & \lambda v.e
\end{aligned}
$$

Fig. 3. Syntax of Redexes, Contexts and Observables

$$
\begin{aligned}
\mathcal{N}[\![v\ e_1 \ldots e_n]\!] \quad &= [e_1, \ldots, e_n] \\
\mathcal{N}[\![c\ e_1 \ldots e_n]\!] \quad &= [e_1, \ldots, e_n] \\
\mathcal{N}[\![\lambda v.e]\!] \quad &= [e] \\
\mathcal{N}[\![con\langle f \rangle]\!] \quad &= [con\langle unfold\ f \rangle] \\
\mathcal{N}[\![con\langle (\lambda v.e_0)\ e_1 \rangle]\!] &= [con\langle e_0\{v := e_1\} \rangle] \\
\mathcal{N}[\![con\langle \textbf{case}\ (v\ e_1 \ldots e_n)\ \textbf{of}\ p_1 \Rightarrow e_1'\ |\cdots|\ p_k \Rightarrow e_k' \rangle]\!] & \\
&= [v\ e_1 \ldots e_n, con\langle e_1'[p_1/v\ e_1 \ldots e_n] \rangle, \ldots, con\langle e_k'[p_k/v\ e_1 \ldots e_n] \rangle] \\
\mathcal{N}[\![con\langle \textbf{case}\ (c\ e_1 \ldots e_n)\ \textbf{of}\ p_1 \Rightarrow e_1'\ |\cdots|\ p_k \Rightarrow e_k' \rangle]\!] & \\
&= [con\langle e_i\{e_1 := v_1, \ldots, e_n := v_n\} \rangle]\ \text{where}\ p_i = c\ v_1 \ldots v_n \\
\mathcal{N}[\![con\langle \textbf{case}\ (\textbf{case}\ e_0\ \textbf{of}\ p_1 \Rightarrow e_1\ |\cdots|\ p_n \Rightarrow e_n)\ \textbf{of}\ p_1' \Rightarrow e_1'\ |\cdots|\ p_k' \Rightarrow e_k' \rangle]\!] & \\
&= [\textbf{case}\ e_0\ \textbf{of} \\
& \qquad p_1 \Rightarrow con\langle \textbf{case}\ e_1\ \textbf{of}\ p_1' \Rightarrow e_1'\ |\cdots|\ p_k' \Rightarrow e_k' \rangle \\
& \qquad \vdots \\
& \qquad p_n \Rightarrow con\langle \textbf{case}\ e_n\ \textbf{of}\ p_1' \Rightarrow e_1'\ |\cdots|\ p_k' \Rightarrow e_k' \rangle]
\end{aligned}
$$

Fig. 4. Normal Order Reduction Rules

Definition 3 (Process Trees). A *process tree* is a directed tree where each node is labelled with an expression, and all edges leaving a node are ordered. One node is chosen as the *root*, which is labelled with the original expression to be transformed. We use the notation $e \rightarrow t_1, \ldots, t_n$ to represent the tree with root labelled e and n children which are the subtrees $t_1, \ldots, t_n$ respectively.

Definition 4 (Driving). Driving in distillation is defined by the following map $\mathcal{D}$ from expressions to process trees:

$$\mathcal{D}[\![e]\!] = e \rightarrow \mathcal{D}[\![e_1]\!], \ldots, \mathcal{D}[\![e_n]\!] \text{ where } \mathcal{N}[\![e]\!] = [e_1, \ldots, e_n]$$

As process trees are potentially infinite data structures, they should be lazily evaluated.

Example 2. A portion of the process tree which would be generated as a result of driving the expression *nrev xs* as defined in Fig. 1 is shown in Fig. 5[1].

4   Generalization

In distillation, as for positive supercompilation, generalization is performed when an expression is encountered which is an *embedding* of a previously encountered expression. The form of embedding which we use to guide generalization is known as *homeomorphic embedding*. The homeomorphic embedding relation was derived from results by Higman [8] and Kruskal [9] and was defined within term rewriting systems [10] for detecting the possible divergence of the term rewriting process. Variants of this relation have been used to ensure termination within positive supercompilation [11], partial evaluation [12] and partial deduction [13,14]. It can be shown that the homeomorphic embedding relation $\trianglelefteq$ is a *well-quasi-order*, which is defined as follows.

Definition 5 (Well-Quasi Order). A well-quasi order on a set S is a reflexive, transitive relation $\leq_S$ such that for any infinite sequence $s_1, s_2, \ldots$ of elements from S there are numbers i, j with $i < j$ and $s_i \leq_S s_j$.

This ensures that in any infinite sequence of expressions $e_0, e_1, \ldots$ there definitely exists some $i < j$ where $e_i \trianglelefteq e_j$, so an embedding must eventually be encountered and transformation will not continue indefinitely.

Definition 6 (Recursive Component). A variable v is called a recursive component of another variable v' (denoted by $v \sqsubset v'$) if v is a sub-component of v' and is of the same type. We also define $v \sqsubseteq v'$ if $v \sqsubset v'$ or $v = v'$.

Definition 7 (Homeomorphic Embedding Relation). The rules for the homeomorphic embedding relation are defined as follows:

---

[1] This process tree, and later ones presented in this paper, have been simplified for ease of presentation by removing some intermediate nodes.

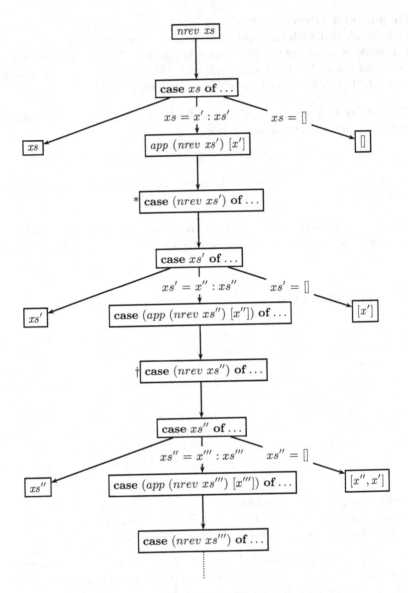

Fig. 5. Portion of Process Tree Resulting From Driving *nrev xs*

$$\frac{e_1 \vartriangleleft e_2}{e_1 \unlhd e_2} \qquad \frac{e_1 \bowtie e_2}{e_1 \unlhd e_2}$$

$$\frac{fv \sqsubseteq fv'}{fv \bowtie fv'} \qquad \frac{bv = bv'}{bv \bowtie bv'}$$

$$\frac{f = f'}{f \bowtie f'} \qquad \frac{c = c' \quad \forall i.e_i \unlhd e_i'}{(c\ e_1 \dots e_n) \bowtie (c'\ e_1' \dots e_n')}$$

$$\frac{e \unlhd (e'\{v' := v\})}{\lambda v.e \bowtie \lambda v'.e'} \qquad \frac{e_0 \bowtie e_0' \quad e_1 \unlhd e_1'}{(e_0\ e_1) \bowtie (e_0'\ e_1')}$$

$$\frac{e \bowtie e' \quad \forall i.p_i \equiv (p_i'\ \theta_i) \wedge e_i \unlhd (e_i'\ \theta_i)}{(\textbf{case } e \textbf{ of } p_1 : e_1 | \dots | p_n : e_n) \bowtie (\textbf{case } e' \textbf{ of } p_1' : e_1' | \dots | p_n' : e_n')}$$

$$\frac{\exists i.e \unlhd e_i}{e \vartriangleleft (c\ e_1 \dots e_n)} \qquad \frac{e \unlhd e'}{e \vartriangleleft \lambda v.e'}$$

$$\frac{\exists i.e \unlhd e_i}{e \vartriangleleft (e_0\ e_1)} \qquad \frac{\exists i.e \unlhd e_i}{e \vartriangleleft (\textbf{case } e_0 \textbf{ of } p_1 : e_1 | \dots | p_n : e_n)}$$

An expression is homeomorphically embedded within another if either *diving* (denoted by $\vartriangleleft$) or *coupling* (denoted by $\bowtie$) can be performed. Diving occurs when an expression is embedded in a sub-expression of another expression, and coupling occurs when two expressions have the same top-level functor and all the corresponding sub-expressions of the two expressions are embedded. Free variables are considered to be embedded if they are related by the $\sqsubseteq$ relation, and the corresponding bound variables within expressions must also match up.

Example 3. Some examples of these embedding relations are as follows:

1. $f_2\ (f_1\ x) \unlhd f_3(f_2\ (f_1\ y))$ 2. $f_1\ (f_2\ x) \unlhd f_1\ (f_2\ (f_3\ y))$
3. $f_2\ (f_1\ x) \vartriangleleft f_3(f_2\ (f_1\ y))$ 4. $f_1\ (f_2\ x) \ntrianglelefteq f_1\ (f_2\ (f_3\ y))$
5. $f_2\ (f_1\ x) \not\bowtie f_3(f_2\ (f_1\ y))$ 6. $f_1\ (f_2\ x) \bowtie f_1\ (f_2\ (f_3\ y))$
7. $\lambda x.x \unlhd \lambda y.y$ 8. $\lambda x.x \not\unlhd \lambda y.x$

Definition 8 (Generalization of Expressions). The generalization of two expressions e and e' (denoted by $e \sqcap_e e'$) is a triple (e_g, θ, θ') where θ and θ' are substitutions such that $e_g\theta \equiv e$ and $e_g\theta' \equiv e'$, as defined in term algebra [10][2]. This generalization is defined as follows:

---

[2] Note that, in a higher-order setting, this is no longer a most specific generalization, as the most specific generalization of the terms $f\ (h\ x)$ and $f\ (g\ (h\ x))$ would be $(f\ (v\ (h\ x)), [(\lambda x.x)/v], [(\lambda x.g\ x)/v])$, whereas $f\ (h\ x) \sqcap_e f\ (g\ (h\ x))$ = $(f\ v, [(h\ x)/v], [(g\ (h\ x))/v])$.

$$e \sqcap_e e' = \begin{cases} (\phi(e_1^g, \ldots, e_n^g), \bigcup_{i=1}^n \theta_i, \bigcup_{i=1}^n \theta_i'), \text{ if } e \bowtie e' \\ \text{where } e = \phi(e_1, \ldots, e_n) \\ \qquad e' = \phi(e_1', \ldots, e_n') \\ \qquad (e_i^g, \theta_i, \theta_i') = e_i \sqcap_e e_i' \\ (v \; v_1 \ldots v_k, \{v := \lambda v_1 \ldots v_k.e\}, \{v := \lambda v_1 \ldots v_k.e'\}), \text{ otherwise} \\ \text{where } \{v_1 \ldots v_k\} = bv(e) \cup bv(e') \end{cases}$$

Within these rules, if both expressions have the same functor at the outermost level, this is made the outermost functor of the resulting generalized expression, and the corresponding sub-expressions within the functor applications are then generalized. Otherwise, both expressions are replaced by the same variable application. The arguments of this application are the bound variables of the extracted expressions; this ensures that these bound variables are not extracted outside their binders. The introduced variable application is a *higher-order pattern* [15]; any term which contains the same bound variables as one of these patterns will therefore be an instance of it, as described in [16].

Definition 9 (Generalization of Process Trees). Generalization is extended to process trees using the $\sqcap_t$ operator which is defined as follows:

$$t \sqcap_t t' = \begin{cases} (e_0^g \to t_1^g, \ldots, t_n^g, \bigcup_{i=0}^n \theta_i, \bigcup_{i=0}^n \theta_i'), \text{ if } e_0 \bowtie e_0' \\ \text{where } t = e_0 \to t_1, \ldots, t_n \\ \qquad t' = e_0' \to t_1', \ldots, t_n' \\ \qquad (e_0^g, \theta_0, \theta_0') = e_0 \sqcap_e e_0' \\ \qquad (t_i^g, \theta_i, \theta_i') = t_i \sqcap_t t_i' \\ (v \; v_1 \ldots v_k, \{v := \lambda v_1 \ldots v_k.e_0\}, \{v := \lambda v_1 \ldots v_k.e_0'\}), \text{ otherwise} \\ \text{where } \{v_1 \ldots v_k\} = bv(e_0) \cup bv(e_0') \end{cases}$$

The following rewrite rule is exhaustively applied to the triple resulting from this generalization to minimize the substitutions by identifying common substitutions which were previously given different names:

$$\begin{pmatrix} e, \\ \{v_1 := e', v_2 := e'\} \cup \theta, \\ \{v_1 := e'', v_2 := e''\} \cup \theta' \end{pmatrix} \Rightarrow \begin{pmatrix} e\{v_1 := v_2\}, \\ \{v_2 := e'\} \cup \theta, \\ \{v_2 := e''\} \cup \theta' \end{pmatrix}$$

5   Folding

In this section, we describe how folding is performed in distillation. This folding is performed on process trees, rather than the flat terms used in positive supercompilation. As process trees are potentially infinite data structures, we use co-induction to define a finite method for determining whether one process tree is an instance of another.

Definition 10 (Process Tree Instance). The following co-inductive rules are used to determine whether one process tree is an instance of another:

$$\frac{\Gamma, con\langle f\rangle \equiv con'\langle f\rangle \ \theta \vdash t \equiv t' \ \theta}{\Gamma \vdash (con\langle f\rangle \to t) \equiv (con'\langle f\rangle \to t') \ \theta} \ \text{IND}$$

$$\Gamma, con\langle f\rangle \equiv con'\langle f\rangle \ \theta \vdash (con\langle f\rangle \ \theta \to t) \equiv (con'\langle f\rangle \ \theta \to t') \ \theta \ \ \text{HYP}$$

$$\frac{\Gamma \vdash e \equiv e' \ \theta, t_i \equiv t'_i \ \theta}{\Gamma \vdash (e \to t_1, \ldots, t_n) \equiv (e' \to t'_1, \ldots, t'_n) \ \theta} \ \text{NON-IND}$$

The environment Γ here relates previously encountered corresponding expressions which have a function as their redex. To match the recursive structure of process trees, the corresponding previously encountered expressions are initially assumed to match if one is an instance of the other in the rule IND. In rule HYP, if corresponding expressions are subsequently encountered which are an instance of previously encountered ones, then we have a recursive match.

Definition 11 (Embedding Process Trees). We define the *embedding process trees* of an expression e within a process tree t (denoted by $e \overset{\emptyset}{\Rightarrow} t$) to be the finite set of subtrees of t where the root expression is coupled with e. This can be defined more formally as follows:

$$e \overset{\sigma}{\Rightarrow} (e_0 \to t_1, \ldots, t_n) = \begin{cases} \emptyset, & \text{if } \exists e'_0 \in \sigma.e'_0 \bowtie e_0 \\ \{e_0 \to t_1, \ldots, t_n\}, & \text{if } e \bowtie e_0 \\ \bigcup_{i=1}^n e \overset{\sigma'}{\Rightarrow} t_i, & \text{otherwise, where } \sigma' = \sigma \cup \{e_0\} \end{cases}$$

The parameter σ contains the set of expressions previously encountered within the nodes of the process tree, and will be empty initially. If the root expression of the current subtree is coupled with an expression in σ, then nothing further is added to the result set. If the root expression of the current subtree is coupled with the given expression, then the subtree is added to the result set and nothing further is added. Otherwise, the subtrees of the current node are searched for embedding process trees, and the expression in the current node is added to σ.

Definition 12 (Folding). Folding in distillation is defined as the map $\mathcal{F}$ from process trees to expressions, as defined in Fig. 6.

Within these rules, the parameter ρ contains a set of newly defined function calls and the previously encountered process trees they replaced. The rules descend through the nodes of the process tree until an expression is encountered in which the redex is a function. If the process tree rooted at this expression is an instance of a previously encountered process tree in ρ, then it is replaced by a corresponding call of the associated function in ρ. If there are no embeddings of the root expression of the current process tree, then this root node is ignored and its subtree is further folded. If there are embeddings of the root expression and at least one of them is not an instance, then the process tree is generalized and further folded; the sub-terms extracted as a result of generalization are then further distilled and substituted back in. If all of the embeddings of the root expression are instances, then a call to a newly defined function is created, and this function call is associated with the current process tree in ρ.

$$\mathcal{F}[\![(v\ e_1 \ldots e_n) \to t_1,\ldots,t_n]\!]\ \rho = v\ (\mathcal{F}[\![t_1]\!]\ \rho)\ldots(\mathcal{F}[\![t_n]\!]\ \rho)$$

$$\mathcal{F}[\![(c\ e_1 \ldots e_n) \to t_1,\ldots,t_n]\!]\ \rho = c\ (\mathcal{F}[\![t_1]\!]\ \rho)\ldots(\mathcal{F}[\![t_n]\!]\ \rho)$$

$$\mathcal{F}[\![(\lambda v.e) \to t]\!]\ \rho = \lambda v.(\mathcal{F}[\![t]\!]\ \rho)$$

$$\mathcal{F}[\![(con\langle(\lambda v.e_0)\ e_1\rangle) \to t]\!]\ \rho = \mathcal{F}[\![t]\!]\ \rho$$

$$\mathcal{F}[\![(con\langle \mathbf{case}\ (c\ e_1 \ldots e_n)\ \mathbf{of}\ p_1 \Rightarrow e'_1\ |\cdots|\ p_k \Rightarrow e'_k\rangle) \to t]\!]\ \rho = \mathcal{F}[\![t]\!]\ \rho$$

$$\mathcal{F}[\![(con\langle \mathbf{case}\ (v\ e_1 \ldots e_n)\ \mathbf{of}\ p_1 \Rightarrow e_1\ |\cdots|\ p_n \Rightarrow e_n\rangle) \to t_0,\ldots,t_n]\!]\ \rho$$
$$= \mathbf{case}\ (\mathcal{F}[\![t_0]\!]\ \rho)\ \mathbf{of}\ p_1 \Rightarrow (\mathcal{F}[\![t_1]\!]\ \rho)\ |\cdots|\ p_n \Rightarrow (\mathcal{F}[\![t_n]\!]\ \rho)$$

$$\mathcal{F}[\![con\langle \mathbf{case}\ (\mathbf{case}\ e_0\ \mathbf{of}\ p_1 \Rightarrow e_1\ |\cdots|\ p_n \Rightarrow e_n)\ \mathbf{of}\ p'_1 \Rightarrow e'_1\ |\cdots|\ p'_k \Rightarrow e'_k\rangle \to t]\!]\ \rho = \mathcal{F}[\![t]\!]\ \rho$$

$$
\begin{aligned}
\mathcal{F}[\![con\langle f\rangle \to t]\!]\ \rho = \ &\mathbf{if}\quad \exists(f'\ v_1\ldots v_n = t') \in \rho.(con\langle f\rangle \to t) \equiv t'\ \theta\\
&\mathbf{then}\ (f'\ v_1 \ldots v_n)\ \theta\\
&\mathbf{else}\quad \mathbf{if}\quad (con\langle f\rangle \overset{\emptyset}{\Rightarrow} t) = \emptyset\\
&\qquad\qquad \mathbf{then}\ \mathcal{F}[\![t]\!]\ \rho\\
&\qquad\qquad \mathbf{else}\quad \mathbf{if}\quad \exists\,t' \in (con\langle f\rangle \overset{\emptyset}{\Rightarrow} t).\nexists\theta.t' \equiv (con\langle f\rangle \to t)\ \theta\\
&\qquad\qquad\qquad\qquad \mathbf{then}\ (\mathcal{F}[\![t^g]\!]\ \rho)\ \theta''\\
&\qquad\qquad\qquad\qquad \mathbf{where}\\
&\qquad\qquad\qquad\qquad (con\langle f\rangle \to t)\ \sqcap_t\ t' = (t^g,\theta,\theta')\\
&\qquad\qquad\qquad\qquad \theta = \{v_i := e_i\}\\
&\qquad\qquad\qquad\qquad \theta'' = \{v_i := \mathcal{F}[\![\mathcal{D}[\![e_i]\!]]\!]\ \rho\}\\
&\qquad\qquad\qquad \mathbf{else}\quad f'\ v_1 \ldots v_n\\
&\qquad\qquad\qquad\qquad \mathbf{where}\\
&\qquad\qquad\qquad\qquad f' = \lambda v_1 \ldots v_n.\mathcal{F}[\![t]\!]\ \rho'\\
&\qquad\qquad\qquad\qquad \rho' = \rho \cup \{f'\ v_1 \ldots v_n = con\langle f\rangle \to t\}\\
&\qquad\qquad\qquad\qquad \{v_1 \ldots v_n\} = fv(con\langle f\rangle \to t)
\end{aligned}
$$

Fig. 6. Folding Rules for Distillation

6   Examples

In this section, we give some examples of the application of the distillation algorithm.

Example 4. The result of applying the driving rules to the expression *nrev xs* defined in Fig. 1 is shown in Fig. 5. When the folding rules are applied to this output, it is found that the subtree with root labelled * is coupled with the subtree with root labelled †. Generalization is therefore performed to obtain the process tree given in Fig. 7, where the extracted variable v has the value *Nil*. The subtree with root labelled † is now an instance of the subtree with root labelled *. Folding is therefore performed to obtain the program shown in Fig. 8. This program has a run-time which is linear with respect to the length of the input list, while the original program is quadratic.

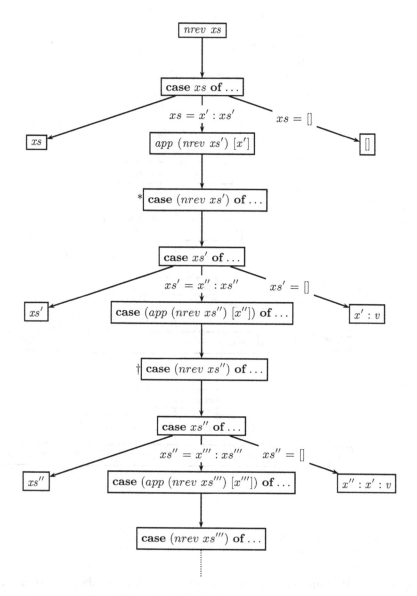

Fig. 7. Result of Generalizing *nrev xs*

Example 5. Consider the expression *app (arev' xs ys) zs* where the functions *app* and *arev'* are as defined in Fig. 1. The result of applying the driving rules to this expression is shown in Fig. 9. When the folding rules are applied to this output, it is found that the subtree with root labelled * is coupled with the subtree with root labelled †. Generalization is therefore performed to obtain the process tree given in Fig. 10, where the extracted variable *v* has the value

$$\textbf{case } xs \textbf{ of}$$
$$[] \qquad \Rightarrow []$$
$$| \ x' : xs' \Rightarrow f \ x' \ xs' \ []$$
$$\textbf{where}$$
$$f = \lambda x'.\lambda xs'.\lambda v.\textbf{case } xs' \textbf{ of}$$
$$[] \qquad \Rightarrow x' : v$$
$$| \ x'' : xs'' \Rightarrow f \ x'' \ xs'' \ (x' : v)$$

Fig. 8. Result of Distilling *nrev xs*

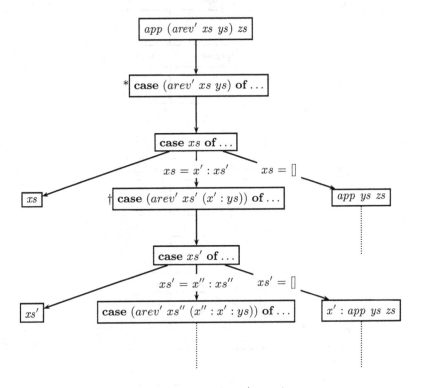

Fig. 9. Result of Driving *app (arev' xs ys) zs*

app ys zs. We can now see that the subtree with root labelled † is an instance of the subtree with root labelled *. Folding is therefore performed to obtain the program shown in Fig. 11. The intermediate list (*arev' xs ys*) within the initial program has therefore been eliminated. This intermediate list is not removed using positive supercompilation.

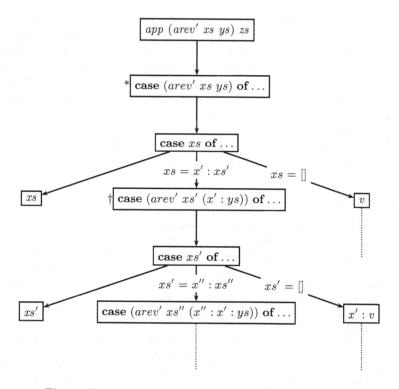

Fig. 10. Result of Generalizing $app \ (arev' \ xs \ ys) \ zs$

$f \ xs \ (g \ ys \ zs)$
where
$f = \lambda xs.\lambda v.\textbf{case } xs \textbf{ of}$
$\qquad\qquad [] \qquad \Rightarrow v$
$\qquad\qquad | \ x' : xs' \Rightarrow f \ xs' \ (x' : v)$
$g = \lambda ys.\lambda zs.\textbf{case } ys \textbf{ of}$
$\qquad\qquad [] \qquad \Rightarrow zs$
$\qquad\qquad | \ y' : ys \Rightarrow y' : (g \ ys' \ zs)$

Fig. 11. Result of Distilling $app \ (arev' \ xs \ ys) \ zs$

7   Conclusion

We have presented the distillation transformation algorithm for higher-order functional languages. The algorithm is influenced by the positive supercompilation transformation algorithm, but can produce a superlinear speedup in programs, which is not possible using positive supercompilation. Of course, this extra power comes at a price. As generalization and folding are now performed on graphs rather than flat terms, there may be an exponential increase in the number of steps required to perform these operations in the worst case.

There are a number of possible directions for further work. Firstly, we intend to incorporate the detection of non-termination into distillation and also into our theorem prover Poitín. Secondly, it has already been shown how distillation can be used to verify safety properties of programs [17]; work is now in progress to show how it can also be used to verify liveness properties. Finally, it is intended to incorporate the distillation algorithm into the Haskell programming language; this will not only allow a lot of powerful optimizations to be performed on programs in the language, but will also allow the automatic verification of properties of these programs. This will also allow the distillation algorithm to be made self-applicable as it has itself been implemented in Haskell.

References

1. Jones, N., Gomard, C., Sestoft, P.: Partial Evaluation and Automatic Program Generation. Prentice Hall, Englewood Cliffs (1993)
2. Wadler, P.: Deforestation: Transforming Programs to Eliminate Trees. In: Ganzinger, H. (ed.) ESOP 1988. LNCS, vol. 300, pp. 344–358. Springer, Heidelberg (1988)
3. Turchin, V.: The Concept of a Supercompiler. ACM Transactions on Programming Languages and Systems 8(3), 90–121 (1986)
4. Sørensen, M., Glück, R., Jones, N.: A Positive Supercompiler. Journal of Functional Programming 6(6), 811–838 (1996)
5. Sørensen, M.: Turchin's Supercompiler Revisited. Master's thesis, Department of Computer Science, University of Copenhagen, DIKU-rapport 94/17 (1994)
6. Wadler, P.: The Concatenate Vanishes. FP Electronic Mailing List (December 1987)
7. Hamilton, G.W.: Distillation: Extracting the Essence of Programs. In: Proceedings of the ACM SIGPLAN Symposium on Partial Evaluation and Semantics-Based Program Manipulation, pp. 61–70 (2007)
8. Higman, G.: Ordering by Divisibility in Abstract Algebras. Proceedings of the London Mathemtical Society 2, 326–336 (1952)
9. Kruskal, J.: Well-Quasi Ordering, the Tree Theorem, and Vazsonyi's Conjecture. Transactions of the American Mathematical Society 95, 210–225 (1960)
10. Dershowitz, N., Jouannaud, J.P.: Rewrite Systems. In: van Leeuwen, J. (ed.) Handbook of Theoretical Computer Science, pp. 243–320. Elsevier, MIT Press (1990)
11. Sørensen, M., Glück, R.: An Algorithm of Generalization in Positive Supercompilation. In: Tison, S. (ed.) CAAP 1994. LNCS, vol. 787, pp. 335–351. Springer, Heidelberg (1994)
12. Marlet, R.: Vers une Formalisation de l'Évaluation Partielle. PhD thesis, Université de Nice - Sophia Antipolis (1994)
13. Bol, R.: Loop Checking in Partial Deduction. Journal of Logic Programming 16(1-2), 25–46 (1993)
14. Leuschel, M.: On the Power of Homeomorphic Embedding for Online Termination. In: Proceedings of the International Static Analysis Symposium, pp. 230–245 (1998)
15. Miller, D.: A Logic Programming Language with Lambda-Abstraction, Function Variables and Simple Unification. In: Schroeder-Heister, P. (ed.) ELP 1989. LNCS, vol. 475, pp. 253–281. Springer, Heidelberg (1991)
16. Nipkow, T.: Functional Unification of Higher-Order Patterns. In: Eighth Annual Symposium on Logic in Computer Science, pp. 64–74 (1993)
17. Hamilton, G.W.: Distilling Programs for Verification. Electronic Notes in Theoretical Computer Science 190(4), 17–32 (2007)

Establishing Linux Driver Verification Process

Alexey Khoroshilov, Vadim Mutilin, Alexander Petrenko,
and Vladimir Zakharov

Institute for System Programming, RAS
Moscow, Russia

Abstract. This paper presents an initiative program aimed at enhancing Linux device driver designing and maintenance by launching a long-
term process that will attend the OS kernel development. This process
includes two adjacent lines of activity: 1) creation and replenishment of a
repository of potential faults and errors that may occur in Linux device
drivers, and 2) development and improvement of special-purpose verification tools for automatic detection of all errors specified in repository. We
describe in some details both lines of activity, present an architecture
of a perspective verification toolset, compare our project with similar
work, and finally discuss the current state of art in Linux device driver
verification.

1 Introduction

Linux is one of the most widespread OS that gains in popularity among both
home and business users. The leading research companies anticipate further open
source software growth. As it was noticed in [1], Linux, which initially was mostly
deployed for infrastructure-oriented workloads (such as print and file services,
DNS serving, DHCP and HTTP), extends its area of service to business-oriented
workloads including ERP, CRM, database applications, and line-of-business solutions. The authors of [1] forecast "that spending on software related to Linux
server platforms is on a compounded annual grow rate of 35.7 percent from 2006
to 2011".

The base of Linux is an open source kernel composed of a kernel core and
drivers. Drivers interact with the kernel core through the application program
interface (API) (Fig. 1). In order for drivers to call API functions correctly,
restrictions are imposed on the interactions of drivers with the kernel core. When
the interaction rules are not observed, this often leads to fatal effects, such as
system crashes, damages of objects under control, material loses. The empirical
data indicates [2,3] that bugs in kernel-space device drivers cause 85% system
crashes. This results from several factors. Firstly, drivers' code constitutes the
major part (up to 70%) of the OS code. Secondly, device drivers are developed
mostly by suppliers of corresponding devices who are not experts in OS kernel.
Therefore, to provide the safety of OS one needs to check that every driver meets
all requirements that specify its interactions with the kernel core.

As a lot of open source projects which progressed to the "bazaar phase" [4],
Linux kernel development falls within the scope of the open source development

A. Pnueli, I. Virbitskaite, and A. Voronkov (Eds.): PSI 2009, LNCS 5947, pp. 165–176, 2010.
© Springer-Verlag Berlin Heidelberg 2010

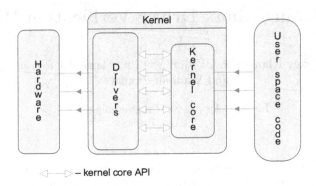

Fig. 1. Interaction between driver and kernel core

model. This model differs from the proprietary one in many aspects. While the development of a proprietary software is a centralized process, the Linux development model is much more distributed. A great number of developers submit proposals (patches). Linux Foundation [5] reports that from the 2.6.11 to the 2.6.24 kernel release (a total of 1140 days) there were, on average, 2.83 patches applied to the kernel tree per hour. It comes to an impressive 3,621 lines added, 1,550 lines removed, and 1,425 lines changed every day for the past $2\frac{1}{2}$ years. Such rate of change exceeds that of any other public software project. Permanent modifications are necessary for continuous kernel improvement, for responding to modern trends, and for supporting new features of architectures and devices. Needless to say that such a vast variety of modifications influences the kernel core API used by drivers. Moreover, as explained in Greg Kroah-Hartman's article [6], kernel core API for drivers is supposed to be unstable and may be changed suddenly. This brings up a difficult task of evolving drivers along with the evolution of the kernel core. Therefore, driver verification process should follow the kernel development process and correspond to all modifications of the kernel.

One of the main advantages of an open source development model is that it offers considerable scope for extensive and thorough code reviewing and testing: availability of the code allows anyone to analyze it. If a software project has a strong community of interested consumers this possibility leads to intensive code review process. Since everyone looks at the code from his own point of view based on his own experience, the effect of "many eyes" [7] allows to fix most if not all of the bugs in a short time. Clearly, this approach does not guarantee the detection of all bugs [8], since only a small number of core developers comprehend in full details the most sophisticated interactions between the components of the kernel and thus can detect difficult-to-find errors that display themselves under rare concourses of circumstances.

Involving volunteer users as testers is especially important in view of modularity and massive concurrent development of kernel. Although originally developed for 32-bit x86-based PCs (386 or higher), today Linux also runs on at least eighteen architectures. Therefore, developers of drivers can hardly test their software in all configurations. Usually, they test their drivers only in some available configurations and leave other configurations to discretion of volunteer testers.

Unfortunately, drivers outside the kernel do not attract so much attention from OS users to benefit from the effect of "many eyes". Developers of such drivers are forced to study all specific features of kernel core API and keep up with modifications. As a rule, these drivers are subject to a greater extent to unexpected bugs and faults. Further testing (unit, system, integration) do not solve the problem of fixing difficult-to-find bugs violating the contract with kernel core API.

Can formal methods be of any use for effective device drivers development? It is believed that the ideal solution is as follows:

1. to describe formally a kernel core API using contract specifications (e.g. in terms of preconditions and postconditions), and
2. to check using automatic verification tools the compliance of driver source code to restrictions on interactions with the kernel core.

But since the development of general-purpose automatic verification tools is not feasible in the nearest future, we suggest more realistic light-weight approaches to this problem. The first approach assumes to describe the API in a formal way and uses a run-time partial verification instead of total formal verification. The second approach is to use formal models (patterns) of the most frequently encountered errors and inefficiencies instead of formal specification of the interface as a whole and to develop a program static analysis toolset that can be able to discover such patterns in source code of device drivers. Since static analysis algorithms are much simpler and faster than formal verification engines, this gives a hope that the corresponding tools can be readily exploited by drivers developers.

The principle drawback of the first approach is that a run-time verification can detect only those violations that happen during the current execution of a program. This means that some problems (e.g. a diversity of configurations) remain unresolved. The main advantage of the approach is that it is free from false positives and detects a violation immediately as it happens.

The advantages of the second approach are as follows:

- it can detect bugs in many configurations simultaneously;
- it can detect bugs without using hardware required to execute the code;
- it can detect even those bugs that occur when several rare events happen simultaneously along a single run.

The principle drawback of the second approach is that it requires a separate model for each kind of violations instead of using universal contract specification. At the same time a development of a set of simple models requires far less efforts than a development of a complex one. Therefore, considering the problem of automatic detection of typical bugs occurred in the interactions of device drivers with kernel core, we believe that the second approach is more promising.

We introduce an initiative program aimed at enhancing Linux device driver designing and maintenance by launching a long-term process that will attend the OS kernel development. This process includes two adjacent lines of activity: 1) creation and replenishment of a repository of potential faults and errors that may occur in Linux device drivers, and 2) development and improvement of special-purpose verification tools for automatic detection of all errors specified in repository. The rest of the paper is organized as follows. In the next section we present the proposed process of Linux device driver verification. Section 3 describes a perspective verification toolset for automatic detection of issues in drivers source code. In the last sections we discuss the related work, summarize the results and overview future directions.

2   Linux Device Driver Verification Process

In this section we outline a procedure which provide the community of Linux device driver developers with an easy-to-use means for automatic verification of their software products. The general scheme of the verification process is presented in Fig. 2.

The key components of the verification system are 1) a repository of templates of potential errors and inefficiencies that may occur in Linux device drivers and 2) a verification toolset aimed at detecting such templates in driver code. Our repository is publicly available at the web site of Linux Verification Center of Institute for System Programming of RAS [9] and contains informal and formal descriptions of rules for well written Linux device drivers. A verification toolset is composed of a set of verification engines operating under the control of a procedure which implements a verification strategy by assigning a specific engine to every error template to be checked.

The Linux device driver verification process consists of the following subprocesses:

- Kernel monitoring;
- Formalization;
- Potential issues detection;
- Result analysis.

The first subprocess is continuously observing the Linux kernel development with the object of revealing and identifying the following events:

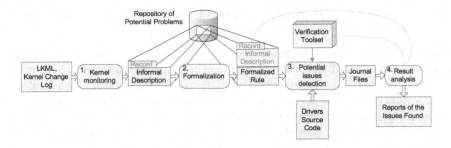

Fig. 2. Linux device driver verification process

- changes in kernel core API that may cause device drivers developed for the former API to erroneous behavior;
- changes in kernel core API that may cause device drivers to inefficient behavior;
- bug fixes and improvement in the kernel/drivers that can be applicable for other drivers as well.

The main activities of kernel monitoring subprocess are 1) analysis of Linux Kernel Mailing List (LKML) and change logs of the kernel, 2) identification of relevant messages, 3) extracting new API interaction rules for well written drivers, and 4) recording into the repository the informal descriptions of these rules and potential consequences of their violation. In case of successful evolvement of the project we hope that the major part of activities on the analysis of changes in kernel core API will be done by kernel developers. It will make the process more efficient, because new verification rules and changes in the old ones are rare in contrast to the rate changes in kernel code.

For example, when analyzing the LKLM message [10] which describes a fix in drivers/firmware/dmi_scan.c, we file the record ID 0060 depicted in Fig. 3. Note, that the rule describes just a part of requirements to the interface functions which are important for the rule, but not the complete requirements. For example, the rule ID 0060 does not describe precondition of *list_add*, which requires non null arguments *head* and *new*.

ID 0060: An element of linked list should not be inserted in the linked list again

DESCRIPTION: A linked list is one of the most widespread data structures in the kernel. They are based on the structure list_head

```
struct list_head
{
  struct list_head *next, *prev;
};
```

The basic operation to add a new element to the list is the list_add() function:

```
static inline void __list_add(struct list_head *new,
                   struct list_head *prev,
                   struct list_head *next)
{
  next→prev = new;
  new→next = next;
  new→prev = prev;
  prev→next = new;
}
static inline void list_add(struct list_head *new,
                struct list_head *head)
{
  __list_add(new, head, head→next);
}
```

The new argument is a pointer to a structure to be added to a list. The head argument is a pointer to the current head of the list.

Let us consider a situation when an element of a list is added to the list again. In this case the __list_add() function modifies next and prev fields of the element and, thus, brakes the old links.

If the list before operation looks like: → a ↔ b ↔ c ↔ d ↔ e ← and we add the element c after the element a, we will have the list: → a ↔ c ↔ b → c{↔ b} ← d ←, where {} means the new link of the element c.

As a result an iteration of the list in the forward direction will lead to the infinite cycle.

LINKS: http://www.mail-archive.com/git-commits-head@vger.kernel.org/msg41536.html

EXAMPLE OF FIX: 2.6.25 → drivers/firmware/dmi_scan.c

Fig. 3. Example of verification rule

The records in the repository are used to track current status of the corresponding problem and to collect all information of it in one place.

These records are analysed within the second subprocess. For each record an expert decides if there exists an available verification tool which can check that all computations of a driver comply with the corresponding rule of its interaction with the kernel. If it is not possible to automatically check such a rule, some feature requests to verification tools are prepared and the rule is marked as "automatically unverifiable" in the repository.

If automatic checking is possible, the most suitable verification engine is identified. Then a formal description (specification) of the rule is prepared and placed to the repository. Each verification engine has its own requirements to formal representation of the rule to be verified. Thus, the specification of a rule depends on the selected verification engine.

The third subprocess performs an automatic verification of Linux device drivers against the current set of formalized rules. As the result the subprocess outputs

- a list of potential problems in source code of drivers;
- a list of recommendations on the improvement of source code of drivers;
- information on compatibility of drivers with various versions of the Linux kernel.

On the early stages of the development the main objective of potential issues detection subprocess is to ensure the quality of verification tools. To achieve it device drivers for the analysis are taken from kernel.org source code repositories and from other public sources as well. Later the objective will be shifted to detection of bugs in actual drivers. In this case the authors of individual drivers and patches will apply the tools to their code independently.

In more details we discuss formalized rules and verification toolset in the next section.

Within the fourth subprocess an expert analyses the results obtained at the previous stages and decides whether an issue detected by a verification toolset can really happens along some run of a driver, or it is a false positive. In the first case the report on the errors detected is sent to the maintainers of the driver. In the second case an expert works out the recommendations on the improvement of verification engines and formalized rules to avoid false positives in future.

Ideally, the role of the fourth subprocess should be reduced to the minimal activity and the work of an expert should be done by maintainer of the driver, but this becomes possible only at some stage of maturity of the verification tools and rule specifications which can be achieved after some time of real operation of the process.

3   Toolset

A verification subprocess is based on a program verification toolset which includes a verification framework and a set of verification engines. An effectiveness of the subprocess depends to a large measure on the ability of choosing an appropriate verification engine for every formalized API interaction rule.

As an input the engine takes a driver source code and a formalized rule from a repository; a rule to be checked is represented by an appropriate failure model, kernel model, traceability descriptor, as well as verification type and list of verification engines.

Failure model should be properly adapted to the data format used in a selected verification engine. Thus, for example, a BLAST-based engine described below can only check that assert statements are not violated. Therefore, a failure model of the rule ID 0060 have to be written in terms of assert statements (see Fig. 4).

The rule ID 0060 in natural language says that an element can be added to the list if it was not added to the list before or was deleted from it. So we should check that the element *new* does not equal to any element in the list, i.e. *for every elem in the list* holds *new* $\neq$ *elem*. Due to lack of precision in analysis of heap graphs and arrays in BLAST we can not simply check if a given element is included in the implementation list *list_head*, as well as we can not model it using an array. So here, for expressing universal quantification over potentially infinite set of dynamically allocated list of elements we use the universal quantification trick. We store one non-deterministically chosen object which was added using *list_add* in the state variable *elem*. If *elem* is *NULL* then no object was chosen in *list_add* or the *elem* was deleted from the list by *list_del*. Hence, verification engine independently check assertion in *list_add* for all single objects which can be added to the list. This technique has been extensively used earlier in SLIC [11] and [12].

To make driver source code independently executable we supply it with a kernel model which is based on original kernel headers, except that simplified model implementations of required functions are provided, and a testbed which models requests to the driver is included. Physically kernel model consists of several C headers and source files. Kernel models can be partially shared between rules, but usually each rule is assigned an individual model. For instance, driver initialization and shutdown procedures invocation is a common part for all kernel models, and spinlocks state tracking is a part specific for proper lock usage rule.

State variable:
```
      struct list_head *elem = NULL;
```
Insert before call to
```
    void list_add(struct list_head *new, struct list_head *head)
    Code:
        assert(new!=elem);
        if(*) elem = new; // * - nondeterministic choice
```
Insert before call to
```
    void list_del(struct list_head *entry)
    Code:
      if(entry==elem) elem=NULL;
```

Fig. 4. Failure model of rule ID 0060

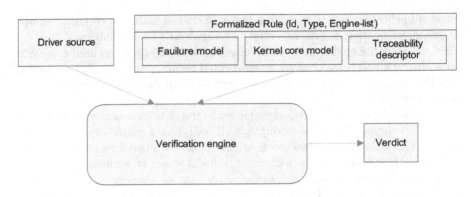

Fig. 5. Potential issues detection subprocess

Traceability descriptor is required to represent an output of a general-purpose verification engine in rule-specific terms.

Verification of a rule is schematically shown in Fig. 5. Given a driver source code and a formalized rule, we choose one of verification engines from the list of engines. The engine takes as input a failure model, a kernel model, and a driver source code, transforms these components into its intermediate representation in which it solves the verification tasks. After getting a solution, the engine outputs a verdict using a traceability descriptor for interpretation of the results.

We distinguish three types of rules: syntactic, safety, liveness. Syntactic rules describe restrictions on usage of syntactic constructs, such as deprecated types, fields and functions. Special cases of other rules are also considered as syntactic if they can be checked using code templates. Safety rules are written in terms of reachability requirements. Liveness rules concern the issues of termination of program runs or that of some progress along code execution.

In most cases each rule can be analyzed with the help of numerous verification engines of appropriate type. Therefore, a rule is usually supplied with some specific information which helps to select the most adequate verification engine.

The simplest utilities like *grep* can be used for checking a part of syntactic rules. For example, search for calls to deprecated functions can be implemented with *grep* by supplying a corresponding regular expression in failure model. But for many other syntactic rules advanced syntactic analyzers are required. An example of such rule is one which do not recommend to use structure initializations in *gcc* style.

At present for checking safety rules we have two verification engines. The first one is a dataflow analysis tool under development which is intended to handle most *gcc* C language extensions that may occur in driver sources. Since this tool is based on the static analysis iteration procedures, it operates much faster than BLAST although this is achieved at the expense of low precision (an abundance of false positives). The second one is a BLAST-based engine which we consider her in more details.

BLAST [13] is an open source tool, which implements counter-example guided abstraction refinement (CEGAR) [14] verification technique for programs written in C programming language. As an input, BLAST takes a program written in C and containing calls to assert function. This function has one Boolean parameter. If there is an execution path where the assert function is called with false, the input program is considered as incorrect, otherwise it is considered as correct.

Drivers are kernel modules containing declarations of initialization and exit functions. Typically, an initialization function registers drivers event handler functions in the kernel. Driver is a reactive program by nature, i.e. operating system calls event handlers in unpredictable order. Since BLAST is aimed to verify sequential programs we developed a special toolset which translates a source code of a driver into a sequential program modeling reactive behavior of the source driver using special nondeterministic operator supported by BLAST. The toolset generates usual entry point *main()* containing calls to initialization, exit functions and event handlers registered by the driver. The translated code is combined with verification model and passed to BLAST for verification.

4   Related Work

To the best of our knowledge the only project which has a verification process is SDV project [15,16] where the development of verification rules coexists with the development of MS Windows kernel. Now they have formalized more than 160 rules. But as it was mentioned above, the development of proprietary software differs from the development of an open source software. So, this process would not be easily applicable to Linux kernel. Moreover, the only thing we know about that process is that the authors of SDV were developing the rules in a close contact with kernel developers.

The necessity of carrying out a verification process in the framework of kernel development is discussed in [17], where a number recommendation on organizing an open source software certification are suggested. In particular, the authors of [17] claim that verification engines should meet the requirements imposed by features of open source development, including huge amount of modifications, distributed development, lack of specifications and impossibility of imposing any style of programming.

There are many work on the development and improvement of verification engines. Thus, SDV team [15,16] uses SLAM engine which is a verification tool intended for checking safety properties of Windows device drivers. It is based on predicate abstraction refinement [18] and is accompanied with specification language SLIC [11] and rule descriptions. SLAM was successfully used to find bugs in Windows drivers [15].

Counterexample guided abstraction refinement is also a principle utilized by BLAST software model checker [13,14]. There are several applications of BLAST for analyzing drivers and other source code in C [19,20,21]. But its practical applicability has been criticized in [22]. The authors of [22] noticed that BLAST needs to instrument driver before verification, and this has been done in our BLAST-based verification engine.

CBMC [23] model checker was successfully used in [12], where they have adapted the SDV approach to the verification of Linux device drivers. To this end they developed an extension of SLIC and a tool which transforms it into C code that uses CBMC's specification and modeling directives. As far as we know they have collected seven rules that can be checked with the help of their verification tool set.

DDVerify is predicate abstraction-based tool is intended for automated verification of Linux device drivers [24] and provides an accurate model of the relevant parts of the kernel [25].

Symbolic approximation can be used to verify large amounts of source code. In [26] it was shown how symbolic approximation can be sharpened to reflect details of C semantics.

Manual program abstraction can be used to facilitate testing [27]. Only relevant parts of a program are inputed to model checker, and its output is transformed into a test trace of the original program. This approach was successfully applied for semi-automatic analysis of kernel sources.

In the practical sense of Linux driver verification it is important to note successful application of Coverity static analysis tool [28], which searches for common errors and inefficiencies such as the existence of dead code, null pointer dereference, use before test, buffer overrun, resource leak, unsafe use of returned values, type and allocation size mismatch, uninitialized values read and use after free. These rules were adapted for Linux kernel so that standard library functions are replaced by kernel API functions. For example, resource leak is described for different kernel resources like *pci_pool*, *usb_urb* etc. In the view of confidential nature of the tool it remains unclear how much far it can be extended for new verification rules.

5   Conclusions

We began to collect rules in the mid of 2007. Since that time we identified API interaction rules for device drivers by analyzing educational resources like books, articles, and by reading Linux kernel source code. At the end of 2007 we gathered 39 rules, but further identification were hard. At the beginning of 2008 we switched to LKML, that increased the rate of identification. Till the middle of 2008 we have collected 71 rules. Today we feel that LKML is inexhaustible source of rules and there is a need to continuously monitor it.

Verification of Linux device drivers is an actual topic from both scientific and industrial points of view. As we discussed in the Section 4 there are several research groups trying to apply different verification techniques to Linux drivers.

We investigate applicability of our verification techniques, but the main goal of the Linux device driver verification program presented in the paper is to build a common framework for cooperation and collaboration of all researches and developers interested in the topic. We believe that sharing common resources such as the repository of potential problems in drivers, kernel core models, etc. will help to achieve a synergetic effect and will be a step forward to an industrial-ready solution.

Also we are designing our verification framework so that it could easily integrate various verification engines. Thus, the framework can be used as a common entry point for device driver developers, who would like to test existing verification tools with their drivers.

References

1. Gillen, A., Stergiades, E., Waldman, B.: The role of Linux servers and commercial workloads (2008),
   http://www.linux-foundation.org/publications/IDC_Workloads.pdf
2. Chou, A., Yang, J., Chelf, B., Hallem, S., Engler, D.: An empirical study of operating systems errors. In: SOSP 2001: Proceedings of the eighteenth ACM symposium on Operating systems principles, pp. 73–88. ACM, New York (2001)
3. Swift, M.M., Bershad, B.N., Levy, H.M.: Improving the reliability of commodity operating systems. In: SOSP 2003: Proceedings of the nineteenth ACM symposium on Operating systems principles, pp. 207–222. ACM, New York (2003)
4. Senyard, A., Michlmayr, M.: How to have a successful free software project. In: 11th Asia-Pacific Software Engineering Conference, pp. 84–91 (2004)
5. Kroah-Hartman, G., Corbet, J., McPherson, A.: Linux kernel development (2008),
   http://www.linux-foundation.org/publications/
   linuxkerneldevelopment.php
6. Kroah-Hartman, G.: The Linux kernel driver interface,
   http://www.kernel.org/doc/Documentation/stable_api_nonsense.txt
7. Raymond, E.S.: The Cathedral and the Bazaar: Musings on Linux and Open Source by an Accidental Revolutionary. O'Reilly, Sebastopol (2001)
8. Glass, R.L.: Facts and Fallacies of Software Engineering, 1st edn. Addison Wesley Professional, Sebastopol (2003)
9. Web-site: Linux Verification Center, http://linuxtesting.ru
10. LKML: Message 41536,
    http://www.mail-archive.com/git-commits-head@vger.kernel.org/
    msg41536.html
11. Ball, T., Rajamani, S.K.: SLIC: A specification language for interface checking. Technical report, Microsoft Research (2001)
12. Post, H., Küchlin, W.: Integrated static analysis for Linux device driver verification. In: Davies, J., Gibbons, J. (eds.) IFM 2007. LNCS, vol. 4591, pp. 518–537. Springer, Heidelberg (2007)
13. Henzinger, T.A., Jhala, R., Majumdar, R., McMillan, K.L.: Abstractions from proofs. SIGPLAN Not. 39(1), 232–244 (2004)
14. Henzinger, T.A., Jhala, R., Majumdar, R.: Lazy abstraction. In: Symposium on Principles of Programming Languages, pp. 58–70. ACM Press, New York (2002)
15. Ball, T., Bounimova, E., Cook, B., Levin, V., Lichtenberg, J., McGarvey, C., Ondrusek, B., Rajamani, S.K., Ustuner, A.: Thorough static analysis of device drivers. SIGOPS Oper. Syst. Rev. 40(4), 73–85 (2006)
16. Ball, T., Cook, B., Levin, V., Rajamani, S.K.: SLAM and Static Driver Verifier: technology transfer of formal methods inside Microsoft. Technical report, Microsoft Research (2004)
17. Breuer, P., Pickin, S.: Open source certification. FLOSS-FM (2008)
18. Ball, T., Majumdar, R., Millstein, T., Rajamani, S.K.: Automatic predicate abstraction of C programs. SIGPLAN Not. 36(5), 203–213 (2001)

19. Henzinger, T.A., Jhala, R., Majumdar, R., Necula, G.C., Sutre, G., Weimer, W.: Temporal-safety proofs for systems code. In: Brinksma, E., Larsen, K.G. (eds.) CAV 2002. LNCS, vol. 2404, pp. 526–538. Springer, Heidelberg (2002)
20. Beyer, D., Henzinger, T.A., Jhala, R., Majumdar, R.: The software model checker Blast: Applications to software engineering. Int. J. Softw. Tools Technol. Transf. 9(5), 505–525 (2007)
21. Beyer, D., Henzinger, T.A., Jhala, R., Majumdar, R.: Checking memory safety with blast. In: Cerioli, M. (ed.) FASE 2005. LNCS, vol. 3442, pp. 2–18. Springer, Heidelberg (2005)
22. Mühlberg, J.T., Lüttgen, G.: Blasting Linux code. In: Brim, L., Haverkort, B.R., Leucker, M., van de Pol, J. (eds.) FMICS 2006 and PDMC 2006. LNCS, vol. 4346, pp. 211–226. Springer, Heidelberg (2007)
23. Clarke, E., Kroening, D., Lerda, F.: A tool for checking ANSI-C programs. In: Jensen, K., Podelski, A. (eds.) TACAS 2004. LNCS, vol. 2988, pp. 168–176. Springer, Heidelberg (2004)
24. Witkowski, T., Blanc, N., Kroening, D., Weissenbacher, G.: Model checking concurrent Linux device drivers. In: ASE 2007: Proceedings of the twenty-second IEEE/ACM international conference on Automated software engineering, pp. 501–504. ACM, New York (2007)
25. Witkowski, T.: Formal verification of Linux device drivers. Master's thesis, Dresden University of Technology (2007)
26. Breuer, P., Pickin, S.: Verification in the light and large: Large-scale verification for fast-moving open source C projects. In: Software Engineering Workshop, Annual IEEE/NASA Goddard, pp. 246–255 (2007)
27. Kim, M., Hong, S., Hong, C., Kim, T.: Model-based kernel tesiting for concurrency bugs through counter example replay. In: Fifth Workshop on Model-Based Testing (2009)
28. Coverity: Linux report (2004), http://scan.coverity.com

A Method for Test Suite Reduction for Regression Testing of Interactions between Software Modules

Dmitry Kichigin

dkichigin@gmail.com

Abstract. In order to reduce the cost of regression testing, researchers have proposed the use of test-suite reduction techniques which aim to reduce the size of a test suite with respect to some criteria. Emerging trends in software development such as complexity of software being developed and increasing use of commercial off-the-shelf components present new challenges for existing test suite reduction techniques. The paper presents results of a new experimental evaluation together with a brief description of our test suite reduction method presented in earlier papers which is not affected by these challenges. The results suggest that the method has a good potential for the use for test suites reduction for software integration testing.

1 Introduction

Raising level of software modularity makes integration and regression integration testing is a vital step in software development and maintenance process. At the same time, high speed of software evolution, and, especially, a big number and high frequency of its modifications, significantly increase the cost of regression integration testing. Test suite reduction [14, 13, 6] is one of possible solutions to this problem.

Test suite reduction looks to reduce the number of test cases in a test suite while retaining a high percentage of the original suite's fault detection effectiveness [14]. Such a reduction decreases the costs of a software execution on the tests as well as the costs of a test suite maintenance [14], thereby reducing the overall cost of regression testing.

A traditional approach to test suite reduction was initially developed for unit testing and is based on filtering individual tests out of an original test suite while preserving original test suite's coverage level (in terms of selected coverage criteria) and involves a static analysis and/or instrumentation of a source code. In case of integration testing, the majority of test suite reduction methods are an adaptation of existing methods for unit testing. The main difference is that they consider coverage not of all code but only a part of it, which is responsible for interactions of software elements being integrated.

Recent trends in software development, such as component-based software development and use of commercial off-the-shelf (COTS) components, and increasing size and complexity of the software being developed, present new challenges for existing test suite reduction techniques that may limit their applicability. The source code is usually unavailable for COTS components, thus making it impossible to use methods which are based on analysis or instrumentation of a source code [14]. It also can be

A. Pnueli, I. Virbitskaite, and A. Voronkov (Eds.): PSI 2009, LNCS 5947, pp. 177–184, 2010.
© Springer-Verlag Berlin Heidelberg 2010

very expensive and hard to conduct source-code based coverage analysis for large software [18, 15]. These problems limit the applicability of existing test suite reduction techniques, thus creating a need for new methods which are able to work without access to a source code.

To resolve this problem, we developed a new test suite reduction technique for regression integration testing which is based on analysis of interactions between modules being integrated and uses sequences of interface functions, invoked during software execution. We considered interactions between two software modules which occur via interface of functions which can take only scalar parameters, however the method can be adapted to handle other parameters as well. Our method does not require source code access or instrumentation for one of two interacting modules and does not require source code analysis for the other module which significantly increases the area of the method's applicability.

This paper is an extension of our earlier work [19] where we presented the method together with results of its experimental evaluation on GNU Assembler test suite. Those experiments showed promising results, however they were not enough in the sense that they did not evaluate the actual gain in resource consumption during the testing using a reduced test suite. In this paper we aim to eliminate this gap and we present the results of an additional experiment which we conducted to measure this characteristic as well.

2 Existing Test Suite Reduction Methods

A traditional approach to test suite reduction consists in building a test suite of a smaller size but equivalent to the original one in terms of a selected coverage metric [7]. Several methods were developed to measure coverage of integration testing.

Interface mutation systematically adds integration errors to part of program's source code which relate to unit interfaces and measures coverage in terms of percentage of errors detected by test cases [4].

Structural metrics examine the ability of a test suite to test software structural elements involved into interactions being tested. These metrics analyze module's source code to discover dependencies between software elements being integrated and build graph models to represent them. By the type of this graph, structural metric are divided into two groups: metrics which use *program control flow model* [17, 12]; and metrics which use *program data flow model* [2, 12]. After a program graph is built, execution of software on test suite modeled as a path in the graph which is called *an execution path*. Structural coverage metrics reflect how well execution paths cover graph's elements thus giving the information about coverage of internal software elements involved into interactions being tested.

Both mutation analysis and structural metrics require an instrumentation or access to source code. This makes it complex and time consuming to use these methods for large software, and even impossible when source code is unavailable as in the case of the component-based development using COTS components.

3 Description of the Method

To solve problems, highlighted in the previous section, we present a new test suite reduction method for regression testing of interactions between two software modules. The method is based on modelling of interactions "behaviour" on a test suite and does not require source code access or instrumentation.

3.1 The Model of Interaction between Two Modules

To model behaviour of interactions between modules, we use sequences of module's interface functions, invoked during the execution of software under test. We take into consideration function names together with parameter values passed to functions on invocation.

Before we start, we need to make some definitions. Let's assume we have two modules, A and B, and we consider interactions between modules which are done via the interface of module B. We define:

Interface functions - functions, which form a part of module's interface.

Interaction trace for a test case t – a sequence of interface functions of module B, which are called by module A during software execution on the test case t. We assume that these functions are represented by their names together with parameter values passed to them on invocation and occur in the trace in the order of their invocation.

K-length sequence of interface functions - an arbitrary continuous sequence of length K, which can be located in an interaction trace.

Set of sequences of interface functions, which corresponds to interaction between modules A and B on the test t, - a set of all possible K-length sequences, which can be located in the interaction trace for the interaction between A and B on t. To construct the set of K-length sequences we use "sliding window" technique [8,19] with window size equal to K.

Having these definitions we define a *model of interaction* between module A and module B on a test t as the set of sequences defined above.

3.2 Equality Relation for Interaction Models

For the model of interaction between modules defined above, we can define an equality relation. As we have shown in [19], we can define equality relation between two interaction behavior models as:

$$\delta(M_1, M_2) = \prod_{s_1 \in M_1} \sum_{s_2 \in M_2} \prod_{k=1}^{K} [\delta(\text{name}(f_{k1}), \text{name}(f_{k2})) \times$$

$$\times \prod_{i=1}^{n} \delta(x_{ki}, y_{ki}) \times \prod_{i=n+1}^{m} \delta(\text{interval}(x_{ki}), \text{interval}(y_{ki}))] \times \qquad (1)$$

$$\times \prod_{s_2 \in M_2} \sum_{s_1 \in M_1} \prod_{k=1}^{K} [\delta(\text{name}(f_{k2}), \text{name}(f_{k1})) \times$$

$$\times \prod_{i=1}^{n} \delta(y_{ki}, x_{ki}) \times \prod_{i=n+1}^{m} \delta(\text{interval}(y_{ki}), \text{interval}(x_{ki}))]$$

where M_1, M_2 – models being compared; s_1, s_2 – K-length sequences, which belong to the models; f_{k1}, f_{k2} – functions, which have m scalar parameters, where first n parameters are nominal and others are numerical; name(f_k) – the name of a function f_k; δ(name(f_i), name(f_j)) – equality relation between names of functions f_i and f_j; x_i, y_i, $i = 1..n$ – values of nominal parameters of functions f_{k1} and f_{k2}; $\delta(x,y)$ – equality relation between nominal parameters x and y; x_i, y_i, $i = n+1..m$ – values of numerical parameters of functions f_{k1} and f_{k2}; interval(x) – the ordinal number of interval to which numerical parameter x belongs; δ(interval(x), interval(y)) – equality relation between numerical parameters x and y.

The detailed explanation of this equality relation is presented in [19]. Here we summarize it as: two given models are equal when their sequence sets are equal and different otherwise. Two sequences of interface functions are considered to be equal when their elements (i.e. function calls) are equal pairwise. Finally, two function calls f_1 and f_2 are equal when 1) the functions have the same names, 2) the values of nominal parameters are the same, and 3) the values of numerical parameters belong to the same intervals.

3.3 The Method's Algorithm

The idea of our test suite reduction method consists in the following. Intuitively, those tests, which initiate the same sequences of interface functions, also repeat themselves in the module interactions they test. Moreover, the tests, which do not initiate any interactions between modules, are also of a little interest to us. Our method is based on these assumptions and "filters out" individual tests which either do not generate new sequences of interface functions, or do not invoke interface functions at all, and so, following our assumptions, do not test an interaction in a new way.

The method uses the model of module interaction built in the previous section and implements the following algorithm:

```
M_T' := Ø;  T' := Ø;
while (T not empty) do begin
        t := get_next_test_from(T);
        M_t := build_interaction_model(t);
        if (M_t is empty) then continue;
        if (M_t ∉ M_T') then begin
                M_T' := M_T' ∪ {M_t};
                T' := T' ∪ {t};
        end;
end
```

where:
T – original test suite;
T' – reduced test suite, $T' \subseteq T$;
t – next test case from the original test suite, $t \in T$;

M_t – model of interaction behaviour on the test case t;
$M_{T'}$ – set of models of interaction behaviour on test cases from T'.
1. First, the next test case is picked up from the original test suite and the program is executed on it;
2. During the program execution, the model M_t of modules' interaction on a test case t is built; if the model is empty, the algorithm returns to the first step;
3. Then, M_t is checked whether it belongs to the set of models $M_{T'}$ or not;
4. If M_t does not belong to $M_{T'}$, then M_t is added to $M_{T'}$ and test case t is added to T';
5. When T is exhausted, the algorithm stops and T' represents the result of algorithm's work, i.e. the reduced test suite.

To check whether model M_t belongs to the set of models $M_{T'}$ or not we will use the equality relation (4). It is important to add that, although we consider only scalar parameters of interface functions, the equality relation (4) can be adapted to take into account any function parameters for which an equality relation can be defined [19]. Therefore our test reduction method can be adapted to handle other types of function parameters.

3.4 Collecting Interaction Traces

In order to implement our method, we need a technique to collect traces of interactions between software components.

The use of a component in the development of software can be represented as an integration of two modules: module A, which is the component itself, and module B, which is the rest of software. In case when a commercial off-the-shelf component is used, only one component, A, comes without source code but with information about its interface (otherwise it would be impossible to use the component).

Many platforms and programming environments provide mechanisms which can be used to collect function call traces without having access to source code. These mechanisms only need information about the functions' signatures and, sometime, access to object or binary code of applications. Examples of such mechanisms can be: in Linux operation system - a mechanism of interception of function calls provided by linker ld [19]; in Windows operation system - Detour tool [1]; .NET and Java platforms have their own built-in mechanisms [11,5] which allow intercepting function calls without even need of instrumentation of program's binary or object code.

In our experiments, where we tested subject applications written in C language and ran in Linux operation system, we used a mechanism provided by linker ld. This mechanism allows intercepting calls to interface functions together with access to values of function parameters. This mechanism only requires information about signatures of interface functions and needs access to object code of only one, caller, module (module B in the example above) and does not require resource-consuming access or instrumentation of a source code of modules.

4 Experimental Evaluation

Test suite reduction methods are characterized by two main characteristics:
1. Percentage of test suite reduction. This characteristic demonstrates the ability of a reduction method to reduce the size of a test suite.

2. Fault detection rate. This characteristic demonstrates fault-detection ability a test suite. It is very important that the fault detection rate of the reduced test suite remain the same or nearly the same as of the original test suite [13].

The previous experiment [19] showed promising results and demonstrated that our method can deliver good level of test suite reduction without loss in fault detection rate, but these results were not enough because they did not show the value of resources which can be saved using reduced test suite for regression testing instead of an original one. In this experiment, in addition to percentage of test suite reduction and fault detection rate, we measured time resources needed to run regression testing. To do this we introduced an additional characteristic which indicates the gain which reduced test suite delivers over the original test suite during regression testing.

4.1 Experiment Setup

For this experiment we took a test suite which was created for certification of candidate operation systems under the Linux Standard Base (LSB) specification: LSB Application Battery v.3.1 [3]. The experiment was conducted in SuSE Linux v10.2 environment. The length K of interface function sequences was the same as in the previous experiment: 6 calls. Xlib library v.11 and the standard C library were used as modules to be integrated.

LSB Application Battery v3.1 test suite is a collection of example LSB compliant applications provided by the LSB project [16] used to test a candidate system if it complies LSB requirements or not. One of specific tasks of LSB Application Battery is to test all libraries specified by LSB specification. For this reason, applications which form LSB Application Battery were selected in a way to collectively exercise all libraries required by LSB specification [16]. Xlib library is one of libraries required by LSB specification v.3.1. The library is a part of X Window System, which is a network-transparent window system. Xlib is a C subroutine library which implements a low-level C language interface to the X Window System protocol [10].

The to-be-tested interaction between Xlib library and the standard C library was carried through a subset of library functions responsible for input/output functionality and defined in stdio.h header file. We used Xlib library which is a part of X Window System version X11R6.9.0; glibc library v 2.8 [9] was taken as an implementation of a standard C library.

To conduct the experiment, we seeded 17 artificial integration errors to the different parts of Xlib library's source code, which are responsible into interactions with the standard C library through its input/output routines. Artificial errors were introduced in the way similar to the one used for mutation integration analysis [4]. Following this way, errors were created by inducing simple changes to functions' input and output parameters, like passing incorrect parameter values or putting values to wrong places in the function parameter list, to disturb the interactions between modules.

To evaluate method's characteristics we used the following indicators:
1. Size of the reduced test suite;
2. Percentage of test suite reduction;
3. Number of detected faults;
4. Fault detection rate (in percent) ;
5. Time of regression testing;
6. Percentage of reduction of time needed for regression testing.

On the first step of the experiment we collected modules interaction traces and built models of modules interaction's behaviour. To do this we recompiled Xlib library to intercept calls to interface functions of glibc library. After that we executed tests from LSB Application Battery test suite and built the interaction behaviour model. Then, using our test suite reduction method, we built a reduced test suite, calculated its characteristics: Size of the reduced test suite and Percentage of test suite reduction; Number of detected faults and Fault detection rate, and compared them with characteristics of the original test suite.

4.2 Experiment Results

Experiment results are summarised in Table 1:

Table 1. Results of the second experiment

Indicator	Original test suite	Reduced test suite
Size of the reduced test suite	81	9
Percentage of test suite reduction	-	88.9%
Number of detected faults	6	6
Fault detection rate	35%	35%
Time of regression testing	1 hour 58 minutes	10 minutes
Percentage of time reduction	-	91.5%

The results show that the method has reduced the original test suite by 88.9% (i.e. by 9 times), which led to reduction of testing time by 91.5% (11.8 times), while the fault detection ability of the test suite was maintained on the same level as of the original test suite: the reduced test suit detected the same number of faults as the original one.

5 Conclusion

In this paper we presented results of a new experimental evaluation of test suite reduction method for regression integration testing. In addition to the main characteristics of the test suite reduction method such as a percentage of reduction of a test suite and a fault detection rate, we measured a gain in resource consumption. The results suggest that the method has a good potential for the use for test suites reduction for software integration testing.

References

1. Hunt, G., Brubacher, D.: Detours: binary interception of Win32 functions. In: Proceedings of the 3rd USENIX Windows NT Symposium, Seattle, WA, July 1999, pp. 135–143 (1999)
2. Harrold, M.J., Soffa, M.L.: Selecting and Using Data for Integration Testing. IEEE Softw. 8(2), 58–65 (1991)

3. Linux Standard Base Application Battery pages,
   `http://www.linuxfoundation.org/appbat/`

4. Delamaro, M.E., Maldonado, J.C., Mathur, A.P.: Interface Mutation: an approach to integration testing. IEEE TSE 27(3), 228–247 (2001)

5. Java™ Virtual Machine Tool Interface (JVM TI),
   `http://java.sun.com/javase/6/docs/technotes/guides/jvmti/`

6. Harrold, M.J., Gupta, R., Soffa, M.L.: A methodology for controlling the size of a test suite. ACM Transactions on Software Engineering and Methodology 2(3), 270–285 (1993)

7. Yu, K.D.: About one test suite reduction method. Collection of papers of The Institute for System Programming of the Russian Academy of Sciences. In: ISP RAS, Moscow (2007); //Кичигин Д.Ю. Об одном методе сокращения набора тестов. Сборник трудов ИСП РАН. М: ИСП РАН (2007)

8. Hofmeyr, S.A., Forrest, S., Somayaji, A.: Intrusion Detection using Sequences of System Calls. Journal of Computer Security 6, 151–180 (1998)

9. GNU C Library, GNU Project, Free Software Foundation (FSF), Inc.,
   `http://ftp.gnu.org/gnu/glibc/`

10. Gettys, J., Scheifler, R.W.: Xlib – C Language X Interface, XWindow System Standard, X Version 11, Release 6.7., `http://www.x.org/docs/X11/xlib.pdf`

11. The .NET Profiling API and the DNProfiler Tool, Matt Pietrek, MSDN Magazine (December 2001),
    `http://msdn.microsoft.com/msdnmag/issues/01/12/hood/default.aspx`

12. Linnenkugel, U., Müllerburg, M.: Test data selection criteria for (software) integration testing. In: Proceedings of the First international Conference on Systems integration on Systems integration 1990, Morristown, New Jersey, United States, pp. 709–717. IEEE Press, Piscataway (1990)

13. Rothermel, G., Harrold, M.J., von Ronne, J., Hong, C.: Empirical studies of test-suite reduction. Journal of Software Testing, Verification, and Reliability 12(4) (December 2002)

14. McMaster, S., Memon, A.M.: Call Stack Coverage for Test Suite Reduction. In: Proceedings of the 21st IEEE international Conference on Software Maintenance (ICSM 2005), September 25 - 30, vol. 00, pp. 539–548. IEEE Computer Society, Washington (2005)

15. Piwowarski, P., Ohba, M., Caruso, J.: Coverage measurement experience during function test. In: Proceedings of the 15th international Conference on Software Engineering, Baltimore, Maryland, United States, May 17 - 21, pp. 287–301. IEEE Computer Society Press, Los Alamitos (1993)

16. Linux Standard Base (LSB) pages. The Linux Foundation,
    `http://www.linuxfoundation.org/en/LSB`

17. Rountev, A., Kagan, S., Sawin, J.: Coverage Criteria for Testing of Object Interactions in Sequence Diagrams. In: Cerioli, M. (ed.) FASE 2005. LNCS, vol. 3442, pp. 282–297. Springer, Heidelberg (2005)

18. Kim, Y.W.: Efficient use of code coverage in large-scale software development. In: Proceedings of the 2003 Conference of the Centre For Advanced Studies on Collaborative Research, Toronto, Ontario, Canada, October 06 - 09. IBM Centre for Advanced Studies Conference, pp. 145–155. IBM Press (2003)

19. Kichigin, D.: Test Suite Reduction for Regression Testing of Simple Interactions between Two Software Modules. In: Proceedings of Spring Young Researchers Colloquium on Software Engineering (SYRCoSE 2007), ISP RAS, vol. 2, pp. 31–37 (2007)

A Java Supercompiler and Its Application to Verification of Cache-Coherence Protocols

Andrei V. Klimov*

Keldysh Institute of Applied Mathematics
Russian Academy of Sciences
4 Miusskaya sq., Moscow, 125047, Russia
klimov@keldysh.ru

Abstract. The Java Supercompiler (JScp) is a specializer of Java programs based on the Turchin's supercompilation method and extended to support imperative and object-oriented notions absent in functional languages. It has been successfully applied to verification of a number of parameterized models including cache-coherence protocols. Protocols are modeled in Java following the method by G. Delzanno and experiments by A. Lisitsa and A. Nemytykh on verification of protocol models by means of the Refal Supercompiler SCP4. The part of the supercompilation method relevant to the protocol verification is reviewed. It deals with an imperative subset of Java.

Keywords: specialization, verification, supercompilation, object-oriented languages, Java.

1 Introduction

Program specialization methods — partial evaluation [10], supercompilation [23,24,25], mixed computation [8], etc. — have been first developed for functional and simplified imperative languages. Later the time has come for specialization of more complex practical object-oriented languages.

There are already a number of works on partial evaluation of imperative and object-oriented languages [3,4,5,15,21]. However, to the best of our knowledge, our work is the first one on supercompilation of a practical object-oriented language [9,11,14]. Inspired by far-reaching results by Alexei Lisitsa and Andrei Nemytykh on verification of protocol models by means of the Refal Supercompiler SCP4 [16,17,18], we extended the Java Supercompiler with the elements of the supercompilation method that were needed to reproduce the results in Java [12] (namely, with restrictions on configuration variables of integral types).

Specialization of operations on objects in JScp is discussed in another paper [11]. Since objects are not used in the protocol models coded in Java, in this paper we review supercompilation of the imperative subset of Java.

* Supported by Russian Foundation for Basic Research projects Nos. 08-07-00280-a, 09-01-00834-a, and 09-07-13598-ofi_ts, and Russian Federal Agency of Science and Innovation project No. 2007-4-1.4-18-02-064.

A. Pnueli, I. Virbitskaite, and A. Voronkov (Eds.): PSI 2009, LNCS 5947, pp. 185–192, 2010.
© Springer-Verlag Berlin Heidelberg 2010

A novelty of this part of the supercompilation method implemented in JScp is that *breadth-first* unfolding of the graph of configurations and recursive construction of the residual code of a statement from the residual codes of nested statements is used rather than *depth-first* traversal of configuration as in other known supercompilers. Another contribution of this paper is reproduction of the results of the experiment on verification of protocols by another supercompiler (JScp instead of SCP4) for a rather different language (the object-oriented Java instead of the functional Refal). This confirms the result is based on the essence of supercompilation rather than on technical implementation details. As a consequence of the experiment the part of supercompilation method relevant to the verification of protocols has been uncovered.

This paper is an extended abstract of the longer version published in the PSI'09 preproceedings [13]. It is organized as follows. In Section 2 the part of the Java supercompilation method that is relevant to verification of protocols is reviewed. In Section 3 experiments on verification of protocol models are described. In Section 4 we conclude.

2   Java Supercompilation

The notion of a configuration While an interpreter runs a program on a ground data, a supercompiler runs the program on a set of data.

A representation of a subject program state in a supercompiler is referred to as a *configuration*. We follow the general rule of construction of the notion of a configuration in a supercompiler from that of the program state in an interpreter that reads as follows: add *configuration variables* to the data domain, and allow the variables to occur anywhere where an ordinary ground value can occur. A configuration represents the set of states that can be obtained by replacing configuration variables with all possible values. Each configuration variable is identified by a unique integer index and carries the type of values it stands for: either one of the Java primitive types, or the reference type along with a class name and some additional information, or the string type. A configuration variable can carry a restriction on the set of values. The configuration variables become the local variables of the residual program.

In the Java virtual machine, a program state consists of *global variables* (`static` fields of Java classes), a representation of *threads* and a *heap*.

In the Java Supercompiler, non-`final` global variables are not represented in a configuration, since at supercompilation time they are considered unknown and no information about them is kept. The values of `final static` fields are evaluated only once at the initialization stage, thus one copy of them is kept for all configurations. As the current version of JScp does not specialize multi-threaded code, the configuration contains only one thread now.

The definition of a *configuration* in the current JScp is as follows:

- a *configuration* is a triple (*thread, restrictions, heap*);
- a *thread* is a *call stack*, a sequence of *frames*;

- a *frame* is a triple (*local environment, evaluation stack, program point*);
- a *local environment* is a mapping of *local variables* to *configuration values*;
- an *evaluation stack* is a sequence of *configuration values*;
- the representation of a *program point* does not matter. It is sufficient to assume it allows us to resume supercompilation from the point;
- a *configuration value* is either a *ground value*, or a *configuration variable*;
- *restrictions* are a mapping *Restr* of configuration variables to predicates on their values. If a configuration variable v is not bound by the mapping, $Restr(v) = \lambda x.\texttt{true}$. In the current version of JScp only restrictions of form $Restr(v) = \lambda x.(x \geq n)$, where n is an integer, on variables of the integral types of the Java language are implemented;
- we leave the notion of a *heap* unspecified here, since this paper does not deal with supercompilation of programs with objects.

The following three operations on configurations are used in JScp.

Comparison. of configurations for inclusion represented by a substitution: we consider $C_1 \subseteq C_2$ if there exist a substitution δ that binds configuration values to configuration variables such that $C_1 = \delta C_2$. Substitutions respect types and restrictions.

Generalization of configurations: a configuration G is the most specific *generalization of two configurations* C_1 and C_2 if $C_1 \subseteq G$ and $C_2 \subseteq G$ and for every G' satisfying this property, $G \subseteq G'$.

Homeomorphic embedding, a well-quasi order used for termination of loop unrolling: $C_1 \trianglelefteq C_2$ if the call stacks of C_1 and C_2 have the same "shape" (the lengths, the program points and the sets of local variables are the same) and $x_1 \trianglelefteq x_2$ holds for all pairs of corresponding configuration values x_1 from C_1 and x_2 from C_2, where $\trianglelefteq$ is the least relation satisfying:

- $v_1 \trianglelefteq v_2$ for all configuration variables v_1 and v_2 of the same type. If the configuration variables have an integral type, their restrictions must embed as well, $Restr(v_1) \trianglelefteq Restr(v_2)$ (see below);
- $x_1 \trianglelefteq x_2$ for all values x_1 and x_2 of the String class unless this is switched off by the user;
- $x_1 \trianglelefteq x_2$ for all ground values x_1 and x_2 of the same floating type;
- $n_1 \trianglelefteq n_2$ for all ground values n_1 and n_2 of the same integral type such that $0 \leq k \leq n_1 \leq n_2$ or $0 \geq -k \geq n_1 \geq n_2$, where k is a user-specified parameter that influences the depth of supercompilation. For verification of the protocols [12] values $k = 0$ and $k = 1$ were used (due to observation by A. Nemytykh);
- embedding of restrictions: $r_1 \trianglelefteq r_2$ if $r_1 = \lambda x.\texttt{true}$, or $0 \leq n_1 \leq n_2$, or $0 \geq n_1 \geq n_2$, where $r_1 = \lambda x.(x \geq n_1)$ and $r_2 = \lambda x.(x \geq n_2)$.

Supercompilation of a method starts with the *initial configuration* comprised of one call stack frame with the method parameters bound to fresh configuration variables.

Driving. In supercompilation, the process of partial execution is referred to as *driving*.

Driving of method invocations. In the current version of JScp method invocations are either inlined, or residualized. No specialized methods are generated as in other supercompilers [19,22,23,24,25] and partial evaluators [10]. Whether to inline or not is controlled by certain JScp options. In our experiments on verification all method invocations were inlined.

Driving of expressions and assignments. Driving of an expression with a current configuration yields the value of the expression, residual code, and a new configuration. Driving is similar to interpretation with the following distinction.

Each unary or binary operation is either evaluated, if there is sufficient information to produce a ground resulting value, or otherwise residualized with a fresh configuration variable v as its value in form of a local variable declaration of form $t\ v\ =\ e$, where e is the expression representing residualized operation with the values of arguments substituted into it.

Integer operations $v+i$ and $v-i$, where i an integer constant, v a configuration variable with restriction $\lambda x.(x \geq n)$, are residualized in form $t\ v' = v + i$ and $t\ v' = v - i$, and a new configuration variable v' with a restriction of form $\lambda x.(x \geq n + i)$ or $\lambda x.(x \geq n - i)$ is added to the configuration.

Integer comparisons $v == i$, $v\ !=\ i$, $v < i$, $v <= i$, $v > i$, $v >= i$ and their commutative counterparts, where i is an integer ground value, v a configuration variable with restriction $\lambda x.(x \geq n)$, evaluate to `true` or `false`, when this is clear from comparison $n > i$ or $n \geq i$.

Driving of conditional statements. Consider a source code if (c) a else b; d, where c is a conditional expression, statements a and b are branches, statements d a continuation executed on exit from the if statement.

If driving of c yields `true` or `false`, the respective branch a or b is used for further driving. Otherwise, let c' be the residual code of the expression c, a configuration variable v its value. Two configurations C_t and C_f corresponding to the `true` and `false` branches are produced by taking into account the last operation of c'. If it is $x == x'$ or $x\ !=\ x'$, where x is a configuration variable, the configuration corresponding to equality is *contracted* [23], that is, substitution $x \mapsto x'$ is applied to the configuration. If the last operation is $x > x'$, $x >= x'$, $x' < x$, or $x' <= x$, where x is a configuration variable of an integral type, x' another variable or nonnegative integer value, the restriction on x is refined with information from x', if possible. Then each of the branches a and b is supercompiled with the respective initial configuration C_t and C_f, producing residual code a' and b' with final configurations C_a and C_b.

Supercompilation of d proceeds either two times with the initial configurations C_a and C_b, or once with C_g being the generalization of C_a and C_b. The choice between the alternatives is made by the JScp user. For the task of protocol verification we used the more aggressive first one.

The residual code of the if statement is either c'; if (v) $\{a'; d'_a\}$ else $\{b'; d'_b\}$, or c'; if (v) $\{a'; \alpha_a\}$ else $\{b'; \alpha_b\}$; d', where d'_a, d'_b, and d' are residual codes of d from C_a, C_b, and C_g respectively, α_a and α_b are assignments that encode in Java the substitutions δ_a and δ_b that emerged from the generalization.

The switch statement is supercompiled analogously.

Configuration analysis of loop statements. Proper configuration analysis is performed only for loops in the current JScp. All kinds of loops in Java are reducible to a loop of form L: while (true) b, where b is a loop body statement.

Four kinds of exits are possible from the source and residual code of a loop body: throw, return, break and continue. The first three kinds are terminal nodes from the viewpoint of supercompilation of the loop statement. A throw statement is just residualized and no more actions are taken on that branch. A return statement is reduced to a break with a label of an appropriate enclosing statement. Processing of breaks and continues to a level higher than the loop statement is postponed until the corresponding level is reached. Statements break L are exits from the residual code of the loop statement. Residual statements continue L along with their configurations are subject to further configuration analysis.

Let a loop statement L: while (true) b be supercompiled with an initial configuration C_0. First, the loop body b is supercompiled with C_0 producing residual code b_0 and the list of statements continue L with configurations C_i, $i \in [1..n_0]$. For those C_i that $C_i \subseteq C_0$, $C_i = \delta_i C_0$, the continue statements are residualized in form α_i; continue L, where α_i are assignments encoding the substitution δ_i.

The remaining configurations C_i, $C_i \not\subseteq C_0$, comprise a current set $Cont$ of to-be-supercompiled continue statements. They are points of further loop unrolling: the loop body b is supercompiled with each $C \in Cont$ and the residual code is analyzed in the same way as for C_0.

This process is repeated and a residual code in form of a tree consisting of residual loop bodies supercompiled with various initial configurations is built. Each new configuration C_i on a leaf of an unfinished tree is checked for looping-back to all of the initial configurations of the residual loop bodies on the path from C_0 to this leaf. The process terminates when the set Cont is empty. However this does not happen in general case.

Generalization and termination. The most popular termination criterion [19,22,25] is based on the well-quasi-ordering. Before supercompiling the loop body with a next configuration C_i, the configuration is compared for homeomorphic embedding $\trianglelefteq$ (described above) with all of the previous initial configurations of the residual loop bodies on the path to it from C_0. If such C_j that $C_j \trianglelefteq C_i$ is found, C_j is generalized with C_i obtaining a configuration G, $C_j \subseteq G$. Then the residual subtree below C_j is erased, a sequence of assignments corresponding to the substitution δ that reduces C_j to G, $C_j = \delta G$, is inserted into the point of C_j, and supercompilation is repeated from the configuration G. This process terminates due to that there can be only a finite number of generalizations for each configuration and that our homeomorphic embedding $\trianglelefteq$ is well-quasi-order.

3 Application to Verification of Cache-Coherence Protocols

A. Lisitsa and A. Nemytykh [16,17,18] have found a nice class of applications solvable by supercompilation. They used the Refal Supercompiler SCP4 developed by A. Nemytkh and V. Turchin [19] and encoded in the functional language Refal the protocol models from Web site [6] developed by G. Delzanno [7]. The code and the results of supercompilation may be found on Web site [17].

Here we demonstrate this method of verification with the use of Java and the Java supercompiler JScp. The protocol models in Java and the results of supercompilation are collected on Web site [12]. The Java code of the models is rather close to the code in the domain-specific language HyTech used in [6].

For the description of the G. Delzanno's approach to the modeling of cache-coherence protocols, see his papers, e.g. [7]. Just the structure of the Java code of models is sufficient for explanation of the use of JScp.The models from [12] match the following pattern. It is commented in more detail in [13] together with a sample model of the MOESI cache-coherence protocol.

```
class model-class-name extends ProtocolModel {
  boolean runModel(int[] actions, int[] pars) throws ModelException {
    int state-var-1 = initial-value-1-or-pars[0]; ...
    require(precondition);
    for (int i = 0; i < actions.length; i++) {
      switch (actions[i]) {
        case 1: require(condition-for-action-1);
          computation-of-next-state; break;
          ...
        default: require(false);
    } }
    if (condition-for-unsafe-state-1) return false; ...
    return true;
  }
  void require(boolean b) throws ModelException {
    if (!b) throw new ModelException();
} }
```

To try to prove the correctness of a model we supercompile the method `runModel` and observe the residual code. If all `return` statements has form `return true`, we conclude the model can never reach an "unsafe" state, a state where the post-condition returns `false`.

4 Conclusion

We demonstrated application of the Java Supercompiler to verification of models belonging to the class of *counter systems*. There are a lot of works on decidability of various properties of these systems including reachability, to which verification reduces, and development of model-checkers for them. An overview can be found in some of the latest papers, e.g., [1]. As compared to these methods, supercompilation can be considered as generalization of forward analysis. The notion of *acceleration* in forward analysis of counter systems corresponds to that of *generalization* in supercompilation. Termination strategies based of well-quasi-orderings are close as well. The Java Supercompiler being a universal program specialization tool for a common object-oriented language is not as efficient and scalable as special-purpose tools and solves less problems from this class. However, its universality is an advantage for the ordinary user, allowing for combing program specialization tasks with verification of program from wider classes.

Supercompilation of the imperative subset of the Java language is worth comparing with works aimed at practical partial evaluation of imperative [3,5] and object-oriented languages [4,15,21]. The main distinctive feature of supercompilation is the explicit notion of a configuration with configuration variables and operations on configurations. This allows for more sophisticated analysis and transformation of programs, which is essential for program verification.

Acknowledgements. The development of the Java supercompiler would not be possible without collaboration with many people. The project was started together with Valentin Turchin and Larry Witte to whom the author is greatly indebted. Special thanks are due to the developers of various parts of the JScp system Arkady Klimov and Artem Shvorin. We are very grateful to our partners Ben Goertzel and Yuri Mostovoy: without their help and support such a complex project as JScp could not be done. It was a pleasure to collaborate with Andrei Nemytykh on application of supercompilation to program verification.

References

1. Bardin, S., Finkel, A., Leroux, J., Petrucci, L.: Fast: acceleration from theory to practice. International Journal on Software Tools for Technology Transfer 10(5), 401–424 (2008)
2. Broy, M., Zamulin, A.V. (eds.): PSI 2003. LNCS, vol. 2890. Springer, Heidelberg (2004)
3. Bulyonkov, M.A., Kochetov, D.V.: Practical aspects of specialization of algol-like programs. In: Danvy, O., Thiemann, P., Glück, R. (eds.) Dagstuhl Seminar 1996. LNCS, vol. 1110, pp. 17–32. Springer, Heidelberg (1996)
4. Chepovsky, A.M., Klimov, And.V., Klimov, Ark.V., Klimov, Y.A., Mishchenko, A.S., Romanenko, S.A., Skorobogatov, S.Y.: Partial evaluation for common intermediate language. In: Broy, Zamulin (eds.) [2], pp. 171–177
5. Consel, C., Lawall, J.L., Le Meur, A.-F.: A tour of Tempo: a program specializer for the C language. Sci. Comput. Program. 52, 341–370 (2004)
6. Delzanno, G.: Automatic Verification of Cache Coherence Protocols via Infinite-state Constraint-based Model Checking,
   http://www.disi.unige.it/person/DelzannoG/protocol.html
7. Delzanno, G.: Constraint-based verification of parameterized cache coherence protocols. Formal Methods in System Design 23(3), 257–301 (2003)
8. Ershov, A.P.: Mixed computation: potential applications and problems for study. Theoretical Computer Science 18, 41–67 (1982)

9. Goertzel, B., Klimov, A.V., Klimov, A.V.: Supercompiling Java Programs, white paper (2002), http://www.supercompilers.com/white_paper.shtml

10. Jones, N.D., Gomard, C.K., Sestoft, P.: Partial Evaluation and Automatic Program Generation. Prentice-Hall, Englewood Cliffs (1993)

11. Klimov, And.V.: An approach to supercompilation for object-oriented languages: the Java Supercompiler case study. In: Nemytykh [20], pp. 43–53 (2008), http://meta2008.pereslavl.ru/accepted-papers/paper-info-4.html

12. Klimov, And.V.: JVer Project: Verification of Java programs by Java Supercompiler (2008), http://pat.keldysh.ru/jver/

13. Klimov, And.V.: A Java Supercompiler and its application to verification of cache-coherence protocols. In: Perspectives of Systems Informatics (Proc. 7th International Andrei Ershov Memorial Conference, PSI 2009), Novosibirsk, Russia, June 15-19, pp. 141–149. Ershov Institute of Informatics Systems (2009)

14. Klimov, And.V., Klimov, Ark.V., Shvorin, A.B.: The Java Supercompiler Project, http://www.supercompilers.ru

15. Klimov, Y.A.: An approach to polyvariant binding time analysis for a stack-based language. In: Nemytykh [20], pp. 78–84, http://meta2008.pereslavl.ru/accepted-papers/paper-info-6.html

16. Lisitsa, A.P., Nemytykh, A.P.: Towards verification via supercompilation. In: COMPSAC (2), pp. 9–10. IEEE Computer Society, Los Alamitos (2005)

17. Lisitsa, A.P., Nemytykh, A.P.: Experiments on verification via supercompilation (2007), http://refal.botik.ru/protocols/

18. Lisitsa, A.P., Nemytykh, A.P.: Reachability analysis in verification via supercompilation. Int. J. Found. Comput. Sci. 19(4), 953–969 (2008)

19. Nemytykh, A.P.: The supercompiler SCP4: General structure. In: Broy, Zamulin (eds.) [2], pp. 162–170

20. Nemytykh, A.P. (ed.): Proceedings of the First International Workshop on Meta-computation in Russia, July 2-5, 2008. Ailamazyan University of Pereslavl, Pereslavl-Zalessky (2008)

21. Schultz, U.P., Lawall, J.L., Consel, C.: Automatic program specialization for Java. ACM Trans. Program. Lang. Syst. 25(4), 452–499 (2003)

22. Sørensen, M.H., Glück, R.: An algorithm of generalization in positive supercompilation. In: Lloyd, J.W. (ed.) International Logic Programming Symposium, Portland, Oregon, December 4-7, pp. 465–479. MIT Press, Cambridge (1995)

23. Turchin, V.F.: The concept of a supercompiler. Transactions on Programming Languages and Systems 8(3), 292–325 (1986)

24. Turchin, V.F.: The algorithm of generalization in the supercompiler. In: Bjørner, D., Ershov, A.P., Jones, N.D. (eds.) Partial Evaluation and Mixed Computation, pp. 531–549. North-Holland, Amsterdam (1988)

25. Turchin, V.F.: Supercompilation: techniques and results. In: Bjorner, D., Broy, M., Pottosin, I.V. (eds.) PSI 1996. LNCS, vol. 1181, pp. 227–248. Springer, Heidelberg (1996)

Proving the Equivalence of Higher-Order Terms by Means of Supercompilation⋆

Ilya Klyuchnikov and Sergei Romanenko

Keldysh Institute of Applied Mathematics
Russian Academy of Sciences

Abstract. One of the applications of supercompilation is proving properties of programs. We focus in this paper on a specific task: proving term equivalence for a higher-order lazy functional language. The "classical" way to prove equivalence of two terms t1 and t2 is to write an equality function equals and to simplify the term (equals t1 t2). However, this works only when certain conditions are met. The paper presents another approach to proving term equivalence by means of supercompilation. In this approach we supercompile both terms and compare supercompiled terms syntactically. Some applications of the technique are discussed. In particular, one of these applications may lead to the development of a more powerful "higher-level" supercompiler.

1 Introduction

The functional style of programming allows developers to write modular, maintainable and elegant programs. However, these advantages do not come for free. Making use of intermediate data structure, higher-order functions, lazy evaluation and function composition may result in a significant overhead during program execution. There are a number of program transformation techniques capable of eliminating this overhead. One of them is *supercompilation*, a technique suggested by V.F. Turchin in early 1970s. Initially, supercompilation was developed as a means of optimizing programs written in a functional language Refal [18,19], but later it was reformulated in more abstract terms [5,9,14,17].
  Supercompilation is based on the following procedures:

- The construction of a labeled "process tree" that represents all possible traces of a computation process, the label (= "configuration") being a representation of the possible states of the computation.
- Decomposing and/or generalizing the configurations in order to turn the (possibly) infinite process tree into a finite graph.
- Generating the target ("residual") program from the graph.

Surprisingly, supercompilation turned out to be applicable not only to program optimization but also to program analysis and verification.

⋆ Supported by Russian Foundation for Basic Research projects No. 08-07-00280-a and No. 09-01-00834-a.

A. Pnueli, I. Virbitskaite, and A. Voronkov (Eds.): PSI 2009, LNCS 5947, pp. 193–205, 2010.
© Springer-Verlag Berlin Heidelberg 2010

Namely, transforming a program by means of a supercompiler may produce an equivalent target program, whose structure is, in a sense, "simpler" than the structure of the source program, so that some subtle properties of the source program may become readily apparent and easy to prove.

Moreover, if some knowledge may be formally expressed in terms of a program, supercompilation may be used for analyzing this knowledge and inferencing and making explicit some non-trivial, hidden facts.

Hence, supercompilation may play a role in program analysis similar to that of X-rays in radiography (at least, potentially).

It should be noted that there is a certain contradiction between the goals of program optimization and program analysis. The main goal of program optimization is to produce a program that is small and fast, but which may be absolutely unreadable for humans, being obscure, messy and ill-structured. Moreover, a program produced by an optimizer does not have to be strictly equivalent to the source one! If the source program successfully terminates for some input data and produces a meaningful result, the optimized program is certainly required to terminate and produce the same result. However, if the source program does not terminate, or terminates abnormally, the optimized program is often allowed to terminate or produce an arbitrary result (especially if this enables the optimizer to produce a faster and/or smaller target program). For example, the supercompiler SCP4 [11,12] often transforms functions extending their domains.

On the contrary, if a program transformation technique is used for program analysis, rather than program optimization, the programs produced by a transformer are not supposed to be executed. Thus, the size and execution speed of a transformed program is not a matter of great importance any more. In particular, the transformer does not have to try hard to avoid code duplication. For example, the following code

let p = f x y **in** g p q p r

can be safely transformed into this:

g (f x y) q (f x y) r

On the other hand, the preservation of program semantics may be highly desirable in cases where program transformation is used for the purposes of program analysis.

The present paper considers the problem of proving term equivalence by means of supercompilation. It is shown that some interesting classes of equivalencies can be proved by supercompiling both terms and comparing the supercompiled terms syntactically. It should be noted that this technique is applicable to languages with infinite data structures and higher-order functions. In addition, this approach does not require that a universal built-in equality predicate be present in the language.

Some applications of the technique are discussed. In particular, one of these applications may lead to the development of a more powerful supercompiler.

2 Why a Lazy Language with Higher-Order Functions?

Suppose there is some knowledge that is going to be encoded as a program, in order to be analyzed by a supercompiler. What programming language should be considered as "good" for this purpose? It could be argued that

1. The semantics of the language should be clearly defined.
2. The language should be easy for a supercompiler to deal with, especially if the supercompiler is required to strictly preserve the semantics of programs.
3. The language should be convenient for encoding knowledge as programs. In particular, infinite data structures are handy for representing infinite sequences of events and similar purposes.
4. The language should provide functions as first-class values. This is useful for formulating and proving "higher-order" assertions quantified over functions.

Since we are interested in reasoning about programs, and this is hardly possible for a language with obscure semantics, the first requirement is quite natural. Thus a functional programming language seems to be a good choice for our purposes.

The second requirement is easier to meet in the case of a lazy functional language, rather than a strict one, because many program transformation techniques (including supercompilation and deforestation) are "call-by-name" in nature. If these techniques are applied to a call-by-value language, the termination properties of programs may be violated. This, certainly, can be avoided by imposing some restrictions on input programs. For example, the termination properties are preserved by supercompilation, if the source program always terminates (see "total functional programming" [21]). Another approach is to impose certain restrictions on the transformations performed during supercompilation, which requires some additional analysis to be perform [9]. However, for the purposes of program analysis, the most straightforward solution is to just assume that the input language is a lazy one. In addition, for a lazy language the third requirement is met in a natural way.

The fourth requirement is motivated by the fact that in almost all programming languages a function's arguments are considered to be universally quantified. So a function definition can be read: for any x, y, ... If we deal with a first-order language then we can abstract over first-order data. But if we deal with a higher-order language, we can abstract over functions, too! Functions may represent rules, transformations, strategies and so forth.

In addition, there are cases where the results of supercompilation are just difficult to represent by a first-order program [16].

For the above reason, we have preferred to deal with a lazy functional language with higher-order functions.

3 HOSC: An Experimental "Higher-Order" Supercompiler

All experiments in program transformation described in the paper have been carried out by means of an experimental open-source supercompiler HOSC, dealing

$$typeDef ::= typeCon = dataCon_1 \mid ... \mid dataCon_n \qquad \text{type definition}$$
$$typeCon ::= tn\ type_1\ ...\ type_n \qquad \text{type constructor}$$
$$dataCon ::= c\ type_1\ ...\ type_n \qquad \text{data constructor}$$
$$type ::= tv \mid typeCon \mid type \rightarrow type \mid (type) \qquad \text{type expression}$$

$$prog ::= typeDef_1...typeDef_n\ e\ \textbf{where}\ f_1 = e_1...f_n = e_n \qquad \text{program}$$

$e ::= v$	variable
$\mid c\ e_1...e_n$	constructor
$\mid f$	function
$\mid \lambda v.e$	abstraction
$\mid e_0\ e_1$	application
$\mid \textbf{case}\ e_0\ \textbf{of}\ p_1 \rightarrow e_1...p_k \rightarrow e_k$	case term
$\mid \textbf{letrec}\ f = \lambda v.e\ \textbf{in}\ e$	local function
$\mid (e)$	term in parenthesis

$$p ::= c\ v_1...v_n \qquad \text{pattern}$$

where tn ranges over type names, tv ranges over type variables, c ranges over constructors.

Fig. 1. HLL grammar

with a lazy language with higher-order functions[1]. HOSC *preserves* the semantics of programs, which is *essential* for the techniques described in the paper.

HOSC transforms programs written in HLL, a simple higher-order lazy language, similar to that used by Hamilton [6,7]. HLL is typed using the Hindley-Milner polymorphic typing system.

A program in HLL consists of a number of data type definitions, a term to be evaluated and a set of function definitions (see Fig. 1).

A left-hand side of a data type definition is a type name (more precisely, a type constructor name) followed by a list of type variables. The right-hand side consists of one or more constructor declarations.

The grammar of HLL is shown in Fig. 1. A term is either a variable, a constructor, a lambda abstraction, an application, a case term, a local function definition or a term in parenthesis. A function definition binds a variable to a lambda abstraction. The intended operational semantics of HLL is the normal-order graph reduction to a weak head normal form. The data analysis is performed by pattern matching with constructors in case terms (as in [17]).

A term in HLL may contain free variables and local function definitions.

Note that the construct **where** is only a syntactic sugar, since the function definitions can always be transformed to **letrec**-s and moved to the term preceding **where**. Hence, any program is essentially a single term (plus a number of type declarations), so that there is no difference between transforming a term and transforming a program. In particular, the equivalence of programs is just the equivalence of terms.

---

[1] See the HOSC web-application and the sources at http://hosc.appspot.com

4 Proving Term Equivalence

4.1 Proving Properties of Terms by Supercompilation

As shown by Turchin [19,20], some properties of programs can be proved by program transformation. For example, suppose there is a function f (represented as a program), and we want to prove that, for any input x, the result returned by f satisfies some property p. Then we may encode p as a program, and try to "simplify" the term $p(f(x))$ by means of a supercompiler. If the structure of the supercompiled term is trivial, so that it can be readily seen that the evaluation of the term never returns **False** and always terminates, we can conclude that the source term $p(f(x))$ always returns **True**. Therefore, the result of evaluating $f(x)$ always satisfies the property p.

The fruitfulness of this approach has been recently shown by Lisitsa and Nemythykh [12], who have succeeded in verifying a number of cache coherence protocols by means of the supercompiler SCP4.

4.2 Equality-Based Approach to Proving Term Equivalence

As pointed out by Turchin [18], proving the equivalence of two terms t1 and t2 can be reduced to proving a property of a single term. Namely, if equals is a function testing values for equality, we can compose the term equals t1 t2 and supercompile it to see whether it always returns **True**.

Consider the program in Fig. 2 in which the function plus takes two natural numbers (in unary system) and returns their sum. We want to prove that

equals (plus (S x) y) (plus x (S y))

or, in more "mathematical" notation, that

$$(x + 1) + y = x + (y + 1)$$

The result of supercompiling the program is shown in Fig. 3. It can be readily seen that the supercompiled program never returns **False**. However, there remain a few subtle points concerning such kind of reasoning!

4.3 Restrictions and Drawbacks of the Equality-Based Approach

Suppose the term equals t1 t2 never returns **False**. Does it mean that t1 and t2 are really "equivalent"?

It depends on what is understood by "equivalence". The "equality-based" approach to proving term equivalence is based on a number of assumptions:

1. There exists a built-in equality function equals, or, at least, equals can be defined for the values returned by t1 and t2.
2. All data structures involved are finite.
3. The evaluation of t1 and t2 always terminates.

Assumption 1 is usually true of first-order strict languages (like Refal [18,12]). However, in the case of a higher-order language there arise some problems, because t1 and t2 may return functional values, which are impossible to test for equality.

```
data number = Z | S number
data boolean = True | False

equals (plus (S x) y) (plus x (S y)) where

plus = λx.λy.
    case x of
        Z → y
        S x1 → S (plus x1 y)

equals = λx.λy.
    case x of
        Z →
            case y of
                Z → True
                S y1 → False
        S x1 →
            case y of
                Z → False
                S y1 → equals x1 y1
```

Fig. 2. Proving $(x + 1) + y = x + (y + 1)$: the source program

```
data number = Z | S number
data boolean = True | False

letrec f = λp2.λr2.
    case p2 of
        Z → letrec g = λs2.
                    case s2 of
                        Z → True
                        S w → g w
                in g r2
        S p1 → f p1 r2
in f x y
```

Fig. 3. Proving $(x + 1) + y = x + (y + 1)$: the supercompiled program

Assumption 2 is not automatically true in the case of a lazy language (even a first-order one).

Assumption 3 may not be true in many interesting cases. For example, if t1 and t2 deal with infinite data structures and, by necessity, never terminate, but are still "equivalent" (i.e. have the same "meaning" according to the language's semantics).

4.4 Normalization-Based Approach to Proving Term Equivalence

In order to get rid of dealing with equality predicates, we need an alternative, more general, definition of term equivalence. Thus, the "contextual equivalence", as defined by Pitt [15], seems to be a reasonable choice:

Loosely speaking, two expressions M and M' of a programming language are contextually equivalent if any occurrences of M and M' in complete programs can be interchanged without affecting the results of executing the programs.

In particular, the above definition implies that two programs are trivially equivalent, if they are "syntactically isomorphic" (i.e. identical, modulo some trivial renaming and/or rearranging of the constructs appearing in the program).

Let $A \Rightarrow_{sc} A'$ mean that A' is semantically equivalent to A and can be produced by supercompiling A, or, in other words, $\Rightarrow_{sc}$ is a "supercompilation relation" (as defined by Klimov [10]).

Let $\approx$ denote equivalence and $\cong$ "syntactic isomorphism" of programs. Then the following holds:

$$A \Rightarrow_{sc} A' \qquad B \Rightarrow_{sc} B' \qquad A' \cong B'$$
$$A \approx B$$

Or, in plain words, if supercompiling A and B results in producing essentially the same residual program, then A and B are equivalent.

Thus, supercompilation can be seen as transformation that, in a sense, "normalizes" terms. Some other program transformation techniques can also be considered as normalizing ones [1,2,3,4].

Note that the general idea of proving equivalence by normalization is a well-known one, being a standard technique in such fields as computer algebra. The idea of using supercompilation for normalization is due to Lisitsa and Webster [13], who have successfully applied supercompilation for proving the equivalence of programs written in a first-order functional language, provided that the programs deal with finite input data and are guaranteed to terminate.

We argue that this techinque is also applicable to higher-order functional programs, even if they deal with inifinite data structures and do not terminate for some inputs.

Let us consider the program in Fig. 4 containing definitions of a few well-known functions over lists. Supercompiling the term `map (compose f g) xs` produces the program shown in Fig. 5. On the other hand, supercompiling the term `(compose (map f) (map g)) xs` results in the same residual program (modulo alpha renaming)! Hence, we have proved that the following holds

```
map (compose f g) xs = (compose (map f)(map g)) xs
```

for all `f`, `g`, and `xs` that are allowed by the type system of the language HLL. Note that this statement holds for all lists `xs` including infinite lists and $\perp$, whose elements may be quite exotic: first-order values, functions, data trees, or $\perp$. Also note that the functions `f` and `g` do not have to terminate.

Therefore, the normalization-based approach enables us to prove statements that are even impossible to formulate in terms of the equality-based approach!

```
data List a = Nil | Cons a (List a)
data Boolean = True | False
data Pair a b = P a b

compose = λf.λg.λx.f (g x)
unit = λx.Cons x Nil
rep = λxs. append xs
abs = λf. f Nil
iterate = λf.λx. Cons x (iterate f (f x))
fp = λp1.λp2.
    case p1 of P a1 a2 →
        case p2 of P b1 b2 → P (a1 b1) (a2 b2)

map = λf.λxs.
    case xs of
        Nil → Nil
        Cons x1 xs1 → Cons (f x1) (map f xs1)

join = λxs.
    case xs of
        Nil → Nil
        Cons x1 xs1 → append x1 (join xs1)

append = λxs.λys.
    case xs of
        Nil → ys
        Cons x1 xs1 → Cons x1 (append xs1 ys)

idList = λxs.
    case xs of
        Nil → Nil
        Cons x1 xs1 → Cons x1 (idList xs1)

filter = λp.λxs.
    case xs of
        Nil → Nil
        Cons x xs1 →
            case p x of
                True → Cons x (filter p xs1)
                False → filter p xs1

zip = λp.case p of P xs ys →
    case xs of
        Nil → Nil
        Cons x1 xs1 →
                case ys of
                    Nil → Nil
                    Cons y1 ys1 → Cons (P x1 y1) (zip (P xs1 ys1))
```

Fig. 4. Example functions over lists

```
data List a = Nil | Cons a (List a)
letrec
  h = λys.
    case ys of
      Nil → Nil
      Cons y1 ys1 → Cons (f (g y1)) (h ys1)
in
  h xs
```

Fig. 5. Supercompilation of *map* (*compose f g*) *xs*

The authors have implemented an equivalence checker based on term normalization and built on top of the specializer HOSC. Following are a number of sample equivalences that have been automatically proved by the checker:

```
compose (map f) unit = compose unit f
compose (map f) join = compose join (map (map f))
append (map f xs) (map f ys) = map f (append xs ys)
append (append xs ys) zs = append xs (append ys zs)
filter p (map f xs) = map f (filter (compose p f) xs)
iterate f (f x) = map f (iterate f x)
map (compose f g) xs = (compose (map f)(map g)) xs
rep (append xs ys) zs = (compose (rep xs) (rep ys)) zs
(compose abs rep) xs = idList xs
map (fp (P f g)) (zip (P x y)) = zip (fp (P (map f) (map g)) (P x y))
append r (Cons p ps) =
  case (append r (Cons p Nil)) of
    Nil → ps
    Cons v vs → Cons v (append vs ps)
```

Note that some of the above equivalences are instances of Wadler's "free theorems" [22,8].

Given the program in Fig. 2, the associativity of addition can be proved by supercompiling both sides of the equation

```
plus (plus x y) z = plus x (plus y z)
```

One might expect that the commutativity of addition

```
plus x y = plus y x
```

could be proved in the same way. However, this is not the case, just because the conjecture is not true! The language HLL is a lazy one, for which reason plus (S Z) $\perp$ = (S $\perp$), but plus $\perp$ (S Z) = $\perp$.

5   Applications of the Technique

5.1   Generating Sets of Equivalent Terms

Since the set of all terms is recursively enumerable, it is possible to write a generator automatically producing sets of equivalent terms. A straightforward procedure may look as follows.

First, a potentially infinite sequence of term can be generated, the terms being ordered according to their size. Then the sequence of terms can be filtered, in order for the terms that are not well-typed to be rejected. Then the well-typed terms can be "normalized" by supercompiling them, and partitioned into equivalence classes by comparing their "normalized" versions.

Certainly, the above procedure is not "complete", because term equivalence is, in general, undecidable. Hence, for any given supercompiler, some equivalences will not be proved by supercompilation. However, an important point is that the above procedure is capable of automatically *discovering* equivalences, rather than just proving them.

5.2   Term Equivalence and Higher-Level Supercompilation

As has been shown above, given a supercompiler, a library of term equivalences can be generated. And this library can be used for increasing the power of supercompilation. In other words, we can build a "higher-level" supercompiler using a "classic" supercompiler as a "lower-level" building block.

Namely, if a "classic" supercompiler encounters two configurations A and B, such that A is homeomorphically embedded into B, the supercompiler tries to fold B to A. This is possible, if B is an instance of A. Otherwise, the supercompiler has to throw B away and replace A with a more general configuration, which may lead to "over-generalization".

However, given a library of equations, a "higher-level" supercompiler may replace B with an equivalent configuration B' that is an instance of A, so that B' can be folded to A.

As an example, let us consider supercompiling a naïve definition of the function `reverse` into one with an accumulating parameter (which is more efficient).

Let us try supercompiling the following term:

```
append (reverse xs) ys
```

After unfolding we get:

$$
\begin{array}{ll}
case \; \texttt{reverse xs} \; of & \\
\quad \texttt{Nil} \; \rightarrow \texttt{ys} & \qquad (1) \\
\quad \texttt{Cons x3 x4} \; \rightarrow \texttt{Cons x3 (append x4 ys)} &
\end{array}
$$

Further unfolding results in:

$$
\begin{array}{ll}
case & \\
\quad case \; \texttt{xs} \; of & \\
\qquad \texttt{Nil} \; \rightarrow \texttt{Nil} & \\
\qquad \texttt{Cons x5 x6} \; \rightarrow \texttt{append (reverse x6) (Cons x5 Nil)} & \qquad (2) \\
of & \\
\quad \texttt{Nil} \; \rightarrow \texttt{ys} & \\
\quad \texttt{Cons x3 x4} \; \rightarrow \texttt{Cons x3 (append x4 ys)} &
\end{array}
$$

Now we have to split the configuration by considering two cases: `xs = Nil` and `xs = Cons x5 x6`. If `xs = Nil`, the configuration is reduced to `ys`, and, in the second case, it is transformed into

```
data List a = Nil | Cons (List a)

letrec reverse1 = λxs1.λys1.
    case xs1 of
        Nil → ys1
        Cons x2 xs2 → reverse1 xs2 (Cons x2 ys1)
in
  reverse1 xs ys
```

Fig. 6. Higher-level supercompilation of append (reverse xs) ys

```
case append (reverse x6) (Cons x5 Nil) of
    Nil → ys
    Cons x3 x4 → Cons x3 (append x4 ys)
```
(3)

The term (3) embeds the term (1), without being an instance of (1). Hence, a "classical" supercompiler would have to generalize (1). But the generalization can be avoided by using the following equation

```
append r (Cons p ps) =
case (append r (Cons p Nil)) of
    Nil → ps
    Cons v vs → Cons v (append vs ps)
```
(4)

Note that this equation can be proved by term normalization.

Applying the substitution $\{r = \text{reverse x6}, p = \text{x5}, ps = \text{ys}\}$ to the above equality, we can replace the term (3) with the equivalent term

```
append (reverse x6) (Cons x5 ys)
```

which is an instance of the initial term append (reverse xs) ys. Hence, a folding can be performed, to produce the final result of this "higher-level" supercompilation shown in Fig. 6.

Therefore, the following equation has been proved

```
append (reverse xs) ys = reverse1 xs ys.
```

which implies that

```
reverse xs = append (reverse xs) Nil = reverse1 xs Nil.
```

The original definition of **reverse** was quadratic in the length of xs, while the transformed one is linear. Hence, the proposed technique is capable of producing results similar to those achieved by "distillation", another approach to "higher-level" supercompilation suggested by Hamilton [6].

6   Conclusions

We have shown that the equivalence of terms can be proved by means of supercompilation without the use of an equality predicate, which makes the technique applicable to lazy languages with higher-order functions. The techniques can be used to increase the power of supercompilation, to achieve the results similar to distillation, which is another approach to "higher-level" supercompilation.

Acknowledgements

An early version of this work was presented as a talk at Copenhagen Programming Language Seminar at DIKU, and we would like to thank Robert Glück, Torben Mogensen and Andrzej Filinski for their useful comments and inspiring advices. The authors are also grateful to Geoff Hamilton, as well as Andrei Klimov and other participants of Refal Seminars at Keldysh Istitute of Applied Mathematics for fruitful discussions.

References

1. Albert, E., Vidal, G.: The narrowing-driven approach to functional logic program specialization. New Generation Computing 20(1), 3–26 (2002)
2. Alpuente, M., Falaschi, M., Vidal, G.: Partial evaluation of functional logic programs. ACM Transactions on Programming Languages and Systems (TOPLAS) 20(4), 768–844 (1998)
3. Cockett, R.: Deforestation, program transformation, and cut-elimination. Electronic Notes in Theoretical Computer Science 44(1), 88–127 (2001)
4. Dybjer, P., Filinski, A.: Normalization and partial evaluation. In: Barthe, G., Dybjer, P., Pinto, L., Saraiva, J. (eds.) APPSEM 2000. LNCS, vol. 2395, pp. 137–192. Springer, Heidelberg (2002)
5. Glück, R., Klimov, A.V.: Occam's razor in metacompuation: the notion of a perfect process tree. In: Cousot, P., Filé, G., Falaschi, M., Rauzy, A. (eds.) WSA 1993. LNCS, vol. 724, pp. 112–123. Springer, Heidelberg (1993)
6. Hamilton, G.W.: Distillation: extracting the essence of programs. In: Proceedings of the 2007 ACM SIGPLAN symposium on Partial evaluation and semantics-based program manipulation, pp. 61–70. ACM Press, New York (2007)
7. Hamilton, G.W., Kabir, M.H.: Constructing programs from metasystem transition proofs. In: Proceedings of the First International Workshop on Metacomputation in Russia (2008)
8. Holst, C.K., Hughes, J.: Towards binding-time improvement for free. In: Functional Programming, Workshops in Computing, Glasgow. Springer, Heidelberg (1990)
9. Jonsson, P.A.: Positive supercompilation for a higher-order call-by-value language. Luleå University of Technology (2008)
10. Klimov, A.V.: A program specialization relation based on supercompilation and its properties. In: Proceedings of the First International Workshop on Metacomputation in Russia, pp. 54–78. Ailamazyan University of Pereslavl (2008)
11. Lisitsa, A., Nemytykh, A.P.: Reachability analysis in verification via supercompilation. International Journal of Foundations of Computer Science 19(4), 953–969 (2008)
12. Lisitsa, A.P., Nemytykh, A.P.: Verification as a parameterized testing (experiments with the scp4 supercompiler). Programming and Computer Software 33(1), 14–23 (2007)

13. Lisitsa, A.P., Webster, M.: Supercompilation for equivalence testing in metamorphic computer viruses detection. In: Proceedings of the First International Workshop on Metacomputation in Russia. Ailamazyan University of Pereslavl (2008)
14. Mitchell, N., Runciman, C.: A supercompiler for core haskell. In: Chitil, O., Horváth, Z., Zsók, V. (eds.) IFL 2007. LNCS, vol. 5083, pp. 147–164. Springer, Heidelberg (2008)
15. Pitts, A.M.: Operationally-based theories of program equivalence. In: Semantics and Logics of Computation, pp. 241–298 (1997)
16. Romanenko, S.A.: Higher-order functions as a substitute for partial evaluation. In: Proceedings of the First International Workshop on Metacomputation in Russia. Ailamazyan University of Pereslavl (2008)
17. Sørensen, M.H., Glück, R., Jones, N.D.: A positive supercompiler. Journal of Functional Programming 6(6), 811–838 (1993)
18. Turchin, V.F.: The Language Refal: The Theory of Compilation and Metasystem Analysis. Department of Computer Science, Courant Institute of Mathematical Sciences, New York University (1980)
19. Turchin, V.F.: The concept of a supercompiler. ACM Transactions on Programming Languages and Systems (TOPLAS) 8(3), 292–325 (1986)
20. Turchin, V.F.: Metacomputation: Metasystem transitions plus supercompilation. In: Danvy, O., Thiemann, P., Glück, R. (eds.) Dagstuhl Seminar 1996. LNCS, vol. 1110, pp. 481–509. Springer, Heidelberg (1996)
21. Turner, D.A.: Total functional programming. Journal of Universal Computer Science 10(7), 751–768 (2004)
22. Wadler, P.: Theorems for free! In: FPCA 1989: Proceedings of the fourth international conference on Functional programming languages and computer architecture, pp. 347–359. ACM, New York (1989)

Unifying the Semantics of UML 2
State, Activity and Interaction Diagrams

Jens Kohlmeyer and Walter Guttmann

Universität Ulm, 89069 Ulm, Germany
jens.kohlmeyer@uni-ulm.de, walter.guttmann@uni-ulm.de

Abstract. We define a formal semantics of the combined use of UML 2 state machines, activities and interactions using Abstract State Machines. The behaviour of software models can henceforth be specified by composing these diagrams, choosing the most adequate formalism at each level of abstraction. We present several reasonable ways to link different kinds of diagrams and illustrate them by examples. We also give a formal semantics of communication between these diagrams. The resulting rules reveal unclear parts of the UML specification and serve as a basis for tool support.

1 Introduction

Ideally, software development proceeds continuously from requirements through specification to implementation, using an integrated formalism, method and tool set. The state-of-the-art proposal aiming at such an integrated approach is to use Model Driven Development as the method and the Unified Modelling Language (UML) [17] as the formalism.

In this paper, we focus on behaviour aspects of software systems. They are represented by several UML language units describing state machines, activities and interactions, as detailed in Section 2. Each type of diagram is useful by itself, offering different facilities to exhibit different properties of a system: State machines emphasise the changes made to a system's state due to the occurrence of events, activities emphasise control and data flow, and interactions emphasise the sequence of messages between the lifelines of objects.

While the UML can be profitably used to describe requirements and specifications, one of its shortcomings is the lack of a precise semantics. This has been addressed in recent years by research formalising the semantics of state diagrams [1,2,5,10], activity diagrams [8,16,19,20] and sequence diagrams [6,15,21]. The frameworks used include Abstract State Machines, graph transformations and basic formalisms such as relations and traces. A semantics of class diagrams is usually implicit, since behaviour applies to objects in the UML. For a detailed discussion of these and further approaches, see [14].

Hence the current state is that formal semantics have been separately defined for the various kinds of diagrams specifying behaviour. What is notably missing, however, is a semantics describing their combined use. This may be due to the

A. Pnueli, I. Virbitskaite, and A. Voronkov (Eds.): PSI 2009, LNCS 5947, pp. 206–217, 2010.
© Springer-Verlag Berlin Heidelberg 2010

fact that the UML specification itself is not very elaborate about this issue, but already the name *Unified* Modelling Language aims at such an integrated use. It is time to give the UML a *unified* semantics.

We use Abstract State Machines (ASM) [3] to define the semantics. ASMs have been used to formalise the semantics of several programming and specification languages, including the UML diagrams for behaviour we are interested in. We can therefore base our unifying work on the existing specifications. At the same time, the resulting ASM rules are precise, comprehensible and executable.

We investigate all UML behaviour diagrams and identify various means to compose them. We formalise the semantics of composition by adding new ASM rules and by modifying appropriate parts of the established ASM specifications. The new rules coordinate the instantiation of the different UML diagrams, the computation of their respective context, and their interplay by communication. We thus achieve an integrated semantics of UML behaviour.

ASMs and the UML language units are briefly introduced in Section 2. In Section 3 we discuss a number of ways to combine different kinds of diagrams and define the corresponding semantics using ASM rules. The communication aspect is elaborated in Section 4.

Our formalisation is high-level enough to reveal problematic issues concerning the UML specification, as we discuss throughout the paper. Besides the exposure of semantical problems, the benefits of a precise semantics are numerous. Among other things, it reduces the space for interpretation and thus clarifies the meaning of models. It also serves as a (necessary) foundation for the implementation of tools supporting model execution, code generation and automated reasoning. For the first time, these advantages are obtained for models combining different kinds of behaviour specifications as intended by the UML.

The present paper extends [13] by the following new contributions. We systematically derive and discuss each of the different ways to compose behaviour, present the corresponding ASM rules in detail, and give examples. We moreover describe the semantics of communication.

2   Basics

In this section we describe the UML language units dealing with the behaviour of software systems, and Abstract State Machines [3] as far as required to understand the rules in this paper. By writing UML we mean UML 2.1.2 as specified in [17] unless stated otherwise.

Higher-level behavioural formalisms of the UML are based on its language unit Common Behaviors, and extended in the units Activities, State Machines and Interactions. Additional units related to behaviour are Actions and Use Cases.

The *Common Behaviors* language unit comprises three subpackages. The BasicBehavior subpackage describes behaviour as the change of an associated context object. In all other respects, behaviour is left abstract, with activities, state machines and interactions as concrete instances. This abstraction is the key to compose behaviour specified by different kinds of diagrams, as detailed in Section 3.1. The Communications subpackage provides the core structure for signal handling and operation calls. It is the basis for our treatment of communication in Section 4. The SimpleTime subpackage is relevant for the semantics of the individual behaviour diagrams, but has no impact on the present paper.

Activity diagrams coordinate lower-level behaviours by specifying their dependences and the allowed execution sequences. They are composed of basic actions connected by edges to indicate (possibly concurrent) control and object flow. Parameterised actions send and receive signals, and invoke behaviour specified elsewhere, for example, in other diagrams. Edges connecting actions may pass through control nodes (decision, merge, fork, join) that coordinate the flows in an activity diagram. Interruptible activity regions support the termination of parts of an activity diagram. Our unifying work uses the ASM semantics of UML 2.0 activities in [19] that sequences actions based on a token flow [20].

State diagrams model discrete behaviour by specifying the states of a system and the transitions between the states. Transitions are triggered by events, resulting in the change of state and the execution of associated behaviour. States may be composed of (orthogonal) subregions and (hierarchical) submachines. Our unifying work uses the ASM semantics of UML 1.4 state machines in [2] extended to UML 2.0 by [9].

We treat the 'most common variant' [17] of *interactions*, namely sequence diagrams. They show how several objects communicate by means of messages. An object's lifeline orders the occurrences of events that include sending and receiving messages, creating and destroying objects, and executing behaviour. In contrast to state machines and activities, which describe behaviour performed by an object, interactions describe *emergent behaviour* resulting from the participant objects. Our unifying work uses the ASM semantics of UML 2.0 sequence diagrams developed in [11].

UML *use case diagrams* capture the high-level requirements of a system, but do not specify behaviour on their own. They are instead linked to behaviour specified by the above language units. UML *actions* specify low-level transformations on the state of the system, and are modelled independently of the behaviours (primarily activities) containing them. Hence an action is likewise not a behaviour on its own. Because of these reasons, it is unnecessary to specially consider use cases and actions for the purposes of this paper.

We have adapted the existing ASM semantics to the same UML version 2.1.2. The modifications necessary to integrate the various diagrams are described in Sections 3.2–3.5 and 4.

The ASMs, used to formalise the semantics of the UML language units, can be read as 'pseudo-code over abstract data' [3]. An ASM comprises transition rules operating on a state composed of functions defined over a base set. The update rule $f(s_1, \ldots, s_n) := t$ modifies the value of f at $(s_1, \ldots, s_n)$ to t. Further constructs include abstractions using **let** ... **in**, multiway conditionals, and rule calls with call-by-name semantics. The rule **forall** x **with** φ **do** R executes R in parallel for each x satisfying φ. The rule **choose** x **with** φ **do** R chooses some x satisfying φ and then executes R. Updates accumulated by these rules are performed in parallel unless sequentialised by **seq**.

In our work we use asynchronous multi-agent ASMs, allowing the concurrent execution of several ASM agents. Each performs its own rules as described above, and they communicate by shared functions. Further details of ASMs, including an operational semantics, are provided by [3].

3 Formal Semantics for Combining Language Units

Before we detail the ways to combine behaviour specifications, we briefly describe our general approach to the semantics of UML. The ASM rules need to access the concrete diagrams of the model whose semantics they define. To this end, we translate the UML syntax, also called the 'meta model', to static ASM domains (for classes) and functions (for attributes and associations). They are initialised to yield the particular values corresponding to the concrete model. Monitored ASM functions are used for information determined by the environment. Individual executions of behaviour are represented by asynchronous multi-agent ASMs. To model their interaction and signal handling, we use shared ASM domains and functions. The semantics is then specified by ASM rules acting on these functions such as those we describe in the following. Further details of this approach are provided in [19], and the complete set of rules in [14].

3.1 Combining Behaviour Specifications

In this section we systematically derive several different ways to combine activities, interactions and state machines. To this end, we investigate the UML meta model, looking for the places where the abstract class Behavior is used to specify behaviour. This way we identify the possible means to combine behaviour, which is then realised by specialising the abstract Behavior to the concrete classes Activity, Interaction or StateMachine.

We find that the occurrences of Behavior fall into two categories. First, behaviour is used for elementary data processing: Data is passed to the behaviour, which is expected to have no side effects; it produces a result that is further processed. Examples are the selection and transformation of tokens at object nodes and flows and decision nodes in activities, and the reduction of a collection by ReduceAction. Typically, this processing is low-level and will be described by code rather than another diagram. The code is easily integrated by specifying the computation directly as an ASM rule or in a language with ASM semantics such as Java or C♯.

Second, behaviour is invoked that can make full use of UML's specification facilities. In this case, we can distinguish the calling and the called behaviour. Typically, the called behaviour is specified by a diagram as discussed in the following. If it is low-level, it may also be given by code and integrated as above.

In principle, each kind of diagram can be used independently to specify the caller and the callee. In practice, it is problematic to call interactions, since they specify emergent behaviour [17, page 482]. This kind of behaviour results from the interaction of all participant objects and is not performed by a particular object [17, page 419]. Hence in general it is not meaningful to let a given object call emergent behaviour. We will investigate this issue in further work, but do not allow interactions to be called in the present paper. However, interactions may appear as the caller, for example, to specify test scenarios as in Section 3.5. For the callee, we are thus left with activities and state machines, and we now argue that these two diagrams can indeed be called from activities, interactions and state machines.

Let us exemplify this argument for state machines as the caller by considering the relevant part of the UML meta model [17, page 525]. It clearly shows that a behaviour may be associated to a state as its entry, exit and do-activity, as well as the effect of a transition. The intended meaning of these behaviours is described by the UML specification in text form. Each of these behaviours can independently be specified as an activity or as a state machine, since they specialise the abstract class Behavior.

We carry out the same procedure for activities and interactions to identify their possible combinations. For activities, we obtain that behaviour is attached to CallBehaviorAction [17, page 245]. This kind of action may be used in activity diagrams, for example, for hierarchical decomposition. For interactions, we obtain that behaviour can be associated to BehaviorExecutionSpecification [17, page 467]. This is a specialisation of InteractionFragment, whose instances are the (partially ordered) constituents of interactions.

We have thus identified the ways to compose UML behaviour diagrams. In the following section, we formalise the calling mechanism of diagrams. It is applied to formally define the semantics of calling behaviour from activities, state machines and interactions, respectively, in Sections 3.3–3.5.

3.2   Calling Mechanism

In the existing ASM semantics of UML behaviour diagrams, there is just one place describing the invocation of behaviour specified by a diagram: The calling of an activity from an activity by a CallBehaviorAction [19]. We abstract the calling mechanism from that description and generalise it to other kinds of diagrams for the caller and the callee. The resulting ASM rule takes as arguments the called behaviour, its context object, its parameters and a flag indicating whether the call is synchronous or asynchronous. Observe that these arguments resemble the ingredients of calling mechanisms in programming languages.

$\text{STARTBEHAVIOUR}(behaviour, context, input, isSynch) \equiv$
    case *behaviour* **in**
        Activity: **if** *behaviour.isSingleExecution* $\land$ *isRunning*(*behaviour*)
                then $\text{RECALL}(behaviour, input)$
                else $\text{CALL}(\text{ACTIVITY}(behaviour, context, input))$
        StateMachine: $\text{CALL}(\text{STATEMACHINE}(behaviour, context, input))$
        Interaction: $\text{CALL}(\text{INTERACTION}(behaviour, input))$
    if *isSynch* **then** *Self.mode* := waiting **else** *Self.mode* := completed

For activities, we distinguish if an existing execution is used or a new one created according to the isSingleExecution attribute [17, page 317]. In the former case, treated by the rule RECALL, we notify the already running execution that new input tokens are available using the internal *StartEvent*. In the remaining cases of STARTBEHAVIOUR, the rule CALL creates a new agent executing the corresponding handler from the ASM semantics for the individual diagrams.

$$\begin{array}{ll}
\text{RECALL}(\textit{activity}, \textit{input}) \equiv & \text{CALL}(\textit{rule}) \equiv \\
\quad \textbf{let } \textit{exec} = \textit{agent}(\textit{activity}) \textbf{ in} & \quad \textbf{let } \textit{exec} = \textit{new}(\textit{Agent}) \textbf{ in} \\
\quad \textit{exec.callers} := \textit{exec.callers} \cup \{\textit{Self}\} & \quad \textit{exec.callers} := \{\textit{Self}\} \\
\quad \text{ADDEVENT}(\textit{exec}, \textit{StartEvent}(\textit{input})) & \quad \text{ASM}(\textit{exec}) := \textit{rule} \\
\quad \textit{Self.calledExec} := \textit{exec} & \quad \textit{Self.calledExec} := \textit{exec}
\end{array}$$

The called behaviour is informed about its callers. This is necessary so that they can be notified about termination even in the case of asynchronous calls (this mechanism is used, for example, to implement the so-called completion transitions in state machines). If the call is synchronous, we put the calling agent into a mode waiting for the called execution to terminate.

Let us finally point to the absence of the context object for interactions in the rule STARTBEHAVIOUR. This reflects the fact that they specify emergent behaviour of several participating objects, as discussed in Section 3.1. Although interactions cannot be called from other diagrams, they are included in STARTBEHAVIOUR to set up the behaviour of the initial objects when the modelled system is started. To this end, we assume that interactions are instantiated as objects and thus run in their own context [17, page 430].

$$\begin{array}{l}
\text{INITIALISEBEHAVIOUR} \equiv \\
\quad \textbf{forall } \textit{object} \textbf{ with } \textit{object} \in \textit{BehaviouredObject} \textbf{ do} \\
\quad\quad \text{STARTBEHAVIOUR}(\textit{object.classOf.classifierBehaviour}, \textit{object}, \emptyset, \textit{false})
\end{array}$$

In the initial case, there are no parameters and the calls are asynchronous since all initial objects act concurrently.

We have thus established the mechanism to call diagrams, namely the rule STARTBEHAVIOUR. It allows for a simple integration of further kind of behaviour having an ASM semantics. The following sections implement the calling of behaviour by this mechanism. To abort a called behaviour, we adapt the termination mechanisms described in [19,9].

3.3   Calling Behaviours from Activities

As our running example, we use a simplified model of an MP3 music player whose behaviour is specified in Figure 1.

The general behaviour is modelled by the activity diagram on the left: Its first action shows a welcome message on the display, then the user can simultaneously edit the play list with the action EditList and listen to music with the action PlayMusic. These actions are instances of CallBehaviorAction, detailed in further UML diagrams. The behaviour EditList is modelled by an (omitted) activity diagram. The calling of activities from activities is described in [19].

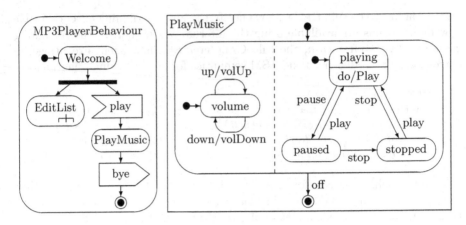

Fig. 1. Simplified MP3 player

In this paper we focus on the right path of the activity diagram which specifies the playing of music. If the play signal is received – generated by the environment, for example, by the user pressing a button – a CallBehaviorAction is executed which activates the behaviour PlayMusic. In our model, this is adequately specified as a state machine on the right of Figure 1. It contains two regions which model the behaviour of volume control and playing music.

The ASM rule EXECUTECALLBEHAVIOURACTION handles the calls of other behaviours. For space reasons we only show the parts of the rule which are relevant for calling another behaviour. The detailed semantics of CallBehaviorAction can be found in [19].

EXECUTECALLBEHAVIOURACTION ≡ ...
  if $Self.mode =$ enabled **then**
    let $cTag = tagValue(Self.node,$ CallContext, context$)$ **in**
      if $cTag = undefined$
        then $context := Self.activityExecution.context$
        else $context := computeContext(Self.activityExecution.context, cTag)$
  seq
  STARTBEHAVIOUR$(Self.node.behaviour, context,$
    $\{(pinToParameter(n), ts) \mid (n, ts) \in Self.input\}, Self.node.isSynchronous)$
  if $Self.mode =$ waiting **then** ...

At first the context object of the called behaviour is computed. This is left unclear by the UML specification [17, page 429], since the called behaviour is not owned by the CallBehaviorAction. We therefore add a context tag as in [19] from which the context is computed. If the tag is not defined, the context of the caller is used. The function $pinToParameter$ maps the inputs, which are provided by the input pins of the calling action, to the parameters of the called behaviour. With these arguments we start the associated behaviour. The waiting mode of the rule waits for the termination of synchronous calls.

In the MP3 player the context of the called state machine is the activity's context. The state machine can thus access attributes of the context object. No parameters are passed and the call is synchronous by default, hence the calling activity waits until the state machine terminates.

The behaviour within the playing state of the MP3 player (do-activity) is specified by the activity diagram Play, not detailed here. Calling activities from state machines is described next.

3.4   Calling Behaviours from State Machines

The state machine on the right of Figure 1 is interpreted by an ASM agent, called 'top agent'. As soon as the composite state is reached, another two agents are started to interpret the orthogonal regions. As described in Section 3.1, calling behaviours from state machines can occur during (internal or external) transitions or when entering, exiting or being in a state. Each agent holds the currently active states and executes the rules required to perform transitions and to call behaviours in its region. Transitions must be performed atomically, including any behaviour invoked while they take place. We can therefore no longer use the rules of [2] since these apply to UML 1.4, which allowed only actions, not behaviours to be executed. To ensure atomic transitions, we introduce appropriate modes for the ASM agents.

First, we select one of the available events and a corresponding, enabled transition. This is done by the selecting and preparing modes of the rule PERFORM-TRANSITION, which we discuss in Section 4. Second, we carry out the selected transition. If it is internal, only its effect has to be executed. In general, the transition crosses several state boundaries, hence a number of steps must be taken to execute the exit, effect and entry behaviours in the given order. Moreover, the running do-activities of the left nodes must be aborted, and new do-activities initiated after each state is entered. The correct sequence of these tasks is delivered iteratively by the rule NEXTTASK, updating the current state and task.

$$
\begin{aligned}
&\text{PERFORMTRANSITION} \equiv \dots \\
&\quad \textbf{if } \textit{Self.mode} = \mathsf{running} \textbf{ then} \\
&\qquad \textbf{case } \textit{currentTask} \textbf{ of} \\
&\qquad\quad \mathsf{exit:}\quad \text{EXIT}(\textit{currentState}) \qquad\quad \mathsf{do:}\quad \text{DO}(\textit{currentState}) \\
&\qquad\quad \mathsf{effect:}\quad \text{EFFECT}(\textit{currentTrans}) \qquad \mathsf{finish:}\ \text{FINISH}(\textit{currentTrans}) \\
&\qquad\quad \mathsf{entry:}\quad \text{ENTRY}(\textit{currentState}) \qquad\qquad\quad \textit{Self.mode} := \mathsf{selecting} \\
&\qquad\quad \text{NEXTTASK}
\end{aligned}
$$

Besides doing the necessary book-keeping, the rules EXIT, EFFECT, ENTRY and DO call the annotated behaviour. We first discuss EFFECT; the rules EXIT and ENTRY are similar. In our example it is invoked when the events up or down trigger a transition in the volume state, and hence the behaviour volUp or volDown. This is performed by a synchronous call since transitions are atomic. In contrast to activities, the context object is clearly specified by the UML as the context of the calling state machine. The parameters are obtained by the monitored function *getEffectParam*, since this is left open by the UML [17, page 574].

$$\text{EFFECT}(trans) \equiv$$
$$\textbf{let } context = trans.container.stateMachine.context \textbf{ in}$$
$$\textbf{let } param = getEffectParam(trans, context) \textbf{ in}$$
$$\text{STARTBEHAVIOUR}(trans.effect, context, param, true)$$

In our example internal behaviour is started when the playing state is entered, either initially or as a result of a transition caused by the play event. This is performed by the rule DO analogously to EFFECT, except that the do-activity (Play) is called asynchronously since it must be performed concurrently; for example, a transition might leave the state while the do-activity is running.

3.5   Calling Behaviours from Interactions

To illustrate the calling of behaviour from interactions, we use them to specify test cases. Figure 2 shows a possible scenario for the MP3 player example. The sequence diagram specifies messages and their sequence between two lifelines, a user and the MP3 player. The events used in the behaviour of the MP3 player are created by the environment, in our case by the user. If the user turns on the player, the activity MP3PlayerBehaviour (see Figure 1) is executed. If the play message is received, the state machine PlayMusic is instantiated. The user then operates the player (for example, higher volume, pause the player) and the player reacts by sending messages to the user (for example, if the play list is finished). These reactions are defined in the do-activity of the playing state. After the user turns off the player, the state machine is terminated immediately and the activity sends the message bye to the user before it is stopped.

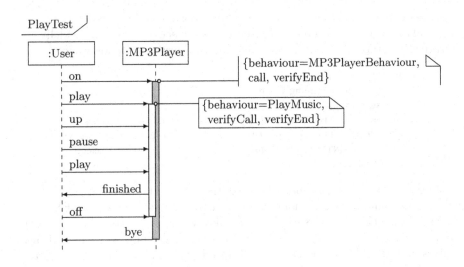

Fig. 2. Interaction defining test cases

A sequence diagram is interpreted by one ASM agent, processing the constituent interaction fragments. For the purposes of test case specification it is sufficient to consider one possible sequence of fragments matching the order imposed by the diagram (conveniently generated by ASM's **choose** rule). The fragments (which may be composed of other fragments) are processed iteratively. For each fragment, a rule defining the semantics according to its kind is executed. We only present the parts of the rule relevant for the combination of behaviours.

In the UML meta model the invocation of behaviour from a lifeline (see Figure 2) is represented as a BehaviorExecutionSpecification associated to two ExecutionOccurrenceSpecifications, namely its start and its finish. Note that both the execution and its two occurrence specifications are interaction fragments according to the UML. We base our semantics on the occurrences, since they offer the finer view. If the current fragment is such an execution occurrence, the following ASM rule is executed.

$\text{CASEBEHAVIOUREXECUTIONEVENT}(fragment) \equiv$
  let $context = fragment.covered$ **in**
    let $param = getBehaviourParam(fragment)$ **in**
      case $behaviourKind(fragment)$ **of**
        call: $\text{STARTBEHAVIOUR}(fragment.behaviour, context, param, false)$
        end: $\text{FINISHBEHAVIOUR}(fragment.behaviour, context)$
        verifyCall: $\text{VERIFYSTARTBEHAVIOUR}(fragment.behaviour, context, param)$
        verifyEnd: $\text{VERIFYFINISHBEHAVIOUR}(fragment.behaviour, context)$

It distinguishes whether the associated behaviour starts or finishes. For test scenarios, we further distinguish who controls the start or finish of the behaviour. This may be the environment; then the behaviour must actually be started or aborted. Alternatively, the behaviour may be started by the specified diagrams under test; we then verify if the appropriate action takes place. The decision is taken according to annotations in the sequence diagram, see Figure 2. We propose that the context object of the behaviour is its lifeline, since this is left unclear by the UML.

4   Communication in UML

In [19] a semantics for the event-based communication between activities is stated. In this section, we describe the necessary modifications due the combination of different kinds of diagrams. The existing semantics uses an event pool for each behaviour execution to store event occurrences (for example, a signal causes an event at its target behaviour). While this suffices for activities, it does not comply with the UML, which requires the context objects (that may have more than one associated behaviour executions) to recognise event occurrences [17, pages 433 and 563].

Thus, we argue that the event pool is located at the context object of a behaviour, not at the behaviour itself. We specify rules to handle the procedure of sending signals via SendSignalAction or BroadcastSignalAction in compliance with the specification. The rules create a request object (several for broadcasts), capturing among other things the sender and the target object. For specifying the target of a signal we use the signal path approach proposed in [18], adapted to our semantics.

Further changes are necessary for the semantics of the particular language units. We exemplify this for the top agent of state machines, which has to perform transitions upon receiving a signal.

> PERFORMTRANSITION $\equiv$ ...
> if $Self.mode =$ selecting then
>   choose e with $e \in Self.context.eventPool$ do
> $dispatched := e$ ...
> if $Self.mode =$ preparing then
>   choose $trans$ with $trans \in fireableTransWithMaxPriority(dispatched)$ do
>   FIRSTTASK($trans$)
> $Self.mode :=$ running

The rule chooses an event from the context object's event pool, the so-called dispatched event. It then chooses a transition fireable with the dispatched event and switches into running mode, see Section 3.4. The agents for the orthogonal regions execute a similar rule, performing transitions enabled by the dispatched event after synchronising with the top agent.

5   Conclusion

As discussed in the introduction, there are a number of works about the semantics of individual types of diagrams. Two further approaches aim at an integrated framework. Subsystems interacting by message passing are described in [12], but this applies to the old UML 1.4 only. Works initiated by the UML Semantics Project [4,5,8] are based on the 'system model' defined in terms of mathematics. However, the combination of different kinds of diagrams is not discussed; for example, activities can only call activities [7].

To overcome these limitations, we have presented a formal semantics of the combined use of activities, state machines and interactions, based on the same UML version 2.1.2. The resulting rules adhere to requirements present in or absent from the UML specification. They also allow the integration of code to implement low-level behaviour.

Based on our semantics, we are currently extending our tool ActiveCharts (http://activecharts.de/), that directly executes UML activities, to simulate models specified by state machines and interactions. The tool can be used to find errors in the modelled system and to obtain a better understanding of it. Examples we have modelled include a lift and a traffic light control.

Acknowledgement. We thank Guido de Melo for his model of the MP3 player.

References

1. von der Beeck, M.: A structured operational semantics for UML-statecharts. Software and Systems Modeling 1(2), 130–141 (2002)

2. Börger, E., Cavarra, A., Riccobene, E.: On formalizing UML state machines using ASMs. Information and Software Technology 46(5), 287–292 (2004)
3. Börger, E., Stärk, R.: Abstract State Machines. Springer, Heidelberg (2003)
4. Broy, M., Crane, M., Dingel, J., Hartman, A., Rumpe, B., Selic, B.: 2nd UML 2 semantics symposium: Formal semantics for UML. In: Kühne, T. (ed.) MoDELS 2006. LNCS, vol. 4364, pp. 318–323. Springer, Heidelberg (2007)
5. Cengarle, M.V., Grönninger, H., Rumpe, B.: System model semantics of statecharts. Informatik-Bericht 2008-04, TU Braunschweig (July 2008)
6. Cengarle, M.V., Knapp, A.: UML 2.0 interactions: Semantics and refinement. In: Jürjens, J., Fernandez, E.B., France, R., Rumpe, B. (eds.) Critical Systems Development with UML, pp. 85–99. TU München (2004)
7. Crane, M.L.: Slicing UML's Three-layer Architecture: A Semantic Foundation for Behavioural Specification. PhD thesis, Queen's University (January 2009)
8. Crane, M.L., Dingel, J.: Towards a UML virtual machine: Implementing an interpreter for UML 2 actions and activities. In: Chechik, M., Vigder, M., Stewart, D. (eds.) Conference of the Centre for Advanced Studies on Collaborative Research, pp. 96–110. ACM Press, New York (2008)
9. Dausend, M.: Entwicklung einer ASM-Spezifikation der Semantik der Zustandsautomaten der UML 2.0. Diploma thesis, Universität Ulm (June 2007)
10. Fecher, H., Schönborn, J.: UML 2.0 state machines: Complete formal semantics via core state machine. In: Brim, L., Haverkort, B.R., Leucker, M., van de Pol, J. (eds.) FMICS 2006 and PDMC 2006. LNCS, vol. 4346, pp. 244–260. Springer, Heidelberg (2007)
11. Fürst, J.: Entwicklung einer ASM-Spezifikation für die Semantik von UML 2 Sequenzdiagrammen als Grundlage zur Anbindung an ActiveCharts. Diploma thesis, Universität Ulm (February 2008)
12. Jürjens, J.: Formal semantics for interacting UML subsystems. In: Jacobs, B., Rensink, A. (eds.) Formal Methods for Open Object-Based Distributed Systems V, pp. 29–43. Kluwer Academic Publishers, Dordrecht (2002)
13. Kohlmeyer, J.: Executing UML 2 diagrams in ActiveCharts: A formal semantics for the combination of behavior specifications in the UML 2. In: Bertelle, C., Ayesh, A. (eds.) ESM 2008, October 2008, pp. 94–101 (2008)
14. Kohlmeyer, J.: Eine formale Semantik für die Verknüpfung von Verhaltensbeschreibungen in der UML 2. PhD thesis, Universität Ulm (July 2009)
15. Li, X., Liu, Z., He, J.: A formal semantics of UML sequence diagram. In: Australian Software Engineering Conference, pp. 168–177. IEEE, Los Alamitos (2004)
16. Marković, S., Baar, T.: Semantics of OCL specified with QVT. Software and Systems Modeling 7(4), 399–422 (2008)
17. Object Management Group. UML 2.1.2 Superstructure Specification (November 2007)
18. Sarstedt, S.: Overcoming the limitations of signal handling when simulating UML 2 activity charts. In: Feliz-Teixeira, J.M., Carvalho Brito, A.E. (eds.) ESM 2005, October 2005, pp. 61–65 (2005)
19. Sarstedt, S.: Semantic Foundation and Tool Support for Model-Driven Development with UML 2 Activity Diagrams. PhD thesis, Universität Ulm (July 2006)
20. Sarstedt, S., Guttmann, W.: An ASM semantics of token flow in UML 2 activity diagrams. In: Virbitskaite, I., Voronkov, A. (eds.) PSI 2006. LNCS, vol. 4378, pp. 349–362. Springer, Heidelberg (2007)
21. Störrle, H.: Semantics of interactions in UML 2.0. In: Symposium on Human Centric Computing Languages and Environments, pp. 129–136. IEEE, Los Alamitos (2003)

Applicability of the BLAST Model Checker: An Industrial Case Study*

Emanuel Kolb[1], Ondřej Šerý[2], and Roland Weiss[1]

[1] Industrial Software Systems, ABB Corporate Research,
ABB AG, Forschungszentrum Deutschland,
Wallstadter Str. 59, D-68526 Ladenburg, Germany
{emanuel.kolb,roland.weiss}@de.abb.com
[2] Charles University in Prague
Malostranske nam. 25, 118 00 Prague 1, Czech Republic
ondrej.sery@dsrg.mff.cuni.cz

Abstract. Model checking of software has been a very active research topic recently. As a result, a number of software model checkers have been developed for analysis of software written in different programming languages, e.g., SLAM, BLAST, and Java PathFinder. Applicability of these tools in the general industrial development process, however, is yet to be shown. In this paper, we present results of an experiment, in which we applied BLAST, a state-of-the-art model checker for C programs, in industrial settings. An industrial strength C implementation of a protocol stack has been verified against a set of formalized properties. We have identified real bugs in the code and we have also reached the limits of the tool. This experience report provides valuable guidance for developers of code analysis tools as well as for general software developers, who need to decide whether this kind of technique is ready for application and suitable for their particular goals.

Keywords: Software analysis, Model checking.

1 Introduction

Is model checking of software ready for application in the industrial development process? The answer to this question is not simple. In some situations, where short time to market and initial budget is more important than correctness, the benefits in the sense of software quality might never outweigh the additional costs of model checking both in time and money. On the other hand, in some very specific scenarios, software model checking has already been used for quite a time, e.g., during development of Windows device drivers [1]. Nevertheless, it is yet to be shown that software model checking can be applied also outside these specific domains.

---

* This work was funded in the context of the Q-ImPrESS research project (http://www.q-impress.eu) by the European Union under the ICT priority of the 7th Research Framework Programme and partially supported by the Grant Agency of the Czech Republic project 201/08/0266.

A. Pnueli, I. Virbitskaite, and A. Voronkov (Eds.): PSI 2009, LNCS 5947, pp. 218–229, 2010.
© Springer-Verlag Berlin Heidelberg 2010

There are potential industrial users. Unfortunately, they often miss the information on which to base their decision of using this technique. Unlike in other fields (e.g., theorem proving and HW model checking), there is no widely accepted collection of problems for software model checking that would allow for comparison of model checking tools against each other and also assessing the strength of the technique as a whole. Therefore, a potential industrial users have to make up their minds based on few available case studies. Moreover, many of these are conducted by the tool's authors in order to point out benefits of a particular technique they use, which gives little information on general applicability. Often, the tools are used to find already discovered errors (e.g., in [14]). This is definitely useful to show that finding a particular type of error is at least possible. However, when manual code simplifications are necessary to do so, it is unclear whether those might have been applied even without knowing the error in advance.

We believe that both potential industrial users and authors of the model checking tools would benefit from more case studies showing applicability and emphasizing limitations of the tools, which are currently available.

1.1 Goal and Structure of the Paper

In this paper, we document a case study in which we have employed the state-of-the-art software model checker BLAST in analysis of an industrial strength C implementation of the OPC UA [13] protocol stack. We have discovered a number of real defects with a reasonable rate of false positives. Our original input was the C source code and a set of informally stated properties to be verified.

The rest of the paper is structured as follows. The OPC UA protocol stack and its C implementation are briefly presented in Section 2. The BLAST model checker is described in Section 3, where we also advocate its choice. In Section 4, the experiment and its results are discussed. In Sections 5 and 6, the related work is listed followed by our conclusions.

2 Case Study: OPC UA Protocol Stack

The OPC Unified Architecture (OPC UA) is a platform-independent standard through which various kinds of systems and devices can communicate by sending messages between clients and servers over various types of networks. OPC UA is applicable to manufacturing software in application areas such as Field Devices, Control Systems, Manufacturing Execution Systems and Enterprise Resource Planning Systems. These systems are intended to exchange information and to use command and control for industrial processes.

It is expected that, over the next years, OPC UA will replace the "classic" OPC protocols, like OPC DA (Data Access), OPC A&E (Alarm and Event) and OPC HDA (Historical Data Access). The classic OPC protocols are widely used in industrial automation, but – due to their specification based on Microsoft's COM and DCOM technology – they can only run on Windows computers. Since OPC UA is based on the web-service paradigm, the protocol is able to run also on non-Windows systems, like Linux or VxWorks. The OPC UA specification is expected to be released by the OPC Foundation [17] in the 1st quarter of 2009.

The specification of the OPC UA protocol is not based on a specific programming language or technology. To access the OPC UA protocol from a specific programming language, a binding of the protocol to the language must be provided. This allows OPC UA applications written in different languages to communicate with each other. Although the OPC Foundation does not specify bindings for programming languages, it makes binding implementations (so called OPC UA Stacks) for C/C++, Java and .Net available. An OPC UA Stack implements the serialization, security and transport of messages exchanged between different UA Applications.

A typical architecture of an OPC UA communication system is depicted in Figure 1. There are two main roles for OPC UA applications: OPC UA client and OPC UA server. An OPC UA client builds up a connection to an OPC UA server and accesses/manages the data that is made available by the server.

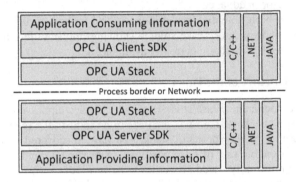

Fig. 1. A typical architecture of an OPC UA communication system

In this paper, we are particularly interested the OPC UA C-stack, which implements the OPC UA protocol binding for the C programming language. The OPC UA C-Stack is programmed in ANSI C (about 150 KLOC) and is split into a platform independent and a platform dependent part (also called platform layer). The platform layer contains the platform specific code that is needed for porting the C-Stack to a specific Operating System. Currently platform layers for Windows and Linux are available. The component is designed for usage in both PC-based and embedded systems.

The internal structure of the OPC UA C-Stack is visualized in Figure 2. Responsibilities of the particular modules are as follows:

- **Server Stub** provides the OPC UA API for OPC UA server applications. Its main functions are: "Managing communication endpoints", "Entry points for OPC UA services" and "Service infrastructure functions".

- **Client Proxy** provides the OPC UA API for OPC UA client applications. Its main functions are: "Managing connections" and "Calling OPC UA Services in synchronous or asynchronous mode".

- **Secure Channel** manages the security layer of the OPC UA protocol. The security layer is on top of the transport layer "Tcp Transport". Its main functions are: "Managing secure connections on client and server side", "Managing the secure data stream" and "Managing security policies".

- **Tcp Transport** is responsible for the binary TCP channel of the OPC UA protocol. Its main functions are: "Managing TCP connections" and "Managing the TCP data stream".

- **Stack Core** contains the core functionality of the C-stack. Its main functions are: "Providing Binary encoders and decoders", "Providing the OPC UA built-in types", "Providing basic cryptographic functions", "Basic stream and connection handling", "Providing the message types used in the OPC UA services" and "Providing a string table type".

- **Core** contains the UA protocol independent basic functionality. Its main functions are: "Basic type handling (Guid, DateTime, Buffer, List, String)", "Basic proxys-tub handling", "Basic memory functions", "Thread and Threadpool management", "Timer functions", "Tracing functions and "Some utility functions (bsearch, qsort,...)".

- **Platform** contains platform specific submodules (Linux, Windows, ...). A platform specific submodule interfaces and abstracts the OS dependent system calls. Its main functions are: "Thread handling", "Mutex/Semaphore functions", "Timer implementations", "Date and Time handling", "Socket handling", "String handling" and "Security functions (interfacing OpenSSL)".

After briefly presenting the BLAST model checker in the next section, we will document its application in analysis of the OPC UA C-Stack source codes.

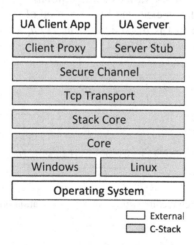

Fig. 2. Internal structure of the OPC UA C-Stack

3 Overview of BLAST

As already mentioned, BLAST is a model checker for analyzing programs written in the C programming language. As well as some other code model checkers designed for C, SLAM [1] and SATABS [7], BLAST utilizes *predicate abstraction* [2] and iterative refinement of the abstraction based on spurious counter-examples. In literature, this technique is often referred to as *counter-example guided abstraction refinement* (CEGAR).

In a nutshell, a coarse existential abstraction (over-approximation) is initially created from the program under analysis. This abstraction is then traversed and sought for any reachable error state. If no reachable error state is found, the use of over-approximation grants that also the original program is error-free. On the other hand, if there is a reachable error state, then this may be either a real error of the original program or a spurious error due to the abstraction. In the second case, the abstraction is refined based on the spurious error in order to avoid it in the future. After such a refinement, the new abstraction is traversed and the process iterates.

Unlike other tools based on CEGAR, BLAST features *lazy abstraction* [11]. This means that BLAST creates the abstraction on-the-fly, and in the refinement step, it refines only the necessary portions of the abstraction, while keeping the rest. Thus, only the reachable part of the abstraction is created and the portions that were previously proven to be error-free are not refined again. This is in contrast to the naïve CEGAR implementation which recreates the whole abstraction in every iteration.

Another useful feature of BLAST is *configurable program analysis* (CPA), published by the BLAST's authors in [5]. The CPA concept stems from *abstract interpretation* [9] and was originally introduced to provide a uniform view on model checking and static analysis. The basic idea is to have multiple CPAs for tracking different kinds of information (e.g., predicates and heap shape) about the program under analysis. Each CPA tracks the information in either a path sensitive or insensitive way. By combining the different CPAs, various configurations of the resulting analysis can be achieved. In [6], this idea is extended by the notion of dynamically adjustable precision of the information that is tracked, yielding *configurable program analysis with dynamic precision adjustment* (CPA+).

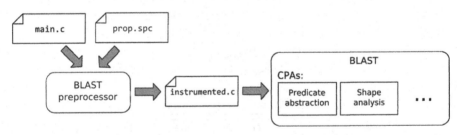

Fig. 3. Original BLAST architecture with property specification preprocessing and configurable program analysis

Building on this work of others, we have proposed an improvement of property specification in CEGAR based tools and implemented an extension in BLAST. Tools like SLAM and BLAST allow for specification of temporal safety properties in a specialized formalism SLIC [3] and BLAST specification language [4], respectively. As depicted in Figure 3, the property specified in such formalism is then used to instrument the original source code of the program under analysis. Artificial variables, their updates, and assertions are added to the source code. The instrumented source code is then analyzed for reachability of error states. This way, the property is encoded into the source code and manifests itself as additional predicates that have to be tracked during the state space traversal, requiring additional theorem proving over-head. Moreover, the instrumentation step has to be repeated after any modification of the original code.

In [16], we proposed an enhancement based on tracking the state of the property explicitly side by side with the program's abstraction, thus, overcoming the need for prior source code instrumentation. In the prototype implementation of the BLAST extension, the property is encoded and tracked in a separate Behavior CPA. The idea is depicted in Figure 4.

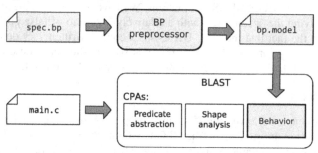

Fig. 4. Extended BLAST architecture when property specification is tracked in a specialized CPA (Behavior CPA)

In the following, we document application of the BLAST model checker enhanced with the abovementioned property specification extension to the C implementation of OPC UA Stack. We have chosen BLAST for this purpose, because, it uses very ad-vanced techniques in comparison to the other CEGAR based tools and it is generally regarded as a state-of-the-art tool in this category. Another reason was our previous positive experience with the tool.

4 Experiment

An important aspect of the OPC UA C-Stack source code we have analyzed is that it is basically a library. In contrast to standalone software, when analyzing a library, there is always the problem of a missing environment. In other words, one cannot simply feed the source code into a model checker tool and hope for meaningful re-sults, because the source code of a library constitutes only a partial model, e.g., there is no main function and the behavior of user code is missing. Moreover, a library is in general used in different environments and analyzing it in a specific one fails to pro-vide guarantees for the others.

There are basically two ways to mitigate this issue. First, one can use the *assume-guarantee principle* [12] and try to formulate the library's assumption about its envi-ronment by creating a very general testing harness, i.e., the *most general environment*. Such an environment should cover both typical usage patterns and border cases. A consecutive analysis of the library in the most general environment would then pro-vide guarantees for any environment subsumed by the most general one (i.e., any environment satisfying the library's assumption).

The second way to cope with the missing environment is to use defensive programming and make no assumptions on the order and the context in which the library's API functions are used, while requiring the library to stay error free and internally consistent at all times. Although the second option gives stronger guarantees and provides for analysis of the API functions in separation, it is also prone to reporting many false positives (due to ignoring potential assumptions), unless the library's source code is written defensively itself.

Although we have originally planned to try both ways, we were unable to complete the first one due to several BLAST limitations. We have, however, achieved satisfactory results in applying the second way with a relatively low ratio of false positives. This is mainly due to the fact that the OPC UA C-Stack code is written very defensively with few implicit assumptions. In the following, this second attempt is described in detail. The discussion of the BLAST's limitations is postponed to Section 4.4.

4.1 Methodology

In our experiments, we have identified three properties (described in Section 4.2) that should be satisfied during calls to the OPC UA C-Stack API functions. Each property was specified using a simple regular language [16]. For each property and each relevant OPC UA C-Stack API function, we have executed the BLAST model checker with the Behavior CPA extension. Although specific functions were used as entry points, BLAST traverses all the states reachable from the specific function in an interprocedural manner (i.e., also functions transitionally reachable from the API functions are considered).

Note also, that some code changes had to be introduced to make the analysis by BLAST possible. Main source of these changes was use of bit operations in error handling code. Although, in principle, BLAST can analyze source code featuring bit operations, it cannot reason about them properly when reachability of an error state depends directly on the result of a bit operation. Note that OPC UA C-Stack was not developed with model checking in mind. Therefore use of some bit operations in the error handling code was superfluous and was rewritten by other means to facilitate analysis. Another change was rewriting of some C macros into functions, so that they survived code preprocessing and BLAST could reason about them. This was the case with mutex locking/unlocking functions, which were originally implemented as macros. After code preprocessing, it was hard to formulate properties concerning proper ordering of mutex locking and unlocking.

It is worth mentioning that majority of the necessary changes have been made in header files. In our settings, this resulted in two versions of header files, the original ones and the "model checking friendly" headers. However, given the rather small amount of changes (tens of lines), this duality would not be strictly necessary if the development was started with model checking and its limitations in mind.

4.2 Properties

Initially, a domain expert identified about eight informal properties to be analyzed. From these, based on experience with model checking tools, we have picked the following three amenable to analysis using BLAST[1].

---

[1] Formalized properties are available at: http://dsrg.mff.cuni.cz/~sery/blast/psi09.tgz

Locking policy. The OPC UA C-Stack is multithreaded by design. Where necessary, access to shared data structures is controlled by locking and unlocking of mutexes. A natural question here concerns correctness of such a locking policy. For example, it is important to see, that any locked lock is always unlocked before returning from an API function call, no matter what exceptional situation might occur.

MessageContext management. Whenever the OPC UA C-Stack implementation manipulates a network message, it uses a message context to hold all necessary data. Before using the message context, the OpcUa_MessageContext_Initialize function has to be called first to initialize it. The message context has to be cleared for other use by invoking the OpcUa_MessageContext_Clear function afterwards.

Encoder management. The OPC UA C-Stack supports secure connection by encoding messages using SSL. This task is carried out by an encoder. Similarly to the previous property, the encoder has to be opened by invoking OpcUa_Encoder_Open before attaching it to a stream. When the encoding is done, the encoder has to be closed by calling the OpcUa_Encoder_Close function in order to free the associated resources and to prevent leaks.

For example, one omitted property is to check that all pointer parameters of an API function are checked for null before use. This task is more suitable for static analysis than for model checking. Another one is to check that all allocated memory is eventually freed, which we consider beyond the power of the current model checkers.

4.3 Experiment Results

All the tests were run on a Linux 2.6.27 system with Intel Pentium 4 CPU at 3.00GHz featuring 2GB of memory[2], with approximately 2 person-months effort[3]. Tables 1-3 summarize running times and number of defects found in the individual tested files for each of the three above listed properties. The error traces reported by BLAST (*reported errors*) were manually inspected to identify real defects (*real errors*). In a few cases, the tool was unable to perform the analysis (*tool failures*). This was mainly due to recursive functions, which are not supported by the tools combination we have used. Of course, such cases have to be considered as potentially erroneous.

A typical spurious error is a situation, where the locking policy is rightfully violated by design. For example, the TcpSecureChannel_GetSecuritySet locks a mutex which is unlocked by the TcpSecureChannel_ReleaseSecuritySet function. In the functions, a missing unlock and a missing lock are reported, respectively. Second type of a spurious error is a situation, where multiple mutexes are manipulated in a single function and they are mismatched by the tool. This is due to the fact that the properties are specified as a correct ordering of function calls, ignoring the function parameters (which identify the distinct mutexes in the code). Similar situation may occur also for the other properties.

---

[2] Although the system supports hyper-threading, BLAST and its process subtree was executed on a single virtual core. This is due to a synchronization issue present in BLAST at the time of writing, which manifested itself on multiprocessors resulting in random deadlocks.

[3] This includes studying the code, identification and formalization of properties, code modifications, analysis and interpretation of error traces.

Table 1. Analysis results of the locking policy property

Filename	time [s]	reported errors	tool failures	real errors
opcua_proxystub.c	2.3	0	0	0
opcua_threadpool.c	2.0	1	0	1
opcua_trace.c	1.2	0	0	0
opcua_thread.c	1.7	0	0	0
opcua_endpoint_ex.c	1.1	0	0	0
opcua_endpoint.c	10.1	0	0	0
opcua_asynccallstate.c	1.1	0	0	0
opcua_channel.c	22.8	4	0	3
opcua_tcpsecurechannel.c	6.3	5	0	2
opcua_securelistener.c	48.2	1	0	0
opcua_secureconnection.c	3:10.4	9	0	1
opcua_binarydecoder.c	1:24.3	0	6	0
opcua_binaryencoder.c	1:54.5	1	8	1
opcua_tcplistener.c	11.1	1	0	0
opcua_tcpconnection.c	7.8	0	0	0
Summary	8:24.9	22	14	8

Table 2. Analysis results of the MessageContext management property

Filename	time [s]	reported errors	tool failures	real errors
opcua_endpoint.c	7.7	0	0	0
opcua_channel.c	14.6	2	0	2
opcua_securelistener.c	16.1	0	0	0
opcua_secureconnection.c	2:15.8	4	0	2
Summary	2:54.2	6	0	4

Table 3. Analysis results of the Encoder management property

filename	time [s]	reported errors	tool failures	real errors
opcua_endpoint.c	7.5	0	0	0
opcua_channel.c	7.1	0	0	0
opcua_securelistener.c	16.1	0	0	0
opcua_secureconnection.c	1:41.0	1	0	1
summary	2:11.7	1	0	1

Let us also describe a typical representative of the real defects that were found. In the OPC UA C-Stack, the API function bodies are typically separated into a business part, which performs the desired activity, and an error handling part, which takes care of exceptional situations and performs the necessary cleanup. Two macros are used to facilitate error handling. The OpcUa_GotoErrorIfBad(uStatus) macro jumps into the error handling code if the preceding activity have failed. In the same situation, the OpcUa_ReturnErrorIfBad(uStatus) macro immediately returns from the function without performing the cleanup. Misuse of the latter one while holding a lock violates the locking policy property and may easily lead to a deadlock.

4.4 Discussion

Above, we have described our findings and it should be clear that, BLAST can be used in the industrial development process to discover real errors that were missed by previous conventional testing. On the other hand, it is also necessary to see what guarantees are really provided by this type of analysis. Or put differently, we should be aware of what we might have missed.

Naturally, BLAST would verify only those properties that were a priori identified by a human user. As a trivial consequence, one should never mistakenly interpret satisfaction of all predefined properties as overall program correctness. There is always a risk that the set of properties is not exhaustive for a particular task.

Even when an exhaustive set of properties is chosen, some of them might be hard or impossible to specify and verify. Let us consider the locking policy property again. A user might want to verify that a specific lock is always locked before a particular data structure is accessed. Unfortunately, BLAST offers no means for this kind of property to be specified. It would require a specification language with deeper understanding to semantics of data structures than BLAST is capable of. Also related to the locking policy is a question of deadlock freedom. Although, the verification approach employed by BLAST, might be used for multithreaded programs in principle, the tool itself has no support for multithreading. As a result, we were able to verify correct locking policy of a single thread (e.g., no pending locks) and even identify some real violations, but there is still a chance that a deadlock may occur (e.g., due to mutexes acquired in different order by distinct threads).

Another issue we have encountered is limitation regarding pointers. First, the OPC UA C-Stack uses function-pointers (unsupported by BLAST) quite heavily. In some situations, this might be overcome by explicit function calls. In others, it cannot. Also quite often, functions accept out-parameters as pointers to values to be modified. Under such circumstances, BLAST often fails to reason about properties directly depending on the modified value. This is the main reason why we were unable to employ an environment that would call the OPC UA API functions in a specific order (as described above in Sect. 4). The API functions depend on out-parameters passed as pointers and modified inside other functions. BLAST failed to analyze this scenario and we have found no workaround, thus, having to abandon the approach entirely.

As a last comment, BLAST would greatly benefit from support during the entire development process. There are typically some changes necessary to the code base in order to make it model checking friendly (e.g., providing dummy versions of some 3rd party libraries, etc.). With no tool support, managing the two versions is an extra burden for the developers. Interpreting the checking results with no graphical support is also very tedious. Unfortunately, there are quite a lot of such minor issues which, in real development, weight against use of this type of formal analysis.

5 Related Work

As already described in Section 3, BLAST is one of the CEGAR based model checkers. Related tools include SLAM [1] and SATABS [7]. A bit different model checker, CBMC [15], is based on bounded model checking. This means that it does not exhaustively traverse the whole state space of a program, but rather limits the search in depth (e.g., by a number of executed code blocks or context switches).

Another direction of related work is application of the model checking tools on case studies. Typically, authors present their tool on examples more or less chosen to manifest its strong points. Quite often, the tools are run on a code with a previously known bug. The source code under analysis is typically manually simplified to make the analysis feasible. Unfortunately, it is hard to see to whether the simplification is driven by some kind of generally applicable guidelines or by the goal of finding the specific bug.

In [14], Muhlberg et al. used BLAST to analyze portions of Linux kernel code for previously reported bugs. Although the bugs were known in advance, substantial manual code changes were introduced in order to make them detectable. The authors conclude that BLAST has several limitations mainly concerning documentation, pointer support and general usability, on which we agree. In contrast to this experiment, our input was source code and an informal list of properties rather than a list of previously known defects. In this respect, we have a more positive experience with identification of previously unknown bugs. However, it would be too optimistic to claim that our verification effort provides strong guarantees regarding the program correctness (as discussed in Section 4.4).

Other techniques than model checking (e.g., static and runtime analysis) are often used for error detection. Nice summaries can be found in [14, 10]. Although these techniques are typically easier to use and they scale much better than model checking, the correctness guarantees are weaker.

6   Conclusion

We have presented an experiment comprising application of the state-of-the-art C code model checker BLAST to an industrial case study. We regard the experiment as successful. We have discovered a number of real issues of the OPC UA C-Stack with a reasonable number of false positives. On the other hand, we have met several limitations that make adoption of these tools in the industrial development process difficult. Some of them follow from the fact that the tools are still research prototypes and might be overcome by additional tool support facilitating day-to-day use. Other ones (e.g., better pointer and multithreading support) are still a hot research topic.

References

1. Ball, T., Bounimova, E., Cook, B., Levin, V., Lichtenberg, J., McGarvey, C., Ondrusek, B., Rajamani, S.K., Ustuner, A.: Thorough static analysis of device drivers. SIGOPS Oper. Syst. Rev. 40(4), 73–85 (2006)
2. Ball, T., Majumdar, R., Millstein, T., Rajamani, S.K.: Automatic predicate abstraction of c programs. SIGPLAN Not. 36(5), 203–213 (2001)
3. Ball, T., Rajamani, S.K.: Slic: A specification language for interface checking. Technical Report MSR-TR-2001-21, Microsoft Research (January 2002)

4. Beyer, D., Chlipala, A., Henzinger, T., Jhala, R., Majumdar, R.: The BLAST query language for software verification. In: Giacobazzi, R. (ed.) SAS 2004. LNCS, vol. 3148, pp. 2–18. Springer, Heidelberg (2004)
5. Beyer, D., Henzinger, T.A., Theoduloz, G.: Configurable Software Verification: Concretizing the Convergence of Model Checking and Program Analysis. In: Damm, W., Hermanns, H. (eds.) CAV 2007. LNCS, vol. 4590, pp. 504–518. Springer, Heidelberg (2007)
6. Beyer, D., Henzinger, T.A., Theoduloz, G.: Program analysis with dynamic precision adjustment. In: Proceedings of the 23rd IEEE/ACM International Conference on Automated Software Engineering (ASE 2008), L'Aquila, September 15-19. IEEE Computer Society Press, Los Alamitos (2008)
7. Clarke, E.M., Kroening, D., Sharygina, N., Yorav, K.: SATABS: SAT-based predicate abstraction for ANSI-C. In: Halbwachs, N., Zuck, L.D. (eds.) TACAS 2005. LNCS, vol. 3440, pp. 570–574. Springer, Heidelberg (2005)
8. Clarke, E.M., Grumberg, O., Jha, S., Lu, Y., Veith, H.: Counterexample-guided abstraction refinement. In: Emerson, E.A., Sistla, A.P. (eds.) CAV 2000. LNCS, vol. 1855, pp. 154–169. Springer, Heidelberg (2000)
9. Cousot, P., Cousot, R.: Abstract interpretation: a unified lattice model for static analysis of programs by construction or approximation of fixpoints. In: POPL 1977: Proceedings of the 4th ACM SIGACT-SIGPLAN symposium on Principles of programming languages, pp. 238–252. ACM, New York (1977)
10. Engler, D., Musuvathi, M.: Static analysis versus software model checking for bug finding. In: Steffen, B., Levi, G. (eds.) VMCAI 2004. LNCS, vol. 2937, pp. 405–427. Springer, Heidelberg (2004)
11. Henzinger, T.A., Jhala, R., Majumdar, R., Sutre, G.: Lazy abstraction. SIGPLAN Not. 37(1), 58–70 (2002)
12. Giannakopoulou, D., Pasareanu, C.S., Cobleigh, J.M.: Assume-guarantee Verification of Source Code with Design-Level Assumptions. In: Proceedings of the 26th International Conference on Software Engineering. IEEE, Los Alamitos (2004)
13. Mahnke, W., Leitner, S.-H., Damm, M.: OPC Unified Architecture. Springer, Heidelberg (2009)
14. Muhlberg, J.T., Luttgen, G.: BLASTing Linux Code. In: Brim, L., Haverkort, B.R., Leucker, M., van de Pol, J. (eds.) FMICS 2006 and PDMC 2006. LNCS, vol. 4346, pp. 211–226. Springer, Heidelberg (2007)
15. Rabinovitz, I., Grumberg, O.: Bounded Model Checking of Concurrent Programs. In: Etessami, K., Rajamani, S.K. (eds.) CAV 2005. LNCS, vol. 3576, pp. 82–97. Springer, Heidelberg (2005)
16. Sery, O.: Enhanced Property Specification and Verification in BLAST. In: Chechik, M., Wirsing, M. (eds.) FASE 2009. LNCS, vol. 5503, pp. 456–469. Springer, Heidelberg (2009)
17. OPC UA Foundation, http://www.opcfoundation.org

Σ_K–constraints for Hybrid Systems[*]

Margarita Korovina[1] and Oleg Kudinov[2]

[1] Centre for Interdisciplinary Computational and Dynamical Analysis,
The University of Manchester and IIS SB RAS Novosibirsk
Margarita.Korovina@manchester.ac.uk
[2] Sobolev Institute of Mathematics, Novosibirsk
kud@math.nsc.ru

Abstract. In this paper we introduce and study computational aspects of Σ_K-constraints which are powerful enough to represent computable continuous data, but also simple enough to be an approach to approximate constraint solving for a large class of quantified continuous constraints. We illustrate how Σ_K-constraints can be used for reasoning about hybrid systems.

1 Introduction

A continuous constraint is a logical formalism which is used extensively in modeling, formal analysis and synthesis of control of hybrid systems [1,5,23,25]. From a mathematical point of view a *continuous constraint* is an expression (well formed formula) in an appropriate language over the reals involving constants, variables (ranging over continuous data i.e. the real numbers, functions), operations, relations, logical connectives and quantifiers. Since continuous constraints involve continuous data such as real numbers, functions and sets, solving of such constraints is already a challenging research problem.

This has resulted in various different approaches to continuous constraint solving. There are at least two main nonequivalent models of continuous constraint solving. The first one is related to model theory and real algebraic geometry (e.g. [4,6,7,24]) where real numbers are considered as basic entities which can be added, multiplied, divided or compared in a single step. Here most of methods for continuous constraint solving are exact and based on quantifier elimination and cylindrical cell decomposition. However, this approach is restricted to special cases such as quantified polynomial constraints.

The second model is closely related to numerical and computable analysis (e.g. [2,22,26]), where continuous data (real numbers, real-valued functions) are given by appropriate representations and computations of the solution sets of continuous constraints are infinite processes which produce inner or outer approximations to the results.

This model conforms to our intuition of reals based on rational approximations to a real number, but depends on representations of continuous data [26]

---

[*] This research was partially supported by EPSRC grant EP/E050441/1, DFG-RFBR (grant No 436 RUS 113/1002/01, grant No 09-01-91334).

A. Pnueli, I. Virbitskaite, and A. Voronkov (Eds.): PSI 2009, LNCS 5947, pp. 230–241, 2010.
© Springer-Verlag Berlin Heidelberg 2010

and particular validated numerical techniques [5]. In this paper we introduce and study Σ_K–constraints which formalise problems involving logical quantifiers bounded by computable compact sets, computable real numbers and computable real-valued functions. A key idea of our approach to approximate solving of Σ_K–constraints is based on a procedure which given a Σ_K–constraint produces an effective sequence of quantifier free formulas (inequality polynomial constraints) defining the solution set. On one hand proposed approach agrees with the second model mentioned above, on the other hand it does not depend on the particular representation of real numbers. We illustrate how Σ_K-constraints can be used for studying reachability problems of switched controlled systems.

The paper is structured as follows. In Section 2 we give the main definitions and notions. We recall properties of Σ-definability and computability over the real numbers. In Section 3 we introduce the notion of Σ_K–constraints and propose an approach to approximate Σ_K–constraint solving. In Section 4 we recall slightly modified **SHS**-specifications of switched controlled systems introduced in [18] and show that under natural assumptions the behaviour of a hybrid system is computable. We illustrate how Σ_K-constraints can be used for studying reachability problems.

2   Basic Notions and Definitions

In order to introduce Σ_K-constraints we propose a basic model, recall the notions and properties of Σ-definability and computability over the reals.

2.1   Basic Model

Our approach to continuous constraints is based on the notion of definability [14,15], where continuous objects and computational processes involving these objects can be defined using finite formulas in a suitable structure. Definability has been a very successful framework for generalised computability theory, descriptive complexity and databases. One of the most interesting and practically important types of definability is Σ-definability, which generalises recursive enumerability over the natural numbers [3,8]. However, the most developed part of definability theory deals with abstract structures with equality (i.e., the natural numbers, trees, automata, etc.). In the case of continuous data, such as real numbers, real-valued functions and functionals, it is reasonable to consider the corresponding structures without equality. This is motivated by the following natural reason. In all effective approaches to exact real number computation via concrete representations [22,26], the equality test is undecidable. In order to do any kind of computation or to develop a computability theory, one has to work within a structure rich enough for information to be coded and stored. For this purpose we extend the structure $\mathbb{R}$ by the set of hereditarily finite sets $HF(\mathbb{R})$. The idea that the hereditarily finite sets over a structure form a natural domain for computation is discussed in [3,8]. Note that such or very similar extensions of structures are used in the theory of abstract state machines [11], in query languages for hierarchic databases [20].

According to this motivation we consider the ordered structure of the real numbers in *the finite predicate language*, $\langle \mathbb{R}, \sigma_P, < \rangle = \langle \mathbb{R}, \sigma_< \rangle$, with $\sigma_P \supseteq \{\mathcal{M}_E^*, \mathcal{M}_H^*, \mathcal{A}_E^+, \mathcal{A}_H^+, \}$, where $\mathcal{M}_E^*, \mathcal{M}_H^*$ are interpreted as an open epigraph and an open hypograph of multiplication respectively, and $\mathcal{A}_E^+, \mathcal{A}_H^+$ are interpreted as an open epigraph and an open hypograph of addition respectively. *We don't assume that the language σ_P contains equality.*

We extend the real numbers by the set of hereditarily finite sets $\mathrm{HF}(\mathbb{R})$ which is rich enough for information to be coded and stored. We construct the set of hereditarily finite sets, $\mathrm{HF}(\mathbb{R})$ over the reals, as follows:

1. $\mathrm{HF}_0(\mathbb{R}) \rightleftharpoons \mathbb{R}$,
2. $\mathrm{HF}_{n+1}(\mathbb{R}) \rightleftharpoons \mathcal{P}_\omega(\mathrm{HF}_n(\mathbb{R})) \cup \mathrm{HF}_n(\mathbb{R})$, where $n \in \omega$ and for every set B, $\mathcal{P}_\omega(B)$ is the set of all finite subsets of B.
3. $\mathrm{HF}(\mathbb{R}) = \bigcup_{m \in \omega} \mathrm{HF}_m(\mathbb{R})$.

We define $\mathbf{HF}(\mathbb{R})$ as the following model: $\mathbf{HF}(\mathbb{R}) \rightleftharpoons (\mathrm{HF}(\mathbb{R}), U, \sigma_<, \emptyset, \in) \rightleftharpoons (\mathrm{HF}(\mathbb{R}), \sigma)$, where the constant $\emptyset$ stands for the empty set and the binary predicate symbol $\in$ has the set-theoretic interpretation. We also add a 1-ary predicate symbol U naming the set of urelements (the real numbers). The natural numbers $0, 1, \ldots$ are identified with the (finite) ordinals in $\mathrm{HF}(\mathbb{R})$ i.e. $\emptyset, \{\emptyset, \{\emptyset\}\}, \ldots$, so in particular, $n + 1 = n \cup \{n\}$ and the set ω is a subset of $\mathrm{HF}(\mathbb{R})$.

The atomic formulas include $U(x), \neg U(x), x < y, x \in s, x \notin s$ where s ranges over sets, and also, for every $Q_i \in \sigma_P$ with the arity n_i, $Q_i(x_1, \ldots, x_{n_i})$ which has the following interpretation:

$$\mathbf{HF}(\mathbb{R}) \models Q_i(x_1, \ldots, x_{n_i}) \text{ if and only if}$$
$$\mathbb{R} \models Q_i(x_1, \ldots, x_{n_i}) \text{ and, for every } 1 \le j \le n_i, x_j \in \mathbb{R}.$$

The set of Δ_0-*formulas* is the closure of the set of atomic formulas under $\wedge, \vee$, bounded quantifiers $(\exists x \in y)$ and $(\forall x \in y)$, where $(\exists x \in y)$ Ψ means the same as $\exists x (x \in y \wedge \Psi)$ and $(\forall x \in y)$ Ψ as $\forall x (x \in y \rightarrow \Psi)$ where y ranges over sets. The set of Σ-*formulas* is the closure of the set of Δ_0-formulas under $\wedge, \vee$, $(\exists x \in y)$, $(\forall x \in y)$ and $\exists$, where y ranges over sets.

Remark 1. It is worth noting that all predicates $Q_i \in \sigma_P$ and $<$ occur only positively in Σ-formulas. Hence, if σ_P does not contain equality then in Σ-formulas we don't allow equality on the urelements (elements from $\mathbb{R}$).

Definition 1. *1. A relation $B \subseteq \mathrm{HF}(\mathbb{R})^n$ is Σ-definable if there exists a Σ-formula $\Phi(\bar{a})$ such that $\bar{b} \in B \leftrightarrow \mathbf{HF}(\mathbb{R}) \models \Phi(\bar{b})$.*

2.2   Basic Properties Σ-definability over the Reals

In this subsection we recall the basic principles for Σ-definability which allow to make effective reasoning about continuous constraints using Σ-formulas.

2.3   Gandy's Theorem and Inductive Definitions

Let us recall Gandy's Theorem for $\mathbf{HF}(\mathbb{R})$ which shows that continuous objects and computational processes involving these objects can be defined using Σ-formulas. Let $\Phi(a_1, \ldots, a_n, P)$ be a Σ-formula, where P occurs positively in Φ and the arity of Φ is equal to n. We think of Φ as defining an *effective operator* $\Gamma : \mathcal{P}(\mathbf{HF}(\mathbb{R})^n) \to \mathcal{P}(\mathbf{HF}(\mathbb{R})^n)$ given by $\Gamma(Q) = \{\bar{a} \mid (\mathbf{HF}(\mathbb{R}), Q) \models \Phi(\bar{a}, P)\}$. Since the predicate symbol P occurs only positively the corresponding operator Γ is monotone, i.e., from $B \subseteq C$ implies $\Gamma(B) \subseteq \Gamma(C)$. By monotonicity, the operator Γ has a least (w.r.t. inclusion) fixed point which can be described as follows. We start from the empty set and apply operator Γ until we reach the fixed point: $\Gamma^0 = \emptyset$, $\Gamma^{n+1} = \Gamma(\Gamma^n)$, $\Gamma^\gamma = \cup_{n < \gamma} \Gamma^n$, where γ is a limit ordinal.

One can easily check that the sets Γ^n form an increasing chain of sets: $\Gamma^0 \subseteq \Gamma^1 \subseteq \ldots$. By set-theoretical reasons, there exists the least ordinal γ such that $\Gamma(\Gamma^\gamma) = \Gamma^\gamma$. This Γ^γ is the least fixed point of the given operator Γ.

Theorem 1. *[15][Gandy's Theorem for $\mathbf{HF}(\mathbb{R})$]*
Let $\Gamma : \mathcal{P}(\mathbf{HF}(\mathbb{R})^n) \to \mathcal{P}(\mathbf{HF}(\mathbb{R})^n)$ be an effective operator. Then the least fixed-point of Γ is Σ-definable and the least ordinal such that $\Gamma(\Gamma^\gamma) = \Gamma^\gamma$ is less or equal to ω.

Definition 2. *A relation $B \subset \mathbb{R}^n$ is called Σ-inductive if it is the least-fixed point of an effective operator.*

Corollary 1. *Every Σ-inductive relation is Σ-definable.*

2.4   Universal Σ-predicate

The following result shows that we can effectively check validity of a Σ-formula on $\mathbf{HF}(\mathbb{R})$. As a corollary there exists a universal Σ-predicate for Σ-formulas over this model.

Theorem 2. *[14] There exists a binary Σ-definable predicate Tr such that for any $n \in \omega$ and $A \in \mathrm{HF}(\mathbb{R})$ we have that $(n, A) \in Tr$ if and only if n is the Gödel number of a Σ-formula Φ, γ_A is a correct interpretation for free variables of Φ and $\mathbf{HF}(\mathbb{R}) \models \Phi[\gamma_A]$.*

2.5   Semantic Characterisation of Σ-definability

The following theorem reveals algorithmic properties of Σ-formulas over $\mathbf{HF}(\mathbb{R})$.

Theorem 3. *[14][Semantic Characterisation of Σ-definability]*
A set $B \subseteq \mathbb{R}^n$ is Σ-definable if and only if there exists an effective sequence of quantifier free formulas in the language $\sigma_<$, $\{\Phi_s(x_1, \ldots, x_n)\}_{s \in \omega}$, such that

$$(x_1, \ldots, x_n) \in B \leftrightarrow \mathbb{R} \models \bigvee_{s \in \omega} \Phi_s(x_1, \ldots, x_n).$$

The proof of this theorem is based on Gandy's theorem and existence of Σ-universal predicate. It is worth noting that both of the directions of this characterisation are important. The right direction gives us an effective procedure which generates quantifier free formulas approximating Σ-relations. The converse direction provides tools for descriptions of the results of effective infinite approximating processes by finite formulas.

2.6 Computability and Σ-definability over $\mathbb{R}$

In order uniformly characterise computability of different continuous data in logical terms, we consider an arbitrary structure $\mathcal{A} = \langle A, \sigma_P, \neq \rangle = \langle A, \sigma_A \rangle$, where A contains more than one element, and σ_P is a finite set of basic predicates. We assume that the existential theory of $\mathcal{A}$ is computably enumerable. For the structure $\mathcal{A}$, we introduce a topology τ_Σ, with the base consisting of the subsets defined by existential formulas with positive occurrences of basic predicates and $\neq$. As examples we can consider the real numbers without equality $\mathbb{R}_< = \langle \mathbb{R}, \sigma_< \rangle$, the real numbers with equality $\mathbb{R}_= = \langle \mathbb{R}, +, *, \leq \rangle$, the real-valued continues functions $C(\mathbb{R}) = \langle C(\mathbb{R}), P_1, \ldots, P_{12}, \neq \rangle$ [12]. We denote Σ-definability in the language σ as Σ-definability in σ. For the definitions of computable real numbers, computable functions, and computable compact sets we refer to [12,19,22,26]. The following theorems connect computable continuous data with validity of Σ–formulas.

Proposition 1. *[17] A real number is computable if and only if the left Dedekind cut and the right Dedekind cut are Σ-definable in $\sigma_<$.*

Theorem 4. *If $f \in C[0,1]$ and its epigrap and hypograph are Σ-definable in $\sigma_=$ then f is computable.*

Proposition 2. *[17] A total function $F : \mathbb{R} \to \mathbb{R}$ is computable if and only if its epigraph and hypograph are Σ-definable in $\sigma_<$.*

Definition 3. *A total continuous function $F : A \times \mathbb{R} \to \mathbb{R}$ is called weakly computable if there exist effective infinite sequences $\{\langle \psi_m^-(x), \phi_m^-(y,z) \rangle\}_{m \in \omega}$ and $\{\langle \psi_m^+(x), \phi_m^+(y,z) \rangle\}_{m \in \omega}$ of Σ-formulas, where $\psi_m^-(x)$ and $\psi_m^+(x)$ are Σ-formulas in σ_A, $\phi_m^-(y,z)$ and $\phi_m^+(y,z)$ are Σ-formulas in $\sigma_=$ such that*

$$F(x,y) < z \leftrightarrow \bigvee_{m \in \omega} (\psi_m^-(x) \wedge \phi_m^-(y,z)) \text{ and}$$

$$F(x,y) > z \leftrightarrow \bigvee_{m \in \omega} (\psi_m^+(x) \wedge \phi_m^+(y,z)).$$

It is worth noting that the computable functions is a proper subclass of the weakly computable functions.

Theorem 5. *Let $F : A \times \mathbb{R} \to \mathbb{R}$ be a weakly computable continuous function. If there exists a computable function $H : A \times \mathbb{R} \to \mathbb{R}$ such that $|F(x,y)| \leq H(x,y)$ for all $x \in A$ and $y \in \mathbb{R}$ then F is computable.*

Proposition 3. *[2] A compact subset $K \subset \mathbb{R}^n$ is computable if and only if the distance function d_K is computable and there exist rational numbers q_1 and q_2 such that $K \subseteq [q_1, q_2]^n$.*

3 Σ_K-constraints

Now we consider the real numbers $\mathbb{R}$ in an extended language σ. Define $\sigma = \sigma_P \cup \sigma_c \cup \sigma_f \cup \sigma_K = (0, 1, \cdot, +, <, c_1, \ldots, c_k, \ldots, f_1, \ldots, f_n, \ldots, K_1, \ldots, K_m, \ldots)$, where c_i is a computable real number, f_j is a computable function, and K_s is a computable compact subset of $\mathbb{R}^n$.

The atomic Σ_K-constraints include $p(\bar{x}) < q(\bar{y})$, $f_i(\bar{x}) < f_j(\bar{y})$, where $\bar{x}$ and $\bar{y}$ range over the real numbers, p and q are polynomials with computable real coefficients, f_i and f_j are computable real functions.

The set of Σ_K-*constraints* is the closure of the set of atomic Σ_K-constraints under $\wedge, \vee$, existential quantifiers $\exists x$ and bounded quantifiers $(\exists x \in K_s)$ and $(\forall x \in K_m)$, where K_s and K_m are computable compact subset of $\mathbb{R}^n$.

Remark 2. By definition, Σ_K–constraints involve continuous data such as variables ranging over the real numbers, computable real constants, computable real-valued functions, the strict inequality relation $<$, logical connectives $\vee, \wedge$ and quantifiers bounded by computable compact sets. It is worth noting that the predicate $<$ occurs only positively in Σ_K–constraints.

Theorem 6. *There is an algorithm which by a Σ_K–constraint φ produces an effective sequence of quantifier free formulas $\{\psi_i\}_{i \in \omega}$ in the language $\sigma_<$ such that*

$$\mathbb{R} \models \varphi(\bar{x}) \leftrightarrow \mathbb{R} \models \bigvee_{i \in \omega} \psi_i(\bar{x}).$$

First we prove the following proposition.

Proposition 4. *For every Σ-formula φ there exists a Σ-formula ψ such that*

$$\mathbf{HF}(\mathbb{R}) \models \forall x \in [a, b] \varphi(x, y_1, \ldots, y_n) \text{ iff } \mathbf{HF}(\mathbb{R}) \models \psi(a, b, y_1, \ldots, y_n),$$

where free variables range over $\mathbb{R}$.

Proof. First we consider the case of $\exists$-formulas in the language $\sigma_{\mathbb{R}}$. Using induction on the structure of a $\exists$-formula φ, we show how to obtain a required formula ψ. Then, based on Theorem 3 we construct a required formula ψ for an arbitrary Σ-formula.

Atomic case. We consider nontrivial subcases.

a) If $\varphi(x, z) \rightleftharpoons x \cdot x > z$ then

$$\psi(a, b, z) \rightleftharpoons z < 0 \vee a > b \vee (a > 0 \wedge b > 0 \wedge a \cdot a > z) \vee (a < 0 \wedge b < 0 \wedge b \cdot b > z).$$

b) If $\varphi(x, z) \rightleftharpoons x \cdot x < z$ then $\psi(a, b, z) \rightleftharpoons a > b \vee (a \cdot a < z \wedge b \cdot b < z)$.

c) If $\varphi(x, y) \rightleftharpoons x \cdot y > x$ then

$$\psi(a, b, z) \rightleftharpoons a > b \vee (a > 0 \wedge b > 0 \wedge y > 1) \vee (a < 0 \wedge b < 0 \wedge y < 1).$$

d) If $\varphi(x) \rightleftharpoons x \cdot x > x$ then $\psi(a, b) \rightleftharpoons a > b \vee (a > 1 \wedge b > 1) \vee (a < 0 \wedge b < 0)$.

e) If $y \cdot z < x$ then $\psi(a, b, y, z) \rightleftharpoons y \cdot z < a \vee b < a$. Other atomic subcases can be considered by analogy.

Conjunction.

If $\varphi \rightleftharpoons \varphi_1 \wedge \varphi_2$ and ψ_1, ψ_2 are already constructed for φ_1, φ_2 then $\psi \rightleftharpoons \psi_1 \wedge \psi_2$.

Disjunction.

Suppose $\varphi \rightleftharpoons \varphi_1 \vee \varphi_2$ and ψ_1, ψ_2 are already constructed. Since $[a, b]$ is compact, validity of the formula $\forall x \in [a, b] (\varphi_1 \vee \varphi_2)$ is equivalent to existence of a finite family of open intervals $\{(\alpha_i, \beta_i)\}_{i=1,\dots,r+s}$ such that $[a, b] \subseteq \bigcup_{i=1}^r (\alpha_i, \beta_i)$, for $i = 1, \dots, r$ $\mathbb{R} \models \varphi_1$ and for $i = r+1, \dots, s$ $\mathbb{R} \models \varphi_2$. Since φ_1 and φ_2 define open sets, this is equivalent to existence of a finite family of closed intervals $\{[\alpha_i', \beta_i']\}_{i=1,\dots,r+s}$ such that $[a, b] \subseteq \bigcup_{i=1}^r [\alpha_i', \beta_i']$, for $i = 1, \dots, r$ $\mathbb{R} \models \varphi_1$ and for $i = r+1, \dots, s$ $\mathbb{R} \models \varphi_2$. It is represented by the following formula.

$$\bigvee_{r \in \omega} \bigvee_{r \in \omega} \exists \alpha_1' \dots \exists \alpha_{s+1}' \exists \beta_1' \dots \exists \beta_{s+1}' \left(\bigwedge_{i=1}^r \forall x \in [\alpha_i', \beta_i'] \varphi_1 \wedge \bigwedge_{j=r+1}^s \forall x \in [\alpha_j', \beta_j'] \varphi_2 \right).$$

By induction hypothesis and Theorem 3, this formula is equivalent to a Σ-formula ψ.

Existential case.

Suppose $\varphi \rightleftharpoons \exists z \varphi_1(z, x_1, \dots, x_n)$. As $[a, b]$ is compact and

$$\{\{x_1 | \mathbb{R} \models \varphi_1(z, x_1, \dots, x_n)\}\}_{z \in \mathbb{R}} = \{V_z\}_{z \in \mathbb{R}}$$

is an open cover, there exists a finite set $J = \{z_1, \dots, z_s\} \subset \mathbb{R}$ such that $[a, b] \subseteq \bigcup_{z \in J} V_z$. So, validity of the formula $\forall x_1 \in [a, b] \exists z \varphi_1(z, x_1, \dots, x_n)$ is equivalent to existence of the finite set $J = \{z_1, \dots, z_s\}$ such that

$$\mathbb{R} \models \forall x_1 \in [a, b] \exists z \varphi_1(z, x_1, \dots, x_n) \leftrightarrow \mathbb{R} \models \forall x_1 \in [a, b] \varphi^s(z_1, \dots, z_s, x_1, \dots, x_n),$$

where $\varphi^s(z_1, \dots, z_s, x_1, \dots, x_n) \rightleftharpoons \varphi_1(z_1, x_1, \dots, x_n) \vee \dots \vee \varphi_1(z_s, x_1, \dots, x_n)$. By induction hypotheses, for every $J = \{z_1, \dots, z_s\}$ there exists a Σ-formula $\psi^s(z_1, \dots, z_s, a, b, x_2, \dots, x_n)$ in the language $\sigma \cup \{P_\lambda' | \lambda : \{1, \dots, n\} \to \{1, \dots, n\}\}$ which is equivalent to $\forall x_1 \in [a, b] \varphi^s(z_1, \dots, z_s, x_1, \dots, x_n)$. Finally,

$$\mathbb{R} \models \forall x_1 \in [a, b] \exists z \varphi_1(z, x_1, \dots, x_n) \leftrightarrow$$
$$\mathbf{HF}(\mathbb{R}) \models \bigvee_{s \in \omega} \exists z_1 \dots \exists z_s (\psi^s(z_1, \dots, z_s, a, b, x_2, \dots, x_n)).$$

A required Σ-formula ψ can be constructed using Theorem 3.

Now we are ready to construct a required formula ψ for a given Σ-formula φ. By Theorem 3, there exists an effective sequence of quantifier free formulas $\{\varphi_i\}_{i \in \omega}$ such that $\mathbf{HF}(\mathbb{R}) \models \varphi \leftrightarrow \mathbf{HF}(\mathbb{R}) \models \bigvee_{i \in \omega} \varphi_i$. As $[a, b]$ is compact and

$\{\{x_1 | \mathbb{R} \models \varphi_i(x_1, \ldots, x_n)\}\}_{i \in \omega} = \{U_i\}_{i \in \omega}$ is its cover, there exist $k \in \omega$ and a finite family $\{U_i\}_{i \leq k}$ such that $[a, b] \subseteq \bigcup_{i \leq k} U_i$. So,

$$\mathbb{R} \models \forall x_1 \in [a, b] \varphi(x_1, \ldots, x_n) \leftrightarrow$$
$$\mathbf{HF}(\mathbb{R}) \models \bigvee_{k \in \omega} \forall x_1 \in [a, b] \bigvee_{i \leq k} \varphi_i(x_1, \ldots, x_n).$$

By induction hypotheses, for every $k \in \omega$ there exists a Σ–formula $\psi_k(a, b, \ldots)$ which is equivalent to $\forall x_1 \in [a, b] \bigvee_{i \leq k} \varphi_i(x_1, \ldots, x_n)$. A required Σ-formula ψ can be constructed using Theorem 3.

Proof (Theorem 6).
We proceed by induction on the structure of the Σ_K-constraint φ.
Atomic Σ_K–constraint case. Suppose $\varphi(\bar{x}) \rightleftharpoons f_1(\bar{x}) < f_2(\bar{x})$, where $f_1(\bar{x}), f_2(\bar{x})$ are computable real-valued functions. It is easy to note that

$$\mathbb{R} \models \varphi(\bar{x}) \text{ iff } \mathbb{R} \models \exists a_1 \exists a_2 \exists b_1 \exists b_2 \forall y_1 \in [a_1, b_1] \forall y_2 \in [a_2, b_2]$$
$$\left(\bigwedge_{1 \leq i \leq 2} (f_i(\bar{x}) < b_i \wedge f_i(\bar{x}) > a_i) \wedge (y_1 < y_2) \right).$$

By Proposition 2, f_i is computable if and only if $f_i(\bar{x}) < z$ and $f_j(\bar{x}) > z$ are Σ-definable. So, we can construct a required sequence of quantifier free formulas $\{\psi\}_{i \in \omega}$ using Proposition 4 and Theorem 3.
Conjunction, Disjunction and *Existential quantifier* cases are straightforward from Theorem 3.
Bounded Existential quantifier case. Suppose $\varphi(\bar{x}) \rightleftharpoons \exists y \in K \phi(y, \bar{x})$, where K is a computable compact subset of $\mathbb{R}^n$. Since ϕ defines effectively open set, the formula φ is equivalent to the formula

$$\exists y' \exists \epsilon > 0 \left(\phi(y', \bar{x}) \wedge d_K(y') < \epsilon \wedge \forall z \in \bar{B}(y', \epsilon) \phi(z, \bar{x}) \right),$$

where $\bar{B}(y', \epsilon)$ is a closed ball. By properties of computable compact sets, the distance function d_K is computable [2], and, as a corollary, the set $\{(y', \epsilon) | d_K(y') < \epsilon\}$ is Σ-definable. By Proposition 4 and Theorem 3, there exists a required sequence of quantifier free formulas $\{\psi\}_{i \in \omega}$.
Bounded Universal quantifier case. Suppose $\varphi(\bar{x}) \rightleftharpoons \forall y \in K \phi(y, \bar{x})$, where K is a computable compact subset of $\mathbb{R}^n$. It is easy to see that φ is equivalent to the formula

$$\forall y \in [-q, q]^n (y \notin K \vee \varphi(y, \bar{x}))$$

for some rational q which can be find effectively by K. By properties of computable closed sets, the distance function d_K is computable [2], and, as a corollary, $\{y | y \notin K\} = \{y | d_K(y) > 0\}$ is Σ-definable. By Proposition 4 and Theorem 3, there exists a required sequence of quantifier free formulas $\{\psi\}_{i \in \omega}$.

Remark 3. It is worth noting that Theorem 6 provides an effective procedure which generates quantifier free formulas approximating the solution set of Σ_K-constraints.

4 Σ_K-constraints for Hybrid Systems

In this section we reconsider reachability problems in terms of Σ_K-constraints for a large class of hybrid systems, where continuous dynamics are represented by computable real-valued functions or functionals. In contrast to special types of hybrid systems such as timed automata or linear hybrid systems, for the considered class of hybrid systems difficulties arise from the fact that we can not exactly compute flow successors, but can only effectively approximate.

4.1   SHS-Specifications of Hybrid Systems

We consider the models of hybrid systems proposed by Nerode, Kohn in [21], called switched controlled systems. A hybrid system is a system which consists of a continuous plant that is disturbed by the external world and controlled by a program implemented on a sequential automaton. In the Nerode–Kohn model a hybrid system is represented by a continuous device given by a collection of dynamical systems parameterised by a control set along with a control automaton for switching among them.

The control automaton has input data (the set of sensor measurements) and the output data (the set of control laws).

The control automaton is modeled by three units. The first unit is a converter which converts each measurement into input symbols of the internal control automaton. The internal control automaton, in practice, is a finite state automaton with finite input and output alphabets. The second unit is the internal control automaton, which has a symbolic representation of a measurement as input and produces a symbolic representation of the next control law to be imposed on the plant as output. The third unit is a converter which converts these output symbols representing control laws into the actual control laws imposed on the plant. The plant interacts with the control automata at discrete times t_i, where the time sequence $\{t_i\}_{i\in\omega}$ satisfies realizability requirements. At time t_i the control automaton gets sensor data, computes the next control law, and imposes it on the plant. The plant will continue using this control law until the next interaction at time t_{i+1}.

The specification $\mathbf{SHS} = \langle TS, \mathbb{X}, \mathbb{U}, \mathbb{D}, Init, \mathbf{F}, Conv1, A, Conv2 \rangle$ of a hybrid system consists of:

- $TS = \{t_i\}_{i\in\omega}$ is an effective sequence of rational numbers which encodes the times of communication of the external world, the plant and the control automata and satisfies realizability requirements.
- $\mathbb{X} \subseteq \mathbb{R}^n$ is a plant state space.
- $\mathbb{U} \subseteq \mathbb{R}^k$ is a set of control parameters.
- $\mathbb{D} \subseteq C(\mathbb{R})$ is a set of acceptable disturbances.
- $\mathbf{F} : \mathbb{D} \times \mathbb{U} \times \mathbb{X} \times \mathbb{R}^+ \to \mathbb{X}$ is a total computable function modeling the behaviour of the plant.
- $Conv1 : \mathbb{D} \times \mathbb{X} \to \omega$ is a weakly computable function. At the time of communication this function converts measurements, presented by $\mathbf{F}$, and the

representation of external world f into finite words which are input words of the internal control automata.

- $A : \omega \to \omega$ is a Σ-definable function. The internal control automata, in practice, is a finite state automata with finite input and finite output alphabets. So, it is naturally modeled by Σ-definable function which has a symbolic representation of measurements as input and produces a symbolic representation of the next control law as output.
- $Conv2 : \omega \to \mathbb{U}$ is a computable function. This function converts finite words representing control laws into control laws imposed on the plant.
- $Init = Init_{\mathbb{U}} \times Init_{\mathbb{X}}$ is a computable compact set of initial conditions.

Definition 4. *The behaviour of a hybrid system is defined by a function $H : \mathbb{D} \times \mathbb{X} \times \mathbb{R}^+ \to \mathbb{X}$ if for any external disturbance $f \in \mathbb{D}$ and initial states $x \in Init_{\mathbb{X}}$ the function $H(f, x, \cdot) : \mathbb{R}^+ \to \mathbb{X}$ defines the trajectory of the hybrid system.*

In order to investigate the behaviour of a hybrid system we consider the spaces $\mathbb{X}$, $\mathbb{U}$ and $\mathbb{D}$ and their products as structures in appropriate languages with induced τ_Σ topologies (see Subsection 2.6).

Theorem 7. *Suppose a hybrid system is specified as above. If the behaviour of the hybrid system is defined by a continuous function $H : \mathbb{D} \times \mathbb{X} \times \mathbb{R}^+ \to \mathbb{X}$ and there exists a computable function $G : \mathbb{D} \times \mathbb{X} \times \mathbb{R}^+ \to \mathbb{R}^n$ such that $\|H(f, x, t)\| \le G((f, x, t))$ for all $f \in \mathbb{D}$, $x \in \mathbb{X}$ and $t \in \mathbb{R}^+$ then H is computable.*

4.2 Σ_K-constraints and Reachability Problems

In this section we illustrate how Σ_K-constraints can be used for reasoning about hybrid systems. Suppose a hybrid system is formalised by

$$\mathbf{SHS} = \langle TS, \mathbb{X}, \mathbb{U}, \mathbb{D}, Init, \mathbf{F}, Conv1, A, Conv2 \rangle$$

which satisfies the conditions of Theorem 7.

Theorem 8. *The set of Σ-definable sets of $\mathbb{X}$ which are reachable by the hybrid system is computably enumerable.*

Proof. Let A be Σ-definable set. The reachability problem can be formalised as follows: $\psi \rightleftharpoons (\exists x \in Init_{\mathbb{X}}) \exists f \exists t H(f, x, t) \in A$. Since the set of polynomials with rational coefficients is dense in $C(\mathbb{R})$ with the compact open topology, Theorem 6 and Theorem 7 imply the equivalence of ψ and a Σ-formula. So, for every Σ-definable set we can effectively check reachability.

Let $\mathcal{D} = \{f_i\}_{i \in \omega}$ be a computable family of acceptable computable disturbances.

Theorem 9. *The set*

$$\{< i, j > | A_i \text{ is reachable by the hybrid system under a disturbance } f_i,$$
$$\text{where } A_i \text{ is } \Sigma\text{-definable and } f_j \in \mathcal{D}\}$$

is computably enumerable.

Theorem 10. *The set*

$\{< i,j > |K_i$ *is unreachable by the hybrid system in bounded time under*
a disturbance f_i, *where* K_i *is a co-semicomputable compact set and* $f_j \in \mathcal{D}\}$

is computably enumerable.

Proof. Let K be co-semicomputable compact set and time bounded by N and f a computable disturbance. The unreachability problem can be formalised as follows: $\varphi \rightleftharpoons \forall a \in Init_X \forall t \in [0, N] H(f, a, t) \notin K$. By properties of co-semicomputable compact sets, the distance function d_K is lower semicomputable [2], and, as a corollary, $\{x | x \notin K\} = \{x | d_K(x) > 0\}$ is Σ-definable. By Theorem 6 and Proposition 2, φ is equivalent to a Σ-formula. So, for every co-semicomputable compact set we can effectively check unreachability.

Now let us fix Σ-definable set A and co-semicomputable compact set K. Let I_r denote a subset of $Init_X$ from which the set A is reachable and I_u denote a subset of $Init_X$ from which the set K is unreachable in bounded time.

Theorem 11. *The sets* I_r *and* I_u *are* Σ-*definable.*

5   Conclusion

We present a methodology that enables the algorithmic analysis of Σ_K-constraints via translation to effective sequences of quantifier free formulas. We hope that proposed results and existing numerical constraint satisfaction techniques (e.g. [5,23]) will lead to new algorithms for effective continuous constraint solving.

References

1. Anai, H., Weispfenning, V.: Reach set computation using real quantifier elimination. In: Di Benedetto, M.D., Sangiovanni-Vincentelli, A.L. (eds.) HSCC 2001. LNCS, vol. 2034, p. 63. Springer, Heidelberg (2001)
2. Brattka, V., Weihrauch, K.: Computability on subsets of euclidean space I: Closed and compact sets. TCS 219, 65–93 (1999)
3. Barwise, J.: Admissible sets and Structures. Springer, Berlin (1975)
4. Basu, S., Pollack, R., Roy, M.-F.: Algorithms in Real Algebraic Geometry. Springer, Heidelberg (2003)
5. Benhamou, F., Goualard, F., Languénou, E., Christie, M.: Interval constraint solving for camera control and motion planning. ACM Trans. Comput. Log. 5(4), 732–767 (2004)
6. Caviness, B.F., Johnson, J.R. (eds.): Quantifier Elimination and Cylindrical Algebraic Decomposition. Springer, Wien (1998)
7. Collins, G.E.: Hauptvortrag: Quantifier elimination for real closed fields by cylindrical algebraic decomposition. In: Brakhage, H. (ed.) GI-Fachtagung 1975. LNCS, vol. 33, pp. 134–183. Springer, Heidelberg (1975)
8. Ershov, Y.L.: Definability and computability. Plenum, New York (1996)

9. Henzinger, T.A., Rusu, V.: Reachability Verification for Hybrid Automata. In: Henzinger, T.A., Sastry, S.S. (eds.) HSCC 1998. LNCS, vol. 1386, pp. 190–205. Springer, Heidelberg (1998)

10. Immerman, N.: Descriptive Complexity. Springer, Heidelberg (1999)

11. Blass, A., Gurevich, Y.: Background, reserve and Gandy machines. In: Clote, P.G., Schwichtenberg, H. (eds.) CSL 2000. LNCS, vol. 1862, pp. 1–17. Springer, Heidelberg (2000)

12. Korovina, M.V., Kudinov, O.V.: Towards Computability over Effectively Enumerable Topological Spaces. Electr. Notes Theor. Comput. Sci. 202, 305–313 (2008)

13. Korovina, M.V., Kudinov, O.V.: Towards computability of higher type continuous data. In: Cooper, S.B., Löwe, B., Torenvliet, L. (eds.) CiE 2005. LNCS, vol. 3526, pp. 235–241. Springer, Heidelberg (2005)

14. Korovina, M.V.: Computational aspects of Σ-definability over the real numbers without the equality test. In: Baaz, M., Makowsky, J.A. (eds.) CSL 2003. LNCS, vol. 2803, pp. 330–344. Springer, Heidelberg (2003)

15. Korovina, M.V.: Gandy's theorem for abstract structures without the equality test. In: Vardi, M.Y., Voronkov, A. (eds.) LPAR 2003. LNCS, vol. 2850, pp. 290–301. Springer, Heidelberg (2003)

16. Korovina, M.V., Kudinov, O.V.: Semantic characterisations of second-order computability over the real numbers. In: Fribourg, L. (ed.) CSL 2001 and EACSL 2001. LNCS, vol. 2142, pp. 160–172. Springer, Heidelberg (2001)

17. Korovina, M.V., Kudinov, O.V.: Formalisation of Computability of Operators and Real-Valued Functionals via Domain Theory. In: Blank, J., Brattka, V., Hertling, P. (eds.) CCA 2000. LNCS, vol. 2064, pp. 146–168. Springer, Heidelberg (2001)

18. Korovina, M.V., Kudinov, O.V.: Generalised Computability and Applications to Hybrid Systems. In: Bjørner, D., Broy, M., Zamulin, A.V. (eds.) PSI 2001. LNCS, vol. 2244, pp. 494–499. Springer, Heidelberg (2001)

19. Korovina, M.V., Kudinov, O.V.: Characteristic properties of majorant-computability over the reals. In: Gottlob, G., Grandjean, E., Seyr, K. (eds.) CSL 1998. LNCS, vol. 1584, pp. 188–203. Springer, Heidelberg (1999)

20. Dahlhaus, E., Makowsky, J.A.: Query languages for hierarchic databases. Information and Computation 101, 1–32 (1992)

21. Nerode, A., Kohn, W.: Models for Hybrid Systems: Automata, Topologies, Controllability, Observability. In: Grossman, R.L., Ravn, A.P., Rischel, H., Nerode, A. (eds.) HS 1991 and HS 1992. LNCS, vol. 736, pp. 317–357. Springer, Heidelberg (1993)

22. Pour-El, M.B., Richards, J.I.: Computability in Analysis and Physics. Springer, Heidelberg (1988)

23. Ratschan, S., She, Z.: Constraints for Continuous Reachability in the Verification of Hybrid Systems. In: Calmet, J., Ida, T., Wang, D. (eds.) AISC 2006. LNCS (LNAI), vol. 4120, pp. 196–210. Springer, Heidelberg (2006)

24. Tarski, A.: A Decidion Method in Algebra and Geometry. University of California Press, Berkeley (1951)

25. Tiwari, A.: Abstractions for hybrid systems. Formal Methods in System Design 32(1), 57–83 (2008)

26. Weihrauch, K.: Computable Analysis. Springer, Berlin (2000)

A Complete Invariant Generation Approach for P-solvable Loops*

Laura Kovács

EPFL, Switzerland

Abstract. We present an algorithm for generating all polynomial invariants of P-solvable loops with assignments and nested conditionals. We prove termination of our algorithm. The proof relies on showing that the dimensions of the prime ideals from the minimal decomposition of the ideals generated at an iteration of our algorithm either remain the same or decrease at the next iteration of the algorithm. Our experimental results report that our method takes less iterations and/or time than other polynomial invariant generation techniques.

1 Introduction

In [14], a systematic method for generating polynomial invariants for P-solvable loops was developed, as follows. (i) First, the body of a P-solvable loop is described by recurrence equations in the loop counter. (ii) Next, recurrence equations of loop variables are solved using symbolic summation techniques, and closed forms of variables are derived as polynomials in the loop counter and some algebraic exponential sequences in the loop counter, where polynomial relations among the exponential sequences are also generated. (iii) Finally, loop counters and algebraic exponential sequences are eliminated using Gröbner basis computation from the polynomial closed form system of loop variables, and polynomial loop invariants are derived. For P-solvable loops with assignments only, the method was proved to be complete: any other polynomial invariant can be derived from the ones inferred by our approach. In the case of P-solvable loops with k conditional branches, completeness was proved only under additional assumptions, by imposing structural constraints on the ideal of polynomial relations after a sequence of k and $k + 1$ P-solvable loops.

The main result of this paper is the proof of completeness of our invariant generation method for P-solvable loops with nested conditionals. For doing so, (i) we generalize the invariant generation algorithm of [14] for P-solvable loops (Section 3) by iterating our algorithm until the polynomial invariant ideal is inferred (i.e. not just 2 iterations as in [14]), and (ii) prove that our approach is sound and complete (Sections 3 and 4). That is, our method infers a *basis* for the polynomial invariant ideal of the P-solvable loop *in a finite number of steps*. The proof relies on showing that the dimensions of the prime ideals from the minimal decomposition of the ideals generated at an iteration of

---

* The author was supported by the Swiss NSF. This research was partly done in the frame of the Transnational Access Programme at RISC, Johannes Kepler University Linz, supported by the European Commission Framework 6 Programme for Integrated Infrastructures Initiatives under the project SCIEnce (contract No 026133).

A. Pnueli, I. Virbitskaite, and A. Voronkov (Eds.): PSI 2009, LNCS 5947, pp. 242–256, 2010.
© Springer-Verlag Berlin Heidelberg 2010

our algorithm either remain the same or decrease at the next iteration of the algorithm. As dimension of ideals are positive integers, our algorithm must terminate after a finite number of iterations. Our approach was implemented in the `Aligator` software package [13]. Our experimental results report that, when compared to existing invariant generation techniques [18,17], our method took less iterations and/or less time in generating polynomial invariant ideals for all examples we tried (Section 5).

Related Work. The problem of synthesizing valid polynomial relations among program variables has received much attention [10,15,17,19]. The works [15,19] derive all polynomial invariants of *a priori fixed degree* in arbitrary polynomial loops, by generating linear constraints on the unknown coefficients of the template invariant of bounded degree. Solutions to these constraints are substituted in the template invariant, and all invariant relations of bounded degree are thus inferred. A similar approach using quantifier elimination was proposed in [10]. Paper [17] combines abstract interpretation with polynomial algebra for inferring polynomial invariants of bounded degree, without restricting the structure of the loops.

Unlike the works mentioned above, our approach does not require a priori a bound on the degree of sought polynomials, but finds all polynomial invariants by *restricting the structure* of the programs that can be treated by the method. This is also the case in [18], where a basis of the polynomial invariant ideal of so-called simple loops is automatically derived. However, unlike [18], we do not limit our technique to loops whose closed form solution may only involve positive rational exponentials. Our approach treats P-solvable loops with arbitrary algebraic exponential sequences in the closed forms of variables. As affine loops are P-solvable [14], note that our approach is able to generate *all polynomial invariants of affine loops* with assignments, nested conditionals and ignored test conditions, which, to the best of our knowledge, is not the case in any of the aforementioned techniques.

2 Preliminaries

We give a short presentation of P-solvable loops, followed by a brief overview on polynomial ideals, recurrences and algebraic dependencies. For more details see [14,2,4].

In what follows, $\mathbb{N}$ and $\mathbb{Q}$ denote respectively the set of natural and rational numbers. Let $\mathbb{K}$ be a field of characteristic zero (e.g. $\mathbb{Q}$) and $\bar{\mathbb{K}}$ denotes its algebraic closure. Throughout this paper, let $X = \{x_1, \ldots, x_m\}$ be the set of loop variables ($m \in \mathbb{N}$). The ring of all polynomials in X over $\mathbb{K}$ is denoted by $\mathbb{K}[X]$. Rings $\mathbb{K}[X]$ and $\bar{\mathbb{K}}[X]$ are integral domains.

P-solvable Loops. We consider loops as below.

$$\texttt{While}[b, s_0; \texttt{If}[b_1 \texttt{ Then } s_1 \texttt{ Else } \ldots \texttt{ If}[b_{k-1} \texttt{ Then } s_{k-1} \texttt{ Else } s_k]\ldots]; s_{k+1}] \quad (1)$$

where $b_0, \ldots, b_{k-1}$ are boolean expressions, and $s_0, \ldots, s_{k+1}$ are sequences of assignments. In our approach for generating polynomial invariants, test conditions b and b_i are ignored, and we deal with non-deterministic programs. Using regular expression like notation, loop (1) can be thus equivalently written as:

$$(S_1|S_2|\ldots|S_k)^*, \text{ where } S_i = s_0; s_i; s_{k+1} \text{ for all } i = 1, \ldots, k. \quad (2)$$

In our work, we identified a class of loops with assignments, sequencing and nested conditionals, called the P-solvable loops [14], for which tests are ignored. Loop (1) is P-solvable iff the *inner* loops S_i^* from (2) are P-solvable. Namely, the values of X at any iteration of S_i^* can be expressed as polynomials of the initial values of variables (those when the loop is entered), the inner loop counter, and some algebraic exponential sequences in the loop counter, where there are polynomial relations among the exponential sequences. We write $S_i^{j_i}$ to mean the j_i-times repeated execution of S_i, where $j_i \in \mathbb{N}$ denotes the loop counter of S_i. In what follows, for $l = 1, \ldots, m$, we denote by $x_l[j_i]$ the value of variable x_l at the j_ith iteration of S_i. As S_i^* is P-solvable, we have $x_l[j_i] = q_l[j_i, \theta_{l1}^{j_i}, \ldots, \theta_{ls}^{j_i}]$, where $\theta_{lk} \in \bar{\mathbb{K}}$, $q_l \in \bar{\mathbb{K}}[j_i, \theta_{l1}^{j_i}, \ldots, \theta_{ls}^{j_i}]$, and the co-efficients of q_l are determined by the initial values of X (i.e. before entering loop S_i^*). Using Hoare-triple notation [8], $p \in \mathbb{K}[X]$ is a polynomial invariant of (2) iff:

$$\{p(X) = 0\} \quad (S_1 | \ldots | S_k)^* \quad \{p(X) = 0\}$$

In our work for generating polynomial invariants of P-solvable loops, we rely on algorithmic methods from polynomial algebra and symbolic summation, as follows.

Polynomial Ideals and Invariants. A non-empty subset $I \subseteq \mathbb{K}[X]$ is an *ideal* of $\mathbb{K}[X]$, and we write $I \trianglelefteq \mathbb{K}[X]$, if $p_1 + p_2 \in I$ for all p_1, $p_2 \in I$, and $pq \in \mathbb{K}[X]$ for all $p \in I$ and $q \in \mathbb{K}[X]$. The *quotient ring* of $K[X]$ by the ideal I is denoted by $\mathbb{K}[X]/I$, and its elements are of the form $q + I$, where $q \in \mathbb{K}[X]$. The ideal I is called a *radical ideal* if $p^t \in I$ implies $p \in I$ for all $p \in \mathbb{K}[X]$, $t \in \mathbb{N}$. I is a *prime ideal* if, for all $p, q \in \mathbb{K}[X]$, $pq \in I$ implies $p \in I$ or $q \in I$. Obviously, any prime ideal is radical. Radical ideals can be uniquely decomposed into prime ideals, as stated below.

THEOREM 2.1 [2] If $\mathbb{K}$ is algebraically closed (i.e. $\mathbb{K} = \bar{\mathbb{K}}$), then every radical ideal $I \trianglelefteq \bar{\mathbb{K}}[X]$ can be written uniquely as a finite intersection of prime ideals, $I = P_1 \cap \ldots P_r$, where $P_i \not\subseteq P_j$ for $i \neq j$. Such a representation of a radical ideal is called a *minimal decomposition*.

For $I \trianglelefteq \mathbb{K}[X]$, there exists a longest descending chain of prime ideals $I \supsetneq P_1 \supsetneq P_2 \supsetneq \ldots$. Its length is called the *dimension* of I and is denoted by $\dim I$.

As observed in [18], the set of polynomials $p \in \mathbb{K}[X]$ such that $p(X) = 0$ is a polynomial loop invariant forms a polynomial ideal, called the *polynomial invariant ideal*. Hilbert's basis theorem asserts that every ideal, and in particular thus the polynomial invariant ideal, has a finite basis. Using the Buchberger Algorithm [1], a special ideal basis, called Gröbner basis $\{p_1, \ldots, p_r\}$ ($p_i \in \mathbb{K}[X]$) of the polynomial invariant ideal can be effectively computed. Hence, the conjunction of the polynomial equations corresponding to the polynomials from the computed basis (i.e. $p_i(X) = 0$) characterizes completely the polynomial invariants of the loop. Namely, any other polynomial invariant can be derived as a logical consequence of $p_1 = 0 \wedge \cdots \wedge p_r = 0$.

Our challenge is thus to compute *a Gröbner basis of the polynomial invariant ideal*. For doing so, we deploy methods from algorithmic combinatorics, as given below.

Recurrences and Algebraic Dependencies. From the assignment statements of a P-solvable loop S_i^*, *recurrence equations* of the variables are built and solved, using the loop counter j_i as the recurrence index. In our work, we only consider P-solvable loops whose assignment statements describe *Gosper-summable* [6] or *C-finite* [16] recurrences. The closed forms of loop variables can be computed by deploying existing symbolic summation algorithms for solving such recurrences [4,16]. As a result, the value of each variable at iteration j_i of the P-solvable loop $S_i^{j_i}$ will be a a polynomial expression in j_i and some algebraic exponential sequences in j_i.

As we are interested in deriving polynomial relations among X, we need to determine the ideal of *algebraic dependencies* among the algebraic exponential sequences in j_i [12], where an algebraic dependency of the algebraic exponential sequences $\theta_1^{j_i}, \ldots, \theta_s^{j_i}$ with $\theta_i \in \bar{\mathbb{K}}$ is a polynomial $p \in \mathbb{K}[j_i, \theta_1^{j_i}, \ldots, \theta_s^{j_s}]$ such that $p((\theta_1^{j_1})^n, \ldots, (\theta_s^{j_s})^n) = 0, \forall n \in \mathbb{N}$. Using the algebraic dependencies so derived, the loop counter j_i and exponential sequences in j_i are then eliminated by Gröbner basis computation from the closed form system of the loop, and polynomial invariants among X are thus inferred.

EXAMPLE 2.2 [3] Consider the loop S^* with iteration counter $j \in \mathbb{N}$, where $S \equiv q := q/4; p := p/2 + q$. The initial values of variables are $p = q = 1$. The (C-finite) recurrence equations of S^j are: $\begin{cases} q[j+1] = q[j]/4 \\ p[j+1] = p[j]/2 + q[j+1] \end{cases}$, yielding the closed form solution system: $\begin{cases} q[j] = q[0] * a_1 \\ p[j] = (p[0] + q[0]) * a_2 - q[0] * a_3 \end{cases}$, where $a_1 = 4^{-j}$, $a_2 = 2^{-j}$, $a_3 = 4^{-j}$, and $q[0]$ and $p[0]$ denote respectively the initial values of q and p (i.e. $p[0] = q[0] = 1$). The algebraic dependencies among a_1, a_2, a_3 are $\{a_1 - a_3 = 0, a_2^2 - a_3 = 0\}$. After eliminating j, a_1, a_2 and a_3, and substituting the initial values of p and q, the polynomial invariant ideal is generated by the invariant $(p+q)^2 - 4q = 0$.

3   Invariant Generation Algorithm

In [14] polynomial invariants of P-solvable loops with $k \geq 1$ conditional branches were inferred by considering polynomial ideals after k and $k + 1$ loop sequences. Although experimental results reported that [14] returned the polynomial invariant ideal for all tried examples, completeness of the approach was only proved under additional assumptions on the structure of the inferred ideals after k and $k + 1$ loop sequences. In this section we generalize the results of [14] by presenting a new algorithm (Algorithm 3.3) for computing *all* polynomial invariants of P-solvable loops with k conditional branches. The algorithm proposed in this paper iteratively computes the ideal of valid polynomial relations after all possible loop sequences of length $k, k+1, k+2, \ldots$, until a fixed point is reached. Namely, if at step $n \geq 1$ of our invariant generation algorithm the ideal of polynomial relations after all possible loop sequences of length $k + n$ is the same as the ideal computed at step $n - 1$, the algorithm terminates with returning the polynomial invariant ideal (Theorem 3.4). Moreover, we also prove termination of our algorithm (Theorem 4.8).

Our method for invariant generations relies on the following two "ingredients": (i) Algorithm 3.1, for deriving the polynomial ideal after an arbitrary sequence of P-solvable loops of length $k + n$, and (ii) Algorithm 3.2, for computing the polynomial ideal after all loop sequences of length $k + n$. In what follows, we first present these "ingredients".

Algorithm 3.1   Polynomial Relations of a P-solvable Loop Sequence [14]
Input: P-solvable loops $S_{w_1}, \ldots, S_{w_k}$ and initial values X_0

Output: The ideal $G \trianglelefteq \mathbb{K}[X]$ of polynomial relations among X after $S_{w_1}^*; \ldots; S_{w_k}^*$
Assumption: S_{w_i} are sequences of assignments, $w_i \in \{1, \ldots, k\}, j_i \in \mathbb{N}, k \geq 1$

1   **for** each $S_{w_i}^{j_i}$, $i = 1, \ldots, k$ **do**
2   Compute the closed form system of $S_{w_i}^{j_i}$:

$$
\begin{cases}
x_1[j_i] = q_{i,1}(j_i, \theta_{w_i 1}^{j_i}, \ldots, \theta_{w_i s}^{j_i}) \\
\vdots \\
x_m[j_i] = q_{i,m}(j_i, \theta_{w_i 1}^{j_i}, \ldots, \theta_{w_i s}^{j_i})
\end{cases}
, \text{ where }
\begin{array}{l}
\theta_{w_i r} \in \bar{\mathbb{K}}, \\
q_{i,l} \in \bar{\mathbb{K}}[j_i, \theta_{w_i r}^{j_i}], \\
r = 1, \ldots, s, \quad l = 1, \ldots, m
\end{array}
$$

3   Compute the ideal $A_{w_i} = I(j_i, \theta_{w_i 1}^{j_i}, \ldots, \theta_{w_i s}^{j_i})$ of algebraic dependencies
4   **endfor**
5   Compute the *merged* closed form of $S_{w_1}^{j_1}; \ldots; S_{w_k}^{j_k}$:

$$
\begin{cases}
x_1[j_{w_1}, \ldots, j_{w_k}] = f_1(j_1, \theta_{w_1 1}^{j_1}, \ldots, \theta_{w_1 s}^{j_1}, \cdots \cdots, j_k, \theta_{w_k 1}^{j_k}, \ldots, \theta_{w_k s}^{j_k}) \\
\vdots \\
x_m[j_{w_1}, \ldots, j_{w_k}] = f_m(j_1, \theta_{w_1 1}^{j_1}, \ldots, \theta_{w_1 s}^{j_1}, \cdots \cdots, j_k, \theta_{w_k 1}^{j_k}, \ldots, \theta_{w_k s}^{j_k})
\end{cases}
, \text{ where }
$$
$$
f_l \in \bar{\mathbb{K}}[j_1, \ldots, j_k, \theta_{w_1 1}^{j_1}, \ldots, \theta_{w_1 s}^{j_1}, \cdots \cdots, \theta_{w_k 1}^{j_k}, \ldots, \theta_{w_k s}^{j_k}],
$$

6    $A = \sum\limits_{i=1}^{k} A_{w_i}$
7    $I = \langle x_1 - f_1, \ldots, x_m - f_m \rangle + A \subset \bar{\mathbb{K}}[j_1, \ldots, j_k, \theta_{w_1 1}^{j_1}, \ldots, \theta_{w_k s}^{j_k}, x_1, \ldots, x_m]$
8   **return** $G = I \cap \mathbb{K}[x_1, \ldots, x_m]$.

Merging of closed forms at step 5 of Algorithm 3.1 is based on the fact that the initial values of the loop variables corresponding to the inner loop $S_{w_{i+1}}^{j_i+1}$ are given by the final values of the loop variables after $S_{w_i}^{j_i}$. We write $x_l[j_{w_1}, \ldots, j_{w_k}]$ to mean the value of x_l after $S_{w_1}^{j_1}; S_{w_2}^{j_2}; \ldots; S_{w_k}^{j_k}$. Based on [12], we note that although the closed form solutions of the P-solvable loops lie in the polynomial ring over $\bar{\mathbb{K}}$, G is an ideal in the ring $\mathbb{K}[X]$.

EXAMPLE 3.1 (GCD COMPUTATION OF INTEGERS x AND y. [3]) Consider the P-solvable imperative loop $(S_1 | S_2)^*$, where:
$S_1 \equiv a := a - b; p := p - q; r := r - s$ and $S_2 \equiv b := b - a; q := q - p; s := s - r$
The initial values of variables are: $a = x$, $b = y$, $p = 1$, $q = 0$, $r = 0$, $s = 1$.
Using Algorithm 3.1, the ideal I_2^1 of valid polynomial relations among the loop variables a, b, p, q, r, s with initial values $a[0], b[0], p[0], q[0], r[0], s[0]$ after the inner loop sequence $S_1^*; S_2^*$ is given below.

$\begin{aligned}
I_2^1 = \langle &-r\,s\,q[0] + s\,q[0]r[0] + q\,r\,s[0] - s\,p[0]\,s[0] - q[0]\,r[0]\,s[0] + p[0]\,s[0]^2, \\
&-r\,q[0] + q[0]\,r[0] + p\,s[0] - p[0]\,s[0], \quad -q\,r + p\,s + q[0]\,r[0] - p[0]\,s[0], \\
&-s\,b[0]\,p[0] + s\,a[0]\,q[0] + q\,b[0]\,r[0] - b\,q[0]\,r[0] - q\,a[0]\,s[0] + b\,p[0]\,s[0], \\
&-r\,s\,b[0] + s\,b[0]\,r[0] + b\,r\,s[0] - s\,a[0]\,s[0] - b[0]\,r[0]\,s[0] + a[0]\,s[0]^2, \\
&-q\,r\,b[0] + s\,b[0]\,p[0] + b\,r\,q[0] - s\,a[0]\,q[0] - b[0]\,p[0]\,s[0] + a[0]\,q[0]\,s[0], \\
&-p\,q\,b[0] + q\,b[0]\,p[0] + b\,p\,q[0] - q\,a[0]\,q[0] - b[0]\,p[0]\,q[0] + a[0]\,q[0]^2, \\
&-r\,b[0] + b[0]\,r[0] + a\,s[0] - a[0]\,s[0], \quad -p\,b[0] + b[0]\,p[0] + a\,q[0] - a[0]\,q[0], \\
&-b\,r + a\,s + b[0]\,r[0] - a[0]\,s[0], \quad -bp + a\,q + b[0]\,p[0] - a[0]\,q[0] \rangle
\end{aligned}$

Closed form computation for inner loops and variable elimination from merged closed forms of inner loops in Algorithm 3.1 are performed as described in Section 2.

Similarly, by Algorithm 3.1, the ideal I_2^2 of polynomial relations after $S_2^*; S_1^*$ is:

$$
\begin{aligned}
I_2^2 = \langle &-s\,p[0] + q\,r[0] - q[0]\,r[0] + p[0]\,s[0], \; -q\,r + p\,s + q[0]\,r[0] - p[0]\,s[0], \\
&-s\,a[0] + b\,r[0] - b[0]\,r[0] + a[0]s[0], \; -q\,a[0] + b\,p[0] - b[0]\,p[0] + a[0]\,q[0], \\
&-r\,b[0]\,p[0] + r\,a[0]\,q[0] + p\,b[0]\,r[0] - a\,q[0]\,r[0] - p\,a[0]\,s[0] + a\,p[0]\,s[0], \\
&-b\,r + a\,s + b[0]\,r[0] - a[0]\,s[0], \; -bp + a\,q + b[0]\,p[0] - a[0]\,q[0] \rangle
\end{aligned}
$$

Polynomial Relations for a Set of P-solvable Loop Sequences. In what follows, we denote by L_l a set of P-solvable loop sequences of length $l \geq 1$ over $S_1, \ldots, S_k$. Namely, $L = \{\{S_{w_1}, \ldots, S_{w_l}\} \mid w_1, \ldots, w_l \in \{1, \ldots, k\}\}$. We write $|L|$ to mean the number of elements of L, and $L[\![s]\!]$ will refer to the sth element of L, where $s = 1, \ldots, |L|$. Furthermore, for a set $L_l = \{\{S_{w_1}, \ldots, S_{w_L}\} \mid w_l \in \{1, \ldots, k\}\}$ and a P-solvable loop S_i, where $i \in \{1, \ldots, k\}$, we write $L_l \circ S_i$ to mean the set of P-solvable loop sequences of length $l + 1$ obtained by appending S_i to each element of L. Namely, $L_l \circ S_i = \{\{S_{w_1}, \ldots, S_{w_l}, S_i\} \mid \{S_{w_1}, \ldots, S_{w_l}\} \in L\}$.

Our algorithm for computing the ideal of valid polynomial relations after all loop sequences from an arbitrary set of loop sequences is presented in Algorithm 3.2. Algorithm 3.2 generalizes the results of [14], as in our previous work we only computed the ideal of valid polynomial relations after all loop sequences of length k. Correctness of Algorithm 3.2 follows directly from [14].

Algorithm 3.2   Polynomial Relations for a Set of P-solvable Loop Sequences
Input: Set L_l of P-solvable loop sequences of length $l \geq 1$ over $S_1, \ldots, S_k$ and initial values X_0
Output: The ideal $G \trianglelefteq \mathbb{K}[X]$ of valid polynomial relations among X after all P-solvable loop sequences of L
Assumption: $S_1, \ldots, S_k$ are sequences of assignments

```
1   G = Algorithm 3.1(L[[1]], X_0)
2   for s = 2 to |L| do
3       G = G ∩ Algorithm 3.1(L[[s]], X_0)
4   endfor
5   return G.
```

EXAMPLE 3.2 For Example 3.1, consider the set $L_2 = \{\{S_1, S_2\}, \{S_2, S_1\}\}$ of P-solvable loop sequences of length 2. Using the notations of Example 3.1, the polynomial relations for L_2 are given by the intersection ideal $G = I_2^1 \cap I_2^2$, and it is generated by 18 polynomials.

Polynomial Invariant Ideal for a P-solvable Loop with Nested Conditionals. Let $\mathfrak{S}_k$ denote the set of permutations of length k over $\{1, \ldots, k\}$. We are now ready to present our invariant generation method in Algorithm 3.3. Unlike [14], Algorithm 3.3 computes a *finite basis* of the polynomial invariant ideal, and thus it is complete.

Algorithm 3.3   Polynomial Relations for P-solvable Loops with Conditionals
Input: P-solvable loop (1) with k conditional branches and assignments
Output: Polynomial invariant ideal $PI \trianglelefteq \mathbb{K}[X]$ for (1)
Assumption: $k \geq 1$

1   Transform loop (1) into loop (2) with k P-solvable inner loops $S_1^*, \ldots, S_k^*$
2   $L_k = \{\{S_{w_1}, \ldots, S_{w_k}\} \mid (w_1, \ldots, w_k) \in \mathfrak{S}_k\}$ and $l = k$
3   $PI = $ Algorithm 3.2(L_l, X_0)
4   **repeat**
5       $PI' = PI$
6       $L_{l+1} = \bigcup\limits_{i=1}^{k} L_l \circ S_i$
7       $PI = $ Algorithm 3.2(L_{l+1}, X_0)
8       $l := l + 1$
9   **until** $PI = PI'$
10 **return** PI.

We denote by PI_n the ideal PI computed at the nth iteration of the loop between lines 4-9 of Algorithm 3.3. PI_0 denotes the ideal computed at step 3 of Algorithm 3.3. Further, we denote by PI_* the polynomial invariant ideal of the P-solvable loop (1). Generalizing the results of [14], the relations between PI_n and PI_* are summarized in Theorem 3.3.

THEOREM 3.3 [14] For any $n \geq 0$, $PI_* \subseteq PI_{n+1} \subseteq PI_n$. If $PI_{n+1} = PI_n$, then $PI_* = PI_n$.

THEOREM 3.4 Algorithm 3.3 is correct. That is, whenever it terminates, $PI = PI_*$.

Proof The returned ideal PI has the property that there exists an $n \geq 0$ such that $PI = PI_n = PI_{n+1}$. By Theorem 3.3, we thus conclude that $PI = PI_n = PI_*$.

EXAMPLE 3.5   Consider Example 3.2. The ideal PI_0 of polynomial relations after loop sequences of length 2 is derived at step 3 of Algorithm 3.3. Using notations of Example 3.2, we have $PI_0 = G$. Next, at step 7 of Algorithm 3.3, the ideal PI_1 of valid polynomial relations after all loop sequences of length 3 is inferred:

$$PI_1 = \langle -b\,p + a\,q + b[0]\,p[0] - a[0]\,q[0],$$
$$-b\,r + a\,s + b[0]\,r[0] - a[0]\,s[0], \quad -q\,r + p\,s + q[0]\,r[0] - p[0]\,s[0],$$
$$-r\,b[0]\,p[0] + r\,a[0]\,q[0] + p\,b[0]\,r[0] - a\,q[0]\,r[0] - p\,a[0]\,s[0] + a\,p[0]\,s[0],$$
$$-s\,b[0]\,p[0] + s\,a[0]\,q[0] + q\,b[0]\,r[0] - b\,q[0]\,r[0] - q\,a[0]\,s[0] + b\,p[0]\,s[0]\rangle$$

As $\langle PI_1 \rangle \neq \langle PI_0 \rangle$, at step 7 of Algorithm 3.3 the ideal PI_2 of valid polynomial relations after all loop sequences of length 4 is next computed:

$$PI_2 = \langle -b\,p + a\,q + b[0]\,p[0] - a[0]\,q[0],$$
$$-b\,r + a\,s + b[0]\,r[0] - a[0]\,s[0], \quad -q\,r + p\,s + q[0]\,r[0] - p[0]\,s[0],$$
$$-r\,b[0]\,p[0] + r\,a[0]\,q[0] + p\,b[0]\,r[0] - a\,q[0]\,r[0] - p\,a[0]\,s[0] + a\,p[0]\,s[0],$$
$$-s\,b[0]\,p[0] + s\,a[0]\,q[0] + q\,b[0]\,r[0] - b\,q[0]\,r[0] - q\,a[0]\,s[0] + b\,p[0]\,s[0]\rangle$$

As $\langle PI_2 \rangle = \langle PI_2 \rangle$, Algorithm 3.3 terminates in 2 iterations, and the returned polynomial invariant ideal is PI_1.

Further we may substitute in PI_1 the concrete values for the symbolically treated initial values $a[0], b[0], p[0], q[0], r[0], s[0]$. The ideal of polynomial invariants is thus generated by the set:

$$\{ -bp + aq + y, \; -br + as - x, \; -1 - qr + ps, \; a - px - ry, \; b - qx - sy \}.$$

4 Termination of the Invariant Generation Algorithm

In this section we prove that Algorithm 3.3 terminates, as follows. (1) We first prove that the polynomial ideals after $k + n$ P-solvable loops are radical, and thus they admit a minimal decomposition (Theorems 4.3, 4.4, and 4.7). (2) Next, we prove that the dimensions of the prime ideals from the minimal decomposition of a polynomial ideal I_{k+n+1} after a P-solvable loop sequence of length $k + n + 1$ are less or equal than the dimensions of prime ideals from the minimal decomposition of ideal I_{k+n} after a P-solvable loop sequence of length $k + n$. If a prime ideal from I_{k+n+1} decreases its dimension wrt a prime ideal of I_{k+n}, it means that some polynomials from the minimal decomposition of I_{k+n} are not invariant (Theorem 4.6 and 4.7). (3) However, the dimension cannot strictly decrease infinitely, and thus our algorithm must terminate in a finite number of steps (Theorem 4.8).

In what follows we state and prove the results enumerated above. For this we need one additional lemma proving the primeness of ideals of algebraic dependencies.

LEMMA 4.1 For every $i \in \{1, \ldots, k\}$, let A_i be the ideal of algebraic dependencies among the exponential sequences from the closed form system of loop S_i^*. For any $i, i_1, i_2 \in \{1, \ldots, k\}$, A_i and $A_{i_1} + A_{i_2}$ are prime.

Proof For $i = 1, \ldots, k$, we denote by $\Theta_i = \{\theta_{i1}^{j_i}, \ldots \ldots, \theta_{is}^{j_i}\}$ the set of exponential sequences from the closed form of the P-solvable loop S_i^* with iteration counter $j_i \in \mathbb{N}$. We only prove that A_i is prime. The primeness of $A_{i_1} + A_{i_2}$ can be done in the similar manner, by using the fact that $A_i + A_j$ generates the ideal of all algebraic dependencies among $j_{i_1}, j_{i_2}, \Theta_{i_1}, \Theta_{i_2}$. Consider $p, q \in \bar{\mathbb{K}}[j_i, \Theta_i]$ such that $pq \in A_i$. We then have $pq = 0$. As $\bar{\mathbb{K}}[j_i, \Theta_i]$ is an integral domain, we conclude that $p = 0$ or $q = 0$, yielding that $p \in A_i$ or $q \in A_i$.

4.1 Polynomial Relations of $k + n$ and $k + n + 1$ Loop Sequences, with $n \geq 0$

For simplicity of notations, let $n = 0$. We consider an arbitrary P-solvable loop sequence of length k, and let I_k denote the ideal of polynomial relations after the P-solvable loop sequence of length k. We build a P-solvable loop of length $k + 1$ by appending a P-solvable loop to the considered loop sequence of length k. Let I_{k+1} denote the ideal of polynomial relations after this sequence of $k + 1$ loops. We show that I_k and I_{k+1} are radical ideals (Theorem 4.4), and the dimensions of prime ideals from the minimal decomposition of I_{k+1} are less or equal than the dimensions of the prime ideals from the minimal decomposition of I_k (Theorem 4.6).

W.l.o.g., for the P-solvable loop sequence of length k we consider the loop sequence $S_1^*; \ldots; S_k^*$, and take $S_1^*; \ldots; S_k^*; S_1^*$ for the P-solvable loop sequence of length $k + 1$. We write $J_k = \{j_1, \ldots, j_k\}$, where $j_i \in \mathbb{N}$ is the loop counter of S_i^* from the loop-sequence $S_1^*; \ldots; S_k^*$. Further, we denote by Θ_k the set of all algebraic exponential sequences in j_i from the polynomial closed forms of all $S_i^{j_i}$. By Algorithm 3.1:

$$I_k = \langle x_1 - q_1, \ldots, x_m - q_m \rangle + \sum_{i=1}^{k} A_i \cap \mathbb{K}[X], \tag{3}$$

where $q_l \in \bar{\mathbb{K}}[\Theta_k, J_k]$, and A_i is the ideal of algebraic dependencies of $S_i^{j_i}$. We write $A_k^* = \sum_{i=1}^{k} A_i$. Similarly, we write $J_{k+1} = J_k \cup \{j_{k+1}\}$, where $j_{k+1} \in \mathbb{N}$ is the loop counter of the $k + 1$th loop from $S_1^*; \ldots; S_k^*; S_1^*$. We denote by Θ_{k+1} the set of all exponential sequences from the polynomial closed forms of each loop of $S_1^*; \ldots; S_k^*; S_1^*$. Note that the polynomial closed form of $S_1^*; \ldots; S_k^*; S_1^*$ is computed by merging the closed form of the $k + 1$th loop with the closed form of $S_1^*; \ldots; S_k^*$. Namely, the initial values of variables X in the polynomial closed form of the $k + 1$th loop are given by the values of variables X after $S_1^*; \ldots; S_k^*$. Let $Y = \{y_1, \ldots, y_m\}$ respectively denote the values of $X = \{x_1, \ldots, x_m\}$ after $S_1^*; \ldots; S_k^*$. By Algorithm 3.1:

$$I_{k+1} = \langle x_1 - p_1, \ldots, x_m - p_m, y_1 - q_1, \ldots, y_m - q_m \rangle + A_k^* + A_{k+1} \cap \bar{\mathbb{K}}[X], \quad (4)$$

where $q_l \in \bar{\mathbb{K}}[\Theta_k, J_k]$ and A_k^* are as in (3), $p_l \in \bar{\mathbb{K}}[j_{k+1}, \Theta_{k+1} \setminus \Theta_k, Y]$, and $A_{k+1} \in \bar{\mathbb{K}}[j_{k+1}, \Theta_{k+1} \setminus \Theta_k]$ is the ideal of algebraic dependencies of $S_1^{j_{k+1}}$. We write $A_{k+1}^* = A_k^* + A_{k+1}$. Observe that considering the polynomials of A_{k+1} in computing the polynomial relations after $S_1^{j_1}; \ldots; S_k^{j_k}$ would yield the same elimination ideal I_k. Hence:

$$I_k = \langle x_1 - q_1, \ldots, x_m - q_m \rangle + A_{k+1}^* \cap \bar{\mathbb{K}}[X].$$

In what follows, we write $\mathfrak{a}_k = \langle x_1 - q_1, \ldots, x_m - q_m \rangle + A_{k+1}^*$ and $\mathfrak{a}_{k+1} = \langle x_1 - p_1, \ldots, x_m - p_m, y_1 - q_1, \ldots, y_m - q_m \rangle + A_{k+1}^*$. Note that $\mathfrak{a}_k \trianglelefteq \bar{\mathbb{K}}[J_{k+1}, \Theta_{k+1}, X]$, $\mathfrak{a}_{k+1} \trianglelefteq \bar{\mathbb{K}}[J_{k+1}, \Theta_{k+1}, X, Y]$, and we have:

$$I_k = \mathfrak{a}_k \cap \bar{\mathbb{K}}[X] \quad \text{and} \quad I_{k+1} = \mathfrak{a}_{k+1} \cap \bar{\mathbb{K}}[X]. \quad (5)$$

Using the notations above, we prove that the ideals $\mathfrak{a}_k, \mathfrak{a}_{k+1}, I_k$ and I_{k+1} are prime (Theorems 4.3 and 4.4). For this, we need Lemma 4.2, which says that extending a ring by an element does not change the ring.

LEMMA 4.2 [11] Let $I \trianglelefteq \mathbb{K}[X]$ be a prime ideal. For all $q \in \mathbb{K}[X]$, the ideal $I' = \langle I \cup \{p\} \rangle \trianglelefteq \mathbb{K}[X, y]$ with $p = y - q$ is prime and $\mathbb{K}[X]/I \cong \mathbb{K}[x, y]/I'$.

THEOREM 4.3 $\mathfrak{a}_k$ and $\mathfrak{a}_{k+1}$ are prime ideals.

Proof
(1) For each $r = 1, \ldots, m$, let $P_r = x_r - q_r \in \bar{\mathbb{K}}[J_{k+1}, \Theta_{k+1}, x_r]$. For each $l = 0, \ldots, m$, we define the ideals $\mathfrak{b}'_l \trianglelefteq \bar{\mathbb{K}}[J_{k+1}, \Theta_{k+1}, x_1, \ldots, x_l]$ recursively:

$$\mathfrak{b}'_l = A_{k+1}^*, \text{ if } l = 0, \quad \text{and} \quad \mathfrak{b}'_l = \langle \mathfrak{b}'_{l-1} \cup \{P_l\} \rangle, \text{ if } 1 \le l \le m.$$

Using Lemma 4.1, we conclude that $\mathfrak{b}'_0 = A_{k+1}^*$ is prime. By Lemma 4.2, the primeness of each $\mathfrak{b}'_l$ implies the primeness of $\mathfrak{b}'_{l+1}$, and observe that $\mathfrak{a}_k = \mathfrak{b}'_m$.
(2) Consider the ring homomorphism $f : \bar{\mathbb{K}}[J_{k+1}, \Theta_{k+1}, X] \to \bar{\mathbb{K}}[J_{k+1}, \Theta_{k+1}, Y]$:

$$x_l \to y_l, \text{ for each } l = 1, \ldots, m \text{ and } c \to c, \text{ for all } c \in \bar{\mathbb{K}}[J_{k+1}, \Theta_{k+1}] \quad (6)$$

Obviously, $\mathfrak{a}_k \cong f(\mathfrak{a}_k)$, and hence $f(\mathfrak{a}_k) \trianglelefteq \bar{\mathbb{K}}[J_{k+1}, \Theta_{k+1}, Y]$ is prime. Note that $\mathfrak{a}_{k+1} = f(\mathfrak{a}_k) + \langle x_1 - p_1, \ldots, x_m - p_m \rangle$.
Further, for each $r = 1, \ldots, m$, let $P_r = x_r - p_r \in \bar{\mathbb{K}}[J_{k+1}, \Theta_{k+1}, Y, x_r]$. For each $l = 0, \ldots, m$, we define the ideals $\mathfrak{b}'_l \trianglelefteq \bar{\mathbb{K}}[J_{k+1}, \Theta_{k+1}, Y, x_1, \ldots, x_l]$ recursively:

$$\mathfrak{b}'_l = f(\mathfrak{a}_k) \text{ if } l = 0 \quad \text{and} \quad \mathfrak{b}'_l = \langle \mathfrak{b}'_{l-1} \cup \{P_l\} \rangle, \text{ if } 1 \le l \le m.$$

By Lemma 4.2, the primeness of each $\mathfrak{b}'_l$ carries over to $\mathfrak{b}'_{l+1}$. As $\mathfrak{a}_{k+1} = \mathfrak{b}'_m$, we conclude that $\mathfrak{a}_{k+1}$ is prime.

THEOREM 4.4 The ideals I_k and I_{k+1} are prime.

Proof We only prove the primeness of $I_k \trianglelefteq \bar{\mathbb{K}}[X]$. Proving that I_{k+1} is prime can be done in a similar manner. Consider $p, q \in \bar{\mathbb{K}}[X]$ such that $pq \in I_k = \mathfrak{a}_k \cap \bar{\mathbb{K}}[X] \subseteq \mathfrak{a}_k$. By Theorem 4.3, $\mathfrak{a}_k$ is prime, and we conclude that $p \in \mathfrak{a}_k$ or $q \in \mathfrak{a}_k$. Thus, $p \in \mathfrak{a}_k \cap \bar{\mathbb{K}}[X]$ or $q \in \mathfrak{a}_k \cap \bar{\mathbb{K}}[X]$, and I_k is prime.

We note that $\mathfrak{a}_k$ and $\mathfrak{a}_{k+1}$ are radical ideals as they are prime. Then, using Theorem 2.1, they admit a minimal decomposition.

THEOREM 4.5 Let $\mathfrak{a}_k = \bigcap_{r=1}^{t} U_r$ be the prime ideal decomposition of $\mathfrak{a}_k$, where $t \in \mathbb{N}$, $U_r \trianglelefteq \bar{\mathbb{K}}[J_{k+1}, \Theta_{k+1}, X]$ are prime ideals, and $U_a \not\subseteq U_b$ for any $a \neq b$. Then there exist prime ideals $V_r \trianglelefteq \bar{\mathbb{K}}[J_{k+1}, \Theta_{k+1}, X, Y]$ with $V_a \not\subseteq V_b$ for any $a \neq b$ such that:

1. $\mathfrak{a}_{k+1} = \bigcap_{r=1}^{t} V_r$;
2. $\bar{\mathbb{K}}[J_{k+1}, \Theta_{k+1}, X, Y]/V_r \cong \bar{\mathbb{K}}[J_{k+1}, \Theta_{k+1}, X]/U_r$;
3. $V_r \cap \bar{\mathbb{K}}[J_{k+1}, \Theta_{k+1}, X]$ is prime and $\dim(V_r \cap \bar{\mathbb{K}}[J_{k+1}, \Theta_{k+1}, X]) \leq \dim U_r$.

Proof Consider $f : \bar{\mathbb{K}}[J_{k+1}, \Theta_{k+1}, X] \rightarrow \bar{\mathbb{K}}[J_{k+1}, \Theta_{k+1}, Y]$ as defined in (6).

(1) For every $r = 1, \ldots, t$, we obviously have $U_r \cong f(U_r)$, and the ideal $f(U_r) \trianglelefteq \bar{\mathbb{K}}[J_{k+1}, \Theta_{k+1}, Y]$ is thus prime. As $\mathfrak{a}_{k+1} = f(\mathfrak{a}_k) + \langle x_1 - p_1, \ldots, x_m - p_m \rangle$, we have $\mathfrak{a}_{k+1} = (\bigcap_{r=1}^{t} f(U_r)) + \langle x_1 - p_1, \ldots, x_m - p_m \rangle = \bigcap_{r=1}^{t} (f(U_r) + \langle x_1 - p_1, \ldots, x_m - p_m \rangle)$. Let us denote by $V_r = f(U_r) + \langle x_1 - p_1, \ldots, x_m - p_m \rangle \trianglelefteq \bar{\mathbb{K}}[J_{k+1}, \Theta_{k+1}, Y, X]$, and we have $\mathfrak{a}_{k+1} = \bigcap_{r=1}^{t} V_r$. The m-fold application of Lemma 4.2 asserts furthermore that V_r is prime, and

$$\bar{\mathbb{K}}[J_{k+1}, \Theta_{k+1}, X, Y]/V_r \cong \bar{\mathbb{K}}[J_{k+1}, \Theta_{k+1}, Y]/f(U_r). \tag{7}$$

Moreover, for any $a, b \in \{1, \ldots, t\}$ such that $a \neq b$ we have $V_a \not\subseteq V_b$, since $U_a \not\subseteq U_b$ implies $f(U_a) \not\subseteq f(U_b)$.

(2) As $\bar{\mathbb{K}}[J_{k+1}, \Theta_{k+1}, Y]/f(U_r) \cong \bar{\mathbb{K}}[J_{k+1}, \Theta_{k+1}, X]/U_r$, using (7) we obtain:

$$\bar{\mathbb{K}}[J_{k+1}, \Theta_{k+1}, X, Y]/V_r \cong \bar{\mathbb{K}}[J_{k+1}, \Theta_{k+1}, X]/U_r \text{ and } \dim V_r = \dim U_r. \tag{8}$$

(3) We denote $W_r = V_r \cap \bar{\mathbb{K}}[\Theta_{k+1}, J_{k+1}, X]$, and hence $W_r \subseteq V_r$. The primeness of V_r implies that W_r is prime. By (8), we then have $\dim W_r \leq \dim V_r = \dim U_r$.

We finally state the theorem relating I_k and I_{k+1}.

THEOREM 4.6 The ideals I_k and I_{k+1} can be written uniquely as:

$$I_k = (\bigcap_{r=1}^{t} U_r) \cap \bar{\mathbb{K}}[X] \quad \text{and} \quad I_{k+1} = (\bigcap_{r'=1}^{t'} W_{r'}) \cap \bar{\mathbb{K}}[X],$$

where $t, t' \in \mathbb{N}$ with $t' \leq t$, and:

- $U_r, W_{r'} \trianglelefteq \bar{\mathbb{K}}[J_{k+1}, \Theta_{k+1}, X]$ are prime ideals;
- $U_a \not\subseteq U_b$ and $W_{a'} \not\subseteq W_{b'}$ for any $a \neq b$ and $a' \neq b'$;
- for every $r' \in \{1, \ldots, t'\}$ there exists $r \in \{1, \ldots, t\}$ such that $\dim W_{r'} \leq \dim U_r$.

Proof Take U_r and W_r as defined in the proof of Theorem 4.5.

We have $I_k = (\bigcap_{r=1}^t U_r) \cap \bar{\mathbb{K}}[X]$ and $I_{k+1} = (\bigcap_{r=1}^t W_r) \cap \bar{\mathbb{K}}[X]$, where $t \in \mathbb{N}$, $U_r, W_r \trianglelefteq \bar{\mathbb{K}}[J_{k+1}, \Theta_{k+1}, X]$ are prime, $U_a \not\subseteq U_b$ for any $a \neq b$, and $\dim W_r \leq \dim U_r$ for every $r = 1, \ldots, t$. However, $W_a \not\subseteq W_b$ for any $a \neq b$ may not be the case. Following the notation from the proof of Theorem 4.5, we have $W_r = V_r \cap \bar{\mathbb{K}}[\Theta_{k+1}, J_{k+1}, X]$, where $V_a \not\subseteq V_b$ for any $a \neq b$. We then take the maximal subset $\{W_1, \ldots, W_{t'}\} \subseteq \{W_1, \ldots, W_t\}$ with $t' \leq t$, satisfying the following properties: (1) for every $r' \in \{1, \ldots, t'\}$ there exists $r \in \{1, \ldots, t\}$ such that $W_{r'} = W_r$, and (2) $W_{a'} \not\subseteq W_{b'}$ for every $a' \neq b'$. In other words, we only keep those prime ideals W_r that are not included in each other. Hence, $I_{k+1} = (\bigcap_{r'=1}^{t'} W_{r'}) \cap \bar{\mathbb{K}}[X]$. From the properties of W_r' so constructed, we finally infer that for every $r' \in \{1, \ldots, t'\}$ there exists $r \in \{1, \ldots, t\}$ such that $\dim W_{r'} = \dim W_r \leq \dim U_r$.

Theorems 4.4 and 4.6 can be obviously generalized to ideals of polynomial relations for $k + n$ and $k + n + 1$ loop sequences, where the loop sequence of length $k + n + 1$ is obtained by appending an arbitrary P-solvable loop to the considered loop sequence of length $k + n$. In the sequel, J_{k+n+1} and Θ_{k+n+1} denote respectively the set of iteration counters and the set of all algebraic dependencies from the closed forms of the considered $k + n + 1$ loops.

THEOREM 4.7 The ideals I_{k+n} and I_{k+n+1} are prime and can be written uniquely as:

$$I_{k+n} = (\bigcap_{r=1}^t U_r) \cap \bar{\mathbb{K}}[X] \qquad \text{and} \qquad I_{k+n+1} = (\bigcap_{r'=1}^{t'} W_{r'}) \cap \bar{\mathbb{K}}[X],$$

where $t, t' \in \mathbb{N}$ with $t' \leq t$, and:

- $U_r, W_{r'} \trianglelefteq \bar{\mathbb{K}}[J_{k+n+1}, \Theta_{k+n+1}, X]$ are prime ideals;
- $U_a \not\subseteq U_b$ and $W_{a'} \not\subseteq W_{b'}$ for any $a \neq b$ and $a' \neq b'$;
- for every $r' \in \{1, \ldots, t'\}$ there exists $r \in \{1, \ldots, t\}$ such that $\dim W_{r'} \leq \dim U_r$.

4.2 Termination of Algorithm 3.3

We now prove termination of Algorithm 3.3.

THEOREM 4.8 Algorithm 3.3 terminates. That is, there exists $n \geq 0$ such that $PI_n = PI_{n+1}$.

Proof Let us first fix some notations. Lines 3 and 7 of Algorithm 3.3 assert:

$$PI_n = \bigcap_{s=1}^{|L_{k+n}|} I_{k+n}^s \qquad \text{for every } n \geq 0 \tag{9}$$

where I_{k+n}^s denotes the ideal of polynomial relations after the P-solvable loop sequence $L_{k+n}[\![s]\!]$ of length $k + n$. For any ideal $I_{k+n}^s \trianglelefteq \bar{\mathbb{K}}[X]$, whose minimal decomposition contains N_d prime ideals of dimension d ($d = 0, 1, 2, \ldots$), we define the vector (in the style of [11] – Theorem 4.5):

$$v(I_{k+n}^s) = (\ldots, N_2, N_1, N_0).$$

Since any radical ideal admits a *finite* decomposition of prime ideals, note that I_{k+n}^s has only a finite number of non-zero entries N_d. Thus for any I_{k+n}^s there exists a $D \in \mathbb{N}$ such that for all $d \geq D$ we have $N_d = 0$. This property allows us to lexicographically compare the vectors $v(I_{k+n}^s)$ and $v(I_{k+n'}^{s'})$ of arbitrary two ideals I_{k+n}^s and $I_{k+n'}^{s'}$, as follows. For two ideals $I_{k+n}^s, I_{k+n'}^{s'} \trianglelefteq \bar{\mathbb{K}}[X]$, we say that $v(I_{k+n}^s) = (\ldots, N_2, N_1, N_0)$ is less than $v(I_{k+n'}^{s'}) = (\ldots, N_2', N_1', N_0')$ and write $v(I_{k+n}^s) \prec v(I_{n'}^{n'})$ iff $N_d < N_d'$ for the maximal d with $N_d \neq N_d'$.

From Theorem 3.3, we have $PI_{n+1} \subseteq PI_n$ for any $n \in \mathbb{N}$. Assume that there exists an $n \in \mathbb{N}$ such that $PI_{n+1} \subsetneq PI_n$. (Otherwise, there is nothing to prove, since $PI_n = PI_{n+1}$ implies termination.) Hence, there exists $p \in \bar{\mathbb{K}}[X]$ such that:

$$p \in PI_n \qquad \text{and} \qquad p \notin PI_{n+1}. \tag{10}$$

From (9), we have:

$$PI_n = \bigcap_{s=1}^{|L_{k+n}|} I_{k+n}^s \qquad \text{and} \qquad PI_{n+1} = \bigcap_{s'=1}^{|L_{k+n+1}|} I_{k+n+1}^{s'}, \tag{11}$$

where I_{k+n}^s and $I_{k+n+1}^{s'}$ denote respectively the ideal of polynomial relations after the P-solvable loop sequences $L_{k+n}[s]$ of length $k+n$, and $L_{k+n+1}[s']$ of length $k+n+1$. By (10), we then have $p \in I_{k+n}^s$ for all $s \in \{1, \ldots, |L_{k+n}|\}$, and there exists an $s_0' \in \{1, \ldots, |L_{k+n+1}|\}$ such that $p \notin I_{k+n+1}^{s_0'}$. From line 6 of Algorithm 3.3, there exists $s_0 \in \{1, \ldots, |L_{k+n}|\}$ and $i \in \{1, \ldots, k\}$ such that $L_{k+n+1}[s_0'] = L_{k+n}[s_0] \circ S_i$. Observe that:

$$p \in I_{k+n}^{s_0} \qquad \text{and} \qquad p \notin I_{k+n}^{s_0'}. \tag{12}$$

Let J_{k+n+1} and Θ_{k+n+1} denote respectively the set of iteration counters and the set of algebraic exponentials from the closed forms of all $k + n + 1$ loops from $L_{k+n+1}[s_0']$. By Theorem 4.7, the minimal decomposition of the ideals $I_{k+n+1}^{s_0'}$ and $I_{k+n}^{s_0}$ is:

$$I_{k+n}^{s_0} = \left(\bigcap_{r=1}^{t} U_r \right) \cap \bar{\mathbb{K}}[X] \qquad \text{and} \qquad I_{k+n+1}^{s_0'} = \left(\bigcap_{r'=1}^{t'} W_{r'} \right) \cap \bar{\mathbb{K}}[X], \tag{13}$$

where $t, t' \in \mathbb{N}$ with $t' \leq t$, $U_r, W_{r'} \trianglelefteq \bar{\mathbb{K}}[J_{k+n+1}\Theta_{k+n+1}, X]$ are prime, $U_a \not\subseteq U_b$ and $W_{a'} \not\subseteq W_{b'}$ for any $a \neq b$ and $a' \neq b'$, and for every $r' \in \{1, \ldots, t'\}$ there exists $r \in \{1, \ldots, t\}$ such that $\dim W_{r'} \leq \dim U_r$.

Let us write $A_r = U_r \cap \bar{\mathbb{K}}[X]$ and $B_{r'} = W_{r'} \cap \bar{\mathbb{K}}[X]$. We thus have $I_{k+n}^{s_0} = \bigcap_{r=1}^{t} A_r$ and $I_{k+n+1}^{s_0'} = \bigcap_{r'=1}^{t'} B_{r'}$. W.l.o.g., we assume that $A_a \not\subseteq A_b$ for any $a \neq b$, and $B_a \not\subseteq B_b$ for any $a \neq b$. (Otherwise, similarly to Theorem 4.6, we only keep those A_a and $B_{a'}$ that are not included in other ideals A_b and $B_{b'}$, respectively). We conclude that A_r and $B_{r'}$ are respectively the prime ideals from the minimal decomposition of $I_{k+n}^{s_0}$ and $I_{k+n+1}^{s_0'}$. Moreover, for every $r' \in \{1, \ldots, t'\}$ there exists $r \in \{1, \ldots, t\}$ such that $\dim B_{r'} \leq \dim A_r$. Then, (12) asserts the existence of $r' \in \{1, \ldots, t\}$ and $r \in \{1, \ldots, t'\}$ such that $\dim B_{r'} < \dim A_r$. It follows that $v(I_{k+n+1}^{s_0'}) \prec v(I_{k+n}^{s_0})$. Furthermore, observe that an infinite sequence

$$\cdots \prec v(I_{k+n+2}^{s_0''}) \prec v(I_{k+n+1}^{s_0'}) \prec v(I_{k+n}^{s_0})$$

cannot exist (Dickson's Lemma). Hence there exits an $n_s \geq 0$ such that $v(I_{k+n+n_s}^{s_0^{(n_s)}}) = v(I_{k+n+n_s+1}^{s_0^{(n_s+1)}})$, which implies $I_{k+n+n_s}^{s_0^{(n_s)}} = I_{k+n_s+n+1}^{s_0^{(n_s+1)}}$, where $s_0^{(n_s)}$ is the short-hand notation for $\overbrace{s_0 \cdots}^{n_s \text{ times}}$. We denoted respectively by $I_{k+n+n_s}^{s_0^{(n_s)}}$ and $I_{k+n+n_s+1}^{s_0^{(n_s+1)}}$ the ideals of polynomial relations after $L_{k+n+n_s}[s_0^{(n_s)}]$ and $L_{k+n+n_s+1}[s_0^{(n_s+1)}]$, with the property that there exists $i \in \{1, \ldots, k\}$ such that $L_{k+n+n_s+1}[s_0^{(n_s+1)}] = L_{k+n+n_s}[s_0^{(n_s)}] \circ S_i$.

Thus, for every n and s_0 with $I_{k+n}^{s_0} \neq I_{k+n+1}^{s_0'}$, there exits $n_s \geq 0$ such that $I_{k+n+n_s}^{s_0^{(n_s)}} = I_{k+n+n_s+1}^{s_0^{(n_s+1)}}$. By taking $n_* = \text{Max}(n_s)$, we have $PI_{n+n_*} = PI_{n+n_*+1}$ (note that $PI_{n+1} \subsetneq PI_n$), which implies that Algorithm 3.3 terminates.

5   Experimental Results

We have implemented our method in the Aligator software package [13] – available from http://mtc.epfl.ch/software-tools/Aligator/. We have successfully tested our approach on a large number of examples. For all examples we tried, a basis of the polynomial invariant ideal was inferred in at most 2 iterations of Algorithm 3.3. When compared to existing invariant generation techniques [18,17], our method reported less time and/or iterations on all examples we tried. We summarize some of our experimental results, obtained on a machine with $1.6GHz$ processor and $1.75Gb$ of memory, in Table 4.2. For more details and examples we refer to the above mentioned URL of Aligator.

For each benchmark example, we present results obtained by our Aligator tool, the Solvable tool implementing the approach described in [18], and the Inv tool implementing the method of [17]. For each tool, we present the required time in generating polynomial invariants, the number of iterations needed by the tool's main algorithm to infer invariants, and the number of invariants that were derived. Aligator and Solvable inferred the basis of the ideal of all polynomial invariants, whereas Inv

Table 1. Experimental Results on Benchmark Examples

		Timing	♯ Iters	♯ Polys			Timing	♯ Iters	♯ Polys
Binary Division [9]	Aligator	0.55 s	1	1	**LCM-GCD** [3]	Aligator	1.23 s	2	1
	Solvable	1.78 s	3	1		Solvable	2.01 s	5	1
	Inv	1.77 s	5	1		Inv	4.32 s	9	1
		Timing	♯ Iters	♯ Polys			Timing	♯ Iters	♯ Polys
Euclid's Alg. [7]	Aligator	9.02 s	2	5	**Binary Product** [7]	Aligator	0.63 s	1	1
	Solvable	3.05 s	5	5		Solvable	1.74 s	4	1
	Inv	4.13 s	8	1		Inv	2.79 s	8	1
		Timing	♯ Iters	♯ Polys			Timing	♯ Iters	♯ Polys
Fermat's Alg. [7]	Aligator	0.24 s	1	1	**Square Root** [18]	Aligator	0.19 s	1	2
	Solvable	1.73 s	4	1		Solvable	1.34 s	2	2
	Inv	2.95 s	8	1		Inv	2.17 s	6	2
		Timing	♯ Iters	♯ Polys			Timing	♯ Iters	♯ Polys
Integer Division [19]	Aligator	0.70 s	1	3	**Wensley's Alg.** [5]	Aligator	0.63 s	1	3
	Solvable	1.78 s	3	3		Solvable	1.95 s	4	3
	Inv	2.54 s	8	3		Inv	3.53 s	8	3

inferred polynomial invariants upto degree 2. We also note that even though the number of loop invariants inferred by Aligator and Solvable differ in some examples, the reduced Gröbner basis of the polynomial invariant ideals returned by Aligator and Solvable coincide, and both tools are complete.

6 Conclusions

We present an algorithm for generating all polynomial invariants of P-solvable loops with assignments and nested conditionals. We prove that our algorithm always terminates. The proof relies on showing that the dimensions of the prime ideals from the minimal decomposition of the ideals generated at an iteration of our algorithm either remain the same or decrease at the next iteration of the algorithm. When compared to existing invariant generation techniques, our method took less iterations and/or less time in generating polynomial invariants in all examples we tried. Future work includes generating polynomial inequalities as invariants, and extending our method to handle nested loops.

Acknowledgements. The author wishes to thank Manuel Kauers for his helpful comments, and for Papa Alioune Ly for collecting experimental data.

References

1. Buchberger, B.: An Algorithm for Finding the Basis Elements of the Residue Class Ring of a Zero Dimensional Polynomial Ideal. J. of Symbolic Computation 41(3-4), 475–511 (2006)
2. Cox, D., Little, J., O'Shea, D.: Ideal, Varieties, and Algorithms. An Introduction to Computational Algebraic Geometry and Commutative Algebra, 2nd edn. Springer, Heidelberg (1998)
3. Dijkstra, E.W.: A Discipline of Programming. Prentice-Hall, Englewood Cliffs (1976)
4. Everest, G., van der Poorten, A., Shparlinski, I., Ward, T.: Recurrence Sequences. Mathematical Surveys and Monographs, vol. 104. American Mathematical Society (2003)
5. German, S.M., Wegbreit, B.: A Synthesizer of Inductive Assertions. IEEE Transactions on Software Engineering 1, 68–75 (1975)
6. Gosper, R.W.: Decision Procedures for Indefinite Hypergeometric Summation. Journal of Symbolic Computation 75, 40–42 (1978)
7. Graham, R.L., Knuth, D.E., Patashnik, O.: Concrete Mathematics, 2nd edn. Addison-Wesley Publishing Company, Reading (1989)
8. Hoare, C.A.R.: An Axiomatic Basis for Computer Programming. Comm. of ACM 12(10), 576–580 (1969)
9. Kaldewaij, A.: Programming. The Derivation of Algorithms. Prentice-Hall (1990)
10. Kapur, D.: A Quantifier Elimination Based Heuristic for Automatically Generating Inductive Assertions for Programs. J. of Systems Science and Complexity 19(3), 307–330 (2006)
11. Kauers, M.: Algorithms for Nonlinear Higher Order Difference Equations. PhD thesis, RISC-Linz, Johannes Kepler University Linz, Austria (2005)
12. Kauers, M., Zimmermann, B.: Computing the Algebraic Relations of C-finite Sequences and Multisequences. J. of Symbolic Computation 43(11), 787–803 (2008)

13. Kovacs, L.: Aligator: A Mathematica Package for Invariant Generation. In: Proc. of IJCAR, pp. 275–282 (2008)
14. Kovacs, L.: Reasoning Algebraically About P-Solvable Loops. In: Ramakrishnan, C.R., Rehof, J. (eds.) TACAS 2008. LNCS, vol. 4963, pp. 249–264. Springer, Heidelberg (2008)
15. Müller-Olm, M., Seidl, H.: Computing Polynomial Program Invariants. Indormation Processing Letters 91(5), 233–244 (2004)
16. Paule, P., Schorn, M.: A Mathematica Version of Zeilberger's Algorithm for Proving Binomial Coefficient Identities. J. of Symbolic Computation 20(5-6), 673–698 (1995)
17. Rodriguez-Carbonell, E., Kapur, D.: Automatic Generation of Polynomial Invariants of Bounded Degree using Abstract Interpretation. Science of Comp. Programming 64(1) (2007)
18. Rodriguez-Carbonell, E., Kapur, D.: Generating All Polynomial Invariants in Simple Loops. J. of Symbolic Computation 42(4), 443–476 (2007)
19. Sankaranaryanan, S., Sipma, H.B., Manna, Z.: Non-Linear Loop Invariant Generation using Gröbner Bases. In: Proc. of POPL (2004)

Standardization and Testing of Mathematical Functions

Victor Kuliamin

Institute for System Programming
Russian Academy of Sciences
109004, Solzhenitsina, 25, Moscow, Russia
kuliamin@ispras.ru

Abstract. The article concerns problems of formulating standard requirements to implementations of mathematical functions working with floating-point numbers and conformance test development for them. Inconsistency and incompleteness of available standards in the domain is demonstrated. Correct rounding requirement is suggested to guarantee preservation of all important properties of functions and to support high level of interoperability between different mathematical libraries and software using them. Conformance test construction method is proposed based on different sources of test data: numbers satisfying specific patterns, boundaries of intervals of uniform function behavior, and points where correct rounding needs much higher precision than in average. Analysis of test results obtained on various implementations of POSIX mathematical library is also presented.

1 Introduction

Computers now are widely used in physics, chemistry, biology, social sciences to model and understand behavior of very complex systems, which can hardly be examined in any other way. Confirmation of such models' correctness by experiments is too expensive and often even impossible. To ensure accurateness of this modeling we need to have adequate models and correctly working modeling systems. The article is concerned with the second problem – how to ensure correct operation of modeling systems. Such systems are often based on very sophisticated and peculiar numeric algorithms, and in any case they use mathematical functions implemented in software libraries or in hardware.

Thus mathematical libraries are common components of most simulation software and correct operation of the latter cannot be achieved without correct implementation of basic functions by the former. In practice software quality is controlled and assured mostly with the help of testing, but testing of mathematical libraries often uses simplistic ad hoc approaches and random test data generation. Specifics of floating-point calculations make construction of both correct and efficient implementations of functions along with their testing a nontrivial task. This paper proposes an approach for standardization of floating-point calculations beyond the bounds of IEEE 754 standard [1] and presents a

A. Pnueli, I. Virbitskaite, and A. Voronkov (Eds.): PSI 2009, LNCS 5947, pp. 257–268, 2010.
© Springer-Verlag Berlin Heidelberg 2010

systematic method of conformance test construction for mathematical functions implemented in software or hardware.

The core of the standardization proposed is correct rounding requirement. It means that an implementation of a function is always required to provide results, which are mathematically precise values correctly rounded to floating-point (FP) numbers according to the current rounding mode. Obeying such a requirement gives an easy way to preserve almost all useful properties of a function implemented, and, more important, it provides an unprecedented interoperability between various mathematical libraries and modeling software using them. Now this interoperability is far from the high level.

The test construction method presented checks correct rounding requirement and uses three different sources of test data – floating-point numbers of specific structure, boundaries of intervals where the function under test behaves in uniform way, and floating-point numbers, for which correct rounding of the function value requires much higher precision of calculations than in average. All these sources are concerned with common errors made by developers of mathematical libraries, which is confirmed both by the practical experience and by the results of tests developed according to this method also presented in the paper.

The main contribution of this article in comparison with [2] and [3] is precise formulation of requirements proposed for standardization and the presentation of considerable testing statistics, which demonstrates rather high error rate of commonly used implementations of mathematical functions and confirms the practical adequacy of the test construction approach proposed.

2   Current Standards' Requirements

Practically significant requirements on the behavior of functions on FP numbers can be found in several standards.

- IEEE 754 [1] (a.k.a IEC 60559) defines representation of FP numbers, rounding modes and describes basic arithmetic operations.
- ISO C [4] and POSIX [5] impose additional requirements on about 40 functions of real and complex variable implemented in standard C library.
- ISO/IEC 10697-2 [6] gives more elaborated requirements for elementary functions.

2.1   Floating-Point Numbers

Standard IEEE 754 defines FP numbers based on various radices. Further only binary numbers are considered, since other radices are used in practice rarely. Nevertheless, all the techniques presented can be extended to FP numbers with different radices.

Representation of binary FP numbers is defined by two main parameters – n, the number of bits in the representation, and $k < n$, the number of bits used to represent an exponent. The interpretation of different bits is presented below.

- The first bit represents the sign of a number.
- The next k bits – from the 2-nd to the $k+1$-th – represent *the exponent* of a number.
- All the rest bits – from $k+2$-th to n-th – represent *the mantissa* or *the significand* of a number.

A number X with the sign bit S, the exponent E, and the mantissa M is expressed in the following way.

1. If $E > 0$ and $E < 2^k - 1$ then X is called *normalized* and is calculated with the formula $X = (-1)^S 2^{(E-2^{k-1}+1)}(1 + M/2^{n-k-1})$. Actual exponent is shifted to make possible representation of both large and small numbers. The last part of the formula is simply 1 followed by point and mantissa bits as the binary representation of X without exponent.

2. If $E = 0$ then X is called *denormalized* and is computed using another formula $X = (-1)^S 2^{(-2^{k-1}+2)}(M/2^{n-k-1})$. Here mantissa bits follow 0 and the point. Note that this gives two zero values $+0$ and -0.

3. Exponent $2^k - 1$ is used to represent positive and negative infinities (zero mantissa) and *not-a-number* NaN (any nonzero mantissa). Infinities represent mathematically infinite values or numbers greater or equal to $2^{2^{k-1}}$. NaN represents results of operations that cannot be considered consistently as finite or infinite, e.g. $0/0 = \text{NaN}$.

IEEE 754 standard defines the following FP number formats: single precision ($n = 32$ and $k = 8$), double precision ($n = 64$ and $k = 11$), and extended double precision ($128 \geq n \geq 79$ and $k \geq 15$, Intel processors use $n = 79$ and $k = 15$). In the current (2008) version of the standard quadruple precision numbers ($n = 128$ and $k = 15$) are added.

2.2 IEEE 754 Requirements

IEEE 754 defines requirements to basic arithmetic operations on numbers (addition, subtraction, multiplication, and division, fused multiplication-addition $x * y + z$), comparisons, conversions between different formats, square root function, and calculation of FP remainder [7]. Since results of these operations applied to FP numbers are often not exact FP numbers, it defines rules of rounding such results. Four rounding modes are defined: to the nearest FP number, up (to the least FP number greater than the result), down (to the greatest FP number less than the result), and to 0 (up for negative results and down for positive ones). If the result is exactly in the middle between two neighbor FP numbers, its rounding to nearest get the one having 0 as the last bit of its mantissa.

To make imprecise and incorrect results more visible IEEE 754 defines a set of FP exception flags.

- Invalid flag should be raised if the result is NaN, while arguments of the operation performed are not NaNs. In addition NaNs are separated in two classes – *signaling NaNs* and *quiet NaNs*. NaN result of an operation on not-NaN arguments is signaling one. If any of arguments of an operation is signaling NaN, then invalid flag is raised. Quiet NaNs can be used as arguments without raising invalid flag with quiet NaN as the result.

- Divide-by-zero flag should be raised if the result is exactly positive or negative infinity, while arguments are finite.
- Overflow flag should be raised if the result absolute value is greater than maximum FP number.
- Underflow flag should be raised if the result is not 0, while its absolute value is less than minimum positive normalized FP number.
- Inexact flag should be raised if the precise result is no FP number, but no overflow or underflow occurs.

2.3 Requirements of ISO C and POSIX

ISO C [4] and POSIX [5] standards provide description of mathematical functions of standard C library, including most important elementary functions (square and cubic roots, power, exponential and logarithm with bases $e, 2$ and 10, most commonly used trigonometric, hyperbolic and their reverse functions) of real or complex variables. Some special functions are added – error function, complementary error function, gamma function, and logarithmic gamma function.

ISO C standard defines points where the specified functions have exact well-known values, e.g. $\log 1 = \sinh 0 = 0, \cos 0 = 1$. It also specifies situations where invalid and divide-by-zero flags should be raised, the first one – if a function is calculated outside of its domain, the second one – if the value of a function is precisely positive or negative infinity. These requirements are specified as normative for real functions and as informative for the complex ones.

POSIX slightly extends the set of described functions; it adds Bessel functions of the first and the second kind of orders $0, 1$, and of an arbitrary integer order given as the second parameter. It also extends ISO C by specifying situations when overflow and underflow flags should be raised for functions in real variables. POSIX specifies that value of **errno** should be set to ERANGE if overflow or underflow occurs or if the result is precise infinity, and **errno** should be set to EDOM if the arguments are out of the domain of a function, excluding arguments for which it returns signed infinite results.

POSIX requires that real functions having asymptotic $f(x) \sim x$ near 0 should return x for each denormalized argument value x. Note, that this would be inconsistent with IEEE 754 rounding requirements if they were applied to such functions.

One more contradiction between POSIX and natural extension of IEEE 754 concerns overflow. IEEE 754 in this case requires to take rounding mode in account – e.g. to return positive infinity for to nearest and up rounding modes and the biggest positive finite FP number for to 0 or down modes. POSIX requires returning in any case one value BIG_VALUE.

Both ISO C and POSIX do not say anything on precision of function calculation in general situation.

2.4   Requirements of ISO 10697

The only standard specifying some calculation precision for rich set of mathematical functions is ISO 10697 [6], standard on language independent arithmetic. It provides the following requirements to implementations of elementary functions.

- Preservation of sign and monotonicity of ideal mathematical function where no frequent oscillation occurs. Frequent oscillation occurs where difference between two neighbor FP numbers is comparable with length of intervals of monotonicity or sign preservation. Trigonometric functions are the only elementary functions that oscillate frequently on some intervals.
- Rounding errors should not be greater than $0.5 - 2.0$ unit of least precision (ulp), depending on the function. Again, this is not applied to implementations of trigonometric functions on arguments greater than some big angle. Note that precision 0.5 ulp is equivalent to the correct rounding to the nearest FP number.
- Preservation of evenness or oddity of implemented functions. For this reason the standard does not support directed rounding modes – up and down. Only symmetric modes – to nearest and to zero – are considered.
- Well-known exact values for functions are specified, extending ISO C requirements. In addition it requires to preserve asymptotic of the implemented function in 0 or near infinity.
- Natural inequalities (e.g. $\cosh(x) \geq \sinh(x)$) should also be preserved.

ISO 10697 provides the most detailed set of requirements including precision requirements. Unfortunately, it has not yet recognized by applied programmers and no widely-used library has declared compliance with this standard. Maybe this situation will improve in future.

3   Correct Rounding Requirement

Analysis of existing standards shows that they are not fully consistent with each other and are usually restricted to some specific set of functions. Trying to construct some systematic description of general requirements based on significant properties of mathematical functions concerned with their computation one can get the following list.

- Exact values and asymptotic near them.
- Preservation of sign, monotonicity, and inequalities with other functions.
- Symmetries – evenness, oddity, periodicity, or more complex properties like $\Gamma(x + 1) = x\Gamma(x)$.
- NaN results outside of function's domain, infinity results in function's poles, correct overflow and underflow detection, raising correct exception flags.
- Preservation of bounds of function range, e.g. $-\pi/2 \leq \arctan(x) \leq \pi/2$.
- Correct rounding according to natural extension of IEEE 754 rules and raising inexact flag on imprecise results.

Correct rounding requirement here is of particular significance.

- It immediately implies almost all other properties in this list. If we want to preserve these properties without correct rounding, much harder work is required, peculiar errors become possible, and thorough testing of such an implementation becomes much harder task.
- It provides results closest to the precise ones. Without correct rounding it is necessary to specify how the results may differ from the precise ones, which is hard and very rarely done in practice. It is supposed usually that correct rounding for sine function on large arguments is too expensive, but none of widely used sine implementations (except for Microsoft's one [9]) explicitly declares its error bounds on various intervals. Users usually don't analyze the results obtained from standard mathematical libraries, and are not competent enough to see the boundaries between areas where their results are relevant and the ones where they become irrelevant due to (not stated explicitly) calculation errors in standard functions. Correct rounding moves most of the problems of error analysis to the algorithms used by the applications, standard libraries become as precise as it is possible.
- Correct rounding implies almost perfect compatibility of different mathematical libraries and precise repeatability of calculation results of modeling software on different platforms, which means very good portability of such applications. This goal is rather hard to achieve without such a requirement – one needs to standardize specific algorithms as it was made by Sun in mathematical library of Java 2. Note that strict precision specification is much more flexible requirement than standardization of algorithms.

High efforts required to develop a function implementation and its resulting ineffectiveness are always mentioned as drawbacks of correct rounding. However, efficient algorithms and resolving techniques are already known for a long time (e.g. see [10,11] for correct argument reduction for trigonometric functions). Work of Arenaire group [12] in INRIA on **crlibm** [13,14] library demonstrates that inefficiency problems can be resolved in almost all cases. So, now these drawbacks of correct rounding can be considered as not really relevant.

More serious issues are contradictions between correct rounding requirement and some other useful properties of mathematical functions. In each case of such a contradiction we should decide how to resolve it.

- Correct rounding can sometimes contradict with boundaries of function range, if they are not precise FP numbers. For example, $\arctan(x) \leq \pi/2$ is an important property. It occurs that single precision FP number closest to $\pi/2$ is greater than it, so if we round arctangent values on large arguments to the nearest FP number, we get $\arctan(x) > \pi/2$, that can radically change the results of modeling of some complex systems. In this case we prefer to give priority to the bounds preservation requirement and do not round values of arctangent (with either rounding mode) to FP numbers out of its range.
- Oddity and some other symmetries using minus sign or taking reciprocal values can be broken by directed rounding modes (up and down), while

symmetric modes (to nearest and to 0) preserve them. In this case it is natural to prefer correct directed rounding if it is chosen, because usually such modes are used to get correct boundaries on exact results.

- Correct rounding for different modes contradicts with two POSIX requirements – that some BIG_VALUE should be always returned in case of overflow, and that a function close to x near 0 should return the value of its argument for denormalized arguments. In both cases correct rounding seems to be more justified.

So, we propose to make correct rounding according to the current rounding mode the main requirement for standardization of any kind of functions working with FP numbers. The single exception is more privileged range preservation requirement in cases where it comes to contradiction with correct rounding. In all other cases correct rounding is sufficient to infer all the properties of an implementation.

In case of overflow a function should return the corresponding infinity for rounding to the nearest and in the direction of the overflow. For rounding in the opposite direction and to 0 maximum positive or negative FP number should be returned. On the arguments outside function's domain it should return signaling NaN, or signed infinity if the sign can be naturally determined by mathematical properties of this function. On infinite arguments a function should return the corresponding limit value, if it has any one, otherwise signaling NaN should be returned. If any of the arguments is signaling NaN, the result should also be signaling NaN. If any of the arguments is quiet NaN and there are no signaling NaNs among them, the result should be quiet NaN.

These requirements should be supplemented with IEEE 754 exception flags raising and setting **errno** to specific values in the corresponding specific situations (see above).

Further we consider test construction to check correct rounding requirement with 4 rounding modes specified by IEEE 754. We also demonstrate that such tests are useful and informative even for implementations that do not satisfy these requirements.

3.1   Table Maker Dilemma

An important issue related with correct rounding requirement is *table maker dilemma* [15,16]. It consists in the fact that sometimes one needs much higher precision of calculations to get correctly rounded value of a function than in average. An example is the value of natural logarithm of a double precision FP number $1.613955DC802F8_{16} \cdot 2^{-35}$ (mantissa is represented in hexadecimals) equal to $-17.F02F9BAF6035\ 7F^{14}9..._{16}$. Here F^{14} means 14 digits F, giving with neighbor digits 60 consecutive units staying after a zero just after the double precision mantissa. This value is very close to the mean of two neighbor FP numbers, and to be able to round it correctly to the nearest FP number we need calculations with relative error bound about 2^{-113} while 0.5 ulp precision corresponds to only 2^{-53} bound.

4   Test Construction Method

Test construction method proposed checks difference between correctly rounded value of a function and the value returned by its implementation in a set of test points. We prefer to have test point selection rules based only on the properties of the function under test and structure of FP numbers, and do not consider specific implementation algorithms. This black box approach appears to be rather effective in revealing errors in practice, and at the same time it does not require detailed analysis of numerous and ever growing set of possible implementation algorithms and various errors that can be made in them.

Test points are chosen by the following rules (see more details in [3]).

1. **FP numbers of special structure**
   First, natural boundary FP numbers are taken as test points: $0, -0, \infty, -\infty$, NaN, the least and the greatest positive and negative denormalized and normalized numbers.
   Second, numbers with mantissa satisfying some specific patterns are chosen. Errors in an algorithm or an implementation often lead to incorrect calculations on some patterns. The notorious Pentium division bug [17] can be detected only on divisors having units as mantissa bits from 5-th to 10-th. Pattern use for testing FP calculations in hardware is already described, e.g. in [18].
   Third, two previous rules are used to get points where reverse function is calculated and pairs of closest FP numbers to its values are taken as test arguments for direct function. So, a function is tested in points satisfying some patterns, and in points where its value is closest to the same patterns.
2. **Boundaries of intervals of specific function behavior**
   All singularities of the function under test, bounds of intervals of its non-overflow behavior, of constant sign, of monotonicity or simple asymptotic determine some partitioning of FP numbers. Boundaries of these intervals and several points on each of them are chosen as test points.
3. **FP numbers, for which calculation of correctly rounded function value requires higher precision**
   Bad cases, which require more than M additional bits for correct rounding (the "badness"), are taken as test points. Two values of M are used: $n-k-10$ for the worst cases and $(n-k)/2$, because some errors can be uncovered in not-very-bad cases. This rule adds test points helping to reveal calculation errors and inaccuracies of various nature.

Implementation of the method is rather straightforward. Test points are gathered into text files, each test point is accompanied with correctly rounded value of the function under test for each rounding mode (only two different values are required at most). Correctly rounded values are calculated with the help of multiprecision implementations of the same functions taking higher precision to guarantee correct results and using both Maple and MPFR library [19] to double check the correctness. A test program reads test data, calls the function under test, and compares its result with the correct one. In case of discrepancy the difference in ulps is counted and reported. In addition the test program checks exception flags raising according to IEEE 754 rules extended to the function under test. Test execution is completely automated.

The hard step of the approach is to compute bad cases. Methods to do this include search based techniques, dyadic method, lattice reduction, and integer secants method (see details in [3]). They do not solve the problem completely, but help to deal with it in many particular cases.

5   Test Results Analysis

The test construction method presented above has been applied to make test suites for POSIX functions **exp, expm1, log, log10, log1b, sin, asin, cos, acos, tan, atan, sinh, asinh, cosh, acosh, tanh, atanh** in double precision. The tests have been executed on the following platforms.

- Platform A – Sun Solaris 10 on UltraSpark III processor.
- Platform B – SUSE Linux Enterprise Server (SLES) 10.0 with **glibc** 2.4 or Debian Linux 4.0 with **glibc** 2.3.6 on Intel Itanium 2 processor.
- Platform C – Red Hat Fedore Core 6 with **glibc** 2.5 or Debian Linux 4.0 with **glibc** 2.7 on Intel Pentium 4.
- Platform D – Windows XP operating system with Microsoft Visual Studio 2005 C runtime library on Intel Pentium 4 processor.
- Platform E – Red Hat Enterprise Linux 4.0 with **glibc** 2.3.4 on Intel Pentium 4 or AMD Athlon 64 processors.
- Platform F – Debian Linux 4.0 with **glibc** 2.7 on 64-bit PowerPC processor.
- Platform G – SLES 10.0 with **glibc** 2.4 on IBM s390 processor.
- Platform H – SLES 10.0 with **glibc** 2.3.5 on 32-bit PowerPC processor.

Platforms E-H being different in minor details are very similar in general picture and demonstrate almost the same numbers of similar errors, so they seem to have almost identical implementations of **glibc** math functions (and actually identical results are demonstrated by platforms F and G for **atan, asinh, atanh, expm1, log1p, log, log10** and by platforms E and H for **atan, log, log10**). Other platforms show more differences and specific errors.

The following errors and "features" were detected.

Table 1. Examples of errors found

Func.	Platf.	Rounding	Argument	Value
exp	E	down, to 0	-1.02338886743052249	1.12533187332226478e+307
exp	F	up	7.07297806243595915e+2	-5.62769256250533586e+306
exp	H	up	-6.59559560885092266e-1	1.00194134452638006
cosh	G	up	7.09150193027364367e+2	-2.35289304846008447e+307
sinh	E	down	6.68578051047927488e+2	-5.48845314236507489e+288
sin	H	up	3.36313335479954389e+1	7.99995094799809616e+22
cos	F	down, to 0	1.62241253252029984e+22	-1.19726021840874908e+52
sin	D	all	-1.79346314152566190e-76	9.80171403295605760e-2

- The most serious bug is numerous and huge calculation errors in implementations of **sin, cos, tan, exp, sinh, cosh** on many platforms. Only platforms A and B implement trigonometric functions without serious errors (with only 1-bit or 2-bit errors). Exponential function and hyperbolic sine and cosine are implemented without big errors on platforms A-D. The salient fact is that on the platforms E-H all these functions work almost correctly for the rounding to nearest (only few 1-bit errors were detected for trigonometric functions, 2-bit ones for hyperbolic functions, and no calculation errors were found for **exp**), but for other rounding modes almost arbitrary inaccuracies are possible. Examples are given in Table 1.

  Implementations of trigonometric functions on platforms C and D, although erroneous, have imprecise argument reduction [10] as the main source of errors, so they show smooth increase of inaccuracies from 0 to infinities, independently of rounding modes.

- Sine is implemented with errors in the interval $(-0.1, -10^{-76})$ on platform D. An example is shown in the last row of Table 1. This error is hard to show due to compiler-implemented transformation $\sin(-x) = -\sin(x)$. To overcome it test data should be generated or loaded dynamically, so that the compiler cannot notice that they are negative numbers.

- The platform B is the only one which preserves oddity or evenness of all the functions tested. **cosh** is implemented as an even function on all the platforms except for D. **atan, cos, sin, tan** also preserve their symmetry on the platform C, **asin** – on the platform D. In all other cases the symmetry is somehow broken.

- Arctangent function for large arguments calculated with up rounding returns the result greater than $\pi/2$ on the platforms A, B, and C.

- Platform C shows big calculation errors in **acos** for rounding up, **tanh** for rounding down, **expm1** for rounding up and down. Also $\mathbf{acos}(-1) = -\pi$ instead of π for rounding up.

- On platform A functions **asin, acos, log, log10** return not-NaN FP number instead of NaN for arguments out of function domain.

- Finite number (actually maximum float value) is returned instead of infinity in case of overflow for **exp, cosh, sinh** and in 0 for **log, log10** on platform A. Maximum finite double value is returned instead of infinity for **exp, cosh, sinh** on platform D. These bugs may be related with POSIX requirement to return some BIG_VALUE in case of overflow independently of rounding mode. This requirement (with BIG_VALUE equal to infinity) is implemented on all platforms except for A and D for **exp**, on platforms B, E, H for **cosh**, on platforms E, H for **expm1**, and only on the platform B for **sinh**.

- On all platforms, except for B, functions that are equivalent to x near 0 "try" to return the argument value for denormal arguments for all rounding modes. That is, POSIX requirement is implemented on most platforms in most cases. However, this requirement is implemented only for positive denormals for **asin, tanh** and **atanh** on the platform C and for **tanh** on the platform G. Platform B implements correct rounding requirement.

– A lot of minor calculation errors were detected. The best accuracy is demonstrated by platform B – maximum errors are only 2-bit and such errors are rather rare, the worst results are shown by **atan,** for which 10% of test points discovered such errors. Platform A shows maximum 3-bit difference from correct results. Sometimes such errors are very often, for example, 99.8% of test points discovered 1-bit errors in **acos** implementation on platform D for rounding up. In some cases probable mistakes in table values used in implementations are uncovered, for example,
  - On platforms E-H **atan** has erroneous 7 last bits of mantissa for rounding up, down or to 0 near -6.25.
  - On platform C **sinh** value for rounding up has erroneous 15 last bits near 1.986821485e-8.
  - On platform D **exp** value has 6 erroneous last bits near -2.56e-9.
– Some errors detected concern incorrect flag (not-)raising and incorrect **errno** values. For example, for almost all implementations of functions that are equivalent to argument near 0 UNDERFLOW flag and ERANGE **errno** value are not set for denormal arguments. For **atanh** in 1 or −1 **errno** value in all implementations is set to domain error, not to range error as it is required by POSIX.

The main result is that tests based on structure of FP numbers and intervals of uniform behavior of the function under test are very good for finding various errors related with mistakes made by programmers, while bad cases for correct rounding help to assess calculation errors in whole and general distribution of inaccuracies.

6   Conclusion

The approach presented in the paper helps to formulate consistent requirements and construct corresponding conformance test suites for floating-point implementations of various mathematical functions in one real variable. Error-revealing power of such test suites is rather high – many errors were found in mature and widely used libraries. Although test suites are intended to check correct rounding requirement, they also give important information about implementations that do not obey this restriction.

Some further research is needed to formulate heuristics or rules that help to make test suites more compact. Now they consists of about $2 \cdot 10^6$ test points and require sometimes several hours to execute. The experiments conducted demonstrated that for exponential function the test suite constructed using the method described and consisting of about $3.7 \cdot 10^6$ test cases, and the reduced test suite of about 10^4 test cases detect all the same errors.

One idea to extend the method proposed for functions in two or more variables is rather straightforward – it is necessary to use not intervals, but areas of uniform behavior of functions. But extension of rules concerning FP numbers of special structure and bad cases seem to be much more peculiar, since their straightforward generalizations gives huge number of tests without any hope to get all the data in a reasonable time. So, some reduction rules should be introduced here from the very beginning to obtain manageable test suites.

The standardization proposed and tests developed with the presented approach can facilitate and simplify construction of correct and portable mathematical libraries giving more adequate and precise means for evaluation of their correctness and interoperability.

References

1. IEEE 754-2008. IEEE Standard for Binary Floating-Point Arithmetic. NY, IEEE (2008)
2. Kuliamin, V.: Standardization and Testing of Implementations of Mathematical Functions in Floating Point Numbers. Programming and Computer Software 33(3), 154–173 (2007)
3. Kuliamin, V.: Test Construction for Mathematical Functions. In: Suzuki, K., Higashino, T., Ulrich, A., Hasegawa, T. (eds.) TestCom/FATES 2008. LNCS, vol. 5047, pp. 23–37. Springer, Heidelberg (2008)
4. ISO/IEC 9899. Programming Languages - C. Geneve: ISO (1999)
5. IEEE 1003.1-2004. Information Technology - Portable Operating System Interface (POSIX). NY, IEEE (2004)
6. ISO/IEC 10967-2. Information Technology - Language Independent Arithmetic - Part 2: Elementary Numerical Functions. Geneve, ISO (2002)
7. Goldberg, D.: What Every Computer Scientist Should Know about Floating-Point Arithmetic. ACM Computing Surveys 23(1), 5–48 (1991)
8. Defour, D., Hanrot, G., Lefevre, V., Muller, J.-M., Revol, N., Zimmermann, P.: Proposal for a standardization of mathematical function implementation in floating-point arithmetic. Numerical Algorithms 37(1-4), 367–375 (2004)
9. http://msdn.microsoft.com/library/wkbss70y.aspx
10. Ng, K.C.: Arguments Reduction for Huge Arguments: Good to the Last Bit (1992), http://www.validlab.com/arg.pdf
11. Kahan, W.: Minimizing $q * m - n$. (1983) (unpublished), http://http.cs.berkeley.edu/~wkahan/testpi/nearpi.c
12. http://www.inria.fr/recherche/equipes/arenaire.en.html
13. de Dinechin, F., Ershov, A., Gast, N.: Towards the post-ultimate libm. In: Proc. of 17th Symposium on Computer Arithmetic, June 2005. IEEE Computer Society Press, Los Alamitos (2005)
14. http://lipforge.ens-lyon.fr/www/crlibm/
15. Lefèvre, V., Muller, J.-M., Tisserand, A.: The Table Maker's Dilemma. INRIA Research Report 98-12 (1998)
16. Lefèvre, V., Muller, J.-M.: Worst Cases for Correct Rounding of the Elementary Functions in Double Precision. In: Proc. of 15th IEEE Symposium on Computer Arithmetic, Vail, Colorado, USA, June (2001)
17. Edelman, A.: The Mathematics of the Pentium Division Bug. SIAM Review 39(1), 54–67 (1997)
18. Ziv, A., Aharoni, M., Asaf, S.: Solving Range Constraints for Binary Floating-Point Instructions. In: Proc. of 16th IEEE Symposium on Computer Arithmetic (ARITH-16 2003), pp. 158–163 (2003)
19. http://www.mpfr.org

Using AOP for Discovering and Defining Executable Test Cases

Philipp Kumar and Thomas Baar

akquinet tech@spree GmbH
Software Reengineering Group
Bülowstraße 66, D-10783 Berlin, Germany
{philipp.kumar,thomas.baar}@akquinet.de

Abstract. The functional specification of software systems is often given in form of use cases. The compliance of a system implementation to a use case specification is validated by system tests, which can nowadays be automated. Unfortunately, system tests run slowly and assume that all needed external systems such as databases and authentication servers are accessible and run correctly. For these reasons, software developers rather rely on module tests, which test the functionality of individual modules. Module tests, however, have the disadvantage of being defined independently of the customer's system specification.

In this paper, we describe an approach to combine the advantages of system and module tests. The core technique is (i) to record the complete information flow between modules during the execution of system tests and (ii) to generate, based on this data, corresponding module tests afterwards. The resulting module tests are fast, they are independent of external systems, and they reflect test scenarios defined in use cases. Our approach is heavily based on aspect-oriented programming (AOP) and implemented by the open-source framework *jautomock*.

Keywords: Aspect-oriented programming (AOP), automated test generation, regression tests.

1 Introduction

Each software project starts with the goal to correctly implement all requirements the customer has formulated. To ensure correct behavior of the system under development, most projects contain, in addition to production code, a considerable amount of test code. Despite this test effort, many projects still fail and do not deliver the expected functionality in time and budget.

In our experience, a major problem of failed projects is that customer requirements have not strictly been taken into account in all project phases. A project typically starts with the documentation of requirements. Then, the overall architecture is developed, including the integration of external systems, and – when a test-based development process has been adopted – the customer's functional requirements are formulated in form of *system tests* (aka. user acceptance tests).

A. Pnueli, I. Virbitskaite, and A. Voronkov (Eds.): PSI 2009, LNCS 5947, pp. 269–281, 2010.
© Springer-Verlag Berlin Heidelberg 2010

Test-based development processes advocate to write a suite of test cases for each module in order to test it individually. Isolated module tests require mock implementations of all components the module communicates with (other modules and external systems). A mock implementation of a component simulates the behavior of this component adequately for the purpose of the test. The development of such mocks and their embedding in a module test can be challenging and usually requires a substantial amount of work. Moreover, module tests require the tested module to be highly configurable (e.g. within the test, the module should communicate with mock implementations and not with the original components), which can pollute the design of the module considerably.

While system tests reflect the customer's requirements very closely, they are often neglected and rarely executed in the development process even if they can be automated. A prominent argument of developers is that running such tests takes too long. Another observation of ours is that system tests are not very accepted by software developers because they tend to be unstable. They fail as soon as an external system is not available or has changed its state in a way that it behaves slightly differently. In other words, system tests rely on test conditions that are out of control of the developer. Once the conditions change, the test might fail though the implemented system still runs correctly. In this case, the software developer has to adapt the test description to the new test conditions, an error-prone and tedious task. Last but not least, if the system failes because of an implementation error, the failed test usually does not give much hints on which parts of the code might be responsible.

Module tests are much more accepted among developers because they avoid the disadvantages of system tests. They are fast to execute, failures can easily tracked back to the source, and they do not depend on the availability or the state of external systems. However, the input data for module tests is usually invented by the software developer herself and not necessarily derived from the original customer's requirements.

The contribution of this paper is to bridge the gap between system and module tests. Our technique generates tests, which are, just like system tests, strictly based on the original customer requirements, while having all the advantages of module tests, such as independence from external systems, fast execution, and easy debugging. The basic idea is to record all communication across module borders while executing a system test. In a second step, this information is used in order to automatically generate a corresponding module test for each module, including all needed mock implementations of the neighboring modules and external systems. Our approach is heavily based on AOP and has been implemented in form of the open-source framework *jautomock*.

The paper is organized as follows. Section 2 briefly explains the most relevant concepts of AOP. Section 3 describes, based on a running example, our approach in detail and Sect. 4 discusses its achievements and limitations. While Sect. 5 reviews related work, Sect. 6 closes the paper with some concluding remarks.

2   Background

2.1   Aspect-Oriented Programming

Aspect-oriented programming (AOP) is a programming paradigm that allows to manipulate the control flow of a given program. A central notion of AOP is the *join point* that can, for the purpose of this paper, be described as a certain location in the source code. Typical join point types are *method call, method execution, constructor call, constructor execution, member variable access* and *throw/catch of exceptions*. Figure 1 shows join points of mentioned types within an exemplary program flow.

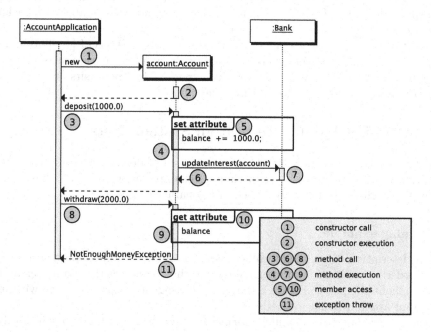

Fig. 1. Join point examples

A set of join points is called *pointcut*. Pointcuts can be defined by the programmer using a selection language. A pointcut is associated with an *advice*. An advice is a set of instructions to be automatically executed whenever a join point from the associated pointcut is reached at runtime. Pointcut-advice combinations are defined within *aspects*.

The goal of AOP is to improve *separation of concerns*. AOP provides the means to implement concerns in a modular way. A common example is the realization of the concern *logging*. Using traditional languages, the programmer has to write logging code at many places within the program. This has a negative impact on readability and maintainability. AOP allows to overcome this deficiency and to encapsulate the implementation code for logging in one separate unit (the aspect).

The paradigm of AOP has been implemented in various ways. There are Java frameworks such as *Spring* and *JBoss Seam* that enable control flow manipulation by so-called *interceptors*. Another realization is in form of programming languages such as AspectJ.

2.2   AspectJ

AspectJ [1,2,3] is a popular aspect-oriented programming language based on Java. It introduces language constructs to define aspects as well as containing advice that can be associated with pointcuts. The defined source code is compiled to Java bytecode executable on any common Java Virtual Machine. For this purpose, AspectJ distributions come with a compiler that is able to translate AspectJ sources as well as Java sources.

In this paper we use the annotation-based syntax of AspectJ [4]. This allows us to create aspects without introducing non-Java language constructs. Aspects are defined by annotating a class with @Aspect, while pointcuts are added by annotating an empty method with @Pointcut.

3   Deriving Module Tests from System Tests

In this section, we detail our two-step approach of deriving module tests from system tests. After introducing a running example as well as prerequisites for the approach, each step is described in a separate subsection.

Running example

The description of our approach is organized around a simple but typical product ordering application written in Java, which will serve as the running example throughout the paper. Figure 2 shows the package and class structure with important attributes and methods.

An *order* is placed by calling anOrderService.placeOrder(..), which takes an XML document as argument and returns the id of the generated order. This document should look similar to that in Listing 1.1. Each order is associated with a certain *customer*, who has a name and may have qualified for a certain discount, and a list of *order items*. An order item is related to a *product* and has an attribute for the quantity with which the product was ordered. Each product knows its price.

There are two use cases of the software system. For each of them, the class OrderService offers a method:

placeOrder – an order is created according to the information passed in argument orderXml.

calculateTotalCharge – the calculation of the total cost of an order depending on the quantity of each order item, the price of the ordered products, and the customer's discount. Products and customers are referenced via ids and managed by databases (ProductDB, CustomerDB).

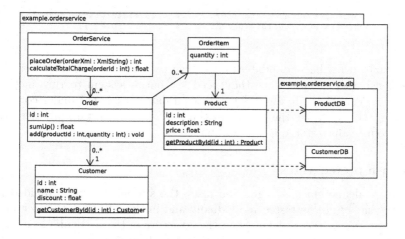

Fig. 2. Class diagram for order service

Listing 1.1. XML input example for the order service

```
1 <order customerId="21">
2    <item productId="7" quantity="5" />
3    <item productId="8" quantity="2" />
4 </order>
```

The example system comes with one system test for the use case *"Calculate total charge for an order"*. It runs against the entire system. The test is shown in Listing 1.2, formulated as a *JUnit* test case[1].

Listing 1.2. System test for `calculateTotalCharge`

```
1  public class SystemTest {
2      private OrderService orderService; // object under test
3      private int orderId;
4
5      @Before
6      public void setUp() throws Exception {
7          this.orderService = new OrderService();
8
9          String inputXml =
10             "<order customerId=\"22\">"
11             + "<item productId=\"7\" quantity= \"5\" />"
12             + "<item productId=\"8\" quantity=\"3\" />"
13             + "</order>";
14
15         /* Place the order */
16         this.orderId = orderService.placeOrder(inputXml);
17     }
18
19     @Test
20     public void testCalculateTotalCharge() {
21         // Assuming that database yields that
22         // product 7 costs $2, product 8 costs $5, customer 22 has
23         // not qualified for a discount,
24         // we expect 5*2 + 3*5 = 25 as return value.
25         double expectedSum = 25;
```

---

[1] In JUnit, `@Before` marks the method that defines the setup procedure to be performed before each test method, while `@Test` marks an actual test method.

```
26        double actualSum = orderService.calculateTotalCharge(orderId);
27        Assert.assertEquals(expectedSum, actualSum, 0.001);
28    }
29 }
```

System tests are bad candidates for frequent regression testing, however. They are expensive to execute since they need the entire system to run, including databases. Also, they are often dependent on data that is not under control of the tester. For example, the test in Listing 1.2 relies on certain product prices and discount values stored in the database.

Approach prerequisites

In order to define efficient regression tests, the system should be divided into modules that are to be tested individually and independently from each other. This partitioning process depends on the structure of the particular system under test, yet there are general criteria that may help to identify modules. One criterion is to specify a particular group of to-be-refactored classes as a module. Another is to define modules on the basis of performance characteristics: Slow system parts shall be omitted and thus be defined outside of to-be-tested modules. Behavior that is not under the control of the tester is also a good candidate for module classification, like database systems.

For our example, we will use a partition that separates business and database classes, effectively defining the following modules:

- Module A: `OrderService`, `Order`, `OrderItem`, `Product`, `Customer`
- Module B: `ProductDB`, `CustomerDB`

3.1   First Step: Recording Phase

In the first step, we obtain data to be used later for testing each module in isolation (module tests). For module tests, we need to know how a module reacts when another module calls a method of it. Thus, we have to monitor the interactions between modules during the acceptance tests and to *record* the data which is exchanged between them. This is basically a logging concern and can be implemented using AOP without touching the production code. An aspect can detect when a module calls another module's method and in that case logs all argument values as well as the return value.

The described process of recording the information flow between modules can be automated by using the framework *jautomock* [5], which has been developed by the authors as an implementation of the approach described in this paper. In order to record the information flow, one has to extend the framework aspect `JAutoMockTestCase` as shown in Listing 1.3. The resulting aspect is a test that acts as a wrapper of the acceptance test from our example application and also specifies the module borders in the AspectJ pointcut language. This is done by overwriting the pointcut `subSystemBorders`[2] of the super aspect.

---

[2] In AspectJ, a pointcut is defined via `@Pointcut`, annotating an empty method and defining the pointcut within the annotation's string argument.

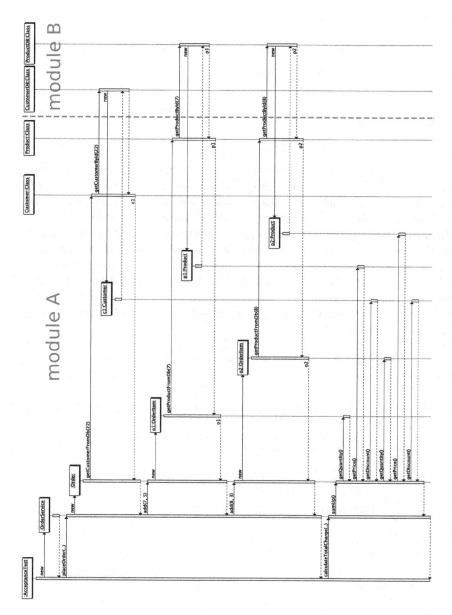

Fig. 3. UML sequence diagram displaying control flow during run of acceptance test

Listing 1.3. Regression test for module Am

```
1  @Aspect
2  public class OrderServiceTest extends JAutoMockTestCase {
3      private OrderService orderService; // object under test
4      private int orderId;
5
6      @Pointcut("within(example.orderservice.*) && ("
7              + "    call(* example.orderservice.db.*.*(..))"
8              + " || call(example.orderservice.db.*.new(..))"
9              + ")")
10     protected void subSystemBorders() {}
11
12     @Test
13     public void testOrderService() {
14         // run system test from here
15     }
16 }
```

The border is here defined to be traversed whenever a method call occurs from module A to module B, i.e. from package *example.orderservice* into package *example.orderservice.db* (including calls to constructors). Figure 3 shows an UML sequence diagram that visualizes the control flow during execution of the test.

When this test is executed, objects passed across the defined border, including method arguments, return values and thrown exceptions, are automatically serialized and persisted to the filesystem. Listing 1.4 shows a section of the corresponding output. A method call is identified by the calling class, the target class, the methods name, its parameter values and a sequence number (to distinguish multiple calls to the same method). Each call is associated with a return value and the parameter values[3].

Listing 1.4. Fragment of the serialized information flow

```
1  <map>
2    ...
3    <entry>
4      <MethodCall>
5        <caller>example.orderservice.Product</caller>
6        <targetMethod class="method">
7          <class>example.orderservice.db.ProductDB</class>
8          <name>getProductById</name>
9          <parameterTypes>
10           <class>int</class>
11         </parameterTypes>
12         <parameterValues class="java.util.Arrays$ArrayList">
13           <a>
14             <int>7</int>
15           </a>
16         </parameterValues>
17       </targetMethod>
18       <invocationSequenceNumber>0</invocationSequenceNumber>
19     </MethodCall>
20     <MethodCallReturnValue>
21       <returnValue class="example.orderservice.Product">
22         <id>7</id>
23         <description>Beer</description>
24         <price>2.0</price>
25       </returnValue>
```

---

[3] As a method can potentially change the state of its parameters, the parameter values are serialized as well after the method has been executed.

```
26        <parameterValues class="java.util.Arrays$ArrayList">
27          <a>
28            <int>7</int>
29          </a>
30        </parameterValues>
31      </MethodCallReturnValue>
32    </entry>
33    ...
34 </map>
```

The serialization is achieved using the open source framework *XStream* [6], capable of serializing a large variety of objects to XML using Java's reflection mechanism.

3.2   Second Step: Playback Phase

In order to test a module individually, all dependencies to other modules must be eliminated through the use of mock objects. A mock object mimics the behavior of the original object in a given context, e.g. during the execution of a test case. For example, a database can be substituted by an ordinary Java object, as long as the object returns the same answers as the original database for the queries issued within the current test.

Using AOP, calls from one module to another can be intercepted and handled by logic defined within an aspect, effectively redefining the semantics of the call in a way that is transparent to the caller. The production code remains unaltered. This mechanism allows us to dispatch method calls across a module border to mock objects instead of actually invoking production logic.

The described interception process has been implemented by the *jautomock* framework. This *playback* phase is automatically performed when we run the test from Listing 1.3 a second time: The framework notices the existence of objects that have been serialized during the first run, and whenever a call across a module border occurs, it is now intercepted. Instead of invoking code of the called module, the framework reconstructs the previously serialized result object for that specific call and returns it. The method call arguments are updated to the state recorded during the previous phase in order to reflect preformed argument state changes. Also, if an exception occurred during the recording phase it is now rethrown.

It is possible to obtain new mock objects by simply discarding the old ones and rerunning the test. Another recording phase will take place, and subsequent runs of the test will perform a playback using the newly recorded mock objects.

4   Limitations

The generated module tests are a good substitute for system tests: They are faster to execute, more stable, independent from external systems and easier to debug.

However, they are not a complete substitute. First of all, some changes within the external systems might require to alter the integration of that external system with our own. Such changes remain undetected, if we rely on the generated module tests only, because the behavior of the external system is "frozen" at a certain point in time.

The second limitation of our approach is the requirement that all calls from a module to its environment remain stable. If a module has indeterministic behavior that causes the parameter values of outgoing method calls to vary (e.g. a random number generator is used), the objects serialized during the recording phase cannot be correctly associated to the arguments of those outgoing calls. And, if the module is refactored to include additional calls to other modules or if these calls are reordered, no suitable prerecorded objects exist during replay phase, causing the module test to fail.

Objects are recorded in association to method calls and their argument values. This implies a necessity to compare deserialized objects to the ones passed as arguments during replay in order to determine if they are equal. In Java, a class must correctly implement the method `equals(..)` to support this.

As our approach relies on object serialization, it shares its restrictions in serializing certain kinds of objects. Such objects become invalid when serialized and deserialized. Examples are thread-like objects and objects keeping system resources such as file handles. In these and similar cases, one should investigate the possibility of implementing custom XStream converters (see [6]) in order to enable XStream to properly serialize and deserialize objects of specific types, e.g. to reinitialize a file handle properly.

The proposed approach does not support cyclic dependencies between the module under test and modules to be replaced by the mocking mechanism. If one of the latter modules calls a method of the module under test, this call is not captured during the recording phase and thus does not occur during the playback phase. It may be possible to track such behavior and replay it accordingly by generating corresponding pointcuts and surrounding aspects as needed instead of defining them manually.

5   Related Work

Elbaum et al. describe in [7] a general technique of extracting module tests from system tests and call this technique "carving and replay differential unit tests (DUTs)". The authors discuss multiple realization variants for simulating the environment of a unit when executing the unit tests (state-based, action-based) but the basic idea is the same as in our approach: Whenever a unit makes a call to its environment, this execution of the call is simulated by a mock, while the simulation might not be restricted on just yielding the return value (as in our approach) but to simulate also side-effects of the called method by update the state of the unit (what overcomes some of the limitations of our approach). Following the taxonomy in [7], our approach would be classified as a "action-state hybrid CR approach". Unlike our approach, their implementation is not based on AOP but employs code instrumentation and the Byte Code Engineering Library (BCEL).

Saff et al. describe in [8] an approach of extracting unit tests from system tests, which is very similar to ours, has similar limitations and which is called *"factoring unit tests"*. The most important difference is the used technique for recording and replaying interactions between modules. While our approach is based on AOP, the tool implemented by Saff et al. relies on Java instrumentation.

Concurrently with Saff et al., Orso and Kennedy developed a similar technique in [9]. While they describe their capture-and-replay approach in a language-agnostic way, the provided implementation of the approach targets Java programs and is, as the other approaches cited above, based on Java instrumentation.

While AOP is not yet used as wide-spread as it was anticipated [10], there are numerous success stories from industry in using this technique. One important application scenario is the enhancement of existing applications aiming at improving its overall quality. Bodkin and Furlong [11] report on adding a component to a widely deployed application at Daimler-Chrysler for monitoring user behavior. The collected data was used to improve both the application and even the overall business process. There is also ongoing research work aiming at combining AOP and testing. This effort, however, is devoted to develop new techniques for testing aspects themselves [12,13], which is a quite different goal from ours.

There are numerous frameworks available that facilitate the automated test of Java code, among them JUnit being the most famous. *EasyMock* is another popular framework, which helps to test a class in isolation from its neighboring classes. Before a test is executed, the neighboring objects of the object under test are substituted by mock objects, whose behavior can be defined programmatically based on dynamic proxies. The technique has limitations when the code under test calls static methods including constructors at neighboring classes, as it was the case in our running example.

Last but not least we have to mention the framework *JMockit* that uses the concept of JVM class redefinition introduced in Java 5. The main idea is to substitute certain classes with mock classes during runtime. This is basically the interceptor technique also realized by AOP. It is possible to formulate JMockit tests that are semantically equivalent to the generated module tests of our approach. One disadvantage of JMockit is the lack of the powerful wildcard notation to define a set of join points where interception should apply. More importantly, JMockit cannot be used for the purpose of tracing production code as required by the first step of our approach.

6   Conclusions

We have applied AOP to define mock tests in which parts of the system under test are substituted by mock objects. One of the biggest problems in writing mock tests is to find an elegant solution for the substitution problem: If the system under test is executed in test mode, then mock objects should be used, while in production mode, mock objects must not be used. The production code itself, of course, must not be aware of the two different execution modes.

Our solution for this substitution problem is based on AOP, which allows to manipulate the control flow of the production code "from outside" in an elegant way, i.e. without altering the production code itself. A definitive advantage over other mock frameworks like EasyMock is that not only calls from the object under test to neighboring objects can be substituted, but also any kind of method call, including calls to static methods and calls that are deeply nested within the production code. This feature of our approach makes it possible to easily define modules of the system under test by simply grouping some classes. Using our AOP-based technique, all outgoing method calls for a group of classes can be captured within a given test scenario.

Future work

Our approach is implemented by the open-source framework *jautomock*. One of its current limitations is the necessity to perform the test generation seperately for each module. Also, one has to define the module borders within the source code of the aspects used. Possible future work includes developing a module-definition language and generating the module borders within aspects automatically.

Ongoing research includes the visualization of generated module tests to facilitate their understanding, particularly the control flow of the system test in the recording phase in form of sequence diagrams. We plan to augment this visualization with other diagrams, e.g. object diagrams for visualizing all involved objects.

Acknowledgement

We would like to express our gratitude to Professor Franz Schweiggert, Ulm University, and to our colleague Michael Bouschen for their input and support.

References

1. Kiczales, G., Hilsdale, E., Hugunin, J., Kersten, M., Palm, J., Griswold, W.G.: An overview of AspectJ. In: Knudsen, J.L. (ed.) ECOOP 2001. LNCS, vol. 2072, p. 327. Springer, Heidelberg (2001)
2. Laddad, R.: AspectJ in Action: Practical Aspect-Oriented Programming. Manning (2003)
3. AspectJ Team. The AspectJ programming guide (2003), http://eclipse.org/aspectj/
4. AspectJ Team. The AspectJ 5 development kit developer's notebook (2004), http://eclipse.org/aspectj/
5. jautomock Homepage, http://sourceforge.net/projects/jautomock/
6. XStream Homepage, http://xstream.codehaus.org/
7. Elbaum, S., Chin, H.N., Dwyer, M.B., Jorde, M.: Carving and replaying differential unit test cases from system test cases. IEEE Transactions on Software Engineering 35(1), 29–45 (2009)

8. Saff, D., Artzi, S., Perkins, J.H., Ernst, M.D.: Automatic test factoring for java. In: ASE 2005: Proceedings of the 20th IEEE/ACM international Conference on Automated software engineering, pp. 114–123. ACM, New York (2005)
9. Orso, A., Kennedy, B.: Selective capture and replay of program executions. In: WODA 2005: Proceedings of the third international workshop on Dynamic analysis, pp. 1–7. ACM, New York (2005)
10. Wiese, D., Hohenstein, U., Meunier, R.: How to convince industry of AOP. In: Industry Track of Sixth International Conference on Aspect-Oriented Software Development, AOSD, Vancouver, British Columbia, Canada (2007), http://aosd.net/2007/program/industry/index.php
11. Bodkin, R., Furlong, J.: Gathering feedback on user behaviour using AspectJ. In: Chapman, M., Vasseur, A., Kniesel, G. (eds.) Industry Track Proceedings of 5th International Conference on Aspect-Oriented Software Development, Technical report IAI-TR-2006-3, Computer Science Department III, University of Bonn, Germany, pp. 58–67 (2006)
12. Alexander, R.T., Bieman, J.M., Andrews, A.A.: Towards the systematic testing of aspect-oriented programs. Technical Report CS-4-105, Colorado State University, Fort Collins, Colorado (2004)
13. Ceccato, M., Tonella, P., Ricca, F.: Is AOP code easier or harder to test than OOP code? In: On-line Proceedings of the First Workshop on Testing Aspect-Oriented Programs (WTAOP 2005), Chicago, Illinois, USA (2005)

Cryptographic Protocols Analysis in Event B⋆

Nazim Benaissa and Dominique Méry

Université Henri Poincaré Nancy 1 and LORIA
BP 239
54506 Vandœuvre-lès-Nancy, France
{benaissa,mery}@loria.fr

Abstract. We consider the proof-based development of cryptographic protocols satisfying security properties. For instance, the model of Dolev-Yao provides a way to integrate a description of possible attacks, when designing a protocol. We use existing protocols and want to provide a systematic way to prove but also to design cryptographic protocols; moreover, we would like to provide proof-based guidelines or patterns for integrating cryptographic elements in an existing protocol. The goal of the paper is to present a first attempt to mix design patterns (as in software engineering) and formal methods (as a verification tool). We illustrate the technique on the well known Needham-Schroeder public key protocol and Blake-Wilson-Menezes key transport protocol. The underlying modelling language is Event B and is supported by the RODIN platform, which is used to validate models.

1   Introduction

To provide a secure communication between two agents over an insecure communication channel, these agents should establish a *fresh key* to use in their subsequent communications. The chosen *session key* must be known only by the two agents involved in the communication, it also needs to be a fresh key to avoid using a key established in a previous session. There are several cryptographic protocols dedicated to key establishment that aim to provide such properties. To be able to prove them on a protocol, we must be able to *model the knowledge of the attacker*. A *pet* model of attacker's behaviour is the Dolev-Yao model [1]; this model is an informal description of all possible behaviours of the attacker as described in section 3.4. We model and prove key establishment protocols using Event B [2,3] as a modelling language. We apply our methodology on two protocols: the well known Needham-Schroeder public key protocol [4] and Blake-Wilson-Menezes key transport protocol [5].

Proving properties on cryptographic protocols such as *secrecy* is known to be undecidable. However, works involving formal methods for the analysis of security protocols have been carried out. Theorem provers or model checkers are usually used for proving properties. For model checking, one famous example is Lowe's

---

⋆ This work is supported by grant No. ANR-06-SETI-015-03 awarded by the Agence Nationale de la Recherche.

A. Pnueli, I. Virbitskaite, and A. Voronkov (Eds.): PSI 2009, LNCS 5947, pp. 282–293, 2010.
© Springer-Verlag Berlin Heidelberg 2010

approach [6] using the process calculus CSP and the model checker FDR. Lowe discovered the famous bug in Needham-Schroeder's protocol. Model checking is efficient for discovering an attack if there is one, but it can not guarantee that a protocol is reliable. We should be carefull on the question of stating properties of a given protocol and it is clear that the modelling language should be able to state a given property and then to check the property either using model checking or theorem proving. Other works are based on theorem proving: Paulson [7] used an inductive approach to prove safety properties on protocols. He defined protocols as sets of traces and used the theorem prover Isabelle [8]. Other approaches, like Bolignano [9], combine theorem proving and model checking taking general formal method based techniques as a framework. Let us remember that we focus on a correct-by-construction approach and we are not (yet) proposing new cryptographic protocols: we analyse existing protocols and show how they can be composed and decomposed using proof-based guidelines. Two protocols illustrate the usefulness of our pattern. We have already developed the MONDEX case study [10] and we have identified a structure for this kind of protocol. Protocols are summarized by diagrams showing the information flows and the interactions among agents. We call these diagrams *interaction diagrams.*

The Blake-Wilson-Menezes key transport protocol is a key transport protocol. Agent B creates a fresh session key K_{BA} and sends it to the agent A. The protocol is based on signed messages using public cryptographic keys in order to provide mutual authentication. The Needham-Schroeder public key protocol provides mutual authentication using exchanged shared nonces N_a, N_b (see figure 1). These nonces can be used as shared secret for key establishment, this is why the last message that contains N_b remains encrypted even if it is not necessary for authentication. We consider in this paper the Lowe's fixed version of the protocol. Lowe discovered an attack on this protocol using *FDR* model checker and proposed a variant protocol where the identifier B was added in the second message of the protocol run.

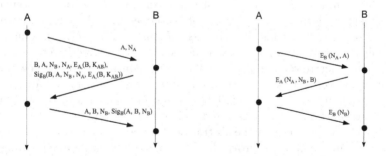

Blake-Wilson-Menezes key transport   Needham-Schroeder public key protocol.
protocol.

Fig. 1. Two protocols

Both protocols can be modelled using interaction diagrams. The proposed guideline is based on this observation and on integration of elements of attack.

2   Development by Step-Wise Refinement

Our event-driven approach [11] is based on the B notation. It extends the methodological scope of basic concepts in order to take into account the idea of *formal models*. Roughly speaking, a formal model is characterized by a (finite) list x of *state variables* possibly modified by a (finite) list of *events*; an invariant $I(x)$ states properties that must always be satisfied by the variables x and *maintained* by the activation of the events. In the following, we briefly recall definitions and principles of formal models and explain how they can be managed by tools [12]. State variables can be modified and we express changes to state variable values, using a general form denoted by the construct $x \; : \mid P(x, x')$. This should be read: "x is modified in such a way that the predicate $P(x, x')$ holds", where x' denotes the *new value* of the vector and x denotes its *old value*. This is clearly non-deterministic in general. In the following, the so-called before-after predicate $BA(x, x')$ describes an event as a logical predicate expressing the relationship linking the values of the state variables just before (x) and just after (x') the "execution" of event evt[1]. Each event has two main parts: a *guard*, which is a predicate built on the state variables, and an *action*, which is a generalized substitution. Proof obligations are produced from events in order to state that an invariant condition $I(x)$ is preserved. Their general form follows immediately from the definition of the before-after predicate, $BA(x, x')$, of each event: $I(x) \wedge BA(x, x') \Rightarrow I(x')$.

The refinement [13,14] of a formal model allows us to enrich a model in a *step-by-step* approach, and is the foundation of our *correct-by-construction* approach. Refinement provides a way to strengthen invariants and to add details to a model. It is also used to transform an abstract model into a more concrete version by modifying the state description. This is done by extending the list of state variables, by refining each abstract event into a corresponding concrete version, and by adding new events. The abstract state variables, x, and the concrete ones, y, are linked together by means of a, so-called, *gluing invariant* $J(x, y)$. A number of proof obligations ensure that (1) each abstract event is correctly refined by its corresponding concrete version, (2) each new event refines $skip$, (3) no new event takes control for ever, and (4) relative deadlock-freeness is preserved. We suppose that an abstract model AM with variables x and invariant $I(x)$ is refined by a concrete model CM with variables y and gluing invariant $J(x, y)$. If $BAA(x, x')$ and $BAC(y, y')$ are respectively the abstract and concrete before-after predicates of the same event, we have to prove the following statement, corresponding to proof obligation (1): $I(x) \wedge J(x, y) \wedge BAC(y, y') \Rightarrow \exists x' \cdot (BAA(x, x') \wedge J(x', y'))$.

---

[1] The prime notation, where we represent the value of a variable x, say, after an event by x' is a fundamental part of the modelling language and is used throughout all the models that follow.

To summarize, refinement guarantees that the set of traces of the abstract model contains (modulo stuttering) the traces of the concrete model.

3   Guidelines for Modelling Protocols

A proof-based guideline is defined by a proof-based development of Event B models which are modelling protocols in a very abstract and general way. A protocol is a system which is controlling the traffic of messages between agents. The first three models are common to protocols where authentication properties have to be established, while the fourth model is dedicated to key establishment protocols. The four models defining the development are as follows:

- In this first model, different steps of the protocol run are modelled using the notion of *abstract transactions*. A transaction has different attributes such as source and destination. These attributes are used to express safety properties we want to prove on our protocol in particular the authentication properties.
- In this first refinement, we add the remaining parts of the protocol that were not modelled in the abstract model. Attacker event preserves (or keeps) the invariant.
- In the second refinement, the attacker knowledge is modelled and used to prove that the safety properties of the model are maintained though attacker's behaviour. This refinement models the behaviour of a Dolev-Yao style attacker. This model can be reused for different protocols.
- This refinement is specific to key establishment protocols, we use the authentication properties and the characterization of the attacker's knowledge proven in the two previous refinements to prove properties over the exchanged keys.

A last data refinement is added where abstract transactions are replaced by concrete nonces. We should recall that the goal is to help the developer in discharging proof obligations and the table of proof obligations for the proof-based guideline applied to the two protocols is given in the tables 1 and 2. Now, we give first a description of the proof-based guideline and then we show how it is applied to model both protocols.

Table 1. Proof obligation of the Needham-Schroeder public key protocol

Model	Total number of PO	Automatics	Interactives
Abstract model	60	60 (100%)	0 (0%)
First refinement	71	71 (100%)	0 (0%)
Second refinement	44	32 (73%)	12 (27%)
Total	175	163 (94%)	12 (6%)

Table 2. Proof obligation of the Blake-Wilson-Menezes key transport protocol

Model	Total number of PO	Automatics	Interactives
Abstract model	50	50 (100%)	0 (0%)
First refinement	50	50 (100%)	0 (0%)
Second refinement	10	7 (70%)	3 (30%)
Total	110	107 (97%)	3 (3%)

3.1 Abstract Model

The proof-based guideline is based on the notion of *abstract transactions*. Safety properties will first be expressed over these abstract transactions. In cryptographic protocols, nonces are used to identify each session or protocol run. Intuitively, each transaction of the abstract model corresponds to a fresh nonce in the concrete model. A transaction has several attributes and, before giving these attributes, we need to introduce the basic sets we will use in our model: T is the set of abstract transactions; $Agent$ is the set of agents; MSG is the set of possible messages among agents; $axm1 : I \in Agent$ expresses the existence of a special agent called the intruder. Note that for most protocols, even if there is more than one dishonest agent in the system, it suffices to consider only one attacker that will combine the abilities and knowledge of all the other dishonnest agents.

In public key protocols, we often have an agent that initiates the protocol run by sending a message to a given agent and then waits for the corresponding answer. This answer is usually encrypted with the source agent public key or signed by the destination agent private key. After receiving this answer, the source agent trusts the authenticity of the destination agent identity, our proof-based guideline captures this idea. A transaction has a source (t_src) and a destination (t_dst). A running transaction is contained in a set *trans*. When a transaction terminates it is added to a set *end*. The answer from the destination agent is transmitted via a channel (*channel*).

$inv1 : trans \subseteq T$
$inv2 : end \subseteq trans$
$inv3 : t\_src \in trans \rightarrow Agent$
$inv4 : t\_dst \in trans \rightarrow Agent$
$inv5 : channel \subseteq MSG$
$inv6 : msg\_src \in channel \rightarrow Agent$
$inv7 : msg\_dst \in channel \rightarrow Agent$
$inv8 : msg\_t \in channel \rightarrow T$
$inv9 : t\_bld\_dst \in trans \rightarrow Agent$

A message from this channel has a source and a destination (msg_src, msg_dst) but also a variable (msg_t) that binds the message to a transaction. To complete the authentication of the destination agent we need an additional variable t_bld_dst that contains the trusted destination agent by the source agent where the variable t_dst contains the real destination agent.

In this case, *to prove authentication, we need to prove that both variables are equal when a transaction terminates*: $inv10 : \forall t \cdot t \in end \Rightarrow t\_dst(t) = t\_bld\_dst(t)$. The diagram describes the model's events. At the beginning of a transaction, the agent A sets the value of the variable t_bld_dst to some agent B and adds the transaction t to the set *trans*. An agent B answers by sending a message to A, the variable *msg_src* is set to the value B.

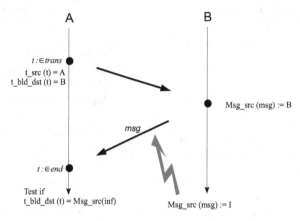

A   **B**

$t : \in trans$
$t\_src\ (t) = A$
$t\_bld\_dst\ (t) = B$

Msg_src (msg) := B

msg

$t : \in end$

Test if
$t\_bld\_dst\ (t) = Msg\_src(inf)$ Msg_src (msg) := I

**Guideline for modelling public
key protocols**

Events of the model are enumerated as follows:

– **EVENT Init**: The transaction source agent initiates the transaction by adding this transaction to the set *trans* and sets the values of the variables t_src to himself and t_bld_dst to the agent he wants to communicate with.

– **EVENT V**: The transaction destination agent answers the source agent by sending a message on the variable *channel* and sets the variable *msg_src* to himself for the sent message.

– **EVENT End**: The transaction source agent receives a message corresponding to this transaction. The variable t_dst is set to the received message source agent contained in the variable *msg_src*.

– **EVENT Attk**: The attacker sends messages to randomly chosen agents to try to mislead them about his identity. The variable *msg_src* is set to the attacker's identity.

EVENT Init
  ANY
    t, A, B
  WHERE
    $grd1 : t \in T \setminus trans$
    $grd2 : A \in Agent \wedge$
       $B \in Agent \wedge A \neq B$
  THEN
    $act1 : trans := trans \cup \{t\}$
    $act2 : t\_src(t) := A$
    $act3 : t\_bld\_dst(t) := B$
  END

EVENT V
  ANY
    A, B, t, msg
  WHERE
    $grd1 : A \in Agent \wedge$
       $B \in Agent \wedge A \neq B$
    $grd2 : t \in T$
    $grd3 : msg \in MSG \setminus channel$
  THEN
    $act1 : channel := channel$
       $\cup \{msg\}$
    $act2 : msg\_src(msg) := B$
    $act3 : msg\_dst(msg) := A$
    $act4 : msg\_t(msg) := t$
  END

When an agent A receives a message corresponding to a transaction, he initiated from an agent B, he sets the variable t_dst to the value B. Thus, the variable t_dst contains the real transaction destination. The value of this variable is not set in the

V event, when the agent B sends the message because many agents may answer to agent A's request and the real transaction destination is known only once A receives one of the messages. Since a message may contain additional informations like a shared session key that B may send to A, when A receives the key, t_dst will contain the identity of the transaction key issuer.

EVENT End
    ANY
        t, A, B, msg
    WHERE
        $grd1 : t \in trans \setminus end$
        $grd2 : A \in Agent \wedge B \in Agent \wedge A \neq B$
        $grd3 : t\_src(t) = A$
        $grd4 : msg \in channel$
        $grd5 : msg\_t(msg) = t$
        $grd6 : msg\_src(msg) = B$
        $grd7 : msg\_dst(msg) = A$
        $grd8 : msg\_src(msg) = t\_bld\_dst(t)$
    THEN
        $act1 : end := end \cup \{t\}$
        $act2 : t\_dst(t) := B$
    END

Depending of the protocol structure, the agent A should know, if the source of the message he receives is the trusted destination of the transaction to guarantee the authentication of the protocol. But in this abstract model, we add the *guard 8* that guarantees this property. We also add in this model the attacker event.

In this event the attacker can add a message with randomly chosen attributes to the *channel*.

EVENT Attk
    ANY
        t, A, msg
    WHERE
        $grd1 : t \in T$
        $grd2 : A \in Agent$
        $grd3 : msg \in MSG \setminus channel$
        $grd4 : A \neq I$
    THEN
        $act1 : channel := channel \cup \{msg\}$
        $act2 : msg\_src(msg) := I$
        $act3 : msg\_dst(msg) := A$
        $act4 : msg\_t(msg) := t$
    END

Another event modelling the loss of messages is added. Messages are removed from the *channel* randomly. This loss can be caused by a malicious attacker action or by an error in the communication channel. To guarantee authentication, the following invariant was added and proved. It states that *for completed transaction, the trusted destination is the real transaction destinations.*

This invariant($inv11 : \forall t \cdot t \in end \Rightarrow t\_dst(t) = t\_bld\_dst(t)$) is easy to prove even for the event **Attk**, because of the *guard 8* of the event **End**.

3.2   Applying the Proof-Based Guideline

In the Needham Schroeder public key protocol (see figure 1) and the Blake-Wilson-Menezes key transport protocol (see figure 1), the agent A first initiates a transaction and waits for the answer from agent B. The agent B does the same, and waits for A's answer. The figure 2 shows how the proof-based guideline is applied two times to model each protocol.

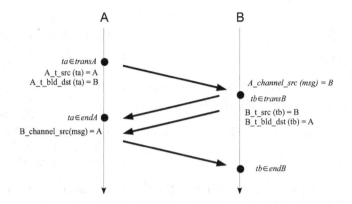

Fig. 2. Proof-based guideline for modelling public key protocols

When the proof-based guideline is applied, the corresponding variables, events and invariants are generated. For both protocols, the following variables are generated: $transA$, $transB$, A_t_src, B_t_src, A_t_dst, B_t_dst, $A\_t\_bld\_dst$, $B\_t\_bld\_dst$. *Invariant10* is generated two times: $\forall t \cdot t \in end \Rightarrow A\_t\_dst(t) = A\_t\_bld\_dst(t) \wedge$, $\forall t \cdot t \in end \Rightarrow B\_t\_dst(t) = B\_t\_bld\_dst(t)$.

3.3   First Refinement

The goal of this first refinement is to understand how authentication is achieved, thus, the remaining details of the modelled protocol messages are added. For instance, in the last step of the Blake-Wilson-Menezes protocol, agent A sends to agent B a signed message containing A, B, N_B. In this message, B is contained in the variable msg_dst and N_B is in the variable msg_t, additional variables are needed for modelling the attribute A and the key K_A in the message. In the second step of the Needham Schroeder public key protocol, agent B sends to agent A a message containing $(B, N_B, N_A)_{KA}$, an additional variable is also needed for modelling the attribute B in the message. This is done exhaustively with all the modelled protocol steps. When keys are used for encryption or signing, a new carrier set is introduced. The relation between the set of agents and keys depends from the type of the encryption used. In the case of public key encryption, each agent has a public key and he is the only agent able to decrypt messages encrypted with this key. Messages attributes are added exhaustively, for any key used to encrypt or sign a message we add the corresponding variable:

Key / ∗ *set of all keys* ∗ /
$inv12 : Agent\_Pc\_key \in Agent \rightarrowtail Key$ / ∗ *Agents public keys* ∗ /
$inv13 : Agent\_Pv\_key \in Agent \rightarrowtail Key$ / ∗ *Agents private keys* ∗ /
$inv14 : msg\_key \in channel \rightarrow Key$

Let MSG_VAR be the set of additional variables. In the abstract model we use the *guard 8* in the **EVENT End** to prove authentication, with this guard agent A could know if the message is authentic or not. In cryptographic protocols it is not possible to perform such tests but the structure of the message itself guarantees authentication.

EVENT End
    ANY
        t, A, B, msg
    WHERE
        $\oplus$ $grd8 : Protocol\_Cond(MSG\_VAR)$
        $\ominus$ $grd8 : msg\_src(msg) = B$
    THEN
        $act1 : end := end \cup \{t\}$
        $act2 : t\_dst(t) := B$
    END

Accordingly, the *guard 8* in the **EVENT End** has to be substituted by a condition over the received message content. This condition is a predicate over the set *MSG_VAR*, we call it *Protocol_Cond(MSG_VAR)*. The predicate is directly derived from the protocol itself.

To prove that the concrete **EVENT End**[2]: refines the abstract event **EVENT End**, the following invariant has to be added:

$inv15 : \forall t, msg, A, B \cdot$
$t \in trans \wedge A \in Agent \wedge B \in Agent \wedge msg \in channel \wedge t\_src(t) = A \wedge$
$t\_bld\_dst(t) = B \wedge msg\_t(msg) = t \wedge Protocol\_Cond(MSG\_VAR)$
$\qquad \Rightarrow \ msg\_src(msg) = t\_bld\_dst(t)$

EVENT Attk
    ANY
        t, A, msg
    WHERE
        $\oplus$ $grd7 : Attk\_Cond$
    THEN
        $act1 : \oplus MSG\_VAR$
    END

The Attacker The next refinement models attackers' knowledge and, in this refinement, the **EVENT Attk** keeps the *invariant15*. To achieve this we call *Attk_Cond* the weakest condition that maintains the *invariant15*. Note that this predicate is obtained from the invariant. We use *Attk_Cond* to refine the *event Attk* as follows:

3.4   Second Refinement: Attacker's Knowledge

To be able to prove properties such as secrecy and authentication on a protocol, we have to be able to model the knowledge of the attacker. To model the knowledge of the attacker, it is necessary to know exactly what the attacker is able to do. One popular model for attacker's behavior is the Dolev-Yao model. This refinement models all the options the attacker has in this attacking model and can be reused for different protocols. One possible modelling is to consider that a part of the attacker knowledge is contained implicitly in the variables modelling the communication channel. The attacker can then try to obtain nonces and keys from the content of the communication channel. The attacker may also have an initial knowledge, or a knowledge he may acquire by means other than analysing the communication channel content. To model all these options, we use variables that contain the crucial information the attacker can obtain. Because of the typing constraints in the

---

[2] $\oplus$ and $\ominus$ are respectively the added and removed guards compared to the refined event.

event-B, we use one variable for each information type : N_Mem for nonces and K_Mem for keys ($N\_Mem \in Agent \rightarrow \mathbb{P}(T)$, $K\_Mem \in Agent \rightarrow \mathbb{P}(Key)$).

We need to answer two issues: What is in the variables N_Mem and K_Mem ?How does the intruder use the knowledge contained in this variable? The answer of the second issue is immediate, the *event Attk* is refined by changing the *guard* 7. Now the attacker uses only transactions or keys that are in his memory and also fragments of encrypted messages contained in the communication channel.

EVENT Attk
   ANY
      t, A, msg
   WHERE
      $\ominus$ $grd7$: $Attak\_Cond$
      $\oplus$ $grd7$: $t \in N\_Mem$
   THEN
      $act1$: $channel := channel \cup \{msg\}$
      $act2$: $msg\_src(msg) := I$
      $act3$: $msg\_Key(msg) := Agent\_Pc\_Key(A)$
      $act4$: $msg\_t(msg) := t$
   END

The *event Attk* is refined into several concrete events that includes all the options, due to lack of space we give here one event that models the attacker when using transactions in his memory (without fragment of encrypted messages). The following invariant is added: $inv18$: $\forall t.t \in N\_Mem \Rightarrow Attak\_Cond$.

To prove this invariant we need to answer the first issue: what is in the attacker memory? This will depend from the chosen attacker model. In the Dolev-Yao one, attacker has full control of communication channel: *He can intercept and remove any message of the channel* or *He can also generate infinite number of messages* or *He can decrypt parts of the message if he has the appropriate key* or *He can split unencrypted messages*. In our model we have already added events where messages are lost no matter if it is done by the attacker or not. And we didn't limit the number of messages the attacker can send. To model the fact that an attacker decrypts parts of the message, if he has the appropriate key, we added the following event where the attacker uses keys he knows to decrypt fragments of messages:

EVENT Attk_Mem
   ANY
      t, A, msg
   WHERE
      $grd1$: $A \in Agent$
      $grd2$: $Agent\_Pv\_key(A) \in K\_Mem$
      $grd3$: $msg \in channel$
      $grd4$: $msg\_t(msg) = t$
      $grd5$: $msg\_Key(msg) := Agent\_Pc\_Key(A)$
   THEN
      $act1$: $N\_Mem := N\_Mem \cup \{t\}$
   END

To prove the invariant *invariant18* we need an additional invariant that gives a characterization of the attacker's knowledge. This invariant is different from a protocol to another. In the case of the Needham-Schroeder public key protocol where the proof-based guideline was applied two times (see figure 2).

We had proven that the attackers's memory contains only transactions that are not in the set *trans* or transactions where the attacker is the source or the trusted destination:

$inv19 : \forall t \cdot t \in N\_Mem \Rightarrow$

$(t \notin transA \cup transB \vee$

$(t \in transA \wedge (I = A\_t\_bld\_dst(t) \vee I = A\_t\_src(t))) \vee$

$(t \in transB \wedge (I = B\_t\_bld\_dst(t) \vee I = B\_t\_src(t))))$

We omit further refinements because of the lack of space. In the third refinement we use the channels where authentication property has been proven to send the session key. The attacker characterization defined in the second refinement is used to prove secrecy property for the session key.

4   Conclusion

We have introduced an Event-B-based guideline for cryptographic key establishment protocols and we have applied it on two different protocols. Properties like authentication, secrecy and key freshness were proved on these protocols. Less than 5% of the proofs of the models were interactive. Our guidelines facilitate proof process by reusing partially former developments; we have not yet designed new cryptographic protocols and it remains to develop other case studies by applying guidelines. Like design patterns, proof-based guidelines are based on real cases; they should help the use of refinement and proof techniques; it is then clear that specific tools should be developed and further works should be carried out using refinement for discovering new guidelines. As a perspective of our work, it is necessary to add new properties that are desired in some situation such as key confirmation where an agent receives an evidence that the other agent involved in the protocol run received the session key. It is also necessary to address questions on extensions of Dolev-Yao models. Finally, we should evaluate impacts of the underlying formalism namely Event B and of the tool namely RODIN, on the discovery of guidelines; it means that we should define what is clearly a guideline or a pattern in the Event B context.

References

1. Dolev, D., Yao, A.: On the security of public key protocols. IEEE Transactions on Information Theory 29(2), 198–208 (1983)
2. Abrial, J.: The B Book - Assigning Programs to Meanings. Cambridge University Press, Cambridge (1996)
3. Cansell, D., Méry, D.: The event-B Modelling Method: Concepts and Case Studies [15], pp. 33–140. Springer, Heidelberg (2007)
4. Needham, R.M., Schroeder, M.D.: Using encryption for authentication in large networks of computers. Commun. ACM 21(12), 993–999 (1978)
5. Blake-Wilson, S., Menezes, A.: Entity authentication and authenticated key transport protocols employing asymmetric techniques. In: Christianson, B., Lomas, M. (eds.) Security Protocols 1997. LNCS, vol. 1361, pp. 137–158. Springer, Heidelberg (1998)

6. Lowe, G.: Breaking and fixing the needham-schroeder public-key protocol using FDR. In: Margaria, T., Steffen, B. (eds.) TACAS 1996. LNCS, vol. 1055, pp. 147–166. Springer, Heidelberg (1996)
7. Paulson, L.C.: The inductive approach to verifying cryptographic protocols. Journal of Computer Security 6, 85–128 (1998)
8. Paulson, L.C. (ed.): Isabelle. LNCS, vol. 828. Springer, Heidelberg (1994)
9. Bolignano, D.: Integrating proof-based and model-checking techniques for the formal verification of cryptographic protocols. In: Hu, A.J., Vardi, M.Y. (eds.) CAV 1998. LNCS, vol. 1427, pp. 77–87. Springer, Heidelberg (1998)
10. Stepney, S., Cooper, D., Woodcock, J.: An electronic purse: Specification, refinement, and proof. Technical monograph PRG-126, Oxford University Computing Laboratory (July 2000)
11. Abrial, J.R., Hallerstede, S.: Refinement, decomposition, and instantiation of discrete models: Application to event-b. Fundamenta Informaticae 77(1-2), 1–28 (2007)
12. Rodin, P.: The rodin project: Rigorous open development environment for complex systems (2006), http://rodin-b-sharp.sourceforge.net/
13. Back, R.J.R.: On correct refinement of programs. Journal of Computer and System Sciences 23(1), 49–68 (1979)
14. Back, R.J., von Wright, J.: Refinement Calculus A Systematic Introduction. Graduate Texts in Computer Science. Springer, Heidelberg (1998)
15. Bjørner, D., Henson, M.C. (eds.): Logics of Specification Languages. EATCS Textbook in Computer Science. Springer, Heidelberg (2007)

A Query Language for Logic Architectures

Anton Malykh and Andrei Mantsivoda

Irkutsk State University, Irkutsk, 664003, Russia

Abstract. In this paper we consider the impact of the Semantic Web and logical means on a wide range of developers solving traditional tasks on the WWW. How to make the 'elite' logic tools acceptable for ordinary developers? How to incorporate a wide range of users in the space of the Semantic Web? These and some other questions are considered here and certain proposals are made. In particular we are based on the conception of a logic architecture as a stratified description logic system, and introduce an ontology query language working within logic architectures.

1 Introduction

The tools of the Semantic Web are successfully applied to solving a number of problems, which demand sophisticated logical descriptions and strong logical inference 'engines'. On the other hand, there is a wide-spread opinion that due to the complexity and heaviness of underlying logics, ontologies can not be successfully applied to solving 'lightweight' problems consisting mostly of object processing. It is true that the existing ontology systems can not compete with, say, data base management systems on this kind of tasks. And it is a pity, because this does not allow the Semantic Web to have a significant impact on 'everyday' web resources development, though it is very important if to keep in mind the initial aims of the SW. If the overwhelming majority of practical applications have nothing in common with the SW, it is impossible to 'reorganize' the Web by the SW's elegant and strong conceptions and tools.

The high comprehension barrier between conventional developers and logics, on which the SW is heavily based, is also a problem, because the things that are done by the ordinary developers should be at least compatible with the SW principles and add value to the SW environment. This means that while producing new data, the conventional developer makes it in the form, which is compatible with the logical formalisms and can be integrated in the SW context.

In [1] we consider a conception of a logic architecture, which in particular tries to tackle the problem outlined above. The idea here is to stratify the general logical formalism (e.g. a strong description logic like $\mathcal{SHOIN}(D)$) in such a way that (1) each stratum is responsible for a specific kind of tasks and/or users (while the higher layers can be used for sophisticated and advanced knowledge management, the lower layers can be employed by the wide range of users and developers); (2) each stratum is supplied with special interfaces and programming methods, which implement the scenarios of work within the stratum; (3) the architecture is supplied with tools/formalisms, which work at each stratum

A. Pnueli, I. Virbitskaite, and A. Voronkov (Eds.): PSI 2009, LNCS 5947, pp. 294–305, 2010.
© Springer-Verlag Berlin Heidelberg 2010

and 'glue' the strata together. Among the tools, which can work at each stratum, a query language plays a key role. The basic feature of this language is to be acceptable for the conventional developers.

In this paper we introduce a query language (named BoxQL), which meets the conditions stated above. BoxQL is designed in the XPath-like style at the both syntactic and operational levels, and looks familiar to many people. The idea behind BoxQL is that it should have identical behavior at any level of the logic architecture. BoxQL is intended for logic architectures, which are based on $\mathcal{SHOIN}(D)$ [2] as a 'maximal' logic. $\mathcal{SHOIN}(D)$ is attractive, because it determines the semantics of the web ontology language OWL DL [3].

2   Preliminaries

The languages and logics we consider in this paper are used to describe the *worlds*, which are habitats for *objects* (individuals like John, planet Jupiter and this paper). Objects can be grouped in *concepts* (or classes like Mammals, Planets and Information resources). Objects are connected with each other through *object properties* (or roles – like hasChild or spouse).

The languages describing the worlds are based on vocabularies. A *vocabulary* is a structure $V = \langle T_C, T_R, Id \rangle$ in which T_C, T_R and Id are finite pairwise disjoint sets. T_C is called the set of concept types, and T_R the set of relations. Id is the set of individual names (identifiers). Each relation $r \in T_R$ is associated with a non-negative integer $\sigma(r)$, which is called the arity of r. T_C and T_R are partially ordered in such a way that T_C has a maximum element $\top$, and the relations with different arities are not comparable in T_R.

Objects can have attributes (e.g. age or price). Attributes are assigned to objects by *datatype properties*. The values of datatype properties are taken in *datatype domains* (e.g. integers or strings). Knowledge about the worlds is stored in various *namespaces*. In order to introduce namespaces and data types we augment the notion of a vocabulary in the following way. Let $NS = \{ns_1, \ldots, ns_k\}$ be the set of namespaces and $D = \{d_1, \ldots, d_m\}$ the set of datatypes.

Definition 1 (A namespaced vocabulary). *Let* $V = \langle T_C, T_R, Id \rangle$ *be a vocabulary. Then* $V_{NS}^D = \langle T_C, T_R, Id, NS, D \rangle$ *is a namespaced vocabulary with names* $L = T_C \cup T_R \cup Id \cup D$, *if the following conditions hold:*

1. *L is divided into k pairwise disjoint subsets* $L = \bigcup_{i=1}^{k} L^{ns_i}$, *such that* $L^{ns_i} = T_C^{ns_i} \cup T_R^{ns_i} \cup Id^{ns_i} \cup D^{ns_i}$. *To indicate that a name nm belongs to a namespace ns_i (that is, $nm \in L^{ns_i}$), we write $ns_i{:}nm$.*
2. *T_R is divided into three pairwise disjoint sets T_R^o, T_R^t, and T_R^d of object properties, datatype properties and domain specific relations, respectively, such that $T_R = T_R^o \cup T_R^t \cup T_R^d$.*
3. *T_C contains a concept type c_{ns} for each $ns \in NS$.*

Informally, a concept type c_{ns} denotes the set of objects with names belonging to the namespace ns. We assume that all c_{ns} belong to the initial vocabulary $\mathcal{V}$. Since we work in the context of $\mathcal{SHOIN}(D)$, we have $\sigma(r) = 2$ for each $r \in T_R^o \cup T_R^t$. The relations of T_R^d can have arbitrary arities.

Definition 2 (A datatype domain). *A datatype domain* $\mathcal{D} = \langle D_1,,\ldots,, D_m; \mathcal{L}_D \rangle$ *is an algebra of the language* $\mathcal{L}_D$*, where each* D_i*,* $1 \leq i \leq m$*, is the set of values of the datatype* d_i*.*

Let $|\mathcal{D}| = D_1 \cup \ldots \cup D_m$. We denote by $\mathrm{Term}_{\mathcal{D}+T}$ the set of all ground terms of the language $\mathcal{L}_D \cup T_R^t \cup \{.\}$, in which elements of $|\mathcal{D}|$, T_R^t and the dot '.' play the role of constants. $\mathrm{Term}_{\mathcal{D}+T}^*$ denotes the set of all finite sequences of elements of $\mathrm{Term}_{\mathcal{D}+T}$, that is, if $v_1,\ldots,v_k \in \mathrm{Term}_{\mathcal{D}+T}$ then $(v_1,\ldots,v_k) \in \mathrm{Term}_{\mathcal{D}+T}^*$.

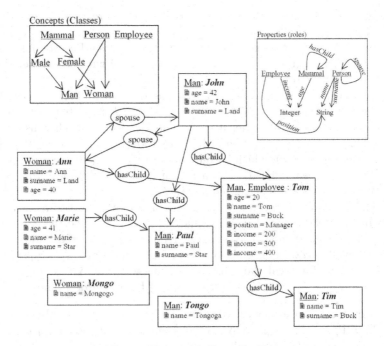

Fig. 1. The world of people $\mathcal{PW}$

Example 1. In figure 1 a simple world of people ($\mathcal{PW}$) is introduced. The vocabulary $\mathcal{V}_{people}$ of this domain consists of

$$T_C = \{\text{Mammal, Female, Male, Person, Man, Woman, Employee}\},$$

with the order Woman $\leq$ Female $\leq$ Mammal, Man $\leq$ Male $\leq$ Mammal, Woman $\leq$ Person, Man $\leq$ Person.

$$T_R = \{\text{spouse, hasChild, age, name, surname, position, income}\}$$

$$Id = \{\texttt{Ann, Marie, Mongo, Tom, Paul, Tim, Tongo, John}\}$$

Let us describe this world in two namespaces `http://people/basic` (in which the basic terminology about people is defined), and `http://people/tribe` (containing only data about two members of a tribe, named Mongogo and Tongoga), plus the datatype namespace `http://www.w3c.org/2001/XMLSchema`. For these namespaces we use the shortcuts (prefixes) p, t and x, respectively. Then, based on $\mathcal{V}_{PW}$ with augmented $T'_C = T_C \cup \{c_p, c_t, c_x\}$, we can construct $\mathcal{V}^D_{PW}$:

$$NS = \{\texttt{p, t, x}\}, D = \{\texttt{x:integer, x:string}\}$$
$$T^o_R = \{\texttt{p:spouse, p:hasChild}\}$$
$$T^t_R = \{\texttt{p:age, p:name, p:surname, p:position, p:income}\}$$
$$T^d_R = \{\texttt{+, >} \text{ and other rels \& ops of } \texttt{x:integer} \text{ and } \texttt{x:string}\}$$
$$Id^p = \{\texttt{p:Ann, p:Marie, p:Tom, p:Paul, p:Tim, p:John}\}$$
$$Id^t = \{\texttt{t:Mongo, t:Tongo}\}, Id^x = \emptyset$$

Definition 3 (The language of $\mathcal{SHOIN}(D)$). *If $c \in T_C$ then c is a named concept of $\mathcal{SHOIN}(D)$. Named concepts are concepts. If a, b are concepts, $id \in Id$, $r \in T^o_R \cup T^t_R$, $p \in T^d_R$ then $a \sqcap b$, $a \sqcup b$, $\neg a$, $\exists r.a$, $\forall r.a$, $\leq_n r$, $\geq_n r$, $\exists(x_1, \ldots, x_n).p$, $\forall(x_1, \ldots, x_n).p$, $\{id\}$ are also concepts. If $r \in T^o_R$ then $\exists r'.a$ and $\forall r'.a$ are concepts, where $r' \in \{r^+, r^-, r^\pm\}$.*

$\mathcal{SHOIN}(D)$ is a description logic, which is very close to the Web ontology language OWL DL. The first $\mathcal{S}$ stands in its name for the basic logic $\mathcal{ALC}$ augmented with transitive roles. In $\mathcal{ALC}$ the basic description logic constructs (concepts, roles, disjunction $\sqcup$, conjunction $\sqcap$, negation $\neg$ and role quantifiers) are introduced. $\mathcal{H}$ stands for role hierarchies, $\mathcal{O}$ denotes objects, which can be represented explicitly, $\mathcal{I}$ stands for inverse roles, and $\mathcal{N}$ for simple number restrictions. (D) means that datatype properties are also allowed.

3   BoxQL: A Query Language

BoxQL is designed in an object-oriented style: it considers the collections of individuals in ontologies as a network of interconnected objects (like in Fig. 1). In [1] we introduce the notion of an object-oriented projection, which formally describes such an understanding of an object network. OO-projections are simple sublogics of $\mathcal{SHOIN}(D)$. The nature of BoxQL is traversal: its queries are 'walking along' the network of objects and collecting necessary data. This style is familiar, intuitively easy and acceptable for many people, because it resembles XPath, directory paths in file systems, and 'dotted' expressions in the object-oriented languages. On the other hand, BoxQL is upward compatible with more sophisticated and elite logic techniques. And the queries in BoxQL are actually 'encoded' formulas of $\mathcal{SHOIN}(D)$, though a flavor of logic is concealed in them. Like in XPath the general structure of BoxQL queries is

$$\texttt{step}_1[\texttt{pred}_1]/\ldots/\texttt{step}_k[\texttt{pred}_k]$$

where predicates in square brackets are optional. A BoxQL query produces a sequence of objects or data values gathered in $\mathcal{KB}$, which satisfy its conditions.

Example 2. Let us take an example from $\mathcal{PW}$. Imagine that we want to find a spouse of some man who is 40 and has a grandson. Here is a BoxQL query

Query: @man/spouse[age = 40 and hasChild/hasChild[@man]]
Result: {Ann}

The main path @man/spouse of this query collects all man's spouses, because the value of a path is always the value of its rightmost step. The names of classes are qualified in BoxQL with '@'. The namespace p is assumed default, thus its prefix is omitted. The predicate in the square brackets allows us to select among the man's spouses those persons who are 40 and for whom the query hasChild/hasChild[@man] produces a non-empty sequence of objects. Now let us compare the above query with the following one:

Query: @man/spouse[age = 40]/hasChild/hasChild[@man]
Result: {Tim}

Here we move along the same path as in the first query. But the result is different, because the main path now is @man/spouse/hasChild/hasChild and its rightmost step gives Tim.

Note that the both queries can be expressed by the formulas of $\mathcal{SHOIN}(D)$:

1. $\exists spouse^-.Man \sqcap \exists age.\{40\} \sqcap \exists hasChild.\exists hasChild.Man$ and
2. $Man \sqcap \exists hasChild^-.\exists hasChild^-.(\exists age.\{40\} \sqcap \exists spouse^-.Man)$

We can see the fundamental difference between the queries and the corresponding DL formulas. The DL formulas just describe the qualities of a searched object, whereas the traversal queries show how to get it from scratch (this is why we need to use the role inversions in the formulas). In practice, the style of writing queries in BoxQL is closer to navigation over description graphs. BoxQL is based on the idea that the user 'walks along' the ontology objects' network, and points out, which data must be collected during this walk. For collecting necessary data the user can employ the *fields*, like in the following example

Query: @p:person as Granparent/hasChild/hasChild
Result: {(Tim, Grandparent=John), (Tim, Grandparent=Ann)}

Now the solution contains not only the value of the rightmost step (Tim) but also the value of the field Grandparent corresponding to Tim. The way of formulating queries in BoxQL is also close to writing dotted expressions in OO programming languages, though the dot itself serves in BoxQL as an analog of Java's 'this':

Query: age[. > 30]
Result: {40, 41, 42}

The result is a datatype sequence, and '>' $\in T_R^d$. We do not distinguish a constant singleton (x) and the value x, so instead of [. > (30)] we can write [. > 30].

An atomic step ns:* selects all objects named within the namespace ns:

Query: t:*/name
Result: {"Tongoga", "Mongogo"}

An atomic step −ns:ro denotes the inverses of object properties:

Query: −hasChild
Result: {John, Marie, John, Ann, Tom}

Intuitively '−' means here that we move from children to parents. John occurs twice, because he is the father of two persons. BoxQL also allows us to explicitly use the names of objects like in

Query: &Tom/income
Result: {200, 300, 400}

Using sequences as steps we can combine the sets of elements like in the following example, in which '*' stands for 'all objects':

Query: (&john, @woman/t:*, *[income])/name
Result: {"John", "Mongogo", "Tom"}

The expression (h ! [r1]) implements in BoxQL the ∀–quantifier of DLs. The next query selects individuals whose children are *all* boys (following the semantics of ∀ in the DLs ! collects also individuals who do not have children):

Query: *[hasChild ! [@man]]
Result: {John, Ann, Marie, Paul, Tom, Tim, t:Tongo, t:Mongo}

Since DLs are based on the open-world paradigm, a BoxQL-query actually produces a sequence of objects, which *are known* to satisfy the query's conditions. Thus, we should be careful with the negation because its use in open knowledge bases can set dangerous non-monotone traps. For instance, the query *[not hasChild] asks to find those *known* objects, which are *unknown* to have children, and further updates in the knowledge base can reduce the resulting sequence. We do not put restrictions on the negation in the general formalism. There are various ways how to tackle such problems, say, with the help of the epistemic operator $\mathcal{K}$ (see [4], section 6.2.3). In particular, we can restrict the negation only to those concepts c, the knowledge about which is complete, i.e. $\neg \mathcal{K} c \sqsubseteq \mathcal{K} \neg c$.

4   The Semantics of BoxQL

First, we formally define the BoxQL syntax.

Definition 4 (BoxQL syntax). *Let $\mathcal{V}_{NS}^D$ be a namespaced vocabulary. We define the sets of steps $\mathcal{S}$, paths $\mathcal{P}$ and predicates $\mathcal{R}$ of BoxQL as follows:*

1. *The atomic steps of BoxQL are: (a) $* \in \mathcal{S}$ and ns:$* \in \mathcal{S}$ for each ns $\in NS$; (b) if ns:c $\in T_C$, then @ns:c $\in \mathcal{S}$; (c) if ns:ro $\in T_R^o$ then ns:ro, -ns:ro $\in \mathcal{S}$; (d) if ns:rd $\in T_R^t$ then ns:rd $\in \mathcal{S}$; (e) if ns:id $\in Id$, then &ns:id $\in \mathcal{S}$.*
2. *$\mathcal{S} \subseteq \mathcal{P}$. If h $\in \mathcal{P}$ and s $\in \mathcal{S}$ then h/s $\in \mathcal{P}$.*
3. *$Term_{D+T}^* \subseteq \mathcal{S}$. If $h_1, \ldots, h_k \in \mathcal{P}$ then the sequence $(h_1, \ldots, h_k) \in \mathcal{S}$. A sequence is called constant if all $h_i \in Id$.*

4. *If* $\mathbf{s} \in \mathcal{S}$ *and* $\mathbf{r} \in \mathcal{R}$, *then* $\mathbf{s}[\mathbf{r}] \in \mathcal{S}$.
5. $\mathcal{P} \subseteq \mathcal{R}$. $\mathrm{Rel}_{\mathcal{D}+T} \subseteq \mathcal{R}$.
6. *If* $\mathbf{h} \in \mathcal{P}$, $\mathbf{r1}$, $\mathbf{r2} \in \mathcal{R}$ *and* $\mathbf{c}$ *is a constant sequence, then* $(\mathbf{r1}$ $\mathbf{and}$ $\mathbf{r2})$, $(\mathbf{r1}$ $\mathbf{or}$ $\mathbf{r2})$, $(\mathbf{not}$ $\mathbf{r1})$, $(\mathbf{r1}$ $=$ $\mathbf{c})$, $(\mathbf{h}$! $[\mathbf{r1}])$ *belong to* $\mathcal{R}$.

A BoxQL-*query* is any $\mathbf{h} \in \mathcal{P}$. A BoxQL-query fetches basic data about objects in the underlying knowledge base $\mathcal{KB}$, in which BoxQL works. In other words, $\mathcal{KB}$ is a parameter of BoxQL. The strength of $\mathcal{KB}$ depends on the stratum of the logic architecture, in which BoxQL works at the moment.

Let $\mathcal{V}_{NS}^{D}$ be a namespaced vocabulary and $\mathcal{KB} = \langle |\mathcal{KB}|, \models \rangle$ a knowledge base of this vocabulary with the interpretation $I : \mathcal{V}_{NS}^{D} \mapsto \mathcal{KB}$. $|\mathcal{KB}|$ is the set of objects stored in $\mathcal{KB}$. We assume that $\models$ allows us to check whether $\mathtt{ns{:}c}^I(o_1)$, $\mathtt{ns{:}ro}^I(o_1, o_2)$, $\mathtt{ns{:}rd}^I(o_1, v)$ are true for any $o_1, o_2 \in |\mathcal{KB}|$, $\mathtt{ns{:}c} \in T_C$, $\mathtt{ns{:}ro} \in T_R^o$, $\mathtt{ns{:}rd} \in T_R^t$ and $v \in |\mathcal{D}|$. Predicates from $\mathrm{Rel}_{\mathcal{D}+T}$ are also evaluated by $\models$.

The (naive) procedural semantics of BoxQL is defined in the form of calculi. Note that the paths of BoxQL focus on collecting objects, while the predicates in square brackets do the opposite work: they filter out the objects not satisfying certain conditions. This means that we need to have separate, though mutually defined, sub-calculi for paths and predicates, which are called the $\star$-calculus and the $\diamond$-calculus, respectively. For technical reasons we treat a path $\mathbf{h}_1/\ldots/\mathbf{h}_k$ as if it is obtained from the empty path ϵ by the multiple applications of the left-associative operator '/': $(\ldots(\epsilon/\mathbf{h}_1)/\mathbf{h}_2)/\ldots/\mathbf{h}_k)$.

The derived objects of the $\star$-calculus have the form $\mathbf{h}\langle \mathcal{C} \rangle$, where $\mathbf{h}$ is a path and $\mathcal{C}$ a finite sequence of elements from $|\mathcal{KB}|$. We say that a sequence $\mathcal{A}$ is the *answer* to a path $\mathbf{h} \in \mathcal{P}$ on a sequence $\mathcal{C}$ (denoted $\mathbf{h}\langle \mathcal{C} \rangle \vdash_\star \mathcal{A}$), if there exists a derivation sequence $\mathbf{h}\langle \mathcal{C} \rangle, \mathbf{h}_1\langle \mathcal{C}_1 \rangle, \ldots, \epsilon\langle \mathcal{A} \rangle$ such that ϵ is the empty path, and every $\mathbf{h}_i\langle \mathcal{C}_i \rangle$ is obtained from the previous one by the application of some $\star$-rule. There are two possibilities: $\mathcal{A} \subseteq |\mathcal{KB}|$ (the result is a sequence of objects), and $\mathcal{A} \subseteq |\mathcal{D}|$ (the result is a sequence of datatype values).

Let $\mathbf{h} \in \mathcal{P}$, $\mathbf{r} \in \mathcal{R}$, $\mathbf{s} \in \mathcal{S}$, $o \in |\mathcal{KB}|$, $x \in |\mathcal{KB}| \cup |\mathcal{D}|$, $\mathcal{C} \subseteq |\mathcal{KB}|$, $\mathcal{A} \subseteq |\mathcal{KB}|$ or $\mathcal{A} \subseteq |\mathcal{D}|$, $\mathtt{ns{:}ro} \in T_R^o$, $\mathtt{ns{:}rr} \in T_R^o \cup T_R^t$. For a ground formula f, $\models f$ means that $\mathcal{KB}$ 'knows' that f is true, and $\not\models f$ means that $\mathcal{KB}$ 'knows' that f is false. Here are the rules of the $\star$-calculus:

$$\star \; \frac{*/\mathbf{h}\langle \mathcal{C} \rangle}{\mathbf{h}\langle \mathcal{C} \rangle} \qquad \star \; \frac{\mathtt{ns{:}*}/\mathbf{h}\langle \mathcal{C} \rangle}{\mathbf{h}\langle \mathcal{C} \cap \{o \mid \models c_{ns}^I(o)\} \rangle} \qquad \star \; \frac{\mathtt{ns{:}c}/\mathbf{h}\langle \mathcal{C} \rangle}{\mathbf{h}\langle \mathcal{C} \cap \{o \mid \models \mathtt{ns{:}c}^I(o)\} \rangle}$$

$$\star \; \frac{\mathtt{ns{:}rr}/\mathbf{h}\langle \mathcal{C} \rangle}{\mathbf{h}\langle \{x \mid \exists o \in \mathcal{C} : \models \mathtt{ns{:}rr}^I(o, x)\} \rangle} \qquad \star \; \frac{-\mathtt{ns{:}ro}/\mathbf{h}\langle \mathcal{C} \rangle}{\mathbf{h}\langle \{o \mid \exists o' \in \mathcal{C} : \models \mathtt{ns{:}ro}^I(o, o')\} \rangle}$$

$$\star \; \frac{\mathbf{s}[\mathbf{r}]/\mathbf{h}\langle \mathcal{C} \rangle}{\mathbf{h}\langle \{o \mid o \in \mathcal{C}' : \mathbf{s}\langle \mathcal{C} \rangle \vdash_\star \mathcal{C}' \text{ and } \mathbf{r}(o) \vdash_\diamond \mathbf{true}\} \rangle} \qquad \star \; \frac{(x_1, \ldots, x_k)/\mathbf{h}\langle \mathcal{A} \rangle}{\mathbf{h}\langle \mathcal{A} \cap \{x_1^I, \ldots, x_k^I\} \rangle}$$

In the next $\diamond$-calculus the derived objects are $\mathbf{true}$ and $\mathbf{false}$, where $\mathbf{true}$ denotes any non-empty set of elements and $\mathbf{false}$ is represented by $\emptyset$. To prove that a predicate $\mathbf{r} \in \mathcal{R}$ holds on an element (an object or a datatype value) x, we need to derive $\mathbf{r}(x) \vdash_\diamond \mathbf{true}$ in the $\diamond$-calculus, and to derive $\mathbf{r}(x) \vdash_\diamond \mathbf{false}$, if we want to refute it. The $\diamond$-rules are:

$$\diamond \; \frac{h\langle\{x\}\rangle \vdash_* \{x_1,\dots,x_k\} \quad \forall i: r(x_i)\vdash_\diamond \texttt{true}}{h \;!\; [r](x)\vdash_\diamond \texttt{true}} \qquad \diamond \; \frac{r_1(x)\vdash_\diamond res_1 \quad r_2(x)\vdash_\diamond res_2}{(r_1 \; \texttt{and} \; r_2)(x)\vdash_\diamond res_1 \wedge res_2}$$

$$\diamond \; \frac{h\langle\{x\}\rangle \vdash_* \{x_1,\dots,x_k\} \quad \exists i: r(x_i)\vdash_\diamond \texttt{false}}{h \;!\; [r](x)\vdash_\diamond \texttt{false}} \qquad \diamond \; \frac{r_1(x)\vdash_\diamond res_1 \quad r_2(x)\vdash_\diamond res_2}{(r_1 \; \texttt{or} \; r_2)(x)\vdash_\diamond res_1 \vee res_2}$$

$$\diamond \; \frac{r(x)\vdash_\diamond res}{(\texttt{not } r)(x)\vdash_\diamond \neg res} \qquad \diamond \; \frac{h\langle\{x\}\rangle \vdash_* \mathcal{A}}{(h=c)(x)\vdash_\diamond \mathcal{A} \cap c^I} \qquad \diamond \; \frac{h\langle\{x\}\rangle \vdash_* \mathcal{A}}{h(x)\vdash_\diamond \mathcal{A}}$$

$$\diamond \; \frac{\exists \, \mathtt{p}_e \uparrow x : \; \models \mathtt{p}_e \uparrow x}{\mathtt{p}_e(x)\vdash_\diamond \texttt{true}} \qquad \diamond \; \frac{\forall \, \mathtt{p}_e \uparrow x : \; \not\models \mathtt{p}_e \uparrow x}{\mathtt{p}_e(x)\vdash_\diamond \texttt{false}}$$

Here $res, res_i \in \{\texttt{true}, \texttt{false}\}$ and $\mathtt{p}_e \in \text{Rel}_{\mathcal{D}+T}$. The first rule also applies if $k = 0$. $\mathtt{p}_e \uparrow x$ is obtained from $\mathtt{p}_e$ by the substitution of all occurrences of the dot '.' by x, and if x is an object, by the substitution of property name occurrences in $\mathtt{p}_e$ with the values of these properties in x. Note that if x contains several values of some property, there can be several such substitutions. $\exists \, \mathtt{p}_e \uparrow x : \models \mathtt{p}_e \uparrow x$ means that there exists a substitution, which makes $\mathtt{p}_e$ true.

Thus, we see that BoxQL is indifferent to the logical mechanisms working in the knowledge base $\mathcal{KB}$, because the procedural semantics of BoxQL uses its checking tool $\models$ as an oracle in a black box. This means that $\models$ can be defined in various ways: as an inference machine for $\mathcal{SHOIN}(D)$, $\mathcal{ALC}$ or whatever we want. In section 6 we consider an experimental implementation, in which BoxQL is used for queries in an object data base, in which $\models$ is implemented as simple check of explicit data. This means that BoxQL can work at any layer of the logic architecture: 'lifting' BoxQL through its layers preserves the compatibility and semantics of the language. In particular this means that, if to be careful enough, the queries that are asked on the lower layer of an object DB, are still valid on the higher logical layers, which subsume this ODB.

Note that the last two $\diamond$-rules show how to handle ordinary relations ($=$, $<$, $>$ etc.) with sequences as arguments. For instance, $*[\texttt{income = 300}]$ selects persons who have the income of 300. Tom has, but he has also incomes of 200 and 400. Thus, we have to check if $\{\texttt{200, 300, 400}\} = \texttt{300}$. In such situations $\diamond$-rules check if *there exist* equal members in the both parts. Of course, sometimes such behavior looks tricky, so BoxQL has special built-ins to treat the sequences in different ways.

The computational complexity of BoxQL depends on the complexity of the underlying $\mathcal{KB}$: by adjusting the checking tools of $\mathcal{KB}$ we can find the necessary ratio of the efficiency and expressiveness. We hope that this can make BoxQL useful in various and very different situations.

5   Translation to DL

In this section we investigate the soundness of BoxQL. First, we show that each BoxQL-query can be translated into a formula of $\mathcal{SHOIN}(D)$ (on the other hand, not any $\mathcal{SHOIN}(D)$ formula can be translated into BoxQL).

To translate BoxQL-queries we augment $\mathcal{SHOIN}(D)$ with a concept non-emptiness construct $\exists c$ [2], which holds if the concept c is non-empty. Also to

h/s	$\mathbb{P}(\text{h/s})$	r	$\mathbb{R}(\text{r})$
ϵ (empty)	$\top$	r1 and r2	$\mathbb{R}(\text{r1}) \sqcap \mathbb{R}(\text{r2})$
h/*	$\mathbb{P}(\text{h})$	r1 or r2	$\mathbb{R}(\text{r1}) \sqcup \mathbb{R}(\text{r2})$
h/ns:*	$c_{ns} \sqcap \mathbb{P}(\text{h})$	not r	$\neg\mathbb{R}(\text{r})$
h/c ($c \in T_C$)	$c \sqcap \mathbb{P}(\text{h})$	h ! [r]	$\forall\mathbb{P}(\text{h}).\mathbb{R}(\text{r})$
h/ro ($\text{ro} \in T_R^o$)	$\exists ro^-.\mathbb{P}(\text{h})$	h $\in \mathcal{P}$	$\exists\mathbb{P}(\text{h})$
h/-ro ($\text{ro} \in T_R^o$)	$\exists ro.\mathbb{P}(\text{h})$	$p_e \in \text{Rel}_{\mathcal{D}+T}$	$\exists(x_1,\ldots,x_k)p_e$
h/rt ($\text{rt} \in T_R^t$)	$rt^* \sqcap \mathbb{P}(\text{h})$	h = c	$\mathbb{P}(\text{h/c})$
h/id ($\text{id} \in Id$)	$\{id\} \sqcap \mathbb{P}(\text{h})$		
h/($\text{h}_1,\ldots,\text{h}_k$)	$\mathbb{P}(\text{h}) \sqcap (\overset{k}{\underset{i=1}{\sqcup}}\,\mathbb{P}(\text{h}_i))$		
h[r]	$\mathbb{P}(\text{h}) \sqcap \mathbb{R}(\text{r})$		
h/v ($v \in |\mathcal{D}|$)	$\{v\} \sqcap \mathbb{P}(\text{h})$		

Fig. 2. The translation operators $\mathbb{P}(\cdot)$ and $\mathbb{R}(\cdot)$

handle queries like */age resulting in sequences of datatype values, we intro-duce a construct rt^* for each datatype property $\text{rt} \in T_R^t$. For any value $v \in |\mathcal{D}|$, $\models rt^*(v)$ iff $\exists o :\models \text{rt}(o,v)$. The connectives $\sqcap, \sqcup, \neg$ behave on 'datatype' propo-sitions as propositional conjunction, disjunction and negation, respectively. Fig-ure 2 defines operators $\mathbb{P}$ and $\mathbb{R}$, which translate paths and predicates, respec-tively, into the formulas of $\mathcal{SHOIN}(D)$ augmented with these two constructs.

Let $\mathcal{T}$ be a $\mathcal{SHOIN}(D)$-description of some world, and $\mathcal{KB}_\mathcal{T}$ a knowledge base, in which $\models$ is interpreted as $\mathcal{SHOIN}(D)$-satisfiability in $\mathcal{T}$. Then the following proposition holds:

Proposition 1 (soundness). *For any* $\text{h} \in \mathcal{P}$, *if* $\text{h}\langle|\mathcal{KB}_\mathcal{T}|\rangle \vdash_\star \mathcal{A}$ *in* $\mathcal{KB}_\mathcal{T}$ *then for each* $x \in \mathcal{A}$, $\mathbb{P}(\text{h})(x)$ *is satisfiable in* $\mathcal{KB}_\mathcal{T}$.

The proof of this proposition is established by induction on the length of a derivation in $\star-$ and $\diamond-$calculi.

6   Implementation and Evaluation

In this section we consider an implementation and evaluation of BoxQL based on an experimental OntoBox module, which we are developing now in Java. In On-toBox, $\models$ is interpreted as an object DB explicit checker. BoxQL is implemented in OntoBox in a naive style based on the $\star$- and $\diamond$-calculi. Also we verified manually some ideas for compilation of BoxQL-queries.

To evaluate the approach, we checked (1) if BoxQL was adequate and reliable for inexperienced developers, and (2) if it could compete with DB management systems on the lower levels of object processing.

To achieve the first goal we had a number of experiments and questionnaires. E.g. we worked with a group of 24 students. The tasks were to develop (after one introductory lecture) reference systems for LaTeX, CSS, HTML, DOM, etc. The students developed ontologies and the corresponding interfaces. 4 advanced tasks were offered to the best students. 14 students were successful, 5 had minor problems with interfaces, 3 had minor problems with BoxQL, 2 had problems with both, 1 failed to solve his task. The questionary showed that in general BoxQL was considered by students as simple and natural. 18 students think that BoxQL is easier than SQL. We also asked the students to write the same queries in $\mathcal{SHOIN}(D)$ and then compare the two styles. All of the students confirmed that writing in BoxQL had been much easier (and more familiar) for them than writing in $\mathcal{SHOIN}(D)$.

As a benchmark for the second goal we took the NCBI taxonomy database [5], which describes the names of all organisms that are represented in the genetic databases with at least one nucleotide or protein sequence. This taxonomy contains 482960 objects. The taxonomy established in a database has been converted into an ontology in which every name is an object of the class node, and the tree structure is represented by the object property parent. In the experiments we asked queries of the form $\underbrace{\texttt{parent/.../parent}}_{n}$ searching for the chains of nodes.

Concurrently we asked the equivalent SQL-queries in the original database (in MySQL):

$$\left.\begin{array}{l} \texttt{select * from nodes where parent\_id in} \\ \quad \texttt{(select id from nodes where parent\_id in} \\ \quad \texttt{... ... ...} \\ \quad \texttt{(select id from nodes))...);} \end{array}\right\} n$$

with indexed columns id and parent_id of taxonomy nodes. Here are the results for Apple Mac OS X 10.5.6, Java 1.6.0_07 (64-Bit Server VM), and MySQL 5.0.51a (MySQL does not allow nestings for $n > 32$):

$n =$	1	5	10	20	30	40
number of collected chains	482959	471762	301503	135297	30736	280
MySQL 5.0.51a (sec)	5.02	42.34	83.25	130.24	148.56	n/a
BoxQL(naive, sec)	1.56	6.62	11.93	17.08	18.94	19.2
BoxQL(compiled, sec)	0.16	0.99	1.54	2.16	2.36	2.41

What we want to say by this example is that on the lower levels of the logic architecture we can develop the tools, which are quite good for 'simple' but efficient knowledge management (especially in object models), while staying compatible (e.g. via the query language BoxQL) with much more expressive methods and tools of the Semantic Web.

7   Related Work and Conclusion

In this paper a new approach to knowledge and data management is introduced, which is targeted at conventional web developers, and based on (1) a new query language designed in the XPath style and compatible with object oriented models; (2) a fast non-memory based implementation of this language.

There are a lot of works, which are focused on the management of large amounts of simple data in the context of the SW. Many researchers consider incorporating the style of relational DBs as the basic way to efficiently handle simple data within SW applications (e.g. see [6][7] etc.). We are convinced that the SW itself can provide quite reliable tools, and 'hybridization' with DBs can be avoided in many cases. The solutions within the SW could be more elegant, coherent and profitable. Concerning the interactions between the object oriented approach and the SW, paper [8] gives the informal case study of interaction between an OO programming language (represented by Java) and OWL. We develop an OO-style query language based on a strictly formal approach, which represents object oriented means as a sublogic of general DLs. In [9] in order to represent structured objects (which are analogous to finite networks of individuals), DL is augmented with description graphs. The basic difference between the approaches is that our aim is to handle with BoxQL the networks of concrete data, whereas in [9] the problem of graph-like object representation is considered on the level of TBoxes. And for this the strength of DL is not sufficient due to the well known tree model property [10].

A lot of query languages have been developed in the context of the SW (see [11]–[18] etc). The basic features, which distinguish BoxQL from them is that it is a traversal language based on the object oriented paradigm, in which triple employing is hidden. E.g. in SPARQL [11] the query to find the capitals of all countries in Africa looks as follows:

```
SELECT ?capital ?country
WHERE {
    ?x :cityname ?capital ;
       :isCapitalOf ?y .
    ?y :countryname ?country ;
       :isInContinent :Africa .
}
```

In BoxQL we have:

```
*[cityname as capital]/
  isCapitalOf[countryname as country and isInContinent = &Africa]
```

The difference is clear. In SPARQL we have to divide the query into a number of triples with auxiliary variables. In BoxQL we just determine a two-step walk along the knowledge graph.

The approach considered in this paper raises a number of questions. Is it possible to use logic architectures and BoxQL for developing SW-technologies, which can compete (and cooperate with) the standard methods of data management (like DBs) on lower levels, but enjoy on the higher levels the full strength of logic? Will such technologies be really interesting to a wider range of users? Shall we manage to preserve compatibility between the lower and higher layers of logical architectures in procedural data management environments? There are no answers yet, but the initial steps look promising.

References

1. Malykh, A., Mantsivoda, A., Ulyanov, V.: Logic Architectures and the Object Oriented Approach. Technical Report (2009)
2. Horrocks, I., Patel-Schneider, P.F.: Reducing OWL entailment to description logic satisfiability. In: Fensel, D., Sycara, K., Mylopoulos, J. (eds.) ISWC 2003. LNCS, vol. 2870, pp. 17–29. Springer, Heidelberg (2003)
3. Horrocks, I., Hayes, P., Patel-Schneider, P.F.: OWL Web Ontology Language Semantics and Abstract Syntax, http://www.w3.org/TR/owl-semantics/
4. Baader, F., Calvanese, D., McGuinness, D.L., Nardi, D., Patel-Schneider, P.F. (eds.): The Description Logic Handbook: Theory, Implementation, and Applications. Cambridge University Press, Cambridge (2003)
5. The NCBI Entrez Taxonomy, http://www.ncbi.nlm.nih.gov/sites/entrez?db=taxonomy
6. Hustadt, U., Motik, B., Sattler, U.: Reasoning in Description Logics by a Reduction to Disjunctive Datalog. Journal of Automated Reasoning 39(3), 351–384 (2007)
7. Haarslev, V., Möller, R.: On the scalability of description logic instance retrieval. Journal of Automated Reasoning 41(2), 99–142 (2008)
8. Puleston, C., Parsia, B., Cunningham, J., Rector, A.L.: Integrating Object-Oriented and Ontological Representations. A Case Study in Java and OWL, pp. 130–145
9. Motik, B., Grau, B.C., Horrocks, I., Sattler, U.: Representing Structured Objects using Description Graphs. In: KR 2008, pp. 296–306 (2008)
10. Vardi, M.Y.: Why Is Modal Logic So Robustly Decidable? In: Proc. DIMACS Workshop. DIMACS Series, vol. 31, pp. 149–184.
11. Prudhommeaux, E., Seaborne, A.: SPARQL Query Language for RDF. W3C Recommendation (2008)
12. Seaborne, A.: RDQL - A Query Language for RDF. W3C Member Submission (2004)
13. Ortiz, M., Calvanese, D., Eiter, T.: Data Complexity of Query Answering in Expressive Description Logics via Tableaux. Journal of Automated Reasoning 41, 61–98 (2008)
14. Bry, F., Furche, T., Linse, B.: Data Model and Query Constructs for Versatile Web Query Languages: State-of-the-Art and Challenges for Xcerpt. In: Alferes, J.J., Bailey, J., May, W., Schwertel, U. (eds.) PPSWR 2006. LNCS, vol. 4187, pp. 90–104. Springer, Heidelberg (2006)
15. Kaplunova, A., Möller, R.: DIG 2.0 Concrete Domain Interface Proposal., http://www.sts.tu-harburg.de/~al.kaplunova/dig-cd-interface.html
16. Frasincar, F., Houben, G.-J., Vdovjak, R., Barna, P.: RAL: An Algebra for Querying RDF. World Wide Web: Internet and Web Information Systems 7, 83–109 (2004)
17. Noy, N., Musen, M.A.: Specifying ontology views by traversal. In: McIlraith, S.A., Plexousakis, D., van Harmelen, F. (eds.) ISWC 2004. LNCS, vol. 3298, pp. 713–725. Springer, Heidelberg (2004)
18. Ogbuji, C.: Versa: Path-Based RDF Query Language, http://www.xml.com/pub/a/2005/07/20/versa.html?page=1

Planet Map Generation by Tetrahedral Subdivision

Torben Ægidius Mogensen

DIKU, University of Copenhagen
Universitetsparken 1, DK-2100 Copenhagen O, Denmark
torbenm@diku.dk

Abstract. We present a method for generating pseudo-random, zoomable planet maps for games and art. The method is based on spatial subdivision using tetrahedrons. This ensures planet maps without discontinuities caused by mapping a flat map onto a sphere.

We compare the method to other map-generator algorithms.

1 Introduction

Computer games have featured (pseudo-)randomly generated maps since at least the 1980s. The best known uses of random maps are in strategy games, such as Sid Meier's Civilization series or Microsoft's Age of Empires series, but random maps have also been used in arcade games and role-playing games. The main advantage of randomly generated maps is replay-ability: The same game can be played on a near infinite number of different maps, providing different challenges each time. Random maps can also contain more detail than it would be realistic to expect from manually created maps.

Nearly all methods for creating pseudo-random maps create a 2D array of values, a so-called *height field*. This can then be rendered in various ways. In the simplest rendering, each altitude is mapped to a colour (like on topographic maps). More complex renderers add shadows or compute a 3D surface from the height field and render this using any 3D rendering algorithm (such as ray tracing). We will in this paper not consider rendering but focus on generation of heights.

Landscapes are fractal of nature [7]. In practise, this means:

1. Maps are continuous, i.e., points close to each other differ little in altitude.
2. There is a similar degree of detail at all levels of magnification (up to a point), i.e., the map is self-similar.

Landscapes are also irregular, so no systematic construction of self-similar maps will give convincing natural maps. Hence, randomness is needed in the process, and the self-similarity is of a statistical rather than exact nature.

One way to make a statistically self-similar map is by generating noise where the power spectral density is inversely proportional to the frequency. This can be done by generating a large number of points in the frequency domain, distributed according to the power density, and then Fourier-transforming this into the amplitude domain to form a height field [1], as illustrated in figure 1. This, however, has a number of disadvantages:

A. Pnueli, I. Virbitskaite, and A. Voronkov (Eds.): PSI 2009, LNCS 5947, pp. 306–318, 2010.
© Springer-Verlag Berlin Heidelberg 2010

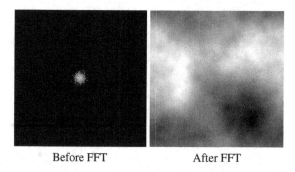

Before FFT   After FFT

Fig. 1. Fourier-transforming $1/n$ noise

1. It is computationally expensive.
2. You can not generate a map of a local region significantly faster than the full map.
3. The map is periodic, i.e., it "wraps around" both vertically and horizontally.

For these reasons, it is more common to use a recursive mid-point displacement method: An initial polygon (or polygon grid) is given height values at its vertices, and is subdivided into smaller polygons where the height values of the new vertices are obtained by adding pseudo-random offsets to the averages of the nearest vertices in the original polygon. By subdividing recursively down to the desired level of detail, a height field can be generated. A common subdivision algorithm is called the *diamond-square* algorithm [5]:

A square grid is given height values at each vertex. This is then subdivided in the following fashion:

Step 1 (diamond). The mid-point of each square is given a height that is an offset from the average of the heights of the four corners. The original square grid points and the new mid-points form a diamond grid.

Step 2 (square). The mid-point of each diamond is given a height that is an offset from the average of the heights of the four corners. The original square grid points plus the points generated in step 1 and 2 now form a square grid with twice the resolution as the original.

Repeat. from step 1 until you get the desired resolution.

Figure 2 illustrates this. The new grid points are shown as filled circles, and the dotted lines connect to the old grid points (shown as outlined circles) used to generate the new.

This is computationally cheap, you can generate a regional map to any detail without computing the full map, and you don't have any undesired wrap-around.[1] Some artefacts may occur in the images due to the use of a regular axis-aligned grid and because the initial vertices are present in the final grid. There are various refinements to the basic algorithm that reduce some of these effects [8]. More algorithms are described briefly in [3].

---

[1] It is still possible to make the map wrap around if this is desired.

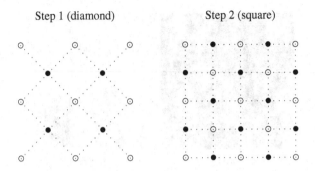

Step 1 (diamond)   Step 2 (square)

Fig. 2. The diamond-square algorithm

Both the Fourier-transform method and the diamond-square algorithm generate height fields: An altitude value assigned to each point on a 2D grid. This means that the generated landscapes can't have overhangs or caves, and since the displacement gets smaller at smaller scales, you don't get vertical cliff faces either. While this limits the type of landscapes that can be created, it is rarely a problem for the typical applications (generating maps for games or landscapes for animation).

The focus of the present article is different: The desire is to make a zoomable map of a full planet. The above methods all generate flat maps, and though they can be made to wrap, this will either create cylindrical or toroidal maps, not spheres. If you wrap these maps on a sphere, you will get distortion and discontinuities (e.g., at the poles). The distortion can be minimised by using *conformal*, i.e., angle-preserving maps, such as stereographic or Mercator projections (in reverse), but these will still give discontinuities in at least one or two points on the sphere. Hence, we will abandon the idea of generating a flat map and wrap this around a sphere, but instead create an everywhere continuous inherently spherical map which (for display purposes) can be projected onto a flat surface.

2   Extending to 3D

To get a full planet map, we need to move to three dimensions. We can easily extend the Fourier-transform to 3D by using a three-dimensional FFT. The result is a cubical grid with a height value at each grid point. To create a spherical map, you embed a sphere in this grid and for each point on the surface of the sphere use a weighted average of values at the nearest grid points.

The altitude values represent displacements of the surface points relative to the centre of the sphere, similar to the way the 2D methods described earlier generate altitudes that represent vertical displacements of points on a 2D grid.

Note that you can embed any surface in the cubical grid, but since worlds tend to be (near) spherical, we will focus on spheres.

Due to the nature of FFT, we can not effectively generate values only for the grid points that are close to the spherical surface, so we generate a lot of values that we never use.

The diamond-square algorithm can also be modified to 3D using a cubical grid and three steps to get to a finer cubical grid:

Step 1. Find a value for the middle of each cube using the values at its eight corners.
Step 2. Find a value for the middle of each face of the cubes using the values at the four corners of the face and at the midpoints (from step 1) of the two adjoining cubes.
Step 3. Find a value for the middle of each edge of the cubes using the values at its two ends and at the midpoints (from step 2) of the four adjoining faces.
Repeat. from step 1 until the desired resolution is obtained.

This, like the Fourier-based method, computes all points in a 3D grid, while we in the end use only small subset of these. It would be natural to subdivide only cubes that contain parts of the spherical surface, which would drastically reduce the required time. However, steps 2 and 3 use information from adjoining cubes, so we can't just omit these. It is possible to modify the algorithms so it in step 2 only uses the four corners of the face and not the adjoining cubes and step 3 so it uses only the two end-points of the edge. This will, however, reduce the quality of the maps.

Additionally, just like the use of a regular square grid in the 2D diamond-square algorithm can produce artefacts that make features orient to the grid, the use of a regular cubical grid in the 3D extension can produce artefacts that make features orient to the 3D grid. This means that, even after rotating the spherical map, it is often possible to visually identify the orientation of the grid.

2.1 Spatial Subdivision

We will now present a method that attempts to address these problems.

Let us say that we wanted to find the height value of just a single point on the surface of a sphere. We can do this using the following algorithm:

1. Embed the sphere inside a polyhedron, where each vertex is assigned a height value
2. Cut the polyhedron into two smaller polyhedra, generating height values for the new vertices from their neighbouring old vertices.
3. Select the polyhedron in which the desired point is located
4. Repeat from step 2 until the polyhedron is small enough
5. Use the average height values of the vertices of the final polyhedron as the height value of the desired point.

When you render a picture of a planet, you find the visible points on the planet surface and apply the above algorithm to each point to find its height value. For example, in ray tracing each ray that hits the surface will define a visible point.

A question is how small is "small enough" in the above algorithm? Basically, you would not want two neighbouring pixels in the image to get the same value because you stop subdivision at the same polyhedron for both pixels. Since the volume of the polyhedron is halved in each step, three steps will double the resolution of the details. So a rough estimate is that a 1000×1000 image will require 30 subdivisions for each pixel (since $2^{10} = 1024$), but this assumes that all pixels represent equal areas on the sphere, which is not typically the case. A better solution is to project the corners of the pixel onto the sphere and stop only when at most one of the projected corner points is inside the polyhedron that holds the desired point (which is the projection of the middle of the pixel). In all but the most extreme cases, this will ensure that neighbouring pixels end in different polyhedra. A somewhat simpler and almost as good method is to estimate the pixel's projected size on the sphere and stop when the polyhedron diameter is smaller than this size. If a standard map projection is used, it is not difficult to make a good estimate of projected pixel diameter without actually projecting the pixel corners to the sphere. For example, in the Mercator projection, the area of a pixel projected to the surface at point (x, y, z) is $\sqrt{1 - y^2}$ times the area if a pixel projected to the equator.[2]

The next question is which type of polyhedron to use and how to subdivide it. The most obvious choice is to use a rectangular box and cut it into two boxes. Indeed, if you choose the proportions correctly,[3] the two new boxes will have the same relative proportions as the original, much like A4 paper is cut into two A5 papers that have the same relative side-lengths. An earlier version of the algorithm presented in this paper did, indeed, use such rectangular boxes. However, using rectangular boxes has several disadvantages:

1. This is equivalent to using a regular axis-aligned grid, which can give artefacts.
2. Four new vertices are created at each subdivision. We would like fewer new vertices at each step to keep the number of calculations per step low.

Our solution is to use a tetrahedron. A tetrahedron can be divided into two tetrahedra by cutting along a plane defined by two vertices and a point on the opposing line, as illustrated in figure 3.

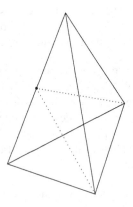

Fig. 3. Cutting a tetrahedron in two

There are no possible proportions of a tetrahedron that will make such a cut produce two tetrahedra with the same relative proportions as the original (even if we allow the two smaller tetrahedra to be of different size). But this is actually an advantage: By

---

[2] If the sphere has radius 1 and the polar axis is the y-axis.
[3] $1 \times 2^{\frac{1}{3}} \times 2^{\frac{2}{3}}$.

Input: A target point p and four vertices $v_1, \ldots, v_4$ of a tetrahedron, each with the following information:

- Coordinates (x_i, y_i, z_i)
- Seed for pseudo-random number generator s_i
- Altitude value a_i

Repeat:

1. Re-order vertices $v_1, \ldots, v_4$ so the longest edge of the tetrahedron is between v_1 and v_2, i.e., such that $(x_1 - x_2)^2 + (y_1 - y_2)^2 + (z_1 - z_2)^2$ is maximised.
2. Define new vertex v_m by

$$(x_m, y_m, z_m) = ((x_1 + x_2)/2, (y_1 + y_2)/2, (z_1 + z_2)/2)$$
$$l = \sqrt{(x_1 - x_2)^2 + (y_1 - y_2)^2 + (z_1 - z_2)^2}$$
$$s_m = random((s_1 + s_2)/2)$$
$$a_m = (a_1 + a_2)/2 + offset(s_m, l, a_1, a_2)$$

3. If p is contained in the tetrahedron defined by the four vertices v_m, v_1, v_3 and v_4, set $v_2 = v_m$. Otherwise, set $v_1 = v_m$.

Until: l is small enough
Return: $(a_1 + a_2 + a_3 + a_4)/4$

Fig. 4. Tetrahedron subdivision

keeping the tetrahedra irregular and different, we avoid the artefacts created by using axis-aligned boxes.

We will use a tetrahedron where all edges are of different lengths and we will always cut the longest edge at its midpoint. The algorithm requires that there is always a unique longest edge to cut. We have no mathematical proof that this is the case with the chosen initial side lengths, but we have tested this uniqueness property down to a large number of subdivisions (by making a full-world map of very high resolution and a large number of detail maps with large magnification) and found no cases where there is no unique longest edge.

With tetrahedron cuts, we now create only one new vertex at each subdivision, so the calculation of new vertices has been cut by four compared to using rectangular boxes. However, extra time is needed to identify the longest edge, and the calculations required to identify in which tetrahedron the goal point is located are more complex, so there is no overall reduction in computational cost. Hence, the main advantage of using tetrahedra is reduction of artefacts caused by using a regular grid.

A more detailed algorithm description can be found in figure 4. Notes:

- The function *random(s)* produces a pseudo-random value from a seed s. The same seed will always give the same result. Note that *random()* is seeded by the average of the seeds of the end points of the edge, so the result is independent of the other vertices and of the order of v_1 and v_2. Since the same edge is shared between several tetrahedrons, all of which may cut this edge, we need to cut the edge in the same way regardless of which tetrahedron it is considered a part of.

- The function $offset(s,l,a_1,a_2)$ provides an offset that depends on the seed s, the length l of the edge and the altitude values a_1 and a_2 at the end-points of the edge. In the simplest case, the offset is simply proportional to l, but more realistic landscapes can be made by making the offset proportional to l^q, where $q < 1$ (since altitudes tend to differ relatively more over short distances than over longer distances), and by adding in a contribution that is proportional to the altitude difference $|a_1 - a_2|$ (since steep areas tend to be less even than flatter areas). Other variations are possible, such as taking the distance from sea-level into account (since areas at higher altitude tend to be more rugged than low-altitude areas).

- The altitude values at the vertices of the initial tetrahedron will affect the altitudes on the surface of the sphere, but since the vertices are outside the sphere, they can not determine exact altitudes of any points on the surface. Hence, while setting these four altitudes to sea level will typically give planet maps with roughly equal parts land and sea, the amount of land and sea can vary greatly if different seeds are used.

- A normal vector of the landscape at a point on the sphere surface can be estimated from the altitude values and coordinates of the four vertices in the final tetrahedron. This can be used for shadow effects and bump maps.

Step 1 (reordering vertices) uses about 50% of the time, 30% is spent in step 2 (calculation of new vertex) and 20% in step 3 (determining in which sub-tetrahedron the point is located).

An optimisation is possible based on the observation that adjacent pixels in a rendered image are likely to correspond to close points on the sphere, so the first many subdivisions will be the same. The idea is that, after a number of subdivisions, we store the vertices of the current tetrahedron before we continue. When we repeat the algorithm for the next pixel, we check if the projected point is inside the stored tetrahedron. If it is, we start subdivision from the stored tetrahedron instead of from the top level. For detailed maps of smaller regions of a planet, this can dramatically reduce the overall calculation time.

3   Implementation and Uses

An implementation in the programming language C of the tetrahedron subdivision algorithm can be found at http://www.diku.dk/~torbenm/. For rendering, a number of standard map projections such as Mercator, Mollweide and Gnomonic are provided. The rendering is otherwise fairly primitive: The colour of a point on the surface depends on the altitude at and the latitude of this point, and shadow effects based on the estimated surface normal can be added. The colouring scheme can be changed by modifying a palette file, and longitude/latitude lines can be added.

Example outputs (rendered in black and white) are shown in figure 5.

Figure 6 shows zooming in on a detail of the map. Each step uses four times the resolution of the previous step, so the last picture is 16384 times as detailed as the first.

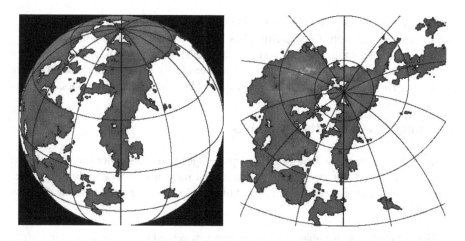

Fig. 5. Maps using orthographic and stereographic projections

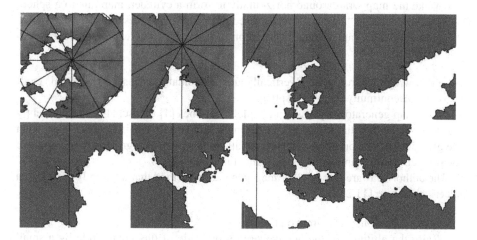

Fig. 6. Zooming in

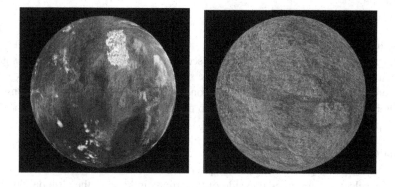

Fig. 7. Planet views from game prototype

While the above program can be used on its own to generate maps for use in role-playing games and such, the algorithm has also been used in open-source computer games, including an upcoming version of a Russian space game [10], where it is one of several planet texture generators. Sample planets rendered by the game engine is shown in figure 7. The clouds and craters are added by additional texture generators.

4   Comparison to Other Methods

We have already mentioned the diamond-square algorithm and Fourier-transform based methods, and noted that these are designed for flat maps and will yield discontinuities if these maps are projected onto spheres. Some tricks are often used to make this less noticeable:

- Force the edges of the map to have certain pre-specified values (such as deep water), so they can meet without discontinuities.
- Make the map wrap around horizontally to form a cylinder, map this to a sphere and add artificial "ice caps" to hide discontinuities at the poles. Fourier-based maps automatically wrap around, and diamond-square algorithm can be made to do so fairly easily.

Note that wrapping around both vertically and horizontally makes a torus, so this can't solve the discontinuity issue on a sphere.

Other map generators try to simulate plate tectonics [4]. These, also, are inherently full-map methods with no way of generating a region map significantly cheaper than the global map. The programs I have seen all use a rectangular grid, so they also have the problems with mapping to a sphere mentioned above.

The author is aware of one other map-generation method that inherently works on a spherical surface [11,2,9]:

1. Select a random great circle on the sphere
2. Raise the altitude for the hemisphere on one side of this great circle by a small amount and lower the altitude for the hemisphere on the other side by the same amount.
3. Repeat this a large number of times.

The method is illustrated in figure 8.

The great-circle algorithm is normally used in a context where the full map is generated in a rectangle that is a projection of the sphere, mapping the great circles to curves in the projection and raising the altitudes on one side of the curve and lowering it on the other side. It is, however, fairly easy to modify this to find the altitude of a single surface point:

1. Start with altitude 0
2. Select a random great circle on the sphere
3. If the selected point is on one side of this great circle, raise the altitude, otherwise lower it.

Fig. 8. Great-circle algorithm

4. Repeat from step 2 N times.
5. Return altitude

If the same initial seed for the pseudo-random number generator is used at every point, you get a consistent result.

In the standard version of the algorithm, the cuts define discontinuities, since all points on one side of the hemisphere are raised by the same amount and all all points on the other side lowered by the same. If this amount is small, this matters little, but at high magnifications, it will be visible. It is easy to modify the algorithm, so the change is more gradual, but that makes the terrain smooth at high magnifications unless you have many cuts, so this doesn't lower the required number of cuts significantly. More seriously, whenever a point on the surface is raised, the point opposite of it on the sphere is lowered, so the maps will have a kind of mirror symmetry: Islands on one side of the planet will have mirror-image lakes on the opposite side, as seen in figure 9, where the right map is centred at the opposite point as the left map and then mirrored. If you raise the waterline above 0 altitude, this is not immediately noticeable, but you can't have land on two opposing points on the sphere. Another way to reduce these artefacts is to make the cuts at smaller circles rather than great circles. There will still be a greater probability for water opposite land than one would expect, but there is no strict mirror-image effect.

To compare running times and results, the great-circle algorithm and the tetrahedron-subdivision algorithm were both run to produce 400×400 pixel full-world and zoomed ($10\times$) maps using the orthogonal projection. The two programs are identical except for the algorithm used to generate altitudes for points on the sphere. The great-circle algorithms pregenerates and stores the cuts, so they don't have to be regenerated for each point. The tetrahedron-subdivision algorithm uses an optimisation where the tetrahedron after k subdivisions is stored and reused for the next point if it is within the same tetrahedron.

Fig. 9. Mirror effect

The number of cuts used for the great-circle algorithm depends on the level of detail required. For the full-world map 2000 great circle cuts suffice, but artefacts are obvious when zooming in. At 10× zoom, ten times as many cuts are needed. This changes the appearance, as all cuts have equal contribution, so even maps at low resolution have to be generated with a high number of cuts if *any* map of the planet is needed at high resolution.

The results can be seen in figure 10.

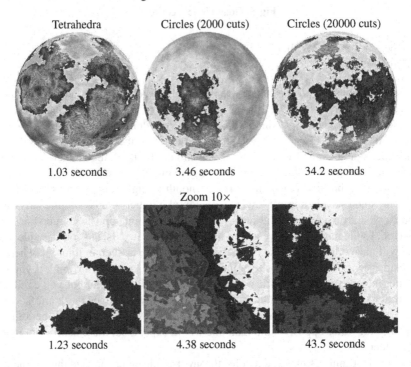

Tetrahedra   Circles (2000 cuts)   Circles (20000 cuts)

1.03 seconds   3.46 seconds   34.2 seconds

Zoom 10×

1.23 seconds   4.38 seconds   43.5 seconds

Fig. 10. Comparing great-circle and tetrahedron-subdivision algorithms

For a full planet map of $n \times n$ pixels, the great-circle algorithm requires time proportional to n^3, as the required number of cuts is proportional to the resolution. In contrast, the tetrahedron subdivision algorithm requires time proportional to $n^2 \log(n)$, as the required number of subdivisions is proportional to the logarithm of the resolution. To generate a map of a detail of the planet at zoom rate z, the great-circle algorithm needs z time more cuts and, hence, z times more time. The subdivision algorithm needs $\log(z)$ more subdivisions, so it needs only $\log(z)$ times more time.

To compare tetrahedron subdivision with recursive subdivision of a rectangular box, figure 11 shows two maps using a "bump map" shading that exaggerates feature details. On the map generated with rectangular box subdivision, there are clear horizontal artefacts at the mid-right and top-middle parts of the map and a noticeable vertical artefact near the middle, while the map on the right doesn't show any clear alignment of features. Subdividing a rectangular box is, in fact, faster than tetrahedron subdivision. This is because it doesn't need to identify the longest edge at each step and because it is simpler to determine in which half-box a point is located.

Rectangular box subdivision: 0.25 seconds   Tetrahedron subdivision: 0.56 seconds

Fig. 11. Comparing rectangular-box and tetrahedron subdivision

5   Conclusion

The tetrahedron subdivision algorithm provides fast and zoomable generation of spherical planet maps. Unlike most other planet map generators, there are no discontinuities nor distortion caused by projecting a flat map onto a sphere. Also, the choice of an inherently irregular tetrahedron subdivision avoids grid-aligned artefacts.

Since single points can be sampled, the method is well suited in contexts where varying levels of detail are needed in the same picture, such as landscape views where the foreground needs more detail than the background: You simply sample points at the required density. Single-point sampling is also well-suited to ray tracing, since you can sample exactly the points that are intersected by rays, thus wasting no time generating details that are not visible.

A limitation with this (and most other fractal map generators) is that there is no erosion, no rivers, no silting and so on – the landscape is everywhere rough, as if newly created by tectonic faulting. Some map generators add erosion, rivers and sedimentation in a post-processing phase, but since these are not local phenomena, you need to perform the process on the full map, which negates the zoomability and variable level of detail. As an example, the map generator Wilbur [6] allows non-local post-processing like flow incision and fill basins to emulate erosion and sedimentation.

There is no obvious solution to the locality problem, though various tricks can be employed to make the map appear more natural, such as making the roughness of terrain depend on the altitude, so areas under or near sea level are smoother than areas of high altitude. Wilbur [6] can remap the generated altitudes according to a user-specified mapping. A standard mapping compresses lower altitudes while higher altitudes are stretched, and a sudden drop in sub-sea altitudes is made to emulate continental shelves.

References

1. Bourke, P.: Frequency synthesis of landscapes, and clouds (1997),
   http://local.wasp.uwa.edu.au/~pbourke/fractals/noise
2. Bourke, P.: Modelling fake planets (2000),
   http://local.wasp.uwa.edu.au/~pbourke/fractals/noise
3. Burke, C.: Generating terrain (1996),
   http://www.geocities.com/Area51/6902/terrain.html

4. Burke, C.: Plate tectonics (1996),
   http://www.geocities.com/Area51/6902/t_plate.html
5. Fournier, A., Fussel, D., Carpenter, L.: Computer rendering of stochastic models. Communications of the ACM 25(6), 371–384 (1982)
6. Layton, J.S.: Wilbur (2009), http://www.ridgecrest.ca.us/~jslayton/wilbur.html
7. Mandelbrot, B.: The Fractal Geometry of Nature. W.H. Freeman & Co, New York (1982)
8. Miller, G.S.P.: The definition and rendering of terrain maps. Computer Graphics 20(4), 39–48 (1986)
9. Olsson, J.: Fractal worldmap generator (2004),
   http://www.lysator.liu.se/~johol/fwmg/fwmg.html
10. Petrov, O.: Babylon 5; i've found her (2008), http://ifh.babylonfive.ru/
11. Voss, R.P.: Random fractal forgeries. Fundamental Algorithms for Computer Graphics 17, 805–835 (1985)

Towards Checking Parametric Reachability for UML State Machines*

Artur Niewiadomski[1], Wojciech Penczek[1,2], and Maciej Szreter[2]

[1] ICS, University of Podlasie, Siedlce, Poland
artur@iis.ap.siedlce.pl
[2] ICS, Polish Academy of Sciences, Warsaw, Poland
{penczek,mszreter}@ipipan.waw.pl

Abstract. The paper presents a new approach to model checking of systems specified in UML. All the executions of an UML system (unfolded to a given depth) are encoded directly into a boolean propositional formula, satisfiability of which is checked using a SAT-solver. Contrary to other UML verification tools we do not use any of the existing model checkers as we do not translate UML specifications into an intermediate formalism. Moreover, we introduce some parametric extensions to the method. The method has been implemented as the (prototype) tool BMC4UML and several experimental results are presented.

1 Introduction

The Unified Modelling Language (UML) [1] is a graphical specification language widely used in development of various systems. The version 2.1 consists of thirteen types of diagrams. The diagrams allows for describing a system from many points of view, with different levels of abstraction. Nowadays, model-checking techniques that are able to verify crucial properties of systems, at a very early stage of the design process, are used in development of IT systems increasingly often. The current paper presents results of our work aiming at development of a novel symbolic verification method that avoids an intermediate translation and operates directly on systems specified in a subset of UML. The method is a version of a symbolic bounded model checking, designed especially for UML systems. All the possible executions of a system (unfolded to a given depth) are encoded into a boolean propositional formula satisfiability of which is checked using a SAT-solver. Contrary to other UML verification systems we do not make use of any existing model checker as we do not translate UML specifications into any intermediate formalism.

There have been a lot of attempts to verify UML state machines - all of them based on the same idea: translate a UML specification to the input language of some model checker, and then perform verification using the underlying model checker. Some of the approaches [2,3] translate UML to Promela and then make

---

* Partly supported by the Ministry of Education and Science under the grant No. N N516 370436.

A. Pnueli, I. Virbitskaite, and A. Voronkov (Eds.): PSI 2009, LNCS 5947, pp. 319–330, 2010.
© Springer-Verlag Berlin Heidelberg 2010

use of the model checker Spin. Others [4,5] exploit timed automata as an intermediate formalism and use UPPAAL for verification. The third group of tools [6,7,8] apply the symbolic model checkers SMV or NuSMV via translating UML to their input languages.

An important advantage of our method consists in an efficient encoding of hierarchical state machines (HSM, for short). Most of other methods, that can handle hierarchy, perform flattening of HSM so they are likely to cause the state explosion of models generated. To the best of our knowledge only the paper [8] handles hierarchies directly without flattening. Another disadvantage of traditional methods follows from the fact that it is hard to reconcile UML semantics with intermediate formalism semantics. This results in a significant growth of the model size caused by adding special control structures that force execution w.r.t. UML semantics.

One of the most serious problems hindering the verification of UML is the lack of its formal semantics. The OMG standard [1] describes all the UML elements, but it deals with many of them informally. Moreover, there are numerous *semantic variation points* having several possible interpretations. Many papers on the semantics of UML have been published so far, but most of them skip some important issues. The interested reader is referred to the surveys [9,10]. The approach of [8], which considers a similar subset of UML, is the closest to our work, but it does not support timed systems.

This paper is an extension of [11] with deferred events added and experimental results for a new benchmark. Moreover, we have introduced some elements of parametric reachability checking. Using our approach, we are able to verify not only that a property is reachable, but also to find a minimal (integer) time c, *when* this is the case.

The rest of the paper is organised as follows. The next section describes the subset of UML considered and formalises its semantics as a labelled transition system. In Section 3, we present a symbolic encoding and describe an algorithm for checking parametric reachability. Preliminary experimental results are discussed in Section 4. Final remarks are given in the last section.

2   Syntax and Semantics of an UML Subset

This section defines the subset of UML considered in the paper and accepted by our tool, along with its operational semantics. Due to the space limitations we give only intuitive explanations of the concepts and the symbols used for defining the semantics. The remaining details and formal definitions can be found in [11].We assume also that the reader is familiar with basic UML state machine concepts.

Overview. We start with an overview of a syntax and a semantics of UML, while in the next section we give a formal operational semantics. The syntax is illustrated with the diagrams of the Generalized Railroad Crossing (GRC) system, which is also used as a benchmark in Section 4.

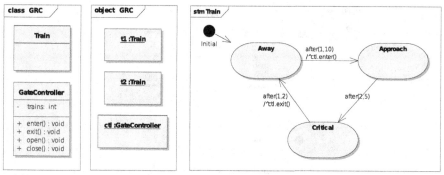

(a) Class and object diagrams   (b) State machine diagram of class Train

Fig. 1. Specification of GRC system

The systems considered are specified by a single class diagram which defines k classes (e.g. see Fig. 1(a)), a single object diagram which defines n objects (e.g. in Fig. 1(a)), and k state machine diagrams (e.g. in Fig. 1(b), 2), each one assigned to a different class of the class diagram.

The class diagram defines a list of attributes and a list of operations (possibly with parameters) for each class. The object diagram specifies the instances of classes (objects) and (optionally) assigns the initial values to variables. All the objects are visible globally, and the set of objects is constant during the life time of the system - dynamic object creation and termination is not allowed. We denote the set of all the variables by $\mathcal{V}$, the set of the integer variables by $\mathcal{V}^{int} \subseteq \mathcal{V}$, and the set of the object variables by $\mathcal{V}^{obj} \subseteq \mathcal{V}$. The values of object variables are restricted to the set of all objects defined in the object diagram, denoted by $\mathcal{O}$, and the special value $NULL$.

Each object is assigned an instance of a state machine that determines the behaviour of the object. An instance of a state machine assigned to ith object is denoted by $\mathcal{SM}_i$. A state machine diagram typically consists of states, regions and transitions connecting source and target states. The set of all states of $\mathcal{SM}_i$ is denoted by $\mathcal{S}_i$, whereas $\mathcal{S} = \bigcup_{i=1}^{n} \mathcal{S}_i$ is the set of all states from all instances of state machines. We consider several types of states, namely: simple states (e.g. *Away* in Fig. 1(b)), composite states, (e.g. *Main* in Fig. 2), final states, and initial pseudo-states, (e.g. *Initial* in Fig. 2). For each object we define the set of *active* states $\mathcal{A}_i$, where $\mathcal{A}_i \subseteq \mathcal{S}_i$, $\mathcal{A}_i \neq \emptyset$, and $i = 1, \ldots, n$. The areas filling the composite states are called *regions*. The regions contained in the same composite state are *orthogonal* (e.g. *Gate* and *Controller* in Fig. 2). The regions contain states and transitions, and thus introduce a *hierarchy* of state machines. We assume that a definition of the hierarchy relation is given, and we implicitly refer to this relation by using the terms ancestor and descendant.

Let $Trig$ be a set of all triggers and $Defer_i : \mathcal{S}_i \longmapsto 2^{Trig}$ - a function returning a set of triggers for each state of $\mathcal{S}_i$. This set defines *deferrable triggers*, i.e., the events matching these triggers can be retained if they fire no transition.

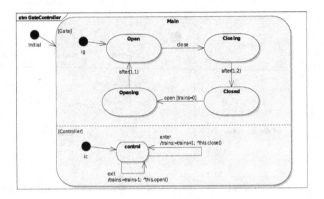

Fig. 2. Specification of GRC system - state machine diagram of class GateController

The labels of transitions are expressions of the form $trigger[guard]/action$, where each of these components can be empty. A transition can be fired if the source state is *active*, the guard (a Boolean expression) is satisfied, and the trigger matching event occurs. An event can be of the following three types: an *operation call*, a *completion event*, or a *time event*. In general, firing of a transition causes deactivation and activation of some states (depending on the type of the transition and the hierarchy of given state machine). We say that the *state machine configuration* changes then.

A time event, defined by an expression of the form $after(\delta_1, \delta_2)$, where $\delta_1, \delta_2 \in \mathbb{N}$ and $\delta_1 \le \delta_2$, can occur not earlier than after passing of δ_1 time units and no later than before passing of δ_2 time units. This is the extension of the standard $after(x)$ expression, which allows one to specify an interval of time in which a transition is enabled. However, we follow the discrete-time semantics where the clock valuations are natural numbers. The time flow is measured from entering the *time state*, which is the source state of a transition with the trigger of the form $after(\delta_1, \delta_2)$. The set of all time states from $\mathcal{SM}_i$ is denoted by Γ_i, and the set of all time states from all instances of state machines is denoted by Γ, where $\Gamma = \bigcup_{i=1}^{n} \Gamma_i$.

The operation calls coming to the given object are put into the *event queue* of the object, and then, one at a time, they are handled. The event from the head of the queue possibly fires a transition (or many transitions), and is consumed. If it cannot fire any transition and the matching trigger is *deferred* in the current state, then the event is deferred, i.e. it will be consumed later. Otherwise, the event is discarded. The transitions with non-empty trigger are called *triggered transitions*. We refer to the processing of a single event from the queue or a time event as the *Run-To-Completion (RTC) step*. Next, an event can be handled only if the previous one has been fully processed, together with all the completion events which eventually have occurred. A completion event (denoted by κ) occurs for a state that has completed all of its internal activities. The completion events fire the *completion transitions*, i.e., transitions without a trigger defined explicitly. The completion transitions have priority over the triggered transitions.

The execution of the whole system follows the interleaving semantics, similar to [5]. During a single step only one object performs its RTC step. If more than one object can execute such a step, then an object is chosen in a non-deterministic way. However, if none of the objects can perform an *untimed action*, then time flows. Note that this happens when all event queues are empty and all the completion events have been handled. The time flow causes occurrences of time events. The time events are processed in the next RTC steps.

Operational semantics. There are two key notions of our semantics, namely, *global states* and a *transition relation*. Below, we recall several definitions from [11], used later to deal with the semantics and extended with deferred events.

Definition 1 (State machine configuration). *A set of states is* consistent *if for each pair of its distinct states these states either belong to orthogonal regions or one is an ancestor of the other. A state is* completed *if a completion event has occurred for this state, but has not been handled yet.*
A configuration *of the state machine of the i-th object is a pair $\langle \mathcal{A}_i, \mathcal{C}_i \rangle$, where $\mathcal{A}_i \subseteq \mathcal{S}_i$ is a consistent set of active states, and $\mathcal{C}_i \subseteq \mathcal{A}_i$ is a set of completed states. The set of all the configurations of the i-th object is denoted by $\widehat{\mathcal{S}}_i$ while $\widehat{\mathcal{S}}$ is the set of all the configurations of all the objects.*

Definition 2 (Valuation). *Let E and $\mathcal{Q}$ denote respectively the set of all the events and the set of all the event queues. Let $\Omega = \mathbb{Z} \cup \mathcal{O} \cup (E \setminus \{\kappa\})^* \cup \widehat{\mathcal{S}}$, where $\mathbb{Z}$ is the set of integer numbers, and $(E \setminus \{\kappa\})^*$ is the set of all finite sequences of events (without completion events).*
A valuation function v *is defined as: $v : \mathcal{V} \cup \mathcal{Q} \cup \mathcal{O} \longmapsto \Omega$, where $v(\mathcal{V}^{int}) \subseteq \mathbb{Z}$, $v(\mathcal{V}^{obj}) \subseteq \mathcal{O} \cup \{NULL\}$, $v(\mathcal{Q}) \subseteq (E \setminus \{\kappa\})^*$ and $v(\mathcal{O}) \subseteq \widehat{\mathcal{S}}$. The function v assigns an integer to each integer variable, an object or $NULL$ to each object variable, a sequence of events to each event queue, and an active configuration to each object.*

The configuration of the i-th object for a given valuation v is denoted by $\langle \mathcal{A}_i^v, \mathcal{C}_i^v \rangle$, whereas $\vartheta(v, \alpha)$ denotes the valuation v' computed from v after the execution of the action α. The *initial valuation* v^0 is a valuation that returns an empty sequence (ε) for all the event queues, the initial states marked as active and completed for all the objects and the initial values for all the variables.

Definition 3 (Clocks valuation). *A clocks valuation function $\mu : \mathcal{S} \longmapsto \mathbb{N}$ assigns a natural number to each time state and zero to any other state. For $s \in \Gamma$, a clock valuation $\mu(s)$ indicates how long ago the system entered the time state s, or how long ago the system started if s has not been active yet.*

Let $\mu + \delta$ (for $\delta \in \mathbb{N}$) denote the clocks valuation such that $\mu'(s) = \mu(s) + \delta$ for $s \in \Gamma$ and $\mu'(s) = 0$ for $s \in \mathcal{S} \setminus \Gamma$. For $Y \subseteq \mathcal{S}$ let $\mu[Y := 0]$ denote the clocks valuation μ' such that $\mu'(s) = 0$ for $s \in Y$ and $\mu'(s) = \mu(s)$ for $s \in \mathcal{S} \setminus Y$. The valuation μ^0 such that $\forall_{s \in \mathcal{S}} \, \mu^0(s) = 0$ is called the *initial clocks valuation*. A pair $g = \langle v, \mu \rangle$ is called a *global state*. It is determined by the active configuration of all instances of state machines, the valuations of all the variables, the contents of all the event queues, and the valuations of all the clocks.

Definition 4 (Operational semantics). *The operational semantics of the systems specified in the selected UML subset is defined by the labelled transition system $\langle \mathcal{G}, g^0, \Sigma, \rightarrow \rangle$, where:*

- $\mathcal{G} = \Omega^{\mathcal{O} \cup \mathcal{V} \cup \mathcal{Q}} \times \mathbb{N}^\Gamma$ *is a set of the global states,*
- $g^0 = \langle v^0, \mu^0 \rangle$ *is the initial state,*
- $\Sigma = \mathbb{N}$ *is a set of the labels equal to time units passing during transitions,*
- $\rightarrow \subseteq \mathcal{G} \times \Sigma \times \mathcal{G}$ *is the transition relation such that for* $g = \langle v, \mu \rangle$, $g' = \langle v', \mu' \rangle$, *and* $\sigma \in \Sigma$ *we have* $g \xrightarrow{\sigma} g'$ *iff one of the following conditions holds:*

  1. $\exists_{i \in \{1,\ldots,n\}} I_i^v \neq \emptyset \ \wedge \ \sigma = 0 \ \wedge \ v' = \vartheta\big(v, \text{discard}(I_i^v)\big)$
     $\wedge \ \mu' = \mu$

  2. $\exists_{i \in \{1,\ldots,n\}} \mathcal{C}_i^v \neq \emptyset \wedge I_i^v = \emptyset \ \wedge \ \sigma = 0 \wedge \ v' = \vartheta\big(v, \lambda(t_\kappa)\big)$
     $\wedge \ \mu' = \mu\big[\Lambda(t_\kappa) := 0\big]$

  3. $\exists_{i \in \{1,\ldots,n\}} \mathcal{C}_i^v = \emptyset \wedge \text{enabled}(g, o_i) \neq \emptyset \wedge \sigma = 0 \wedge v' = \vartheta\big(v, \lambda(\varphi)\big)$
     $\wedge \ \mu' = \mu\big[\Lambda(\overline{\varphi}) := 0\big]$

  4. $\exists_{i \in \{1,\ldots,n\}} \mathcal{C}_i^v = \emptyset \wedge v(q_i) \neq \varepsilon \wedge \text{enabled}(g, o_i) = \emptyset \wedge \text{isDeferred}(g, o_i) \wedge \sigma = 0 \wedge \ v' = \vartheta\big(v, \text{defer}(q_i)\big) \wedge \mu' = \mu$

  5. $\exists_{i \in \{1,\ldots,n\}} \mathcal{C}_i^v = \emptyset \ \wedge \ v(q_i) \neq \varepsilon \ \wedge \text{enabled}(g, o_i) = \emptyset \ \wedge \ \neg\text{isDeferred}(g, o_i) \wedge$
     $\sigma = 0 \wedge \ v' = \vartheta\big(v, \text{cons}(q_i)\big) \wedge \mu' = \mu$

  6. $\forall_{i \in \{1,\ldots,n\}} \mathcal{C}_i^v = \emptyset \wedge v(q_i) = \varepsilon \wedge \ \sigma = x \wedge 0 < X_1 \leq x \leq X_2 \wedge v' = v$
     $\wedge \ \mu' = \mu + x$

*where: (i) the set $I_i^v \subseteq \mathcal{C}_i^v$ contains the completed states of the i-th object that are the source states for the completion transitions not enabled in the state g, (ii) discard(I_i^v) is the action of removing the elements of the set I_i^v from $\mathcal{C}_i^v$, (iii) $\lambda(t_\kappa)$ is the sequence of actions w.r.t. the specification of the completion transition t_κ executed, (iv) $\Lambda(t_\kappa)$ is the set of states activated as a result of firing the transition t_κ, (v) enabled(g, o_i) is the set of triggered transitions of i-th object enabled in the state g, (vi) isDeferred(g, o_i) is a function returning **true** if the first event in the i-th queue matches a deferrable trigger in state g, (vii) defer(q_i) is the action of deferring the first event of the i-th queue, (viii) $\lambda(\varphi)$ is the sequence of actions w.r.t. the specifications of the sequence of triggered transitions φ executed, (ix) $\Lambda(\overline{\varphi})$ is the set of states activated as a result of firing the set of transitions $\overline{\varphi} \subseteq$ enabled(g, o_i), (x) $v(q_i)$ is the content of the i-th event queue in the state g, (xi) cons(q_i) is the action of removing an event from the head of i-th event queue, (xii) $X_1, X_2 \in \mathbb{N}$ are the starting time of the earliest time event and the earliest expiration time of the considered time events resp.*

It follows from Def. 4 that at a state $g = \langle v, \mu \rangle$ the system can perform one of the following transitions (the ordering follows the priorities of the transitions):
1. Consumption of the completion events. Removes all the completion events that cannot fire a completion transition for the i-th object in the state g.
2. Execution of a completion transition. Handles one completion event κ causing a firing of one completion transition t_κ, and changes the valuation according to the sequence of actions $\lambda(t_\kappa)$, that is: exit actions and deactivation of leaving states, the transition action, the entry actions and activation of the

entered states, and producing completion events for some of the activated states. Moreover the clocks of the entered timed states are reset.

3. Execution of triggered transitions. Firing of the set of non-conflicting triggered transitions enabled by the event in the head of the event queue. The resolution of conflicts is based on the nesting level of the source states of transitions. We deal with changes of the valuation in a way similar to 2. If a transition is triggered by an event from the queue, then it is additionally consumed. The second possibility is the firing of a timed transition triggered by a time event. In this case the enabling condition depends rather on the clock valuation than the queue contents. Moreover, in the presence of orthogonal (concurrent) regions more than one transition can be fired in the single RTC step, so the action sequence $\lambda(\varphi)$ which changes the valuation contains the actions caused by all executed transitions (the set $\overline{\varphi}$).

4. Deferring an event. An event is deferred, i.e., it cannot be dispatched while staying at the current state, but it will be considered again after leaving this state.

5. Discarding of an event. Discards an event from the head of the i-th event queue, when it does not enable any transition.

6. Time flow. If all the event queues are empty and all completion events have been processed, then x time units pass, where $0 < X_1 \leq x \leq X_2$. We compute a set of the allowed values of x by subtracting of, respectively, the lower and upper bound of the time events specifications from all the time transitions with guard expressions satisfied and with active states as sources ($\mu(s) - \delta_1$ and $\mu(s) - \delta_2$). The set is bounded by the starting time of the earliest time event (X_1) and the earliest expiration time of the considered time events (X_2).

3   Symbolic Encoding

Below we present a symbolic encoding of the operational semantics introduced in the previous section. First the encoding of the global states is defined in order to give the symbolic transition relation.

As usual, the global states are represented by sequences of bits. To this aim each global state g is represented by n binary sequences, where each sequence stands for a state of one object. The representation of a single object consists of five binary sequences that encode respectively a set of active states, a set of completed states, a contents of the event queue, a valuation of the variables, and a valuation of the clocks.

Observe that the following conditions hold:

1. The number of bits r needed to encode one global state is given as follows:
$$r = \Sigma_{i=1}^{n}\left(|\mathcal{S}_i| + |C(o_i)| + m * b(i) + 2 * \lceil \log_2 m \rceil + (|\mathcal{V}_i| + |Reg(\Gamma_i)|) * int_{size}\right)$$
2. The number of clocks sufficient for representation of a state of ith object is equal to number of regions that directly contain time states.

The symbols $C(o_i)$, m, $b(i)$, and $Reg(\Gamma_i)$ denote respectively the set of *completion sensitive* states (the states being the source states for completion transitions,

$C(o_i) \subseteq S_i$), the size of the event queues, the maximum size of a single element of a queue, and the set of regions that directly contain time states. By int_{size} we denote the number of bits used to encode an integer number. From now on, we identify a global state with its binary representation.

Symbolic transition relation. Now, we give the encoding of the symbolic transition relation. The description is structured in a top-down manner, i.e., first we provide an encoding of the symbolic path, then the transition relation, and finally we describe in detail the encoding of some transition types. In order to encode all the executions of length k for a given system as the formula $path_k$, we work with vectors of propositional variables, called *state variables*. Denote by S_v a set of state variables, containing the symbols **true** and **false**. Each state of a k-path can be symbolically represented as a valuation of a vector of state variables $\mathbf{w} = (w_1, \ldots, w_r)$.

Definition 5 (Valuation of state variables). *Let us define a valuation of the state variables as $\mathcal{V} : S_v \longmapsto \{0,1\}$. Then, a valuation of the vectors of r state variables $\mathcal{V} : S_v{}^r \longmapsto \{0,1\}^r$ is given as: $\mathcal{V}(w_1, \ldots, w_r) = (\mathcal{V}(w_1), \ldots, \mathcal{V}(w_r))$.*

All the k-paths can be encoded over a symbolic k-path, i.e., $k+1$ vectors of state variables $\mathbf{w}_j$ for $j = 0, \ldots, k$. Each vector $\mathbf{w}_j$ is used for encoding global states of a system. Specifically, $\mathbf{w}_0$ encodes the initial state (g^0) whereas $\mathbf{w}_k$ encodes the last states of the k-paths.

Let $\mathbf{w}$ and $\mathbf{w}'$ be vectors of state variables, and $\mathcal{V}$ - a valuation of state variables, as discussed above. Define the following formulae:

- $\mathfrak{I}(\mathbf{w})$ is a formula s.t. for every valuation $\mathcal{V}$ have we that $\mathcal{V}$ satisfies $\mathfrak{I}(\mathbf{w})$ iff $\mathcal{V}(\mathbf{w})$ is equal to the initial state g^0 of the transition system.
- $\mathfrak{T}(\mathbf{w}, \mathbf{w}')$ - a formula s.t. for every valuation $\mathcal{V}$ we have that $\mathcal{V}$ satisfies $\mathfrak{T}(\mathbf{w}, \mathbf{w}')$ iff $\mathcal{V}(\mathbf{w}) \xrightarrow{x} \mathcal{V}(\mathbf{w}')$, for $x \in \mathbb{N}$.

Hence the formula encoding a symbolic k-path is defined as follows:

$$path_k(\mathbf{w}^0, \ldots, \mathbf{w}^k) = \mathfrak{I}(\mathbf{w}^0) \wedge \bigwedge_{i=0}^{k-1} \mathfrak{T}(\mathbf{w}^i, \mathbf{w}^{i+1}) \tag{1}$$

Next, we give the detailing encoding of the transition types. We start with a set of helper formulae that encode enabling conditions and execution of transitions of types 1 - 6, given in Def. 4. We define propositional formulae for transitions of types $1 \leq i \leq 5$ that encode their preconditions over the vector $\mathbf{w}$ for the object o: $EOi(o, \mathbf{w})$. We define also the propositional formulae encoding an execution of these transitions over the vectors $\mathbf{w}, \mathbf{w}'$ for the object o: $XOi(o, \mathbf{w}, \mathbf{w}')$ for $1 \leq i \leq 5$ and the formula encoding the time flow $X6(\mathbf{w}, \mathbf{w}')$.

The transitions of types 1–5 are called *local* as their execution does not depend on which type of transition can be fired by other objects. The execution of local transitions for object o over the vectors of state variables $\mathbf{w}$ and $\mathbf{w}'$ is recursively encoded as (we set $XO(o, \mathbf{w}, \mathbf{w}') = f_1(o, \mathbf{w}, \mathbf{w}')$):

$$f_5(o, \mathbf{w}, \mathbf{w}') = EO5(o, \mathbf{w}) \wedge XO5(o, \mathbf{w}, \mathbf{w}')$$
$$f_i(o, \mathbf{w}, \mathbf{w}') = EOi(o, \mathbf{w}) \wedge XOi(o, \mathbf{w}, \mathbf{w}') \qquad (2)$$
$$\vee \neg EOi(o, \mathbf{w}) \wedge f_{i+1}(o, \mathbf{w}, \mathbf{w}') \text{ for } i \in [1, 4]$$

We ensure that a transition of each level becomes enabled only if the transitions of the preceeding levels cannot be executed, by nesting the conditions for the consecutive levels. Then, iterating over the objects of class c, we encode the execution of local transitions for the class c:

$$XC(c, \mathbf{w}, \mathbf{w}') = \bigvee_{o \in Objects(c)} XO(o, \mathbf{w}, \mathbf{w}') \qquad (3)$$

Now we are ready to give the encoding of the transition relation:

$$\mathfrak{T}(\mathbf{w}, \mathbf{w}') = \bigvee_{c \in Classes} XC(c, \mathbf{w}, \mathbf{w}') \vee E6(\mathbf{w}) \wedge X6(\mathbf{w}, \mathbf{w}') \qquad (4)$$

where $E6(\mathbf{w})$ encodes the enabling conditions of the time flow transition.

Dealing with deferred events: queues. In this subsection we describe some ideas behind the symbolic encoding of event queues. In particular, we explain how the queues of [11] have been extended to deal with the deferred events. We describe informally the general ideas, skipping implementation details of the Boolean formula encoding each concept.

The queues are implemented as cyclic buffers (Fig. 3). The index i (p) shows the inserting (removing, resp.) position. Both the indices are incremented (modulo the queue length) when performing the respective operations. The third index d points at the first deferred event.

Referring to Fig. 3, the implementation of event queues can be explained as follows: a) shows the case without deferred events, the event pointed to by p is to be removed first and a new event will be inserted at the place pointed to by i. If $p = i$, then the queue is empty. For b), the pointer d points at the first event deferred in the current state, so all the events between d and p are deferred (red/gray fields). As shown in c), consuming a non-deferred event $E3$ requires performing a left-shift of the non-deferred events. This is necessary to ensure that the events in the queue are kept without empty fields between them. Figure 3 d) shows that when leaving the state with deferrable triggers we set $p = d$, so all the previously deferred events are now at the beginning of the queue.

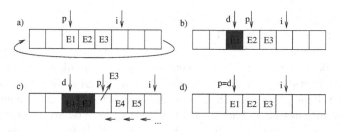

Fig. 3. Implementing event queues

Symbolic encoding: some details. In this section we introduce a symbolic encoding of transition type 1, leaving the remaining definitions in [12] and [11]. We give the encoding of the preconditions of particular transition types as formulae denoted with labels beginning with E, and the encoding of postconditions (execution) as formulae denoted with labels beginning with X.

Transitions of type 1 (discarding of completion events). A precondition for a transition of level one for object o ($EO1$) is satisfied if in a symbolic state $\mathbf{w}$ there exists a completion sensitive state s that is completed and there does not exist any completion transition, outgoing from s, having the guard satisfied.

$$ES1(s, \mathbf{w}) = \left(cpl(s, \mathbf{w}) \wedge \bigwedge_{t \in outC(s)} \neg(grd(t, \mathbf{w}))\right), EO1(o, \mathbf{w}) = \bigvee_{s \in C(o)} ES1(s, \mathbf{w})$$

where $cpl(s, \mathbf{w})$ is evaluated to **true** iff state s is completed in $\mathbf{w}$, $outC(s)$ is a set of all completion transitions outgoing from the state s, and the formula $grd(t, \mathbf{w})$ encodes the guard of transition t over the state variables from $\mathbf{w}$. The execution of this transition is encoded as the formula:

$$XO1(o, \mathbf{w}, \mathbf{w}') = \bigwedge_{s \in C(o)} \left(ES1(s, \mathbf{w}) \implies \neg cpl(s, \mathbf{w}')\right) \wedge cpRest(\mathbf{w}, \mathbf{w}')$$

The UML states satisfying the precondition $ES1$ are marked as not completed in the state $\mathbf{w}'$, and the formula $cpRest(\mathbf{w}, \mathbf{w}')$ encodes the copying of unchanged state variables from $\mathbf{w}$ to $\mathbf{w}'$.

Parametric Reachability. Now, we introduce an algorithm for finding a minimal (integer) time c, when a reachable property α holds in the model:

1. Run BMC for finding a minimal k s.t. α is reachable on a k-path.
2. Add a global clock X to the model to find the time x of reaching α at the k-path. Let $n := x - 1$.
3. Run BMC for checking $\alpha \wedge X \leq n$ over the extended model.
4. If BMC returns SAT, then let $n := n - 1$ and goto 3.
5. If BMC returns UNSAT, then $c := n + 1$, STOP.

We present some preliminary results in the next section.

4   Experimental Results

Our prototype implementation has been tested on 3 example specifications. The first one is Aircraft Carrier (AC) [12]. AC consists of a ship and a number of aircraft taking off and landing continuously, after issuing a request being accepted by the controller. The events of answering these requests may be marked as deferred. Each aircraft refills fuel while on board and burns fuel while airborne. We check the property whether an aircraft can run out of fuel during its flight.

Table 1. Results of verification of Aircraft Carrier system (defer/no defer)

N	k	Hugo+Uppaal [s]	BMC4UML [s]	Parametric [s], c = 4
3	19	1.32 / 1.25	67.59 / 51.26	31.34 / 22.64
4	20	13.15 / 11.41	101.58 / 81.28	45.44 / 42.38
5	21	147.43 / 95.67	155.63 / 132.34	60.49 / 37.01
6	22	Out of mem	257.08 / 216.42	52.23 / 75.08
7	23	- / -	686.06 / 421.85	101.86 / 199.09

The second benchmark - Master-Slave system [12] - is an untimed specification of a simple system consisting of one instance of class Master and some number (N) instances of class Slave. The objects of type Slave send requests to the object of type Master (m) that handles the messages and decreases the variable *resources*. When the variable is equal to 0 the object m enters the state *deadlock*. Table 2 presents our experimental results of testing the reachability of the *deadlock* state for N objects of class Slave. The column k contains the depth of the symbolic path for SMUML and our tool. The tests have been performed on the computer equipped with Pentium M 1.73 GHz CPU and 1.2 GB RAM running Linux.

Table 2. The experimental results of verification of Master-Slave

N	k	Hugo+Uppaal [s]	SMUML+NuSMV [s]	BMC4UML [s]
3	24	17.74	35.62	167.44
4	22	110.05	36.77	59.24
5	22	Out of memory	55.16	65.73
7	22	-	282.03	131.44
9	22	-	2 402.96	666.41

The third specification tested is a variant of the well known Generalised Railroad Crossing (GRC) benchmark (Fig. 1, 2). The system, operating a gate at a railroad crossing, consists of a gate, a controller and N tracks which are occupied by trains. Each track is equipped with sensors that indicate a position of a train and send appropriate message to the controller. Depending on the track occupancy the controller can either open or close the gate.

Table 3. The experimental results of verification of GRC (c = 6 for Param. columns)

N	k	Hugo+Uppaal[s]	BMC4UML[s]	BMC4UML*[s],k=18	Param.[s]	Param.*[s]
3	24	2.89	86.07	40.44	140.87	27.51
4	25	175.41	139.39	50.41	83.45	85.01
5	26	>2500	221.4	59.9	240.85	131.54
6	27	-	1354.89	75.21	365.37	175.63
7	-	-	-	92.6	-	191.46
20	-	-	-	448.64	-	620.66

Table 3 presents the results of verification of GRC, where N denotes the number of trains, and k the depth of symbolic path at which the tested property is satisfiable. The results in the column marked with asterisk concern the symbolic paths of length 18 that start not from the initial state of the GRC system, but from the state where all trains are in the states *Away* and object *ctl* is in the states *Main*, *Open*, and *control* (see Fig. 1, 2). In other words the paths have been shorted by the "initialization part". Although this trick can be applied to all systems, it guarantees an improvement only for those where the initialisation part of all objects *always* takes place before any other transitions.

5   Final Remarks

In this paper we described a new approach to Bounded Model Checking for UML. Instead of dealing with a translation to a standard formalism of timed automata, we encoded the verification problem directly into SAT. We believe that this is a way in which symbolic methods can be used to handle high-level languages. Our preliminary results are very promising. A future work is to enlarge the subset of the UML state machines handled, and to introduce some more optimisations at the level of symbolic encoding and implementation.

References

1. OMG: Unified Modeling Language (2007), http://www.omg.org/spec/UML/2.1.2
2. Lilius, J., Paltor, I.P.: vUML: A Tool for Verifying UML Models. In: 14th IEEE international conference on Automated Software Engineering, Washington DC, pp. 255–258. IEEE Computer Society, Los Alamitos (1999)
3. Jussila, T., Dubrovin, J., Junttila, T., Latvala, T., Porres, I.: Model Checking Dynamic and Hierarchical UML State Machines. In: 3rd Workshop on Model Design and Validation, pp. 94–110 (2006)
4. Knapp, A., Merz, S., Rauh, C.: Model Checking - Timed UML State Machines and Collaborations. In: Damm, W., Olderog, E.-R. (eds.) FTRTFT 2002. LNCS, vol. 2469, pp. 395–416. Springer, Heidelberg (2002)
5. Diethers, K., Goltz, U., Huhn, M.: Model Checking UML Statecharts with Time. In: Proc. of the UML 2002 workshop, TU München, pp. 35–52 (2002)
6. Compton, K., Gurevich, Y., Huggins, J., Shen, W.: An Automatic Verification Tool for UML. Technical Report CSE-TR-423-00, University of Michigan (2000)
7. Gutiérrez, M.E.B., Barrio-Solórzano, M., Quintero, C.E.C., de la Fuente, P.: UML Automatic Verification Tool with Formal Methods. Electr. Notes Theor. Comput. Sci. 127(4), 3–16 (2005)
8. Dubrovin, J., Junttila, T.: Symbolic Model Checking of Hierarchical UML State Machines. Technical Report B23, HUT TCS, Espoo, Finland (2007)
9. Bhaduri, P., Ramesh, S.: Model Checking of Statechart Models: Survey and Research Directions. ArXiv Computer Science e-prints, cs/0407038 (2004)
10. Crane, M.L., Dingel, J.: On the Semantics of UML State Machines: Categorization and Comparison. Technical Report 2005-501, Queen's University (2005)
11. Niewiadomski, A., Penczek, W., Szreter, M.: A New Approach to Model Checking of UML State Machines. Fundamenta Informaticae 93 (1-3), 289–303 (2009)
12. Niewiadomski, A., Penczek, W., Szreter, M.: Towards Checking Parametric Reachability for UML State Machines. In: 7th International Ershov Memorial Conference Perspectives of System Informatics, pp. 229–240 (2009)

A Flexible Approach to Automated Development of Cross Toolkits for Embedded Systems

Nikolay Pakulin and Vladimir Rubanov

Institute for System Programming of the Russian Academy of Sciences,
Moscow, Russia
npak@ispras.ru, vrub@ispras.ru

Abstract. Cross toolkits (assembler, linker, debugger, simulator, profiler) play a key role in the development cycle of embedded systems. Early creation of cross toolkits and possibility to quickly adapt them allows using them as early as at the hardware/software codesign stage, which shortens time-to-market and becomes an important success factor for the entire project. Challenging issues for cross toolkits development is efficiency of simulation and ability to adapt to CPU instruction set ongoing changes at the design phase. Developing cross toolkits in C/C++ produces highly efficient tools but requires extensive rework to keep up with instruction set changes. Approaches based on automatic toolkit generation from some top level specifications in Architecture Description Languages (ADLs) are less sensitive to this problem but they produce inefficient tools, especially simulators. This paper introduces a new approach to cross toolkit development that combines the flexibility of ADL and efficiency of C/C++ based approaches. This approach was implemented in the MetaDSP framework, which was successfully applied in several industrial projects.

1 Introduction

Nowadays we witness emerging of various embedded systems with rather tough requirements on their charateristics (chip size, power consumption, performance) not only for aerospace and military applications but also for industry and even consumer electronics. The progress in reducing cost and schedule of microelectronics hardware design and development makes it reasonable to develop customized computing systems for particular applications and gives new momentum to the market of embedded systems. Such systems consist of a dedicated hardware platform developed for a particular application domain and problem-specific software optimized for that hardware.

The process of simultaneous design and development of hardware and software components of an embedded system is usually referred to as *hardware/software codesign and codevelopment*. This general term covers a number of subprocesses or activities related to embedded system creation:

A. Pnueli, I. Virbitskaite, and A. Voronkov (Eds.): PSI 2009, LNCS 5947, pp. 331–343, 2010.
© Springer-Verlag Berlin Heidelberg 2010

1. design phase, including functional design, when requirements are studied and transformed into functional architechture, and hardware/software partitioning, when functions are divided between hardware and software components;
2. development phase or software/hardware codevelopment when both hardware and software teams develop their components; both development activities may influence each other;
3. verification; it spans from unit and module tests to early integration testing in simulator/emulator.

Hardware/software codesign and codevelopment are crucial factors for success of embedded systems. They reduce time-to-market by better parallelization of the development wrokflows and improve the quality by enabling early identification of design flaws and fine optimization of the product performance.

Cross toolkits play an important role in hardware/software codesign and codevelopment. Primary components of such cross toolkits are assembler, linker, simulator, debugger, and profiler. Unlike chip production, development of cross toolkits does not require precise hardware design description; it is sufficient to have just a high-level definition of the target hardware platform: the memory/register architecture and the instruction set with a timing specification. This allows developing cross tools as soon as at the early design stages even if the detailed VHDL/Verilog specification is not ready yet. Cross tools could be used in the following scenarios:

- Hardware prototyping and design space exploration (e.g. [1] and [2]) – early development, execution and profiling of sample programs allows easy assessment of the overall design adequacy as well as efficiency of particular design ideas such as adding/removing instructions, functional blocks, registers or whole co-processors.
- Early software development including development, debugging and optimizing the software *before* the target hardware production.
- Hardware design validation. The developed cross-simulator could be used to run test programs against VHDL/Verilog-based simulators. This capability could not be overestimated for the quality assurance before the actual silicon production.

1.1 Paper Overview

In this paper, we present a new approach to cross toolkit development to be used in hardware/software co-development environments. The method enables software developers to follow even frequent hardware design changes, most notably instruction set modifications, thus reducing the overall time frame of the design phase.

The article is organized as follows. Section 2 discusses generic requirements to cross toolkit develpment that hardware/software codevelopment imposes. Section 3 presents the new ADL language for defining instruction set called *ISE*. Section 4 introduces MetaDSP framework for cross toolkit development that uses hybrid hardware description with both high-level ADL part and fine-detail

C/C++ part. Section 5 briefly overviews several industrial applications of the ISE and MetaDSP framework. Conclusion summarizes the lessons learned and gives some perspectives for future development.

2   Hardware/Software Codesign Requirements for Cross Toolkit Development

Let us consider a typical co-development process depicted at the fig. 1. The development process involves at least two teams - one is working on the hardware part of the system while another one focuses on software development.

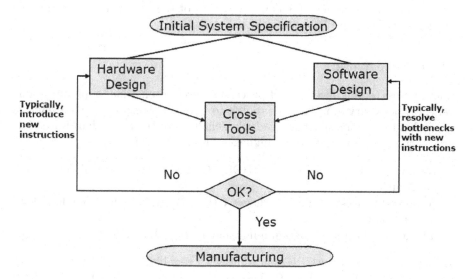

Fig. 1. Co-development process

Cross tools make it possible to run software on simulators or emulators of the target hardware early in the development process. Bottlenecks and performance problems identified during running the software might require modifications of both software and hardware design parts, e.g. adding new instructions and rewriting software to use them.

Frequent alterations in hardware design are typical for co-development process in the industry. In section 5, we provide basic statistics on several industrial projects. The number of *major changes* in hardware specification varies from 25 to 39 with the average of 31 changes per project.

In order to make the process seamless and continious, cross toolkit developers must rapidly react to such changes and produce new versions of the toolkit in short terms. Changes in the instruction set require consistent updates in every tool of the cross toolkit. Cross tookit developers must be very careful not to introduce errors during the modification process.

Another critical issue for cross-toolkits application in the co-development process is performance of the tools. Special attention should be paid to the performance efficiency of the simulator. High-performance simulators are required to perform validation and profiling of the target software on real-life data within reasonable time. For instance, processing a 10-second long speech sample on a DSP board takes about $7 \cdot 10^{11}$ CPU cycles. Running this sample on a simulator slower that 10 MCPS (millions of cycles per second) results in more that 2-hour long test execution, which could be hardly considered acceptable.

Simulator must be cycle-accurate to guarantee correctness of profiling data for fine optimizations. But simulator does not need to model the internal structure of hardware. Only the externally observable effects (e.g. values of registers and memory) of the simulator must be equivalent to that of the actual hardware while the internal design need not follow the design of the target hardware (pipline structure, ALU and FPU, internal buses, etc.)

2.1   Related Work

Efficient cross toolkit development process requires automation to minimize time and effort necessary to update the toolkit to frequent changes. Such automation can be built around a machine-readable definition of the target hardware platform. There are three groups of languages suitable for this purpose:

- Hardware Definition Languages (HDL, [3]) used for detailed definition of the hardware;
- Architecture Description Languages (ADL, [4] and [5]) used for high-level description of the hardware;
- and general purpose programming languages (such as C/C++).

HDL specifications define CPU operations with very high level of detail. All three major modern HDLs – VHDL [6], Verilog [7], and SystemC [8] – have execution environments that can serve as a simulator to run any assembly language programs for the target CPU: Synopsys VCS, Mentor Graphics ModelSim, Cadence NC-Sim and others. Still, low performance of HDL-based simulators is one of the major obstacles for HDL application in cross toolkit development. Another issue is the late moment of HDL description availability: it appears after completing the detailed instruction set design and functional decomposition. Furthermore, HDL does not contain an explicit instruction set definition that makes automated development of assembler/disassembler impossible. These issues prevent from using HDL to automate cross toolkit development.

Architecture Description Languages (such as nML [9], ISDL [10], EXPRESSION [11]) are under active development during the recent decade. There are tools for rapid hardware prototyping at the high level including cross toolkit generation. Corresponding approaches are really good for early design phase since they help to explore key design decisions. Unfortunately, at the later design stages details in an ADL description become smaller, the size of the description grows and sooner or later it comes across the limitations of the language. As a result, is breaks the efficiency of the simulator generated from the ADL description and makes the profiler to give only rough performance estimates without clear picture of bottlenecks. Cross toolkits completely generated from an ADL description are not applicable for industrial-grade software development yet.

Manual coding with C or C++ language gives full control over all possible details and allows creation of cross toolkits of industrial quality and efficiency. Many companies offer services on cross toolkit development in C/C++ (e.g. TASKING, Raisonance, Signum Systems, ICE Technology, etc.). Still it requires significant efforts and (what is more important) time to develop the toolkit from scratch and maintain it aligned with the requirements. Long development cycle makes it almost impossible to use cross toolkits developed in C/C++ for hardware prototyping and design space exploration.

3   ISE Language

We developed ISE (*Instruction Set Extension*) language to specify hardware design elements that are subject to most frequent changes: memory architecture and CPU instruction set. ISE description is used to generate assembler and disassembler tools completely and to generate components of the linker, debugger and simulator tool.

The following considerations guided the language design:

- the structure of an ISE description should follow the typical structure of an instruction set reference manual (like [12] or [13]) that usually serve as the input for the ISE description development;
- support for irregular encoding of instructions typical for embedded DSP applications including support for large number of various formats, distributed encoding of operands in the word, etc.;
- operational definition of data types, logic and arithmetic instructions, other executable entities should be specified in a C-like programming language.

ISE module consists of 7 sections:

1. **.architecture** defines global CPU architecture properties such as pipeline stages, CPU resources (buses, ALUs, etc.), initial CPU state;
2. **.storage** defines memory structure including memory ranges, I/O ports, access time;
3. **.ttypes** and **.otypes** define data type to represent registers and instruction operands;
4. **.instructions** defines CPU instruction set (see 3.1);
5. **.aspects** defines various aspects of binary encoding of CPU instructions or specifies additional resources or operational semantics of instructions;
6. **.conflicts** specifies constraints on sequential execution of instructions such as potential write after read register or bus conflict; assembler uses conflict constraints to automatically insert NOP instructions to prevent conflicts during software execution.

3.1 Instruction Definition

.instruction section is the primary section an ISE module. It defines the instruction set of the target CPU. For each instruction cross toolkit developers can specify:

- mnemonics and binary encoding;
- reference manual entry;
- instruction properties and resources used;
- instruction constraints and inter-instruction dependencies;
- definition of execution pipeline stage.

Mnemonics part of an instruction definition is a template string that specifies fixed part of mnemonics (e.g. ADD, MOV), optional suffixes (e.g. ADDC or ADDS) and

```
/*
 * This is a C-style block comment.
 */
// This is a C++-style one-line comment.
// <ALU001> - the identifier of the definition.
// ADD[S:A][C:B]   - instruction mnemonics with optional parts.
//   Actually defines 4 instructions: ADD, ADDS, ADDC, ADDSC.
//   GRs, GRt - identifiers of a general-purpose register.
//     Rules for binary encoding of GRs and GRt are defined in
//     .otypes section.
<ALU001>  ADD[S:A][C:B] {GRs}, {GRt}
    // Binary encoding rule.
    // For example, "ADDC R0, R1" is encoded as
    // 0111-0001-1000-1001
    0111-0A0B-1SSS-1TTT
    // The reference manual string.
    "ADD[S][C] GRs, GRt"
    // instruction properties:
    //   reads the registers GRs and GRt,
    //   writes the register GRs.
    properties [ wgrn:GRs, rgrn:GRs, rgrn:GRt ]
    // Operation of the EXE pipeline stage
    // specifies using ISE-C language.
    action {
      alu_temp = GRs + GRt;
      // If the suffix 'C' is set in mnemonics
      // use 'getFlag' function from the core library.
      if (#B) alu_temp += getFlag(ACO);
      // If the suffix 'S' is set in mnemonics
      // use 'SAT16' function from the core library.
      if (#A) alu_temp = SAT16(alu_temp);
      GRs = alu_temp;
    }
```

Fig. 2. An example of instruction specification

operands. A singe instruction might have several definitions depending on the operand types. For example, MOV instruction could have different definitions for register-register operation, register-memory and memory-memory operations.

Binary encoding is a template that specifies how to encode/decode instructions depending on the instruction name, suffixes and operands.

Reference manual entry is a human-readable specification of the instruction.

Properties and resources specify external aspects of the instruction execution such as registers that it reads and writes, buses that the instruction accesses, flags set etc. This information is used to detect and resolve conflicts by the assembler tool. Besides this the instruction definition might specify explicit dependencies on preceding or succeeding instructions in the constraints and dependencies section.

ISE language contains an extension of C programming language called ISE-C. This extension is used to specify execution of the operation on each pipeline stage. ISE-C has extra types for integer and fixed point arithmetic of various bit length, new built-in bit operators (e.g. shift with rotation), built-in primitives for bit handling. ISE-C has some grammar extension for handling operands and optional suffixes in mnemonics. Furthermore ISE-C expression can use a large number of functions implemented in ISE core library.

An example of instruction specification is presented at figure 2.

Please note that unlike classic ADL languages ISE specification does not provide the complete CPU model. The purpose of ISE is to simplify definition of the elements that are subject to the most frequent changes. All the rest of the model is specified using C/C++ code. This separation allows for flexible and maintainable hardware definition along with high performance and cycle-precise simulation.

4   Application to the Codevelopment Process

The proposed hybrid ADL/C++ hardware definition is supported by the *MetaDSP* framework for cross-toolkit development. The framework is intended for use by software developers. Typical use case is as following:

1. hardware developers provide the software team with hardware definition in the form of ISE specification;
2. software developers generate cross tools from the specification;
3. software team develops the software in Embedded-C[14] and build using the generated cross-assembler and cross-compiler;
4. the machine code is executed and profiled in simulator.

To support this use case the framework includes:

- ISE translator that generates components of cross tools from the ISE specification;
- pre-defined components for ISE development (e.g. ISE-C core functions library);

– an IDE for hardware definition development (in ISE and C++), target software development (in Embedded C and assembly languages), controlled execution within simulator; the Embedded C compiler supports a number of optimizations specific for DSP applications[15].

MetaDSP toolkit uses ISE specification to generate cross tools and components. For example, the MetaDSP tools generate assembler and disassembler tools completely from the ISE specification. For linker MetaDSP generates information about instruction binary encodings, instruction operands and relocatable instructions. Debugger and profiler use memory structures and operand types from the ISE specification.

The cycle-precise simulator is an important part of the toolkit. Figure 3 presents its architecture. MetaDSP tools generate several components from the ISE specification: memory implementation (from .storage section), resources (from .architecture section), instruction implementations and decoding tables (from .instruction section), as well as conflicts detector and instruction metadata.

Within the presented approach certain components are specified in C++:

– control logic, including pipeline control (if any), address generation, instruction decoder;

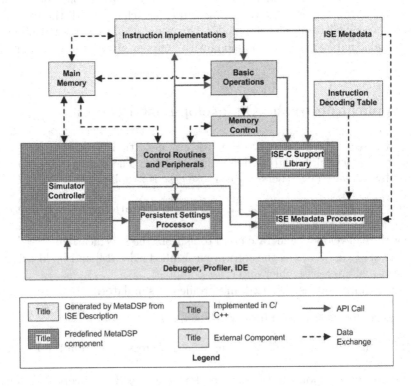

Fig. 3. MetaDSP simulator architecture

- memory control;
- model of the peripheral devices including I/O ports.

For most of the manual components MetaDSP tools generate stubs or some basic implementation in C++. Developers may use the generated code to implement peculiarities of the target CPU, such as jumps prediction, instruction reordering, etc.

Using C/C++ to implement CPU control logic and memory model facilitates high performance of the simulator. Another benefit of using C/C++ compared to true ADL languages is an early development of the cross toolkit: it might start before completing the function decomposition of the target CPU; thus the simulator could be used to experiment with design variations.

Figure 4 presents the snapshot of OSCAR Studio, the IDE for target software development within the MetaDSP framework. Red numbers mark various windows of the IDE:

1. Project Navigator window. It displays the tree of the source files and data files.
2. Source Code Editor window. The editor supports syntax highlight and instruction autocompletion (from the ISE specification). The editor window

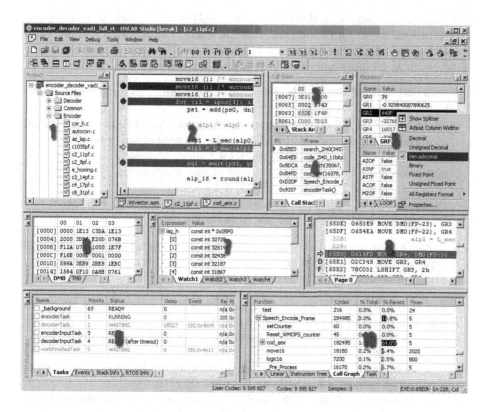

Fig. 4. OSCAR Studio: the IDE for MetaDSP framework

is integrated with the debugger - it marks break points, frame count points and trace points.

3. Stack Memory window displays the contents of the stack.
4. Call Stack window displays the enclosing frames (both assembly subroutines and C functions).
5. Register window displays the contents of the CPU registers.
6. Memory dump window displays contents of various memory regions.
7. Watch window displays the current value of arbitrary C expressions.
8. Code Memory window displays the instructions being executed. It supports both binary and disassembly forms as well as displaying the current pipeline stage (fetch, decode, execute, etc.).
9. OS debugger window displays the current state of the execution environment (OS): list of the current tasks, semaphores, mutexes, etc.
10. Profiler window displays various profiling data. The profiler is integrated with the editor window as well – the editor can show profiling information associated with code elements.

5   Industrial Applications

The approach presented in this paper and MetaDSP framework were applied to five industrial projects. Please note that the each "major releases of the cross toolkit" mentioned in the project list below is caused by a major change in CPU design such as modification of the instruction set or memory model alteration.

- 16-bit RISC DSP CPU with fixed point arithmetic. Produced 25 major releases of the cross-toolkit.
- 16-bit RISC DSP CPU with support for Adaptive Multi-Rate (AMR) sound compression algorithm. Produced 25 major releases of the cross-toolkit.
- 32-bit RISC DSP CPU with support for Fourier transform and other DSP extensions. Produced 39 major releases of the cross-toolkit.
- 16/32-bit RISC CPU clone of ARM9 architecture.
- 16/32-bit VLIW DSP CPU with support for Fourier transform, DMA, etc. Produced 33 major releases of the cross-toolkit.

The following list summarizes lessons learned from the practical applications of the approach. We compared time and effort needed in a pure C++ development cycle of cross toolkits with the ISE-enabled process:

- size of assembler, disassembler and simulator sources (excluding generated code), in lines of code: reduced by 12 times;
- cross-toolkit development team (excluding C compiler development): reducing from 10 to 3 engineers;
- number of errors detected in the presentation of hardware specifications in cross tools: reduction by the factor of more than 10;
- average duration of the toolkit update: reduced from several days to hours (even minutes in many cases).

5.1   Performance Study

This section presents a performance study of a production implementation of the AMR sound compression algorithm. The study was performed on Intel Core 2 Duo 2.4 GHz.

The size of the implementation was 119 C source files and 142 C header files, and 25 files in the assembly language; total size of sources was 20.2 thousand LOC without comments and empty lines. The duration of the audio sample (10 seconds voice speech) lasted 670 million of cycles on the target hardware.

Table 1 presents elapsed time measurements of the generated cross tools for the AMR case study. Table 2 presents measurements of the generated simulator in MCPS (millions of cycles per second).

Table 1. AMR sample – cross toolkit performance

Operation	Duration, sec.
Translation (.c → .asm)	22
Assembly (.asm → .obj)	14
Link (.obj → .exe)	1
Build, total	**37**
Execution on the audio sample (fast mode)	53
Execution on the audio sample (debug mode with profiling)	93

Table 2. AMR sample – simulator performance

Execution mode	MCPS
Fast mode	12.6
Debug mode with profiling	7.2
Peak performance on a synthetic sample	25.0

6   Conclusion

The paper presents an approach to automation of cross toolkit development for special-purpose embedded systems such as DSPs and microcontrollers. The approach aims at creation of the cross tools (assembler/disassembler, linker, simulator, debugger, and profiler) at the early stages of system design. Early creation of the cross tools gives opportunity to prototype and estimate efficiency of design variations, co-development of the hardware and software components of the target embedded system, and verification and QA of the hardware specifications before silicon production.

The presented approach relies on a two-part description of the target hardware: description of the most flexible part – the instruction set and memory model – using the new ADL language called *ISE* and description of complex fine grained functional aspects of CPU operations using a general purpose programming language (C/C++). Having ADL descriptions along with a framework to generate components of the target cross toolkit and common libraries brings high level of responsiveness to frequent changes in the initial design that are a common issue for modern industrial projects. Using C/C++ gives cycle-accurate simulation and high overall efficiency of the cross toolkits that meets the needs of industrial developers. The approach is supported by a family of tools comprising MetaDSP framework.

The approach is applicable to various embedded systems with RISC core architectures. It supports simple pipelines with fixed number of stages, multiple memory banks, instructions with fixed and variable cycle count. These facilities cover most of modern special purpose CPUs (esp. DSP) and embedded systems. Still some features of modern general purpose high performance processors lay beyond the capabilities of the presented approach: superscalar architectures, microcode, instruction multi-issue, out-of-order execution. Besides this, the basic memory model implemented in MetaDSP does not support caches, speculative access, etc.

Despite the limitations of the approach mentioned above it was successfully applied in a number of industrial projects including 16 and 32-bit RISC DSPs and 16/32 ARM-like CPUs. The number of major design changes (with corresponding releases of separate cross toolkit versions) ranged in those projects from 25 to 40. The industrial applications of the presented approach proved the concept of using the hybrid ADL/C++ description for automated development of production quality cross toolkits even in case of volatile design process of the target embedded systems.

References

1. Hartoog, M., Rowson, J., Reddy, P.: Generation of Software Tools from Processor Descriptions for Hardware/Software Codesign. In: Design Automation Conference, DAC (1997)
2. Yung-Chia, L.: Hardware/Software Co-design with Architecture Description Language. Programming Language Lab. NTHU (2003)
3. Navabi, Z.: Languages for Design and Implementation of Hardware. In: The VLSI Handbook, 2nd edn. CRC Press, Boca Raton (2007)
4. Mishra, P., Dutt, N.: Architecture description languages for programmable embedded systems. IEEE Proceedings Computers and Digital Techniques 152(3) (May 2005)
5. Tomiyama, H., Halambi, A., Grun, P., Dutt, N., Nicolau, A.: Architecture Description Languages for Systems-on-Chip Design. In: Proc. Asia Pacific Conf. on Chip Design Language, pp. 109–116 (1999)
6. VHDL Language Reference Manual. IEEE Std 1076-1987
7. Hardware Description Language Based on the Verilog Hardware Description Language. IEEE Std 1364-2005
8. System C Language Reference Manual. IEEE Std 1666-2005
9. Fauth, A., Van Praet, J., Freericks, M.: Describing instruction set processors using nML. In: Proc. of EDTC (1995)

10. Hadjiyannis, G., Hanono, S., Devadas, S.: ISDL: An Instruction Set Description Language for Retargetability. In: Design Automation Conference, DAC (1997)
11. Halambi, A., Grun, P., Ganesh, V., Khare, A., Dutt, N., Nicolau, A.: EXPRESSION: A Language for Architecture Exploration through Compiler/Simulator Retargetability. In: DATE 1999 (1999)
12. MicroDSP 2 Instruction Set Description. VIA Technologies Manual (2005)
13. TMS320C6000 CPU and Instruction Set Reference Guide. Texas Instruments Literature Number SPRU189F,
    http://focus.ti.com/lit/ug/spru189g/spru189g.pdf
14. ISO/IEC TR 18037:2008. Programming languages – C – Extensions to support embedded processors (2004)
15. Rubanov, V., Grinevich, A., Markovtsev, D.: Programming and Computing Software 32(1), 19–30 (2006)

A Technique for Information Retrieval from Microformatted Websites[*]

J. Guadalupe Ramos[1], Josep Silva[2], Gustavo Arroyo[2], and Juan C. Solorio[1]

[1] Instituto Tecnológico de La Piedad
Av. Tecnológico 2000, La Piedad, Mich., México. CP 59300
guadalupe@dsic.upv.es, juancsol@hotmail.com
[2] DSIC, Universidad Politécnica de Valencia
Camino de Vera s/n, E-46022 Valencia, Spain
{jsilva,garroyo}@dsic.upv.es

Abstract. In this work, we introduce a new method for information extraction from the semantic web. The fundamental idea is to model the semantic information contained in the microformats of a set of web pages, by using a data structure called *semantic network*. Then, we introduce a novel technique for information extraction from semantic networks. In particular, the technique allows us to extract a portion—a *slice*—of the semantic network with respect to some criterion of interest. The slice obtained represents relevant information retrieved from the semantic network and thus from the semantic web. Our approach can be used to design novel tools for information retrieval and presentation, and for information filtering that was distributed along the semantic web.

1 Introduction

The Semantic Web is considered an evolving extension of the World Wide Web in which the semantics of information and services on the web is made explicit by adding metadata. Metadata provides the web contents with descriptions, meaning and inter-relations. The Semantic Web is envisioned as a universal medium for data, information, and knowledge exchange.

Recently, a new initiative has emerged that looks for attaching semantic data to web pages by using simple extensions of the standard tags currently used for web formatting in (X)HTML[1], these extensions are called *microformats* [1,2]. A microformat is basically an open standard formatting code that specifies a set of attribute descriptors to be used with a set of typical tags.

Example 1. Consider the XHTML of the left that introduces information of a common personal card:

---

[*] This work has been partially supported by the Spanish *Ministerio de Ciencia e Innovación* under grant TIN2008-06622-C03-02, by the *Generalitat Valenciana* under grant ACOMP/2009/017, by the *Universidad Politécnica de Valencia* (Programs PAID-05-08 and PAID-06-08) and by the Mexican *Dirección General de Educación Superior Tecnológica* (Programs *CICT 2008* and *CICT 2009*).
[1] XHTML is a sound selection because it enforces a well-structured format.

A. Pnueli, I. Virbitskaite, and A. Voronkov (Eds.): PSI 2009, LNCS 5947, pp. 344–351, 2010.
© Springer-Verlag Berlin Heidelberg 2010

```
<h2>Directory</h2>                    <h2>Directory</h2>
<p> Vicente Ramos <br>                <div class="vcard">
   Software Development <br>            <span class="fn">Vicente Ramos</span>
   118, Atmosphere St. <br>            <div class="org">Software Development </div>
   La Piedad, México <br>              <div class="adr">
   59300 <br>                             <div class="street-address">Atmosphere 118</div>
   +52 352 52 68499 <br>                  <span class="locality">La Piedad, México</span>
</p>                                      <span class="postal-code">59300</span>
<h4>His Company</h4>                   </div>
<a href="page2.html">                 <div class="tel">+52 352 52 68499</div>
   Company Page </a>                      <h4>His Company</h4>
                                         <a class="url" href="page2.html">Company Page </a>
                                      </div>
```

Now, observe the code on the right which shows the same information but using the standard hCard microformat [3], which is useful for representing data about people, companies, organizations, and places. The class property qualifies each type of attribute which is defined by the hCard microformat. The code starts with the required main class vcard and classifies the information with a set of classes which are auto-explicative: fn describes name information, adr defines address details and so on.

In this paper we propose the use of *semantic networks* which is a convenient simple model for representing semantic data; and we define a slicing technique for this formalism in order to analyze and filter the semantic web.

2 From the Semantic Web to the Semantic Network

The concept of *semantic network* is fairly old, and it is a common structure for knowledge representation, which is useful in modern problems of artificial intelligence. A semantic network is a directed graph consisting of nodes which represent *concepts* and edges which represent *semantic relations* between the concepts [4,5].

In order to represent semantic information in a semantic network we consider the microformats, i.e., classes as convenient entities for modeling, and then, for indexing or referencing. If we focus on the relations between classes we identify two kinds of relations, namely[2]:

strong relations. that are the relations which come from hypertext links between pages or sections of a page by using anchors.

weak relations. that can be *embedding relationships*, for classes that embeds other classes or *semantic relationships* among classes of the same type, for instance, between two vcard.

Example 2. Consider the semantic network depicted in Figure 1 (the grey parts of the figure do not belong to the semantic network and thus they can be ignored for the time being). It is composed of two webpages (*P*1 and *P*2), and *P*1 represents the microformatted code of Example 1.

In the figure, the nodes of the first page are labeled with *P*1 and the nodes of the second page are labeled with *P*2. Thus, nodes (i.e., concepts) are unique. We

---

[2] In this paper, without loss of generality, we only consider weak relations (i.e., only semantic relations), thus we analyze semantic networks without taking into account the labels associated to the edges.

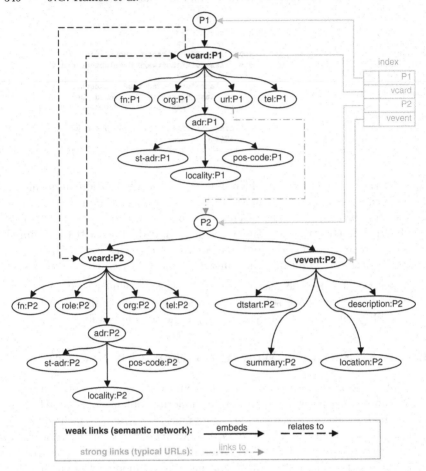

Fig. 1. Example of semantic network

observe three kinds of edges: The `locality` class from Example 1 is embedded in the `adr` class. Thus, there is an embedding relationship from node `adr` to node `locality`. Furthermore, `vcard` in $P1$ and `vcard` in $P2$ are linked by a semantic relationship. Besides, there is one strong hyperlink to $P2$ generated by the micro-formatted tag `<a class="url" href="page2.html">`. Observe that the graph only contains semantic information and their relations; and it omits content or formatting information such as the $<strong></strong>$ labels. Observe that we add to the graph two additional concepts, $P1$ and $P2$, which refer to web pages. This is very useful in practice in order to make explicit the embedding relation between microformats and their web page containers.

3   A Technique for Information Retrieval

We introduce first some preliminary definitions.

Definition 1 (semantic network). *A directed graph is an ordered pair* $\mathcal{G} = (\mathcal{V}, \mathcal{E})$ *where* $\mathcal{V}$ *is a finite set of vertices or nodes, and* $\mathcal{E} \subseteq \mathcal{V} \times \mathcal{V}$ *is a set of ordered pairs* $(v \to v')$ *with* $v, v' \in \mathcal{V}$ *called edges. A semantic network is a directed graph* $\mathcal{S} = (\mathcal{V}, \mathcal{E})$ *in which nodes have been labeled with names of web pages and microformatting classes of these pages.*

As an example of semantic network consider the directed graph in Figure 1 (omitting the grey parts) where nodes are the set of microformatted classes provided by two semantic web pages.

A semantic network is a profuse mesh of information. For this reason, we extend the semantic network with an *index* which acts as an interface between the semantic network and the potential interacting systems. The index contains the subset of concepts that are relevant (or also visible) from outside the semantic net. It is possible to define more than one index for different systems and or applications. Each element of the index contains a key concept and a pointer to its associated node. Artificial concepts such as webpages (See $P1$ and $P2$ in Figure 1) can also be indexed. This is very useful in practice because it is common to retrieve the embedded (microformatted) classes of each semantic web page.

Let $\mathcal{K}$ be a set of concepts represented in the semantic network $\mathcal{S} = (\mathcal{V}, \mathcal{E})$. Then, $rnode : (\mathcal{S}, k) \to \mathcal{V}$ where $k \in \mathcal{K}$ (for the sake of clarity, in the following we will refer to k as the *key concept*) is a mapping from concepts to nodes; i.e., given a semantic network $\mathcal{S}$ and a key concept k, then $rnode(\mathcal{S}, k)$ returns the node $v \in \mathcal{V}$ associated to k.

Definition 2 (semantic index). *Given a semantic network* $\mathcal{S} = (\mathcal{V}, \mathcal{E})$ *and an alphabet of concepts* $\mathcal{K}$, *a semantic index* $\mathcal{I}$ *for* $\mathcal{S}$ *and* $\mathcal{K}$ *is any set* $\mathcal{I} = \{(k, p) \mid k \in \mathcal{K} \text{ and } p \text{ is a mapping from } k \text{ to } rnode(\mathcal{S}, k)\}$

We can now extend semantic networks by properly including a semantic index. We call this kind of semantic network *indexed semantic network* (IS).

Definition 3 (indexed semantic network). *An indexed semantic network IS is a triple* $IS = (\mathcal{V}, \mathcal{E}, \mathcal{I})$, *such that* $\mathcal{I}$ *is a semantic index for the semantic network* $\mathcal{S} = (\mathcal{V}, \mathcal{E})$.

Now, each semantic index allows us to visit the semantic network from a well defined collection of entrance points which are provided by the *rnode* function.

Example 3. An IS with a set of nodes $\mathcal{V} = \{a, b, c, d, e, f, g\}$ is shown in Figure 2 (a). For the time being the reader can ignore the use of colors black and grey and consider the graph as a whole. There is a semantic index with two key concepts a and c pointing out to their respective nodes in the semantic network.

Similarly, the semantic network of Figure 1 has been converted to an IS by defining the index with four entries $P1$ (page1.html), $P2$ (page2.html), *vcard* and *vevent* and by removing the strong links. Thus, for instance, *vcard* entry points to the cycle of *vcard* nodes.

Given a graph $\mathcal{G} = (\mathcal{V}, \mathcal{E})$ and two nodes $v_1, v_n \in \mathcal{V}$, if there is a sequence $v_1, v_2, \ldots, v_n$ of nodes in $\mathcal{G}$ where $(v_i, v_{i+1}) \in \mathcal{E}$ for $1 \leq i \leq n-1$, then we say that there is a *path* from v_1 to v_n in $\mathcal{G}$. Given $u, v \in \mathcal{V}$ we say that the node v is *reachable* from u if there is a path from u to v.

Definition 4 (semantic sub-net). *Let $IS = (\mathcal{V}, \mathcal{E}, \mathcal{I})$ be an indexed semantic network. Then, a semantic sub-net of IS with respect to concept k, with $(k, p) \in \mathcal{I}$ for some p, is $\mathcal{S}_k = (\mathcal{V}', \mathcal{E}')$ such that $\mathcal{V}' = \{rnode((\mathcal{V}, \mathcal{E}), k)\} \cup \{v | v \in \mathcal{V}$ and v is reachable from $rnode((\mathcal{V}, \mathcal{E}), k)\}$ and $\mathcal{E}' = \{(u, v) | (u, v) \in \mathcal{E}$ and $u \in \mathcal{V}'\}$.*

Example 4. Figure 2 (a) shows in black color the semantic sub-net extracted from the whole IS with respect to concept c.

Definition 5 (semantic relationship). *Given a semantic network $\mathcal{S} = (\mathcal{V}, \mathcal{E})$ and a node $v \in \mathcal{V}$, the semantic relationships of v are the edges $\{v \rightarrow v' \in \mathcal{E}\}$. We say that a concept v is semantically related to a concept u if there exists a semantic relationship $(u \rightarrow v)$.*

The semantic relations in our semantic networks are unidirectional. The semantics associated to the edges of a semantic network is not transitive because edges can have different meanings. Therefore, the semantic relation of Definition 5 is neither transitive.

Given a node n in a semantic network, we often use the term *semantically reachable* to denote the set of nodes which are reachable from n through semantic relationships. Clearly, semantic reachability is a transitive relation.

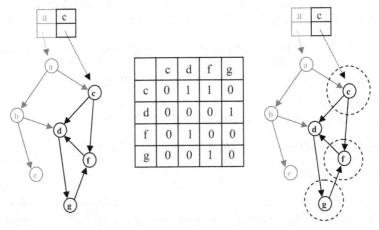

Fig. 2. a) A semantic sub-net. b) The sub-net's adjacency matrix. c) A backward slice.

3.1   Semantic Sub-net Slicing

In this section we present a procedure that allows us to extract a portion of a semantic sub-net according to some criterion. The procedure uses an *adjacency matrix* to represent the semantic sub-net.

The adjacency matrix m of a directed graph $\mathcal{G}$ with n nodes is the $n \times n$ matrix where the non-diagonal entry m_{ij} contains 1 if there is an edge such that $m_i \rightarrow m_j$.[3]

---

[3] Note that we could write a label associated to the edge in the matrix instead of 1 in order to also consider other relationships between nodes.

Example 5. Consider the semantic sub-net in Figure 2 (a). Node c has two directed edges, one to node d and other to node f. Thus, in the entry m_{cd} and m_{cf} we write 1, and 0 in the other cells.

Now, we are in a position to introduce our slicing based method for information recovering from semantic sub-nets. Firstly, we can select a concept in the index. From this concept we can extract a semantic sub-net as described before. Next, in the resultant semantic sub-net we can select the node of interest. Hence, our slicing criterion consists of a pair formed by a key concept and a node. Formally:

Definition 6 (slicing criterion). *Let $IS = (\mathcal{V}, \mathcal{E}, \mathcal{I})$ be an indexed semantic network. Then a slicing criterion $\mathcal{C}$ for IS is a pair of elements $\langle k, v \rangle$ such that $(k, p) \in \mathcal{I}$ for some p, $v \in \mathcal{V}'$ and $S_k = (\mathcal{V}', \mathcal{E}')$ is the semantic sub-net of IS with respect to concept k.*

Given a semantic sub-net, we can produce two different slices by traversing the sub-net either forwards or backwards from the node pointed out by the slicing criterion. Each slice gives rise to different semantic information.

Example 6. Consider the slicing criterion $\langle c, d \rangle$ for the IS in Figure 2 c). The first level of slicing uses c to extract the semantic sub-net highlighted with black color. Then, the second level of slicing performs a traversal of the semantic sub-net either forwards or backwards from d. In Figure 2 c) the backward slice contains all nodes whereas the forward slice would only contain {d, f, g}.

Example 7. Consider the semantic network in Figure 1 together with the slicing criterion $\langle P1, adr{:}P1 \rangle$. With $P1$ we can perform the first level of slicing to recover a semantic sub-net which is composed by the nodes $\{P1, vcard{:}P1, vcard{:}P2\}$ and all of their descendant (semantically reachable) nodes. Then, from node $adr{:}P1$ we can go forwards and collect the information related to the address or backwards and collect nodes $vcard{:}P1$, $P1$ and $vcard{:}P2$. The backward slicing illustrates that the node $adr{:}P1$ is semantically reachable from $P1$, $vcard{:}P1$, and $vcard{:}P2$, and thus, there are semantic relationships between them. Hence, we extract a slice from the semantic network and, as a consequence, from the semantic web.

We can now formalize the notion of forward/backward slice for semantic sub-nets. In the definition we use $\to^*$ to denote the reflexive transitive closure of $\to$.

Definition 7 (forward/backward slice). *Let $IS = (\mathcal{V}, \mathcal{E}, \mathcal{I})$ be an indexed semantic network with $(k, p) \in \mathcal{I}$ for some p. Let $S_k = (\mathcal{V}', \mathcal{E}')$ be the semantic sub-net of IS with respect to k and $\mathcal{C} = \langle k, node \rangle$ a slicing criterion for IS. Then a slice of IS is $\mathcal{S}' = (\mathcal{V}_1, \mathcal{E}_1)$ such that*

forward $\mathcal{V}_1 = \{node\} \cup \{v | v \in \mathcal{V}' \text{ and } (node \to^* v) \in \mathcal{E}'\}$
backward $\mathcal{V}_1 = \{node\} \cup \{v | v \in \mathcal{V}' \text{ and } (v \to^* node) \in \mathcal{E}'\}$

and $\mathcal{E}_1 = \{(u \to v) \mid (u \to v) \in \mathcal{E}' \text{ with } u, v \in \mathcal{V}_1\}$

The algorithm of Figure 3 shows the complete slicing based method for information extraction from semantic networks. Roughly speaking, given an IS and a

Input: An indexed semantic network $IS = (\mathcal{V}, \mathcal{E}, \mathcal{I})$
      and a slicing criterion $\mathcal{C} = \langle k, node \rangle$ where $(k, p) \in \mathcal{I}$ for some p
Output: A slice $\mathcal{S}' = (\mathcal{V}', \mathcal{E}')$
Initialization: $\mathcal{V}' := \{node\}, \mathcal{E}' := \{\}, Visited := \{\}$
Begin
    Compute $S_k = (\mathcal{V}_k, \mathcal{E}_k)$ a semantic sub-net of IS
        whose adjacency matrix is $\mathcal{M}$
  Repeat
    let $s \in (\mathcal{V}' \setminus Visited)$
    let $c := column(s, \mathcal{M})$
    For each $s' \in \mathcal{V}_k$ with $r = row(s', \mathcal{M})$ and $\mathcal{M}_{r,c} = 1$
      $\mathcal{V}' := \mathcal{V}' \cup \{s'\}$
      $\mathcal{E}' := \mathcal{E}' \cup \{(s' \to s)\}$
    $Visited := Visited \cup \{s\}$
  Until $\mathcal{V}' = Visited$
End
Return: $(\mathcal{V}', \mathcal{E}')$

Fig. 3. An algorithm for semantic network backward slicing

slicing criterion, (i) it extracts the associated semantic sub-net, (ii) it computes the sub-net's adjacency matrix, and (iii) it extracts (guided by the adjacency matrix) the nodes and edges that form the final slice.

The algorithm uses two functions $row(s, \mathcal{M})$ and $column(s, \mathcal{M})$ which respectively return the number of row and column of concept s in matrix $\mathcal{M}$. It proceeds as follows: Firstly, the semantic sub-net associated to IS and the adjacency matrix of the sub-net are computed. Then, the matrix is traversed to compute the slice by exploiting the fact that a cell $\mathcal{M}_{i,j}$ with value 1 in the matrix means that the concept in column j is semantically related to the concept in row i. Therefore, edges are traversed backwards by taking a concept in a column and collecting all concepts of the rows that have a 1 in that column.

4   Related Work and Conclusions

In [6], three prototype hypertext systems were designed and implemented. In the first prototype, an unstructured semantic net is exploited and an authoring tool is provided. The prototype uses a knowledge-based traversal algorithm to facilitate document reorganization. This kind of traversing algorithms is based on typical solutions like depth-first search and breadth-first search. In contrast, our IS allows us to optimize the task of information retrieval.

[7] designed a particular form of a graph to represent questions and answers. These graphs are built according to the question and answer requirements. This is in some way related to our work if we assume that our questions are the slicing criteria and our answers are the computed slices. In our approach, we conserve a general form of semantic network, which is enriched by the index, so, it still permits to represent sub-graphs of knowledge.

To the best of our knowledge this is the first program slicing based approach to extract information from the semantic web. The obtained answers are semantically correct, because since, the information extraction method follows the paths of the source semantic tree, i.e., the original semantic relationships are preserved. Furthermore, semantic relationships contained in sets of microformatted web pages can also be discovered and extracted.

Program slicing has been previously applied to data structures. For instance, Silva [8] used program slicing for information extraction from individual XML documents. He also used a graph-like data structure to represent the documents. However semantic networks are a much more general structure, that could contain many subgraphs, while XML documents are always a tree-like structure. In contrast to this method, our approach can process groups of web pages.

This method could be exploited by tools that feed microformats. Frequently, these tools take all the microformats in the semantic web and store them in their databases in order to perform queries. Our representation improves this behavior by allowing the system to determine what microformats are relevant and what microformats can be discarded. Another potential use is related to automatic information retrieval from websites by summarizing semantic content related to a slicing criterion. Similarly, web search engines could use this method to be able to establish semantic relations between unrelated links.

References

1. Microformats.org. The Official Microformats Site (2009),
   http://microformats.org/
2. Khare, R., Çelik, T.: Microformats: a Pragmatic Path to the Semantic Web. In: WWW 2006: Proceedings of the 15th International Conference on World Wide Web, pp. 865–866. ACM, New York (2006)
3. hCard. Simple, Open, Distributed Format for Representing People, Companies, Organizations, and Places (2009), http://microformats.org/wiki/hcard
4. Sowa, J.F. (ed.): Principles of Semantic Networks: Explorations in the Representation of Knowledge. Morgan Kaufmann, San Francisco (1991)
5. Sowa, J.F.: Semantic Networks. In: Shapiro, S.C. (ed.) Encyclopedia of Artificial Intelligence. John Wiley & Sons, Chichester (1992)
6. Wang, W., Rada, R.: Structured Hypertext with Domain Semantics. ACM Transactions on Information Systems (TOIS) 16(4), 372–412 (1998)
7. Mollá, D.: Learning of Graph-based Question Answering Rules. In: Proc. HLT/NAACL 2006 Workshop on Graph Algorithms for Natural Language Processing, pp. 37–44 (2006)
8. Silva, J.: A Program Slicing Based Method to Filter XML/DTD Documents. In: van Leeuwen, J., Italiano, G.F., van der Hoek, W., Meinel, C., Sack, H., Plášil, F. (eds.) SOFSEM 2007. LNCS, vol. 4362, pp. 771–782. Springer, Heidelberg (2007)

From Dynamic to Static and Back: Riding the Roller Coaster of Information-Flow Control Research

Andrei Sabelfeld and Alejandro Russo

Dept. of Computer Science and Engineering, Chalmers University of Technology
412 96 Göteborg, Sweden, Fax: +46 31 772 3663

Abstract. Historically, dynamic techniques are the pioneers of the area of information flow in the 70's. In their seminal work, Denning and Denning suggest a static alternative for information-flow analysis. Following this work, the 90's see the domination of static techniques for information flow. The common wisdom appears to be that dynamic approaches are not a good match for security since monitoring a single path misses public side effects that could have happened in other paths. Dynamic techniques for information flow are on the rise again, driven by the need for permissiveness in today's dynamic applications. But they still involve nontrivial static checks for leaks related to control flow.

This paper demonstrates that it is possible for a purely dynamic enforcement to be as secure as Denning-style static information-flow analysis, despite the common wisdom. We do have the trade-off that static techniques have benefits of reducing runtime overhead, and dynamic techniques have the benefits of permissiveness (this, for example, is of particular importance in dynamic applications, where freshly generated code is evaluated). But on the security side, we show for a simple imperative language that both Denning-style analysis and dynamic enforcement have the same assurance: termination-insensitive noninterference.

1 Introduction

Historically, dynamic techniques are the pioneers of the area of information flow in the 70's (e.g., [9]). They prevent explicit flows (as in *public := secret*) in program runs. They also address *implicit* [8] flows (as in if *secret* then *public := 1*) by enforcing a simple invariant of no public side effects in *secret context*, i.e., in the branches of conditionals and loops with secret guards. These techniques, however, come without soundness arguments.

In their seminal paper, Denning and Denning [8] suggest a static alternative for information-flow analysis. They argue that static analysis removes runtime overhead for security checks. This analysis prevents both explicit and implicit flows statically. The invariant of no public side effects in secret context is ensured by a syntactic check: no assignments to public variables are allowed in secret context. Denning and Denning do not discuss soundness, but Volpano et al. [26] show soundness by proving *termination-insensitive noninterference*, when they cast Denning and Denning's analysis as a security type system. Termination-insensitive noninterference guarantees that starting with two initial memories that agree on public data, two terminating runs of a

A. Pnueli, I. Virbitskaite, and A. Voronkov (Eds.): PSI 2009, LNCS 5947, pp. 352–365, 2010.
© Springer-Verlag Berlin Heidelberg 2010

program result in final memories that also agree on public data. Denning-style analysis is by now the core for the information-flow tools Jif [14], FlowCaml [21], and the SPARK Examiner [4, 7].

The 90's see the domination of static techniques for information flow [18]. The common wisdom appears to be that dynamic approaches are not a good match for security since monitoring a single path misses public side effects that could have happened in other paths [18].

Dynamic techniques for information flow are on the rise again [24, 13, 20, 12, 23] driven by the need for permissiveness in today's dynamic applications. But they still involve nontrivial static checks for leaks related to control flow.

In this light, it might be surprising that it is possible for purely dynamic enforcement to be *as secure as Denning-style static analysis*. The key factor is termination. Program constructs introduce *channels* for information transfer (recall the explicit and implicit flows above that correspond to channels via assignments and branching). The termination channel is introduced by loops: by observing the termination of program while *secret* do skip, the attacker learns that *secret* was 0. Denning-style static analyses are typically termination-insensitive. They ignore leaks via the termination behavior of programs. Thus, they satisfy termination-insensitive noninterference [26], as previously mentioned. Monitors supervise the execution of programs to guarantee security properties. Executed instructions are first analyzed by the monitor to determine if they are safe to run. In the presence of unsafe instructions, monitors can take several countermeasures: block the execution of programs or transform the unsafe instruction into a safe one. If the monitor can introduce nontermination by blocking the underlying program, this feature can be used for collapsing high-bandwidth information channels into low-bandwidth ones. Turning the high-bandwidth implicit-flow channel into the low-bandwidth termination channel is one example: blocking the execution at an attempt of a public assignment in secret context (note the similarities to the techniques from the 70's!) is in fact sufficient for termination-insensitive security.

This paper demonstrates the above insight for a simple imperative language. We present a Denning-style static analysis in the form of a security type system by Volpano et al. [26] and a simple monitor. We show that a monitor is strictly more permissive than the type system, and both the type system and the monitor satisfy termination-insensitive noninterference.

Sections 2–5 consider a batch-job model: programs run until completion before the produce a result (which is the final memory). Termination-insensitive noninterference [26] for batch-job programs simply ignores diverging runs. However, Section 6 generalizes our results to a language with output, a natural extension [1] of the type system by Volpano et al. [26] with output, and *progress-insensitive* noninterference [1], a generalization of termination-insensitive noninterference to reason about programs with output, which does not ignore diverging runs, but ignores (the lack of) progress at each step.

2 Semantics

Figure 1 presents the semantics for a simple imperative language. Configurations have the form $\langle c, m \rangle$, where c is a *command* and m is a *memory* mapping variables to values.

$$\langle \text{skip}, m \rangle \xrightarrow{nop} \langle stop, m \rangle \qquad \frac{m(e) = v}{\langle x := e, m \rangle \xrightarrow{a(x,e)} \langle stop, m[x \mapsto v] \rangle}$$

$$\frac{\langle c_1, m \rangle \xrightarrow{\alpha} \langle stop, m' \rangle}{\langle c_1; c_2, m \rangle \xrightarrow{\alpha} \langle c_2, m' \rangle} \qquad \frac{\langle c_1, m \rangle \xrightarrow{\alpha} \langle c_1', m' \rangle \quad c_1' \neq stop}{\langle c_1; c_2, m \rangle \xrightarrow{\alpha} \langle c_1'; c_2, m' \rangle}$$

$$\frac{m(e) \neq 0}{\langle \text{if } e \text{ then } c_1 \text{ else } c_2, m \rangle \xrightarrow{b(e)} \langle c_1; end, m \rangle} \qquad \frac{m(e) = 0}{\langle \text{if } e \text{ then } c_1 \text{ else } c_2, m \rangle \xrightarrow{b(e)} \langle c_2; end, m \rangle}$$

$$\frac{m(e) \neq 0}{\langle \text{while } e \text{ do } c, m \rangle \xrightarrow{b(e)} \langle c; end; \text{while } e \text{ do } c, m \rangle} \qquad \frac{m(e) = 0}{\langle \text{while } e \text{ do } c, m \rangle \xrightarrow{b(e)} \langle end, m \rangle}$$

$$\langle end, m \rangle \xrightarrow{f} \langle stop, m \rangle$$

Fig. 1. Command semantics

Semantic rules have the form $\langle c, m \rangle \xrightarrow{\alpha} \langle c', m' \rangle$, which corresponds to a small step between configurations. If a transition leads to a configuration with the special command *stop* and some memory m, then we say the execution *terminates* in m. Observe that there are no transitions triggered by *stop*. The special command *end* signifies exiting the scope of an if or a while. Observe that *end* is executed after the branches of those commands. Commands *stop* and *end* can be generated during execution of programs but they are not used in initial configurations, i.e., they are not accessible to programmers. For simplicity, we consider simple integer expressions in our language (i.e., constants, binary operations, and variables). The semantics for expressions is then standard and thus we omit it here. We note the result of evaluating expression e under memory m as $m(e)$. The semantics are decorated with *events* α for communicating program events to an execution monitor. Event *nop* signals that the program performs a skip. Event $a(x, e)$ records that the program assigns the value of e in the current memory to variable x. Event $b(e)$ indicates that the program branches on expression e. Finally, event f is generated when the structure block of a conditional or loop has finished evaluation.

Assume $cfg, cfg', \ldots$ range over command configurations and $cfgm, cfgm', \ldots$ range over monitor configurations. For this work, it is enough to think of monitor configurations as simple stacks of security levels (see below). The semantics are parametric in the monitor μ, which is assumed to be described by transitions between monitor configurations in the form $cfgm \xrightarrow{\alpha}_\mu cfgm'$. The rule for monitored execution is:

$$\frac{cfg \xrightarrow{\alpha} cfg' \quad cfgm \xrightarrow{\alpha}_\mu cfgm'}{\langle cfg \mid_\mu cfgm \rangle \longrightarrow \langle cfg' \mid_\mu cfgm' \rangle}$$

The simplest example of a monitor is an all-accepting monitor μ_0, which is defined by $\epsilon \xrightarrow{\alpha}_{\mu_0} \epsilon$, where ϵ is its only state (the empty stack). This monitor indeed accepts all events α in the underlying program.

$$pc \vdash \texttt{skip} \qquad \frac{lev(e) \sqsubseteq \Gamma(x) \qquad pc \sqsubseteq \Gamma(x)}{pc \vdash x := e} \qquad \frac{pc \vdash c_1 \qquad pc \vdash c_2}{pc \vdash c_1; c_2}$$

$$\frac{lev(e) \sqcup pc \vdash c_1 \qquad lev(e) \sqcup pc \vdash c_2}{pc \vdash \texttt{if } e \texttt{ then } c_1 \texttt{ else } c_2} \qquad \frac{lev(e) \sqcup pc \vdash c}{pc \vdash \texttt{while } e \texttt{ do } c}$$

Fig. 2. Typing rules

$$st \xrightarrow{nop} st \qquad \frac{lev(e) \sqsubseteq \Gamma(x) \qquad lev(st) \sqsubseteq \Gamma(x)}{st \xrightarrow{a(x,e)} st} \qquad st \xrightarrow{b(e)} lev(e) : st \qquad hd : st \xrightarrow{f} st$$

Fig. 3. Monitoring rules

3 Type System

Figure 2 displays a Denning-style static analysis in the form of a security type system by Volpano et al. [26]. Typing environment Γ maps variables to security levels in a security lattice. For simplicity, we assume a security lattice with two levels L and H for low (public) and high (secret) security, where $L \sqsubseteq H$. Function $lev(e)$ returns H if there is a high variable in e and otherwise returns L. Typing judgment for commands has the form $pc \vdash c$, where pc is a security level known as the *program counter* that keeps track of the context. Explicit flows (as in $l := h$) are prevented by the typing rule for assignment that disallows assignments of high expressions to low variables. Implicit flows (as in $\texttt{if } h \texttt{ then } l := 1 \texttt{ else } l := 0$) are prevented by the pc mechanism. It demands that when branching on a high expression, the branches must be typed under high pc, which prevents assignments to low variables in the branches.

4 Monitor

Figure 3 presents monitor μ_1 (we omit the subscript μ_1 in the transition rules for clarity). The monitor either accepts an event generated by the program or blocks it by getting stuck. The monitor configuration st is a stack of security levels, intended to keep track of the current security context: the security levels of the guards of conditionals and loops whose body the computation currently visits. This is a dynamic version of the pc from the previous section. Event nop (that originates from a $\texttt{skip}$) is always accepted without changes in the monitor state. Event $a(x, e)$ (that originates from an assignment) is accepted without changes in the monitor state but with two conditions: (i) that the security level of expression e is no greater than the security level of variable x and (ii) that the highest security level in the context stack (denoted $lev(st)$ for a stack st) is no greater than the security level of variable x. The former prevents *explicit* flows of the form $l := h$, whereas the latter prevents implicit flows of the form $\texttt{if } h \texttt{ then } l := 1 \texttt{ else } l := 0$, where depending on the high guard, the execution of the program leads to different low events.

Events $b(e)$ result in pushing the security level of e onto the stack of the monitor. This is a part of implicit-flow prevention: runs of program if h then $l := 1$ else $l := 0$ are blocked before performing an assignment l because the level of the stack is high when reaching the execution of the assignment. The stack structure avoids overrestrictive enforcement. For example, runs of program (if h then $h := 1$ else $h := 0$); $l := 1$ are allowed. This is because by the time the assignment to l is reached, the execution has left the high context: the high security level has been popped from the stack in response to event f, which the program generates on exiting the if.

We have seen that runs of programs like if h then $l := 1$ else $l := 0$ are rejected by the monitor. But what about a program like if h then $l := 1$ else skip, a common example for illustrating that dynamic information-flow enforcement is delicate? If h is nonzero, the monitor blocks the execution. However, if h is 0, the program proceeds normally. Are we accepting an insecure program? It turns out that the slight difference between unmonitored and monitored runs (blocking in case h is nonzero) is sufficient for termination-insensitive security. In effect, the monitor prevents implicit flows by *collapsing the implicit-flow channel into the termination channel*; it does not introduce any more bandwidth than what the termination channel already permits. Indeed, implicit flows in unmonitored runs can be magnified by a loop so that secrets can be leaked bit-by-bit in linear time in the size of the secret. On the other hand, implicit flows in monitored runs cannot be magnified because execution is blocked whenever it attempts entering a branch with a public side effect. For example, one implication for uniformly-distributed secrets is that they cannot be leaked on the termination channel in polynomial time [1].

5   Results

This section presents the formal results. We assume μ_0 is the monitor that accepts all program events, and μ_1 is the monitor from Section 4. First, we show that the monitor μ_1 is strictly more permissive than the type system. If a program is typable, then all of its runs are not modified by the monitor.

Theorem 1. *If* $pc \vdash c$ *and* $\langle\langle c, m \rangle |_{\mu_0} \epsilon\rangle \longrightarrow^* \langle\langle c', m' \rangle |_{\mu_0} \epsilon\rangle$, *then* $\langle\langle c, m \rangle |_{\mu_1} \epsilon\rangle \longrightarrow^* \langle\langle c', m' \rangle |_{\mu_1} st'\rangle$.

Proof. We prove a generalization of the theorem (see the appendix). Intuitively, the theorem holds because (i) the requirements for assignments in the type system and the monitor μ_1 are essentially the same; and (ii) there is a tight relation between the join operations for pc and pushing security levels on the stack st.   □

Further, there are programs (e.g., if $l > l$ then $l := h$ else skip) whose runs are always accepted by the monitor, but which are rejected by the type system. Hence, the monitor is strictly more permissive than the type system.

We now show that both the type system and monitor enforce the same security condition: termination-insensitive noninterference [26]. Two memories m_1 and m_2 are *low-equal* (written $m_1 =_L m_2$) if they agree on the low variables. Termination-insensitive noninterference demands that starting with two low-equal initial memories, two terminating runs of a typable program result in low-equal final memories.

$$\frac{m(e) = v}{\langle \text{output}(e), m \rangle \xrightarrow{o(e)}_v \langle \text{stop}, m \rangle} \qquad \frac{lev(e) \sqcup pc \sqsubseteq L}{pc \vdash \text{output}(e)} \qquad \frac{lev(e) \sqcup st \sqsubseteq L}{st \xrightarrow{o(e)} st}$$

Fig. 4. Semantics, typing, and monitoring rules for outputs

Theorem 2. *If* $pc \vdash c$, *then for all* m_1 *and* m_2, *where* $m_1 =_L m_2$, *whenever we have* $\langle\langle c, m_1 \rangle |_{\mu_0} \epsilon \rangle \longrightarrow^* \langle\langle \text{stop}, m_1' \rangle |_{\mu_0} \epsilon \rangle$ *and* $\langle\langle c, m_2 \rangle |_{\mu_0} \epsilon \rangle \longrightarrow^* \langle\langle \text{stop}, m_2' \rangle |_{\mu_0} \epsilon \rangle$, *then* $m_1' =_L m_2'$.

Proof. By adjusting the soundness proof by Volpano et al. [26] (see the appendix). □

Termination-insensitive noninterference also holds for the runs monitored by the monitor from Section 4:

Theorem 3. *For all* m_1 *and* m_2, *where* $m_1 =_L m_2$, *whenever* c *contains no end commands and* $\langle\langle c, m_1 \rangle |_{\mu_1} \epsilon \rangle \longrightarrow^* \langle\langle \text{stop}, m_1' \rangle |_{\mu_1} st_1' \rangle$ *and* $\langle\langle c, m_2 \rangle |_{\mu_1} \epsilon \rangle \longrightarrow^* \langle\langle \text{stop}, m_2' \rangle |_{\mu_1} st_2' \rangle$, *then* $m_1' =_L m_2'$.

Proof. By induction on $\longrightarrow^*$. The details can be found in the appendix. □

6 Incorporating Output into the Language

This section introduces outputs to the language. For simplicity, we only consider public outputs. The semantics, typing, and monitoring rules for outputs are described in Figure 4. Command $\text{output}(e)$ outputs the value of expression e on a public channel. Semantically, configurations might now trigger *externally observable* events with an additional label (v) indicating an output value. Public outputs can be considered as special assignments to low variables. In this light, the typing and monitor rules (adapted from [1] and [2], respectively) for this command are similar to the ones applied when modifying low variables. Event $o(e)$ conveys information that expression e is output by the program. Monitored configurations need to be adapted to synchronize with output events. Formally, a monitor transition $\langle cfg |_\mu cfgm \rangle \longrightarrow_\gamma \langle cfg' |_\mu cfgm' \rangle$ is possible if the program and monitor transitions $cfg \xrightarrow{\alpha}_\gamma cfg'$ and $cfgm \xrightarrow{\alpha}_\mu cfgm'$ are also possible. Event α can be $o(e)$ or any of the events described in Section 4. Event γ stands for an externally observable event: it can be an output (v) or an empty event (ϵ).

We present the adaptation of Theorems 1–3 for a language with outputs (proved in an accompanying technical report [19]). The next theorem looks the same as Theorem 1 except for the presence of a vector of output events ($\vec{\gamma}$).

Theorem 4. *If* $pc \vdash c$ *and* $\langle\langle c, m \rangle |_{\mu_0} \epsilon \rangle \longrightarrow_{\vec{\gamma}}^* \langle\langle c', m' \rangle |_{\mu_0} \epsilon \rangle$, *then there exists* st' *such that* $\langle\langle c, m \rangle |_{\mu_1} \epsilon \rangle \longrightarrow_{\vec{\gamma}}^* \langle\langle c', m' \rangle |_{\mu_1} st' \rangle$.

As before, there are programs (e.g., `if` $l > l$ `then` $l := h$ `else skip`) whose runs are always accepted by the monitor, but which are rejected by the type system. Hence, the monitor for the extended language is strictly more permissive than the extended type system.

As explained in Section 1, Sections 2–5 consider a batch-job model: programs run until completion before the produce a result (which is the final memory). Termination-insensitive noninterference [26] for batch-job programs simply ignores diverging runs. This condition is not appropriate for reasoning about programs with output since a program that outputs a secret and then diverges would be accepted by the condition [3, 1]. Thus, the security condition guarantee for the extended type system establishes *progress-insensitive* noninterference [1], a generalization of termination-insensitive noninterference to reason about programs with output, which does not ignore diverging runs, but ignores (the lack of) progress at each step. We show that given two low-equivalent initial memories, and the two sequences of outputs generated by monitored executions in these memories, then either the sequences are the same or one of them is a prefix of the other, in which case the execution that generates the shorter sequence produces no further public output events. Formally:

Theorem 5. *If* $pc \vdash c$, *then for all* m_1 *and* m_2, *where* $m_1 =_L m_2$, *whenever we have* $\langle\langle c, m_1 \rangle |_{\mu_0} \epsilon\rangle \longrightarrow_{\vec{\gamma_1}}^* \langle\langle stop, m_1' \rangle |_{\mu_0} st_1'\rangle$, *then there exists* c', m_2', st_2', $\vec{\gamma_2}$ *such that* $\langle\langle c, m_2 \rangle |_{\mu_0} \epsilon\rangle \longrightarrow_{\vec{\gamma_2}}^* \langle\langle c', m_2' \rangle |_{\mu_0} st_2'\rangle$ *where* $|\vec{\gamma_2}| \leq |\vec{\gamma_1}|$, *and*

a) *If* $|\vec{\gamma_2}| = |\vec{\gamma_1}|$, *then* $\vec{\gamma_1} = \vec{\gamma_2}$.
b) *If* $|\vec{\gamma_2}| < |\vec{\gamma_1}|$, *then* $prefix(\vec{\gamma_2}, \vec{\gamma_1})$ *holds and* $\langle\langle c', m_2' \rangle |_{\mu_0} st'\rangle \Rightarrow_H$.

The number of events in $\vec{\gamma}$ is denoted by $|\vec{\gamma}|$. We also define predicate $prefix(\vec{x}, \vec{y})$ to hold when list $\vec{x}$ is a prefix of list $\vec{y}$. We write $\langle\langle c, m\rangle |_\mu cfgm\rangle \Rightarrow_H$ to denote a monitored execution that does not produce any public output. Generalized termination-insensitive noninterference also holds for the extended monitor. More precisely, we have the following theorem.

Theorem 6. *For all* m_1 *and* m_2, *where* $m_1 =_L m_2$, *whenever* c *contains no end commands and* $\langle\langle c, m_1 \rangle |_{\mu_1} \epsilon\rangle \longrightarrow_{\vec{\gamma_1}}^* \langle\langle stop, m_1' \rangle |_{\mu_1} st_1'\rangle$ *then there exists* c', m_2', st_2', $\vec{\gamma_2}$ *such that* $\langle\langle c, m_2 \rangle |_{\mu_1} \epsilon\rangle \longrightarrow_{\vec{\gamma_2}}^* \langle\langle c', m_2' \rangle |_{\mu_1} st_2'\rangle$ *where* $|\vec{\gamma_2}| \leq |\vec{\gamma_1}|$, *and*

a) *If* $|\vec{\gamma_2}| = |\vec{\gamma_1}|$, *then* $\vec{\gamma_1} = \vec{\gamma_2}$.
b) *If* $|\vec{\gamma_2}| < |\vec{\gamma_1}|$, *then* $prefix(\vec{\gamma_2}, \vec{\gamma_1})$ *holds and* $\langle\langle c', m_2' \rangle |_{\mu_1} st_2'\rangle \Rightarrow_H$.

The proofs of the above two theorems are by adjusting the soundness proofs from [1] and [2], respectively, to model that attacker that does not observe changes in low memories, but only observes public output.

7 Discussion

On joint points The monitor critically relies on the joint-point information for each branching point (in conditionals in loops). This allows the monitor to discover that the execution has left a secret context, and relax restrictions on assignment to public variables. When branching, the command *end* is inserted at the joint point by the semantics in Figure 1. At the time of execution, *end* communicates information that a joint point has been reached to the monitor.

In a more complex language, we would expect the interpreter/compiler to extract the information about joint points from the scopes in the program text. This might be natural in a structured language. We remark, however, that in a low-level languages, or in a language with breaks and continues, this might require a separate static analysis.

On flow sensitivity Another point to emphasize is regarding *flow sensitivity*, i.e., possibility for variables to store values of different sensitivity (low and high) over the course of computation. Although it might be against the intuition, if we consider a *flow-sensitive* type system [11], then it is actually impossible to have a purely dynamic sound mechanism that is more precise than the type system. We give the formal details in a separate paper [16], and illustrate the issue with an example (similar examples have been discussed in the literature [23, 6]). In the program in Figure 5, assume *secret* is a high variable containing a boolean secret (either 0 or 1). Imagine a simple purely dynamic monitor that keeps track of security levels of variables and updates them on each assignment in the following way. The monitor sets the level of the assigned variable to high in case there is a high variable on the right-hand side of the assignment or in case the assignment appears inside of a high context. The level of the variable is set to low in case there are no high variables in the right-hand side of the assignment and the assignment does not appear in high context. Otherwise, the monitor does not update the the level of the assigned variable. This is a straightforward extension of the monitor from Section 4 with flow sensitivity.

$$public := 1; temp := 0;$$
$$\texttt{if } secret \texttt{ then } temp := 1;$$
$$\texttt{if } temp \neq 1 \texttt{ then } public := 0$$

Fig. 5. Example

This monitor labels *public* and *temp* as low after the first two assignments because the variables receive low information (constants). If *secret* is nonzero, variable *temp* becomes high after the first conditional. In this case the guard in the second conditional is false, and so the then branch with the assignment *public* := 0 is not taken. Therefore, the monitor allows this execution. If *secret* is zero, then *temp* is not relabeled to high, and so the second if is also allowed by the monitor even though the then branch is taken: because it branches on an expression that does not involve high variables. As a result, the value of *secret* is leaked into *public*, which is missed by the monitor.

This illustrates that flow sensitivity introduces a channel that poses a challenge for purely dynamic enforcement.

8 Related Work

Fenton [9] presents a monitor that takes into account program structure. It keeps track of the security context stack, similarly to ours. However, Fenton does not discuss soundness with respect to noninterference-like properties. Volpano [24] considers a monitor that only checks explicit flows. Implicit flows are allowed, and therefore the monitor does not enforce noninterference. Boudol [5] revisits Fenton's work and observes that the intended security policy "no security error" corresponds to a safety property, which is stronger than noninterference. Boudol shows how to enforce this safety property with a type system.

Mechanisms by Venkatakrishnan et al. [22], Le Guernic et al. [13, 12], and Shroff et al. [20] combine dynamic and static checks. They have a number of attractive features, for example, the mechanism by Le Guernic et al. [13, 12] is flow-sensitive: security levels of variables may change during the program execution. We take a deeper look at the impact of flow sensitivity on the trade off between static and dynamic information-flow enforcement in a separate paper [16] (cf. discussion in Section 7).

Tracking information flow in web applications is becoming increasingly important (e.g., recent highlights are a server-side mechanism by Huang et al. [10] and a client-side mechanism for JavaScript by Vogt et al. [23], although they do not discuss soundness). Dynamism of web applications puts higher demands on the permissiveness of the security mechanism: hence the importance of dynamic analysis.

Yet, all the mechanisms from the above two paragraphs involve nontrivial static analysis for side effects in conditionals and loops, whereas our proof-of-concept monitor is purely dynamic.

The monitor presented here is at core of (i) the termination-insensitive part of the enforcement of information-release (or *declassification*) policies by Askarov and Sabelfeld [2] for a language with dynamic code evaluation and communication and (ii) the monitor by Russo and Sabelfeld [17] to secure programs with timeout instructions.

9   Concluding Remarks

When it comes to information-flow tracking, static techniques have benefits of reducing runtime overhead, and dynamic techniques have the benefits of permissiveness (this, for example, is of particular importance in dynamic applications, where freshly generated code is evaluated). But on the security side, we have demonstrated that both Denning-style analysis and dynamic enforcement have the same guarantees: termination-insensitive noninterference. Another way to interpret the result is that neither Denning-style analysis nor termination-insensitive noninterference itself offer strong guarantees (as also hinted in previous findings [1]).

However, when *termination-sensitive* noninterference is desired, the absence of side effects of traces not taken is hard to ensure dynamically.

But which policy should be the one of choice, termination-insensitive noninterference or termination-sensitive noninterference? Termination-sensitive noninterference is attractive, but rather difficult to guarantee. Typically, strong restrictions (such as no loops with secret guards [25]) are enforced. Program errors exacerbate the problem. Even in languages like Agda [15], where it is impossible to write nonterminating programs, it is possible to write programs that terminate abnormally: for example, with a stack overflow. Generally, abnormal termination due to resource exhaustion, is a channel for leaks that can be hard to counter.

As mentioned earlier, the information-flow tools Jif [14], FlowCaml [21], and the SPARK Examiner [4, 7] avoid these problems by targeting termination-insensitive noninterference. The price is that the attacker may leak secrets by brute-force attacks via the termination channel. But there is formal assurance that these are the only possible attacks. Askarov et al. [1] show that if a program satisfies termination-insensitive noninterference, then the attacker may not learn the secret in polynomial running time in the size of the secret; and, for uniformly-distributed secrets, the probability of guessing the secret in polynomial running time is negligible.

Acknowledgments. Thanks are due to Gurvan Le Guernic and Rustan Leino for the interesting discussions. This work was funded by the Swedish research agencies SSF and VR.

References

[1] Askarov, A., Hunt, S., Sabelfeld, A., Sands, D.: Termination-insensitive noninterference leaks more than just a bit. In: Jajodia, S., Lopez, J. (eds.) ESORICS 2008. LNCS, vol. 5283, pp. 333–348. Springer, Heidelberg (2008)

[2] Askarov, A., Sabelfeld, A.: Tight enforcement of information-release policies for dynamic languages. In: Proc. IEEE Computer Security Foundations Symposium (July 2009)

[3] Banerjee, A., Naumann, D., Rosenberg, S.: Expressive declassification policies and modular static enforcement. In: Proc. IEEE Symp. on Security and Privacy (May 2008)

[4] Barnes, J., Barnes, J.: High Integrity Software: The SPARK Approach to Safety and Security. Addison-Wesley Longman Publishing Co., Inc., Boston (2003)

[5] Boudol, G.: Secure information flow as a safety property. In: Degano, P., Guttman, J., Martinelli, F. (eds.) FAST 2008. LNCS, vol. 5491, pp. 20–34. Springer, Heidelberg (2009)

[6] Cavallaro, L., Saxena, P., Sekar, R.: On the limits of information flow techniques for malware analysis and containment. In: Zamboni, D. (ed.) DIMVA 2008. LNCS, vol. 5137, pp. 143–163. Springer, Heidelberg (2008)

[7] Chapman, R., Hilton, A.: Enforcing security and safety models with an information flow analysis tool. ACM SIGAda Ada Letters 24(4), 39–46 (2004)

[8] Denning, D.E., Denning, P.J.: Certification of programs for secure information flow. Comm. of the ACM 20(7), 504–513 (1977)

[9] Fenton, J.S.: Memoryless subsystems. Computing J. 17(2), 143–147 (1974)

[10] Huang, Y.-W., Yu, F., Hang, C., Tsai, C.-H., Lee, D.-T., Kuo, S.-Y.: Securing web application code by static analysis and runtime protection. In: Proc. International Conference on World Wide Web, May 2004, pp. 40–52 (2004)

[11] Hunt, S., Sands, D.: On flow-sensitive security types. In: Proc. ACM Symp. on Principles of Programming Languages, pp. 79–90 (2006)

[12] Le Guernic, G.: Automaton-based confidentiality monitoring of concurrent programs. In: Proc. IEEE Computer Security Foundations Symposium, July 2007, pp. 218–232 (2007)

[13] Le Guernic, G., Banerjee, A., Jensen, T., Schmidt, D.: Automata-based confidentiality monitoring. In: Okada, M., Satoh, I. (eds.) ASIAN 2006. LNCS, vol. 4435, pp. 75–89. Springer, Heidelberg (2008)

[14] Myers, A.C., Zheng, L., Zdancewic, S., Chong, S., Nystrom, N.: Jif: Java information flow. Software release (July 2001), http://www.cs.cornell.edu/jif

[15] Norell, U.: Towards a practical programming language based on dependent type theory. PhD thesis, Department of Computer Science and Engineering, Chalmers University of Technology, SE-412 96 Göteborg, Sweden (September 2007)

[16] Russo, A., Sabelfeld, A.: Dynamic vs. static flow-sensitive security analysis (April 2009) (Draft)

[17] Russo, A., Sabelfeld, A.: Securing timeout instructions in web applications. In: Proc. IEEE Computer Security Foundations Symposium (July 2009)

[18] Sabelfeld, A., Myers, A.C.: Language-based information-flow security. IEEE J. Selected Areas in Communications 21(1), 5–19 (2003)

[19] Sabelfeld, A., Russo, A.: From dynamic to static and back: Riding the roller coaster of information-flow control research (full version) (2009), http://www.cse.chalmers.se/~russo/

[20] Shroff, P., Smith, S., Thober, M.: Dynamic dependency monitoring to secure information flow. In: Proc. IEEE Computer Security Foundations Symposium, July 2007, pp. 203–217 (2007)

[21] Simonet, V.: The Flow Caml system. Software release (July 2003),
   http://cristal.inria.fr/~simonet/soft/flowcaml

[22] Venkatakrishnan, V.N., Xu, W., DuVarney, D.C., Sekar, R.: Provably correct runtime enforcement of non-interference properties. In: Ning, P., Qing, S., Li, N. (eds.) ICICS 2006.
   LNCS, vol. 4307, pp. 332–351. Springer, Heidelberg (2006)

[23] Vogt, P., Nentwich, F., Jovanovic, N., Kirda, E., Kruegel, C., Vigna, G.: Cross-site scripting
   prevention with dynamic data tainting and static analysis. In: Proc. Network and Distributed
   System Security Symposium (February 2007)

[24] Volpano, D.: Safety versus secrecy. In: Cortesi, A., Filé, G. (eds.) SAS 1999. LNCS,
   vol. 1694, pp. 303–311. Springer, Heidelberg (1999)

[25] Volpano, D., Smith, G.: Eliminating covert flows with minimum typings. In: Proc. IEEE
   Computer Security Foundations Workshop, June 1997, pp. 156–168 (1997)

[26] Volpano, D., Smith, G., Irvine, C.: A sound type system for secure flow analysis. J. Computer Security 4(3), 167–187 (1996)

A Appendix

Before proving the theorems described in body of the paper, we need to introduce some
auxiliary lemmas. We describe the most important ones here. We start by showing lemmas related to sequential composition of monitored executions.

Lemma 1. *If* $\langle\langle c, m\rangle \mid_\mu st\rangle \longrightarrow^* \langle\langle stop, m'\rangle \mid_\mu st'\rangle$, *then* $st = st'$, *where* $\mu \in \{\mu_0, \mu_1\}$.

Lemma 2. *Given that* $stop; c'$ *denotes* c', *if* $\langle\langle c_1, m\rangle \mid_\mu st\rangle \longrightarrow^* \langle\langle c', m'\rangle \mid_\mu st'\rangle$, *then*
$\langle\langle c_1; c_2, m\rangle \mid_\mu st\rangle \longrightarrow^* \langle\langle c'; c_2, m'\rangle \mid_\mu st'\rangle$, *where* $\mu \in \{\mu_0, \mu_1\}$.

Lemma 3. *If* $\langle\langle c_1; c_2, m\rangle \mid_\mu st\rangle \longrightarrow^* \langle\langle c', m'\rangle \mid_\mu st'\rangle$ *and* c_1 *contains no end instructions, then there exists* c^*, m'', *and* st^* *such that* $c' = c^*; c_2$ *and* $\langle\langle c_1, m\rangle \mid_\mu st\rangle \longrightarrow^*$
$\langle\langle c^*, m'\rangle \mid_\mu st^*\rangle$; *or* $\langle\langle c_1, m\rangle \mid_\mu st\rangle \longrightarrow^* \langle\langle stop, m''\rangle \mid_\mu st\rangle$ *and* $\langle\langle c_2, m''\rangle \mid_\mu st\rangle \longrightarrow^*$
$\langle\langle c', m'\rangle \mid_\mu st'\rangle$, *where* $\mu \in \{\mu_0, \mu_1\}$.

These lemmas can be proved by a simple induction on $\longrightarrow^*$. Before proving Theorem
1, we prove a generalization of it described in the following lemma.

Lemma 4. *If* $pc \vdash c$, $\langle\langle c, m\rangle \mid_{\mu_0} \epsilon\rangle \longrightarrow^* \langle\langle c', m'\rangle \mid_{\mu_0} \epsilon\rangle$, *then it holds* $\forall\ lev(st) \sqsubseteq$
$pc \cdot \exists\ lev(st') \cdot \langle\langle c, m\rangle \mid_{\mu_1} st\rangle \longrightarrow^* \langle\langle c', m'\rangle \mid_{\mu_1} st'\rangle$.

Proof. By induction on $\longrightarrow^*$ and the number of sequential instructions in c. We only
show the most interesting cases.

$x := e$) Given a st such that $lev(st) \sqsubseteq pc$, we need to prove that exists st' such
   that $lev(st')$ and $\langle\langle x := e, m\rangle \mid_{\mu_1} st\rangle \longrightarrow \langle\langle stop, m'\rangle \mid_{\mu_1} st'\rangle$. Let's take $st' =$
   st. Then, the transition under μ_1 is possible provided that $lev(e) \sqsubseteq \Gamma(x)$ and
   $lev(st) \sqsubseteq \Gamma(x)$. By the typing rules, it holds that $lev(e) \sqsubseteq \Gamma(x)$ and $pc \sqsubseteq \Gamma(x)$.
   By these two facts, and having that $lev(st) \sqsubseteq pc$, it holds that $lev(e) \sqsubseteq \Gamma(x)$ and
   $lev(st) \sqsubseteq \Gamma(x)$.

if e **then** c_1 **else** c_2) Let's assume that $m(e) \neq 0$ (the proof follows the same structure when $m(e) = 0$). We omit the proof when $\longrightarrow_0$ since it holds trivially. By semantics, we know that

$$\langle\langle \text{if } e \text{ then } c_1 \text{ else } c_2, m\rangle \mid_{\mu_0} \epsilon\rangle \longrightarrow \langle\langle c_1; end, m\rangle \mid_{\mu_0} \epsilon\rangle \qquad (1)$$

$$\langle\langle c_1; end, m\rangle \mid_{\mu_0} \epsilon\rangle \longrightarrow^* \langle\langle c', m'\rangle \mid_{\mu_0} \epsilon\rangle \qquad (2)$$

By definition of the monitor, we know that

$$\langle\langle \text{if } e \text{ then } c_1 \text{ else } c_2, m\rangle \mid_{\mu_1} st\rangle \longrightarrow \langle\langle c_1; end, m\rangle \mid_{\mu_1} lev(e) : st\rangle \qquad (3)$$

If $\longrightarrow^*$ is $\longrightarrow_0$ in (2), the result follows from (3). Otherwise, by applying Lemma 3 on (2) and semantics, we have that there exists m'', c^*, and st^* such that
$c' = c^*; end$) In this case, we have that

$$\langle\langle c_1, m\rangle \mid_{\mu_0} \epsilon\rangle \longrightarrow^* \langle\langle c^*, m'\rangle \mid_{\mu_0} st^*\rangle \qquad (4)$$

We know that $st^* = \epsilon$ from the definition of μ_0. We apply IH on $lev(e) \sqcup pc \vdash c_1$ (obtaining from the typing rules) and (4), then we obtain that $\forall\ lev(st_1) \sqsubseteq lev(e) \sqcup pc \ \cdot\ \exists\ lev(st_1') \ \cdot\ \langle\langle c_1, m\rangle \mid_{\mu_1} st_1\rangle \longrightarrow^* \langle\langle c^*, m'\rangle \mid_{\mu_1} st_1'\rangle$. Let's instantiate this formula by taking $st_1 = lev(e) : st$. We then have that

$$\langle\langle c_1, m\rangle \mid_{\mu_1} lev(e) : st\rangle \longrightarrow^* \langle\langle c^*, m'\rangle \mid_{\mu_1} st_1'\rangle \qquad (5)$$

By Lemma 2 applied to (5) and end, we obtain $\langle\langle c_1; end, m\rangle \mid_{\mu_1} lev(e) : st\rangle \longrightarrow^* \langle\langle c', m'\rangle \mid_{\mu_1} st_1'\rangle$. The result follows from this transition and (3).
$c' \neq c^*; end$)

$$\langle\langle c_1, m\rangle \mid_{\mu_0} \epsilon\rangle \longrightarrow^* \langle\langle stop, m''\rangle \mid_{\mu_0} \epsilon\rangle \qquad (6)$$

$$\langle\langle end, m''\rangle \mid_{\mu_0} \epsilon\rangle \longrightarrow^* \langle\langle c', m'\rangle \mid_{\mu_0} \epsilon\rangle \qquad (7)$$

By IH on $lev(e) \sqcup pc \vdash c_1$ (obtaining from the typing rules) and (6), we have that $\forall\ lev(st_1) \sqsubseteq lev(e) \sqcup pc \ \cdot\ \exists\ lev(st_1') \ \cdot\ \langle\langle c_1, m\rangle \mid_{\mu_1} st_1\rangle \longrightarrow^* \langle\langle stop, m''\rangle \mid_{\mu_1} st_1'\rangle$. Let's instantiate this formula with $st_1 = lev(e) : st$. We then have that

$$\langle\langle c_1, m\rangle \mid_{\mu_1} lev(e) : st\rangle \longrightarrow^* \langle\langle stop, m''\rangle \mid_{\mu_1} st_1'\rangle \qquad (8)$$

At this point, we do not know the shape of st_1', but we can deduced it by applying the Lemma 1 to it: $st_1' = lev(e) : st$. Then, by Lemma 2 on (8) and semantics for end, we have that

$$\langle\langle c_1; end, m\rangle \mid_{\mu_1} lev(e) : st\rangle \longrightarrow^* \langle\langle end, m''\rangle \mid_{\mu_1} lev(e) : st\rangle \qquad (9)$$

In the case that $\longrightarrow^*$ is $\longrightarrow_0$ in (7), the result holds from (3) and (9). Otherwise, from semantics rules in (7), we know that $c' = stop$ and $m' = m''$. By monitor semantics, we know that

$$\langle\langle end, m''\rangle \mid_{\mu_1} lev(e) : st\rangle \longrightarrow \langle\langle stop, m''\rangle \mid_{\mu_1} st\rangle \qquad (10)$$

The result then follows from (3), (9), and (10).
while e **do** c) Similar to the previous case. $\qquad\qquad\square$

We can then prove the first theorem.

Theorem 1. *If $pc \vdash c$ and $\langle\langle c, m\rangle \mid_{\mu_0} \epsilon\rangle \longrightarrow^* \langle\langle stop, m'\rangle \mid_{\mu_0} \epsilon\rangle$, then $\langle\langle c, m\rangle \mid_{\mu_1} \epsilon\rangle \longrightarrow^*$ $\langle\langle stop, m'\rangle \mid_{\mu_1} st'\rangle$.*

Proof. By Lemma 4, we obtain that $\forall\ lev(st) \sqsubseteq pc \cdot \exists\ lev(st') \cdot \langle\langle c, m\rangle \mid_{\mu_1} st\rangle \longrightarrow^*$ $\langle\langle stop, m'\rangle \mid_{\mu_1} st'\rangle$. The result follows by instantiating the formula with $st = \epsilon$ since $lev(\epsilon) = L$. $\qquad\square$

To prove Theorem 2, we firstly prove that, for terminating programs, there is an isomorphism between the command semantics and executions under μ_0.

Lemma 5. *Given command c that contains no end instructions, $\langle c, m\rangle \longrightarrow^* \langle stop, m'\rangle$ $\Leftrightarrow \langle\langle c, m\rangle \mid_{\mu_0} \epsilon\rangle \longrightarrow^* \langle\langle stop, m'\rangle \mid_{\mu_0} \epsilon\rangle$.*

Proof. Both directions of the implication are proved by a simple induction on $\longrightarrow^*$. $\quad\square$

Now, we are in conditions to prove the mentioned Theorem.

Theorem 2. *If $pc \vdash c$, then for all m_1 and m_2, where $m_1 =_L m_2$, whenever we have $\langle\langle c, m_1\rangle \mid_{\mu_0} \epsilon\rangle \longrightarrow^* \langle\langle stop, m_1'\rangle \mid_{\mu_0} \epsilon\rangle$ and $\langle\langle c, m_2\rangle \mid_{\mu_0} \epsilon\rangle \longrightarrow^* \langle\langle stop, m_2'\rangle \mid_{\mu_0} \epsilon\rangle$, then $m_1' =_L m_2'$.*

Proof. By Lemma 5, we have that $\langle c, m_1\rangle \longrightarrow^* \langle stop, m_1'\rangle$ and $\langle c, m_2\rangle \longrightarrow^* \langle stop, m_2'\rangle$. The result follows by applying the soundness theorem from [26] to $pc \vdash c$, $\langle c, m_1\rangle \longrightarrow^*$ $\langle stop, m_1'\rangle$, and $\langle c, m_2\rangle \longrightarrow^* \langle stop, m_2'\rangle$. $\qquad\square$

We need two auxiliary lemmas in order to prove Theorem 3. They express that public variables cannot be affected when the security level of the monitor's stack is H.

Lemma 6. *If c contains no end instructions, $lev(st) = H$, and $\langle\langle c, m\rangle \mid_{\mu_1} st\rangle \longrightarrow^*$ $\langle\langle stop, m'\rangle \mid_{\mu_1} st'\rangle$, then $m =_L m'$.*

Proof. By induction on $\longrightarrow^*$. $\qquad\square$

Lemma 7. *If c contains no end instructions, and $\langle\langle \mathtt{while}\ e\ \mathtt{do}\ c, m\rangle \mid_{\mu_1} st\rangle \longrightarrow^*$ $\langle\langle stop, m'\rangle \mid_{\mu_1} st'\rangle$, then $m =_L m'$.*

Proof. By performing one small-step in the semantics and then applying Lemma 6. $\quad\square$

The next lemma is a generalization of Theorem 3.

Lemma 8. *For all m_1 and m_2, where $m_1 =_L m_2$, whenever c contains no end commands and $\langle\langle c, m_1\rangle \mid_{\mu_1} st\rangle \longrightarrow^* \langle\langle stop, m_1'\rangle \mid_{\mu_1} st_1'\rangle$ and $\langle\langle c, m_2\rangle \mid_{\mu_1} st\rangle \longrightarrow^*$ $\langle\langle stop, m_2'\rangle \mid_{\mu_1} st_2'\rangle$, then $m_1' =_L m_2'$.*

Proof. By induction on $\longrightarrow^*$. We list the most interesting cases.

if e **then** c_1 **else** c_2) We consider the case when $lev(e) = H$ and that $m_1(e) \neq m_2(e)$. Otherwise, the proof follows by simply applying IH and Lemmas 2 and 3. We assume, without loosing generality, that $m_1(e) \neq 0$. Consequently, by semantics, we have that

$$\langle\langle \text{if } e \text{ then } c_1 \text{ else } c_2, m_1\rangle \mid_{\mu_1} st\rangle \longrightarrow \langle\langle c_1; end, m_1\rangle \mid_{\mu_1} lev(e) : st\rangle \tag{11}$$

$$\langle\langle c_1; end, m_1\rangle \mid_{\mu_1} lev(e) : st\rangle \longrightarrow^* \langle\langle stop, m_1'\rangle \mid_{\mu_1} st_1'\rangle \tag{12}$$

$$\langle\langle \text{if } e \text{ then } c_1 \text{ else } c_2, m_2\rangle \mid_{\mu_1} st\rangle \longrightarrow \langle\langle c_2; end, m_2\rangle \mid_{\mu_1} lev(e) : st\rangle \tag{13}$$

$$\langle\langle c_2; end, m_2\rangle \mid_{\mu_1} lev(e) : st\rangle \longrightarrow^* \langle\langle stop, m_2'\rangle \mid_{\mu_1} st_2'\rangle \tag{14}$$

By applying Lemma 3 on (12) and (14), we have that there exists m_1'' and m_2'' such that

$$\langle\langle c_1, m_1\rangle \mid_{\mu_1} lev(e) : st\rangle \longrightarrow^* \langle\langle stop, m_1''\rangle \mid_{\mu_1} lev(e) : st\rangle \tag{15}$$

$$\langle\langle end, m_1''\rangle \mid_{\mu_1} lev(e) : st\rangle \longrightarrow^* \langle\langle stop, m_1'\rangle \mid_{\mu_1} st_1'\rangle \tag{16}$$

$$\langle\langle c_2, m_2\rangle \mid_{\mu_1} lev(e) : st\rangle \longrightarrow^* \langle\langle stop, m_2''\rangle \mid_{\mu_1} lev(e) : st\rangle \tag{17}$$

$$\langle\langle end, m_2''\rangle \mid_{\mu_1} lev(e) : st\rangle \longrightarrow^* \langle\langle stop, m_2'\rangle \mid_{\mu_1} st_2'\rangle \tag{18}$$

By applying Lemma 6 on (15) and (17), we have that $m_1'' =_L m_1 =_L m_2 =_L m_2''$. By semantics, (16), and (18), we have that $m_1' = m_1''$ and $m_2' = m_2''$. Consequently, we have that $m_1' =_L m_2'$ as expected.

while e **do** c) The proof proceeds similarly as the previous case but also applying Lemma 7 when needed. $\qquad\square$

We prove our last last theorem as follows.

Theorem 3. *For all m_1 and m_2, where $m_1 =_L m_2$, whenever c contains no end commands and $\langle\langle c, m_1\rangle \mid_{\mu_1} \epsilon\rangle \longrightarrow^* \langle\langle stop, m_1'\rangle \mid_{\mu_1} st_1'\rangle$ and $\langle\langle c, m_2\rangle \mid_{\mu_1} \epsilon\rangle \longrightarrow^* \langle\langle stop, m_2'\rangle \mid_{\mu_1} st_2'\rangle$, then $m_1' =_L m_2'$.*

Proof. By applying Lemma 8 with $st = \epsilon$. $\qquad\square$

History-Dependent Stochastic Petri Nets

Helen Schonenberg, Natalia Sidorova, Wil van der Aalst, and Kees van Hee

Eindhoven University of Technology,
Den Dolech 2, 5600 MB Eindhoven, The Netherlands
{m.h.schonenberg,n.sidorova,w.m.p.v.d.aalst,k.m.v.hee}@tue.nl

Abstract. Stochastic Petri Nets are a useful and well-known tool for performance analysis. However, an implicit assumption in the different types of Stochastic Petri Nets is the Markov property. It is assumed that a choice in the Petri net only depends on the current state and not on earlier choices. For many real-life processes, choices made in the past can influence choices made later in the process. For example, taking one more iteration in a loop might increase the probability to leave the loop, etc. In this paper, we introduce a novel framework where probability distributions depend not only on the marking of the net, but also on the history of the net. We also describe a number of typical abstraction functions for capturing relevant aspects of the net's history and show how we can discover the probabilistic mechanism from event logs, i.e. real-life observations are used to learn relevant correlations. Finally, we present how our nets can be modelled and simulated using CPN Tools and discuss the results of some simulation experiments.

1 Introduction

The use of Petri net-based models for business process modelling as workflows has become a standard practice both in academia and in industry. These models allow for both parallelism and choices, which makes them very suitable for the performance analysis of concurrent systems and for the evaluation of possible changes in the process design. To provide the information needed for the performance analysis, Petri nets are then extended with the information about the (distributions of) task durations or costs and the probabilities of choices that can be made. Stochastic Petri nets (SPN) [3,10,15] and Generalised Stochastic Petri nets (GSPN) [9,8] have become very popular due to the nice theoretical basis they provide for the analysis of systems by using Markovian techniques.

A natural question arising when people start using Stochastic Petri nets for practical applications is how to obtain a model that can be used for the analysis they want to perform. In the "easy" cases, the basic Petri net for the process is already known (e.g. the model can be given by the workflow schema running at the organisation in question), and one "only" needs to define the values of stochastic elements there. In more difficult cases, the process is also unknown, and Process Mining techniques [1] can be used to discover the model, after which the problem is in principle reduced to the "easy" case.

A. Pnueli, I. Virbitskaite, and A. Voronkov (Eds.): PSI 2009, LNCS 5947, pp. 366–379, 2010.
© Springer-Verlag Berlin Heidelberg 2010

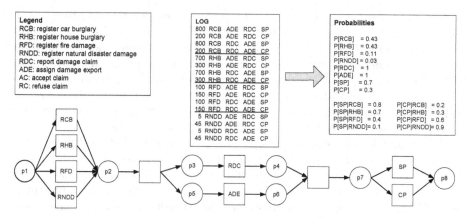

Fig. 1. Insurance claim example

A natural source of information about the process behaviour in the past is the log where the execution of the handled cases is registered. The straightforward approach for estimating probability distributions based on the log is to define distributions assuming that they do not depend on the context, i.e. assuming that the basic model to which the stochastic elements are being added has the Markov property [13]. Often, this is actually not the case.

Figure 1 gives a simplistic example of a Petri net that models the handling of claims in an insurance company and its execution log[1]. A simple procedure (SP) or a complex procedure (CP) can be chosen to handle a claim. According to the log, 70% of the cases has been handled by the simple procedure and 30% by the complex procedure. The probability overview shows a clear difference between the probability for selecting the procedure (SP or CP), given the initial claim (RCB, RHB, RFD or $RNDD$). So, it is not sufficient to increase the flood rate ($RNDD$) to estimate the performance of this process in times of severe flooding. The change should also be propagated to the associated parts of the process. The effect of increased floods is not reflected in unconditional probabilities $P(SP)$ and $P(CP)$ and their use in the model will result in wrong conclusions about the process performance. According to the logged information the number of complex procedures should increase, since complex procedures occur in 90% of cases where $RNDD$ occurred (cf. conditional probability $P(CP|RNDD)$).

In this paper we provide a Petri net extension that exibits history-dependent probability distributions, estimated from the execution log. Simulation of these nets allows a *"what if"* type of performance analysis of workflows, based on observations and correlations discovered from the log. First we investigate the problem of constructing a stochastic model for a workflow based on a given classical Petri net. Like in [13], we assume that each event recorded in the log refers to a task from the model and to the case in whose context it has been

---

[1] For sake of readability, events from the same case have been grouped into traces and equal traces have been aggregated and equipped with a counter indicating the frequency of the trace.

executed. In this paper we ignore time aspects and concentrate on probabilistic choices only. Our framework is based on the extension of classical Petri nets with the notion of global history[2] [4], i.e. we use history-dependent transition guards. We generalise it by defining a history-dependent probability mechanism for making choices. We discuss some abstractions on history that allow to reduce the process to a finite-state process (for bounded nets). Then we show how we can discover correlations between choices and estimate the history-dependent probabilistic mechanism by using the information from the log.

The remainder of the paper is organised as follows. In Section 2 we provide some basic definitions. In Section 3 we introduce History-Dependent Stochastic Petri nets (HDSPNs) and describe techniques for the estimation of history-dependent probabilities. In Section 4 we show how HDSPNs can be represented in CPN Tools and discuss some simulation experiments. Section 5 concludes the paper by discussing directions for future work.

2   Preliminaries

$\mathbb{N}$ denotes the set of natural numbers. Let P be a set. A *bag (multiset)* m over P is a mapping $m : P \to \mathbb{N}$, with $dom(m) = P$. We identify a bag with all elements occurring only once with the set containing the elements of the bag. The set of all bags over P is denoted by $\mathbb{N}^P$. We use $+$ and $-$ for the sum and the difference of two bags and $=, <, >, \leq$ and $\geq$ for the comparison of bags, which are defined in the standard way. We overload the set notation, writing $\emptyset$ for the empty bag and $\in$ for the element inclusion. We write e.g. $m = 2[p] + [q]$ for a bag m with $m(p) = 2$, $m(q) = 1$, and $m(x) = 0$ for all $x \notin \{p, q\}$. As usual, $|m|$ and $|S|$ stand for the number of elements in bag m and in set S, respectively.

For (finite) *sequences* of elements over a set P we use the following notation: The empty sequence is denoted with ϵ; a non-empty sequence can be given by listing its elements. The concatenation $\sigma; s$ of sequence $\sigma = \langle a_1, a_2, \ldots, a_n \rangle$ with element s is the sequence $\langle a_1, a_2, \ldots, a_n, s \rangle$, and the concatenation $\sigma; \gamma$ of σ with sequence $\gamma = \langle b_1, b_2, \ldots, b_n \rangle$ is the sequence $\langle a_1, a_2, \ldots, a_n, b_1, b_2, \ldots, b_n \rangle$.

The characteristic function $\mathcal{X}$ is defined as usual, i.e. $\mathcal{X} : \{\text{false}, \text{true}\} \to \{0, 1\}$ with $\mathcal{X}(\text{false}) = 0$ and $\mathcal{X}(\text{true}) = 1$.

2.1   Petri nets

Definition 1 (Petri net). *A Petri net N is a tuple $\langle P, T, F \rangle$, where: (1) P and T are two disjoint non-empty finite sets of* places *and* transitions *respectively; we call the elements of the set $P \cup T$* nodes *of N; (2) $F : (P \times T) \cup (T \times P) \to \mathbb{N}$ is a* flow relation *mapping pairs of places and transitions to the naturals.*

We present nets with the usual graphical notation. For any pair of nodes x, y with $F(x, y) \geq 1$, we say that (x, y) is an arc with *weight* $F(x, y)$.

---

[2] In many practical cases, like workflow engines, the global history is available in a log.

Given a transition $t \in T$, the *preset* $^\bullet t$ and the *postset* $t^\bullet$ of t are the *bags* of places where every $p \in P$ occurs $F(p, t)$ times in $^\bullet t$ and $F(t, p)$ times in $t^\bullet$. Analogously we write $^\bullet p, p^\bullet$ for pre- and postsets of places.

A marking m of N is a bag over P; markings are states (configurations) of a net. A pair (N, m) is called a *marked* Petri net. A transition $t \in T$ is *enabled* in marking m if and only if $^\bullet t \leq m$. An enabled transition t may *fire*. This results in a new marking m' defined by $m' = m - {}^\bullet t + t^\bullet$. A marking is called dead if there are no enabled transitions for this marking.

Definition 2 (Incidence matrix). *Let N be the set $\langle P, T, F \rangle$. The incidence matrix $\mathbf{N} : (P \times T) \to \mathbb{Z}$ of N is defined by $\mathbf{N}(p, t) = F(t, p) - F(p, t)$.*

Definition 3 (Parikh Vector). *Let $\langle P, T, F \rangle$ be a net and σ be a finite sequence of transitions. The Parikh vector $\vec{\sigma} : T \to \mathbb{N}$ of σ maps every transition t of T to the number of occurrences of t in σ.*

We will use the following well-known lemma:

Lemma 1 (Marking Equation). *Let $N = \langle P, T, F \rangle$ be a Petri net with the incidence matrix $\mathbf{N}$. Given a finite firing sequence $\sigma \in T^*$ in N leading from a marking m to a marking m', the following equation holds: $m' = m + \mathbf{N} \cdot \vec{\sigma}$.*

A class of particular practical interest for us are free-choice Petri nets [2]. In these nets, choice and synchronisation are separated like in many other graphical process modelling notations. Moreover, as motivated in [1], many process mining algorithms produce free-choice nets.

Definition 4 (Free-choice nets). *A Petri net $N = \langle P, T, F \rangle$ is* free-choice *if for any transitions $t_1, t_2 \in T$, $^\bullet t_1 \cap {}^\bullet t_2 \neq \emptyset$ implies that $^\bullet t_1 = {}^\bullet t_2$.*

Definition 5 (Clusters [2]). *Let x be a node of a Petri net $N = \langle P, T, F \rangle$. The cluster of x, denoted by $[x]$, is the minimal set of nodes such that (1) $x \in [x]$; (2) for any $p \in P$, if $p \in [x]$, then any transition $t \in p^\bullet$ belongs to $[x]$, and (3) for any $t \in T$, if $t \in [x]$, then any place $p \in {}^\bullet t$ belongs to $[x]$.*

An important property of free-choice nets is that when a transition t is enabled in a marking m, then all other transitions of $[t]$ are enabled as well (see [2]).

2.2 Stochastic Processes

A function $f : A \times B \to [0, 1]$, where A and B are finite or countable sets, is called a *transition probability function* if for all $b \in B : f(., b)$ is a probability over A, i.e. for all $b \in B : \sum_{a \in A} f(a, b) = 1$.

A discrete *stochastic process* is a finite or infinite sequence of random variables $X_0, X_1, X_2, \ldots$ with values in some domain X, defined on some probability space $(\Omega, \mathfrak{F}, \mathbb{P})$, where Ω is the sample space, $\mathfrak{F}$ is a σ-algebra on Ω and $\mathbb{P}$ is a probability (measure) on $\mathfrak{F}$, such that $\mathbb{P}(\emptyset) = 1 - \mathbb{P}(\Omega) = 0$. We characterise $\mathbb{P}$ without explicit construction of Ω and $\mathfrak{F}$, by conditional probabilities:

$$\mathbb{P}[X_{n+1} = y | X_0 = x_0, \ldots, X_n = x_n] = f(y, \langle x_0, \ldots, x_n \rangle)$$

for $y \in X$ and $x_i \in X$, $i = 0, 1, 2, \ldots, n$. We assume that transition probability f is a *computable function* on $X \times X^*$. Note that by the theory of Ionescu Tulcea (see [11]) the transition probability function characterises the probability measure $\mathbb{P}$ completely. In fact, this is a generalisation of the result of A. Kolmogorov presented in [7].

Definition 6 (Markov Chain). *If there is a computable function f such that $\mathbb{P}[X_{n+1} = y | X_0 = x_0, \ldots, X_n = x_n] = f(y, \langle x_n \rangle)$ for all $y, x_0, \ldots, x_n \in X$, then the process is called a* Markov chain. *For a finite X we call it a* finite Markov chain. *If there is a $k \in \mathbb{N}$ such that $\mathbb{P}[X_{n+1} = x_{n+1} | X_0 = x_0, \ldots, X_n = x_n] = \mathbb{P}[X_{n+1} = x_{n+1} | X_{n-k} = x_{n-k}, \ldots, X_n = x_n]$ this process is called a k-order* Markov chain.

It is well-known that any discrete stochastic process $\{X_n | n = 0, 1, \ldots\}$ can be transformed into a Markovian discrete stochastic process $\{Y_n | n = 0, 1, \ldots\}$, where the domain of Y is X^*. It can be defined as $Y_n = \langle X_0, \ldots, X_n \rangle$. Note that $\{Y_0 = \langle x_0 \rangle, \ldots, Y_n = \langle x_0, \ldots, x_n \rangle\} = \{X_0 = x_0 \ldots, X_n = x_n\}$. Also note that $\mathbb{P}[X_{n+1} = x_{n+1} | X_0 = x_0, \ldots, X_n = x_n] = \mathbb{P}[X_{n+1} = x_{n+1} | Y_n = \langle x_0, \ldots, x_n \rangle] = \mathbb{P}[Y_{n+1} = \langle x_0, \ldots, x_{n+1} \rangle | Y_n = \langle x_0, \ldots, x_n \rangle]$, which proves that $\{Y_n | n = 0, 1, \ldots\}$ is a Markov chain, however, with an infinite domain (Y).

Similarly, we can make a finite Markov chain of a discrete stochastic process $\{X_n | n = 0, 1, \ldots\}$ if there is a $k \in \mathbb{N}$ such that $\mathbb{P}[X_n = x_n | X_0 = x_0, \ldots, X_{n-1} = x_{n-1}] = \mathbb{P}[X_n = x_n | X_{n-k} = x_{n-k}, \ldots, X_{n-1} = x_{n-1}]$. So only the last k random variables have influence on the next step. This process is called a k-order *Markov chain* and in case it is finite, it can be transformed into a *finite* Markov chain $\{Y_n | n = 0, 1, \ldots\}$ where Y_n is defined as $Y_n = \langle X_{n-k+1}, \ldots, X_{n-1}, X_n \rangle$. Thus $\mathbb{P}[X_n = x_n | X_{n-k} = x_{n-k}, \ldots, X_{n-1} = x_{n-1}] = \mathbb{P}[X_n = x_n | Y_{n-1} = \langle x_{n-k}, \ldots, x_{n-1} \rangle] = \mathbb{P}[Y_n = \langle x_{n-k+1}, \ldots, x_n \rangle | Y_{n-1} = \langle x_{n-k}, \ldots, x_{n-1} \rangle]$.

3 History-Dependent Stochastic Petri Nets

Now we introduce a class of stochastic Petri nets where the probability of an enabled transition to fire depends on the execution history. Moreover, we explain how these probability measures can be estimated based on the execution log.

3.1 Definition of History-Dependent Stochastic Petri Nets

We base our definition on Petri nets extended with history [4] and define history-dependent probability measures. Let (N, m_0) be a marked Petri net N with initial marking m_0. X_n is the stochastic variable corresponding to the nth transition that fires from m_0; domain $X = T \cup \{\iota, \delta\}$ is the set of transition from N extended with transitions ι and δ ($\iota, \delta \notin T$). The dummy transitions are isolated from the marked net N, m_0 and only serve the purpose of providing a convenient mapping to an infinite stochastic process. When N is in a dead marking, dummy transition δ becomes enabled and the process remains in the same state forever. This way we model a finite workflow process as infinite process starting with ι

$(X_0 = \iota)$ and ending with absorbing[3] state δ: if $X_n = \delta$, then $X_{n+1} = \delta$. In Markov chains the transition to move to a state is sometimes identified with the state, as is the case here for δ. We consider finite histories[4] and we introduce a short hand notation for the history at step n by $H_n = \langle X_0, \ldots, X_n \rangle$ and $H = X^*$ denotes the set of all possible histories.

Definition 7 (Transition Probability for Petri Nets). *For $t \in (T \cup \{\iota, \delta\})$, $h \in H$, we define transition probability function $f : (T \cup \{\iota, \delta\}) \times H \to [0, 1]$. We assume function f to be computable and having the following properties: (1) $\forall h \in H : \sum_{t \in (T \cup \{\iota, \delta\})} f(t, h) = 1$, (2) $\forall h \in H : f(\iota, h) = X(h = \epsilon)$, (3) $f(\delta, h) = X(\forall t \in T : m_0 + \mathbf{N}\overrightarrow{h} < {}^\bullet t)$, and (4) $\forall h \in H, t \in T : m_0 + \mathbf{N}\overrightarrow{h} < {}^\bullet t \Rightarrow f(t, h) = 0$.*

The first condition means that the sum of probabilities over all transitions, including ι and δ, equals 1; the second condition assures that ι fires iff no transition has fired yet; the third condition means that δ will fire iff there are no other enabled transitions in the net; and the fourth condition means that the probability to fire for not enabled transitions equals 0, i.e. our nets are a true extension of the classical Petri nets.

Definition 8 (History-Dependent Stochastic Petri Net). *A history-dependent stochastic Petri net (HDSPN) N is a tuple $\langle P, T, F, m_0, f \rangle$, where $N = \langle P, T \cup \{\iota, \delta\}, F \rangle$ is a Petri net with ${}^\bullet\iota = \iota^\bullet = \emptyset$, ${}^\bullet\delta = \delta^\bullet = \emptyset$, m_0 is an initial marking, and $f : (T \cup \{\iota, \delta\}) \times H \to [0, 1]$ is a transition probability function.*

Firings of ι and δ do not change the marking of the net. A free-choice Petri net extended with ι and δ remains a free-choice Petri net, with $[\delta] = \{\delta\}$ and $[\iota] = \{\iota\}$. An HDSPN defines an infinite stochastic process $X_0, X_1, \ldots$, where $\mathbb{P}[X_{n+1} = t | H_n = h] = f(t, h)$. We assume that $f(t, h)$ exists. Usually $f(t, h)$ is unknown and then we can use the log to estimate $f(t, h)$.

Figure 2 shows the stochastic process $\{X_n | n = 0, 1, \ldots\}$ for the HDSPN based on the Petri net from Figure 1. The concrete values for $f(t, h)$, given for different h's, are defined from the observations in the log, as we will explain in Section 3.2. We transform this process into a stochastic process $\{Y_n | n = 0, 1 \ldots\}$ that has the Markovian property. The state of the Y process is the history, i.e. action sequence, of the X process, see Figure 3.

We can further specialise our definition for the case of free-choice Petri nets. Let C be the set of clusters of $\langle P, T, F, m_0, f \rangle$. Recall that whenever a transition t of cluster $[t]$ is enabled, all transitions in $[t]$ are enabled. The firing of a transition from $[t]$ leaves all transitions from other clusters enabled. For this reason we move to a "two-phase selection" of the transition to fire: first we choose a cluster, and then a transition from this cluster. Since $\mathbb{P}[X_{n+1} = t | H_n = h] = \mathbb{P}[X_{n+1} = t | H_n = h \land X_{n+1} \in [t]] \cdot \mathbb{P}[X_{n+1} \in [t] | H_n = h]$, we can represent $f(t, h)$ as

$$f(t, h) = p(t, h) \cdot q(t, h),$$

---

[3] The process remains in this state with probability 1.
[4] Estimations are based on finite traces contained in a log.

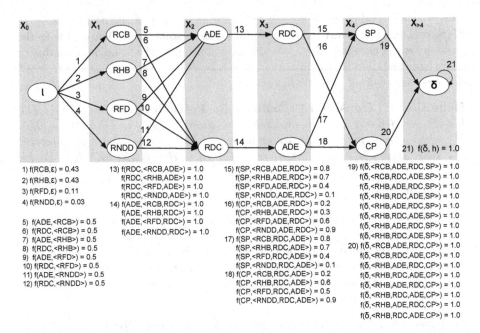

1) f(RCB,ε) = 0.43
2) f(RHB,ε) = 0.43
3) f(RFD,ε) = 0.11
4) f(RNDD,ε) = 0.03

5) f(ADE,<RCB>) = 0.5
6) f(RDC,<RCB>) = 0.5
7) f(ADE,<RHB>) = 0.5
8) f(RDC,<RHB>) = 0.5
9) f(ADE,<RFD>) = 0.5
10) f(RDC,<RFD>) = 0.5
11) f(ADE,<RNDD>) = 0.5
12) f(RDC,<RNDD>) = 0.5

13) f(RDC,<RCB,ADE>) = 1.0
f(RDC,<RHB,ADE>) = 1.0
f(RDC,<RFD,ADE>) = 1.0
f(RDC,<RNDD,ADE>) = 1.0
14) f(ADE,<RCB,RDC>) = 1.0
f(ADE,<RHB,RDC>) = 1.0
f(ADE,<RFD,RDC>) = 1.0
f(ADE,<RNDD,RDC>) = 1.0

15) f(SP,<RCB,ADE,RDC>) = 0.8
f(SP,<RHB,ADE,RDC>) = 0.7
f(SP,<RFD,ADE,RDC>) = 0.4
f(SP,<RNDD,ADE,RDC>) = 0.1
16) f(CP,<RCB,ADE,RDC>) = 0.2
f(CP,<RHB,ADE,RDC>) = 0.3
f(CP,<RFD,ADE,RDC>) = 0.6
f(CP,<RNDD,ADE,RDC>) = 0.9
17) f(SP,<RCB,RDC,ADE>) = 0.8
f(SP,<RHB,RDC,ADE>) = 0.7
f(SP,<RFD,RDC,ADE>) = 0.4
f(SP,<RNDD,RDC,ADE>) = 0.1
18) f(CP,<RCB,RDC,ADE>) = 0.2
f(CP,<RHB,RDC,ADE>) = 0.6
f(CP,<RFD,RDC,ADE>) = 0.5
f(CP,<RNDD,RDC,ADE>) = 0.9

19) f(δ,<RCB,ADE,RDC,SP>) = 1.0
f(δ,<RCB,RDC,ADE,SP>) = 1.0
f(δ,<RHB,ADE,RDC,SP>) = 1.0
f(δ,<RHB,RDC,ADE,SP>) = 1.0
f(δ,<RHB,ADE,RDC,SP>) = 1.0
f(δ,<RHB,RDC,ADE,SP>) = 1.0
f(δ,<RHB,ADE,RDC,SP>) = 1.0
f(δ,<RHB,RDC,ADE,SP>) = 1.0
20) f(δ,<RCB,ADE,RDC,CP>) = 1.0
f(δ,<RCB,RDC,ADE,CP>) = 1.0
f(δ,<RHB,ADE,RDC,CP>) = 1.0
f(δ,<RHB,RDC,ADE,CP>) = 1.0
f(δ,<RHB,ADE,RDC,CP>) = 1.0
f(δ,<RHB,RDC,ADE,CP>) = 1.0
f(δ,<RHB,ADE,RDC,CP>) = 1.0
f(δ,<RHB,RDC,ADE,CP>) = 1.0

21) f(δ, h) = 1.0

Fig. 2. The discrete stochastic process defined by the HDSPN for N from Figure 1

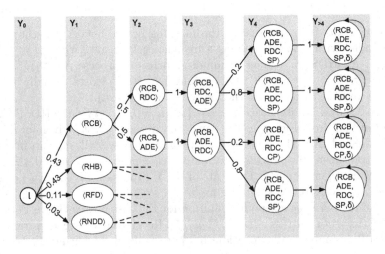

Fig. 3. The Markov Chain (partly) for the stochastic process from Figure 2

where $p(t,h)$ gives the estimated probability of transition t within cluster $[t]$, and $q(t,h)$ the estimated probability to choose cluster $[t]$.

The probability $f(t,h)$ for ι and δ is known and straightforward. Since $[\iota] = \{\iota\}$ and $[\delta] = \{\delta\}$, there are no other transitions to fire and $p(\iota,h) = p(\delta,h) = 1$. The cluster probability is defined by $q(\iota,h) = \mathcal{X}(h = \epsilon)$ and similarly

$q(\delta, h) = \chi(\forall t \in T : m_0 + \mathbf{N}\overrightarrow{h} < {}^\bullet t)$, due to Def. 7. These clusters are selected iff the history is empty, or when there are no other enabled transitions, respectively.

For the remainder of the paper we assume that when transitions of multiple clusters are simultaneously enabled, a choice between these clusters is made with equal probabilities, which is justified by the cluster independency.[5]

Assumption 1 (Equal Probabilities for Clusters). *Let C be the set of all clusters in $N = \langle P, T, F \rangle$. $\forall c_i, c_j \in (C \setminus \{[\iota], [\delta]\}) : (\forall t \in ((c_i \cup c_j) \cap T) : (m_0 + \mathbf{N}\overrightarrow{h}) \geq {}^\bullet t)) \Rightarrow \mathbb{P}[X_{n+1} \in c_i | H_n = h] = \mathbb{P}[X_{n+1} \in c_j | H_n = h]$.*

Assumption 1 implies the following definition of $q(t, h)$:

$$
q(t, h) = \begin{cases} 0 \text{ , if } q(\iota, h) = 1. \\ 0 \text{ , if } q(\delta, h) = 1. \\ \dfrac{\chi(m_0 + \mathbf{N}\overrightarrow{h} \geq {}^\bullet t)}{\displaystyle\sum_{c \in (C \setminus \{[\iota], [\delta]\})} \chi(\forall u \in (c \cap T) : (m_0 + \mathbf{N}\overrightarrow{h}) \geq {}^\bullet u)} \text{ , otherwise.} \end{cases}
$$

$$(1)$$

Next we will give some simple examples of possible $p(t, h)$ definitions.

Example 1. Let transitions in a cluster be chosen with equal probabilities $p(t, h) = |[t] \cap T|^{-1}$. Note that in this case not all enabled transitions in the net have the same probability.

Example 2. We can use the observed firing frequency of transition t in h for defining its probability. The more often t has fired, the higher the probability becomes:

$$
p(t, h) = \frac{\overrightarrow{h}(t) + 1}{\displaystyle\sum_{x \in ([t] \cap T)} (\overrightarrow{h}(x) + 1)}.
$$

The latter example shows that in some cases we cannot aggregate the history to a k-order finite Markov chain.

Among other typical examples are nets where reaching some threshold of the occurrence of a transition t increases or decreases the probability of some transition(s) in the net. For example, error-handling transitions can be more likely to become enabled after the occurrence of a number of errors. Also the time spent in the process or the resources involved in the process can be part of the characterisation. It is not our intention here to be complete, nor to discuss how to get the best characterisation. In this paper we limit ourselves to the definition of the framework and showing some example characterisations.

---

[5] Different assumptions can be made. However, since we abstract from time and the firing in one cluster does not disable transitions in another cluster, this is less relevant.

3.2   Discovery of $p(t, h)$

In real life, $p(t, h)$ is normally unknown. When $p(t, h)$ is unknown, we use the log to estimate $\hat{p}(t, h)$. Let $[t] = \{t_1, \ldots, t_k\}$. The multinomial distribution for the transitions is the probability distribution of n independent observations $X1, \ldots, X_n$, where each possible outcome $X_i \in \{t_1, \ldots, t_n\}$ occurs with probability π_i, with $\pi_1, \ldots, \pi_k \geq 0$ and $\sum_{i=1}^{k} \pi_i = 1$. For n observations we denote the number of times that t_i fired by n_i. $X1, \ldots, X_n$ follows a multinomial distribution with parameters n and $\pi = (\pi_1, \ldots, \pi_k)$. We estimate $f(t_i, h)$ by estimating parameter $\hat{\pi}_i = \frac{n_i}{n}$ for the multinomial distribution of $[t_i]$ from the log.

A naive approach for the estimation would be to look in L how often t was chosen after h. However, the requirement $H_n = h$ might exclude (too) many cases from the execution log resulting in a sample from which no reliable estimation can be made. Abstractions on history can be used to still obtain meaningful results. Note that we did use history abstractions in the examples above: in Example 1 the history is completely disregarded, in Example 2 the Parikh vector abstraction is taken, i.e. the order of transitions in h is ignored. Other examples of abstractions are finite horizon abstractions and abstractions that consider the net structure, for example by counting formulae [4]. Note that the definition of $q(t, h)$ is already an abstraction.

Here we consider one of the possible abstractions in more detail, where we concentrate on the correlation between the choice of a transition from cluster c and the last fired transition from cluster $R(c)$, assuming we know a function R mapping c to a cluster that has the strongest correlation with c. This abstraction is interesting for practical applications since the choices in some clusters (which might also be human made choices) can be strongly correlated e.g. due to data dependencies, that might not be visible in the log. We introduce the history abstraction function $\alpha : H \times C \to T$ as follows.

$$\alpha(h, c) = \begin{cases} t\,, & \text{if } h = (\sigma; t; \gamma) \text{ and } t \in (c \cap T) \text{ and } \sigma \in T^* \text{ and } \gamma \in (T \setminus c)^*, \\ \bot\,, & \text{if } h \in (T \setminus c)^*. \end{cases}$$

Now we estimate for every t the probability to choose t under the condition that s was the last choice in cluster $R([t])$. If no transition from $R([t])$ has fired yet, s is undefined ($s = \bot$). Under this condition we obtain the samples from the log to estimate $p(t, h)$, for every t, given h. For this purpose we divide $\phi(t, s)$ by $\psi(t, s)$, where $\phi(t, s)$ is the number of positive observations in the sample, i.e. the frequency of $s \in R[t] \cup \{\bot\}$ being the last transition of the cluster $R([t])$ occurring before t and $\psi(t, s)$ is the sample size, i.e. the frequency of s being the last transition of $R([t])$ before *some* transition of the cluster of t:

$$\phi(t, s) = \sum_{h \in L} L(h) \cdot |\{\tilde{h} \mid \exists \tilde{h}, \gamma \in T^* : h = (\tilde{h}; t; \gamma) \wedge \alpha(\tilde{h}, R([t])) = s)\}|,$$

$$\psi(t, s) = \sum_{h \in L} L(h) \cdot |\{\tilde{h} \mid \exists \tilde{h}, \gamma \in T^*, x \in [t] : h = (\tilde{h}; x; \gamma) \wedge \alpha(\tilde{h}, R([t])) = s)\}|.$$

In case the denominator is 0 (i.e. s was never seen before any transition from cluster $[t]$ in cases registered in the log), we take the history-independent estimation of the probability of t by dividing the number $\overline{\phi}(t)$ of occurrences of t in the log by the number $\overline{\psi}(t)$ of the occurrences of transitions from $[t]$ in the log.

$$\overline{\phi}(t) = \sum_{h \in L} L(h) \cdot |\{\tilde{h} \mid \exists \tilde{h}, \gamma \in T^* : h = (\tilde{h}; t; \gamma)\}|, \qquad (2)$$

$$\overline{\psi}(t) = \sum_{h \in L} L(h) \cdot |\{\tilde{h} \mid \exists \tilde{h}, \gamma \in T^*, x \in [t] : h = (\tilde{h}; x; \gamma)\}|. \qquad (3)$$

In cases where there are no occurrences of transitions from $[t]$ in the log at all, we assume that each transition from $[t]$ fires with equal probability. Now $\hat{p}(t, h)$ takes the following form:

$$\hat{p}(t, h) = \begin{cases} \dfrac{\phi(t, \alpha(h, R([t])))}{\psi(t, \alpha(h, R([t])))} & , \text{if } \exists h \in L, x \in [t] : x \in h \wedge \psi(t, \alpha(h, R([t]))) \neq 0, \\[2ex] \dfrac{\phi(t)}{\psi(t)} & , \text{if } \exists h \in L, x \in [t] : x \in h \wedge \psi(t, \alpha(h, R([t]))) = 0, \\[2ex] |[t] \cap T|^{-1} & , \text{if } \forall h \in L, x \in [t] : x \notin h. \end{cases}$$

This idea can be straightforwardly generalised for several correlated clusters. Note that for this abstraction we could easily extend the marking to include the dependencies with the past, but then the net loses its free-choice property and becomes more difficult to understand and maintain, especially for more complex dependencies.

3.3   Discovery of the Correlations between Clusters

In the reasoning above, we assumed that the function R is known. In some cases R can be defined based on judgements of experts; in many cases R should be discovered based on the information from the log. Here we describe a simple procedure for checking whether the choice made in cluster C_2 is a significant correlated with the choice already made in cluster C_1.

We introduce two random variables: X and Y, representing the choices in clusters C_1 and C_2 respectively. The 0-hypothesis is that X and Y are independent. Let C_1 contain transitions $x_1, \ldots, x_l$ and C_2 transitions $y_1, \ldots, y_m$.

From the log we derive the depicted matrix. The test statistic is: $\mathbf{T} = \sum_{i=1}^{l} \sum_{j=1}^{m} \dfrac{(n_{ij} - E_{ij})^2}{E_{ij}}$, which is χ^2-distributed with parameter $(m-1)(l-1)$.

We reject the 0-hypothesis if $\mathbf{T}$ is sufficiently large. For example if $l = m = 7$ we reject the independency hypothesis with confidence 99% if the test statistic is greater than 58.6 and with confidence 95% if it is greater than 51.

	$y_1 \ldots$	y_j	$\ldots y_m$	
x_1				r_1
.				
x_i		n_{ij}		r_i
.				.
x_l				r_l
	$k_1 \ldots$	k_j	$\ldots k_m$	N

Here n_{ij} is the number of the occurrences of transition x_i before transition y_j, $r_i = \sum_{j=1}^{m} n_{ij}$, $k_j = \sum_{i=1}^{l} n_{ij}$ and $\sum_{i=1}^{l} r_i = \sum_{j=1}^{m} k_j = N$.

Under our 0-hypothesis, the expected value E_{ij} of a cell is $E_{ij} = p_i \cdot q_i \cdot N$, where $p_i = \dfrac{r_i}{N}$ and $q_i = \dfrac{k_j}{N}$. So

$$E_{ij} = \frac{r_i \cdot k_j}{N}.$$

4 Simulation with HDSPNs

In this section we show how to simulate HDSPNs using CPN tools [6], which is a well established tool for modelling and analysis of Coloured Petri nets (CPNs) [5] with support for simulation. We also show some results of simulation experiments showing the benefits of HDSPNs.

4.1 HDSPNs in CPN Tools

To represent a HDSPN in CPN tools we start with its basis (classical) Petri net and then add the history and the probability information as follows:

Global History. The *global history* (or its abstraction) is kept in a special place that contains a token with the history information. Initially it contains a token containing the empty history. Every transition of the Petri net is then linked to the history place, and transition firings update the history token by adding the information about the firing. If a history abstraction is used, some firings might leave the history token value unchanged.

For the abstraction described in Section 3.2, the colour set of the history token can be the set of transitions from the range of function R, i.e. $R[T]$. The set contains at most one transition per cluster. Whenever from some cluster where $c \in R[T]$ a transition $t \in c$ fires, a transition from c is removed from the history token (if it was there) and t is added instead.

History-Dependent Probabilities. CPN Tools has the possibility to define probabilities but these probabilities are history-independent. To introduce a history-dependent probability mechanism, we add place *random* that contains a token whose value is a randomly chosen between 0 and 1. Every firing of a transition results in updating the value of this token with a new random number.

Within each cluster we define transition guards capturing the probability mechanism as follows: Let cluster c contain transitions $t_1, \ldots, t_n$ and given history h, the probability to choose transition t_i under condition that cluster c is chosen is $p(t_i, h)$. Then the guard for t_i is defined as $\sum_{j=1}^{i-1} p(t_j, h) \leq r < \sum_{j=1}^{i} p(t_j, h)$ (for transition t_1, the lower border is 0), where r is the value of the token on *random*. This definition of the guards implies that in every cluster at every moment at most one transition can enabled. Due to the semantics used by CPN Tools[6], the default choice of the transition is made between the enabled transitions with equal probability. In our case this actually becomes the choice of the cluster, from which the transition will fire, thus implementing Equation 1.

To measure relevant performance indicators, necessary information like costs of actions is added to the transitions of the net.

4.2   Simulation Experiments

One of the intended practical applications for the HDSPN framework is the evaluation of process execution recommenders [14]. These recommenders assist users in deciding which enabled activity to execute next, according to some strategy. We can compare different recommender strategies by performing the simulation with the user actions being chosen followed the recommender advises and the system choices (as opposite to the choices of the user) being made according to history-dependent probabilities, taking into account the most significant correlations (estimated based on the past performance of the system). The goal of our experiments below is to show the impact of history-dependent probabilities on the simulation outcome.

We start with a model M_0, which is a CPN model with data-dependent transition guards and case data generated according to some distributions. We use this model to produce an execution log of the system before the use of the recommender. Data dependencies in the model induce the existence of correlations between the choices of transitions in certain clusters. (In real life, data dependencies are often fuzzy or unknown, so the model with data and data operations defined is actually not available and cannot be used for simulations; the log is available.) Then we use this execution log to discover history-dependent probabilities by applying the abstraction from Subsection 3.2. Finally, we construct model M_1 from M_0 by removing data and adding the discovered history-dependent probabilities as defined in Section 3.2.

For comparison, we additionally construct two models: M_2 obtained from M_0 by removing data and without adding any probabilities (i.e. the default probability mechanism of CPN Tools is used in the simulations), and M_3 where static (not history-dependent) probabilities are added as $\dfrac{\overline{\phi}(t)}{\overline{\psi}(t)}$ (with $\overline{\phi}$ and $\overline{\psi}$ defined by Equations 2 and 3) for every transition t. We define performance metrics, e.g. costs, for each transition. Finally, we ran the recommender with all the four models and compared the obtained results.

We characterise the differences between the approaches by considering the differences in transition occurrence ratios, because they are independent from the actual values of the performance metrics. In the simulation on M_0 with a recommender, 381 out of 500 (76,2%) traces of the execution log contained transition t_9. In our HDSPN M_1 this number was almost the same: 361 (72,2%),

---

[6] For automatic simulation CPN tools uses random number generation to chose between enabled transitions

in M_2 that was only 237 (47,4%) and in M_3 233 (46,6%). Similar ratios were found for the other transitions as well. As expected, our model gave the most precise approximation of the behaviour of M_0.

In this experiment we have changed the simulation settings by using recommendations. For history-independent approaches we have shown that such changes do not affect the simulation, i.e. the probabilities for the remainder of choices remain equal, even though there is a correlation with the part that has been changed. This is not the case for HDSPNs, due to history-dependency. Simulation of HDSPNs yields the best estimations for the number of transition occurrences, making these nets most suitable for the evaluation of recommenders.

5   Conclusion

In this paper we introduced stochastic Petri nets with history-dependent probability distributions. We also gave an example showing how the probability distributions can be estimated based on the execution log. In this paper we concentrated on untimed nets, where the execution of transitions would have fixed costs. To allow for timed performance analysis, we will extend our framework with time. An additional research question arising there is the estimation of the history influence on the distributions of the execution times of the transitions. Our experiments showed the potential usefulness of our framework for performance analysis of workflows. History-dependency of probabilistic distributions facilitates analysis of the effect of different executions (choices). This makes the framework suitable for the evaluation of process execution recommenders. Currently, we are comparing several strategies for process recommenders by using simulations on HDSPNs based on real-life logs.

For the future work we also plan systematic investigation of the possible abstractions of history and methods for the discovery of most significant correlations to obtain better estimations of the probability distributions. Another direction of this research is combining our framework with the theory of Markov Decision Processes (MDPs) [12] to control the process execution by minimizing cost, or maximizing reward.

References

1. van der Aalst, W.M.P., van Dongen, B.F., Herbst, J., Maruster, L., Schimm, G., Weijters, A.J.M.M.: Workflow Mining: A Survey of Issues and Approaches. Data and Knowledge Engineering 47(2), 237–267 (1996)
2. Desel, J., Esparza, J.: Free Choice Petri Nets. Cambridge Tracts in Theoretical Computer Science, vol. 40. Cambridge University Press, Cambridge (1995)
3. Florin, G., Natkin, S.: Les Reseaux de Petri Stochastiques. Technique et Science Informatiques 4(1), 143–160 (1985)
4. van Hee, K.M., Serebrenik, A., Sidorova, N., van der Aalst, W.M.P.: History-Dependent Petri Nets. In: Kleijn, J., Yakovlev, A. (eds.) ICATPN 2007. LNCS, vol. 4546, pp. 164–183. Springer, Heidelberg (2007)

5. Jensen, K.: Coloured Petri Nets. Basic Concepts, Analysis Methods and Practical Use. EATCS monographs on Theoretical Computer Science. Springer, Heidelberg (1992)
6. Jensen, K., Kristensen, L.M., Wells, L.: Coloured Petri Nets and CPN Tools for Modelling and Validation of Concurrent Systems. International Journal on Software Tools for Technology Transfer 9(3-4), 213–254 (2007)
7. Kolmogorov, A.: Moscow Univ. Math. Bull. 1 (1937)
8. Ajmone Marsan, M., Balbo, G., Chiola, G., Conte, G.: Generalized Stochastic Petri Nets Revisited: Random Switches and Priorities. In: PNPM 1987: The Proceedings of the Second International Workshop on Petri Nets and Performance Models, Washington, DC, USA, pp. 44–53. IEEE Computer Society, Los Alamitos (1987)
9. Ajmone Marsan, M., Balbo, G., Conte, G., Donatelli, S., Franceschinis, G.: Modelling with Generalized Stochastic Petri Nets. ACM SIGMETRICS Perform. Eval. Rev. 26(2), 2 (1998)
10. Molloy, M.K.: On the Integration of Delay and Throughput Measures in Distributed Processing Models. PhD thesis, University of California, Los Angeles (1981)
11. Neveu, J.: Mathematical Foundations of the Calculus of Probability. Holden-day (1965)
12. Ross, S.M.: Introduction to Probability Models, 9th edn. Academic Press, Inc., Orlando (2006)
13. Rozinat, A., Mans, R.S., Song, M., van der Aalst, W.M.P.: Discovering Colored Petri Nets From Event Logs. International Journal on Software Tools for Technology Transfer 10(1), 57–74 (2008)
14. Schonenberg, H., Weber, B., van Dongen, B.F., van der Aalst, W.M.P.: Supporting Flexible Processes Through Recommendations Based on History. In: Dumas, M., Reichert, M., Shan, M.-C. (eds.) BPM 2008. LNCS, vol. 5240, pp. 51–66. Springer, Heidelberg (2008)
15. Symons, F.J.W.: Modelling and Analysis of Communication Protocols Using Numerical Petri Nets. 152, Ph.D. Thesis, Univ. of Essex, Dep. of Electr. Engineering Science, Telecommunication Systems Group (May 1978)

Privacy Preserving Modules for Ontologies

Thomas Studer

Universität Bern, Institut für Informatik und angewandte Mathematik,
Neubrückstrasse 10, CH-3012 Bern, Switzerland
tstuder@iam.unibe.ch

Abstract. Data privacy is an important application of ontology modularization. The aim is to publish one module while keeping the information of another module private. We show how locality and partitioning - two basic concepts in the theory of modular ontologies - naturally lead to privacy preserving query answering over modular ontologies.

1 Introduction

Recently, big effort has been made to understand modules in the context of ontologies and description logic. The problems studied in that context are to find formalisms for combining OWL ontologies as well as methods for decomposing ontologies. These issues mainly are investigated in order to enable safe ontology reuse and to obtain better reasoning algorithms.

We believe that there is another important application of ontology modularization, namely data privacy for ontologies. If we are given a modular ontology, then it should be possible to publish a module while keeping the information of another module private. We show how concepts of modular ontologies, such as *locality* and *partitioning*, naturally lead to privacy preserving modules.

The privacy notion we study is *provable data privacy* which has been introduced in the context of relational database systems [1]. This notion has later been extended to logic based systems in [2]. Assume we are given a set of axioms T (which can be seen as general public background knowledge, the database schema, or an ontology) and a public view definition V. A view V_I is possible if it may be the answer an agent obtains when issuing the queries of V. We say privacy is preserved for a query C if for no possible view V_I the agent can infer from T and V_I that an individual a belongs to the answer of C. In database systems this is formalized as the set of certain answers to C is empty with respect to T and V_I. For logic based systems this is equivalent to saying that T and V_I do not entail $a : C$ for any a.

This paper is organized as follows. In the next section we introduce the expressive description logic $\mathcal{SHOIQ}$ for which we will state our privacy results. Further we recall the definitions of provable data privacy in the context of description logic. In Section 3, we present a first privacy result which is based in the notion of locality. Intuitively, a concept C is local with respect to a signature S if we can interpret C by the empty set no matter how S is interpreted. This leads immediately to a privacy result since having an interpretation I where

A. Pnueli, I. Virbitskaite, and A. Voronkov (Eds.): PSI 2009, LNCS 5947, pp. 380–387, 2010.
© Springer-Verlag Berlin Heidelberg 2010

C^I is empty means that $a : C$ cannot be inferred for any a. Then in Section 4 we investigate data privacy based on partitioning of ontologies. This allows us to include in the public view definition other queries than in the locality based approach. Finally we discuss related work and conclude.

2   Technical Preliminaries

In the first part of this section we introduce the description logic $\mathcal{SHOIQ}$, see [3], which underlies modern ontology languages such as OWL. In the second part we recall the notion of provable data privacy from [1].

A $\mathcal{SHOIQ}$ signature S is the disjoint union of a set of role names R, a set of concept names C, and a set of nominals I. A $\mathcal{SHOIQ}$ role is either $R \in \mathsf{R}$ or an inverse role R^- for $R \in \mathsf{R}$. The set of $\mathcal{SHOIQ}$ concepts C is given by the following grammar

$$C ::= A \mid j \mid \neg C \mid C \sqcap C \mid \exists R.C \mid \geq nS.C$$

where $A \in \mathsf{C}$, $j \in \mathsf{I}$, and R, S are roles where S is a simple role[1], and n is a positive integer. We use the abbreviations: $C \sqcup D := \neg(\neg C \sqcap \neg D)$, $\forall R.C := \neg \exists R.\neg C$, and $\leq nS.C := \neg(\geq n+1S.C)$.

A $\mathcal{SHOIQ}$ TBox is a finite set of role inclusion axioms $R_1 \sqsubseteq R_2$ where R_i are roles, transitivity axioms $\mathsf{trans}(R)$ where $R \in \mathsf{R}$, and general concept inclusion axioms $C_1 \sqsubseteq C_2$ where C_i are concepts. The signature $\mathsf{sig}(T)$ of a TBox T is the set of symbols occurring in T. Similarly, we define the signature of an axiom and of a concept, respectively.

An *interpretation* I for the signature S is a par $(\Delta^I, \cdot^I)$ where Δ^I is a non-empty set (called the domain) and $\cdot^I$ is the interpretation function such that $R^I \subseteq \Delta^I \times \Delta^I$ for each $R \in \mathsf{R}$, $C^I \subseteq \Delta^I$ for each $C \in \mathsf{C}$, and j^I is a singleton subset of Δ^I for each $j \in \mathsf{I}$. The interpretation function extends to complex roles by $(R^-)^I := \{(y, x) : R^I(x, y)\}$ and to concepts by:

$$(\neg C)^I := \Delta^I \setminus C^I$$
$$(C \sqcap D)^I := C^I \cap D^I$$
$$(\exists R.C)^I := \{x : \exists y(R^I(x, y) \wedge C^I(y))\}$$
$$(\geq nR.C)^I := \{x : \#\{y : R^I(x, y) \wedge C^I(y)\} \geq n\}.$$

We say $I \models R_1 \sqsubseteq R_2$ iff $R_1^I \subseteq R_2^I$, $I \models \mathsf{trans}(R)$ iff R^I is transitive, and $I \models C \sqsubseteq D$ iff $C^I \subseteq D^I$. An interpretation I is a *model of a TBox* T $(I \models T)$ iff it is a model of all axioms of T. A TBox is *consistent* if it has a model. A TBox T *entails* an axiom α $(T \models \alpha)$ iff $I \models T$ implies $I \models \alpha$ for each I.

In this paper we restrict ourselves to the case of data privacy with respect to retrieval queries. Since our ontology language includes nominals, we do not need to introduce individuals. Informally, the statement that an individual a belongs to a concept C can be expressed as $\{a\} \sqsubseteq C$. Therefore we will treat nominals as individuals and write $j : C$ for $j \sqsubseteq C$ when $j \in \mathsf{I}$.

---

[1] See [3] for a precise definition of simple roles.

Definition 1 (Query, answer, view)

1. *A retrieval query is a concept C.*
2. *The answer to a query C with respect to a TBox T is the set of all nominals $a \in I$ for which $T \models a : C$.*
3. *A view definition is a finite set of queries.*
4. *A view V_I of a view definition V is a finite set of axioms of the form $a : C$ such that if $a : C$ is an element of V_I, then $C \in V$.*
5. *A view V_I is possible with respect to a TBox T and a view definition V, if V_I is a view of V and $T \cup V_I$ is consistent.*

In [1] we introduced the notion of provable data privacy. It turned out that for the setting we introduced above, provable data privacy can be reduced to entailment, see [2]. We make use of this fact here to give the following definition of data privacy.

Definition 2 (Data privacy)

1. *Given a TBox T, a view V_I, and a query C, we say that privacy is preserved for C with respect to T and V_I if the set of answers to C with respect to $T \cup V_I$ is empty.*
2. *Given a TBox T, a view definition V, and a query C, we say that privacy is preserved for C with respect to T and V if for all views V_I that are possible with respect to T and V we have that privacy is preserved for C with respect to T and V_I.*

3   Locality Based Privacy

We prove a first privacy theorem based on the notion of locality which was first introduced in [4] in order to provide a logical framework for modular ontologies. A similar theorem for subsumption queries and $\mathcal{SHIQ}$ TBoxes is shown in [5].

Definition 3 (Trivial expansion). *An S-interpretation $J = (\Delta^J, \cdot^J)$ is an expansion of an S'-interpretation $I = (\Delta^I, \cdot^I)$ if $S' \subseteq S$, $\Delta^J = \Delta^I$, and $X^J = X^I$ for every $X \in S'$. A trivial expansion of I to S is an expansion J of I such that $X^J = \emptyset$ for every role name and concept name $X \in S \setminus S'$.*

Definition 4 (Locality). *Let S be a signature.*

1. *A concept A is positively local wrt. S if for every trivial expansion J of any S-interpretation to any $S' \supseteq S \cup \text{sig}(A)$ we have $A^J = \emptyset$.*
2. *An axiom α is local wrt. S if every trivial expansion J of any S-interpretation to any $S' \supseteq S \cup \text{sig}(\alpha)$ is a model of α.*

Note that the definition of locality implies that an axiom containing a nominal j cannot be local wrt. S if $j \notin S$.

Grau et al. [6] show how locality can be tested by standard DL reasoners. Although for $\mathcal{SHOIQ}$ this is a NEXPTIME-complete problem, the locality test will often perform well in practice. However, they also present a tractable approximation to the locality condition which is based on the syntactic structure of concepts.

In order to state our first privacy theorem we make the following assumptions. Let P and S be two signatures with P $\subseteq$ S. Let T be a TBox over S and let $T_P \subseteq T$ be those axioms of T that are built from the signature P only. Further, we assume that all axioms of $T \setminus T_P$ are local wrt. P.

Theorem 1. *Let C be a positive local query wrt. P. Let V be a view definition which contains only queries over P. Then data privacy is preserved for C with respect to the TBox T and the view definition V.*

Proof. Let

$$V_I \text{ be a possible view with respect to } T \text{ and } V. \tag{1}$$

Since V contains only concepts of P, we find that $\mathsf{sig}(V_I) \setminus P$ consists of nominals only. Therefore

$$C \text{ is positively local wrt. } P \cup \mathsf{sig}(V_I), \tag{2}$$

$$\text{all axioms of } T \setminus T_P \text{ are local wrt. } P \cup \mathsf{sig}(V_I). \tag{3}$$

Because of (1) there exists a $P \cup \mathsf{sig}(V_I)$-interpretation I such that $I \models T_P$ and $I \models V_I$. Let J be a trivial expansion of I to $S \cup \mathsf{sig}(C)$. Thus by (3) and the definition of locality we immediately get for each $\alpha \in T \setminus T_P$ that $J \models \alpha$. Therefore we have $J \models T \cup V_I$. Moreover, by (2) we find $C^J = \emptyset$. Since V_I was arbitrary, we conclude that privacy is preserved for C. $\square$

4   Partition Based Privacy

The assumption in the previous theorem that the view only consists of queries over P may be too restrictive in practice. In this section, we will present a privacy result that is based on partitioning an ontology T in a public part T_P and a private (hidden) part T_H. The public view definition V may now contain queries that access T_H. However, this access will occur only via quantifiers and these quantifiers serve the purpose of information hiding. Therefore privacy will be preserved for positively local concepts of T_H.

Definition 5 (Safe TBox)

1. *A TBox is called* safe *if all its axioms are local with respect to $\emptyset$.*
2. *A concept is* positively local *if it is positively local with respect to $\emptyset$.*

In [7] an algorithm is presented to generate modules from a safe ontology. We use this algorithm to produce a partitioning of a TBox T such that $T = T_P \cup T_H$ where T_H and T_P are disjoint. Moreover this algorithm gives a function $\mathcal{V}$ such that

1. $\mathcal{V}$ assigns to each concept A in $\mathsf{sig}(T)$ either 1 or 2, and
2. $\mathcal{V}$ assigns to each role R in $\mathsf{sig}(T)$ a pair (i, j) with $i, j \in \{1, 2\}$.

The semantic counterpart of the partitioning of a TBox is given by the following construction which is used in the proof of Theorem 3 in [7]. Let $I = (\Delta^I, \cdot^I)$ be a model for the TBox T. We define an interpretation J as follows.

1. For each $x \in \Delta^I$ we generate two new objects x_1 and x_2. We then set $\Delta^J_1 := \{x_1 : x \in \Delta^I\}$, $\Delta^J_2 := \{x_2 : x \in \Delta^I\}$, and $\Delta^J := \Delta^J_1 \cup \Delta^J_2$.
2. For each concept name A with $\mathcal{V}(A) = i$ we set $A^J := \{x_i : x \in A^I\}$.
3. For each role name R with $\mathcal{V}(R) = (i, j)$ we set $R^J := \{(x_i, y_j) : (x, y) \in R^I\}$.

It is easy to see that

1. $\Delta^J_1 \cap \Delta^J_2 \neq \emptyset$,
2. $A^J \subseteq \Delta^J_i$ for each concept name A with $\mathcal{V}(A) = i$, and
3. $R^J \subseteq \Delta^J_i \times \Delta^J_j$ for each role name R with $\mathcal{V}(R) = (i, j)$.

As in [7] we can show the following lemma.

Lemma 1. *For every concept C with $\mathcal{V}(C) = i$ we have:*

1. *if C is positively local, then $C^J = \{x_i : x \in C^I\}$,*
2. *if C is not positively local, then $C^J = \Delta^J_{j \neq i} \cup \{x_i : x \in C^I\}$.*

From this we immediately get the following theorem, again see [7] for a proof.

Theorem 2. *Let T be a safe TBox and I be a model of T. Let J be the interpretation given above. Then J also is a model of T.*

Next we introduce the notion of an open concept. We will then prove that privacy is preserved for positively local concepts C with $\mathcal{V}(C) = 2$ with respect to the TBox T and any view definition which consists of open concepts only. This privacy result is based on the fact that the view definition (consisting of open concepts) accesses private information only via quantifiers. These quantifiers serve the purpose of information hiding.

Definition 6. *Let T, T_P, T_H, and V as above. The open concepts are inductively defined by the following clauses.*

1. *A concept C is open if $\mathcal{V}(C) = 1$.*
2. *$C \sqcup D$ and $C \sqcap D$ are open if both C and D are open.*
3. *$\neg C$ is open if C is a positively local concept with $\mathcal{V}(C) = 2$.*
4. *$\exists R.C$ and $\geq nR.C$ are open if $\mathcal{V}(R)) = (1, 2)$ and $\mathcal{V}(C) = 2$.*
5. *$\exists R.C$ and $\geq nR.C$ are open if $\mathcal{V}(R)) = (1, 1)$ and C is an open concept.*
6. *$\forall R.C$ and $\leq nR.C$ are open if $\mathcal{V}(R)) = (1, 2)$ and $\mathcal{V}(C) = 2$.*
7. *$\forall R.C$ and $\leq nR.C$ are open if $\mathcal{V}(R)) = (1, 1)$ and C is an open concept.*

An open view definition is a view definition that consists of open concepts only.

Theorem 3. *Let T be a safe TBox as above. Let V be an open view definition. Let C be a positively local concept with $\mathcal{V}(C) = 2$. Then privacy is preserved for C with respect to T and V.*

Proof. Assume we are given a view V_I based on V and a model I of T and V_I. We define the interpretation J as above where we additionally define

$$a^J := \{x_1 : \{x\} = a^I\} \text{ for each nominal } a \in \mathsf{sig}(V_I). \tag{4}$$

By Theorem 2, we know that J models T. We now show that J also is a model of V_I. Let $a : D$ be an assertion on V_I for an open concept D. We show by induction on the structure of D that $\{x_1 : x \in D^I\} \subseteq D^J$.

1. D is a concept with $\mathcal{V}(D) = 1$. In this case our claim follows from Lemma 1.
2. D is of the form $E \sqcup F$ or $E \sqcap F$ with E and F being open. The claim is an immediate consequence of applying the induction hypothesis to E and F.
3. D is of the form $\neg E$ where E is a positively local concept with $\mathcal{V}(E) = 2$. We find by Lemma 1 that $\Delta_1^J \subseteq D^J$. Therefore we have $\{x_1 : x \in D^I\} \subseteq D^J$.
4. D is of the form $\exists R.E$ or $\geq nR.E$ for (i) a role name R with $\mathcal{V}(R) = (1, 2)$ and a concept E with $\mathcal{V}(E) = 2$ or (ii) R with $\mathcal{V}(R) = (1, 1)$ and an open concept E. Assume there are x, y such that $R^I(x, y)$ and $E^I(y)$. In case (i) we find $R^J(x_1, y_2)$ by the definition of J and by Lemma 1 we find $E^J(y_2)$. In case (ii) we find $R^J(x_1, y_1)$ and applying the induction hypothesis to E yields $E^J(y_1)$. Therefore in both cases we conclude $x_1 \in (\exists R.E)^J$. The cases for $\geq nR.E$ are similar.
5. D is of the form $\forall R.E$ or $\leq nR.E$ for (i) a role name R with $\mathcal{V}(R) = (1, 2)$ and a concept E with $\mathcal{V}(E) = 2$ or (ii) R with $\mathcal{V}(R) = (1, 1)$ and an open concept E. Assume $x \in (\forall R.E)^I$. Let y be such that $R^J(x_1, y)$. In case (i) we have that y is of the form z_2 for some z with $R^I(x, z)$. Thus we have $z \in E^I$ and Lemma 1 yields $E^J(y)$. In case (ii) we have that y is of the form z_1 for some z with $R^I(x, z)$. Thus we have $z \in E^I$ and by the induction hypothesis we obtain $y \in E^J$. Therefore in both cases we conclude $x_1 \in (\forall R.E)^J$. The cases for $\leq nR.E$ are similar.

From $\{x_1 : x \in D^I\} \subseteq D^J$ and (4) we conclude that $J \models a : D$. Thus J is a model of T and V_I such that for each nominal $a \in \mathsf{sig}(V_I)$ we have $a^J \in \Delta_1^J$. Since $C^J \subseteq \Delta_2^J$ by Lemma 1, we conclude that privacy is preserved for C. $\square$

Remark 1. We have to be careful when we try to enlarge the class of open concepts. The following examples show that privacy will be violated if we allow additional open concepts. Let C be a concept with $\mathcal{V}(\neg C) = 1$ and $\mathcal{V}(C) = 1$. Further let D be a positively local concept with $\mathcal{V}(D) = 2$. We consider the following cases:

1. Suppose $E \sqcap F$ is open if E is open. Then $V = \{C \sqcap D\}$ is an open view definition. However, the view $a : C \sqcap D$ entails $a : D$.
2. Suppose $E \sqcup F$ is open if E is open. Then $V = \{C \sqcup D, \neg C\}$ is an open view definition. However, $\{a : C \sqcup D, a : \neg C\}$ is a possible view with respect to V which entails $a : D$.
3. Suppose $\neg E$ is open if E is open. Then $V = \{\neg\neg D\}$ is an open view definition. However, the view $\{a : \neg\neg D\}$ entails $a : D$.

Thus in all three cases, there is a possible view with respect to which the set of answers to D is non-empty. Therefore in all three cases privacy is not preserved for D with respect to V.

5   Related Work and Conclusion

We have introduced the problem of provable data privacy with respect to *views* in [1,2]. An investigation of privacy with respect to *view definitions* in the context of $\mathcal{ALC}$ ontologies is provided in [8]. Provable data privacy is a privacy notion which corresponds to entailment. Of course there are also other - more fine grained - notions, most prominently perfect privacy [9]. Unfortunately, lack of space does not permit a discussion of them here.

Locality has been introduced in [4] in order to support safe merging of ontologies. That means an ontology can be integrated with a foreign ontology without changing the meaning of the foreign ontology. Later, locality has also been used to support partial reuse of ontologies [6]. There the problem is to find a fragment of an ontology which captures completely the meaning of some terms. The problem of extracting modules from a given ontology has also been addressed in [7] where the partitioning algorithm is presented which is the core to our results in Section 4. It is worth mentioning that the result of partitioning an ontology can be seen as a knowledge base in the language of E-connections [10]. In fact, all models of an E-connection ontology have the form required for Theorem 3.

A basic notion for the study of modularity is the one of a conservative extension, see for instance [11]. Grau and Horrocks [12] establish a tight connection between conservative extensions and privacy guarantees for logic-based information systems. Privacy aware access to ontologies is also addressed in [13] in the context of view-based query answering over ontologies.

Summing up, we have established two privacy theorems stating that given a modular ontology T, a view definition V, and a query C, privacy is preserved for C wrt. T and any possible view of V. Our first result is based on the notion of locality whereas the second one relies on a partitioning algorithm for ontologies.

References

1. Stoffel, K., Studer, T.: Provable Data Privacy. In: Andersen, K.V., Debenham, J., Wagner, R. (eds.) DEXA 2005. LNCS, vol. 3588, pp. 324–332. Springer, Heidelberg (2005)
2. Stouppa, P., Studer, T.: A formal model of data privacy. In: Virbitskaite, I., Voronkov, A. (eds.) PSI 2006. LNCS, vol. 4378, pp. 400–408. Springer, Heidelberg (2007)
3. Horrocks, I., Sattler, U.: A tableau decision procedure for $\mathcal{SHOIQ}$. J. Autom. Reason. 39(3), 249–276 (2007)
4. Grau, B.C., Horrocks, I., Kazakov, Y., Sattler, U.: A logical framework for modularity of ontologies. In: Veloso, M.M. (ed.) IJCAI 2007, pp. 298–303 (2007)
5. Bao, J., Slutzki, G., Honavar, V.: Privacy-preserving reasoning on the semantic web. In: WI 2007, pp. 791–797 (2007)

6. Grau, B.C., Horrocks, I., Kazakov, Y., Sattler, U.: Just the right amount: extracting modules from ontologies. In: WWW 2007, pp. 717–726. ACM, New York (2007)
7. Grau, B.C., Parsia, B., Sirin, E., Kalyanpur, A.: Modularity and web ontologies. In: KR 2006, pp. 198–209. AAAI Press, Menlo Park (2006)
8. Stouppa, P., Studer, T.: Data privacy for $\mathcal{ALC}$ knowledge bases. In: Artemov, S., Nerode, A. (eds.) LFCS 2009. LNCS, vol. 5407, pp. 409–421. Springer, Heidelberg (2008)
9. Miklau, G., Suciu, D.: A formal analysis of information disclosure in data exchange. In: SIGMOD (2004)
10. Kutz, O., Lutz, C., Wolter, F., Zakharyaschev, M.: E-connections of abstract description systems. Artifical Intelligence 156(1), 1–73 (2004)
11. Kontchakov, R., Wolter, F., Zakharyaschev, M.: Modularity in DL-Lite. In: DL 2007. CEUR Workshop Proceedings, vol. 250 (2007)
12. Cuenca Grau, B., Horrocks, I.: Privacy-preserving query answering in logic-based information systems. In: ECAI 2008 (2008)
13. Calvanese, D., De Giacomo, G., Lenzerini, M., Rosati, R.: View-based query answering over description logic ontologies. In: KR 2008, pp. 242–251 (2008)

Symbolic Bounded Conformance Checking of Model Programs

Margus Veanes and Nikolaj Bjørner

Microsoft Research, Redmond, WA, USA
{margus,nbjorner}@microsoft.com

Abstract. Model programs are high-level behavioral specifications typically representing Abstract State Machines or ASMs. Conformance checking of model programs is the problem of deciding if the set of traces allowed by one model program forms a subset of the set of traces allowed by another model program. This is a foundational problem in the context of model-based testing, where one model program corresponds to an implementation and the other one to its specification. Here model programs are described using the ASM language AsmL. We assume a background $\mathcal{T}$ containing linear arithmetic, sets, and tuples. We introduce the Bounded Conformance Checking problem or BCC as a special case of the conformance checking problem when the length of traces is bounded and provide a mapping of BCC to a theorem proving problem in $\mathcal{T}$. BCC is shown to be highly undecidable in the general case but decidable for a class of model programs that are common in practice.

1 Introduction

We consider behavioral specifications given in the form of model programs. Model programs are mainly used to describe protocol-like behavior of software systems, and the underlying update semantics is based on ASMs [17]. However, model programs usually depend on additional parameters that are needed for executability. At Microsoft, model programs are used in the Spec Explorer tool in the Windows organization as an integral part of the *protocol quality assurance process* [16] for model-based testing of public application-level network protocols. A central problem in the context of model-based testing is to determine if an implementation *conforms* to a given specification, meaning that the traces that are observed from the implementation under test do not contradict the model. Traditionally, model-based testing is used at system-level, as a black-box testing technique where the implementation code is not visible to the tester. White-box testing on the other hand, is used at the unit-level by the developers of the code and is based on different techniques. Here we assume that the implementation is also given or abstracted as a model program and consider the conformance checking problem as a theorem proving problem between the implementation and the model. The general conformance checking problem is very hard but can be approximated in various ways. One way is to bound the length of the traces,

A. Pnueli, I. Virbitskaite, and A. Voronkov (Eds.): PSI 2009, LNCS 5947, pp. 388–400, 2010.
© Springer-Verlag Berlin Heidelberg 2010

```
type Vertex = Integer
type Edge = (Vertex, Vertex)
IsSource(v as Vertex, E as Set of Edge) as Boolean
   return not exists e in E where Second(e) = v
Sources(E as Set of Edge) as Set of Vertex
   return {First(e) | e in E where IsSource(First(e),E)}
```

Model program P	Model program Q

`var` E `as Set of` $Edge$
`var` V `as Set of` $Vertex$ =
          $\{x,y \mid (x,y)$ `in` $E\}$
`[Action]`
$Step(v$ `as` $Vertex)$
   `require` v `in` V `and` $IsSource(v,E)$
   `forall` w `in` V
      `remove` (v,w) `from` E
   `remove` v `from` V
	`var` D `as Set of` $Edge$
	`var` S `as Set of` $Vertex$ = $Sources(D)$
	
	`[Action]`
	$Step(v$ `as` $Vertex)$
	   `require` S`<>{}` `and` v`=`$Min(S)$
	   D' = $\{e \mid e$ `in` D `where First(e)<>`$v\}$
	   S := $(S\backslash\{v\})$ `union` $Sources(D')$
	   D := D'

Fig. 1. P specifies a topological sorting of a directed graph $G = (V, E)$ as follows. The $Step$-action of P requires that the vertex v has no incoming edges and removes all outgoing edges from v. Thus, starting from a given initial graph G with n vertices, a trace $Step(v_1), Step(v_2), \ldots, Step(v_n)$ is allowed in P if and only if $(v_1, v_2, \ldots, v_n)$ is a topological sorting of G. Similarly, the model program Q describes a particular implementation where during each step the vertex with minimum integer id is selected. As in ASMs, the top-level loop of a model program is implicit: while there exists an enabled action, one enabled action is chosen and executed.

which leads to the Bounded Conformance Checking problem, or BCC, and is the topic of this paper.

Model programs typically assume a rich background universe including tuples (records) and sets, as well as user defined data structures. Moreover, unlike traditional sequential programs, model programs often operate on a more abstract level, for example, they use set comprehensions and parallel updates to compute a collection of elements in a single atomic step, rather than one element at a time, in a loop. The definition of model programs here extends the prior definitions to *nondeterministic* model programs, by allowing internal choices. Two model programs, written in AsmL [4,18], are illustrated in Figure 1.

In Section 2 we define model programs. In Section 3 we define the problem of *bounded conformance checking* or *BCC* and show its reduction to a theorem proving problem in $\mathcal{T}$. Section 4 discusses the complexity of *BCC*. Section 5 is about related work.

2   Model Programs

We consider a background $\mathcal{T}$ that includes linear arithmetic, Booleans, tuples, and sets. All values in $\mathcal{T}$ have a given *sort*. Well-formed expressions of $\mathcal{T}$ are

$$T^\sigma \qquad ::= x^\sigma \mid \mathit{Default}^\sigma \mid \mathit{Ite}(T^\mathbb{B}, T^\sigma, T^\sigma) \mid \mathit{TheElementOf}(T^{\mathbb{S}(\sigma)}) \mid$$
$$\pi_i(T^{\sigma_0 \times \cdots \times \sigma_{i-1} \times \sigma \times \cdots \times \sigma_k})$$

$$T^{\sigma_0 \times \sigma_1 \times \cdots \times \sigma_k} ::= \langle T^{\sigma_0}, T^{\sigma_1}, \ldots, T^{\sigma_k} \rangle$$

$$T^\mathbb{Z} \qquad ::= k \mid T^\mathbb{Z} + T^\mathbb{Z} \mid k * T^\mathbb{Z}$$

$$T^\mathbb{B} \qquad ::= \mathit{true} \mid \mathit{false} \mid \neg T^\mathbb{B} \mid T^\mathbb{B} \wedge T^\mathbb{B} \mid T^\mathbb{B} \vee T^\mathbb{B} \mid T^\mathbb{B} \Rightarrow T^\mathbb{B} \mid \forall x\, T^\mathbb{B} \mid \exists x\, T^\mathbb{B} \mid$$
$$T^\sigma = T^\sigma \mid T^{\mathbb{S}(\sigma)} \subseteq T^{\mathbb{S}(\sigma)} \mid T^\sigma \in T^{\mathbb{S}(\sigma)} \mid T^\mathbb{Z} \leq T^\mathbb{Z}$$

$$T^{\mathbb{S}(\sigma)} \qquad ::= \{T^\sigma \mid_{\bar{x}} T^\mathbb{B}\} \mid \emptyset^{\mathbb{S}(\sigma)} \mid T^{\mathbb{S}(\sigma)} \cup T^{\mathbb{S}(\sigma)} \mid T^{\mathbb{S}(\sigma)} \cap T^{\mathbb{S}(\sigma)} \mid T^{\mathbb{S}(\sigma)} \setminus T^{\mathbb{S}(\sigma)}$$

$$T^\mathbb{A} \qquad ::= f^{(\sigma_0, \ldots, \sigma_{n-1})}(T^{\sigma_0}, \ldots, T^{\sigma_{n-1}})$$

Fig. 2. Well-formed expressions in $\mathcal{T}$. Sorts are shown explicitly here. An expression of sort σ is written T^σ. The sorts $\mathbb{Z}$ and $\mathbb{B}$ are for integers and Booleans, respectively, k stands for any integer constant, x^σ is a variable of sort σ. The sorts $\mathbb{Z}$ and $\mathbb{B}$ are *basic*, so is the *tuple sort* $\sigma_0 \times \cdots \times \sigma_k$, provided that each σ_i is basic. The *set sort* $\mathbb{S}(\sigma)$ is not basic and requires σ to be basic. All quantified variables are required to have basic sorts. The sort $\mathbb{A}$ is called the *action sort*, $f^{(\sigma_0, \ldots, \sigma_{n-1})}$ stands for an *action symbol* with fixed arity n and argument sorts $\sigma_0, \ldots, \sigma_{n-1}$, where each argument sort is a set sort or a basic sort. The sort $\mathbb{A}$ is *not* basic. The only atomic relation that can be used for $T^\mathbb{A}$ is equality. *Default*$^\mathbb{A}$ is a nullary action symbol. Boolean expressions are also called *formulas* in the context of $\mathcal{T}$. In the paper, sort annotations are mostly omitted but are always assumed.

shown in Figure 2. Each sort corresponds to a disjoint part of the universe. We do not add explicit sort annotations to symbols or expressions but always assume that all expression are well-sorted. A value is *basic* if it is either a Boolean, an integer, or a tuple of basic values.

The expression $\mathit{Ite}(\varphi, t_1, t_2)$ equals t_1 if φ is true, and it equals t_2, otherwise. For each sort, there is a specific *Default* value in the background. In particular, for Booleans the value is *false*, for set sorts the value is $\emptyset$, for integers the value is 0 and for tuples the value is the tuple of defaults of the respective tuple elements.

The function *TheElementOf* maps every singleton set to the element in that set and maps every other set to *Default*. Note that *extensionality* of sets: $\forall v\, w\, (\forall y(y \in v \leftrightarrow y \in w) \rightarrow v = w)$, allows us to use set comprehensions as terms: the *comprehension term* $\{t(\bar{x}) \mid_{\bar{x}} \varphi(\bar{x})\}$ represents the set such that $\forall y(y \in \{t(\bar{x}) \mid_{\bar{x}} \varphi(\bar{x})\} \leftrightarrow \exists \bar{x}(t(\bar{x}) = y \wedge \varphi(\bar{x})))$. We make use of explicit definitions in terms of $\mathcal{T}$ such as *Min* (used in Figure 1), that returns the minimum element from a set of integers, or 0 when the set is empty, $Min(X) \stackrel{\text{def}}{=} \mathit{TheElementOf}(\{y \mid y \in X \wedge \forall z(z \in X \Rightarrow y \leq z)\})$. In the general case, model programs also use *maps*. We assume a standard representation of maps as function graphs, maps are needed to represent dynamic ASM functions, see [7], maps are not used in the current paper.

Actions. There is a specific *action sort* $\mathbb{A}$, values of this sort are called *actions* and have the form $f(v_0, \ldots, v_{\mathrm{arity}(f)-1})$. *Default*$^\mathbb{A}$ has arity 0. Two actions are equal if and only if they have the same action symbol and their corresponding arguments are equal. An action $f(\bar{v})$ is called an f-action. Every action symbol f with arity $n > 0$, is associated with a unique *parameter variable* f_i for all i, $0 \leq i < n$.[1]

Choice variables. A *choice variable* is a variable[2] χ that is associated with a formula $\exists x \varphi[x]$, called the *range condition* of χ, denoted by $\chi^{\exists x \varphi[x]}$. The following axiom is assumed to hold for each choice variable:

$$IsChoice(\chi^{\exists x \varphi}) \stackrel{\text{def}}{=} (\exists x\, \varphi[x]) \Rightarrow \varphi[\chi^{\exists x \varphi}]). \tag{1}$$

In the general case, the sort of χ may be non-basic and χ is a map (a Skolem function), in which case the range condition must hold for the elements in the range of the map, see [7].

Model programs. The following definition extends the former definition of model programs by allowing nondeterminism through *choice variables*. An *assignment* is a pair $x := t$ where x is a variable and t is a term (both having the same sort). An *update rule* is a finite set of assignments where the assigned variables are distinct.

Definition 1 (Model Program). A *model program* is a tuple $P = (\Sigma, \Gamma, \varphi^0, R)$, where

- Σ is a finite set of variables called *state variables*;
- Γ is a finite set of *action symbols*;
- φ^0 is a formula called the *initial state condition*;
- R is a collection $\{R_f\}_{f \in \Gamma}$ of *action rules* $R_f = (\gamma, U, X)$, where
  - γ is a formula called the *guard of f*;
  - U is an update rule $\{x := t_x\}_{x \in \Sigma_f}$ for some $\Sigma_f \subseteq \Sigma$, U is called the *update rule of f*,
  - X is a set of *choice variables of f*
  All unbound variables that occur in an action rule, including the range conditions of choice variables, must either be state variables, parameter variables, or choice variables of the action. The sets of parameter variables, state variables and choice variables must be disjoint.

Intuitively, choice variables are "hidden" parameter variables, the range condition of a choice variable determines the valid range for its values. For parameter variables, the range conditions are typically part of the guard. We often say *action* to also mean an action rule or an action symbol, if the intent is clear from the context. The case when all parameter variables and choice variables of a model program are basic is an important special case when symbolic analysis becomes feasible, which motivates the following definition.[3]

---

[1] In AsmL one can of course use any formal parameter name, such as v in Figure 1, following standard conventions for method signatures.

[2] Pronounced "chi".

[3] The standard notion of basic ASMs is more restrictive, in particular model programs allow unbounded exploration, quantifiers may be unbounded.

Definition 2 (Basic Model Programs). An update rule is *basic* if all pa-rameter variables and choice variables that occur in it are basic. An action rule is *basic* if its update rule is basic. A model program is *basic* if its action rules are basic and the initial state condition implies that all nonbasic state variables are empty sets.

Representing standard ASMs as model programs. Standard *ASM update rules* can be translated into update rules of model programs. A detailed translation from standard ASMs to model programs is given in [7]. Intuitively, a forall-statement (such as the one used in Figure 1) translates into a comprehension expression, and each choose-statement introduces a new choice variable. An im-portant property of the translation is that, if choose statements are not allowed to occur inside forall statements in the ASM update rules, then the transla-tion yields a basic model program. When a choose-statement is nested inside a forall-statement, the resulting model program will depend on a non-basic choice variable or a *choice function* (Skolem function). In the general case, the trans-lation also adds an additional state variable that indicates collisions of updates and in this way captures "error" states. We assume here that update rules of actions in a model program correspond to ASM update rules where some choice variables occur as parameters of the action, in which case their range conditions are typically part of the guard.

States. A *state* is a mapping of variables to values. Given a state S and an expression E, where S maps all the free variables in E to values, E^S is the *evaluation of E in S*. Given a state S and a formula φ, $S \models \varphi$ means that φ is true in S. A formula φ is *valid* (in $\mathcal{T}$) if φ is true in all states. *Since $\mathcal{T}$ is assumed to be the background theory we usually omit it, and assume that each state also has an implicit part that satisfies $\mathcal{T}$, e.g. that $+$ means addition and $\cup$ means set union.* In the following let P be a fixed model program.

Definition 3. Let a be an action $f(v_0, \dots, v_{n-1})$ and S a state. A *choice ex-pansion of S for a* is an expansion S' of $S \cup \{f_i \mapsto v_i\}_{i<n}$ with choice variables of f.

Definition 4. An f-action a is *enabled* in a state S if there exists a choice expansion of S for a that satisfies the guard of f.

Definition 5. An f-action a *causes a transition* from a state S_1 to a state S_2, if a is enabled in S_1, S_1' is a choice expansion of S_1 that satisfies the guard of a, for each assignment $x := t$ of f, $x^{S_2} = t^{S_1'}$, and for any other state variable x, $x^{S_2} = x^{S_1}$.

Example 1. Let P be the model program in Figure 1. The set of initial states of $[\![P]\!]$ includes for example the state $S_0 = \{V \mapsto \{1, 2, 3\}, E \mapsto \{\langle 1, 2\rangle, \langle 2, 3\rangle\}\}$. The action $Step(1)$ is enabled in S_0 because $S_0 \cup \{v \mapsto 1\} \models v \in V \wedge \neg\exists w(w \in V \wedge \langle w, v\rangle \in E)$. The action $Step(1)$ causes a transition from S_0 to $S_1 = \{V \mapsto \{2, 3\}, E \mapsto \{\langle 2, 3\rangle\}\}$. ⊠

A *labeled transition system* or *LTS* is a tuple $(\mathcal{S}, \mathcal{S}_0, L, T)$, where $\mathcal{S}$ is a set of states, $\mathcal{S}_0 \subseteq \mathcal{S}$ is a set of *initial states*, L is a set of labels and $T \subseteq \mathcal{S} \times L \times \mathcal{S}$ is a *transition relation*.

Definition 6. Let $P = (\Sigma, \Gamma, \varphi^0, R)$ be a model program. The *LTS of P*, denoted by $[\![P]\!]$ is the LTS $(\mathcal{S}, \mathcal{S}_0, L, T)$, where $\mathcal{S}_0 = \{S \mid S \models \varphi_0\}$; L is the set of all actions over Γ; T and $\mathcal{S}$ are the least sets such that, $\mathcal{S}_0 \subseteq \mathcal{S}$, and if $S \in \mathcal{S}$ and there is an action a that causes a transition from S to S' then $S' \in \mathcal{S}$ and $(S, a, S') \in T$.

Definition 7. A model program P is *deterministic* if forall transitions (S, a, S_1) and (S, a, S_2) in $[\![P]\!]$, $S_1 = S_2$.

Clearly, any model program without choice variables is deterministic.

Definition 8. A *run* of P is a sequence of transitions $(S_i, a_i, S_{i+1})_{i<\kappa}$ in $[\![P]\!]$, for some $\kappa \leq \omega$, where S_0 is an initial state of $[\![P]\!]$. The sequence $(a_i)_{i<\kappa}$ is called an *(action) (κ-)trace* of P.

3   Symbolic Bounded Conformance Checking

We are now ready to define the central problem of the paper in Definition 10. Let P and Q be fixed model programs with the same set of action symbols. Let $k \geq 0$ be a fixed bound. We assume here that P and Q have initial state conditions that require that all the state variables are initially equal to *Default*. Under this assumption, we drop the initial state condition from the definition. This assumption is needed in order to avoid tedious special cases, when for example the initial conditions are false, etc. Note that, by adding an additional initialization action, any values can be assigned to the state variables.

Definition 9. Q *k-conforms to* P, $Q \sqsubseteq_k P$, if for all $l \leq k$, all *l*-traces of Q are *l*-traces of P. Q *conforms to* P, $Q \sqsubseteq P$, if $Q \sqsubseteq_k P$ for all k.

If $Q \sqsubseteq_k P$, then P is more liberal by allowing more traces up to length k. Intuitively, when P is a specification model program and Q is an implementation model program and $Q \sqsubseteq_k P$, then Q behaves as expected by P within k steps. Conformance testing is an approximation of k-conformance up to some k, where k depends on the maximum length of the test cases. In the more general case, when one distinguishes between *observable* and *controllable* actions in the context of asynchronous systems, one needs to consider a more general form of conformance notion, such as alternating refinement [2] or ioco [26], that is outside the scope of this paper, see [28]. Note that a most general model program is one where all actions have an empty update rule and all guards are *true*, such a model program is trivially conformed to by any other model program.

Example 2. Let P and Q be the model programs in Figure 1. Assume that there is an additional *Init*-action in both P and Q that first initializes the state variables to a concrete graph G and then enables the *Step*-action. One can show that $Q \sqsubseteq_k P$ for all k and thus $Q \sqsubseteq P$. In this particular case, if one shows that, for all input graphs with k vertices $Q \sqsubseteq_{k+1} P$, then $Q \sqsubseteq P$ follows. Note also that $P \not\sqsubseteq_2 Q$. ⊠

Definition 10 (BCC). *Bounded Conformance Checking* or *BCC* is the problem of deciding if $Q \sqsubseteq_k P$.

In order to reduce BCC into a theorem proving problem, we construct a special formula from given P, Q and k, as defined in Definition 11. Given an expression E and a step number $i > 0$, we write $E[i]$ below for a copy of E where each (unbound) variable x in E has been uniquely renamed to a variable $x[i]$. We assume also that $E[0]$ is E.

Definition 11 (Bounded Conformance Formula). Let P and Q be model programs $(\overline{x_\star}, \Gamma, (\gamma_{f,\star}, U_{f,\star}, X_{f,\star})_{f \in \Gamma})$, for $\star = P, Q$. Assume that $\overline{x_Q} \cap \overline{x_P} = \emptyset$ and that the choice variables in P and Q are disjoint.[4] Assume also that each action rule includes an assignment for all the state variables.[5] The *bounded conformance formula* for P, Q, and k is:

$$BCC(Q, P, k) \stackrel{\text{def}}{=} (\overline{x_Q} = \overline{Default} \wedge \overline{x_P} = \overline{Default}) \Rightarrow Conforms(0, k)$$

$$Conforms(k, k) \stackrel{\text{def}}{=} true$$

$$(i < k)\ Conforms(i, k) \stackrel{\text{def}}{=} \bigwedge_{f \in \Gamma} (\forall \overline{f_j[i]}\, \overline{\chi_{f,Q}[i]}(\gamma_{f,Q}[i] \wedge \overline{IsChoice(\chi_{f,Q}[i])}) \Rightarrow$$

$$\exists \overline{\chi_{f,P}[i]}(\gamma_{f,P}[i] \wedge \overline{IsChoice(\chi_{f,P}[i])} \wedge$$

$$(\bigwedge_{x := t_x \in U_{f,Q} \cup U_{f,P}} x[i+1] = t_x[i]$$

$$\Rightarrow Conforms(i+1, k)))))$$

where $\overline{f_j[i]} = f_0[i] \dots f_{\text{arity}(f)-1}[i]$ are the parameter variables of action f for step i (the parameter variables of f are shared between P and Q), and $\overline{\chi_{f,P}[i]}$ and $\overline{\chi_{f,Q}[i]}$ are the choice variables of f in P and Q, respectively, for step i.

Notice that all parameter variables, and choice variables have distinct names in each step. This implies that all oracles and parameters are local to a single step, and do not carry over from one step to the next. The only connection between the steps happens via the state variables. Note also that if both P and Q are deterministic, then the resulting formula is essentially a universal formula. If P has choice variables then the bounded conformance formula has a k-depth quantifier alternation.

The following theorem allows us to check k-conformance by proving that the corresponding bounded conformance formula is valid in $\mathcal{T}$.

---

[4] Alternatively rename those variables in Q for example.
[5] Add an assignment $x := x$ for each state variable x that is not assigned.

Theorem 1. $BCC(Q, P, k)$ *is valid in* $\mathcal{T}$ *if and only if* $Q \sqsubseteq_k P$.

Proof (Sketch). For $k = 0$ the statement holds trivially. Assume $k > 0$. Both directions are proved separately. For the direction ($\Longrightarrow$) we assume that $Q \not\sqsubseteq_k P$ and get a shortest run of length $l \leq k$ where the last action is enabled in Q but not in P. From the run we can construct a state where $\neg BCC(Q, P, l)$ is true. Note that if $\neg BCC(Q, P, l)$ is satisfiable then so is $\neg BCC(Q, P, l')$, for $l' > l$. The proof of the direction ($\Longleftarrow$) is similar.   ⊠

4   Complexity of BCC

Here we look at the complexity of BCC. First we note that the problem is effectively equivalent to the validity problem of formulas in second-order Peano arithmetic with sets (Π_1^1-complete). This implies that there exists no refutationally complete procedure for checking k-conformance in general (even for $k = 1$). Second, we note that, even if we restrict the background universe to *finite* sets, the problem is still undecidable, by being co-re-complete. Third, we show that BCC is decidable over *basic* model programs. The reason for this is that for basic model programs, the set variables can be eliminated, and the problem reduces to Presburger arithmetic.

Undecidability of BCC. We use the result that the validity problem of formulas in Presburger arithmetic with unary relations is Π_1^1-complete [1,19]. The Π_1^1-hardness part is an immediate consequence of the results in [1,19], by considering model programs that have one action with a set-valued parameter and a linear arithmetic formula as the guard. The inclusion in Π_1^1 can be shown similarly to the proof of the Σ_1^1-completeness of the BMPC problem in [7].

Corollary 1. *BCC is* Π_1^1-*complete*.

Now suppose that the sets in the background are finite and consider the satisfiability problem in $\mathcal{T}$ over finite sets that is re-complete [7].

Corollary 2. *BCC over finite sets is co-re-complete.*

Decidability of BCC over basic model programs. Basic model programs are common in practical applications. The two main reasons for this are: 1) actions typically only use parameters that have basic sorts, see for example the Credits model in [32]. 2) the initial state is usually required to have fixed initial values or default values for all the state variables. Let $\mathcal{T}^0$ stand for the fragment of $\mathcal{T}$ where all variables are basic. We use decidability of $\mathcal{T}^0$, that follows as a special case from the decision procedure for $\mathcal{T}^{\prec}$ in [7], that is by reduction to linear arithmetic.

Theorem 2. *BCC of basic model programs is decidable.*

Proof (Sketch). Let P and Q be basic model programs and k a step bound. Let $\psi = BCC(Q, P, k)$. The subformula $\bigwedge_{x \in \Sigma} x[i+1] = t_x[i] \Rightarrow Conforms(i+1, k)$ of ψ is equivalent to the formula $Conforms(i+1, k)\{x[i+1] \mapsto t_x[i] \mid x \in \Sigma\}$ where $x[i+1]$ has been replaced by $t_x[i]$. Apply this transformation successively to eliminate each occurrence of $x[i+1]$ for $i < k$. Finally, eliminate each (initial) state variable by replacing it with the default value. The resulting formula, say φ, is equivalent to ψ and does not use any state variables. Moreover, since P and Q are basic, φ is in T^0. The statement follows from Theorem 1 and decidability of T^0.   ⊠

It is possible to carry out the reduction in Theorem 2 in polynomial time in the size ψ. First, the formula ψ is translated into logic without sets but with unary relations, by replacing set variables with unary relations and by eliminating set comprehensions and set operations in the usual way, e.g., $t \in S$, where S is a set variable, becomes the atom $R_S(t)$, where R_S is a unary relation symbol. It is easy to show by induction over expressions that such a translation can be done in polynomial time in the size of ψ and preserves the structure of ψ.

We iterate the following transformation on the resulting formula, say ψ_i, starting with $i = k$, repeating the transformation for $i := i - 1$, until $i = 0$. For ease of exposition assume also that there is a single set valued state variable S.

The formula ψ_i has a subformula of the form (2) where $\mathbf{Q}\bar{y}\rho$ is assumed to be on Prenex form so that ρ is quantifier free,

$$\forall x(R_{i+1}(x) \Leftrightarrow \varphi[x]) \Rightarrow \mathbf{Q}\bar{y}\rho[R_{i+1}(t_1), \ldots, R_{i+1}(t_n)] \tag{2}$$

where R_{i+1} corresponds to the value of S at step $i+1$ and φ as well as each t_j may only contain values of S from step i. The formula (2) is equivalent to (3) where we may assume that $\bar{y}$ do not occur free in φ.

$$\mathbf{Q}\bar{y}(\forall x(R_{i+1}(x) \Leftrightarrow \varphi[x]) \Rightarrow \rho[R_{i+1}(t_1), \ldots, R_{i+1}(t_n)]) \tag{3}$$

The formula (3) is equivalent to (4) (where $\bar{z}$ are Boolean).

$$\mathbf{Q}\bar{y} \forall \bar{z}(\underbrace{(\bigwedge_{j=1}^{n} z_j \Leftrightarrow \varphi[t_j]) \Rightarrow \rho[z_1, \ldots, z_n])}_{\delta} \tag{4}$$

Formula δ is equivalent to (5) by using the encoding in [15, p 129],

$$\forall x \forall w (\underbrace{(\bigvee_{j=1}^{n} (x = t_j \wedge w = z_j)) \Rightarrow (w \Leftrightarrow \varphi[x])}_{\Phi[w \Leftrightarrow \varphi]}). \tag{5}$$

Now consider the formula $\Phi[w \Leftrightarrow \varphi]$, where φ is $\mathbf{Q}\bar{u}\gamma[\bar{u}]$ in Prenex form. The formula $\Phi[w \Leftrightarrow \varphi]$ is equivalent to

$$\mathbf{Q}\bar{u}\mathbf{Q}^c\bar{u}'\Phi[(w \wedge \gamma[\bar{u}]) \vee (\neg w \wedge \neg\gamma[\bar{u}'])] \tag{6}$$

where $\mathbf{Q}^c$ is the complement of quantifier prefix $\mathbf{Q}$; (6) is equivalent to

$$\mathbf{Q}\bar{u}\mathbf{Q}^c\bar{u}'\forall b\forall b'((\underbrace{\gamma[\bar{u}] \Leftrightarrow b \wedge \gamma[\bar{u}'] \Leftrightarrow b'}_{\gamma'}) \Rightarrow \Phi[(w \wedge b) \vee (\neg w \wedge \neg b')]) \qquad (7)$$

Using the same encoding from [15] as above, γ' is equivalent to

$$\forall\bar{v}\forall d(((\bar{v} = \bar{u} \wedge d = b) \vee (\bar{v} = \bar{u}' \wedge d = b')) \Rightarrow (d \Leftrightarrow \gamma[\bar{v}])) \qquad (8)$$

Combining the above equivalences, it follows that (2) is equivalent to

$$\mathbf{Q}\ldots((8) \Rightarrow \Phi[(w \wedge b) \vee (\neg w \wedge \neg b')]) \Rightarrow \rho[\bar{z}]) \qquad (9)$$

The reduction from (2) to (9) shows that no t_j or φ needs to be duplicated and clearly the Prenex form of (9) has the same size as (9). The formula (2) is replaced in ψ_i with (9) to get ψ_{i-1}.

Finally, recall that the initial values of set variables are empty sets, which means that $\forall x\,(R_0(x) \Leftrightarrow \text{false})$, so each occurrence of an atom $R_0(t)$ is replaced in ψ_0 with false.

The above reduction can also be carried out in a more general setting, independent of the background theory, by first introducing auxiliary predicates that define all the subformulas of ψ, by applying a transformation similar to [27] or [24], and then eliminating the predicates (as a form of deskolemization) by equivalence preserving transformations similar to the transformations shown above.

The overall reduction shows that the computational complexity of BCC of basic model programs, regarding both the lower and the upper bound, is the same as that of Presburger arithmetic, stated here as a corollary of the above reduction and [15].

Corollary 3. *The upper bound of the computational complexity of BCC of basic model programs is $2^{2^{2^{cn}}}$ and the lower bound is $2^{2^{cn}}$, where c is a constant and n is the size of the input (P, Q, k) for BCC.*

5   Related Work

The bounded model program checking problem or BMPC [7,29,31] is a bounded path exploration problem of a given model program. BMPC is a generalization of bounded model checking to model programs. The technique of bounded model checking by using SAT solving was introduced in [5] and the extension to SMT was introduced in [14], a related approach is described in [3]. BMPC reduces to satisfiability modulo $\mathcal{T}$. Unlike BCC, the resulting formula for a BMPC problem is typically existential with no quantifier alternation, even for nondeterministic model programs, since choice variables and parameter variables are treated equally. BMPC is therefore better suited for analysis using the SMT approach. General reachability problems for transition systems as theorem proving problems are also discussed in [25].

Formulating a state refinement relation between two symbolic transition systems as a theorem proving problem, where one system describes an implementation and the other one its specification, has a long standing in automatic verification of hardware, with seminal work done in [11] for verifying control properties of pipelined microprocessors. In particular the work generated interest in the use of uninterpreted functions for hardware verification problems [10]. Refinement techniques related to ASMs are discussed in [8]. Traditionally, such techniques are based on state transitions, rather than action traces and use untyped ASMs; the main motivation is incremental system design. Various refinement problems between specifications are also the topic of many analysis tools, where sets and maps are used as foundational data structures, such as RAISE, Z, TLA+, B, see [6]. The ASM method is also described in [6]. In some cases, like in RAISE, the underlying logic is three-valued in order to deal with undefined values in specifications. In many of those formalisms, frame conditions need to be specified explicitly, and are not implicit as in the case of model programs or ASMs. In Alloy [20], the analysis is reduced to SAT, by finitizing the data types. A file system case study of a refinement problem using Alloy is discussed in [22].

As future and ongoing work, we use the state of the art SMT solver Z3 [13] for our experiments on satisfiability problems in $\mathcal{T}$. Our current experiments use a lazy quantifier instantiation scheme that is on one hand not limited to basic model programs, but is on the other hand also not complete for basic model programs, some of the implementation aspects are discussed in [32] in the context of BMPC. In particular, the scheme discussed in [32] is inspired by [9], and extends it by using model checking to implement an efficient incremental saturation procedure on top of Z3. The saturation procedure is similar to CEGAR [12], the main difference is that we do not refine the level of abstraction, but instead lazily instantiate axioms in case their use has not been triggered during proof search. Implementation of the reduction of BCC of basic model programs to linear arithmetic is future work. In that context the reduction to Z3 does not need to complete all the reductions to linear arithmetic, but can take advantage of built-in support for *Ite* terms, sets, and tuples.

Model programs are used as high-level specifications in model-based testing tools such as Spec Explorer [30] and NModel [23]. In Spec Explorer, one of the supported input languages is the abstract state machine language AsmL [17,18]. In that context, sanity checking or validation of model programs is usually achieved through simulation and explicit state model checking and search techniques [21,30].

References

1. Alur, R., Henzinger, T.A.: A really temporal logic. In: Proc. 30th Symp. on Foundations of Computer Science, pp. 164–169 (1989)
2. Alur, R., Henzinger, T.A., Kupferman, O., Vardi, M.: Alternating refinement relations. In: Sangiorgi, D., de Simone, R. (eds.) CONCUR 1998. LNCS, vol. 1466, pp. 163–178. Springer, Heidelberg (1998)

3. Armando, A., Mantovani, J., Platania, L.: Bounded model checking of software using SMT solvers instead of SAT solvers. In: Valmari, A. (ed.) SPIN 2006. LNCS, vol. 3925, pp. 146–162. Springer, Heidelberg (2006)
4. AsmL, http://research.microsoft.com/fse/AsmL/
5. Biere, A., Cimatti, A., Clarke, E., Zhu, Y.: Symbolic model checking without BDDs. In: Cleaveland, W.R. (ed.) TACAS 1999. LNCS, vol. 1579, pp. 193–207. Springer, Heidelberg (1999)
6. Bjørner, D., Henson, M. (eds.): Logics of Specification Languages. Springer, Heidelberg (2008)
7. Bjørner, N., Gurevich, Y., Schulte, W., Veanes, M.: Symbolic bounded model checking of abstract state machines. Technical Report MSR-TR-2009-14, Microsoft Research (February 2009) (Submitted to IJSI)
8. Börger, E., Stärk, R.F.: Abstract State Machines: A Method for High-Level System Design and Analysis. Springer, Heidelberg (2003)
9. Bradley, A.R., Manna, Z., Sipma, H.B.: What's decidable about arrays? In: Emerson, E.A., Namjoshi, K.S. (eds.) VMCAI 2006. LNCS, vol. 3855, pp. 427–442. Springer, Heidelberg (2005)
10. Bryant, R.E., German, S.M., Velev, M.N.: Exploiting positive equality in a logic of equality with uninterpreted functions. In: Halbwachs, N., Peled, D.A. (eds.) CAV 1999. LNCS, vol. 1633, pp. 470–482. Springer, Heidelberg (1999)
11. Burch, J.R., Dill, D.L.: Automatic verification of pipelined microprocessor control. In: Dill, D.L. (ed.) CAV 1994. LNCS, vol. 818, pp. 68–80. Springer, Heidelberg (1994)
12. Clarke, E.M., Grumberg, O., Jha, S., Lu, Y., Veith, H.: Counterexample-guided abstraction refinement. In: Emerson, E.A., Sistla, A.P. (eds.) CAV 2000. LNCS, vol. 1855, pp. 154–169. Springer, Heidelberg (2000)
13. de Moura, L., Bjørner, N.S.: Z3: An efficient SMT solver. In: Ramakrishnan, C.R., Rehof, J. (eds.) TACAS 2008. LNCS, vol. 4963, pp. 337–340. Springer, Heidelberg (2008)
14. de Moura, L., Rueß, H., Sorea, M.: Lazy theorem proving for bounded model checking over infinite domains. In: Voronkov, A. (ed.) CADE 2002. LNCS (LNAI), vol. 2392, pp. 438–455. Springer, Heidelberg (2002)
15. Fisher, M.J., Rabin, M.O.: Super-exponential complexity of presburger arithmetic. In: Caviness, B.F., Johnson, J.R. (eds.) Quantifier Elimination and Cylindrical Algebraic Decomposition, pp. 122–135. Springer, Heidelberg (1998); Reprint from SIAM-AMS Proceedings, vol. VII, pp. 27-41 (1974)
16. Grieskamp, W., MacDonald, D., Kicillof, N., Nandan, A., Stobie, K., Wurden, F.: Model-based quality assurance of Windows protocol documentation. In: ICST 2008, Lillehammer, Norway (April 2008)
17. Gurevich, Y.: Evolving Algebras 1993: Lipari Guide. In: Specification and Validation Methods, pp. 9–36. Oxford University Press, Oxford (1995)
18. Gurevich, Y., Rossman, B., Schulte, W.: Semantic essence of AsmL. Theor. Comput. Sci. 343(3), 370–412 (2005)
19. Halpern, J.Y.: Presburger arithmetic with unary predicates is Π_1^1 complete. Journal of Symbolic Logic 56, 637–642 (1991)
20. Jackson, D.: Software Abstractions. MIT Press, Cambridge (2006)
21. Jacky, J., Veanes, M., Campbell, C., Schulte, W.: Model-based Software Testing and Analysis with C#. Cambridge University Press, Cambridge (2008)
22. Kang, E., Jackson, D.: Formal modeling and analysis of a flash filesystem in Alloy. In: Börger, E., Butler, M., Bowen, J.P., Boca, P. (eds.) ABZ 2008. LNCS, vol. 5238, pp. 294–308. Springer, Heidelberg (2008)

23. NModel, http://www.codeplex.com/NModel (public version released, May 2008)
24. Plaisted, D.A., Greenbaum, S.: A structure-preserving clause form translation. J. Symb. Comput. 2(3), 293–304 (1986)
25. Rybina, T., Voronkov, A.: A logical reconstruction of reachability. In: Broy, M., Zamulin, A.V. (eds.) PSI 2003. LNCS, vol. 2890, pp. 222–237. Springer, Heidelberg (2004)
26. Tretmans, J.: Model based testing with labelled transition systems. In: Hierons, R.M., Bowen, J.P., Harman, M. (eds.) FORTEST. LNCS, vol. 4949, pp. 1–38. Springer, Heidelberg (2008)
27. Tseitin, G.S.: On the complexity of derivations in the propositional calculus. Studies in Mathematics and Mathematical Logic, Part II, pp. 115–125 (1968)
28. Veanes, M., Bjørner, N.: Input-output model programs. In: Leucker, M., Morgan, C. (eds.) ICTAC 2009. LNCS, vol. 5684, pp. 322–335. Springer, Heidelberg (2009)
29. Veanes, M., Bjørner, N., Raschke, A.: An SMT approach to bounded reachability analysis of model programs. In: Suzuki, K., Higashino, T., Yasumoto, K., El-Fakih, K. (eds.) FORTE 2008. LNCS, vol. 5048, pp. 53–68. Springer, Heidelberg (2008)
30. Veanes, M., Campbell, C., Grieskamp, W., Schulte, W., Tillmann, N., Nachmanson, L.: Model-based testing of object-oriented reactive systems with Spec Explorer. In: Hierons, R.M., Bowen, J.P., Harman, M. (eds.) FORTEST. LNCS, vol. 4949, pp. 39–76. Springer, Heidelberg (2008)
31. Veanes, M., Saabas, A.: On bounded reachability of programs with set comprehensions. In: Cervesato, I., Veith, H., Voronkov, A. (eds.) LPAR 2008. LNCS (LNAI), vol. 5330, pp. 305–317. Springer, Heidelberg (2008)
32. Veanes, M., Saabas, A., Bjørner, N.: Bounded reachability of model programs. Technical Report MSR-TR-2008-81, Microsoft Research (May 2008)

Multi-level Virtual Machine Debugging Using the Java Platform Debugger Architecture*

Thomas Würthinger[1], Michael L. Van De Vanter[2], and Doug Simon[2]

[1] Institute for System Software
Johannes Kepler University Linz
Linz, Austria
[2] Sun Microsystems Laboratories
Menlo Park, California, USA
wuerthinger@ssw.jku.at, michael.vandevanter@sun.com, doug.simon@sun.com

Abstract. Debugging virtual machines (VMs) presents unique challenges, especially *meta-circular* VMs, which are written in the same language they implement. Making sense of runtime state for such VMs requires insight and interaction at multiple levels of abstraction simultaneously. For example, debugging a Java VM written in Java requires understanding execution state at the source code, bytecode and machine code levels. However, the standard debugging interface for Java, which has a platform-independent execution model, is itself platform-independent. By definition, such an interface provides no access to platform-specific details such as machine code state, stack and register values. Debuggers for low-level languages such as C and C++, on the other hand, have direct access only to low-level information from which they must synthesize higher-level views of execution state. An ideal debugger for a meta-circular VM would be a hybrid: one that uses standard platform-independent debugger interfaces but which also interacts with the execution environment in terms of low-level, platform-dependent state.

This paper presents such a hybrid architecture for the meta-circular Maxine VM. This architecture adopts unchanged a standard debugging interface, the Java Platform Debugger Architecture (JPDA), in combination with the highly extensible NetBeans Integrated Development Environment. Using an extension point within the interface, additional machine-level information can be exchanged between a specialized server associated with the VM and plug-in extensions within NetBeans.

1 Introduction

Higher level programming languages are increasingly implemented by a *virtual machine* (VM), which is implemented in a lower-level language, which is in turn compiled into the machine language of each target platform. Standard debuggers for the VM *implementation language*, often C or C++, suffice in simple situations, but not when parts of the VM (for example critical libraries) are written

---

* This work was supported by Sun Microsystems, Inc.

A. Pnueli, I. Virbitskaite, and A. Voronkov (Eds.): PSI 2009, LNCS 5947, pp. 401–412, 2010.
© Springer-Verlag Berlin Heidelberg 2010

in the *implemented language*. This is also the case for applications written in the Java™ programming language [4] that combine Java and C code via the Java Native Interface(JNI) [5]. This creates a demand for *mixed-mode debuggers* that support both languages: implementation and implemented.

The debugging challenge is even more complex and subtle for meta-circular VM implementations where the implementation and implemented languages are *one and the same*. A solution requires what we call *multi-level debugging*. A VM developer would like to debug at the source-level of the implementation language, but since that language is also being implemented by the VM, one must often drop to a lower level: the *machine language* of the platform into which the implementation is compiled. At this lower level one must be able to examine every aspect of machine state (registers, stacks, data layouts, compiled code, etc.) and to interpret that state in terms of the implementation language, even when the implementation may be broken. Such a tool is necessarily specialized, with the consequence that the many advantages of debugging with a modern Integrated Development Environment (IDE) are unavailable.

For example, the *Maxine Inspector* is a multi-level debugger that is of necessity highly specialized for the meta-circular *Maxine Virtual Machine* [6], for which Java is both the implementation and implemented language. The Maxine Inspector is an out-of-process, machine-level debugger that has the additional ability to interpret machine data at multiple levels of abstraction; it does this through extensive code sharing with and knowledge of the Maxine VM implementation. For example, Java objects can be viewed either abstractly or in terms of a concrete memory layout that may vary across implementation platforms and VM configurations. Java methods can be viewed as source code, bytecodes, or machine code produced by one of Maxine's compilers. Register values and memory words can be interpreted either as bits, as primitive values, as addresses, or as pointers to known Java objects. Figure 1 shows a Java object and a Java method, each viewed in both in source- and machine-level representations.

There are Java debuggers as well as machine code debuggers, but to the best of our knowledge, no system successfully combines both worlds as does the Maxine Inspector. The original Inspector, however, stood alone and lacked both the productivity features and sophisticated user interface that Java programmers expect. As an alternative to replicating those advantages, we explored integrating the core of the Inspector, the out-of-process *Inspector Debugging Agent* that reads and interprets machine state, with the extensible *NetBeans IDE* [14].

This has been made possible through development of a new framework for integration that depends on NetBeans support for the *Java Platform Debugger Architecture* (JPDA) [13], which specifies contracts between a Java VM and a Java debugger. This framework depends on JPDA's *Java Debug Interface* (JDI) [11] and uses JPDA's *Java Debug Wire Protocol* (JDWP) [12] to communicate with the debugged process over a network stream. This approach emphasizes Java-level functionality and is extended when needed for displaying additional machine-level information. A new "protocol within the JDWP protocol" enables

Java-Level View ◄─────────────► **Machine-Level View**

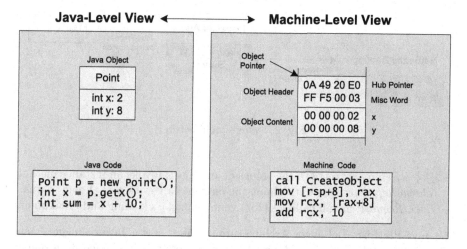

Fig. 1. Multiple view levels on a Java object and Java code during debugging

the transfer of extended kinds of information via JDWP, a technique of general interest to VM developers seeking such extensions to debugging support.

Section 2 introduces this technique in the context of the Maxine VM and Inspector. Section 3 describes the extended JDWP server implementation added to the Inspector, along with a new mechanism using Java dynamic proxy classes [10] to transmit additional information via the unchanged JDWP protocol. Section 4 shows how a new "protocol with the JDWP protocol" communicates with NetBeans, in particular with plug-in extensions that allow the debugger to use the mechanism. Section 5 comments on the advantages of this approach, Section 6 reviews related work, and Section 7 concludes.

2 System Architecture

The Maxine Inspector requires almost no active support from the Maxine VM; this is necessary because there is no separate implementation language whose own implementation can be relied upon. The Inspector runs in its own process, reads VM memory via inter-process communication, and implements basic debugging commands by managing the VM process. The original Inspector internally comprises two software layers: an *agent* that both communicates with the VM and interprets its state, and a *front end* that adds graphical views and user interaction.

The alternative architecture developed for multi-level Maxine debugging with NetBeans uses JDWP: an asynchronous protocol that defines a standard for communication between Java debugger and VM. Important JDWP command groups are:

- *VirtualMachine*: get general information, loaded classes, current threads.
- *ReferenceType*: reflective information about types, class fields and methods.

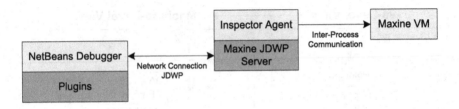

Fig. 2. System architecture

- *ObjectReference*: retrieve the values of an object; invoke an instance method.
- *ThreadReference*: get data about the current call stack and thread status.
- *EventRequest*: install callbacks for events, e.g. class loading and breakpoints.

The Java Platform Debugger Architecture specifies how a Java debugger, using a standard interface (JDI) and wire protocol (JDWP), can connect to a remote server for debugging Java programs via a network connection.

Figure 2 shows how Maxine system components interact in this architecture; new components are dark gray, and the others are unchanged. The new Maxine JDWP Server delegates commands to the existing Maxine Inspector Agent. New plugins extend the NetBeans debugger and communicate directly with the JDWP server. These plugins use both the standard JDWP protocol and a new technique, described in Section 4, to access additional information not directly supported by JDWP. Examples of such information include the address of objects in memory and compiled machine code for a Java method.

3   The Maxine JDWP Server

Most JDWP commands are *queries* from the client (debugger) that produce answers from the server (agent), for example to gather information about loaded classes and thread state. Events that originate in the VM are transmitted to the client only when the client has *registered* for the events with a JDWP command. Current Maxine VM limitations delayed a complete implementation of the JDWP protocol by the server, but the implemented subset already suffices for debugging the Maxine VM using NetBeans.

In addition to standard Java debugging operations, the Maxine JDWP Server can set machine code breakpoints, perform a machine code single-step, examine memory contents, and more. When a breakpoint is reached, the server transmits information about threads and their instruction pointers. The NetBeans debugger always needs a correct Java bytecode position, which is then matched back to the source code and highlighted as the current line in the program. The server calculates the bytecode position based on the current machine code address; the position can be either exact or approximate, depending on which Maxine compiler produced the code. For setting a breakpoint in the Java source code, the server performs the reverse approximation, because the command sent by the client Java debugger contains the bytecode location only.

The Maxine JDWP Server holds information about all loaded classes. Requests for object field access are delegated to the Maxine Inspector Agent, which reads the raw bytes and converts them, if possible, to valid JDWP types. This allows IDE windows that display watch expressions and local variables to work as expected. Current implementation restrictions in the Inspector Agent prevent evaluation of method calls in watch expressions, but all other kinds of watch expressions work as expected.

The Maxine JDWP Server creates *artificial fields* for the transmission of additional, implementation-related information about Java objects. It can do this because the server controls class layout information transmitted to the client. Requests for read access to artificial fields are handled directly by the server, whereas access to other fields requires reading from VM memory via the Inspector Agent. Figure 3 shows an example Java object and how it would appear in the debugger client. At this time the server simulates fields for the address and the header word of an object, both of which are machine-level VM implementation artifacts. The server also simulates a field that points to an object's *hub*: a Maxine VM implementation object describing the type and other meta-data related to the object. The client debugger requires no modification to display artificial fields, since they appear as ordinary Java fields.

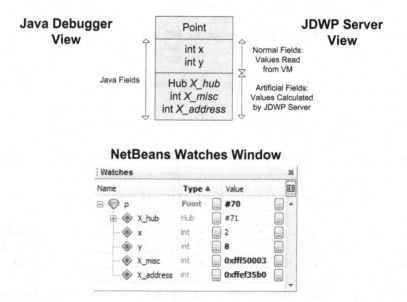

Fig. 3. Artificial object fields help transmitting additional information about objects to the debugger

Shared Interface

```
interface A {
  String foo();
}
```

Implementation on Server Side

```
class AImpl implements A {
  String foo() {
    return "Hello world!";
  }
}
```

Access on Client

```
// Obtain JDI object reference
ObjectReference reference = getReference();

A a = createProxy(reference, A.class);
String s = a.foo();
```

```
class DynamicProxy implements InvocationHandler {

  // Encapsulated JDI reference
  ObjectReference reference;

  public Object invoke(Object proxy,
                       Method method,
                       Object[] args) {
    ...
    // Send JDWP Invoke command
    ...
  }
}
```

Fig. 4. Code example for the Java dynamic proxy mechanism combined with JDWP

4   A Protocol within the JDWP Protocol

Although artificial fields permit the display of additional information about objects without modification to the JDWP debugger client, a more general mechanism is also needed. This is done without change to the protocol by leveraging the JDWP invoke command, which was originally intended to support method calls in watch expressions. Java's *dynamic proxy* mechanism [10] makes it possible to create proxy objects behind an interface, objects that delegate method calls to JDWP invoke commands. The Maxine JDWP Server creates *artificial methods* that provide access to machine-level information via reflective delegation to appropriate methods in the Inspector Agent. The net effect is a kind of specialized "remote method invocation" available to the client through an interface.

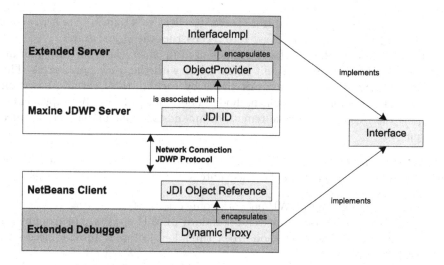

Fig. 5. Dynamic proxy objects for implementing a protocol within the protocol

Code samples in Figure 4 show how the dynamic proxy mechanism is implemented. Interface **A** is defined on both server and client. On the server it is implemented by class **AImpl**; on the client a dynamic proxy object is created. The client-side proxy implements the interface **InvocationHandler**, which allows the delegation of Java calls; it delegates method calls to the **invoke** method.

Figure 5 diagrams the interaction among objects in this architecture. The client implements the interface with a Java dynamic proxy object; it is based on a JDI Object Reference to which it delegates method calls. This JDI Object Reference is also known to the NetBeans Debugger and can be referenced in JDWP commands. The Maxine JDWP Server delegates **invoke** commands on a specific JDWP ID to the corresponding Java object. In conventional usage, server-side **invoke** commands are delegated to the VM via the Inspector Agent, but in this case they are redirected via reflective call to the implementer of the interface. Glue code for these interactions is automated, so neither the user of the interface nor the implementer need any special handling.

Three important optimizations address performance concerns:

- *State Change:* The client normally presumes that a conventional JDWP **invoke** invalidates previously retrieved VM state. We can guarantee, however, that an **invoke** on an artificial method in the Maxine JDWP Server executes no VM code. In these cases Java reflection is used to bypass the built-in refresh mechanisms of JDI, thus avoiding unnecessary overhead on the client.
- *Multiple Objects:* Although transmitting data is typically fast, the round trip needed to perform a JDWP **invoke** is not. Some return values (e.g. the information about all registers of a thread) are represented by multiple objects, and transmitting them individually could introduce undesirable latency. Such

values are instead returned from server to client as a unit: a byte array containing the serialized data needed to reconstruct the object graph.
- *Cache:* Many of the interface methods used in this architecture are guaranteed to return the same result when called with the same parameters. The client further optimizes network traffic by caching these results, based on annotations applied to such methods. This grants client side implementations the freedom to invoke remote commands without undue performance concerns.

This approach, by virtue of specialization, has advantages over Java RMI or other Java remote technologies in this context:

- It shares an existing JDWP network connection.
- Interfaces can be used to extend standard JDWP objects. For example, a special interface adds methods to a thread object that provide access to register state.
- JDWP objects can appear as method parameters and return types.

Figure 6 diagrams the interactions that follow when the client invokes an artificial method on the Maxine JDWP Server. The client's dynamic proxy implements the call, checking first whether the result is cached and can be returned immediately. If not cached, the client marshalls parameters as JDI values for transmission via

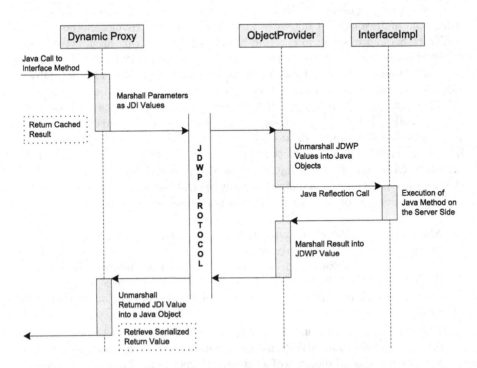

Fig. 6. Example sequence of a call to an interface

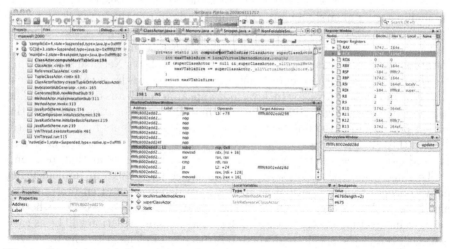

Fig. 7. Screenshot of the enhanced NetBeans debugger showing both machine code and Java source code position

JDWP `invoke`. Primitive types are marshalled by encapsulation in a JDI data object, reference types by JDWP identifiers managed on the server. Array types are simply copied to the server and filled with marshalled primitive or reference values.

The Maxine JDWP Server first unmarshalls the `invoke` parameters, using a map to convert JDWP identifiers to object references. The call is then delegated via Java reflection to the implementer of the interface. Finally the server marshalls the return value into a JDWP value for return to the client.

The client's dynamic proxy receives the return value as a JDI object and converts it to a Java object. In case of an array this can again require additional JDWP commands to retrieve array contents. In case of a byte array containing the serialized form of a Java object, the bytes are retrieved and deserialized. The original caller receives a normal Java object in return without special treatment.

5   Status and Results

The architecture of our approach makes it possible for any client that implements JDWP to debug the Maxine VM at the Java-level. Multi-level debugging, however, requires additional functionality, for which we chose to extend NetBeans. NetBeans already implements JDWP, has a flexible plugin architecture, and provides standard techniques for extending debugger functionality without modification.

Our approach succeeds in making it simple to transport additional information between the Maxine Inspector Agent and the NetBeans IDE. Client-side code for displaying data can use simple interfaces that are implemented on the server.

The Java dynamic proxy mechanism hides the complications implied by data marshalling and unmarshalling to transmit the data over the network.

The Maxine JDWP server implements both a useful subset of the standard source-level JDWP protocol and access to the VM's machine-level state. We have prototyped additional machine-level views; Figure 7 shows NetBeans debugging the Maxine VM with these extensions enabled. The Java-level call stack, local variables, and current position in Java code appear in NetBeans components. The Maxine Code View highlights the current machine code location based on the current position in Java code. Also shown are register contents for the currently selected thread. The address of each Java object appears in an artificial field, and this address can be used to retrieve the raw memory contents at that location.

The full reuse of the NetBeans Java debugger frees us from implementing many concepts that are part of a modern Java debugger, and ensures ongoing benefit as NetBeans evolves. On the other hand, it remains to be seen whether the tight integration among views at different levels of abstraction will be as easy as it has been in the specialized Maxine Inspector. Implementing the prototype described here has already required the use of Java reflection in order to access NetBeans functionality for which no public API is provided. This difficulty is not a limitation of the transport architecture described in this paper, but rather the nature of an IDE for which this type of extension was perhaps not anticipated.

The prototype described here is integrated into the Maxine open source project. We plan to continue exploring this approach to multi-level debugging for the Maxine VM with work on additional components and mutli-level views.

6   Related Work

Ungar et al. developed a meta-circular VM for the Self programming language [15], which they debugged with a debug server written in C++. Remote debugging in Self relies upon a custom network protocol as well as a custom debugger.

The meta-circular Jikes Research Virtual Machine is also written in Java [1]; it uses a remote reflection technique for accessing VM data that is similar to ours [7]. The Jikes debugger itself however, is not based on an existing Java debugger.

Simon et al. [9] developed the Squawk VM, a small Java VM written mostly in Java that runs on a wireless sensor platform. Squawk includes a debug agent that implements a subset of JDWP, but there are no extensions of the sort that permit multi-level debugging.

Printezis and Jones created GCspy framework for the analysis of VM memory management behavior [8]. They considered and rejected using an enhanced version of JDWP for transmitting their data for two reasons: GCspy data has nothing to do with debugging, the focus of the JDWP protocol, and its use would needlessly confine GCspy technology to Java applications. These, however, are actually advantages in the context of Maxine debugging.

Dimitriev extended the JDWP protocol with additional commands for redefining classes in the VM [2][3]. Although this approach is reasonable for functionalities that are of general interest for virtual machines, it would complicate the protocol significantly in our case. By defining a protocol within the JDWP protocol, we retained flexibility and avoided the need for further standardization.

7   Conclusions

Multi-level debugging for a meta-circular VM presents technical challenges that are not easily met with conventional development tools, even mixed-mode tools designed to support multiple languages. Faced with the choice between the development cost of a specialized, isolated tool (our original approach), and the challenges of directly extending an existing IDE, we have explored an alternate approach. Leveraging a single-level standard architecture (JPDA) for remote debugging, we were able to transport information at additional levels of abstraction by implementing a remote invocation protocol within the JPDA's Java Debugging Wire Protocol (JDWP). The advantages of this approach, prototyped using the Maxine Inspector Agent on the server side and NetBeans as the client, are that a wide array of rich functionality becomes available for debugging the Maxine VM at the Java-level. This dramatically reduces Maxine development cost for this level of functionality, both present and future as the NetBeans platform evolves.

Solving the transport problem, however, is only part of the solution. The next challenge is to provide the advantages of tightly integrated multi-level views, easily developed in the stand-alone Maxine Inspector, in a rich platform that was originally designed for single-level debugging.

Acknowledgements

The authors would like to thank Maxine team members Ben Titzer and Bernd Mathiske for their support and many helpful suggestions.

References

1. Alpern, B., Attanasio, C.R., Cocchi, A., Hummel, S.F., Lieber, D., Mergen, M., Shepherd, J.C., Smith, S.: Implementing jalapeño in Java. In: OOPSLA 1999: Proceedings of the 14th ACM SIGPLAN conference on Object-oriented programming, systems, languages, and applications, pp. 314–324. ACM Press, New York (1999)
2. Dmitriev, M.: Safe class and data evolution in large and long-lived Java^{TM} applications. Technical report, Sun Microsystems Laboratories (2001)
3. Dmitriev, M.: Towards flexible and safe technology for runtime evolution of Java language applications. In: Proceedings of the Workshop on Engineering Complex Object-Oriented Systems for Evolution, in association with OOPSLA 2001 International Conference (2001)
4. Gosling, J., Joy, B., Steele, G., Bracha, G.: Java^{TM} Language Specification, 3rd edn. Java Series. Addison-Wesley Professional, Reading (2005)
5. Liang, S.: The Java Native Interface: Programmers Guide and Specification. Addison-Wesley Publishing Co., Inc., Reading (1999)

6. Mathiske, B.: The maxine virtual machine and inspector. In: OOPSLA Companion 2008: Companion to the 23rd ACM SIGPLAN conference on Object oriented programming systems languages and applications, pp. 739–740. ACM, New York (2008)

7. Ngo, T., Barton, J.: Debugging by remote reflection. In: Bode, A., Ludwig, T., Karl, W.C., Wismüller, R. (eds.) Euro-Par 2000. LNCS, vol. 1900, pp. 1031–1038. Springer, Heidelberg (2000)

8. Printezis, T., Jones, R.: Gcspy: an adaptable heap visualisation framework. In: OOPSLA 2002: Proceedings of the 17th ACM SIGPLAN conference on Object-oriented programming, systems, languages, and applications, pp. 343–358. ACM, New York (2002)

9. Simon, D., Cifuentes, C., Cleal, D., Daniels, J., White, D.: Java^{TM} on the bare metal of wireless sensor devices: the squawk Java virtual machine. In: VEE 2006: Proceedings of the 2nd international conference on Virtual execution environments, pp. 78–88. ACM, New York (2006)

10. Sun Microsystems, Inc.: Java Dynamic Proxy Classes (1999),
    `http://java.sun.com/j2se/1.5.0/docs/guide/reflection/proxy.html`

11. Sun Microsystems, Inc.: Java Debug Interface (2004),
    `http://java.sun.com/javase/6/docs/jdk/api/jpda/jdi/index.html`

12. Sun Microsystems, Inc.: Java Debug Wire Protocol (2004),
    `http://java.sun.com/javase/6/docs/technotes/guides/jpda/`
    `jdwp-spec.html`

13. Sun Microsystems, Inc.: Java Platform Debugger Architecture (2004),
    `http://java.sun.com/javase/6/docs/technotes/guides/jpda/`

14. Sun Microsystems, Inc.: NetBeans (2009), `http://www.netbeans.org`

15. Ungar, D., Spitz, A., Ausch, A.: Constructing a metacircular virtual machine in an exploratory programming environment. In: OOPSLA 2005: Companion to the 20th annual ACM SIGPLAN conference on Object-oriented programming, systems, languages, and applications, pp. 11–20. ACM, New York (2005)

Anti-unification Algorithms and Their Applications in Program Analysis*

Peter E. Bulychev, Egor V. Kostylev, and Vladimir A. Zakharov

Faculty of Computational Mathematics and Cybernetics,
Moscow State University, Moscow, RU-119899, Russia
peter.bulychev@gmail.com, jegor_kostylev@hotmail.com, zakh@cs.msu.su

Abstract. A term t is called a *template* of terms t_1 and t_2 iff $t_1 = t\eta_1$ and $t_2 = t\eta_2$, for some substitutions η_1 and η_2. A template t of t_1 and t_2 is called *the most specific* iff for any template t' of t_1 and t_2 there exists a substitution ξ such that $t = t'\xi$. The anti-unification problem is that of computing the most specific template of two given terms. This problem is dual to the well-known unification problem, which is the computing of the most general instance of terms. Unification is used extensively in automatic theorem proving and logic programming. We believe that anti-unification algorithms may have wide applications in program analysis. In this paper we present an efficient algorithm for computing the most specific templates of terms represented by labelled directed acyclic graphs and estimate the complexity of the anti-unification problem. We also describe techniques for invariant generation and software clone detection based on the concepts of the most specific templates and anti-unification.

The anti-unification problem is that of finding the most specific template (pattern) of two terms. It is dual to the well-known unification problem, which is the computing of the most general instance of terms. Unification is extensively used in automatic theorem proving, logic programming, typed lambda calculus, term rewriting, etc. The unification problem has been studied thoroughly in many papers and a wide variety of efficient unification algorithms have been developed by many authors (see [1] for survey). The anti-unification problem attracted far less attention. It has been first considered by G.D. Plotkin [12] and J. Reynolds [13]. The algebraic properties of anti-unification operation have been studied in [6,11]. To the extent of our knowledge all anti-unification algorithms introduced so far (see [12,13,15]) deal with tree-like representation of terms. It is obvious that the anti-unification problem for terms represented by labelled trees can be solved in linear time. However, if one needs to deal with large sets of sizable terms then it is more suitable to represent such sets of terms by labelled directed acyclic graphs (dags). One of the aims of this paper is to develop an efficient algorithm for computing the most specific templates and estimate the complexity of anti-unification problem for terms represented by labelled dags.

Only few papers concern the application of anti-unification. R. Gluck and M.H. Sorensen used anti-unification (the most specific generalization) of terms

---

* The research is supported by RFBR grants 09-01-00277 and 09-01-00632.

A. Pnueli, I. Virbitskaite, and A. Voronkov (Eds.): PSI 2009, LNCS 5947, pp. 413–423, 2010.
© Springer-Verlag Berlin Heidelberg 2010

to guarantee the termination of a positive supercompilation algorithm developed in their paper [15]. The utility of anti-unification in the setting of symbolic mathematical computing has been studied in [10,17]. We believe that anti-unification algorithms may have wide applications in many areas of computer science and software engineering. In this paper we study the perspectives of using the concepts of the most specific templates and anti-unification for invariant generation and software clone detection.

The generation of invariants is the key technique in the analysis and verification of programs, since the effectiveness of automated program verification is highly sensitive to the ease with which invariants, even trivial ones, can be automatically deduced. Much efforts (see [8,16]) are directed towards the development of powerful invariant generating techniques for particular classes of programs. As opposed to these attempts, we present a light-weight technique for invariant generation. Our anti-unification based algorithm for invariant generation operates on the syntactic level. Therefore, it is of little sensitivity to program semantics and can reveal only trivial invariants. But, due to the efficiency of anti-unification algorithms, this technique provides a way for processing large pieces of code in short time.

Anti-unification algorithms can be of significant value in software refactoring. One of the major activities in this area is the detection and extraction of duplicate code. Code duplication can be a serious drawback, leading to bad design, and increased probability of bug occurrence and propagation. Consequently, duplicate code detectors are a useful class of program analysis tools (see [14]). We describe a anti-unification based algorithm for finding software clones. The algorithm checks fragments of code (sequences of program statements) and assign two pieces of code to the same clone if they are not too different from their most specific template.

1   Preliminaries

Given a set of variables $\mathcal{Y}$ and a set of functional symbols $\mathcal{F} = \{f_1^{(m_1)}, \ldots, f_k^{(m_k)}\}$, we define the set of terms $Term[\mathcal{Y}, \mathcal{F}]$ as the smallest set of expressions that contains $\mathcal{Y}$ and satisfies the following property: if $f^{(m)} \in \mathcal{F}$ and $t_1, \ldots, t_m \in Term[\mathcal{Y}, \mathcal{F}]$ then $f^{(m)}(t_1, \ldots, t_m) \in Term[\mathcal{Y}, \mathcal{F}]$.

Let $\mathcal{X} = \{x_1, \ldots, x_n\}$ and $\mathcal{Y} = \{y_1, y_2, \ldots\}$ be two sets of variables. The set $Subst[\mathcal{X}, \mathcal{Y}, \mathcal{F}]$ of $\mathcal{X}$-$\mathcal{Y}$-substitutions is the set of mappings $\theta : \mathcal{X} \to Term[\mathcal{Y}, \mathcal{F}]$. A $\mathcal{X}$-$\mathcal{Y}$-substitution θ can be represented as the set of bindings $\theta = \{x_1/\theta(x_1), \ldots, x_n/\theta(x_n)\}$. We denote by $Range(\theta)$ the set of all variables in terms $\theta(x_1), \ldots, \theta(x_n)$. An *application* of a substitution θ to a term $t = t(x_1, \ldots, x_n)$ yields the term $t\theta = t(\theta(x_1), \ldots, \theta(x_n))$ obtained from t by replacing all variables x_i with the terms $\theta(x_i)$, $1 \leq i \leq n$. The *composition* $\eta = \theta\xi$ of substitutions $\theta \in Subst[\mathcal{X}, \mathcal{Y}, \mathcal{F}]$ and $\xi \in Subst[Range(\theta), \mathcal{Y}, \mathcal{F}]$ is defined as follows: $\eta(x) = (\theta(x))\xi$ holds for every variable x from $\mathcal{X}$.

The set of substitutions $Subst[\mathcal{X}, \mathcal{Y}, \mathcal{F}]$ is supplied with a quasi-order $\sqsubseteq$ and an equivalence relation $\sim$: a relation $\theta_1 \sqsubseteq \theta_2$ holds iff there exists $\xi \in$

$Subst[Range(\theta_1), \mathcal{Y}, \mathcal{F}]$ such that $\theta_2 = \theta_1\xi$, and $\theta_1 \sim \theta_2$ holds iff $\theta_2 = \theta_1\rho$ holds for some bijection ρ from $Range(\theta_1)$ to $Range(\theta_2)$. Let $\top$ be a new element such that $\theta \sqsubseteq \top$ holds for every substitution θ. Quasi-order $\sqsubseteq$ induces the partial order $\preceq$ on the quotient set $Subst^\sim[\mathcal{X}, \mathcal{Y}, \mathcal{F}] = (Subst[\mathcal{X}, \mathcal{Y}, \mathcal{F}] \cup \{\top\})/\sim$. Poset $(Subst^\sim[\mathcal{X}, \mathcal{Y}, \mathcal{F}], \preceq)$ has been studied in [6,11]. It is a complete lattice, and the least element of the lattice is the equivalence class of the *empty substitution* $\varepsilon = \{x_1/y_1, \ldots, x_n/y_n\}$. The least upper bound $\theta_1^\sim \uparrow \theta_2^\sim$ is called the *most general instance* of substitutions θ_1 and θ_2, whereas the greatest lower bound $\theta_1^\sim \downarrow \theta_2^\sim$ is called the *most specific template* of θ_1 and θ_2. The operation $\downarrow$ of computing the most specific template of substitutions is called *anti-unification* (or *generalization*). For the sake of simplicity we will often skip the superscript $\sim$ in our notation. The anti-unification operation can be naturally extended to the terms. The term t is called the most specific template of terms t_1 and t_2 ($t = t_1 \downarrow t_2$ in symbols) if $\{x/t\} = \{x/t_1\} \downarrow \{x/t_2\}$.

2   Anti-unification Algorithms

In this section we study the complexity of anti-unification of substitutions represented as labelled directed acyclic graphs (dags). Dags are the most suitable structures for succinct representation of substitutions. A node V that has no incoming arcs is called a *root* of a dag. A labelled single-rooted dag $\mathcal{G}(t)$ associated with a term t, $t \in Term[\mathcal{Y}, \mathcal{F}]$, is arranged as follows. If t is a constant or a variable then $\mathcal{G}(t)$ is single node labelled with t (this node is the root of $\mathcal{G}(t)$). If $t = f^{(m)}(t_1, \ldots, t_m)$ then the root of $\mathcal{G}(t)$ is labelled with $f^{(m)}$ and has m outgoing arcs labelled with integers from 1 to m; the arc labelled with i, $1 \leq i \leq m$, leads to the root of $\mathcal{G}(t_i)$ associated with the subterm t_i. Given a node V of such a dag, we denote by $mark(V)$ the label of V and by $desc(V, i)$ the i-th descendant of V (i. e., the node that is at the end of the arc outgoing from V and labelled with i). A labelled dag $\mathcal{G}$ represents a substitution $\theta = \{x_1/t_1, \ldots, x_n/t_n\}$ if it contains dags $\mathcal{G}(t_1), \ldots, \mathcal{G}(t_n)$ associated with the terms $t_1, \ldots, t_n$ as subgraphs, and the root of each subgraph $\mathcal{G}(t_i)$ has an extra label x_i. We denote these roots by $V_\mathcal{G}(x_1), \ldots, V_\mathcal{G}(x_n)$, respectively. Two nodes V and U of a dag $\mathcal{G}$ associated with a substitution θ are said to be *equivalent* if the subgraphs rooted at V and U are associated with the same term. A dag $\mathcal{G}$ is called *reduced* if every node is reachable from a root extra labelled with a variable x, $x \in \mathcal{X}$, and all nodes of $\mathcal{G}(\theta)$ are pairwise non-equivalent. Every substitution θ is associated with the unique reduced dag, which is denoted by $\mathcal{G}(\theta)$. The *size* $N(\theta)$ of a substitution θ is the number of nodes in the reduced dag $\mathcal{G}(\theta)$ associated with θ.

A sequential anti-unification algorithm MST, which computes the most specific templates of substitutions represented by reduced labelled dags, is depicted in Fig. 1. The algorithm gets as input a pair of reduced dags $\mathcal{G}(\theta')$ and $\mathcal{G}(\theta'')$ associated with substitutions θ' and θ'' and outputs the reduced dag $\mathcal{G}$ associated with the most specific template η of θ' and θ''. Every node W in $\mathcal{G}$ matches some pair of nodes (subterms) V' and V'' in the dags $\mathcal{G}(\theta')$ and $\mathcal{G}(\theta'')$, respectively. Such a node W is specified by a 3-tuple (y, V', V''), where y is a variable from

```
procedure MST (G(θ'), G(θ''))
   set G := G({x₁/y₁, ..., xₙ/yₙ}), Q := ∅, Q̂ := ∅;
   for i := 1 to n do
       if exists y, such that (y, V_{G(θ')}(xᵢ), V_{G(θ'')}(xᵢ)) ∈ Q
          then remove V_G(xᵢ) from G; set mark(mem(y)) := xᵢ
          else set Q := Q ∪ {(yᵢ, V_{G(θ')}(xᵢ), V_{G(θ'')}(xᵢ))}, mem(yᵢ) := V_G(xᵢ)
       fi
   od;
   while exists (y, V', V'') ∈ Q such that mark(V') = mark(V'') do
       set Q := Q\{(y, V', V'')}, Q̂ := Q̂ ∪ {(y, V', V'')};
       if mark(V') = f^(m) ∈ F then
          set mark(mem(y)) := f^(m);
          for i := 1 to m do
              if exists z such that (z, desc(V', i), desc(V'', i)) ∈ Q ∪ Q̂ then
                 let Wᵢ = mem(z)
              else
                 let Wᵢ be a new node in G and z be a new variable in Y;
                 set mark(Wᵢ) := z, mem(z) := Wᵢ, Q := Q ∪ {(z, desc(V', i), desc(V'', i))}
              fi;
              set desc(mem(y), i) := Wᵢ
          od
       fi
   od;
   return G(θ' ↓ θ'') := G
end of MST.
```

Fig. 1. Anti-unification algorithm MST

$\mathcal{Y}$ used as a unique identifier of W. A node named y is denoted by $mem(y)$. The algorithm MST operates with two sets Q and $\widehat{Q}$. The set Q is a worklist of nodes to be handled. When handling a node W specified by (y, V', V'') the algorithm assigns the corresponding label to W, checks all its descendants, and moves W from the worklist Q to the list of processed nodes $\widehat{Q}$.

Theorem 1. *The algorithm MST correctly computes a reduced dag associated with the most specific template $\eta = \theta' \downarrow \theta''$ of substitutions θ' and θ'' in time $O(n \log n)$, where $n = N(\eta)$.*

Since every node in $\mathcal{G}$ matches subterms corresponding to exactly one pair of nodes in $\mathcal{G}(\vartheta')$ and $\mathcal{G}(\vartheta'')$, the size $N(\eta)$ of η does not exceeds $N(\vartheta') \times N(\vartheta'')$. Hence, we arrive at the corollary.

Corollary 1. *The most specific template of substitutions θ' and θ'' represented by reduced dags can be computed in time $O(n^2 \log n)$, where $n = \max(N(\theta'), N(\theta''))$.*

As can be seen from the assertions below, the upper bound can not be substantially improved.

Theorem 2. *Suppose that $\mathcal{F}$ contains a functional symbol of arity $m > 1$. Then there exists an infinite sequence of pairs of substitutions (θ'_i, θ''_i), $i \geq 1$, such that $\frac{1}{6} N(\theta'_i) \times N(\theta''_i) \leq N(\theta'_i \downarrow \theta''_i)$.*

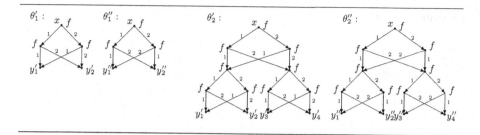

Fig. 2. Dags for substitutions θ'_i and θ''_i, $i = 1, 2$

Proof. Suppose that $\mathcal{F}$ contains a symbol f of arity 2, and $\mathcal{X} = \{x\}$. Suppose also that $\mathcal{Y}' = \{y'_1, y'_2, \ldots\}$ and $\mathcal{Y}'' = \{y''_1, y''_2, \ldots\}$ are subsets of $\mathcal{Y}$. Consider two sequences of substitutions $\vartheta'_i = \{x/t'_i(y'_1, \ldots, y'_{2^i})\}$ and $\vartheta''_i = \{x/t''_i(y''_1, \ldots, y''_{2^i})\}$, $i \geq 1$, such that

$$t'_1(y'_1, y'_2) = f(f(y'_1, y'_2), f(y'_1, y'_2)), \qquad t''_1(y''_1, y''_2) = f(f(y''_1, y''_2), f(y''_2, y''_1)),$$
$$t'_{i+1}(y'_1, \ldots, y'_{2^{i+1}}) = t'_1(t'_i(y'_1, \ldots, y'_{2^i}), t'_i(y'_{2^i+1}, \ldots, y'_{2^{i+1}})),$$
$$t''_{i+1}(y''_1, \ldots, y''_{2^{i+1}}) = t''_1(t''_i(y''_1, \ldots, y''_{2^i}), t''_i(y''_{2^i+1}, \ldots, y''_{2^{i+1}})), i \geq 1.$$

The dags associated with θ'_i and θ''_i, $i = 1, 2$, are presented in Fig. 2 (for the sake of clarity they are nonreduced). It is easy to see that $N(\vartheta'_i) = 3 \cdot 2^i - 2$ and $N(\vartheta''_i) = 4 \cdot 2^i - 3$, $i \geq 1$, but the reduced dags for substitutions $\theta_i = \theta'_i \downarrow \theta''_i$, $i \geq 1$, are full binary trees such that $N(\theta_i) = 2 \cdot 4^i - 1$.

Corollary 2. *If $\mathcal{F}$ contains a functional symbol of arity $m > 1$ then time complexity of the anti-unification problem for two substitutions represented by reduced dags of the size n is $\Omega(n^2)$.*

3 Generating Invariants with the Help of Anti-unification

In this section we demonstrate how to generate program invariants with the help of anti-unification algorithms. We introduce a nondeterministic formal model of sequential programs and show that the most specific invariants of the form $x_1 = t_1 \wedge x_2 = t_2 \wedge \ldots \wedge x_n = t_n$ can be computed by conventional static analysis techniques (see [9]) adapted to the lattice of finite substitutions.

Let $\mathcal{V} = \{v_1, \ldots, v_n\}$ be a finite set of variables and $\mathcal{F}$ be a set of functional symbols. Then a *program* is a pair $\Pi = \langle L, E \rangle$, where L is a finite set of program points (non-negative integers) and E is a finite set of assignment statements. We will assume that L includes 0 which is the *entry point* of Π. Every *assignment statement* e of a program Π is an expression of the form $l_{in} : v \Leftarrow t : l_{out}$, where $v \in \mathcal{V}$, $t \in Term[\mathcal{V}, \mathcal{F}]$, and l_{in}, l_{out} are program points. The integer l_{in} is called the *entry point* of e (denoted $in(e)$) and the integer l_{out} is called the *exit point* of e (denoted $out(e)$). Any finite sequence of statements $tr = e_1, e_2, \ldots, e_m$ is called a *trace* of a program Π if $in(e_1) = 0$ and $out(e_i) = in(e_{i+1})$ for every

```
program test(z)
  x1 = z;
  z = z+1;
  x2 = z;
  while x2==x1+1 do
    x1 = z;
    if prime(z)
      then z = x2+1
      else x1 = 2*z;  z=2*x2+1
    fi;
    x2 = z
  od
end.
```

program Π_0:
$$0 : x_1 \Leftarrow z : 1,$$
$$1 : z \Leftarrow f(z, c_1) : 2,$$
$$2 : x_2 \Leftarrow z : 3,$$
$$2 : x_2 \Leftarrow z : 7,$$
$$3 : x_1 \Leftarrow z : 4,$$
$$4 : z \Leftarrow f(x_2, c_1) : 6,$$
$$4 : x_1 \Leftarrow g(c_2, z) : 5,$$
$$5 : z \Leftarrow f(g(c_2, x_2), c_1) : 6,$$
$$6 : x_2 \Leftarrow z : 7,$$
$$6 : x_2 \Leftarrow z : 3.$$

Fig. 3. An example of sequential program

i, $1 \leq i < m$. We say that such a trace tr leads to the point $out(e_m)$. The set of all traces of a program Π leading to a point l will be denoted by $Tr_\Pi(l)$.

The semantics of our programs is defined on the first-order structures $M = \{D_M, \overline{f}_1, \ldots, \overline{f}_k, =\}$, where D_M is a semantic domain with equality relation $=$, and functions $\overline{f}_1, \ldots, \overline{f}_k$ are interpretations of the functional symbols from $\mathcal{F}$. A *data state* σ is a mapping $\mathcal{V} \rightarrow D_M$. We write $t[\sigma]$ to denote the value of a term t in the data state σ. Let M be a structure, σ_0 be a data state, and $tr = e_1, e_2, \ldots, e_m$ be a trace of Π such that $e_i = l_i : v_i \Leftarrow t_i : l_{i+1}$. Then the *run* of a program Π for the data state σ_0 and the trace tr is the finite sequence $(e_1, \sigma_1), (e_2, \sigma_2), \ldots, (e_m, \sigma_m)$, such that the data state σ_i agrees with σ_{i-1} except for the variable v_i, where the value $v_i[\sigma_{i-1}]$ is changed to $t_i[\sigma_{i-1}]$, for every i, $1 \leq i \leq m$. The final state σ_m of this run is called the result of the run and denoted by $r(\sigma_0, tr)$.

Example 1. A conventional pseudo-code depicted in Fig. 3 (left side) can be translated into the set of labelled assignment statements (right side). To this end every condition checking is replaced by a nondeterministic choice between two assignment statements that have the same entry point. The same abstraction is used in [8]. □

A first-order formula $\Phi(v_1, \ldots, v_n)$ is called an *M-invariant* of a program Π at a point l iff $M, r(\sigma_0, tr) \models \Phi(v_1, \ldots, v_n)$ holds for every data state σ_0 and trace $tr \in Tr_\Pi(l)$. If $\Phi(v_1, \ldots, v_n)$ is an M-invariant for every structure M then it is called a *strong invariant*. An invariant Φ is called *the most specific strong invariant* if, for every strong invariant Ψ, the formula $\Phi \rightarrow \Psi$ is valid. We restrict our consideration only with *equality invariants* $\Phi(v_1, \ldots, v_n)$ of the form $\exists y_1 \ldots \exists y_k (v_1 = t_1 \wedge v_2 = t_2 \wedge \ldots \wedge v_n = t_n)$.

Theorem 3. *Let H be an Herbrand structure. Then a formula $\Phi(v_1, \ldots, v_n)$ is a strong equality invariant of Π at a point l iff $\Phi(v_1, \ldots, v_n)$ is an H-invariant of Π at the same point.*

We are in a position to show how anti-unification can be used in generating the most specific strong equality invariants. Every statement $e = l_{in} : v_i \Leftarrow t : l_{out}$ gives rise to a $\mathcal{V}$-$\mathcal{V}$-substitution $\theta_e = \{v_1/v_1, \ldots, v_{i-1}/v_{i-1}, v_i/t, v_{i+1}/v_{i+1}, \ldots v_n/v_n\}$. The substitutions introduced thus provide a way of characterizing the equality invariants of programs. With every trace $tr = e_1, e_2, \ldots, e_m$ of a program Π we associate a substitution $\eta_{tr} = \theta_{e_m} \ldots \theta_{e_2} \theta_{e_1} \varepsilon$ which is a composition of substitutions associated with the statements $e_m, \ldots, e_2, e_1$ and the empty substitution ε. Then, given a program Π and a point l of Π, we denote by $\theta_{\Pi,l}$ the substitution $\downarrow_{tr \in Tr_{\Pi}(l)} \eta_{tr}$ which is the most specific template of all substitutions associated with the traces of Π leading to the point l.

Theorem 4. *Suppose that* $\theta_{\Pi,l} = \{v_1/t_1, v_2/t_2, \ldots, v_n/t_n\}$. *Then the formula*

$$\Phi_{\Pi,l} = \exists y_1 \ldots \exists y_k (v_1 = t_1 \wedge v_2 = t_2 \wedge \ldots \wedge v_n = t_n),$$

where $\{y_1, \ldots, y_k\}$ *is the set of all variables occurred in the terms* $t_1, t_2, \ldots, t_n$, *is the most specific strong equality invariant of the program* Π *at the point* l.

To effectively compute the substitutions $\theta_{\Pi,l}$ consider the system of equations

$$\Omega(\Pi) : \begin{cases} \Theta_l = \downarrow_{e \in E, out(e)=l} \theta_e \Theta_{in(e)}, \; l \in L, l \neq 0, \\ \Theta_0 = \varepsilon, \end{cases}$$

where the Θ_l, $l \in L$, are the unknown substitutions.

Theorem 5. *For every program* $\Pi = \langle L, E \rangle$, *the set of substitutions* $\{\theta_{\Pi,l} : l \in L\}$ *is the least solution to the system* $\Omega(\Pi)$ *in the lattice of substitutions* $Subst[\mathcal{V}, \mathcal{Y}, \mathcal{F}]$.

It is easy to check (see [6,11]) that composition of substitutions is left-distributive over anti-unification, i. e. $\eta(\theta_1 \downarrow \theta_2) = \eta\theta_1 \downarrow \eta\theta_2$. This theorem relies upon this property of substitutions. To solve the system $\Omega(\Pi)$ one can involve anti-unification algorithms and any iterative technique used in program static analysis for computing the least fixed points of monotonic operators on lattices (see [9]). By applying this technique to the system of equations Ω_{Π_0} corresponding to the program Π_0 presented in Example 1 one can readily compute a substitution $\theta_{\Pi_0,3} = \{x_1/y, x_2/g(y, c_1), z/g(y, c_1)\}$. Thus, by Theorem 4, $\Phi = \exists y(x_1 = y \wedge x_2 = y+1 \wedge z = y+1)$ is the most specific strong invariant of the program Π_0 at the point 3 (loop invariant). Since Φ implies $x_2 = x_1 + 1$, we draw a conclusion that the source program test never terminates.

4   Duplicate Code Detection Using Anti-unification

Two sequences of program statements form duplicate code if they are similar enough according to a selected measure of similarity. Different researchers report that the amount of duplicate code in software systems varies from 6.4% - 7.5% to 13% - 20% [14]. Code duplication can be a significant drawback, leading to bad design, and increased probability of bug occurrence and propagation. As a result, it can significantly increase maintenance cost (for instance, any bug in the original has to be fixed in all duplicates), and form a barrier for software evolution. Consequently, duplicate code detectors are a useful class of software analysis tools. Such tools can aid in measuring the quality of software systems and in the process of refactoring.

Detecting duplicate pieces of program code is another task that can be effectively solved with the help of anti-unification. Although there is a huge amount of papers dealing with the duplicate code detection problem (see [14] for survey), so far as we know, no generally recognized definitions of code cloning has been developed yet. Pieces of code can be viewed as similar based on syntactic criteria or at the semantic level.

The authors of the paper [7] came up with a proposal for detecting code clones by analyzing the patterns of program expressions. We think that this is one of the most simple yet effective approach to checking the similarity code pieces. Following this line of research we have developed a new anti-unification based duplicate code detection algorithm. Its key idea is as follows. Given two expressions E_1 and E_2, one need to compute their most specific template $E = E_1 \downarrow E_2$ and estimate how much E_1 and E_2 differs from E. The latter can be done based on anti-unification distance: if $E_1 = E\eta_1$ and $E_2 = E\eta_2$ then *anti-unification distance* $\rho(E_1, E_2)$ is the total number of leaves in dag representations of substitutions η_1 and η_2. We count leaves only because their number is equal to the number of lexems covered by the substitutions and thus it is independent of the program graph's representation. Anti-unification distance $\rho(E_1, E_2)$ can be seen as a variant of tree edit distance introduced in [3]. If $\rho(E_1, E_2)$ is less than some threshold d_1, and the sizes of both expressions are greater than another threshold d_2, then E_1 and E_2 belong to the same clone. The efficiency of anti-unification algorithms guarantees that this approach is applicable to large programs independent of the source language.

Example 2. Let $E_1 = Add(Name(i), Name(j))$ and $E_2 = Add(Name(n), Const(1))$. These terms have the most specific template $E = Add(Name(x_1), x_2)$ such that $E_1 = E\eta_1$, $E_2 = E\eta_2$, where $\eta_1 = \{x_1/i, x_2/Name(j)\}$ and $\eta_2 = \{x_1/n, x_2/Const(1)\}$. Then $\rho(E_1, E_2) = 4$.

In order to separate real clones that are composed of several statements from a huge amount of similar small pieces of code we developed a compound algorithm that consists of three stages. In the beginning anti-unification is used to partition all statements of a program under analysis into clusters. Such clusterization makes it possible to view the code as a sequence of cluster identifiers. At the second stage the algorithm finds all pairs of identical sequences of cluster identifiers. Finally, the matching pairs of sequences having similar statements in corresponding positions are checked once again for global similarity. This checking also involves the computation of anti-unification distance. Two sequences of program statements are assigned to the same clone if the distance between them is below some certain threshold.

Now we discuss the stages of our duplication detection algorithm in some detail. In the very beginning of the whole algorithm an abstract syntax tree for the analyzed program is built. For the sake of efficiency and memory saving, this tree can be transformed into a reduced dag. Every statement is associated with a subgraph (a tree or a dag) in an abstract syntax graph, and anti-unification algorithm is used to compute a distance between any pair of program statements. Clusterization of program statements is performed in two passes. During the first pass the most frequent templates of program statements in the source code are discovered and a preliminary clusterization is performed. Every cluster C is characterized by the template $E_C = \downarrow_{E \in C} E$. Each new statement E' is compared with the templates E_C of all existing clusters. If the distance $\rho(E', E_C)$ is below some threshold d_3 then the updated template of C becomes equal to $E_C \downarrow E'$. If no such clusters are found then E' forms a new cluster. During the second pass all statements are processed again. For every statement E' the algorithm chooses the cluster C from the set produced at the first pass whose template E_C is the most similar to E'. When such cluster C is found, E' is assigned to C.

After the first stage of our algorithm all statements are assigned to clusters and marked with corresponding clusters identifiers. At the second stage the algorithm searches for long enough pairs of sequences of statements which are labelled identically, i.e. the statements at the same position in both sequences are marked with the same ID. Detected pairs are considered as clone candidates and their similarity have to be checked at the next stage. This checking is performed at the third stage as follows. Every sequences $B = E_1, E_2, \ldots, E_n$ is treated as a whole expression. If anti-unification distance $\rho(B', B'')$ between sequences B' and B'' is below a certain threshold then this pair is reported as a clone.

The algorithm described above has been implemented in a software tool Clone Digger aimed at detecting similar code in Python and Java programs (see [4]). This tool is provided under the GNU General Public License and can be downloaded from the site http://clonedigger.sf.net. In [5] we compared Clone Digger with two clone-detection tools: DuDe [18] and CloneDR^{TM}[2]. The tool DuDe [18] deals with the textual representation of programs. As expected, the quality of clone candidates reported by our tool was better than those discovered by DuDe. For instance, some of the clones reported by DuDe cover the end of one function and the beginning of the next function; such clones can't be refactored. If we split them, the size for one or both parts are far below the chosen threshold. Another expected observation is that DuDe is significantly faster than Clone Digger, because DuDe uses a very simple suffix tree based algorithm for finding clones. Next, Clone Digger has been compared with the commercial abstract syntax tree based clone detection tool CloneDR^{TM}[2]. The main observation was that Clone Digger was able to detect all the clones that were reported by CloneDR^{TM}. Moreover, some clones detected by Clone Digger can not be detected by CloneDR^{TM} in principle. There are mainly two types of valuable additional clones. First, CloneDR^{TM} is only able to handle renamings, while Clone Digger handles replacements of subexpressions using the anti-unification based algorithm. Second, Clone Digger supports parametrization of variable names and counts several equal renamings as one (appropriate for refactoring), thus resulting in smaller clone distances.

Thus, the anti-unification based approach gives us a possibility to develop a high-speed clone detection tool, which is able to detect more real clones than the available commercial tools.

5   Conclusion

The main contribution of our work is twofold.

1. We introduced an anti-unification algorithm for computing the most specific templates (patterns) of expressions represented as labelled directed acyclic graphs. All previously known anti-unification algorithms operate only with tree-like structures. Since the size of tree representation of some expressions is exponent of the size of their dag representation, our algorithms extend the field of application of anti-unification techniques. We also proved that time complexity of our anti-unification algorithms is close to the optimal one. This provides a firm foundation for the development of various anti-unification based techniques for program analysis.

2. We also showed that anti-unification machinery can be successfully applied to the solution of two important problems in program analysis — generation of program invariants and duplicate code detection. Since anti-unification deals with program expression on syntactic level only, our techniques for invariant generation and clone detection are insensitive to any semantical properties of functions and predicates involved in programs. Thus, program invariants computed with the help of anti-unification capture only primitive relationships between data structures, and even a small modification of a program (say, a transposition of program statements) makes similar pieces of code unrecognizable by our duplicated code detection algorithm. This is the principal drawback of any anti-unification based technique for program analysis. On the other hand, anti-unification algorithms are very efficient and simple, they provide a way for processing large pieces of code in reasonable time. Non-trivial relationships and structures (program invariants and clones) revealed by these means can be used as a raw material for more advanced program analysis procedures. Therefore, anti-unification based techniques for program analysis can find practical use in the front end of many tools for program optimization and verification.

References

1. Baader, F., Snyder, W.: Unification theory. In: Robinson, J.A., Voronkov, A. (eds.) Handbook of Automated Reasoning, vol. 1, pp. 447–533 (2001)
2. Baxter, I., Yahin, A., Moura, L.M., Sant'Anna, M., Bier, L.: Clone Detection Using Abstract Syntax Trees. In: Proc. of the 14th IEEE International Conference on Software Maintenance, pp. 368–377 (1998)
3. Bille, P.: A survey on tree distance and related problems. Theoretical Computer Science 337(1-3), 217–239 (2005)
4. Bulychev, P.: Duplicate code detection using Clone Digger. PythonMagazine 9, 18–24 (2008)

5. Bulychev, P., Minea, M.: An evaluation of duplicate code detection using anti-unification. In: Proc. of the 3rd Int. Workshop on Software Clones, pp. 22–27 (2009)
6. Eder, E.: Properties of substitutions and unifications. Journal of Symbolic Computations 1, 31–46 (1985)
7. Evans, W., Fraser, C., Ma, F.: Clone detection via structural abstraction. In: Proc. of 14th Working Conference on Reverse Engineering, pp. 150–159 (2007)
8. Kovac, L.I., Jebelean, T.: An algorithm for automated generation of invariants for loops with conditionals. In: Proc. of the 7th Int. Symp. on Symbolic and Numeric Algorithms for Scientific Computing, pp. 245–250 (2005)
9. Nielson, F., Nielson, H.R., Hankin, C.: Principles of program analysis, 446 p. Springer, Heidelberg (1999)
10. Oancea, C.E., So, C., Watt, S.M.: Generalization in Maple. In: Maple Conference, pp. 277–382 (2005)
11. Palamidessi, C.: Algebraic properties of idempotent substitutions. In: Paterson, M. (ed.) ICALP 1990. LNCS, vol. 443, pp. 386–399. Springer, Heidelberg (1990)
12. Plotkin, G.D.: A note on inductive generalization. Machine Intelligence 5(1), 153–163 (1970)
13. Reynolds, J.C.: Transformational systems and the algebraic structure of atomic formulas. Machine Intelligence 5(1), 135–151 (1970)
14. Roy, C.K., Cordy, J.R.: A survey on software clone detection research. Technical Report N 2007-541, School of Computing Queen's University at Kingston Ontario, Canada
15. Sorensen, M.H.: Gluck. R. An algorithm of generalization in positive supercompilation. In: Proc. of the 1995 Int. Symposium on Logic Programming, pp. 465–479. MIT Press, Cambridge (1995)
16. Tiwari, A., Rueb, H., Saidi, H., Shankar, N.: A technique for invariant generation. In: Margaria, T., Yi, W. (eds.) TACAS 2001. LNCS, vol. 2031, pp. 113–127. Springer, Heidelberg (2001)
17. Watt, S.M.: Algebraic generalization. ACM SIGSAM Bulletin 39(3), 93–94 (2005)
18. Wettel, R., Marinescu, R.: Archeology of Code Duplication: Recovering Duplication Chains From Small Duplication Fragments. In: Proc. of the 7th Int. Symb. on Symbolic and Numeric Algorithms for Scientific Computing, pp. 63–70 (2005)

Author Index